ECSTASY

ECSTASY

A Study of some Secular and Religious Experiences

By Marghanita Laski

BLOOMINGTON
INDIANA UNIVERSITY PRESS

First published in the U.S. in 1962

Printed in Great Britain by Butler & Tanner Ltd., Frome and London

TO MY HUSBAND

ACKNOWLEDGEMENTS

My first thanks must be to the people who generously answered my questionnaires or wrote me letters describing their experiences. They provided my raw material; without them I would have had no book.

Next I must thank those who so kindly helped me to collect material or made material available to me: especially Mrs. Eirlys Cullen, Mr. Christopher Mayhew, M.P., Mrs. Lorna Pegrim, Miss Joanna Scott-Moncrieff, Miss Joie Macaulay, Miss Yona Swain, and Dr. Hilde Himmelweit to whom I am also indebted for much valuable advice on questioning and arrangement.

I welcome the opportunity to express my thanks to Mr. John Hayward for his persistent attempts to teach me to write better English; and to Mrs. Philippa Foot for some arguments which have been of the greatest value. I am grateful to Mr. R. W. Burchfield for his useful advice on the layout of bibliographical references, and to the printers whose perspicacious queries at every stage have been a great help. I thank my husband for his unfailing encouragement during the writing of this book, and for his professional help in its making.

I lack words to say how much I owe to Mr. Frank Blackaby and to Mr. Rupert Crawshay-Williams. Mr. Blackaby evolved the method of presenting my analyses in statistical form and has with endless patience striven to overcome my natural preference for first unchecked results. Mr. Crawshay-Williams, with patience and kindness beyond all possible claims of friendship, has not ceased to try to make me understand what it is that I am trying to say and not to say more than I can justify. Few people can have had, in writing a book, the immense gift of such stern and unfailing help as Mr. Blackaby and Mr. Crawshay-Williams have given me; neither is to be held responsible for any errors of fact or judgement which I have made and which they would be the first to deplore.

My gratitude is also due to those people who have kindly allowed me to quote from material in which they hold the copyright:

Messrs. George Allen and Unwin Ltd.: *Mysticism, Christian and*

Buddhist by D. T. Suzuki. Messrs. Edward Arnold (Publishers) Ltd.: *Howard's End* by E. M. Forster. Messrs. Cassell & Company Ltd.: *Christ Stopped at Eboli* by Carlo Levi. Messrs. Chatto and Windus Ltd.: *The Doors of Perception* and *Heaven and Hell* by Aldous Huxley; *A Writer's Notes on his Trade* by C. E. Montague; *Swann's Way* by Marcel Proust, translated by C. K. Scott Moncrieff. The Clarendon Press: *Enthusiasm* by Ronald Knox; *Mysticism Sacred and Profane by* R. C. Zaehner. Messrs. Constable and Company Ltd.: *Aesthetics and History* by Bernard Berenson; *Western Mysticism* by Dom Cuthbert Butler. The Cresset Press: *A Land* and *Man on Earth* by Jacquetta Hawkes. Messrs. J. M. Dent and Sons Ltd.: *The Mystic Way* by Evelyn Underhill. Messrs. Faber and Faber Ltd.: *The Timeless Moment* by H. Warner Allen. Messrs. Victor Gollancz Ltd.: *Wisdom, Madness and Folly* by J. Custance; *A Drug-Taker's Notes* by R. H. Ward. Messrs. W. Heffer and Sons Ltd.: *An Anatomy of Inspiration* by Rosamond E. M. Harding. The Hogarth Press Ltd.: *A Writer's Diary* by Virginia Woolf. Messrs. Longmans, Green & Co. Ltd.: *The Vision of God* by Kenneth E. Kirk. Messrs. Macmillan & Co. Ltd.: *The Search* by C. P. Snow. Messrs. Methuen & Co. Ltd.: *Christian Mysticism* by W. R. Inge; *Mysticism* by Evelyn Underhill. The Oxford University Press: *A Study of History* by Arnold Toynbee. Messrs. A. D. Peters: *Arrow in the Blue* by Arthur Koestler (Hamish Hamilton). Messrs. Laurence Pollinger Ltd.: *Over the Bridge* by Richard Church (William Heinemann); *The Rainbow* and *Sons and Lovers* by D. H. Lawrence (William Heinemann). Messrs. Routledge and Kegan Paul Ltd.: *The Psychology of Religious Mysticism* by James H. Leuba; *The Graces of Interior Prayer* by A. Poulain, S.J.; *Practical Criticism* and *Principles of Literary Criticism* by I. A. Richards. The Joseph Rowntree Charitable Trust: *Studies in Mystical Religion* by Rufus Jones (Macmillan). Messrs. David Higham Associates Limited: *Autobiography* by Margiad Evans (Arthur Barker).

A NOTE ON REFERENCES AND TEXTS

The books I have most frequently referred to, and the abbreviations under which I refer to them are as follows:

Butler: W.M.	Dom Cuthbert Butler, *Western Mysticism* (London, 1922; 2nd edn., 1926).

(NOTE: The arrangement of the second edition of this book differs substantially from that of the first, and the page references I give are therefore useless for the first edition; there is no index to either.)

Harding: A.I.	Rosamond E. M. Harding, *An Anatomy of Inspiration* (Cambridge, 1940; 3rd edn., 1948).
Hügel: M.E.R.	Friedrich von Hügel, *The Mystical Element in Religion* (London, 1908).
Inge: C.M.	W. R. Inge, *Christian Mysticism* (London, 1899; 8th edn., 1948).
James: V.R.E.	William James, *The Varieties of Religious Experience* (London, 1902; 1952 edn.).
Jones: S.M.R.	Rufus Jones, *Studies in Mystical Religion* (London, 1909).
Kirk: V.G.	Kenneth E. Kirk, *The Vision of God* (London, 1931; 2nd edn., 1932).
Leuba: P.R.M.	James H. Leuba, *The Psychology of Religious Mysticism* (London, 1925; 2nd edn., 1929).
O.D.C.C.	*The Oxford Dictionary of the Christian Church*, ed., F. L. Cross (Oxford, 1957).
Poulain: G.I.P.	A. Poulain, S.J., *The Graces of Interior Prayer*, trans. Leonora L. Yorke Smith (London, 1910; 1950 edn.).
Richards: *Principles*	I. A. Richards, *Principles of Literary Criticism* (London, 1924; 2nd edn., 1926).
Richards: P.C.	I. A. Richards, *Practical Criticism* (London, 1929).
Sanctis: R.C.	Sante de Sanctis, *Religious Conversion*, trans. Helen Augur (London, 1927).
Teresa: *Life*	*The Life of Saint Teresa*, trans. J. M. Cohen (Penguin, 1957).

Thurston: P.P.M.	Herbert Thurston, S.J., *The Physical Phenomena, of Mysticism*, ed. J. H. Crehan, S.J. (London, 1952).
Thurston: S.M.	Herbert Thurston, S.J., *Surprising Mystics*, ed. J. H. Crehan, S.J. (London, 1955).
E.U: M.	Evelyn Underhill, *Mysticism* (London, 1911; 1930 edn.).
E.U: M.W.	Evelyn Underhill, *The Mystic Way* (London, 1913).
W.W: Prel.	William Wordsworth, *The Prelude*, ed. Ernest de Selincourt (Oxford, 1926; 2nd corrected imp. 1928).
W.W: P.W.	William Wordsworth, *Poetical Works*, ed. Ernest de Selincourt (Oxford, 1940; 2nd corrected imp., 1952).
Zaehner: M.S.P.	R. C. Zaehner, *Mysticism Sacred and Profane* (Oxford, 1957).

References to the dictionary are, unless otherwise stated, to the Oxford English Dictionary (O.E.D.), 1933 edition.

In cited texts, widely spaced dots (. . .) indicate cuts in the original, closely spaced dots (...) cuts made by me. Square brackets in texts indicate interpolations made by me. All italics in the texts are, except where stated, in the original.

I have generally referred to the people I quote by their surnames only for simplicity sake, not from any lack of respect.

CONTENTS

Introduction   1

PART ONE

I   The questionnaire and the texts   5
II   The analyses   16
III   Criteria for ecstasies   37

PART TWO

IV   Intensity and withdrawal   47
V   The duration of ecstasies   57
VI   Up, down, light, dark   67
VII   Physical claims in general   77
VIII   Varieties and values   89
IX   Adamic and time ecstasies   103
X   Knowledge   116
XI   Contact   122
XII   Ecstasy in children   134
XIII   Ecstasy and childbirth   138
XIV   Ecstasy and sexual love   145
XV   Revelation ecstasies   154
XVI   Desolation   160
XVII   Nomenclature   171
XVIII   Anti-triggers   176
XIX   Some common triggers   187
XX   Some Desolation triggers   207
XXI   Some qualities of triggers   213
XXII   Language and ecstatic experience   226
XXIII   Inducing ecstatic experiences   249
XXIV   Mescalin and ecstasy   263
XXV   The distribution of ecstatic experience   274

xi

PART THREE

XXVI	Inspiration	279
XXVII	Conversion	289
XXVIII	Primary overbelief (i): The seeds of utopia	294
XXIX	Primary overbelief (ii): Communication and contact	305
XXX	Primary overbelief (iii): Ecstasy and conduct	312
XXXI	The formation of overbelief (i): The general process	319
XXXII	The formation of overbelief (ii): The asking of the question	335
XXXIII	The formation of overbelief (iii): The collection of material	339
XXXIV	The formation of overbelief (iv): The fusing of the material	343
XXXV	The formation of overbelief (v): The translation	346
XXXVI	The formation of overbelief (vi): Testing the answer	350
XXXVII	Some critical judgements	360

PART FOUR

XXXVIII	Conclusions	369
	Appendices	375
	Index	534

And if any have been so happy as truly to understand Christian annihilation, ecstasies, exolution, liquefaction, transformation, the kiss of the spouse, gustation of God, and ingression into the divine shadow, they have already had an handsome anticipation of heaven; the glory of the world is surely over, and the earth in ashes unto them.

SIR THOMAS BROWNE, *Hydriotaphia*

To be forced by desire into any unwarrantable belief is a calamity.

I. A. RICHARDS,
Principles of Literary Criticism

Introduction

In 1953 I wrote a novel in which, by means of an experience I believed was known as ecstasy, I translated my heroine from present to past time. This seemed to me to be credible in a fictional context and it must have seemed credible to readers since the book was well received and no one questioned the device. But later I began to wonder why anything so extraordinary should be accepted as within the bounds of even fictional possibility, and this led me to speculate on ecstatic experiences in general.

I had then read nothing about these experiences and did not know how common and indeed commonplace my original speculations were. An ecstatic experience gave a feeling of being outside time; did this mean that time was illusory and timelessness, perhaps, the reality? An ecstatic experience sometimes felt like translation to a simpler, purer state; was it? Sometimes it felt like a state in which one received new knowledge, wonderful beyond possible rendering into words; was ecstasy perhaps a foretaste of a next development of man when knowledge would be wordless and greater? And sometimes ecstasy felt like contact with a transcendental spirit.

One can accept only the answers one needs. At this point I reached the conclusion that my speculations were nonsense, and that it would be interesting to know what ecstasy felt like to other people.

A very few inquiries were enough to establish that other people knew these experiences, and their descriptions of them were similar in so many ways that it seemed they might be capable of systematization. So I drew up a list of standardized questions and proceeded to put them to people with a view to systematizing the answers.

I had not, at that stage, any intention of writing a book about ecstatic experiences. I wanted only to satisfy my own curiosity, but this seemed persistently to expand. As is always the case when one becomes interested in a subject, I began to notice references that had hitherto passed me by, and I also started to read books about these kinds of experiences. It was after I had begun to evolve methods of systematizing the results of my own inquiries that it occurred to me to try the same methods on other experiences, both those I had come across in general reading and the experiences of classic religious mystics. Whatever the source of the experiences I examined, similar results were attained.

The books I read proffered one or other of two explanations of the experiences I was calling ecstatic. The majority, which were books on religious mysticism written by religious believers, assumed a supernatural origin for these experiences. A few other books, which were equally about religious mysticism but written by people who were not religious believers, sought the origin of these experiences in morbid conditions, whether physical or psychological or both. Both kinds of writers usually assumed that the experiences of ordinary people were a simpler form of supernatural or of morbid experiences, though sometimes the experiences of classic religious mystics were given a supernatural origin and those of other people a morbid one.

That some such experiences had morbid origins seemed certain; that some were supernaturally caused it was not my temperamental bias to believe. There seemed to be room for an empirical investigation of ecstatic experiences that was based on neither of these presuppositions. I did not and do not know of any such study and so felt justified in trying to make one. The difficulties confronting an amateur attempt to deal with such a subject are of course immense, but no professional has undertaken it or, so far as I know, considered doing so. More, it is hard to see under what professional discipline such a study would properly fall. I have consistently felt the lack of specialized training in philosophy, theology, psychology, physiology, semantics, and statistics. All I could hope to do was to produce a limited study, leaning heavily on authorities.

The authorities I have used are of two kinds. In the first place I have had advice and criticism from specialist friends; the thanks I have given them in my Acknowledgements are an insufficient measure of my gratitude. Secondly, I have relied on books. Originally I picked these at random from the shelves of libraries, but gradually I came to use some more than others and it was a considerable relief to me to be confirmed in my choices when the *Oxford Dictionary of the Christian Church* appeared in 1957, giving, in the brief bibliography to its entry under 'Mysticism', all the books I had principally used.

The plan of the book is as follows:

The first part discusses the methods by which texts were obtained and analysed. Based on the results of the analyses I put forward criteria for the experiences I shall accept as ecstatic ones.

In the second part of the book I examine ecstatic experiences in detail, drawing, for evidence, principally upon my texts but also on other accounts of similar experiences. The objects of examination are determined by the nature of the material, and include, for instance, the duration of ecstatic experiences, the physical claims made, the different varieties of ecstatic experiences, the circumstances inducing such experiences, the most useful ways of naming them, their probable availability, and so on.

The third part is largely speculative. In it I discuss the results of ecstatic experiences with particular reference to beliefs that arise as a result of these experiences.

Finally I summarize my findings and make suggestions for further specialized study.

Although my book is far longer than I originally intended—prudence, though not pleasure, would have dictated ending it after Chapter III—I have tried to restrain most of it within the proper limits of empirical inquiry and to curb though not wholly to suppress an inveterate lust for speculation; enjoyment is a strong spur to writing and I enjoy speculation more than in these disciplined days I should. There are however many aspects of the subject that I have been able to mention only with misleading brevity. My comments on what appear to be the obverse experiences to ecstatic ones are sadly superficial, and I should like to be more sure than I am that I am substantially correct in what I have said about the form of ecstatic experience I have called withdrawal; but in order to be more sure I would have had to make a considerable study of eastern mysticism, and this would have been to transgress beyond permissible limits the bounds of the amateur. But every writer imagines ideal readers, and my ideal readers are those specialists who can, by empirical methods, refute my findings or confirm and extend them.

PART ONE

CHAPTER I

The Questionnaire and the Texts

Before drawing up a questionnaire I had to decide under what name I would ask people to identify and describe the experiences I wanted to investigate, and finally decided that *ecstasy*, which I had assumed was the name most properly given to the experience described in my novel, was in fact the name most usually used for the range of experiences I was interested in.[1]

The usage I had in mind was one in which *ecstasy* named a range of experiences characterized by being joyful, transitory, unexpected, rare, valued, and extraordinary to the point of often seeming as if derived from a praeternatural source. It did not seem to me that we would naturally speak of a sad ecstasy, or of a trivial or worthless ecstasy, or would apply the name to experiences that could reasonably be expected to follow from known causes. Thus, I would normally expect pleasure from, say, hearing certain music or making love; I would normally expect my heart to leap up when I beheld a rainbow in the sky; but I would not speak of these expected pleasures as ectasies.

'Extraordinary to the point of often seeming as if derived from a praeternatural source' is, I think, essential to this concept of ecstasy. One might attain a joyful experience in many ways similar from, say, drink or drugs; but the cause being understood, I think one would name such an experience *euphoria* rather than ecstasy or say that it was 'like ecstasy'. *Ecstasy* is, it seems to me, applied to experiences

[1] Among names given to experiences which seemed, at first glance, as if they might be of the kind I was looking for, were mystical experience, cosmic consciousness, soul-life, infused contemplation, timeless moments, the oceanic feeling, etc. Apart from an initial feeling of distaste for many of these, most of them were linked with particular explanations or were initially too descriptive. The most possible seemed to be mystical experience, but when I later used this phrase on a B.B.C. Brains Trust and asked people to write to me about their mystical experiences, it appeared that for many people this name covered experiences of widely different kinds, many of them beyond the range of my interests; see Appendix J.

that are different from those we could expect in the normal course of events and different in seeming to lie outside the normal course of events.

I am less sure that the name should be applied only to transitory experiences, lasting, say, a matter of moments, but I do rather feel that a state of joy of considerable duration would tend to be described as 'like a continuous ecstasy' rather than *ecstasy, tout court*.[1] The phrase 'a moment of ecstasy' is a common one and, as we shall see, many people are specific about the momentary nature of their ecstatic experiences.

But the word ecstasy has other usuages and I had to consi der how far these might modify this concept in the minds of my respondents.

Catholic theologians use 'ecstasy' to refer to a prolonged trance-like state which may be of frequent occurrence, that is, to experiences not transitory and not necessarily rare;[2] John Donne's poem *The Extasie* presumably refers to an experience of this kind. In the event it did not appear that any of my respondents knew of this special usage or recalled Donne's poem in this context. When I have occasion to refer to 'ecstasy' in this sense, I shall do so in inverted commas, and prefaced by the adjective *religious*, i.e. religious 'ecstasy'.

Then ecstasy can refer to a state of madness. When Ophelia spoke of Hamlet's sweet reason as being 'blasted with extasie'[3] she referred to an experience neither valued nor transitory nor, necessarily, joyful or unexpected. Again when John Donne was described as being 'in such an Extasie, and so alter'd as to his looks' when he saw a vision of his ailing wife and dead child, an experience described by Donne himself as 'a dreadful Vision',[4] we may be sure this was not a joyful experience and doubt whether it could fairly be described as a valuable one. *Ecstasy* has moreover many trivial usages. When Elizabeth Bennet described as 'exstacy' the moment of her release from dancing with Mr. Collins, she meant only that she felt considerable relief.[5] And latterly the word *ecstasy* has been widely used by advertisers and popu-

[1] E.g. 'There were two B.B.C. interviews last week which had more effect on me than anything I have yet seen... One was a continuous ecstasy lasting fifty-five minutes'. Maurice Richardson in the *Observer*, April 2, 1961.

[2] Poulain says of these that 'it is the exception when they do not last more than half an hour' and instances 'ecstasies' that lasted from several hours to forty days; and that for some of the saints 'their life has been little else than a series of ecstasies'. G.I.P., ch. xviii, 7-10.

[3] *Hamlet*, III. i.

[4] Izaac Walton, *Lives* (1640; World's Classics edn., 1950), pp. 39-40.

[5] Jane Austen, *Pride and Prejudice* (1813; Oxford, 1932), ch. xviii, p. 90.

lar writers to refer to states that can normally be expected as a result of using advertised products or of being in love.[1] In such usages the concept of ecstasy does not include the qualities of being unexpected or rare or extraordinary to the point of often seeming as if derived from a praeternatural source, since the source is known and the experience, given the right stimulus, is to be expected—and, in the case of advertised products, attained at will. Nor are such experiences necessarily transitory. Finally, the related adjective and adverb, *ecstatic* and *ecstatically* are nowadays used in smart—or perhaps slightly outmoded—feminine argot to mean little more than 'very nice'—for instance, an ecstatic hat, an ecstatic party; compare similar uses of 'enchanting' and 'divine'.

If there is a common quality to all these usages it is no more than a reference to being in a state of mind other than one's usual one; this is, of course, implied by the derivation of the word *ecstasy*. And although I sought a name for the experiences I had in mind that should be as little descriptive as possible, the basic concept of being in a state of mind other than one's usual one was insufficiently definite to pinpoint a concept of ecstasy as joyful, transitory, unexpected, etc. and to exclude the others I have instanced which, rightly or wrongly, I thought likely to be known to such people as those I would question. I therefore decided that I would ask them not if they had known an experience of ecstasy but if they had known an experience of transcendent ecstasy. This adjective involved the danger that my respondents would suppose that only experiences accepted by them as of praeternatural origin were wanted. But in the event it appeared that—as I had hoped—they took transcendent to mean (as the dictionary allows it to mean) only 'surpassing', 'excelling'.[2] The use of this adjective did, I think, entail that only joyful and valuable experiences would be proffered, experiences of a kind to which it would not seem odd to attribute a praeternatural origin, and thus would eliminate the concepts of ecstasy as states of madness, as dreadful experiences, and as trivial experiences normally to be expected once the right stimuli had been applied. It did not eliminate the possibility that the prolonged trance-like condition known as 'ecstasy' was being referred to, but, as I have explained, it did

[1] E.g., 'O then, O gee, I'm in ecstasy When I dance with my girl'; popular song.

[2] The first meaning of *transcendent* given by O.E.D. is 'Surpassing or excelling others of its kind; going beyond the ordinary limits; pre-eminent; superior or supreme; extraordinary. Also, loosely, Eminently great or good'.

not appear that any of my respondents knew of this usage. I do not think that the use of *transcendent* necessarily had any further effect on the answers. More or less prolonged dionysiac transports—Keats's 'wild ecstasy'— remained a possible interpretation, but was not one given by any of my respondents.

There was however one disadvantage to 'transcendent ecstasy' which I could not eliminate and this is that it was embarrassing, and this embarrassment is worth some comment since it is likely to affect the reader as it did me and the people I questioned. I suspect it has many sources. In part it may spring from what Coleridge suggests is 'a cowardice of all deep feeling, even though pleasurable'.[1] Some of it is undoubtedly due to the fact that many amateurs interested in subjects which go by names such as this hold views which are widely regarded as eccentric or silly. Some of it may be due to the association of feelings identified with this name with explanations that people would like to be able to believe without being forced to defend. But whatever the reasons for the embarrassment, it certainly exists. I felt it every time I asked my first question and my respondents obviously felt it too. But it was, to my surprise and relief, very quickly dissipated as answers were given, only two of the people I asked being unwilling to answer and most being noticeably eager.

The questionnaire, which was built up after much trial and error, was deliberately kept as unstructured and flexible as possible. I wanted to know the circumstances in which ecstatic experiences took place in order to see whether these circumstances could be limited and defined. I wanted people to tell me what ecstasy felt like for them because it was largely from these answers that I hoped to make a systematization. I wanted to know my respondents' religious positions to see whether these affected their answers in any consistent ways. Some questions on inspiration were added because I shared what seemed to be the common assumption that inspiration and ecstatic experiences were in some way related, and I hoped I might obtain answers that could throw some light on the relationship, particularly as many of the people I questioned were engaged in creative work. When and only when people said that they believed ecstasy and inspiration to be identical, or, in answering on inspiration, referred back to ecstasy, I have felt justified in using answers from the second part of the questionnaire in the analyses.

[1] *Anima Poetae*, October 21, 1803.

The questions asked were as follows:

1. Do you know a sensation of transcendent ecstasy?
   (If people asked, as they sometimes did, 'What do you mean by transcendent ecstasy?' I replied, 'Take it to mean whatever you think it means.' If they answered *No* to the first question, I omitted questions 2 to 4 and went on to question 5.)
2. How would you describe it?
3. What has induced it in you?
4. How many times in your life have you felt it—in units, tens, hundreds?
5. What is your religion or faith?
6. Do you know a feeling of creative inspiration?
7. How would you describe it?
8. Does it seem to you to have anything in common with ecstasy?
9. What is your profession?

My first desire was to know whether these experiences were rare or common. I had no means of questioning a balanced sample of the population, nor, in the early stages, did I see any advantages in doing so. *People I knew* seemed to me to constitute a group that would give me adequate answers for my initial purposes.

So the people questioned consisted of friends and acquaintances and other people I met in circumstances that allowed me to put my questions without intolerable embarrassment. The questionnaires were collected over a period of three years, and in order to obtain 60 affirmative answers to the first question, 63 people were questioned. These 63 people consisted of 26 males and 27 females, including a boy of ten, a girl of fourteen and a girl of sixteen.[1]

These people will be referred to collectively as the questionnaire group or Group Q. All agreed that I might make what use I pleased of the material they gave me so long as identities were suppressed. I have

[1] The professions of the adults included 20 writers of various kinds and, as described by themselves, 3 Civil Servants, 3 secretaries, 3 housewives, 2 publishers, 2 economists, 2 B.B.C. producers, 2 cameramen, a medical student, a doctor, a psychologist, a biologist, a scientist, a social scientist, a mathematician, an engineer, a geographer, an actor, a composer, a musicologist, a sculptor, a potter, a music teacher, a commercial artist, a literary agent, a salesman, an administrator, a lecturer, a floor manager, a cosmetician, and a Trades Union official. I later came to think it a pity that no people engaged in commerce were included in this group.

therefore given the people in this group numbers—Q 1, Q 2, etc.—by which I shall refer to them, and, in reproducing their answers, have omitted the individual professions and also place-names where these might serve to identify people to their friends.

Since my sole evidence for the feelings people identified with the name *transcendent ecstasy* lay in the words they used to describe them, it was essential that I should take down as nearly as I could (not knowing shorthand) the actual words they used. So I did not try to tidy their usually groping, disconnected phrases into syntactical sentences. To those unaccustomed to the often great differences between spoken and written English, it will probably seem that these answers must have come from people exceptionally inarticulate rather than from people of whom a high proportion was skilled in the written language. Those who were so skilled did not prove any more able to speak articulated sentences than those who were not. Readers may try for themselves the experiment of putting into spoken English, without pen in hand, feelings they have never before tried to describe orally.

It was of course necessary to consider possible sources of falsification. All the questionnaires were completed in personal interviews, and I soon began to wonder whether the often substantial similarities between different people's answers could be in any way unconsciously influenced by myself. To test this, a friend undertook some questioning for me (these answers are headed *Compiled by E. C.*). Her results were not in any significant way different from my own.[1]

It was also necessary to ask whether respondents could have falsified their answers: whether, perceiving that an affirmative answer to the first question was wanted, could, generously or naughtily or even unconsciously, have given orthodox and conventional answers to the following questions even though such answers did not correspond with their own experiences.

Certainly it is possible that some of the people questioned might have studied religious experiences sufficiently closely to have been able to produce, on the spur of the moment, condensed versions of such experiences—always assuming that they associated the phrase *transcendent ecstasy* with religious experiences, as very few did. I do not think this is likely. Little or no evidence of such study appears, and apart from religious experiences there is no source from which orthodox

[1] That the questioner did not noticeably influence the answers was confirmed by later postal questionnaires; see Appendix J.

and conventional answers could have been derived, for none exists. No such collection of people as those in the questionnaire group have, so far as I know, been questioned before about their ecstatic experiences.

Many people in this group confirm each other's honesty by giving answers similar to those of other people in the group but not obtainable from any written source. For instance, several women gave childbirth as a circumstance inducing ecstasy in them; I do not know of any written ecstatic experience, whether secular or, less probably, religious induced by childbirth. Then several people, men and women, gave sexual love as a circumstance inducing ecstasies (this they could hardly have derived from religious sources) but showed no tendency to claim a higher occurrence of ecstasy than people who named other circumstances. Since many of these people were sexually experienced and must have known the experience of sexual orgasm, they clearly distinguished between this and the transcendent ecstasy they were being asked about. And since sexual success is known to be an aspect of life about which most people will, when questioned, lie in the directions most likely to enhance their prestige, it may be taken as evidence of good faith that these people did not claim that sexual intercourse had induced ecstasy in them more often than the limited number of times claimed by people who named other circumstances.

It should be remembered that the people questioned did not know why the information was sought. Very generously they did their often halting best to describe, on the spur of the moment, feelings for which no model descriptions exist. Often it is possible that some information that might usefully have filled out the picture was omitted, not because it was not available but because it was lost in the immediately felt importance of another statement. Sometimes people spontaneously proffered additional information later, often several years later, and in two cases I have appended this to the original answers (see Q 22 and Q 26); in both cases the later comments considerably extend both the range of inducing circumstances named and the information given about the actual experiences. This possibility, that we are being told only a part of what might have been said, applies to all descriptions of experiences whether oral or written, but it is obviously more likely when someone is trying, unprepared, to answer a question verbally than when they have of their own accord decided to communicate an experience in writing. But in the event the principal differences between the accounts of those who described their experiences to me and those who wrote them down for posterity lie more in the style of the language used than in its matter.

Since similar things were said by a number of those interviewed, it was possible to group what they said under various headings, which were, therefore, established not by *a priori* hypotheses but by the material brought up by the respondents themselves. These groupings were checked by other people and general agreement reached on the classifications. Some simple statistical analysis was then attempted.

At this stage it occurred to me that the same method of analysis might be usefully applied to other accounts of experiences—experiences which had been written down spontaneously and not proffered in response to a questionnaire. So I collected two more groups of texts, one from literary sources, the other from books about religious experience. These I call the literary group and the religious group; the texts in each have been numbered and are referred to briefly as L 1, R 1, etc. These texts were similarly analysed, and it thus became possible to compare the statistical patterns derived from each of the three groups.

Of texts in the literary group I demanded only that they had been published. I was looking for experiences superficially similar to those of the questionnaire group which their authors had thought worth communicating to the public.

With the single exception of classic religious experiences (which would appear in the religious group) I wanted to be as eclectic as possible. I wanted experiences from writers of much reputation and of little, from different periods, and from autobiography, poetry or fiction (for there is no less reason to trust novelists than other writers to communicate experience honestly). I confined myself largely to English writers because language was my material for analysis and I feared the loss of verbal shades in translation; but where a translation particularly interested or pleased me I put it in.

As I have explained in the Introduction, once I became interested in ecstasies, apparent ecstasies seemed to confront me almost wherever I looked, and I deliberately did not look far afield for my literary texts but took the first thirty suitable ones that I came across in what I happened to be reading at the time. And by *suitable*, I mean seeming before analysis to describe one of the experiences I was interested in, no matter how the experience was interpreted or the circumstances in which it took place. At this stage I had not evolved the concepts of triggers or of different varieties of ecstasies, or, save in rudimentary form, the statistical analyses. In three cases in the literary texts (and in the religious texts) I took two texts from one writer. I was collecting and comparing experiences, not people, and I thought—as proved to be the case—that this might be helpful in examining the range of experiences available to one person. But on the whole I now think this a mistaken decision, particularly in view of the fact that in one case both texts proved dubious in several respects.[1] But I could not know they were dubious until I had established normality, and they were useful for raising the queries they did. Certainly hindsight could have chosen texts with greater discrimination; but hindsight was not available.

The twenty-four texts in the religious group were deliberately taken from secondary sources, from the books of writers on religious mysticism who cited these experiences to illustrate one or other aspect of their subject. Not all these texts were presented by their commentators as representing commendable or orthodox experiences; in my penultimate chapter I have commented on some of the often interesting and enlightening criticisms that have been made.

Many of these religious texts are quoted by several writers, often using different translations and making different extracts from the same sources. In these cases I have chosen the version best suited to my purpose. That most of the texts in this group are translations is, from the nature of the material, unavoidable.

In contrast with the questionnaire group, the writers in the religious and literary groups were proffering their experiences by their own choice. This means that each account is as complete a description of the experience in question as the writer, for his immediate purposes, chose to make it, and explains why, on the average, more entries were made for each text in the literary and religious groups than for each text in the questionnaire group.[2] It also means that the language used is a literary as opposed to a spoken one, and in many cases the language is elaborately rhetorical. It is however striking to what a large extent the images produced spontaneously by the people in the

---

[1] See p. 73 and pp. 148–53.
[2] In the analysis of descriptions of feeling, each pers
averaged 4·8 entries; in the literary group 12·6 ent
13·0 entries.

questionnaire group are similar to the more considered images of the people in the literary and religious groups.

This is the more impressive when we remember one important respect in which the texts in the religious group differ from those in the questionnaire group and, to a considerable extent, from those in the literary group. All the people in the religious group believed that they knew the explanation of their experiences, and that this explanation was that their experiences had been given them by God; none of them found his experience inconsonant with his previous beliefs. Practically all of them knew by hearsay of such experiences, even if they had not previously encountered them themselves, and knew, too, an accepted vocabulary of description for such experiences. Thus Suso (text R 1) admitting, perhaps, a scintilla of doubt in his phrase, 'If that which I see and feel be not the Kingdom of Heaven, I know not what it can be', still stamped his own assurance of what it was with his echo of St. Paul's phrase in II *Cor.* xii. 2–3, 'whether his soul were in or out of the body, he could not tell'. Again, Louis of Blois's not uncommon image of swift flow, 'like a living fountain, flowing with streams of eternal sweetness' (text R 20) almost certainly derives from *Jeremiah* ii. 13 and *Revelation* vii.17. To a substantial extent the people in the religious group knew the vocabulary for such experiences before they knew the experiences; inevitably, when the experiences *are* known, they tend to be recounted in the vocabulary already accepted as appropriate. When this special knowledge of the religious group is borne in mind the similarities of expression as between the three groups is the more striking.

But such undeniable borrowing of images, by one group at least, may well lead to the suspicion that in many of the texts cited writers are, consciously or unconsciously, rather using a borrowed vocabulary to convey a conventional account than attempting to describe an individual experience. This is obviously possible, but there are arguments, which the development of this book may clarify, to suggest that it is improbable.

In the first place, it is sometimes possible to detect in 'faked' ecstasies—that is, ecstasies known on other than internal evidence to be ma̲ ̲ ̲ ̲ ̲ducts and not genuine reports of feelings—many ̲ ̲ ̲ ̲ ̲types. It is apparently less easy than it might ̲ ̲ ̲ ̲l get it right. There are, as we shall see, many ̲ ̲ ̲e and these can be distinguished one from the other by the ways in which they are described; some images are appropriate to one kind of experience, some to another. The self-consistency, in this respect, of almost all my texts is hardly to be expected were people selecting their descriptive phrases virtually at random, knowing that such phrases belonged to these experiences as a whole, but not knowing, from personal experience, which were appropriate to this or that variety.[1]

Then, among accounts of the ecstatic experiences of the religious, there are many which describe experiences unacceptable to orthodox religious opinion. Since the degree of borrowing in the religious texts shows considerable academic interest in ecstatic experiences, it seems reasonable to suppose that if orthodox religious people sought, consciously or unconsciously, to fake accounts of ecstatic experiences, they would turn to orthodox and not to heterodox models. To some extent all vocabulary is borrowed, but people may still choose to borrow that which most nearly expresses their own feelings and this, I suppose, is what the writers of most if not all my religious texts have done.

For the literary figures far less of a stereotyped and accepted vocabulary is readily available. And it might seem to be of the nature of creative writers, both those in the literary group and those in the questionnaire group, to seek original language for individual experience rather than to borrow the language and perhaps even the experiences of other people. But how far one accepts this as true must be a matter of personal judgement, and my own is that in all but two texts in the literary group and throughout the questionnaire group people were trying, even struggling to express genuine personal experience, and that common language derives from common experience rather than from deliberate or unconscious borrowing with the intention of faking or elaborating experience.

The texts of all three groups will be found in Appendix A.

[1] See also the argument on pp. 348–9.

CHAPTER II

The Analyses

The content analysis was divided into two main parts, the first (Section I) classifying the circumstances in which the experiences took place (the triggers), the second (Sections II to V) what people said about their experiences. Some factual or putatively factual information, mostly about the experiences in the questionnaire group, was also classified.

When asked 'What has induced [ecstasy] in you?' almost all the people in the questionnaire group named one or more objects, events and ideas in a range sufficiently limited for classification; that is to say, of the circumstances in which they found themselves when ecstasy took place, they identified certain objects, events, and ideas as standing in some kind of a causal relationship to their ecstatic experiences. These objects, events, and ideas I am calling *triggers*.

In the literary and religious groups people do not necessarily suggest that there is any kind of causal relationship between their circumstances and their experiences. Where the circumstances are given—and often, in the religious group, they are not—I have none the less noted those that seem to fall under one or other of the headings made on the basis of the answers in the questionnaire group. Where, which rarely happens, the attendant circumstances do not fit any of these headings, I have noted any particular circumstances which seem as if they might have been significant in inducing the experience.

Obviously in choosing such a name as *trigger*, I am supposing that these circumstances can in some way act as a release mechanism in inducing ecstatic experience. I am not suggesting that encounter with a trigger provides a sufficient cause for an ecstasy, only that encounter with a trigger is, as the material shows, almost always a necessary pre- ecstasy, except where ecstatic states are deliberately in- disciplines or where they accompany recognizably

The headings in this as in the other sections of the analysis were made on the basis of the material of the questionnaire group (with two exceptions in later sections which will be pointed out). Triggers were entered under the following headings:

Natural scenery, objects, etc.; sexual love; childbirth; exercise, movement; religion; art; scientific or exact knowledge; poetic knowledge; creative work; recollection, introspection; 'beauty'; miscellaneous.

Where people have given, as inducing a single ecstasy, circumstances involving more than one of these headings, I have made an entry under each of the headings to which the circumstances refer. I call these *compound triggers*.

The next four sections (II to V), under the general title of *What they said they felt*, classify people's descriptions of their experiences. Several attempts were made before arriving at the classification now presented, but from the start three sub-groups (Sections II to IV) seemed to be imposed by the fact that people seemed to be saying three kinds of things. They said that they had lost a sense of (something); that they had gained a sense of (something); and that they had feelings which seemed to refer to physical as opposed to mental sensations, whether spoken of with apparently literal or apparently figurative intention.

It was not my business at this stage to make any judgements of the feelings said to be lost or gained beyond deciding how most conveniently to group them. But after several attempts a pattern of relationship between loss and gain statements seemed to emerge and this I accepted as the most convenient for purposes of classification. There was no such pattern in my first attempt at grouping and it only gradually appeared. One must be wary of improperly imposing patterns which may improperly impose explanations, but this undoubtedly proved the most convenient arrangement, and my initial concern was with convenience rather than with significance.

Statements referring to loss were entered under the following headings:

Feelings of loss of: difference; time; place; limitation; worldliness; desire;[1] sorrow; sin; self; words and/or images; sense.

[1] The negative or loss form of this statement does not appear in the questionnaire group.

Statements referring to gain were entered under the following headings:

Feelings of gain of: unity and/or 'everything'; timelessness; an ideal place, heaven; release; a new life, another world; satisfaction; joy; salvation, perfection; glory; contact; mystical knowledge; new knowledge; knowledge by identification.

Statements about feelings of ineffability were entered separately.

Under the general heading *Quasi-physical feelings* I have entered expressions that seem to refer to physical happenings in the ecstatic.[1] Sometimes such references are clear and direct; sometimes they are implied by choice of metaphors and figurative language; often it is difficult to be sure whether an expression is used with literal or figurative intention. I realize that the inclusion of phrases in which the metaphor can hardly be perceived any more will need much defence, and later on several appropriate occasions I attempt this. For the moment I will cite authority to support my belief that the implications of the limited range of metaphors used may be taken as probably significant:

'a word never—well, hardly ever—shakes off its etymology and its formation. In spite of all changes in and extensions of and additions to its meaning, and indeed rather pervading and governing these, there will still persist the old idea.'[2]

Quasi-physical feelings are entered under the following headings: Up-words and phrases; inside-words and phrases; light and/or heat words and phrases; dark-words and phrases;[3] enlargement and/or improvement words and phrases; pain-words and phrases; liquidity words and phrases; calm and peace-words and phrases.

The last section under the general title 'What they said they felt' has two headings, *intensity* and *withdrawal*. It seemed to me, on reading the texts, that there were basically two ways of approaching ecstatic experiences, and I chose these names to distinguish them.

For most people ecstasy seemed to be an experience of tumescence and release, and it is for such experiences that I use the name *intensity*.

---

[1] I use the noun *ecstatic* throughout to indicate a person who has had an ecstatic experience, and not, as the dictionary has it, one who is subject to fits of ecstasy.

[2] J. L. Austin, 'A Plea for Excuses, *Proceedings of the Aristotelean Society*, 1956–7, pp. 27–8.

[3] Dark-words and phrases do not appear in the questionnaire group.

To describe what I mean by it I offer a modification of Havelock Ellis's description of tumescence:

> The organism is wound up and force accumulated, then the accumulated force is let go and something is felt to be liberated.[1]

The stress is on the winding-up, the accumulation of force to the point at which it is let go and the liberation achieved. I have omitted the word *slowly* used in Ellis's description, because it seems to me that people who use the word *suddenly* or imply a sudden seizure are describing ecstasies at the point of release only, which suggests that the preceding tumescence may often be very rapid indeed. On the other hand, the words used to describe withdrawal ecstasies suggest that these take place slowly, not suddenly.

In all three groups we find intensity described in any of three ways. Some speak of both tumescence and release (e.g. 'like a great climax which has built up—this thing has been seething inside you and suddenly it comes out' (Q 34)); some speak of tumescence only (e.g. 'something wells up...grows like a spring' (Q 26)); and some speak of release only (e.g. 'it sort of overwhelms you, it hits you..., and it's all-powerful' (Q 60)).

Ecstasies achieved by this kind of process I call *intensity ecstasies*.

I find it harder to describe what I mean by *withdrawal*, but perhaps the easiest method is by way of my description of the intensity approach. This I described as the accumulation of force which seems to be built up to the point of breakdown and then released.

By *withdrawal* I mean a method of reaching an ecstatic condition not by accumulation but by subtraction. Feelings of force and energy are stilled rather than intensified. Withdrawal experiences are felt as taking place slowly not suddenly. Where, in intensity ecstasies, images implying a rapid gush or flow of water are frequent, in withdrawal ecstasies images of slow movement of water are widely used, and particularly images of an out-flowing into something larger or infinitely large. Texts Q 1, L 7 (the second part), and R 21 are usefully illustrative models of withdrawal ecstasies.

Out of 114 texts only 6 (5 per cent.) are solely and clearly withdrawal ecstasies as compared with 52 (46 per cent.) which are solely and

---

[1] Havelock Ellis, speaking specifically of sexual tumescence, wrote: 'In tumescence the organism is slowly wound up and force accumulated ; in the act of detumescence the accumulated force is let go, and by its liberation the sperm-bearing instrument is driven home.' *Psychology of Sex* (London, 1933), p. 16.

clearly intensity ecstasies. I therefore regard intensity ecstasies as the more usual form among the people who supplied my texts, and I take intensity ecstasies as my main subject for study. I shall consider withdrawal ecstasies only in so far as they throw light on the general subject of intensity ecstasies. A few texts include both withdrawal and intensity phrases, and these will obviously require some consideration.

How all phrases in all texts were entered under the general headings of *triggers* and *what they said they felt* will be found in the analyses in Appendix B; these facilitate comparison of the phrases used by different people and by different groups.

In making entries under the general heading of *what they said they felt*, I have tried to elicit the general sense of the statement made, ignoring, for purposes of analysis, implications of specific beliefs. This is the method of approach that William James thought proper in considering religious experiences, that of 'disregarding the over-beliefs, and confining ourselves to what is common and generic'.[1]

The too-little-known word *overbelief* is so useful for my purposes throughout that I must explain it. *Overbelief* made its first dictionary appearance in the 1933 supplement to the *Oxford English Dictionary* where it was defined as: 'Belief in more than is warranted by the evidence or in what cannot be verified.' The first use cited is in 1900, but the best-known example of its use is William James's in *Varieties of Religious Experience* first published in 1902. Here James uses *overbelief* as I shall principally use it, to name the subjective gloss or interpretation placed by people on their experiences, and although he believed, as he put it, that 'the most interesting and valuable things about a man are usually his over-beliefs', he still thought it proper, in trying to discover the nature of religious experience, to disregard the overbeliefs and confine himself to what was common and generic.

And this is what, in analysing the descriptions given, I have tried to do. Thus, when we find one person saying that ecstasy feels 'as if being borne into heaven itself' and another saying of it 'very happy—floating', I take it that both these people are speaking of feelings of joy and of up-feelings. Again, people speak of feeling as if they had made contact with a variety of named persons and things; for my present purposes what is common and generic is the feeling of contact.

Later it will be necessary to consider not only what is common and generic but the particular forms of overbelief implied by the expres-

[1] V.R.E., p. 505.

sions chosen. As explained, I have used the word as James used it, but it is worth considering briefly what is implied by the dictionary definition of 'belief in more than is warranted by the evidence'.

The evidence warranted by people's descriptions of their ecstasies is that this is what the experiences felt like to them, and of that only. If they say—I take three examples from the questionnaire group—that ecstasy felt like being borne into heaven, being in touch with the Creator, understanding everything, then we have warrant for believing that for these people it felt like being borne into heaven, being in touch with the Creator, and understanding everything. We have no warrant for believing that these people were borne into heaven, in touch with the Creator, and understood everything. Not even those who most fervently believe in a divine source for religious experience maintain that personal interpretations of such experiences have any validity save for the person who proffers them:

> 'With regard to the special revelations that have been made to the saints, **belief** in them is **not required** by the Church, even when she approves them.' [1]

The general heading to Sections II–V is 'What they said they felt' and in classifying what they said they felt I have been concerned only to elicit what, as James put it, is common and generic beneath the particular forms of overbelief that appear.

It must already be clear that under the general title of *what they said they felt*, some phrases must be entered under more than one heading. Sometimes this is because different headings are implied by different words in a single phrase; sometimes it is because the same words have two or more different and equally appropriate points of entry. I can best illustrate this point, which is an important one for my purposes. with some examples:

EXAMPLE I: 'removed from consideration of earthly things' (Q 14), This phrase is entered under:
Loss of feelings of worldliness, because it is of *earthly* things that consideration is said to be lost.
Loss of feelings of sense, because *consideration* is said to be lost.
Up-words and phrases, with regard to the fact that to be removed from

[1] Poulain, G.I.P., ch. xxi, 2.

consideration of *earthly* things is, by implication, to be removed in an upward direction.[1]

EXAMPLE II: 'great joy bubbling up inside' (Q 49).
This phrase is entered under:
Gain of feelings of joy, because *joy* is specifically mentioned.
Up-words and phrases, because the joy is said to bubble *up*.
Inside-words and phrases, because the bubbling is said to take place *inside*.
Enlargement/improvement words and phrases, because both *great* and *bubbling up* imply something larger than the previous condition.
Intensity, because *bubbling up* implies tumescence. It will be apparent that an implication of intensity will often be present in *enlargement* phrases.

EXAMPLE III: 'soaring up to something you've always wanted, always known was there' (Q 3).
This phrase is entered under:
Gain of feelings of satisfaction, because what is approached is *something you've always wanted*.
Gain of feelings of contact, because *something* is felt to have been approached.
Gain of feelings of knowledge by identification, because what is approached is identified as *something you've always wanted, always known was there*.
Up-words and phrases, justified by *soaring up*.

This method was applied to the literary and religious as well as the questionnaire texts, with only this difference, that in the questionnaire group virtually all phrases used were classified, while in the literary and religious groups there were so many repetitions that to classify all phrases used would have been supererogatory.

Obviously there is room for argument about the right place or places to enter certain phrases. Let us take as an example 'as if being borne into heaven itself' (Q 15). I have entered this phrase under:

Gain of feelings of an ideal place/heaven; gain of feelings of a new life/another world; gain of feelings of joy; gain of feelings of knowledge by identification; up-words and phrases.

[1] Compare 'it will be thought a great absurditie to talke of heaven and point downwarde to the earth.' Thomas Morley. *A Plaine and Easie Introduction to practicall Musicke*, 1597 (quoted by Harding, A.I., p. 83).

Now it could be argued that *heaven* implies salvation, eternity, contact with God; and that it also implies many kinds of loss, such as loss of sorrow, sin, worldliness. But if I am right in supposing that the statements made describe aspects of a range of experiences to any one of which almost all the statements under the various headings could be felt applicable, then many phrases used may well imply many more parts of a putatively full description than they actually state; the consistency of the metaphors used supports this contention and is part of my justification for regarding even almost dead metaphors as significant. But I have still tried to confine the entry of phrases to the headings that seem appropriate in view of what the phrases actually state or *unavoidably* imply. Thus, in the example given above, I have taken *heaven* as unavoidably implying joy in modern speech, but not as unavoidably implying eternity or salvation.

I have tried to be consistent in my treatment of doubtful phrases, and so long as such phrases *are* consistently treated—indeed, so long as all phrases are consistently treated—the patterns of experience shown by the three groups are found to be essentially similar. It should be remembered that one of the main purposes of the analysis is to produce systematic patterns that enable the three groups to be compared with each other. For the present, the headings should be regarded as based on convenience rather than significance.

In addition to the analysis of texts according to triggers and what people said they felt, I have, where possible, noted some factual or putatively factual information.[1]

In the questionnaire group people were asked how often they had known the experience—'in units, in tens, in hundreds?' Their answers will be found in the texts. (The purpose in so framing the question was to set some simple limits to the answers; I did not then know that the most likely result of a question so framed would be a tendency to choose the middle possibility, i.e. *tens*. That most people in fact chose *units* may be taken as evidence of their sincerity.)

In the literary and religious groups evidence as to frequency was seldom available, though sometimes it seems evident that an unique experience is being described. Where however such evidence is

---

[1] I much regret that I did not note the ages of people in the questionnaire group. These ranged from ten years old to over sixty. I have the impression that the answers of adults were in no noticeable way affected by age, but am sorry I cannot confirm this.

available, either from the text or from another source, I have noted
this at the end of the text.

Unfortunately I did not think to ask the people in the questionnaire
group how long their experiences had lasted. Often, however, they
mentioned 'a moment' as did people in the other groups. Where, in all
groups, any statements indicative of duration appear, I have italicized
them.

People in the questionnaire group were asked their religious positions.[1] I do not know the religious positions of most of the people in
the literary group. In the religious group all but one person (Plotinus
—R 4) are Christians.

The categorization of people according to their kind is necessarily
tentative but proved unexpectedly valuable. I first extracted from the
questionnaire group those people who were creative by profession—
writers, artists, etc.—and classified them as *creative*. Of the rest I made
a subjective assessment based on Coleridge's distinction between those
who aim 'almost solely to convey insulated facts' and those who
chiefly seek

> 'to discover and express those connections of things, or those
> relative bearings of fact to fact, from which some more or less general
> law is deducible.'[2]

The latter I have classified as *intellectual*, and to the former I have given
the designation 'O'. The appropriate designation, expressed as 'C'
(*creative*), 'I' (*intellectual*), or 'O', will be found at the head of each text
in the questionnaire group.

Most though not all of the creative people in the questionnaire
group are also intellectuals in the modern sense of the word; they
are all, of course, concerned with expressing the connexions or relative
bearings of things, though not necessarily of fact to fact. In the literary
and religious groups these distinctions are irrelevant, since all people
who have chosen to write down their experiences and communicate
them to the world are to some extent creative.

---

[1] Of the 63 people in the questionnaire group, 19 said that they were atheists or
had no faith and 6 said they were agnostics; 17 were Christians (among whom
6 specified 'C. of E.', 3 'Protestant', and 2 'Catholic'); 4 people said they believed
in God and 2 that they believed in good; there were 3 pantheists, 2 Jews, 2 believers
in reincarnation, and 1 in Zen; 7 people gave statements of belief that I could not
classify.

[2] *Biographia Literaria* (1817; Everyman edn., 1956), ch. xvii, pp. 196–7.

In Appendix C I give sample analyses of half a dozen texts from the questionnaire group. All texts from all groups were similarly analysed.

There follows a list of all the headings used in the analysis, with examples of entries from all groups and some brief notes.

For each group, the number of entries made under each heading in Sections II to V of the analysis (that is, statements of loss and of gain, quasi-physical statements, references to intensity or withdrawal) was expressed as a percentage of the total number of entries in all those sections. Thus for each group there emerged a pattern of the frequency with which different feelings were mentioned (see Table I, Appendix D).

The patterns of all groups proved to be very similar; that is to say, people in the three groups expressed the same sorts of feelings with the same sort of frequency. This can be clearly seen in the bar-charts on pp. 34–6. Here I have simplified the more detailed classification and have grouped together statements which seem to be of a similar kind.[1]

[1] The simplified table on which this bar-chart is based will be found in Appendix D as Table 2. I explain there my justification for this simplification; subsequent tables are drawn up on the same basis as this simplified one.

I. TRIGGERS[1]

Heading	Examples
1. Natural scenery, objects, etc.	fine weather; being in hills near the sea (Q 48)
2. Sexual love	love in its fullest sense, spiritual and physical (Q 31)
3. Childbirth	the first sight of my first baby (Q 28)
4. Exercise, movement	swimming, flying (Q 16)
5. Religion	watching vespers in (a foreign) cathedral (Q 56); the Bodhisatta in the British Museum (Q 26)
6. Art	the Flemish primitive paintings in the National Gallery; any Brandenburg, especially the Sixth (Q 19)
7a. Scientific knowledge	solving mathematical problems (Q 45)
7b. Poetic knowledge	realization of profound truth...like in Greek tragedy (Q 25)
8. Creative work	suddenly able to express something in permanent form (Q 46)
9. Recollection, introspection	Giorgione's *Tempest*...and recollections of that picture—I can call it up (Q 27)
10. 'Beauty'	in a word, beauty (Q 7)
11. Miscellaneous	seeing Stalin and Churchill shaking hands in the Bolshoi Theatre (Q 32); wine at exactly the right moment (Q 48)

[1]Where people have given, as inducing ecstasy, circumstances involving more than one heading, I have made an entry under each of the headings to which the circumstances refer.

Natural is used here in the sense of 'not man-made'.[1] This heading covers all references to country-side, scenery, plants, animals, weather, time of day, etc.

This heading covers both sexual intercourse and 'being in love' without intercourse.

This heading covers both the cases where the person concerned was taking exercise immediately before the ecstasy and also where he was being moved as in a motor-car, aeroplane, boat, etc.

Art with inescapably religious connotations is included here.

This heading covers references to scientific (or exact or neutral or referential) knowledge.

This heading is used when the trigger is an idea without exact reference which is felt to have the compelling force of truth.[2]

This heading is used when ecstasy is said to have been induced by something not physically present at the time; it excludes the prayers and meditations of religion.

This heading was justified by the considerable number of people who said 'beauty' or who used the adjective 'beautiful' of the things that induced ecstasy in them.

Here I entered, from the questionnaire group any mention of circumstances said to induce ecstasy which does not fit into the other headings; and from the other two groups any miscellaneous circumstances I thought might have been influential in inducing the ecstasy.

---

[1] *Natural* was used in this sense by J. S. Mill and defined by him as 'What takes place without the agency, or without the voluntary and intentional agency, of man'; I take this from *The Religion of Nature* by Basil Willey (London, 1957), pp. 11–12.
[2] Where a passage from literature is given as a trigger without its being said or implied to have this force of truth, the trigger is entered under *Art*.

II. *Feelings of loss of*   *Examples*

1. difference	the hard lines round one's individuality are gone (Q 1); undefin'd existence (L 2); (the soul) loses all...distinction of things (R 20)
2. time	complete absence of a sense of specific time (Q 40); far from time (L 12); no consciousness of time (R 8)
3. place	you're not anywhere (Q 34); detached from every earthly thing and place (L 12); I know not where I am (R 12)
4. limitation	transcend your normal limitations (Q 5); when...the flesh (begins) to feel the chain (i.e. afterwards) (L 21); the soul quite transcends the limits of her natural way of existence (R 21)
5. worldliness	removed from consideration of earthly things (Q 14); detached from every earthly thing (L 12); the soul forgets all earthly things (R 14) [1]
6. desire	all human desires and purposes shrivelled (L 13); seeking nought, desiring nought (R 12)
7. sorrow	complete separation from trouble (Q 18); the vicissitudes of life had become indifferent to me (L 26); all my past wretchedness and pain is forgot (R 12)
8. sin	mostly kept from transcendent living by sin (Q 46); as long as one of those half-hours spent by Adam and Eve...before their Disobedience set the clocks ticking (L 23a); there...is...(no) iniquity (R 19)
9. self	a loss of the sense of being yourself (Q 40); I lost myself (L 13); temporary loss of my own identity (R 6)
10. words, images	(i) I don't know how to put it into words (Q 34); the more I seek words ...the more I feel the impossibility of describing the thing by any of our usual images (R 11); (ii) Shirley says nothing...she is quite mute (L 14); the tongue does not speak; except as the abundance of the heart will sometimes permit it (R 2); [2] (iii) hard to distinguish between thought and feeling (L 24); (iv) sense of certitude about nothing I can define (Q 56); each failing sense...grew thrillingly distinct and keen (L 2); she understands, but otherwise than by the senses (R 10a)
11. sense	overwhelming all other senses and superseding thought (Q 38); sensation...melted...thought was not (L 1b); all her powers are at rest (R 10a)

[1] The word *things* is often used in a pejorative sense by ecstatics as referring to what is perceived by and of concern to the animal senses.

[2] This and other examples of involuntary speech and cries are discussed on p. 84.

I have taken *timeless* to imply gain rather than loss since it seems generally to be so intended, e.g. by Q 18 with 'timeless bliss' and by L 11 quoting the phrase 'the timeless moment'.

I have chosen the word *worldliness* to cover those feelings we normally and exclusively associate with our everyday, mundane, temporal life in society, accepting the *Concise Oxford Dictionary's* definition of *worldly* as 'concerned with or devoted to the affairs of this life'.

The questionnaire group provides no entries here; is this because people in our materialistic and post-Freud age seldom look on desire as evil but rather as likely to bring commendable satisfactions?

The single entry in the questionnaire group (and that from a non-conformist Welshman) may remind us of Gladstone's lament: 'Ah, the sense of sin—that is the great want in modern life.' (Lionel A. Tollemache, *Talks with Mr. Gladstone* (London, 1898), p. 96.) On the questionnaire group's paucity of entries in this and the preceding three sections, see pp. 103-4.

Soul as used seems sometimes to be synonymous with the self, sometimes with the *mens*, that 'essence of the soul, the root of its powers or faculties' (Butler: W.M., pp. xlvii–xlviii). Where the self is mentioned (e.g. R 4 speaks of the soul ceasing to be itself) an entry is made here. In other cases I have made a largely intuitive decision as to whether to make an entry here or under *loss of sense*, and can only plead, with St. Teresa, that 'I cannot understand what *mind* is, or how it differs from *soul* or *spirit*. They all seem one to me' (*Life*, ch. xviii, pp. 122-3).

Four kinds of statements are included here: (i) that the ecstatic is unable to describe his feelings; (ii) that the ability or wish to verbalize is lost; (iii) that thought and feeling become one in a way they usually are not; (iv) that while ordinary means of expression are lost, inexpressible knowledge is gained; the entries here refer to the loss rather than the gain which finds its place under 11a of the next section.

Loss of sense is claimed both generally and specifically, e.g. loss of bodily powers, feeling, intellectual capacity. All are subsumed under this single heading.

[3] I have twice when in complete uncertainty entered a phrase both here and under *loss of sense* —L 27 and R 5b.

1. unity, everything	a sense of the oneness of things (Q 20); you understand everything (Q 54); reality...is one thing (L 8); saw nothing and everything (L 27); all the separate notes have melted into one swelling harmony (R 3); I saw and knew the being of all things (R 16)
2. Timelessness, eternity	sensation of timelessness (Q 31); 'timeless moment' (L 11); felt the Eternal (R 3)
3. an ideal place, heaven	as if being borne into heaven itself (Q 15); (comparison with Adam and Eve in Eden) (L 23a); now was I come up in spirit...into the paradise of God (R 9)
4. release	complete sense of liberation (Q 44); new doors...beginning to open—liberation (L 20); glory seemed to open (R 13)
5. a new life, another world	double realization of perfection with life (Q 26); soaring up to something you've always wanted, always known was there (Q 3); the vision of life as she wishes it (L 14); its home, its harbour found (L 21); all the creation gave another smell unto me than before (R 9); it seemed to him that he returned from another world (afterwards) (R 1)
6. satisfaction	complete satisfaction (Q 15); satisfaction (L 5); great satisfaction (R 10a)
7. joy	extreme happiness (Q 59); immense happiness (L 12); exultation—immense joyousness (R 17)
8. salvation, perfection	something being perfected (Q 35); gave me authority over the horrors ...the guilt complexes (L 23b); knew nothing but pureness, innocency and righteousness (R 9)
9. glory	sudden glory (Q 24); pass from gloom to glory (L 2); unspeakable glory—Divine glory (R 13)
10. contact	a sense of being in touch with the Creator (Q 15); communion with something else (Q 27); visitation from the living God (L 1b); had become...part of the truth I sought (L 25); joined to God (R 20); the universe is...a living Presence (R 17)
11a. mystical knowledge	sense of certitude about nothing I can define (Q 56); each failing sense... grew thrillingly distinct and keen (L 2); she understands, but otherwise than by the senses (R 10a)
11b. new knowledge	immensely creative, full of ideas (Q 57); I had only to yield...to discover a poem—I was being told something (L 5); in one quarter of an hour I saw and knew more than if I had been many years together at an university (R 16)
11c. knowledge by identification	in touch with the Creator (Q 15); knowledge of the reality of things (Q 63); the inner and outer meaning of the earth and sky and all that is in them, fit exactly (L 4); I perceived the heavenly godhead (L 22); it appeared to be Divine glory (R 13); I saw that the universe is...a living presence (R 17)
Ineffability	indescribable (Q 25); I have failed to describe it, because language cannot form the thought (L 4); ineffable—impossible fully to describe the experience (R 3)

Included here are both claims to see everything and to see that everything is one.

Whether the changed vision is felt to have been achieved by a change in the self or in the surrounding world or by sight of something wholly other, there is almost always the imputation that what is revealed is what 'ought' habitually to be—as Q 18 put it, 'life should be like this for ever'.

Sometimes the self is said to be perfected—i.e. salvation—sometimes that something or everything is good and perfect.

Glory is an interesting word in an ecstasy context owing to earlier associations with light and fire. I discuss these on pp. 246–7 and explain why I did not think it proper to assume that mentions of *glory* in the texts were necessarily light/fire references.

Entries include all statements in which contact with someone or something is said to be made. I am not concerned here with establishing distinctions between the various second parties to the contact.

'Spiritual apprehension of truths beyond the understanding' says the *Concise Oxford Dictionary of the mystic's belief*, and this is the meaning of *mystical* I accept here. This heading includes those entries also made under *loss of words/images* which claim that while ordinary means of expression are lost, inexpressible knowledge is gained, the reference here being to the gain and not to the loss.

Here come feelings of enhanced mental capacity and of new knowledge which could, at least putatively, be expressed. Often there is no proof that the knowledge claimed *could* be expressed, and sometimes it is, of its nature, inexpressible, e.g. you understand everything to which you turn your mind (Q 54); but the claims are made without reservations, and sometimes they are justified.

Many people felt themselves able to name or recognize what they believed they had encountered in their experience or what they felt it revealed to them. I am not here concerned with the nature of what was felt to have been encountered, recognized or revealed, only with the fact that it was named.

The entries here are those where the experience is said to be, of its nature, indescribable; as opposed to those under *loss of words/images*, where the failure is said to be that of the person and not necessarily because of the nature of the experience. Demonstrably these experiences are *not* ineffable; few kinds of experiences can have been so fully and so consistently described. But such experiences obviously *feel* ineffable, and to say that they are ineffable (or indescribable, etc.) is a typical part of their description.

31

1. Up-words & phrases	a floating sensation (Q 51); heightened awareness (Q 17); unutterable buoyancy (L 2); elevated thoughts (L 1a); walked on air (R 1); the intellect, elevated (R 2)
2. Inside-words & phrases	an enormous bubble swelling inside the chest (Q 55); full of force (Q 31); the hieroglyphics upon the waters seemed to flash through me— filled with an immense and pure emotion (L 5); the fire was within myself (R 17); goodness and power...penetrating me altogether (R 11)
3. Light/heat-words & phrases	sudden flash of an idea (Q 31); whitening, flashing, ebbing light (L 2); wonderful enlightenments (L 20); heavenly lightings passed and repassed in the deeps of his being (R 1); burning with ardent love (R 20)
4. Darkness-words & phrases	leapt clear into the darkness above (L 17a); the brightness of most lucid darkness (R 20)
5. Enlargement/im-provement-words & phrases	transcend your normal limitations, capacity for experience, burst into a wider one (Q 5); largeness of feeling (L 3); the soul...almost bursting with its own emotion (R 3)
6. Pain-words & phrases	so intense in its joy as to be almost painful (Q 38); unbearable knowledge (Q 63); great agony once; and always some terror (L 8); moves me with such sweetness and violence (R 12)
7. Liquidity-words & phrases	bubbling up inside (Q 49); the cup is being filled (Q 35); that spring... bubbling in her heart (L 14); the inspiration flowed...like blood (L 27); like a living fountain, flowing with streams of eternal sweetness (R 20)
8. Peace/calm-words & phrases	complete peace (Q 1); a hush of peace, a soundless calm (L 21); sensations of silence and of rest (R 1)

V. *Intensity, Withdrawal*

1. Intensity	like a great climax which has built up—this thing has been seething inside you and suddenly it comes out (Q 34); like a thundering pulse in my head it strikes (L 9); a rushing together—one swelling harmony— almost bursting (R 3)
2. Withdrawal	a sort of merging into the experience—the hard lines...are gone, one flows over them (Q 1); relaxed quietude and self-dissolving stillness (L 7); she does not spring out of herself by a sudden leap...but gently glides...into the Divinity (R 21)

[1] In suitable cases an example of apparently literal and apparently figurative intention is given from each group.

Two kinds of expression appear here: (i) the ecstatic feels that something is happening inside him, whether spontaneously or through outside influence; (ii) he feels he is inside someone or something else—e.g. engulfed in her God (R 21).

The most striking difference between the questionnaire group and the other two is the questionnaire group's low proportion of entries under this heading; for comments relating to this see pp. 189–90, 246–7, and p. 480.

There are no *darkness* entries for the questionnaire group and only one for the literary group. For reasons given later (see pp. 72–6) I came to the conclusion that *darkness* words and phrases do not relate to the particular kinds of ecstatic experience I am trying to isolate.

Enlargement phrases almost always imply improvement; some *improvement* phrases do not imply enlargement, but they never imply any kind of diminishment.

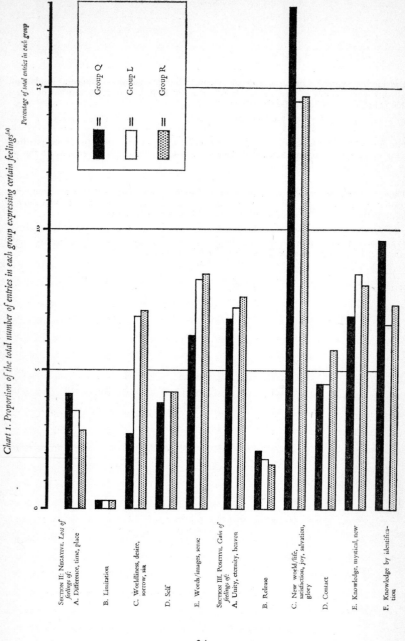

Chart 1. Proportion of the total number of entries in each group expressing certain feelings[a]

Percentage of total entries in each group

Group Q =

Group L =

Group R =

SECTION II: NEGATIVE. Loss of feelings of:
A. Difference, time, place

B. Limitation

C. Worldliness, desire, sorrow, sin

D. Self

E. Words/images, sense

SECTION III. POSITIVE. Gain of feelings of:
A. Unity, eternity, heaven

B. Release

C. New world/life, satisfaction, joy, salvation, glory

D. Contact

E. Knowledge, mystical, new

F. Knowledge by identification

34

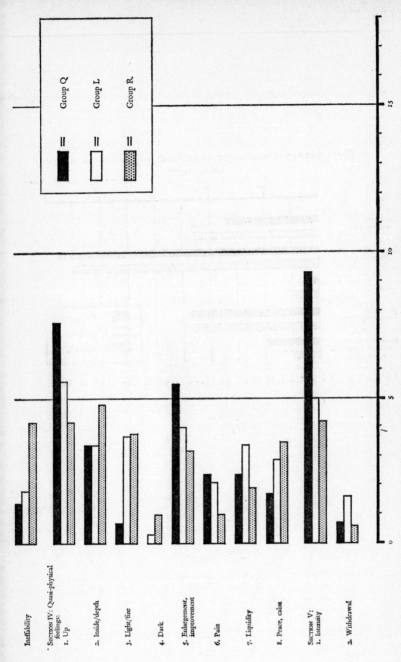

(a) See Table 2, Appendix D, for the figures on which these charts are based.

35

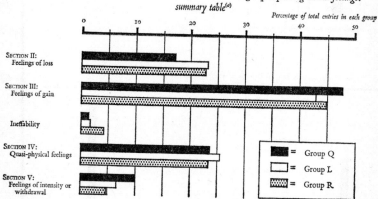

Chart 2. Proportion of the total number of entries in each group expressing certain feelings: summary table[a]

(a) See Table 2, Appendix D, for the figures on which these charts are based.

CHAPTER III

Criteria for Ecstasies

If there are no other kinds of experience of which 114 examples would, when similarly analysed, fall into patterns similar to those I have derived from accounts of ecstasies, then I am justified in drawing from my analyses criteria for ecstasies.

The obvious way to show this would be to collect a number of accounts of other kinds of experience and then show that they would not, when similarly analysed, fall into similar patterns. But I do not think it necessary to do this because I believe the point can easily be made on the basis of common sense.

It is hard to know what feelings it would be fairest to consider as possibly giving results similar to those of ecstasy, but I think that three of the most likely are the feelings aroused by anger, the feelings aroused by worldly pleasure and the feelings aroused, *as a rule*, by sexual intercourse.

Feelings of the last kind are discussed in Chapter XIV, where I hope I have shown that descriptions of the feelings aroused, *as a rule*, by sexual intercourse would, when similarly analysed, almost certainly make a different pattern from that made by descriptions of ecstasies.

Descriptions of feelings of anger do often have much in common with descriptions of ecstatic feelings, particularly where what I have called quasi-physical feelings are concerned. But even here there are considerable divergencies, and other sections of the analysis are barely relevant. Certainly one might find an occasional description of anger that could be fully analysed under my headings: an angry person might feel himself lost to his surroundings and to reason as he swelled with emotion that finally burst out. But this is a devised not a typical description of anger, and however many genuine descriptions of anger are amassed and analysed, such analyses would not result in charts similar to those of my three groups; it is improbable that there would be any entries for feelings of knowledge, of joy, of salvation, of

37

contact, of oneness. Nor, of course, would the triggers to anger fall into the same range as the triggers to ecstasy.

Though ecstasies are undoubtedly pleasurable, it is not to be supposed that any and all accounts of experiences of pleasure would, when analysed, give the same results as ecstasies. Descriptions of the feelings of worldly pleasure certainly would not. Loss of the world is a very usual feeling of ecstasies, and the world that is lost is variously described, by people in the groups, as a place of everyday desires and purposes, animal being, cares, commerce, ridiculous desires and purposes, conventionalities, worldly enjoyments, a place where there are crowds and people can 'get at you', a place of cares and vicissitudes and disasters.

Now while some of these things are obviously 'bad', others can give much pleasure. From most of them derive the pleasures of social life and worldly success, of making money and acquiring possessions. But though one could, as with anger, devise or possibly find descriptions of feelings of worldly pleasure that could be analysed in an ecstasy pattern, it does not seem probable that some twenty descriptions of worldly pleasure would give a pattern principally characterized by feelings of joy of a kind that includes feelings of a new life, another world, salvation; or by feelings of new or mystical knowledge, or of unity or eternity. Nor would the triggers to feelings of worldly pleasure fall into the same range as that of the triggers to ecstasies.

The likelihood that the pattern revealed by the analyses refers uniquely to the kinds of feelings I am calling ecstasies seems to me sufficiently great to justify the assumption that this is so, and to allow the conclusion that the people in the three groups were speaking of feelings that can, for many purposes, be treated as similar to each other and different from other kinds of feelings.[1] In particular it seems likely that they can be treated as a distinct and largely homogeneous class for the purpose of working out how and by what they are usually induced, what results they have, and what are their relations to other kinds of experience.

I propose therefore to use the information made available by the analyses as a basis for some tentative generalizations along these lines, and at the same time to identify the main varieties of ecstatic experience.

In attempting this I shall draw, as far as possible, on the material

[1] This general conclusion is not invalidated by the presence of a few doubtful texts which will gradually be commented upon and, where proper, discarded.

supplied by my texts, since these experiences, with a few exceptions, I feel justified in calling ecstasies. But I shall also want to consider experiences not included in these groups, and so must state my criteria for deciding that any experience outside them may be counted as an ecstasy. These criteria must, of course, be drawn from my analyses.

It cannot be demanded that all experiences which are to be accepted as ecstasies must have in common at least one characteristic which can be shown to be present in all experiences in the groups, which has justified giving the name *ecstasy* to all these experiences, and which would justify withholding the name from any experience that lacked it. Having shown that ecstasies form a family or group with family likenesses that overlap, what can be demanded of any other experience is that it should show sufficient of these family likenesses to make it reasonable to treat it as belonging to the group called ecstasies rather than to any other group.[1]

The characteristics of the family or group of experiences I am calling ecstasies are shown by the statistical tables (Appendix D, Tables 1 and 2) and by the bar-chart on p.p.34-6. If the arguments on the first pages of this chapter be accepted, these are not the characteristics of groups of other kinds of experiences. The question is, what characteristics should we demand of any single experience to justify calling it an ecstasy?

There is not, in fact, in the three groups, any single characteristic capable of being brought out by verbal analysis which is common to all these experiences and can be shown to be unique to them. But there are many features characteristic of many or most of these experiences, and the more of these that were present in any other experience the more we should feel justified in treating that experience as an ecstasy.

On the material so far presented we should seek, in any described experience, evidence to justify the name *ecstasy* in what was said about the conditions in which the experience took place and what it felt like.

As already explained, I am giving the name *trigger* to the circumstances in which an ecstasy takes place, assuming—as was assumed by everyone in the questionnaire group and by some people in the other

---

[1] 'We are inclined to think that there must be something in common to all games, say, and that this common property is the justification for applying the general term "game" to the various games; whereas games form a *family* the members of which have family likenesses. Some of them have the same nose, others the same eyebrows and others again the same way of walking; and these likenesses overlap.' Ludwig Wittgenstein, *The Blue and Brown Books* (Oxford, 1958), p. 17.

groups—that certain circumstances play a causal part in inducing ecstasies. Triggers were named in 59 out of the 60 texts in the questionnaire group, and in 57 (95 per cent.) of these cases could be categorized under ten headings: nature, sexual love, childbirth, exercise and movement, religion, art, scientific knowledge, poetic knowledge, creative work, recollection and introspection, and 'beauty'. The circumstances in which the experiences took place were indicated in all texts in the literary group and in all cases fell wholly or partly under the same ten headings. In the religious group, the circumstances were indicated in only 10 texts, which in 8 cases fell under the same ten headings. But the experiences of this group are, in any case, shown by the statistical analyses to be similar to those of the other two groups.

Thus an experience need not be rejected as an ecstasy only because the circumstances in which it took place are not described. But in order to err on the side of strictness I will not, in general, call any experience outside the groups an ecstasy where the circumstances in which it took place are not given; or, where such circumstances *are* given, if they do not fall under one or more of the ten headings I have used in my analyses.

There are a couple of reasonable exceptions to be made. In some cases a person may not indicate the circumstances in which an experience took place or may indicate circumstances that do not fall under my headings; but may say that this experience was similar to another or others that did take place under what I accept as trigger conditions and which were acceptable as ecstasies. I would accept any such experience as an ecstasy.[1] Then one or other of the sets of circumstances that I have classified as *miscellaneous* in my analysis may be shown to have been present in several other experiences in all other respects acceptable as ecstasies; the range of common triggers may be enlarged by such cases.[2] For the present the more common trigger situations must be accepted as such because they have been named as inducing ecstasy by several people in the questionnaire group and largely confirmed by the literary group who had similar experiences in similar conditions.

I shall sometimes want to refer to experiences which are in many ways similar to ecstasies but which are deliberately self-induced or

---

[1] Two examples, one from Wordsworth, the other from Toynbee, are to be found on p. 114.

[2] This applies, for example, to ruins; see pp. 112 and n.

induced by drugs or which arise when the subject is in a morbid condition of health. I shall not use the name *ecstasy* without qualification for any such experience, but shall call it, if it seems in context to be an ecstasy, a self-induced, drug-induced, or morbidly-induced ecstasy.

What ecstatic experiences feel like were described in the following terms:

feelings of new life, satisfaction, joy, salvation, purification, glory; new and/or mystical knowledge; loss of words, images, sense; knowledge by identification; unity, eternity, heaven; loss of worldliness, desire, sorrow, sin; up-feelings; contact; enlargement and/or improvement; loss of self; inside-feelings; loss of difference, time, place; light and/or heat feelings; peace, calm, liquidity feelings; ineffability; release; pain-feelings; dark-feelings; loss of limitation.[1]

No one of these feelings is named in all experiences in all groups, or even in all experiences in any one group. One cannot, then, insist on the presence of any one of them before accepting an experience as an ecstasy.

But it does seem reasonable to insist, on the basis of the analyses, that certain groups of these feelings be mentioned in certain proportions. In each of the three groups nearly half the entries under the general heading of *what they said they felt* are statements of feelings of gain; about one-fifth are of feelings of loss; and about one quarter are of quasi-physical feelings.[2] In the literary and religious groups, which contain more entries per person than does the questionnaire group,[3] only in one case is there only one entry under *feelings of gain*. So when considering as possible ecstasies experiences spontaneously communicated in writing I shall demand, in order to call them ecstasies, that they contain statements which, when analysed as my texts were analysed, would provide two entries under the heading *feelings of gain*, and at least one entry either under the heading *feelings of loss* or under the heading *quasi-physical feelings*.

[1] The order is that of frequency of mention of the mean of the three groups. Of the 112 people in the three groups, over half mentioned feelings of: new life, etc.; knowledge by identification; new and/or mystical knowledge; loss of words, etc.; unity, etc.; and up-feelings. Between a quarter and a half mentioned feelings of: contact; loss of worldliness, etc.; enlargement, improvement; loss of self; inside-feelings; loss of difference, etc.; light/fire feelings. See Tables 4*a* and 4*b*, Appendix D.

[2] See Table 2, Appendix D.

[3] See p. 13n.

Thus any spontaneously communicated experience, to be accepted as an ecstasy, must claim at least two of the following feelings:

unity, eternity, heaven; new life, satisfaction, joy, salvation, perfection, glory; contact; new or mystical knowledge,

and at least one of the following feelings:

loss of difference, time, place; of worldliness, desire, sorrow, sin; of self; of words and/or images and/or sense; up-feelings; inside-feelings; light and/or heat feelings; enlargement and/or improvement feelings; liquidity feelings; feelings of calm, peace.[1]

But since so many fewer entries were made for the questionnaire group I shall, when considering answers given to questions, demand only one statement of gain and one of either loss or quasi-physical feelings.

If however a person says of an experience that it was similar to others that do fulfil my criteria, I should naturally accept it as an ecstasy even though its own description was deficient in some of these requirements. I will not of course accept as an ecstasy any experience claiming feelings inconsistent with any of my headings, such as feelings of dryness, constriction, etc.

How far can the fact that a person calls an experience an ecstasy be taken as indicating that it is an ecstasy in my sense? From what has already been said (see p. 6) it is clear that mention of 'ecstasy' by an informed Catholic makes it unlikely that the experience in question is ecstasy in my sense.[2] Owing to varied meanings of the word in the past, its use before contemporary times is no sure indication that it is being used in my sense. Despite some contemporary debasement of the word, I do think that a contemporary use in a reasonably serious context is likely to refer to an experience of this kind; that my adjective *transcendent* was not prepotent in conveying this sense is suggested by the fact that similar results were obtained in a later though much smaller questionnaire, using *ecstasy* without qualification.[3] But though contemporary use of the word *ecstasy* may be taken as an indication that this kind of experience is intended, I shall

---

[1] I have excluded the following which were negligible entries in all groups: feelings of release, of loss of limitation, dark-feelings, pain-feelings. I have also excluded knowledge by identification; see pp. 116–17.

[2] But it should be noted that the two Catholics in the questionnaire group, Q 44 and Q 63, apparently do not know this special meaning and take *ecstasy* to mean the kind of experiences I am investigating.

[3] See Appendix J.

not take it as a sufficient indication but shall expect other criteria to be satisfied.

It is worth considering how far the experiences in the groups show the defining characteristics I originally gave for the word *ecstasy* (see p. 5). *Ecstasy*, I supposed, referred to experiences characterized by being joyful, transitory, unexpected, rare, valued, and extraordinary to the point of often seeming as if derived from a praeternatural source. I think there can be little doubt that most if not all the people in the questionnaire group would have accepted this definition, and that nearly all the experiences in the other two groups are properly named by a word so defined. To obtain empirical confirmation of the qualities of rarity and transitoriness is, in particular, useful when considering whether other experiences should or should not be treated as ecstasies.

In the literary and religious groups one can sometimes gather, from internal or external evidence, how often the experience in question has been known, and often it is implicit that an unique experience is being described. In the questionnaire group, out of 58 people[1]

29 (50 per cent.) claimed the experience in units; of these, 6 people claimed it once only, 4 people twice only.

22 (38 per cent.) claimed the experience in tens; of these, 9 people specified an occurrence of 25 times or less.

7 (12 per cent.) claimed the experience in hundreds or constantly.[2]

Ecstasies are, then, typically rare, and I shall not treat as ecstasy any experience outside the groups which is said to be frequent or which is said or implied to be the normal consequence of contact with a trigger·

The people in the questionnaire group were not asked how long their experiences had lasted but sometimes they gave indications of duration as did some people in the other groups. In all, such indications were given by 31 people, and of these 20 (65 per cent.) gave a moment (or an instant or a split second, etc.) as the duration of their experience. The other durations named were: a very short time (2 people), quarter of an hour, ten minutes to half an hour, half an hour, half an hour to an hour, an hour, a summer evening till dusk, and a day or two; two people spoke both of a moment and a longer period—one of half an hour, the other of an hour.

From this it appears that the duration of an ecstasy is unlikely to be

---

[1] I forgot to put this question to two people.
[2] For a possible explanation of this claim, see p. 97.

more than an hour and is most likely to be a moment. I should, then, be predisposed to regard as ecstasies experiences said to last only a moment.[1]

I shall, then, on the results of the analyses treat as ecstasies almost all experiences in the three groups. Outside the groups I shall treat as ecstasies experiences conforming to the criteria stated above, that is, experiences taking place under common trigger conditions whose descriptions include at least two of the gain-feelings of my headings and at least one either of the loss-feelings or of the quasi-physical feelings; and whose occurrence, if given, is said to be infrequent, and whose duration, if given, is said to be short.

My description of ecstatic experience is intended to apply to all ecstasies whether they have a religious content or not. Most descriptions of mystical experience refer only to religious experiences—taking *religious* to mean, here, having a content claimed to supply or correspond with or justify religious belief. As I have explained, the term *mystical experience* includes though it does not correspond with the term *ecstasy* as I am using it. But it may still be interesting to compare my description with some descriptions of religious mystical experience, and of these probably the best-known is William James's description of what he calls 'mystical states'.

James cites four 'marks' that an experience should have in order to 'justify us in calling it mystical for the purpose of the present lectures';[2] these marks are,

1. Ineffability, which James calls a 'negative' mark. 'In this peculiarity mystical states are more like states of feeling than like states of intellect.' The subject says that the mystical state 'defies expression, that no adequate report of its content can be given in words.'
2. Noetic quality: 'mystical states seem to those who experience them to be also states of knowledge. They are states of insight into depths of truth unplumbed by the discursive intellect.'

'These two characters', says James, 'will entitle any state to be called

---

[1] For a possible explanation of the discrepancy between the comparatively frequent mention of a moment and the occasional mention of longer periods, see pp. 57–63.

[2] V.R.E., pp. 371–2.

mystical, in the sense in which I use the word.' He adds two other marks, 'less sharply marked' but 'usually found' which are:

3. Transiency: 'Except in rare instances, half an hour, or at most an hour or two, seems to be the limit'. [1]
4. Passivity: Although the oncoming of mystic states can be voluntarily facilitated, once the characteristic sort of consciousness has set in, 'the mystic feels as if his own will were in abeyance'.

If we take only the first two and more important of these marks, noetic quality and ineffability, we may reasonably represent them, in terms of my headings, as *new and/or mystical knowledge* and by either *loss of words, images, sense* or by *ineffability*. We find these mentioned in combination (together with other mentions) by 5 out of 60 people in the questionnaire group, by 19 out of 30 people in the literary group, and by 15 out of 24 people in the religious group. Among people in the religious group who would not qualify, by this test, as having 'mystic states' are a clergyman (R 3) whose experience is cited by James as being of this kind, another man (R 6) also cited by James as having an experience of this kind, and St. Francis of Sales (R 21), whose experience is cited by Butler as that of a representative Catholic mystic. [2]

Thus though James may well be justified in claiming that the two marks of ineffability and noetic quality 'will entitle any state to be called mystical' for his purpose, it appears that there are, in fact, states he would accept as mystical which do not show these characteristics. States showing these characteristics may, if they fulfil other criteria too, fairly be called ecstasies; but James's description of mystical states would not suffice for a description of ecstasies.

Leuba, a sceptic in matters of religion, defines mystical experience as

'any experience taken by the experiencer to be a contact (not through the senses, but "immediate," "intuitive") or union of the self with a larger-than-self, be it called the World-Spirit, God, the Absolute, or otherwise.' [3]

Contact is often spoken of as if it were the keynote of religious experience; Poulain states that the real difference between ordinary

---

[1] James does not point out, which seems as apparent from his texts as from mine, how often the duration is said to be a moment or an instant or a second.
[2] W.M., p. 5.   [3] P.R.M., p. 1.

prayer and mystical states is that in the latter '[God] makes us feel that we really enter into communication with Him'.[1] But a feeling of contact is not present in all religious experiences accepted as mystical (that of St. Ignatius Loyola (R 15), for instance, has no feeling of contact); nor do all theologians accept a feeling of contact as a necessary characteristic of mystical states. Butler, for instance, says that 'Poulain is mistaken in making such experience [i.e. "real experimental perception of God's presence"] the characteristic feature of all grades of infused contemplation and of all mystical states'. Though some other theologians agree with Poulain, there are, says Butler, 'many experiences certainly mystical without such direct sense of God'.[2]

More, Leuba's description does not cover experiences he himself adduces as being of the same kind as religious experiences, such as the experience of Tennyson when eating a mutton-chop after a period of vegetarianism—'I shall never forget the sensation. I never felt such joy in my blood.'[3] Leuba's explanation, that Tennyson, had he been ignorant of the cause of his feelings, would have classed this experience with his religious, mystical illuminations, seems to suggest that feelings of contact are no more than a matter of overbelief. But that this is not so is borne out by the people in the questionnaire group who, in experiences wholly without religious overbelief and often themselves without religion, still have feelings of contact. One must say of Leuba's description that while experiences that conform with it may often be ecstasies in my sense, there are many ecstasies (as there are many experiences accepted as religious mystical experiences) that it does not cover.

I do not find that I can equate my criteria for ecstasies with anyone else's criteria for mystical states. I can only say that experiences that fulfil the criteria stated in this chapter are, for my purposes, ecstasies, and that I shall draw on such experiences, as well as on my texts, in trying to establish what I can about the range of experiences I am calling ecstasies.

[1] G.I.P., ch. v, 3.   [2] W.M., p. xliv and p. xlv.
[3] P.R.M., pp. 214-15.

PART TWO

CHAPTER IV

Intensity and Withdrawal

On the basis of their far greater incidence[1] I have accepted tumescent experiences as the norm among the texts I have examined and as my principal subject for study; it is such experiences that I call intensity ecstasies. Out of 114 texts, only six showed clearly and exclusively the characteristic phrases I associate with what I call withdrawal ecstasies, the phrases about slow and gentle merging, melting, liquefying, dissolving, usually into something else.[2]

There are however four texts in which both withdrawal *and* intensity phrases occur—the texts of Q 5 from the questionnaire group, of Joël and of Emily Brontë from the literary group (L 9 and L 21), and of Louis of Blois from the religious group (R 20).

In the case of Q 5, the contradiction is apparent, not real. It is clear, on reading the text, that this woman is contrasting a single withdrawal experience with more usual experiences of intensity ecstasy; as will become increasingly clear, many people enjoy a wide range of experiences which they regard as basically similar.

But in the other cases both intensity and withdrawal phrases appear in single texts. And it will be useful to examine these apparent anomalies since withdrawal ecstasies (though not my main subject) are of considerable interest and it is impossible fully to study intensity ecstasies without frequent reference to them.

Louis of Blois uses *first* intensity phrases and *later* withdrawal phrases—first, 'burning with ardent love...carried above itself', then 'liquefied by love, it melts away into...' I have no other example of this order of phrases and no explanation of it.[3]

Both Joël and Emily Brontë, however, precede intensity phrases

[1] See pp. 19–20.
[2] These texts are Q 1, L 1b, L 7, L 13, L 15, R 21. For the relevant phrases, see p. 469 of the content analyses, Appendix B.
[3] But see p. 175n.

with withdrawal phrases. First comes 'lulling to sleep' (L 9); 'a hush of peace, a soundless calm descends; the struggle of distress and fierce impatience ends' (L 21). Then come the intensity phrases: 'like a thundering pulse in my head it strikes' (L 9); 'measuring the gulf it stoops and dares the final bound' (L 21). In both cases it seems that what begins as withdrawal, as detumescent experience ends as intensity, as tumescent experience.

Two other texts may be relevant in this context, though the phrases used were not sufficiently indicative of withdrawal for me to have entered them under that heading in the analyses. Levi speaks of 'a great feeling of peace' followed by 'all of a sudden... a flow of fulfilment' (L 12). Charlotte Brontë describes the ecstatic as having 'a still, deep, inborn delight' followed by the figurative climb to the heights where 'the swift glory spreads out, sweeping and kindling' (L 14).

Four texts, then, describe ecstatic experiences which seem to take the form of an initial withdrawal or detumescent experience followed by an intensity or tumescent experience. In three of these cases, those of Joël, Levi, and Charlotte Brontë, it is clear that the whole process is involuntary. In Emily Brontë's case I wonder whether the initial part of the process, that of withdrawal, may not be self-induced.

Emily Brontë says that this experience happens 'every night'. Ecstasies are typically rare (see p. 43). Emily Brontë may be unusual in experiencing ecstasy more often than other people or she may be exaggerating the frequency with which she knows it. But it is also possible that she would try deliberately to induce withdrawal ecstasy, whether for its own sake or in the hope that intensity ecstasy, which cannot be induced, might follow. This seems to be a fairly common procedure among mystics.

There are, says Underhill,

'[two] complementary modes of apprehending that which is One. A. The usually uncontrollable, definitely outgoing, ecstatic experience; the attainment of Pure Being, or "flight to God." B. The more controllable ingoing experience'. [1]

Her first mode corresponds with what I have called approach by intensity, her second with what I have called approach by withdrawal. She continues:

'Yet it is probable...that these two experiences, in their most sub-

[1] E.U: M., p. 304.

lime forms, are but opposite aspects of one while... In that consummation of love which Ruysbroeck has called "the peace of the
summits" they meet'. [1]

Underhill tells her readers how to achieve contemplation, the first
step on the controllable road to experiences which are usually, in my
terms, withdrawal ecstasies. Her directions are so clear, so explicit
and, in my present context, so significant, that it is worth quoting
them at some length:

'All that is asked is that we shall look for a little time, in a special
and undivided manner, at some simple, concrete, and external thing.
This object of our contemplation may be almost anything we please:
a picture, a statue, a tree, a distant hillside, a growing plant, running
water, little living things.[2] ...Wilfully yet tranquilly refuse the messages which countless other aspects of the world are sending... Do
not think, but as it were pour out your personality towards it: let
your soul be in your eyes. Almost at once, this new method of perception will reveal unsuspected qualities in the external world. First,
you will perceive about you a strange and deepening quietness; a
slowing down of our feverish mental time. Next, you will become
aware of a heightened significance, an intensified existence in the
thing at which you look... It seems as though the barrier between its
life and your own, between subject and object, had melted away.
You are merged with it, in an act of true communion: and you *know*
the secret of its being...in a way which you can never hope to
express.' [3]

The description is of an experience that is, in my terms, a withdrawal
ecstasy. Thought is stilled, subject and object melt into one; there is
Emily Brontë's hush of peace as she watches the night sky. Joël's
lulling to sleep as he lies beside the sea. The experience, up to this point,
may be readily induced by anyone who cares to try the experiment.
But, insists Underhill,

'I do not suggest that this simple experiment is in any sense to
be equated with the transcendental contemplation of the mystic. Yet
it exercises on a small scale... the same natural faculties... But whilst

[1] E.U: M., p. 304.
[2] Notice that the examples of 'almost anything we please' are all what the
questionnaire and literary groups have shown to be common triggers. It is not
explained why we should not choose for our 'simple, concrete, and external
thing(s)' say, an advertisement, a chair, a suitcase.
[3] E.U: M., pp. 301–2.

the contemplation of Nature entails an outgoing towards somewhat indubitably external to us, and has as its material the world of sensible experience: the contemplation of Spirit...requires a deliberate refusal of the messages of the senses, an ingoing or "introversion" of our faculties, a "journey towards the centre".... In mystical language he [*sc.* the mystic] must "sink into his nothingness": into that blank abiding place where busy, clever Reason cannot come.' [1]

Butler quotes a passage from St. Gregory which shows what is presumably, in Underhill's terms, the approach to 'the transcendental contemplation of the mystic':

'And so the first step is that it collect itself within itself (recollection); the second, that it consider what its nature is so collected (introversion); the third, that it rise above itself and yield itself to the intent contemplation of its invisible Maker (contemplation). But the mind cannot recollect itself unless it has first learned to repress all phantasmata of earthly and heavenly images, and to reject and spurn whatever sense impressions present themselves to its thoughts, in order that it may seek within itself as it is without these sensations.' [2]

If we are to accept Underhill, it would seem that 'ordinary people' can achieve an inferior state of contemplation by concentration on a suitable external object, while religious mystics achieve a superior condition by deliberate introversion. But leaving aside judgements as to the comparative value of experiences gained by one or other of these methods, it is not in fact the case that the religious mystics necessarily use the one method and 'ordinary people' the other.

St. Teresa, for instance, says that she could not attain the first stage of prayer by use of her imagination, like some people 'who can induce recollection by calling up mental images'.[3] She herself 'found it helpful to look at fields, water, or flowers',[4] to take a walk in the country,[5] found 'a book is useful' and was 'fond of pictures' as means of bringing this state about.[6]

In contrast, Butler compares with the passage from St. Gregory

[1] E.U: M., pp. 302–3.　　　　　　　　[2] W.M., p. 70.
[3] *Life.* ch. ix, p. 68.　　　　　　　　[4] Ibid.
[5] Ibid., ch. xi, p. 82.
[6] Ibid., p. 68. Notice that St. Teresa's pre-conditions, like Underhill's, are all common trigger situations.

quoted above one from Richard Jefferies which, as he says, it strikingly resembles:

'Sometimes I have concentrated myself, and driven away by continued will all sense of outward appearances, looking straight with the full power of my mind inwards on myself. I find "I" am there; an "I" I do not wholly understand or know—something is there distinct from earth and timber, from flesh and bones. Recognising it, I feel on the margin of a life unknown...on the verge of powers which if I could grasp would give me an immense breadth of existence'. [1]

It seems clear that both the religious and the non-religious can induce such states as those I call withdrawal ecstasies either by interior contemplation or by contemplation of a suitable external object. There seems to be agreement that such acts of withdrawal or contemplation can be deepened with practice. But the well-known fact that eastern mystics practise disciplines to achieve their chosen mystical experiences —which are usually, I believe, of the kind I have called withdrawal experiences—makes it essential for Christians to show that it is something other than the eastern mystical states that Christians achieve by these means.

Thus Butler, commenting on the passage from Jefferies quoted above, says that its likeness to the passage from St. Gregory

'shows that the process is no Asiatic or neo-Platonic infusion, but the natural process whereby the soul tries to enter into itself and get into touch with higher realities.' [2]

Underhill also takes pains to point out that the process she advises is 'not an opportunity of pretty and pantheistic meditation'.[3]

The Christian mystic is in duty bound to prevent the withdrawal from becoming too deep. If the introversion goes too far, it can lead only to what Inge calls 'the emptiness of the undifferentiated Godhead' [4] and of which Kirk writes,

'And when...Cassian introduces the phrase "prayer without images," and characterises it as a condition in which the mind is void, of "every image of the divinity, every memory of things said, every picture of things done, every impress or experience of every kind,"

---

[1] W.M., p. 230.
[2] Ibid.
[3] E.U: M., p. 301.
[4] C.M., p. 70.

we have reached the threshold of a point of view from which spiritual vacancy and spiritual fulness are almost indistinguishable.' [1]

This might seem to be Underhill's 'consummation of love' in which the two modes of approach meet (see p. 49 above), but generally Christian writers insist that some degree of consciousness must be retained. Inge says that for Indian mystics the highest stage is one of absolute inertness, knowing nothing whatsoever;[2] this 'introspective Mysticism' or 'Asiatic Mysticism' or 'Asiatic nihilism' as he variously calls it, he regards as a *via negativa*, natural in the break-up of civilization the medieval Christian mystics knew, but 'foreign to the temper of Europe' and properly giving way to 'energetic and full-blooded activity in the Renaissance and Reformation'. Inge considers that St. Teresa's teaching about passivity and the prayer of quiet falls into this negative and quietist error, and that St. John of the Cross took this negative road. ' We must be conscious of ourselves in God, and conscious of ourselves in ourselves,' he insists,[3] and objects, as do other Christian writers, to the mystics' use of phrases that could imply total absorption, total self-loss, total annihilation.[4]

Withdrawal ecstasy may, then, be achieved naturally or be self-induced. To learn to achieve it is a matter of practice,[5] and practice can deepen the degree of withdrawal achieved; but Christians may not so far lose themselves as to lose all sense of their own personalities or all mental capacities, though they accuse oriental mystics of doing so and admit that this fault has been committed by certain Christian mystics.

But, as the four texts under consideration show, after an initial approach by withdrawal an intensity ecstasy may supervene, and that an intensity ecstasy *should* supervene would seem to be the hope of many who deliberately practise this method. To follow St. Teresa's stages of prayer is in many points to be reminded of the experiences described by Emily Brontë and the other people in question.

After St. Teresa's first stage—the one induced by a walk in the country, a book, a picture, contemplation of natural objects (see p. 50 above)—comes the second, the prayer of quiet, where the soul comes

---

[1] V.G., p. 199.   [2] C.M., p. 113 et seq.   [3] Ibid., p. 170.
[4] Compare Poulain's strictures, quoted on p. 59 and p. 123.
[5] Notice, in text L 15, Daniel Deronda's speculation on 'how far it might be possible habitually to shift his centre, till his own personality would be no less outside him than the landscape'.

into touch with the supernatural, achieves joy and calm, and begins
to lose the desire for earthly things. To this state, she says, the soul
could not possibly attain by its own efforts.[1] She is emphatic about
the limitations of human effort in procuring mystical conditions:

'Anyone who tries to pass on [from the first stage] and raise his
spirit to taste the pleasures that are denied him will, in my opinion,
lose in a double sense',

by which, as her editor explains, she means she will lose the prayer
of recollection and fail to gain the prayer of quiet.[2] Of her major
visionary experiences she writes,

'however much I desire and strive for it, and annihilate myself to
get it, it is only when His Majesty pleases... that I can attain even a
single spark of it.' [3]

But St. Teresa did find that when she had recollected herself so as to
reach the first stage of prayer, other states, independent of her efforts,
might follow. There is the joy and quiet of the second stage (which
most people accept as attainable by effort), and this, I suggest, is similar
to Emily Brontë's 'hush of peace' and 'soundless calm', to Levi's 'great
feeling of peace', etc. Then follows St. Teresa's third stage which is,
as she describes it, a state of tumescence:

'on the point of dying the death he desires...takes unutterable delight
in the enjoyment of its agony...a glorious bewilderment, a heavenly
madness...The soul...is in a sweet unrest, and cannot contain itself.' [4]

[1] *Life*, ch. xiv, p. 98. There is apparently much dispute among theologians as to
whether any state of prayer that can be attained by one's own efforts can properly
be called mystical; see Butler: W.M., p. xv et seq. St. Teresa took the view that
one can only dispose oneself to receive supernatural prayer, not achieve it by one's
own efforts, and so speaks of her second stage as supernatural prayer. But this
would seem to correspond with the stage which, according to the people quoted
earlier, *can* be achieved by one's own efforts.

[2] Ibid, ch. xii, p. 85 and note.

[3] Ibid, ch. xxxix, p. 304. Notice of St. Teresa's use of the decried phrase about
self-annihilation.

[4] Ibid., ch. xvi, pp. 112–13. This, says St. Teresa, is the state in which true wisdom is acquired, a state in which she once suddenly composed some stanzas. We
shall later have ample evidence that inspiration or a feeling that wisdom is
acquired takes place at a stage of ecstasy universally regarded as less than the
greatest; we may contrast this with the complete non-productiveness of the
latest stages, whether achieved by intensity or by the *via negativa* of withdrawal,
and may begin to wonder whether we have here some part of the European
Christian's abhorrence of these conditions.

This third stage of St. Teresa's we may, I suggest, equate with the later stages in the experiences of Joël, Levi, and the two Brontës, where, after calm and peace, feelings of tumescence are described. St. Teresa's third stage is followed by the prayer of union, the state of complete absorption described in text R 10b. This, I suggest, is what lay on the other side of Emily Brontë's 'final bound', Joël's state in which 'the world exales in the soul and the soul dissolves in the world', the meeting point of the two modes posited by Underhill.

In so far as the experiences discussed here consist of the attainment (whether deliberately or involuntarily) of a state of calm followed by tumescent ecstasy, capable of reaching a climax of total self-loss, St. Teresa's experiences are similar to those of Joël and Emily Brontë; and to those of Levi and Charlotte Brontë in that initially achieved calm is succeeded by tumescent climax, though not to the point of total self-loss. The initial state can, as has been shown, be self-induced, and there is no reason why Emily Brontë should not have succeeded in inducing it 'every night'; but that it should every night have been succeeded by intensity ecstasy is distinctly unusual.[1]

The fact that withdrawal ecstasies can be self-induced should not obscure the fact that they may arise spontaneously, and may for some people (though not for most of the people of my texts) be a more usual form of ecstatic experience than intensity ecstasy. I think that this may be the case with Koestler (L 7).

Koestler identifies his experience with Freud's 'oceanic feeling' and says that it is the opposite of Moral or Chronic Indignation. Q 44, on the other hand, said that the opposite of his ecstatic feeling was ennui.

---

[1] I had shared what seemed to be the general assumption that eastern mystics were content with deep withdrawal ecstasies and did not hope, as Christians do, that initial withdrawal would be succeeded by intensity ecstasy. That I was wrong seems to be shown by a recent article which states that for Zen Buddhists 'the state of objectlessness...is not the final one; an ancient Master warns us not to mistake the state of unconsciousness or objectlessness for the truth. While in this state, however, you happen to hear a sound or perceive an object, and then, all of a sudden, the whole thing bursts upon you: you have at last touched the ultimate reality...crossed the final barrier.' (A Chinese Zen Master quoted by Richard Rumbold in *Encounter*, January 1959.) This and other statements in Mr. Rumbold's article suggest that for Zen Buddhists self-induced withdrawal ideally leads to momentary intensity ecstasy. He says of his own experience, 'One has to learn to die—to oneself and to thought, to the world and everything in it—and out of the dying embers came—to unitive spark! A cry, a shout, a sudden interjection—and the spirit is released from its prison, and in the illuminating moment everything stands open to its gaze.'

So far as intensity ecstasies are concerned, Q 44 is undoubtedly right.[1]

But Koestler knows what he feels, and if he says that for him indignation seems to be the opposite of feelings which I accept as ecstatic, then I must try to find out what he means.

An obvious suggestion is that Koestler's experience should not be counted as an ecstasy in my sense. I believe that it should be and that what Koestler describes is a spontaneously achieved withdrawal ecstasy, rare in my texts but not difficult to find elsewhere.

This is how Koestler describes his 'opposite' feeling, his state of chronic indignation:

'I can feel, during an attack, the infusion of adrenalin into the bloodstream, the craving of the muscles, flooded with blood-sugar, for violent action. As the case may be, you begin to tremble, or throw a choleric fit, or write a revolutionary tract, or start growing an ulcer.'

The indignation that Koestler regards as the opposite to his oceanic feeling is, then, a tumescent experience that has its proper forms of release.[2] For most of the people in my texts it is ecstasies that involve tumescent feelings, but, as we have already seen, for some people ecstasy can be a detumescent or withdrawal experience. This, I suggest, may habitually be the case for Koestler. The symbol of the ocean is common in withdrawal ecstasies,[3] and the association of the oceanic feeling with 'retreats' may also be significant.

It is also interesting that Koestler regards 'Yogi' as the word appropriate to describe the attitude to life induced by the oceanic feeling, since withdrawal ecstasies seem to be far more typical of eastern than of western experience.

Gissing's experience (L 13) is one that seems to me to be in many ways similar to Koestler's. In both cases a state of angry disturbance is transformed into what both men speak of as 'nirvana', a word whose connotations are with eastern, not western mysticism. For Gissing,

[1] The experiences that seem to be the opposite to intensity ecstasies are discussed in Ch. XVI.

[2] Although, as I have said, I do not believe that analyses of several descriptions of outbursts of anger would show similar patterns to analyses of ecstasies (see pp. 37-8), there do seem to be several resemblances between outbursts of anger and intensity ecstasies.

[3] See p. 69.

'the idea of vastness in geological time' reduces his former racking and rending passion to 'ridiculous unimportance'; for Koestler, the idea of infinite time dissolves his former choking indignation, reducing its causes to 'microscopic insignificance'.

CHAPTER V

The Duration of Ecstasies

Where in the texts the duration of an ecstasy is indicated, this is usually said to be a moment. Outside the texts, a moment (or some similar word or phrase) is by far the most usual duration indicated. Religious mystical experiences, which can often be accepted as ecstasies on other evidence than that of duration, are frequently said to last a moment. Butler, with many examples from St. Augustine, St. Gregory, St. Bernard, shows that 'the soul can maintain itself in the act of contemplation only for a brief moment'.[1] Von Hügel speaks of the similarity of experience between St. Paul and St. Catherine of Genoa: 'in both cases, everything leads up to, or looks back upon, a great culminating, directly personal experience of shortest clock-time duration'.[2]

But as against this we find in the texts Q 5 saying that after her son was born her ecstasy lasted from ten minutes to half an hour; Richard Church speaking of half an hour (L 23a) and Suso of half an hour to an hour (R 1); M.E. says 'it may have lasted 4 or 5 minutes' (R 11), Boehme that it lasted for quarter of an hour (R 16).[3]

There are three possible explanations of these occasional reports of intensity ecstasies of extended duration, none of which need exclude the others. The first is that occasionally the actual tumescence and discharge is not momentary but prolonged. This is obviously possible but it seems to me improbable. To try to show by analogy what I mean: such actions as an eye-blink, a heart-beat, a sneeze, a sexual

---

[1] W.M., p. 81; see also pp. 47, 73, 108.

[2] M.E.R., Vol. II, pp. 78–9.

[3] None of these is a case of religious 'ecstasy' which is not said to be momentary; see p. 6. Descriptions of religious 'ecstasies' are however often similar to those of the brief or momentary experiences I am investigating, and without some indication of duration or of trance, it may sometimes be impossible to know which kind of experience is in question. The experience of Suso (text R 1) may, I think, be either.

orgasm has each its own functional duration and cannot, whether by will or involuntarily, be prolonged. In the context of physiological function the discharge of intensity ecstasy seems to me to be an event probably similar to these.

Then the extended time may be that of an ecstatic period before the tumescence and discharge take place. This may well be the case when the experience is of the withdrawal-intensity kind discussed in the last chapter. Withdrawal intensities are never said to last a moment and, as described, seem to take longer than 'a moment' to reach their state of maximum loss and to be able to be sustained for longer, whether spontaneously achieved or self-induced.[1]

Finally, the extended period may be one of ecstatic feelings *after* tumescence and discharge. I shall show that such a state does often occur after an ecstatic moment, lasting up to an hour or so, sometimes more, sometimes less, and that in this period the ecstatic moment may be realized, appreciated, interpreted, while the ecstatic recovers from the shock of the climactic moment.

For some people the period immediately after an ecstatic experience is clearly one of mental bemusement and physical incapacity. The author of text R 11 describes both the ecstatic moment and its aftermath. After the 'throb of emotion' he sat down and his eyes filled with tears; he thanked God that he had been allowed to know him:

'Then, slowly, the ecstasy left my heart; that is, I felt that God had withdrawn the communion which he had granted, and I was able to walk on, but very slowly, so strongly was I still possessed by the emotion.'

Suso recovered consciousness after his experience asking, 'Oh, my God, where was I and where am I?' and then realized that the words of St. Paul were appropriate to his own experience.

'He walked, but it was but his body that walked, as a machine might do...his soul and his spirit were full of marvels... He was like a vase from which one has taken a precious ointment, but in which the perfume long remains' (R 1).

Forster seems to intend to convey a similar but less intense state in his Helen Schlegel. Like Suso she breathed deeply; like the author of text R 11 she walked slowly; and 'The notes meant this and that to

---

[1] See, for instance, text L 15 where a comparatively slight and incomplete withdrawal ecstasy seems to be extended over several minutes and possibly longer.

her, and they could have no other meaning, and life could have no other meaning' (L 18).

If it is indeed this period immediately after an ecstatic moment that is included by some people in their assessments of an ecstasy's duration, this could help to resolve a difficulty that has been raised by many people who have experienced or been interested in ecstasy, the question of how it is possible to know what ecstasy felt like or to receive information in an ecstasy if ecstasy is or can be a state when the means of perception are in abeyance. 'But you will say, how can the soul see and comprehend that she is in God and God in her, if during this union she is not able either to see or understand?' asks St. Teresa (R 10b). This obvious difficulty is one of the reasons why Christian theologians have insisted that the intensity of an ecstatic experience shall not be so great that the mystic reports that all sense was lost.

Poulain is emphatic that the mystic must not say 'The person thinks of *nothing*' or 'he loves God and possesses Him without knowing *anything* about it'; the 'right expression', he says, is 'The mind *does nothing*, save that it adheres to the divine action'. He insists,

> 'all the schoolmen are in agreement upon this point, namely, that there is *neither love nor enjoyment without knowledge*. Again, if it were not so in your prayer, if you were not *thinking* of God in it, how would you know whether it is He whom you love or whether you are praying at all?' [1]

Notwithstanding such objurgations many Christians do use the forbidden forms of words and yet claim afterwards that their souls have been with God. But even at a lesser stage of ecstasy than that in which all sense is lost, it is still characteristic of ecstasies that normal perceptions are more or less in abeyance. 'She understands, but otherwise than by the senses', says St. Teresa (R 10a), and St. Augustine, 'without any image of body the perspicuous truth is perceived' (R 19). Those who are not disposed to accept the validity of mystical truth may well ask how one can speak of 'thinking' or 'understanding' or 'perceiving' when the faculties by which we think, understand, perceive are not functioning.

But with the postulated period of ecstatic afterglow the difficulty can be resolved, for we can suppose that it was in this period that the

[1] G.I.P., ch. ix, 15.

ecstatic 'knew' what it was he believed he had felt during the sense-disordered moment of ecstasy.

> 'how can the soul see and comprehend that she is in God and God in her, if during this union she is not able either to see or understand? I reply, that she does not see it at the time, but that afterwards she perceives it clearly: not by a vision, but by a certitude which remains in the heart which God alone can give.' [1]

St. Teresa says elsewhere that she believes that voices and visions occur after the experience itself, whether this be ecstasy (in my sense) or religious 'ecstasy':

> 'It should be noted that if we see visions and hear words like this [i.e. from God], it is never, in my opinion, at a time when the soul is in union or during the rapture itself. For then...all the senses are completely lost and, as I believe, there can be no seeing or understanding or hearing at all... But when this *brief time* [my italics] is over, and the soul is still enraptured, then is the time I am speaking of.' [2]

Many ecstatics agree with St. Teresa that it is after the experience that they understand what it was about. H. Warner Allen writes that 'the mysterious event itself' which took place in 'an infinitesimal fraction of a split second' he learned *afterwards* [my italics] from St. Teresa to call the Union with God. Then came Illumination, 'a *wordless* stream of complex feelings . . . that was continually swollen by tributaries of associated Experience'. This is the condition that I call the ecstatic afterglow when, with returning consciousness, the realization, appreciation, and interpretation of the experience begins. It is after the 'wordless' state that he calls Illumination that, for Allen, comes Enlightenment, 'the recollection in tranquillity of the whole complex of Experience as it were embalmed in thought-forms and words' (L 11).

This impression, that interpretation followed the ecstatic moment and was not simultaneous with it, is given by several other people in the groups. 'I continued in this state of inward joy, peace, and astonishing till near dark, without any sensible abatement; and then began to think and examine what I had seen,' wrote Brainerd (R 13). Of the experience itself the author of text R 6 says only that he felt 'a tem-

---

[1] St. Teresa in text R 10b.   [2] *Life*, ch. xxv, pp. 175-6.

porary loss of my own identity, accompanied by an illumination which revealed to me a deeper significance than I had been wont to attach to life'. This is a minimal statement of overbelief—little more than the expression of feelings of loss of self and gain of knowledge. 'It is in this,' he continues, 'that I find my justification for saying that I have enjoyed communication with God.' The justification is made after the experience; it is what he afterwards interpreted his feelings as having implied.

The clergyman of text R 3 says very much the same thing:

'My most assuring evidence of [God's] existence is deeply rooted in that hour of vision, in the memory of that supreme experience, and in the conviction, gained from reading and reflection, that something the same has come to all who have found God.'

Notice that in this passage he speaks of an hour of vision, whereas in his account of the actual experience ('a rushing together of two worlds') he wrote,

'The ordinary sense of things around me faded. For the *moment* [my italics] nothing but an ineffable joy and exultation remained.'

I do not think that 'a moment' is a likely metaphor for a period as long as an hour.[1] It seems to me more likely that the 'moment' of 'ineffable joy and exultation' is to be distinguished from the 'hour of vision' afterwards during which the experience was appreciated, realized, interpreted.

In all such cases it would be very natural, when both the ecstatic moment and the afterglow had passed, to believe that it was in the moment of ecstasy itself that the new knowledge both came and was fully understood, and some ecstatics do maintain this. Virginia Woolf believes that during her experience she learns what 'reality' is, but that it is nearly impossible to set it down afterwards (L 8). Jacquetta Hawkes believes that during her experience her thoughts had been given an extraordinary clarity and truth which could not be translated into 'everyday terms' (L 19). Boehme, again, believed that it was during his experience that he was able to understand 'all things' but that afterwards 'I could very hardly apprehend the same in my external man' (R 16).

---

[1] It does not so refer in any of the examples given in the dictionary.

Tennyson, however, is uncertain what to believe. Though he believes that the experience itself brought illumination and clarity:

> *I know not if I shape*
> *These things with accurate similitude*
> *From visible objects, for but dimly now,*
> *Less vivid than a half-forgotten dream,*
> *The memory of that mental excellence*
> *Comes o'er me, and it may be I entwine*
> *The indecision of my present mind*
> *With its past clearness*

He is still forced to doubt whether, at the time of the experience, he was in a position to receive coherent communications:

> *yet it seems to me*
> *As even then the torrent of quick thought*
> *Absorbed me from the nature of itself*
> *With its own fleetness* (L 2).

It should be noted that where coherent knowledge is claimed to have been received during ecstasy, there is no evidence of more than a *feeling* of coherent knowledge unless such knowledge can be coherently communicated later. I believe it possible to explain the feelings of these last examples, that the ecstatic moment was one of clarity that could not be retained, with reference to the general nature of ecstatic experiences, but must defer this until I come to consider overbelief as a whole (see, especially, p. 334). But whether or not clear communications can be perceived in the ecstatic moment itself does not affect the present arguments for regarding the tumescence and discharge of intensity ecstasy as generally momentary.

There is no reason to suppose that all ecstatic experiences should be taken as including a period of ecstatic afterglow; that full mental and physical capacities return only slowly to all ecstatics or that all ecstastics use this period to interpret their experiences. Some—indeed most of the people in the questionnaire group—barely interpret them at all. Outside this group, Nichols says specifically that his could have remained a state 'for the expression of which words were neither sought nor found' had not the light on the water suggested hieroglyphics to him (L 5). Charlotte Brontë upbraids her character Shirley for not taking a pen, fixing the apparition, telling the vision received 'while the recollection of such *moments* [my italics] was yet fresh on her spirit'; but Shirley, she complains, has no understanding of what it is she has been told.

I shall accept intensity ecstasies as being generally momentary in their tumescence and discharge, possibly sometimes preceded by a longer than momentary period of withdrawal, probably often followed by a period—up to an hour or so—of ecstatic afterglow. We must next consider some other states whose duration can be considerable but which, in other respects, have many similarities to intensity ecstasies. Such a state is described in text R 22.

This passage describes a continuous state in which ecstatic feelings are not brief or momentary but sustained. Thus descriptions of these states, usually called by theologians unitive states or the unitive life, differ from descriptions of ecstatic experiences in the matter of duration; and in the fact that complete or substantial loss of sense cannot be claimed—though people may speak, as Suso does in text R 22, of inebriation or intoxication—since the unitive life is still a life to be lived.

Like all other aspects of mystical experience, religiously viewed, this one has been thoroughly systematized. Poulain describes it as

1. A union that is almost *permanent*, persisting even amidst exterior occupations, and this in such a manner that the two different occupations do not interfere with one another.

2. A *transformation* of the higher faculties as to their manner of operation (hence the name of transforming union).

3. Generally a permanent *intellectual vision* of the Blessed Trinity or of some divine attribute.[1]

Thus we may describe the unitive state as an almost continuous extension[2] of the feelings of a mystical experience which are often, as in Suso's case, similar to those of an ecstatic experience. To attain such a condition is the aim of most people who have assumed a supernatural origin for ecstasies. Such a condition, when habitual, must clearly involve some such transformation of 'the higher faculties' as Poulain speaks of, and it seems probable that the way to it must be one of such

[1] G.I.P., ch. xix, 2.
[2] Kirk is emphatic that to speak of a continuous state is heretical; what should be spoken of is a condition 'habitual, but by no means continuous.' V.G., p. 452n.

unremitting and systematized mental discipline as all mystical religions and philosophies have evolved for those who seek it.[1]

But without such a disciplined search it seems that many people have spontaneously known periods—a few hours, a day, a week, perhaps more—when they lived in what seemed like an almost continuous state of ecstasy. As we shall see, there are different varieties of ecstasy and these seem to be reflected in different varieties of continuous states of ecstatic feeling.

A good example of such a state without any religious connotations is provided by George Gissing. He tells of the indigent young man forced to spend the summer in London,

'when my health had begun to suffer from excess of toil, from bad air, bad food and many miseries; then awoke the maddening desire for countryside and sea-beach—and for other things yet more remote.'

For six years he 'trod the pavement, never stepping once upon mother earth' then,

'On an irresistible impulse, I suddenly made up my mind to go into Devon, a part of England I had never seen. At the end of March I escaped from my grim lodgings, and, before I had time to reflect on the details of my undertaking, I found myself sitting in sunshine...

I had stepped into a new life. Between the man I had been and that which I now became there was a very notable difference...I suddenly entered into conscious enjoyment of powers and sensibilities which had been developing unknown to me. To instance only one point: till then I had cared very little about plants and flowers, but now I found myself eagerly interested in every blossom, in every growth of the wayside... To me the flowers became symbolical of a great release, of a wonderful awakening... So intense was my delight in the beautiful world about me that I forgot even myself; I enjoyed without retrospect or forecast; I, the egoist in grain, forgot to scrutinise my own emotions, or to trouble my happiness by comparison with others' happier fortune. It was a healthful time; it gave me a new lease of life, and taught me—in so far as I was teachable—how to make use of it.'[2]

[1] Underhill gives some comparisons of the times taken by various religious mystics to attain this state. St. Paul and St. Catherine of Siena each took three years, Suso sixteen years, St. Teresa thirty years, while 'that flaming thing which was the soul of Jesus burned its way to full expression' in 'forty days of solitary communion'. M.W., p. 95.

[2] *The Private Papers of Henry Ryecroft* (London, 1903; 1928 edn.), p. 16 et seq.

In this case trigger conditions were needed to bring about the state as, I suspect, for such temporary non-religious states, they usually are. The similarities to momentary ecstasies are plain—loss of feelings of self, of worldliness, of time, gain of feelings of new life, joy, knowledge.

Most blue-prints for utopia postulate such states of mind as the natural condition of the inhabitants. H. G. Wells provides an example when he describes how people feel after the comet has destroyed the wicked old world and changed the minds of men who can now build a world of perfection:

> 'For the fluctuating, uncertain, passion-darkened thought and feeling of the old time came steady, full-blooded, wholesome processes. ...The dominant impression I would convey in this account of the Change is one of enormous release, of a vast substantial exaltation. There was an effect, as it were, of light-headedness that was also clear-headedness...a new detachment from the tumid passions and entanglements of the personal life.' [1]

This new and lasting feeling is said by Wells to be similar to that of 'glowing moments' induced 'by histories and music and beautiful things, by heroic instances and splendid stories'.

The change of heart, so often spoken of as 'all that is needed' to bring about, say, world peace or a classless society, is surely envisaged as the change to such states as these.

Among the extra-utopian conditions that may bring about such states for ordinary people are periods of creative work,[2] of holidays (as Gissing suggests), of being in love; indeed, it would seem reasonable to regard the honeymoon as the institutionalized recognition of such states. One condition that sometimes seems for women to bring about such a state is childbirth.

In Chapter XIII I discuss letters received by the B.B.C. from women, several of whom describe prolonged periods of something that sounds very like ecstasy after the birth of their children. Two of these letters told of the writers staying awake all night after their babies were born, 'wonderfully happy, spiritually elated, and free of my body', wrote one, and the other 'marvelling at the wonderful feeling of being a mother'. Another woman, who enjoyed momentary ecstasy at the

---

[1] *In the Days of the Comet* (London, 1906), pp. 185-6.
[2] Examples will be found on pp. 87-8 and p. 95.

first birth-pang, wrote, 'the calmness never left me throughout my labour. I gave birth to my baby girl with the Magnificat truly in my heart.' Another wrote, 'the miracle of seeing my two babies born and the satisfaction of the days after were on a plane far above the level of normal life'. From another source I quote the experience of a woman who for several days after the birth of her baby enjoyed a condition very similar to that described by Gissing above.

Whether we call such states ecstatic afterglows or unitive states might be allowed to depend on circumstances and duration. If such a state immediately succeeds an ecstasy and lasts anything from a few minutes to an hour or two—which was James's limit for his mystical states (see p. 45)—we may conveniently call it an ecstatic afterglow and look on it as the period in which a momentary ecstasy is realized, appreciated, interpreted.[1] If such a state lasts for longer than this, having succeeded an ecstasy, we might regard up to the first hour or so as ecstatic afterglow and the later period as a unitive state. And if such a state lasts for hours or days without having been preceded by a single ecstasy (as seems to have been the case for Gissing), then we may conveniently call this a unitive state.

[1] Thus when Q 5 says that after the birth of her baby ecstasy lasted from ten minutes to half an hour, I would consider this an ecstatic afterglow.

CHAPTER VI

Up, Down, Light, Dark

Up-feelings are the most common of the quasi-physical feelings recorded in my texts and appear in half of them. Sometimes these feelings are claimed with apparently literal intention; for instance, 'associated with sensations of physical flying' (Q 29), 'I experienced a feeling of being raised above myself' (R 11). Sometimes the intention is apparently figurative, with the use of expressions about soaring up, being airborne, carried away, reaching the highest point of bliss, etc. And sometimes I infer up-feelings from the use of words and phrases deriving from metaphors about up-feelings—exalted, elevated, supreme, uplifted, etc.[1]

Broadly, these up-feelings can be divided into two kinds: feelings of upward thrust or positive movement upwards, which are by far the more numerous; and feelings of floating.

The former I associate exclusively with intensity ecstasies, in which they are a very usual form of expression. Sometimes the upward thrust is said to take place inside the ecstatic and is often associated with the heart. 'The heart...leaps like a fountain', said Q 24, quoting Cassian, and 'their sweetness and unusual beauty made my heart to leap, and almost mad with ecstasy', said Traherne of trees that 'transported and ravished' him when a child.[2] To feel that one's heart is lightened or uplifted or leaping with joy is commonly said of ecstasy as of less intense experiences of joy.

Ecstatics often associate upward feelings with a gush or flow of liquid, sometimes specifically sited in the heart as it is in the phrase of Q 24 quoted above, 'the heart...leaps like a fountain'; and Charlotte Brontë speaks of 'that spring...bubbling in her heart' (L 14). Others who believe they feel this upward gush of liquid are not specific about

[1] For a detailed division of the words and phrases entered under this heading, see Appendix E, 1.
[2] From *Centuries of Meditation. The Third Century*, 3.

its location beyond its taking place 'inside'. 'Something wells up in one...grows like a spring', says Q 26 of inspiration which she relates closely to ecstasy. 'Great joy bubbling up inside', says the child Q 49.

More frequent than these upward feelings felt as taking place inside are people's feelings that they themselves are borne upwards. 'Soaring up to something', said Q 3; 'as if being borne into heaven', said Q 15; '[my] soul is being wafted upwards' said a clergyman (R 3), and Joseph Salmon 'sprang up far above my earthly centre' (R 18). Q 29 says that ecstasy for her is 'associated with feelings of physical flying, like going to sleep or in dreams'.[1]

Other feelings of upward thrust are occasionally connected, more or less figuratively, with the mind or intellect or spirit. Tennyson seems to be referring to physical sensation when he writes that he felt his spirit 'With supernatural excitation bound' (L 2), but unfortunately does not say where he supposed or felt his spirit to be. St. Catherine of Siena says that her intellect was elevated (R 2).

These feelings of upward thrust or positive upward movement do not seem to occur in ecstasies that are in all other respects withdrawal ones. Less common than these are feelings of floating. Two people in the questionnaire group speak of floating, one of hovering and one of weightlessness. The author of text L 24 speaks of 'bodily lightness...as if one's limbs had no weight', and St. Catherine of Siena speaks of feeling 'raised from the earth almost as if the heavy body became light' (R 2).

I know from experience that to induce a floating sensation is easy. I need only lean back in a chair or lie on a bed with my eyes shut and 'think myself light' and I will quickly feel that I am floating and incapable of coherent thought. Sometimes this is moderately pleasant and restful; more often it makes me feel slightly sick, which makes me wonder whether Q 51, at least, is not speaking of a similar feeling when she says of her floating sensation that 'it can make me feel sick'. I should myself associate this floating sensation, which has no more feeling of *up* about it than floating on water has, with withdrawal rather than intensity ecstasy.

[1] Many mystics who believed they had been levitated felt that a force had lifted them up despite themselves. St. Teresa wrote 'It seemed to me when I tried to resist that a great force...was lifting me up from beneath my feet.' *Life*, ch. xx, p. 137.

A feeling of floating on or sinking into water is recorded and does seem to be connected with withdrawal rather than with intensity ecstasies. Q 1 speaks of flowing, Koestler of dissolving (L 7), Louis of Blois of melting (R 20) and St. Francis of Sales of gliding, as a fluid and liquid thing, into the Divinity (R 21). More specifically St. Catherine of Genoa wrote

'I am so placed and submerged in His immense love, that I feel as though in the sea entirely under water, and could on no side touch, see, or feel anything but water.' [1]

This is typical of many of her statements which Von Hügel later describes as

'quasi-Pantheism, of immense expansion. Here the crushed plant expands in boundless air, light and warmth; the parched seaweed floats and unfolds itself in an immense ocean of pure waters—the soul, as it were, breathes and bathes in God's peace and love.' [2]

Here feelings of light, warmth and breathing and expanding into air are treated as if similar to feelings of floating on water. I suspect that they are not, that the former are associated with intensity ecstasies, the latter with withdrawal ecstasies.[3] I believe that references to *floating* might indicate either form of ecstasy, and that one should look for supplementary evidence to decide whether the feeling is of upward floating into air—probably an intensity ecstasy—or of floating on water—almost certainly a withdrawal ecstasy. Koestler, it will be remembered, found the appropriate image for the feelings of his withdrawal ecstasy in Freud's phrase, 'the oceanic feeling' (see p. 54).

The heading *inside-words and phrases* represents something of a rag-bag which I must now try to sort out.

[1] Quoted by Hügel: M.E.R., Vol. I, p. 274.   [2] Ibid., Vol. II, p. 39.

[3] Many of St. Catherine's experiences are, as Von Hügel admits, dubious from the Christian point of view (see pp. 125n. and 311n.) and Von Hügel is constantly concerned to present them in as favourable a light as possible. He writes that St. Paul conceived of Christ or the spirit 'as it were an ocean of ethereal light, in which souls are plunged and which penetrates them' (M.E.R., Vol. II, p. 70) and this, he says, is the source of some of Catherine's perceptions.   But St. Paul himself does not, on the evidence of the texts Von Hügel quotes, introduce anything like this 'oceanic' vision of Christ; more, as I hope to show in the course of this chapter, *light* and *down* are never associated in ecstasies. Does Von Hügel attribute this image to St. Paul so as to link St. Paul's feelings with those of Catherine who so often felt as if she was floating on or in water, and thus to purge Catherine's image of questionable connotations?

By far the most common in all three groups are expressions indicating that something is felt as happening inside the ecstatic, whether by spontaneous generation (e.g. 'something wells up in one...grows like a spring' Q 26) or by penetration from without (e.g. 'goodness and power...penetrating me altogether' R 11). Such expressions may be accepted as usual in intensity ecstasies.

Rarely in the texts, the ecstatic feels that he is inside someone or something else—e.g. 'penetrated the very heart of the universe' (L 12), 'engulfed in her God' (R 21). These phrases, which seem to refer to a particular stage of ecstatic experience, are further discussed in Ch. XI.

We sometimes find apparently ecstatic experiences in which there are indications of a feeling of *down* in the dictionary sense of 'In a descending direction; from above, or towards that which is below.' There are, I believe, various possible explanations of such usages.

We occasionally find both *down-* and *up*-phrases in an account of an experience, the phrases being used in this chronological order. In such cases the *down*-phrases may refer to a state of feeling very different from and, indeed, the opposite of the ecstatic state that supersedes it. these varieties of experience are discussed in Chapter XVI.

Then, as we have already seen and shall increasingly see, *down*-phrases may indicate not intensity but withdrawal ecstasy;[1] thus, *down*-phrases followed by *up*-phrases may indicate such ecstasies as were discussed in Chapter IV, where initial withdrawal is followed by later tumescence.

It is however important to distinguish down-words and phrases used in the dictionary sense of 'from above or towards that which is below' from apparently down-words and phrases where the intended meaning is 'inwards towards a centre'.

I believe that we can see a confusion of this kind resulting from Meister Eckhart's use of the German word *grund* meaning the essence or core or *synteresis* of the soul. Where this is translated as *ground* (as it is, for instance, by Aldous Huxley,[2] there may arise an image of the 'ground' of the soul being *down* in the dictionary sense, and this may account for the persistent feeling of *down* in Huxley's admittedly contrived ecstasy, referred to on p. 73n. But in mystical usuage *grund* is not properly translated as *ground*. D. T. Suzuki, for instance, trans-

---

[1] Cp. St. Catherine of Genoa, quoted on p. 69 : 'I am so...submerged...that I feel...entirely under water.'

[2] See *The Devils of Loudun* (London, 1952), p. 371.

lates Meister Eckhart's *grund* by *core*, and speaks of 'the inmost core (*grund*) of the divine nature'. In contrast, he quotes someone else's translation, 'When I go back into the ground, into the depths, into the well-spring of the Godhead'; it is obvious what a different impression would have been conveyed by using *core* and not *ground*.[1]

Suzuki is Japanese. I have already said that I associate down-phrases with withdrawal ecstasies and withdrawal ecstasies with eastern experiences. It is then interesting to notice that down-words and phrases are usual in his own descriptions of mystical experiences—'I must plunge into "the vast emptiness of the Absolute Tao" ', 'leaping or plunging into the silent valley of Absolute Emptiness', 'plunge right into the abyss of nameless nothingness'.[2] He quotes from Lao-Tzu,

> *The Way...is bottomless...*
> *It is like a deep pool that never dries.*[3]

There can be little doubt that Suzuki's own mystical experiences are most naturally described in *down*-words, for Eckhart's 'Hie muoz kommon in ein vergezzen und ein nihtwizzen', which has no *down* indications, Suzuki translates as 'sinking into oblivion and ignorance'.[4]

But in Eckhart, as in other Christian mystics who have incurred the suspicion and censure of the Church as being what is stigmatized as buddhistic, pantheistic, negativistic, etc., we not very frequently find not only such inside-words and phrases as may indicate feelings of movement towards a core or centre but also unmistakably down-words and phrases in the dictionary sense of 'from above, or towards that which is below'.[5]

The assumptions on which I shall work are that phrases with an unmistakable feeling of upward movement or thrust refer to intensity ecstasies; that phrases indicating unmistakable downward movement

---

[1] *Mysticism, Christian and Buddhist* (London, 1957), pp. 76–7 and p. 16. The core of the soul is not necessarily associated only with words carrying *down* or *inward* implications: thus Inge, citing earlier writers, uses the phrase *apex mentis*. C.M., p. 185 and p. 360.

[2] Ibid., pp. 17, 23, 61   [3] Ibid., p. 18.   [4] Ibid., p. 23.

[5] This *down* phraseology is found in the writings of the later Jewish Merkabah or Throne mystics (so-called with reference to the vision of *Ezekiel* x, in which a throne-chariot was seen 'in the firmament that was above the head of the cherubims'), who, from about A.D. 500 onwards, referred to the visionary journey of the soul to heaven as the 'descent to the Merkabah', and called themselves *Yorde Merkabah*, the descenders to the Merkabah; see Gershom G. Scholem, *Major Trends in Jewish Mysticism* (Jerusalem, 1941; New York, 1946), pp. 46–7.

refer either to withdrawal ecstasies or to those experiences I regard as the opposite to intensity ecstasies and shall discuss in Chapter XVI; and that phrases indicating floating or hovering, and inside-words and phrases must be considered in their total context.

The number of entries under *light/heat* show the greatest disparity as between the three groups, the questionnaire group contributing far fewer entries than either of the other two.

The light-references are of two kinds: references to flashes of light, which are by far the more frequent, and references to sustained brightness. Both flashes and sustained brightness may be spoken of in a single experience, as they are by Tennyson (L 2) and by Suso (R 1).

Light seen in ecstasies, whether as sustained light or in flashes, never seems to be any other colour than white.[1] Apparent contradictions to this cannot usually be sustained. Von Hügel, for instance, speaks of 'The yellow light-image, which all but alone typifies God's friendliness in the Bible';[2] I cannot find any references to yellow (or golden) light in the Bible. Ovid, in the translation I give for my text L 22, is made to speak of purple light; but my translator was young and inexperienced, and though I have gratefully reproduced his text, I gather that *purpureus* may and even should sometimes be translated as *shining white*, as, for example, in Horace's phrase *purpureis . . . oloribus*[3]—the (something) swans.[4]

References to feelings of warmth are less frequent than to feelings of light. Both references to light and to heat may be apparently literally or apparently figuratively intended. References to seeing light are often connected, as they are in common usage, with feelings of mental illumination.

---

[1] 'This *white* is a recurring idea which holds much more than blankness,' writes Gerald Bullett (*The English Mystics* (London, 1950), p. 105). He says that the latest biographer of Vaughan relates the poet's fondness for the word 'to the rich connotations of the Welsh word *gwyn*, which signifies not only white, but fair happy, holy, blessed'. We may also compare English *white* and French *blanc* which both have connotations of shining brightness.

[2] M.E.R., Vol. II, ch. x, p. 70.

[3] *Carmina*, 4. 1. 10.

[4] A dream-ecstasy which was sent to me is interestingly insistent on this point of whiteness. The ecstatic, who wrote down the dream immediately on waking, spoke of 'streams, showers, of silver-white light...unlike fireworks this light was white, silver...very, very white, light or silver.' See Appendix J, p.p. 532–3. 'White flame' is an essential constituent of an ecstatic dream described by J. B. Priestly in his autobiographical book *Rain Upon Godshill* (London, 1939), pp. 305–6).

Next to *loss of feelings of limitation*, darkness-words and phrases represent the smallest entry of all. There are no mentions of darkness in the questionnaire group; in the literary group darkness is mentioned only by Lawrence (L 17a), and in the religious group by Angela of Foligno (R 5b), by Ruysbroeck (R 7), and by Louis of Blois (R 20).

In all these four texts *dark* is associated with *up*. Now, of the possible combinations of light/dark with up/down; we find the following:

Light is mentioned in 25 texts (excluding the two texts by Lawrence and mentions of heat without light). 18 times it is mentioned in conjunction with *up*-words and phrases; that is to say, in 72 per cent. of cases feelings of seeing light appear in association with up-feelings. It is my strong impression that this is sustained in other ecstasies outside my texts, and I regard mentions of light as indicating intensity ecstasies.

Light does not appear with down-words and phrases in my texts or in any other accounts of ecstatic experiences that I know of.[1]

Down and *darkness* in combination I associate with withdrawal ecstasies. Certainly *dark* would seem to be implied by the depths of the pools, valleys, abysses into which the eastern mystic plunges or sinks (see p. 71). *Down* and *darkness* also appear in combination in those opposite experiences to intensity ecstasies which I shall discuss in Chapter XVI.

Apart from Lawrence no secular mystic, so far as I know, associates *dark* and *up*. About the use of *dark* with *up* by the religious mystics, there are several points to be made.

Ruysbroeck and Louis of Blois both contrast dark with light, the dark being the ultimate and valued destination. Louis of Blois speaks of 'the brightness of most lucid darkness', Ruysbroeck of being carried 'above the light, into the Divine Dark'. Such phrases are common among certain religious mystics, notably Dionysius the Areopagite who first spoke of 'Divine Darkness' and those whose mystical experiences seem to have been patterned on his. This group of mystics

---

[1] *Light* and *down* do however appear together in the admittedly contrived ecstasy with which Aldous Huxley ended his novel *Eyeless in Gaza* (London, 1936). He explains in *The Doors of Perception* (London, 1954, p. 31) that before taking mescalin he had never known mystical experience, but even without this explanation I should not have found it possible to accept this as an account of an ecstasy, for it presents too many atypical features: the frenetic repetition of 'peace' which conveys the opposite of peaceful feelings; the obviously intellectual image of the two inverted cones which has, so far as I know, no parallel in mystical literature; the sustained image of *down* for 'good', *up* for 'bad' and the finding of light at a depth below darkness.

who often use darkness-phrases include such people as Eckhart, Boehme, Ruysbroek, who have often been charged, as Inge charged Dionysius, with developing a *via negativa* that can lead, in Inge's phrase, only to 'Asiatic nihilism'.[1]

Some commentators however accept references to darkness as allowable in Christian experience. Poulain says that 'even ecstatic contemplation is a mixture of light and darkness'[2] and Underhill that dark-images arise because 'God in His absolute Reality is unknowable —is dark—to man's intellect' and so, in mystical experience, man's reason 'finds itself..."in the dark"—immersed in the Cloud of Unknowing'.[3]

One might, then, accept that though secular mystics do not seem to find 'dark' in intensity experiences (for Lawrence's experiences present too many other odd features to allow me to accept them as ecstasies in my sense), yet certain religious mystics do find darkness in 'up' experiences. But there is, in this group of mystics, a special use of language which adds to the difficulty. Of Eckhart Professor Clark writes,

> 'Since God is brighter than any earthly light, He is called "darkness", not to denote the absence of light but the presence of something brighter than light as we know it, superabundant light or excess of light.'[4]

Similarly, says Clark, Eckhart calls God 'Nothing' not to suggest that he does not exist, but rather to postulate for him 'a fuller, richer existence than that of any created thing in the universe'. He points out that the mystical usages of words like *nothing, darkness, desert*, were taken from the Neoplatonists and especially from Dionysius. There is, then, a long tradition for this use of a negative to express a supposedly supreme positive, and it must remain possible that references to darkness are cryptic references to light. It will be noticed that Clark's argument presupposes that light is the normal destination and that darkness-references require explanation.

But Clark goes on to say,

> 'These negative names are very popular with Eckhart, as with many other mystics, so much so that one cannot help thinking there must be some particular reason for this. Certainly God is thus described

[1] C.M., p. 110 et seq.   [2] G.I.P., ch. xviii, 64.   [3] E.U: M., p. 348.
[4] James M. Clark, *Meister Eckhart* (Edinburgh, 1957), p. 28.

because of the limitations of human speech and of the human intellect, but quite apart from this, these words must correspond to something in Eckhart's experience.'[1]

This is my own supposition. I do not find darkness-words used in ecstasies that also use up-words, except among those mystics who have persistently been accused of negativism; or in accounts of experiences that present other unusual features.

As to the 'other unusual features' in the darkness-texts in my groups: Louis of Blois's text, as already pointed out (see p. 47), is the only one in which withdrawal phrases *follow* intensity phrases. Lawrence in no way suggests a contrast of light and dark, as do the mystics discussed above; more, his sense of direction in text L 17b—onwards and upwards, an apparently oblique rise—is idiosyncratic, and his relation of sexual intercourse to ecstasy strange to a degree (see Ch. XIV). Angela of Foligno's experience is not, in my terms, ecstasy at all.

Underhill offers this text as an example of 'the "dark contemplation" by which alone selves of the transcendent and impersonal type claim that they draw to the Unconditioned One'.[2] The examples she gives as being similar to this text (including Dionysius the Areopagite) are all couched in darkness-and-light terms. But Angela's text contains no light-references at all.

More, Underhill seems to be speaking of a deliberate, not an involuntary approach to 'dimness and lostness of the mind', of a 'deliberate inhibition of discursive thought and rejection of images', achieved by the 'orison of quiet' or by 'personal surrender or "self-naughting"'[3]—which may perhaps be taken as indicating that darkness-ecstasies are, as I suspect, likely to be withdrawal ones. But Angela's experience is in no way deliberately self-induced; it takes place 'suddenly' in the middle of a working conversation with her secretary.[4]

Angela's experience is, in fact, an example of religious 'ecstasy', and it is as such that Poulain cites it.[5] More, it is the special form of 'ecstasy' known as rapture, which is 'sudden and violent'. In 'ecstasy'

[1] *Meister Eckhart*, p. 28.   [2] E.U: M., pp. 346-7.   [3] Ibid., pp. 348-9.
[4] That is to say, it lacks a trigger within the range so far established. Some kinds of conversation can induce ecstasy—see p. 196—but in these cases both conversations and relationships are different from those of Angela with her secretary.
[5] He cites it, however, under the heading 'That even ecstatic contemplation can be a mixture of light and darkness' (G.I.P., ch. xviii, 64). But, as already pointed out, Angela's experience contains no reference to light.

75

the senses cease to act, the limbs become immovable and coldness sets in at the extremities of the limbs.[1] Some people have the impression of there being a fog or mist before their eyes. When the state is at its deepest, people feel as though they are in complete darkness. During the rapture, which may last several hours or days, the body continues in the position it was in when the rapture came upon it.[2] After it is over there may, for several days, be a difficulty in resuming ordinary occupations; or the person may continue the conversation he was having when the rapture overtook him.[3]

Angela's experience does not, then, confirm Lawrence's assertion of attaining darkness without light by a strong upward thrust in a momentary experience.

To summarize: there seems to be a tendency for light and upward movement to be feelings of intensity ecstasy and for darkness and downward feelings to appear in withdrawal ecstasies. The experiences of a special group of mystics, where darkness and light are combined with upward movement, I shall, as far as possible, ignore. Secular experiences are my principal interest and in secular experiences which in other respects confirm to my criteria I have not encountered this particular combination.

[1] Poulain: G.I.P., ch. xiii, 2–4.

[2] St. Thomas of Villanova was seized by an 'ecstasy' while reading the office for Ascension Day and remained suspended in the air for twelve hours. This fact was cited in the Bull for his canonization; ibid., ch. xviii, 7.

[3] The reader may suspect a connexion between religious 'ecstasies' and ill health, and in Angela's case this seems probable. Poulain says that she had one 'ecstasy' that lasted for three days (ibid., ch. xviii, 7), that she had more than a thousand raptures (ibid., ch. xviii, 75), and that she suffered infirmities in her body, all her members suffering horribly; at times she could hardly restrain herself from striking herself or tearing at herself, and sometimes did so (ibid., ch. xiv, 90).

CHAPTER VII

Physical Claims in General

The headings for quasi-physical claims in the analyses were made on the basis of what people seemed most often to say when describing their experiences. Quasi-physical claims accounted in each group for about a quarter of all mentions, and in the three groups 78 per cent. of people made one or more such claim.[1] Many of the headings used in the analyses can usefully be sub-divided (as has just been done with claims to up-feelings, seeing lights, etc.) and, in addition, a few other claims not included in the analyses are sometimes made. Although in most of these cases there is no evidence of any physical events corresponding to the descriptions given, these descriptions are sufficiently self-consistent to make it reasonable to say that any experience described in ways inconsistent with them should not be regarded as an ecstatic one.

Many descriptions of physical or quasi-physical events involve common figures of speech often used to describe experiences which, although regarded as valuable, would not fulfil my criteria for calling an experience an ecstasy. In the next chapter I discuss what I believe to be the relation of such experiences to ecstatic ones; and the similarity of language, as regards quasi-physical as well as other feelings, is part of the evidence on which I base my postulated relationship.

Broadly speaking, the physical events described are most often (*a*) to do with the heart; (*b*) to do with breathing; (*c*) to do with tinglings and flashes and stabs and shocks; and in each of these cases the events described seem to amount to processes covering the periods of tumescence, climax, and detumescence. There are, in addition, some other claims more or less frequently made which seem to pertain to one or other of these periods.

The picture given of the heart is that from being comparatively cold,

[1] How often the claims included in the analyses were made can be seen in Table 4*b*, Appendix D.

hard, small, low and dry, it becomes progressively warmer, softer, larger, higher, and finally releases a flow of liquid. Almost the complete picture is given in the following passage from St. Bernard:

> 'Often we...begin to pray with a heart lukewarm and dry. But if we steadily persist, grace comes steadily in a flood upon us, our breast grows full of increase, a wave of piety fills our inward heart; and if we press on, the milk of sweetness conceived in us will spread over us in fruitful flood.' [1]

Several people provide one or more parts of this general picture. Thus Charlotte Brontë says of her reading that it has 'refreshed, refilled, rewarmed her heart' (L 14); Hugh of St. Victor says that his intellect is illuminated and his heart afire (R 12).[2]

Sometimes the flow of liquid is given no specific location beyond taking place 'inside'. Proust writes that he has the sensation of being filled with a precious essence (L 26); compare Q 35's more figurative 'the cup is being filled'. Several people in the questionnaire group give the picture of liquid seething and bubbling inside until eventually released to surge upwards like a spring or fountain or wave; for instance, 'something wells up...grows like a spring' (Q 26); 'this thing has been seething inside you and suddenly it comes out' (Q 34); 'great joy bubbling up inside' (Q 49). Several other people give the picture of swift, torrential flow which seems to be felt as release, for instance: Carlo Levi's 'happiness...swept over me with a flow of fulfilment' (L 12); Church's 'The result was like that of opening a weir' (L 23a); and L 27's 'the inspiration flowed...like blood...The passion rushed out of him!'

The flow is often said or implied to be a warm one. This is implicit in St. Bernard's account. Two very similar statements giving the same impression are from Charlotte Brontë and from Louis of Blois:

---

[1] Quoted by Butler: W.M., p. 100.

[2] In a form of mystical experience which does not usually fulfil my criteria for ecstasy but is often discussed in the same context, the mystic insists that his heart does literally grow warm. Suso, after feeling 'a flame of intense heat in his heart', cut the name of Jesus deeply into his breast at the place where he felt the heat (C.M., pp. 174-5). Richard Rolle of Hampton insists that the heat which he often feels in his heart is felt 'truly, not imaginingly' (E.U: M., p. 193). Thurston gives many instances of the mystical phenomenon known as *incendium amoris*; the burning pain is always sited in the heart, which is sometimes said to be hot even after death (P.P.M., ch. viii).

'delight glows in her young veins—the swift glory spreads out, sweeping and kindling—that spring...bubbling in her heart' (L 14)[1] 'feels a certain glow of quiet love...like a living fountain, flowing with streams of eternal sweetness' (R 20).

Feelings of slow, gentle flow seem to be associated with withdrawal not intensity ecstasies, and feelings of flowing into something or someone else are all of this kind. Often the ecstatic feels he is floating or melting or dissolving, for instance: 'the hard lines round one's individuality are gone, one flows over them' (Q 1); Koestler's 'self-dissolving —oceanic feeling—dissolution' (L 7); St. Francis of Sales's 'the soul lets herself pass or flow into What she loves—gently glides, as a fluid and liquid thing—The outflowing of a soul into her God' (R 21).

In the last example God is named as the larger body into which individuality flows. For Wordsworth and George Eliot it is different modes of sensibility in the individual which melt or flow together. Wordsworth writes, 'sensation, soul, and form, All melted into him' (L 1b), and George Eliot, 'thinking and desiring melt together imperceptibly' (L 15). Some triggers seem to have inherent qualities that correspond with feelings of the kinds of experiences they can arouse: Wordsworth was looking down on 'ocean's liquid mass', and Daniel Deronda was watching the river at his favourite hour of 'deepening stillness'.

The impression given by mention of changes in breathing seems to be—though this is very tentative—of a deep breath before the ecstasy, a holding of the breath at or up to the point of climax, and a need to take deep breaths afterwards. There is most evidence for the last. A respondent to a later questionnaire described the experience he identified as ecstasy as being 'accompanied by a little heavier breathing' (see J 1, Appendix J). Suso, when he came to, was 'heaving great sighs from the depth of his soul' (R 1). St. Augustine, after describing an ecstasy he experienced with his mother, continues,

> 'We sighed, and there we leave bound *the first fruits of the Spirit*; and returned to vocal expressions of our mouth.' [2]

Forster's Helen, as she walked out of the Albert Hall after her ecstasy, was 'breathing the autumnal air' (L 18); Fox writes that 'all creation

---

[1] Charlotte Brontë may well have associated *glory* with fire; see the comment on this word on pp. 246–7.
[2] *Confessions* (Everyman edn., 1949), ix. 24.

gave another smell unto me than before' (R 9) which must, I think, imply breathing more deeply to notice the smell just as one must breathe more deeply to notice the autumnal air. Jefferies, after one of his ecstasies, rested, sitting down and 'inhaling the richness of the sea'.[1]

A need to breathe more deeply afterwards might suggest a momentary cessation of breathing earlier, and this is occasionally implied. Q 24 speaks of a 'terrific constriction' in her throat, and so does A. E. Housman, speaking of more frequent, less intense experiences.[2] Wordsworth, rapt in the experience of text L 1b, says, 'No thanks he breathed'; Meredith says that when Richard Feverel's experience was over, 'he looked out from his trance on the breathing world' (L 16), which I think implies that the 'breathing' of the world is being contrasted with a previous non-breathing of the observer. R. H. Ward writes that

> 'In those approaches to ecstasy which are sometimes experienced under the stimulus of nature (for instance), breathing deepens, slows, tends to become like that of a person anaesthetized or otherwise "entranced";' [3]

This also implies deeper breathing before the experience; and the same suggestion appears in text L 3 where Jefferies writes that before he was lost in his moment of exaltation, 'Involuntarily I drew a long breath, then I breathed slowly.' [4]

Some feelings of enlargement seem to be connected with the idea of inflation as by air. James quotes an ecstatic conversion:

> 'Suddenly there seemed to be a something sweeping into me and inflating my entire being'. [5]

This recalls Q 47's 'great joyful gusts and a burst' and Q 55's 'like an enormous bubble swelling inside the chest, bursting into a soundless shout'. In considering this feeling of inflation by air, the origin of the

---

[1] *The Story of My Heart* (London, 1883; Swan Library edn., 1936), ch. vi, p. 113. In my own experience, the immensely refreshing quality of post-ecstatic breathing is one of the most noticeable physical effects of these experiences.

[2] *The Name and Nature of Poetry* (Cambridge, 1933), p. 47.

[3] *A Drug-Taker's Notes* (London, 1957), p. 94.

[4] Edward Thomas, Jefferies's biographer, says that Jefferies would try to induce these experiences by 'the long breath, followed by slow breathing' (*Richard Jefferies, His Life and Work* (London, 1909), p. 182). But the experience of my text was an early one and Jefferies specifically says that the deep breath was involuntary; of course it may be that, having found it effective, he later used it deliberately.

[5] V.R.E., p. 247.

word *inspiration* must come to mind, with the many beliefs that accept inspired utterances as the result of a breathing-in by a divine breath.[1]

It would be a pity to ignore Lewis Carroll who suggests that a deep breath may be a helpful preliminary to experiences that facilitate credulity:

' "I ca'n't believe *that!*" said Alice. "Ca'n't you?" the Queen said in a pitying tone. "Try again: draw a deep breath, and shut your eyes." ' [2]

The third process that can, I believe, be discerned in descriptions of ecstasies is of tinglings leading up to feelings variously described as shocks, stabs, shudders, flashes—though I am far from certain how far feelings described in these various ways should properly be assimilated to each other.

References to tinglings, shivers, etc. are common. Q 44 speaks of 'a tingling that goes on', Q 54 of 'an electric sensation in the chest, spreading over your whole body', Q 57 of 'something creeping up your spine'; Berenson refers to 'an ideated tingling on and in my own skin' (L 10), Church of 'the hair on my head tingling' (L 23b).

Shudders and shocks sometimes appear as the climax. Proust felt that a shudder ran through his whole body as he tasted the cake (L 26). Meredith says of Richard Feverel that 'his strength went out of him and he shuddered' and then 'Vivid as lightning the Spirit of Life illumined him' (L 16). And a music critic tells how at a performance of the *Götterdämerung*, which was 'on an ecstatic height', the swearing of the oath on the sword

'reduced me to a single electric current, something near to dissolution into electricity, pure electricity.' [3]

The flashes of light, spoken of in the last chapter and mentioned in the quotation from Meredith above, are often compared, apparently for speed and brilliance but perhaps also for sensation, with lightning, for instances, 'flashes of lightning' (L 6), 'flashed up lightning-wise' (L 11). Sometimes these flashes are associated with feelings of thrills,

---

[1] De Selincourt comments that 'It is worth noting how often Wordsworth's imagination conceives of the coming of creative energy to the soul as a "breeze" ' (*Prel.*, p. 500).

[2] *Through the Looking-Glass* (London, 1871; 1910 edn.), ch. v., p. 100.

[3] Vincent Sheean, *First and Last Love* (London, 1957), p. 103.

shudders, etc. Tennyson says that 'Each failing sense, As with a momentary flash of light Grew thrillingly distinct and keen' (L 2)[1] and Nietzsche that 'The grey sky of abstraction seems thrilled with flashes of lightning' (L 6). Nichols wrote of the hieroglyphics he discerned in the lights on the water that

> '[they] seemed to flash through me, that is to say, to pass through my body without occasioning any pain' (L 5).

St. Augustine implies that the flashes are felt as warm,[2] and links these and the shudders referred to above with feelings in the heart:

> 'What is this which gleams through me, and strikes my heart without hurting it; and I shudder and kindle?' [3]

It seems to me that it may be of similar feelings that St. Teresa is speaking when she refers to a fire-tipped spear that pierces through her heart so deeply that it penetrates to her entrails.[4] Ecstasies provide few claims of feelings below the chest: Q 24 spoke of feelings of constriction in her stomach as well as her throat, and Housman said, of lesser experiences, that the sensation of something going through one like a spear is located in the pit of the stomach (see p. 88). The few descriptions of this kind that do appear tend to be seized upon and generalized from by people who seek explanations of a sexual kind for these experiences. Thus Leuba explains St. Teresa's experience as being 'the participation of sex organs tormented by an insufficient stimulation'.[5] But many such stabs in the heart do *not* penetrate to the entrails:[6] entrails are not sex-organs; and Q 24 is a happily married woman.[7]

The flashes are often associated by ecstatics with feelings of mental

---

[1] The derivation of *thrill* is interesting here. It is a variation of *thirl*, whose first definition in O.E.D. is 'To pierce, to run through or into (a body) as a sharp-pointed instrument does', and whose other definitions all carry connotations of *penetrating*, *passing through*, as, indeed, do most of the definitions of *thrill* itself.

[2] Warm flashes also appear in an account of an ecstasy triggered by music: 'White-hot lines of melody sear across the dark sky of his being.' Paul Jennings in the *Observer*, October 23, 1956.

[3] *Confessions*, xi. 11.   [4] *Life*, ch. xxix, p. 210.

[5] P.R.M., p. 145.

[6] St. Augustine's, quoted above, does not; nor does Jacopone da Todi imply this when he writes, 'Love rises to such ardour that the heart seems to be transfixed as with a knife'; (quoted by Hügel: M.E.R., Vol. II, p. 107.

[7] These piercings to the heart recall the common image of being pierced by Cupid's dart at the first sight of the loved one, especially as the first sight of the loved one is a not uncommon trigger to ecstasy; see p. 155.

illumination, and relevant to this may be the fact that several people locate them in the 'sky' of their spirit or being.

Some other physical or quasi-physical feelings claimed by ecstatics are as follows:

We find several general statements about feelings of enlargement other than by inflation by air or by a head of fluid building up. The impression given is usually that of pressure from inside. Some such general statements are Q 16's 'an enlarging', Q 44's 'tremendous expansion', and the phrase used by the clergyman of text R 3, 'one swelling harmony—his soul…almost bursting with its own emotion'.[1]

Some general feelings of enlargement are connected with mental illumination. Tennyson associates enlargement with soul, spirit, mental eye, brain:

> I felt my soul grow mighty, and my spirit
> With supernatural excitation bound
> Within me, and my mental eye grew large
> With such a vast circumference of thought…
>
> A maze of piercing, trackless, thrilling thoughts…
> Expanding momently…
> The issue of strong impulse, hurried through
> The riv'n rapt brain (L 2).[2]

Charlotte Brontë says that 'the swift glory spreads out…faster than Thought can effect his combinations' (L 14), and Nichols, before his poem came to him, was 'filled with an immense and pure emotion—a regular and growing central excitement' (L 5).

There are some claims of throbbing or pulsation, often said to increase to a climax, and usually sited in the head or, more specifically, the ear.[3] What Tennyson believed to be 'the hum of men, Or other

---

[1] Such feelings should be distinguished from those of slow gentle expansion into something else, so typical of withdrawal ecstasies, described by Q 1 as 'the hard lines round one's individuality are gone, one flows over them' and by Von Hügel as 'quasi-Pantheism…immense expansion' (see p. 69).

[2] Notice that Tennyson is pierced by thrilling thoughts as others are by flashes.

[3] 'People in a state of strong religious emotion sometimes become conscious of a throbbing sound in their ears, due to the increased force of their circulation. An organist, by opening the thirty-two foot pipe, can create the same sensation, and can thereby induce in the congregation a vague and half-conscious belief that they are experiencing religious emotion' (Graham Wallas: Human Nature in Politics (London, 1908), p. 103). It is common experience that deep notes on an organ

things talking in unknown tongues... Beat like a far wave on my anxious ear' (L 2). L 27 heard a note in his ears which he compares with a rushing wind and waves on sand, and the visitant to St. John (whose experience has many resemblances to Tennyson's) had a voice like 'the sound of many waters'.[1] To Joël the waves seemed to strike like a thundering pulse in his head (L 9). R 11 speaks of 'the throb of emotion.'

It will be noticed that these, like some other of the quasi-physical feelings of ecstasy, are associated with waves.

Very occasionally one finds indications of involuntary speech or cries, apparently during tumescence; a possible parallel might be the involuntary cries of sexual tumescence. St. Teresa, of her third and noticeably tumescent stage of prayer, writes,

> 'O my God, what must a soul be like when it is in this state! It longs to be all one tongue with which to praise the Lord. It utters a thousand pious follies, in a continuous endeavour to please Him who thus possesses it.' [2]

Angela of Foligno reported that 'through excess of marvelling, the soul cried with a loud voice, saying "This whole world is full of God!"' (R 5a). St. Catharine of Siena says that during her experience,

> 'the tongue does not speak; except as the abundance of the heart will sometimes permit it, for the alleviation of the heart' (R 2).[3]

Fire-images occasionally appear and seem often to be linked with feelings of mental illumination. Hugh of St. Victor says that his intellect is illuminated and his heart afire (R 12), St. Catherine of Siena that her intellect is elevated and her bodily powers enflamed (R 2). Bucke momentarily thought that he was wrapped in a flame-coloured cloud;[4] the next instant,

may also induce thrills and shudders; so may gazing at a point of bright light and so may thundery weather.

[1] *Rev.* i. 15.   [2] *Life*, ch. xvi, p. 113

[3] St. Catherine's experience is taken by Underhill to be religious 'ecstasy'; but involuntary cries seem surprising in a state of trance.

[4] In connexion with Bucke's unusual flame-coloured cloud, it is worth mentioning Church's almost equally unusual 'curtain of red blood' that appeared to fall before his eyes (L 23b). Both, apparently, blur or blot out vision before a moment of illumination.   D. H. Lawrence speaks of being blinded by crimson blood floating up from his swelling heart in his poem 'Snap-Dragon'; but I do not think the experience there described can count as an ecstasy.

'I knew that the fire was within myself. Directly afterwards there came upon me a sense of exultation, of immense joyousness accompanied or immediately followed by an intellectual illumination impossible to describe.' (R 17).

Tennyson described his thoughts as being 'rapid as fire' (L 2).[1]

A felt achievement of pattern or harmony is common in ecstasy, and sometimes, and noticeably in my questionnaire group, the achievement of this pattern or harmony is described in what seem to be quasi-physical terms; for instance, 'suddenly clicked, perception of a pattern' (Q 6); 'sensation of absolute oneness, rightness, the same thing—the whole world falls into place, matches, fits' (Q 19). Compare Nietzsche's 'unexpectedly answers drop into my lap, a small hailstorm of ice and wisdom' (L 6); a similar phrase was used by Wordsworth about the making of a poem: 'While thoughts press on, and feelings overflow, And quick words round him fall like flakes of snow'.[2] These phrases about *dropping, falling* in connexion with mental patterns being formed are the only association of ecstasy (or inspiration) with anything to do with falling; and the images of ice and snow used by Nietzsche and Wordsworth are the only instances I know of associations with coldness.

Feelings of increasing calm, stillness, peace are, of course, of the nature of withdrawal ecstasies, but there are some suggestions of an instant of calm at or immediately after the climax of an intensity ecstasy; for instance, 'suddenly overwhelms without expectation—standstill feeling' (Q 30); 'great joyful gusts and a burst, a sudden feeling of complete calm' (Q 47). Suso speaks of 'sensations of silence and of rest' apparently at the heart of his experience (R 1), and Hugh of St. Victor of peace, apparently after he had been carried away but before he returned to a more ordinary state (R 12).

The analyses have made it clear that it is characteristic of ecstasies that during their brief duration normal faculties of perception are felt to be diminished or in abeyance.

A common claim is that after these experiences the ecstatic finds

[1] Heat or fire images are not uncommon in descriptions of inspiration; for instance, Wordsworth, after hearing Dorothy read Milton's sonnets aloud, 'took fire...and produced three Sonnets that same afternoon' (P.W., Vol. III, p. 417).
[2] 'The Warning', P.W., Vol. IV, p. 110, ll. 20-1.

himself in tears or with tears in his eyes. A later respondent spoke of a feeling of wanting to close the eyes and cry, and another from the same group said that the experience sometimes leads to tears (J 1 and J 2, Appendix J). Q 56's tears were caused, he felt, by the *force* (my italics) of beauty; R 11's eyes were filled with tears after the experience was over; Tennyson's eyes were filled with tears after his climax (L 2).

Those people—not always very reliable witnesses—who have observed religious mystics in or just after mystical states—which may or may not be ecstasies—have commented on such changes in appearance as shining or rosy or flushed faces and bright or sparkling eyes.[1] Eyes might well seem bright or sparkling because tear-washed.

A common effect of ecstasy, presumably connected with the eyes, is an apparent cleansing of the doors of perception, a feeling that after an ecstasy the world appears fresh and new and gleaming—'I felt myself in a new world, and everything about me appeared with a different aspect from what it was wont to do' (R 13).

Ecstasies usually give rise to feelings of vitality and well-being. The improvement claimed may be mental or physical or both. I give an example of each type from each group: first, of increased general vitality,

'awareness of being so alive' (Q 46); 'some deeply felt vitality' (L 19); 'as one inspired with a supernatural life' (R 18),

of increased physical well-being,

'intense physical well-being' (Q 54); 'an extraordinary physical exhilaration' (L 5); 'a great bodily comfort' (R 10a),

of increased mental capacity,

'transcend your normal limitations, capacity for experience, burst into a wider one' (Q 5); 'our faculties...enhanced—keener perceptions' (L 20); 'my intellect is illumined' (R 12).

A prime test for religious mystical experience is that it should 'leave the soul, and the very body, as its instrument, strengthened and improved'.[2]

---

[1] See, for instances, E.U: M.W., pp. 121–2; Hügel: M.E.R., Vol. I, p. 161; and on the possibility that light may in literal fact stream from some faces, Thurston: P.P.M., ch. v.

[2] Hügel: M.E.R., Vol. II, p. 47. In many cases it clearly does not do so, and some excuses are provided. It is said, for instance, that a certain tender psycho-physical make-up seems to be especially apt for these experiences (E.U: M., p. 59), and, says Von Hügel, even if mystical experiences do sometimes exact 'a

An enhancement of well-being, both mental and physical, is usual in unitive states. 'There is given to man a divine strength and a divine power,' said Suso (R 22) of the religious state, and for the secular we may take Gissing's statement that 'It was a healthful time; it gave me a new lease of life and taught me...how to make use of it' (see p. 64).

Sometimes however the immediate effect of an ecstatic experience is exhaustion or near-collapse. R 11 had to sit down and only after a time was able to walk on, 'but very slowly, so strongly was I still possessed by the emotion'. Suso walked afterwards 'as a machine might do' (R 1). Jefferies, after one of his ecstatic experiences, 'rested, sitting by the wheat...By the dry wheat I rested, I did not think'.[1] In text L 27 Ray, still dazed after his experience, 'lurched' to the centre of the dais. Tennyson seems to have collapsed: 'thick night Came down upon my eyelids, and I fell' (L 2).

Some feelings of pain are spoken of in connexion with ecstasies. First we have accounts of what seem to be the usual pain/pleasure feelings of many tumescent experiences: for example, 'so intense in its joy as to be almost painful' (Q 38); 'moves me with such sweetness and violence' (R 12). Then there are the thrills, shudders, shocks apparently felt at the climax of the experience; the heart-piercing experiences, also referred to earlier, are sometimes said to be painful, though usually delightfully so. Finally, impaired capacity after the experience seems sometimes to be accompanied with pain during the return to normal. This is implied by both Emily Brontë (L 21) and by Suso (R 1).

Some ecstatics claim none of these feelings, and some claim several. Tennyson, for instance, speaks of roarings in his ears, flashes of light, general feelings of enlargement, tears; Joël of pulsation and of liquidity. Several of these may similarly be claimed in unitive states; Benjamin Haydon's account of a period of inspiration brings together up-feelings, flashes, shudders, and feelings of breathing intoxicating air:

'This week has really been a week of great delight. Never have I had such irresistible, perpetual continued urgings of future greatness.

serious physical tribute', so do mining, warfare, hospital work, and the preparation of many chemicals; yet no one thinks of abolishing these 'if the end to be attained is found to be necessary or obviously helpful, and unobtainable by other means' (M.E.R., Vol. II, pp. 57–8.).

[1] *The Story of My Heart*, ch. vi, p. 113.

I have been like a man with air balloons under his arm pits, and ether in his soul. While I was painting or walking, or thinking, these beaming flashes of energy followed and impressed me!... They came over me, & shot across me, & shook me, & inspired me to such a degree of intensity, that I lifted up my heart, & thanked God.' [1]

Similar accounts of quasi-physical feelings, whether singly or in groups, also occur in descriptions of experiences similar to ecstatic ones but more frequent and less intense (these will be discussed in the next chapter). Housman writes,

'Experience has taught me, when I am shaving of a morning, to keep watch over my thoughts, because, if a line of poetry strays into my memory, my skin bristles so that the razor ceases to act. This particular symptom is accompanied by a shiver down the spine; there is another which consists in a constriction of the throat and a precipitation of water to the eyes; and there is a third which I can only describe by borrowing a phrase from one of Keats's last letters, where he says, speaking of Fanny Brawne, "everything that reminds me of her goes through me like a spear". The seat of this sensation is the pit of the stomach.' [2]

And, says Housman, poetry that is lofty, magnificent or intense will stab the heart, shake the soul and take the breath away.[3]

Some of these symptoms claimed—tears, for instance, sighs, shudders —could be verified by simple observation—apart, of course, from the improbability of ecstasies taking place when there are people there to observe them. Others could not, and it would be interesting to know how far, if at all, ecstatics' accounts of their symptoms correspond with actual physical events that may accompany, if only incidentally, experiences of ecstasy.

---

[1] Quoted by Dorothy Hewlett, *A Life of John Keats* (London, 1949; 2nd edn., 1950), p. 60.

[2] *The Name and Nature of Poetry*, p. 47. Housman cites confirmatory evidence from *Job* iv, 19: 'Then a spirit passed before my face; the hair of my flesh stood up.'

[3] Ibid., p. 12.

CHAPTER VIII

Varieties and Values

Among the general range of intensity ecstasies several variant forms appear, and people who have known more than one form often indicate that they consider one more valuable than another.

Some people in the questionnaire group do this without indicating the bases for their judgements. Thus Q 30 says she has known ecstasy 'perfectly only about twelve times', which implies that she has more often known less perfect experiences; but she does not say in what she believes the difference between perfect and less perfect experiences to consist. Q 25 distinguishes between very rare transcendental experiences and more frequent approaches to such experiences without achieving them.

Other people in the questionnaire group both distinguish between different forms of ecstasy and explain why they consider one form more valuable than another. Q 26, in a note added to her original answers, said,

'if you're conscious of the state when you're in it, it's not so terrific. But with the great ones, you don't realize till you come back that you were in heaven.'

Q 22, also in a later communication, wrote,

'I do not think it is ecstasy unless you are literally lifted out of yourself, unless you have left yourself behind,'

and described the lesser state as 'the sensation of a poet in the act of creation'.

Still in the questionnaire group, many of the people who believed there was a relationship between ecstasy and inspiration described that relationship in terms of ecstasy being better than inspiration though of the same kind. Thus, Q 16, contrasting ecstasy and inspiration, said that ecstasy was a self-losing, and inspiration 'the opposite'; this is similar to Q 22's belief that ecstasy, in which the self is lost, is better than the creative state in which self is not lost. Q 34 said that inspiration was a minor form of ecstasy, and that ecstasy involved 'feeling in unity with everything'. Q 58 said that inspiration was not so mysterious and exciting as ecstasy but gave a feeling that 'the day has been lived, not just passed through'. Several others indicated that they thought inspiration similar to but less than ecstasy.

This widespread feeling in the questionnaire group that inspiration is less than ecstasy or can be felt at a stage of ecstasy less than the best is confirmed by St. Teresa for whom the third of her four stages of prayer (from less to best) was apt for creation:

> 'I know someone' [i.e. herself] 'who, although no poet, yet suddenly composed some stanzas, full of feeling'. [1]

The clergyman of text R 3 implies that his supreme (and unique) experience gave feelings of contact with God, other lesser experiences giving feelings of vision and of eternity. Wordsworth implies that feelings of restoration and sweet sensations from which may result little acts of kindness and love are less sublime than though similar to experiences which enable us to 'see into the heart of things'.[2]

Fox usefully describes what he regards as more valuable—or, as he puts it, more steadfast—stages of ecstasy. My text R 9 shows the first stage, the feeling that both he and the world around him have been purified and renewed so that he feels himself to be in the state of Adam before the Fall. My text contains only what was quoted by Knox from whom I took it, but in Fox's *Journal* the account continues:

> '[before he fell]. The creation was opened to me; and it was shewed me how all things had their names given them according to their nature and virtue. I was at a stand in my mind whether I should practise physic for the good of mankind, seeing the nature and virtues of the creatures were so opened to me by the Lord. But I was immediately taken up in spirit, to see into another or more steadfast state than Adam's in innocency, even into a state in Christ Jesus that should never fall. And the Lord shewed me that such as were faithful to Him, in the power and light of Christ, should come up into that state in which Adam was before he fell; in which the admirable works of the creation, and the virtues thereof, may be known through the openings of that divine Word of wisdom and power by which they

[1] *Life*, ch. xvi, p. 113.
[2] *Lines composed a few miles above Tintern Abbey*, P.W., Vol. II, p. 260, ll. 22–49.

were made. Great things did the Lord lead me into, and wonderful depths were opened unto me beyond what can by words be declared; but as people come into subjection to the Spirit of God, and grow up in the image and power of the Almighty, they may receive the word of wisdom, that opens all things, and come to know the hidden unity in the Eternal Being.' [1]

Thus Fox first enters the state of Adam, the Adamic state of innocency in which both he and the material world feel purified and renewed. He gains knowledge of the material world, communicable knowledge that he feels he could turn to practical effect.[2] He passes from the stage in which communicable knowledge is gained to one in which, through contact with God, incommunicable knowledge is felt to have been gained.

Not only is this stage felt to be better than the one in which communicable knowledge is gained; incommunicable knowledge is itself felt to be better than communicable knowledge. Both beliefs are common among religious mystics. Thus St. Augustine speaks of perceiving the brightness of the Lord 'not by any symbolic vision, whether corporeal or spiritual'; of perceiving the perspicuous truth, 'without any image of body'; and of this state being higher than one in which 'images of body' may be seen by the spirit (R 19). Suso believed that the less imagery there was in experiences of apprehending the divinity, 'the higher they are and the nearer to absolute reality is the knowledge they impart'.[3] St. John of the Cross, setting 'infinite incomprehension' above 'visions, revelations, locutions, and spiritual impressions', writes,

'One of the greatest favours, bestowed transiently on the soul in this life, is to enable it to see so distinctly and to feel so profoundly, that it cannot comprehend Him at all.' [4]

Thus knowledge of its nature incommunicable—mystical knowledge—is felt to derive from experiences better than those in which communicable knowledge is gained. And it follows that knowledge of *all* or *everything*—a very usual claim—which cannot of its nature

[1] George Fox, *Journal* (Everyman edn., 1948), p. 17.
[2] For most people, the state of Adam (a common expression in mystical experience) is one of innocency without knowledge. But Fox regards it as proper in this state to be able to see how 'things' were given names, presumably because the naming of created things was one of the functions given to Adam; see *Gen.* ii. 19–20.
[3] Quoted by Leuba: P.R.M., p. 65.   [4] Quoted by Hügel: M.E.R., Vol. II, p. 51.

be communicated, is derived from experiences felt to be better than those in which knowledge of *something* is gained. In what is generally regarded as the best stage of ecstasy there is no ability to understand even mystical knowledge, for all the senses are lost.[1]

From the evidence put forward I postulate as a working model the following pattern for what are believed to be progressively better stages of ecstasy:

At the least stage at which ecstatics identify experiences as being of a kind, we find feelings that life is joyful, purified, renewed. Ecstasies principally characterized by feelings of this kind I shall call *adamic ecstasies*. It is to this stage, I believe, that there belong those feelings of kindness and love spoken of by Wordsworth, Fox's desire to benefit mankind.

At a stage regarded as better we find feelings of creativity or of knowledge gained. These I shall call *knowlegde ecstasies*. Often the knowledge is felt to be gained through a contact felt to be made, and these I shall call *knowledge-contact* ecstasies.

That knowledge may come at a stage less than that in which contact is felt to be made is suggested by the feelings often reported that where knowledge is gained, self is not felt to be lost; but where contact is made, self *is* often felt to be lost, and it is generally agreed that ecstasies in which self is lost are better than those in which feelings of self are not lost.

The more complete the knowledge is felt to be and the more incommunicable, the better the ecstasy.

At the stage regarded as the best, ecstasies may involve complete or almost complete loss of sensibility, coupled with a feeling (necessarily afterwards) that any contact made has been complete. Ecstasies with these characteristics I shall call *union ecstasies*.

The postulation is tentative because the evidence is insufficient. But this scale of values, which has emerged from a very few comparative statements made by people in the groups, substantially corresponds with the scales systematized by many Christian writers to differentiate the kinds of experiences that may be progressively expected along the

[1] But it is usually the mystics rather than the theologians who regard this stage as the best; Inge remarks tartly 'There is nothing Divine about a *tabula rasa*' (C.M., p. 114n).

Christian's road to God. The *Oxford Dictionary of the Christian Church* (under 'Unitive Way'), following St. Teresa, St. John of the Cross, and others, names the first stage of the spiritual life 'The Purgative Way' (in which the soul is purified), the next stage 'The Illuminative Way' (in which the soul is enlightened), and the final stage 'The Unitive Way' (where the soul enters on the 'Way of Union' with God).[1] Inge says that the social and civic virtues belong to the lowest or purgative stage where they occupy the lowest place:[2] I think this is some support of my suggestion that feelings of kindness and love to other people belong to this stage.

It is agreed by most systematizers that any such classifications are necessarily rough-and-ready and arbitrary, and that many experiences fail to be clearly distinctive of one or other stage. 'It is generally held, however,' says the *Oxford Dictionary of the Christian Church*, 'that there is no hard-and-fast dividing line, and elements from the illuminative and even purgative stages may appear also in the unitive life'; and Underhill comments that in some people some stages are left out, while for others they are reversed. Thus not even disciplined Christians, knowing of the existence of such systematizations, need necessarily either have experiences clearly distinctive of one or other stage or progress from experiences of the first stage through those of the second to the third.

This is as true of the ecstasies I am examining in relation to the scale I have empirically established for them. It is already clear that some people at least enjoy different experiences on different occasions.[3] Something of the possible range of experiences open to the religious is shown by the following:

'Sometimes, like guests at a royal feast, they are satiated with indescribable enjoyments; sometimes they are filled with a divine and intimate delight, like that of the bride when she rejoices in the presence of the bridegroom . . . sometimes the communication of the divine mysteries induces in them a holy inebriation. Sometimes they are seized by a lively compassion at the sight of human misery,

---

[1] My suggestion that feelings of knowledge may be regarded as lesser than feelings of contact is implicit in the above but is explicitly supported by Proclus's 'Knowledge leads, then follows proximity, and then union' (Hügel: M.E.R., Vol. II, p. 98).

[2] C.M., p. 10.

[3] Both St. Teresa and Fox seem to have enjoyed progressively greater experiences on single occasions; see pp. 52–4 and pp. 90–1.

and, in the ardour of their charity, they give themselves wholly to prayers and tears... At other times, he immerses himself in a profound silence; and then his soul enjoys great peace, and tastes in its quietude of ineffable delights. Or else the Holy Spirit illuminates his intelligence, and communicates to him a supernal wisdom, and high knowledge which human speech cannot express.' [1]

The scale I have described is intended to apply only to intensity ecstasies. I have not attempted to systematize withdrawal ecstasies. It seems, however, that to the religious the final stage of both is believed to be similar, what Underhill calls the meeting of the two approaches in 'the peace of the summits' (see p. 49) and Kirk, 'a point of view from which spiritual vacancy and spiritual fulness are almost indistinguishable'. [2]

For Christian mystics the experiences regarded as more valuable are also generally accepted as rarer. I have not enough evidence to say whether this is so with ecstasies, though several people in the questionnaire group do imply that experiences regarded as more valuable are rarer than others regarded as less valuable; for instance, Q 30 who said she had known the experience 'perfectly only about twelve times'.

We now have a tentative scale of ecstasies—adamic, knowledge-contact, union—which I shall accept as a working model and which on the evidence of ecstatics is a scale of increasing value. It is hard to escape the conclusion that ecstatic experiences become more *something* as they progress along this scale. I do not know what this something is; I suspect it may have a physical referent. But I shall want to refer to ecstasies as being more or less *something* without necessarily implying that they are—as ecstatics regard them—more or less valuable. No comparative epithets that have occurred to me are sufficiently neutral; I shall use *greater* and *less* in italics to refer, as unemotionally

---

[1] St. Macarius of Egypt, quoted E.U : M.W., pp. 326–7.

[2] V.G., p. 199. Although in her later book *The Mystic Way*, Evelyn Underhill pleads for acceptance of the condition in which mystics claim total oneness with the divine involving total loss of sense, in *Mysticism* she tries to avoid the difficulty by postulating a fourth stage on the mystic way, which is accepted by 'Oriental Mysticism' but 'decisively rejected by all European mystics'. This is 'the total annihilation or reabsorption of the individual soul in the Infinite' and she explains that though the language of some of the 'more Orientally-minded mystics' such as Dionysius the Areopagite, may suggest that they are trying to describe this state, they are not really trying to do so, but only the permissible third stage (pp. 170–2). But I should have thought that to postulate on a scale of progressively increasing value a final stage impermissible to Christians led her only into greater difficulties.

as possible, to this postulated quality of being more or less *something*. Thus I shall say that knowledge ecstasies are *greater* than adamic ecstasies, *less* than knowledge-contact ecstasies.

Not only momentary ecstasies but also unitive states—those prolonged ecstatic states discussed in Chapter V—can usefully be called adamic, knowledge or knowledge-contact, and union. The passage from Wells describing the feelings of the man who awakes in a new utopian world (see p. 65) shows close correspondence with the feelings characteristic of adamic ecstasies—loss of worldliness, joy, release, up-feelings, feelings of enlargement—and one of the characters does, indeed, exclaim 'I feel like a new Adam'. Such states of mind are attributed to the inhabitants by almost all the creators of this kind of utopia. The Gissing extract, on the same page, shows rather a unitive state similar to a knowledge ecstasy, with its feelings of loss of time, of self, of joy, release, renewal in a new world, new and expanding knowledge. So does the passage from Haydon's diary quoted on p.87-8, though here the emphasis is rather on quasi-physical symptoms. And Bowra's description of the poet in a period of creativeness suggests a unitive state closely resembling a knowledge-contact ecstasy:

> 'The poet unaccountably finds himself dominated by something which absorbs his being and excludes other interests from his mind ...though at first it is too indefinite for intellectual analysis, it imposes itself on the poet with the majesty and authority of vision. Even if he does not fully understand it, he feels it and almost sees it... While such a fit is on him, the poet has a sense of inexhaustible abundance and does not question that the visitation will give him all, and more than all, that he needs for his task...this condition is one of joy...the poet not only forgets anything outside the immediate object of his vision but loses his sense of time. Past and future no longer exist for him and he enjoys a timeless condition. Nor is this condition negative, a mere state of omissions and absences. It is strikingly positive. In it the poet feels that his whole being is enlarged and that he is able to enjoy in an unprecedented completeness what in his ordinary life he enjoys only in fragments...in such circumstances they [*sc.* poets] feel they have passed into eternity.
>
> This condition is often also one of an extraordinary illumination, for which the poets use the imagery of light.' [1]

[1] C. M. Bowra, *Inspiration and Poetry* (London, 1955), pp. 4-10; I have made considerable cuts, but the whole passage is worth reading in this context.

The feeling of expanding knowledge, so strongly expressed here, is not confined to those engaged in creative work, whether artistic or scientific. It is expressed in the Gissing extract; and I think we see a similar state in Wesley in the days just after his conversion, when he wrote, 'All these days I scarce remember to have opened the Testament, but upon some great and precious promise.' [1]

An example of a unitive state corresponding with the third or union stage of ecstasy is provided by Suso in text R 22 which showed, in analysis, feelings of loss of worldliness and of self, gain of joy, etc., and of contact and feelings of ineffability, but with no claims to new or even mystical knowledge. I quote a few phrases which give an impression of the whole:

> 'he is no longer conscious of his selfhood; he disappears and loses himself in God... All human desires are taken from [such people].'

People do not compare unitive states one with the other, so it is not possible to say whether these differences are, as with momentary ecstasies, regarded as corresponding with different degrees of value.

There is widespread agreement that momentary ecstatic experiences may vary in intensity as well as in kind. Often in religious writing there is the assumption that 'ordinary people' may have ecstatic experiences differing from those of the classic mystics in being less intense.[2] Sometimes this assumption is echoed by the ordinary people themselves. For instance Q 46, a practising non-conformist, assumed that a question about transcendent ecstasy referred to religious experience and replied that he had not known experiences like those of the religious ecstatics; yet apart from matters of overbelief it is not possible to say that the experiences he describes differ in substance from those of many classic mystics. Again, a devout Roman Catholic woman said of her experiences, 'I know enough about mysticism to know that they are not the ecstasies the saints experience' (see J 6, Appendix J, p. 531); her own momentary experiences included feelings of being uplifted, oblivious of what was around her, and praise to God.

---

[1] *The Journal of the Rev. John Wesley*, June 4, 1738 (Everyman edn., 1921).
[2] For instance: 'Few people pass through life without knowing what it is to be at least touched by this mystical feeling...But we do not call every one who has these partial and artistic intuitions of reality a mystic'. E.U: M., pp. 73 and 75; see also my p. 274.

Of experiences that fulfil my criteria for ecstasy it is not possible to distinguish, by study of the words used, whether any experience of any one person is more or less intensely felt than any experience of another. It might conceivably be possible to find referents for a physical scale by which experiences fundamentally similar could be judged as more or less intense, but failing this, one must rely on the evidence of people who compare their own experiences in terms of intensity or in what can reasonably be taken to imply intensity.[1]

Such comparisons are made by several people in the questionnaire group. Q 34 says that ecstasy 'varies in intensity—one can induce it in oneself, not very intensely, if one's in a suitable mood, place, etc.' Q 26 says she has known ecstasy something under a hundred times— 'say, between fifty and a hundred, but really intensely, real spiritual ecstasy, say, between twenty to thirty times'. Q 50 says she has known transcendent ecstasy in units—'I've often had it nearly, but not the real fire'. Q 61, who said he had known ecstasy in units, added,

'sometimes here [in a London office] because the sky is blue and the building is white, you look at it and feel that life is worthwhile, the same kind of feeling, but much less.'

The greater frequency of these less intense experiences may help to explain why a few people said they had known ecstasy hundreds of times; they may have taken the name *transcendent ecstasy* to refer to experiences less intense than most people supposed it to refer to, or they may have been lumping more and less intense experiences together. But clearly most people did *not* regard these less intense, more frequent experiences as fitted by the name ecstasy. They did, however, regard them as being of the same general kind.

There are some purposes for which it may be useful to trace the same general kind of experiences to still lower levels of intensity, and one such purpose is to allow consideration of the possibility that ecstatic experiences represent rare exaggerations of other experiences commonly known to at least some people.

I have specifically excluded from my criteria for ecstasies experiences

[1] The differences between adamic, knowledge-contact, and union ecstasies do not seem to be felt as differences in intensity. The comparisons were based, by people in the groups or cited in this chapter, on experiences being more or less great (this was the most frequent), mysterious, exciting, ecstatic, high, sublime, steadfast; *intense*, which might seem an obvious word, is used only by Q 58.

which are said to be people's normal and habitual response to triggers
(see p. 43). I now want to consider whether it is reasonable to regard
ecstasies as exaggerations of these habitual experiences.

I have found in talking to people that some take it for granted that
ecstasies are an exaggerated form of experiences normally expected
from encounter with triggers, while others are equally sure that the
two kinds of experience are basically different; and that people holding
the second point of view are usually religious while those holding the
first are not. It would, I imagine, be generally agreed that on contact
with at least some triggers some if not most people expect to have responses they regard as beneficial and valuable. This is, I think, indicated
by the prestige accorded to all the more common triggers, and the
widespread feelings of outrage when triggers are felt to be rendered
ineffective by intrusive action (see Ch. XVIII). Ecstasies are so very
infrequent and so rarely (if ever) induced twice by the same trigger
that one may suppose this respect and solicitude justified by the likelihood of more frequent benefits than the extreme off-chance of an
ecstatic experience.

Though I have not collected and analysed any substantial number of
the experiences people say they normally expect on encounter with
triggers, examination of the language in which only a few are described does support the view that such experiences may often if not
usually be considered as similar to ecstatic ones but less intense. What
the expected benefits from such encounters may be is often most
easily shown by giving a few instances of occasions when people
feel that they have been denied, and my first is from Byron, telling
of his feelings at the conclusion of his tour of Switzerland in
1816:

'neither the music of the shepherds, the crashing of the avalanche,
nor the torrent, the mountain, the glacier, the forest, or the cloud,
have for one moment lightened the weight upon my heart, nor
enabled me to lose my wretched identity in the majesty, and the
power, and the glory around, above and beneath me.' [1]

What Byron expected from these various trigger conditions was at
least a momentary lightening of the heart and loss of identity.

[1] From note to Canto III, lxviii of *Childe Harold*, ed. E. H. Coleridge (London,
1898), p. 258.

My next example is from Wordsworth who presents Peter Bell as extraordinary in that he is unmoved by nature, that

> A primrose by a river's brim
> A yellow primrose was to him,
> And it was nothing more.[1]

What more, we must ask, should it have been? In another poem Wordsworth explains that what primroses should give is

> genial promises to those who droop
> Sick, poor, or weary, or disconsolate,
> Brightening at once the winter of their souls.[2]

Wordsworth, again, describes in a short poem his usual response to a rainbow:

> My heart leaps up when I behold
> A rainbow in the sky:
> So was it when my life began;
> So is it now I am a man;
> So be it when I shall grow old,
> Or let me die![3]

And after so many years of this expected response Wordsworth was very much aware of his loss when he later found that though 'The Rainbow comes and goes', yet there has passed away a glory from the earth.[4]

Another kind of trigger is involved in this quotation from Jefferies:

'O beautiful human life! Tears come in my eyes as I think of it. So beautiful, so inexpressibly beautiful… How willingly I would strew the paths of all with flowers; how beautiful a delight to make the world joyous!'[5]

We may fairly take it that Jefferies would have been surprised had he thought of beautiful human life and *not* found tears come to his eyes and magnanimity to his soul.

From only these few examples—but many more could be adduced—

---

[1] *Peter Bell*, P.W., Vol. II, p. 341, ll. 248–50.
[4] 'The Tuft of Primroses', P.W., Vol. V, p. 348, ll. 34–6.
[3] P.W., Vol. I, p. 226.
[4] *Intimations of Immortality*, P.W., Vol. IV, p. 279 et seq.
[5] *The Story of My Heart*, ch. vii, pp. 128–9.

we find that the feelings that some people expect from contact with at least some triggers are those of glory and joy and lightening or leaping of the heart, perception of pattern, enhanced well-being, loss of self. These are some of the feelings of ecstasy. Cumulatively they would, in analysis, provide enough for me to call an ecstasy any experience that included them all. But no one of these experiences provides enough of my criteria for ecstasy, and experiences normally expected from contact with triggers were not those proffered by most people in the questionnaire group when asked about transcendent ecstasy.[1]

But experiences such as these do confirm the suggestion that the feelings expected by many people on contact with at least some triggers are less intense forms of the feelings I am calling ecstasy; that at the very least these people expect, on encounter with triggers, to feel benefited.

It is noticeable that where, in accounts of such experiences, physical or quasi-physical feelings are described, these fall into the same range as those described in accounts of ecstatic experiences.[2]

I think it surprising that experiences so widely known and so often recounted should have no name. I shall want to refer to them again and shall call them—for lack of a better name—*response experiences*. I shall not call any experience a response experience unless it is preceded by encounter with a trigger and is either said to be similar to but less intense than ecstasy, or is described in some of the terms of ecstasy and in none inconsistent with these. Whether different types of response experiences correspond with different types of ecstasies will be further considered in connexion with inspiration (see pp. 284–5).

Before leaving the subject of less intense experiences it is worth noting Leuba's suggestion that the beneficial results of mystical experiences—that is, increased vitality and moral energy—may at least to some extent be obtained by 'commonplace means of physical and moral refreshment'. Fear of the trivial, he writes, should not lead one to avoid, in this connexion,

'the mention of coffee, of tea, of a hot bath[3]...Nothing is trivial which

---

[1] It may however have been such experiences that Q 35 and Q 46 were referring to; the former said that any aesthetic experience was liable to induce ecstasy, and the latter, that he knew ecstasy 'endlessly, in a sense'.

[2] Tears coming to the eyes are, as a matter of fact, much more common in accounts of these lesser experiences than in accounts of ecstasies.

[3] Suzuki, modifying an illustration given by a Zen master, brings the refreshment afforded by mountains and by tea into the same context: 'I have been read-

alters so radically mood and outlook as a cup of tea sometimes does. There are neuropathic persons who describe their transformation after a cup of tea in terms which fall little short of those fittingly used to characterise the results of a religious ecstasy. A hot bath improves not only the general well-being but also the moral attitude: restlessness, mental dispersion, irritability, malevolence, pessimism, may vanish and be replaced by peace, mental unification, benevolence, optimism.' [1]

I have no wish to avoid the trivial, and suggest that unitive states may, like ecstasies, vary in intensity to the low point where we might more properly speak of something like response states. After a long winter, after a period of intensive and commonplace work, after an illness, someone—a doctor, a friend, less probably one's own good sense—will suggest that a change is needed. The good results that may stem from this change will very likely be described in terms similar to but less intense than those used to describe unitive states—feelings of rest, peace, refreshment, being taken out of oneself, forgetting the clock and one's day-to-day mundane worries, being mentally and physically renewed.

Indeed it is possible—but here my speculations must end—that both ecstasies and unitive states represent only unusually intense varieties of experiences and states inseparable from being healthily alive and human.

An experience which does not fit into any of the patterns so far described is related in text Q 57. There are, says this respondent, two feelings: one, 'you experience while it's happening', and the other is 'the liberation of relief'. It is to the latter, it seems, that she ascribes feelings of 'gratified vanity'.

Many ecstatics claim loss of feelings of self; many, equally, do not, though no one in my texts claims feelings so positively incompatible with loss of self as feelings of gratified vanity must be. Yet Q 57, while differentiating between them, still calls both feelings 'transcendent ecstasy'.

ing all day, confined to my room, and feel tired. I raise the screen and face the broad daylight. I move the chair on the verandah and look at the blue mountains. I draw a deep breath, fill my lungs with fresh air and feel entirely refreshed. I make tea and drink a cup or two of it. Who would say that I am not living in the light of eternity?' (*Mysticism, Christian and Buddhist*, p. 111).

[1] P.R.M., pp. 261–2.

This distinction seems very similar to one made by C. P. Snow in his novel *The New Men*:[1]

> 'So far as I could distinguish, there were two kinds of scientific experience, and a scientist was lucky if he was blessed by a visitation of either just once in his working life. The kind which most of them, certainly Martin, would have judged the higher was not the one he had just known: instead, the higher kind was more like (it was in my view the same as) the experience that the mystics had described so often, the sense of communion with all-being. Martin's was quite different, not so free from self, more active: as though, instead of being one with the world, he held the world in the palm of his hand; as though he had, in his moment of insight, seen the trick by which he could toss it about.'

In the experience regarded as less high, the self is neither lost nor ignored; as Snow describes it, 'gratified vanity' would not seem an inappropriate term. Tennyson, early in text L 2, speaks of 'vanity' as he stands alone on a height and seems to survey the universe; this, if it is indeed an experience basically similar to those of Q 57 and Snow's character, appears to pass into the more genuinely ecstatic kind of experience. Both Snow and Q 57 describe these 'different' experiences in the context of others which it is reasonable to call ecstatic.[2] Both attribute to these 'different' experiences some of the characteristics of ecstasy. Snow says that they are rare, momentary, and accompanied by feelings of insight. Q 57 says that both experiences include feelings of being immensely light, of enhanced capacity, of 'something creeping up your spine', as well as that they are rare and, by implication, momentary.

I think that they may, perhaps at varying levels of intensity, be very well known; the common phrase, 'on top of the world' seems perfectly appropriate to these feelings, and the picture this gives, of supremacy over the world as it is, is very different from the ecstatic up-picture of soaring away from the world-as-it-is towards something supreme. Worldly success can be very pleasing and gratifying and perhaps these two experiences represent the acme of pleasure obtainable in relation to worldly success.

[1] *The New Men* (London, 1954), pp. 50–1.
[2] Text L 25 undoubtedly represents Snow's impression of the 'higher' feeling which, there as here, he associates with religious mystical experience.

CHAPTER IX

Adamic and Time Ecstasies

Adamic ecstasy is, as I explained in the last chapter, the name I am giving to ecstatic experiences principally characterized by feelings that life is joyful, purified, renewed, but which lack feelings of knowledge gained or contact made. In terms of my analyses, these ecstasies are distinguished by entries implying feelings of new life, another world, joy, salvation, perfection, satisfaction, glory (the entries that, in the simplified analyses, were grouped together under III C), but with no entries under feelings of contact or feelings of knowledge (except of knowledge by identification).

Several of my texts fall into this pattern. In the questionnaire group there are seventeen such texts; in the literary group, four, those of Jefferies, Charlotte Brontë, Proust, and the earlier of the texts of Richard Church;[1] in the religious group there is one such text, that from George Fox (R 9).

If these twenty-two ecstasies are analysed as a group, they show interesting divergencies from the analyses of the groups as wholes.[2] Although an entry under one of the headings grouped together with *new life*, etc. is a defining characteristic, the number of entries here is very high (25·9 per cent. of all entries, contrasted with 15·5 per cent. for the mean). The proportion of entries under *loss of worldliness, desire, sorrow, sin*, is higher than in any of the groups, and this is particularly interesting in view of the fact that most of the adamic ecstasies come from the questionnaire group whose entry under this heading was

---

[1] Texts L 3, 14, 26, and 23a. The text by Charlotte Brontë does, in analysis, show an entry under *gain of knowledge*; but this refers to what Charlotte Brontë herself would have made of such an experience, contrasted with her character's inability to do the same. She wished to show that Shirley's experience was inferior to one that could be used creatively; or that Shirley, being inferior, could not make the best use of such experience.

[2] See Appendix D, Table 5, where the analyses of adamic ecstasies are compared with those of knowledge-contact ecstasies and of the mean.

noticeably lower than those of the other two groups. In one case only is there an entry for *loss of self* (0·8 per cent. of all entries contrasted with 4·1 per cent. for the mean); I think we may take it that to feel loss of self is not characteristic of this type of ecstasy. It will be remembered that many ecstatics felt *loss of self* to pertain only to their *greater* ecstasies (see p. 92 above).

The quasi-physical feelings show entries rather larger than the mean of the three groups under *inside-feelings* and *enlargement/improvement* feelings. But the differences are not great; in whatever ways I have divided and analysed the texts, the proportion of entries for the different quasi-physical feelings remains fairly constant.

As explained earlier (see p. 24) I had originally categorized people in the questionnaire group on the basis of whether they were creative, intellectual, or neither. It now appeared that though people who were creative or intellectual might have adamic ecstasies, people whom I had categorized as neither did not have ecstasies containing feelings of knowledge or of contact. The two younger children in the questionnaire group described adamic ecstasies. In the literary group the experiences of Jefferies, Church, and Proust are all recollected experiences of childhood or youth;[1] while Shirley is regarded with some contempt by Charlotte Brontë for her inability to use her experience creatively.

Thus in my texts adamic ecstasies seem principally to be associated with people who are neither intellectual nor creative, or with experiences of childhood; and generally, to be regarded as something less than other more valuable forms of ecstatic experience, those including feelings of knowledge and/or contact.

The condition of the adamic ecstasy is one in which the ecstatic feels that he himself and his environment are joyfully changed or renewed while freed from all that is distastefully characteristic of his everyday self in the real world. But it is important to notice that in adamic ecstasies both a sense of self and a sense of environment are typically present. The ecstatic's self and his world are changed not lost, and it is this feeling of changed self in a changed environment, often back to a self and an environment once known and later lost, that are characteristic of adamic ecstasy.

There are various models for this state of feeling, and in the Christian

---

[1] Jefferies says of this experience that it is of an earlier period than anything else narrated in his book, 'So long since that I have forgotten the date'. *Story of My Heart*, ch. v, p. 75.

world the model is usually that of Adam before the Fall. Adam was, as people feel themselves in this state to be, happy and innocent, knowing nothing of sin or toil or change or sorrow. He lost this state because through sin he acquired knowledge.[1] This model is used by Fox in text R 9 and by Church in text L 23a; other examples from literature will readily come to mind.

But the state of Adam is not the only type for the feelings of adamic ecstasies. What is needed for a model is some creature that can be seen as perfectly happy, uncorrupted by knowledge, and in a lower state than one believed to be possible after perfect knowledge has been attained. The model must be one from the past rather than the future, since in adamic experiences the ecstatic feels he has been renewed, regenerated, restored to a condition once known now lost, rather than brought to a state more perfect than any yet known. Other models often used by ecstatics for the states to which they feel they are brought by adamic ecstasy include the Noble Savage, primitive man, the Arcadian shepherd, the craftsman, the Worker of the World, certain animals, the innocent child—though this last was barely possible until the Christian conception of the child as born in sin had been weakened.[2]

Ecstasies of this general type are so easy to find that I shall allow their

---

[1] In this connexion a recent Catholic theory is of interest. This suggests that mystical knowledge and its adjuncts are not natural or supernatural but praeternatural, '*i.e.* this knowledge was not acquired naturally nor given by grace but was akin to that which Adam had in his state of integrity'. This theory was put forward by Abbot Chapman in 1928 to account for the epiphenomena that may accompany purported mystical experiences of people whom the Church cannot accept as receiving divine revelations. (See Thurston: S.M., p. 99n.)

Professor Zaehner, who explains that he had not seen this theory when he wrote his book, independently puts forward a theory which relates the experiences he cannot accept as of divine origin to the putative state of Adam before the Fall (M.S.P., p. 101 and note), and later interprets the creation of Adam as 'an original infusion of the divine essence into what had previously been an anthropoid ape'. The natural bliss of Adam, he explains, is often mistaken for the final bliss of heaven (ibid., p. 191–2).

One can see the usefulness to Christians of such postulations. Here is a state at least as praeternatural as it feels and known to be capable of being mistaken for the highest Christian experience; yet not this, but only the state of Adam.

[2] The change to this view of the child is interestingly discussed in *Poor Monkey* by Peter Coveney, a study of the child in literature (London, 1957).

Before the concept of Original Sin was introduced, Jesus had used the child as a type of the individual who had been regenerated and renewed, when he said 'Except ye be converted and become as little children, ye shall not enter into the kingdom of heaven' (*Matt.* xviii. 3).

existence to make a modification in my original criteria (see p.42) and accept as an ecstasy any experience that would provide only one entry in my analysis under *feelings of gain*, provided that the ecstatic refers to one of the models indicated above—the state of Adam, of childhood, etc.

Ideally, according to the religious systems, experiences of the kind I have called adamic should be known first, the *greater* ecstasies coming later, and this would suggest that adamic ecstasies are likely to be more common than those of the *greater* kinds. Certainly their influence seems to be substantial, and overbeliefs apparently deriving from adamic models may still be used where ecstasies contain elements of knowledge or contact or both. It is not, of course, possible to sort experiences of these kinds into tidy compartments (see p.93), and an ecstasy may be predominantly adamic in feeling and still contain some feelings of knowledge or contact. It is, to say the least of it, likely that the fairly elaborate models I shall instance derive from experiences containing some feelings of knowledge gained as well as of life renewed and perfected.

All these models derive from the ecstatic's belief that he has been united or re-united with another point in time—almost invariably in past time. Sometimes all that is intended is to create or use an image felt adequately to represent the feelings of an ecstasy; sometimes the belief seems to be seriously held. The former can easily become the latter and—a persistent difficulty in assessing ecstasies—it is often impossible to know whether the ecstatic himself believes he is making a figurative or a literal statement.

An interesting variety of these adamic models is that in which the point of time chosen is much further back than that of the putative Adam. Such beliefs are necessarily of fairly recent date; just as the child could not be used as a model while the Christian belief in Original Sin held sway, so belief of reversion to a primitive form was impossible before Darwin had established the descent of man.

Ecstasies of this kind are almost always triggered by what I call a *unitive symbol*—an object, event, or idea that can be seen as far older than the life of a man or, in the case of these primitive reversions, than the life of mankind. Obvious and basic symbols often found triggering this type of ecstasy are sea, earth, mountains, etc., but frequently, instead of or in addition to these, there is reference to a more particular symbol, usually a primitive form that can be seen as having existed

from distant time until the moment when the ecstatic encounters it.
A poem by Frances Cornford significantly entitled 'Pre-Existence',
will provide a useful first example:

> I laid me down upon the shore
>   And dreamed a little space;
> I heard the great waves break and roar
>   The sun was on my face.
>
> My idle hands and fingers brown
>   Played with the pebbles grey;
> The waves came up, the waves went down,
>   Both thundering and gay...
>
> The sun shone down upon us all,
>   And so my dream began:
>
> How all of this had been before,
>   How ages far away
> I lay on some forgotten shore
>   As here I lie today.
>
> The waves came shining up the sands,
>   As here today they shine;
> And in my pre-Pelasgian hands
>   The sand was warm and fine.
>
> I have forgotten whence I came
>   Or where my home might be...
>
> I only know the sun shone down
>   As still it shines today,
> And friendly in my fingers brown
>   The little pebbles lay.[1]

Here the sea and the sunshine are the primary triggers, with the
pebbles as the secondary unitive symbol. The joy felt by the ecstatic
is transferred to the waves. There is loss of place, loss of sense, and the
feeling of timelessness, of infinitely extended existence, becomes belief
in a recaptured moment of far-extended memory stretching back to a
primitive ancestry, an interpretation that has an obvious affinity to
Jung's conception of the collective unconscious.

A very much less sophisticated interpretation of what seems a very

---

[1] *Collected Poems* (London, 1954). pp. 18–19.

similar experience is shown in the following essay or prose-poem spontaneously written by a girl of eight and a half:

'It rises, it falls, it breaks upon the beach; it splashes against worn rocks. Oh! How I wish I were a wave. Alas, I was not born with the tide; yet, as I sit in deep meditation, my heart beats hard; I feel as if I could leap one hundred times and become a wave' (from a school magazine).

Here, I suggest, the worn rocks are the unitive symbol corresponding with Frances Cornford's pebbles. This, and the wish to become a wave, communicate the feeling of infinite duration, of timelessness. The initial withdrawal of deep meditation is succeeded by the intensity and up-feelings of repeated leaping.

Both these experiences have much in common with that of Joël (L 9). He too is lying by the sea. As with the child, initial withdrawal is succeeded by intensity; the child's heart beat hard as Joël's pulse thundered in his head. Joël's thoughts 'hark back dimly through eons of existence', to a pre-conscious existence like that of the jelly-fish—in my terms, the unitive symbol—dreaming 'of the primitive life'.[1]

Jacquetta Hawkes, a professed follower of Jung, recounts several ecstatic experiences with overbeliefs of this kind. She begins her book *A Land* by describing an ecstasy enjoyed while lying, at night, on the ground of a garden in Primrose Hill and explains how at night she feels that cats, 'perfectly formed while men were still brutal...represent the continued presence of the past'. A little further on she uses birds and their song as the unitive symbol:

'Perhaps [this emotion] is evoked by the singing, whistling and calling that fell into millions of ancestral ears and there left images that we all inherit.'

She then describes an earlier ecstatic experience evoked by bird-calls in the country, and writes:

'It seemed to me that I had my ear to a great spiral shell and that these sounds rose from it. The shell was the vortex of time, and as the birds themselves took shape, species after species, so their distinctive songs were formed within them and had been spiralling up ever since.'[2]

---

[1] The jelly-fish is further discussed on p.p. 363-4.
[2] *A Land* (London, 1951), pp. 8-9.

In her later book *Man on Earth* she suggests how this feeling of relationship with the past may be induced, using the human hand as the unitive symbol:

'Let anyone who wishes really to grasp and accept the continuity of life hold out his hand, look at it with unaccustomed eyes, feel its bones and nails, and see if, from somewhere at the base of memory, he cannot recover the feeling of the dark, warm mud squeezing between scaly claws.' [1]

But acceptance of Jung's postulations is not necessary for feelings of links with the infinitely distant past. For Gissing's hero geological strata provide the unitive symbol but no supposition of extended memory is made: imagination suffices:

'Escaping from the influence of personality, his imagination wrought back through eras of geologic time, held him in a vision of the infinitely remote, shrivelled into insignificance all but the one fact of inconceivable duration.' [2]

Jung himself, in an experience that has wild animals for the unitive symbol, uses the model of Adam, but with a difference:

'Standing on a little hill in the East African plains, I saw herds of thousands of wild beasts, grazing in soundless peace, beneath the breath of the primaeval world, as they had done for unimaginable ages of time, and I had the feeling of being the first man, the first being to know that all this *is*. The whole world around me was still in the primitive silence and knew not that it was. In this very moment in which I knew it the world came into existence, and without this moment it would never have been.' [3]

For the first man to acquire self-awareness is, in Jung's model, his function not his sin, and this experience, like that of Joël (L 9), is finally something of a knowledge ecstasy.

But where mindlessness, lack of self-awareness is a necessary characteristic of the chosen model, ecstatics may find themselves in something of a difficulty.

Thus Jacquetta Hawkes asks

'Is it possible that the collective unconscious...functions from the Thalamus?' [4]

[1] *Man on Earth* (London), 1954, p. 50.
[2] *Born in Exile*, Pt. I, ch. iii; cp. the very similar phraseology of text L 13.
[3] From an essay 'On a Higher State of Consciousness', in *Eranos Jahrbuch*, 1938.
[4] *Man on Earth*, p. 134 et seq.

from, that is to say, what she calls the Old Brain,

> 'that organ evolved by the amphibians and shared by us with all our fellow creatures who are not more lowly than the frogs'

as distinguished from the Cortex or New Brain which relates to the intellect and consciousness of the ego. The Old Brain, in this picture, is figuratively the brain of Adam before he acquired knowledge and self-consciousness, and so a state of adamic ecstasy could be called a thalamic state.

The difficulty is that models once postulated tend to become exclusively accepted and differentiation inhibited. Thus a model based on feelings of reversion to a more primitive state has to stand not only for adamic ecstasies but also for those *greater* ecstasies in which knowledge is felt to be gained. Thus Miss Hawkes is led into the awkward position of regarding as supremely valuable a regressive rather than a progressive condition, a difficulty from which she could extricate herself if she limited her model; if she acknowledged varieties of experience and saw the adamic state, as the Christians do, as a negative rather than a positive condition, a reversion to something which—though more joyful than the condition in which we now find ourselves—is still less than that to which we can attain when knowledge is perfected and man perfectly individuated.

It has for some time now been very common to picture childhood as a continuous state of ecstasy—a unitive state. Here is a typical description of that condition as re-created by an adult:

> *Happy those early dayes! when I*
> *Shin'd in my Angell-infancy.*
> *Before I understood this place*
> *Appointed for my second race,*
> *Or taught my soul to fancy ought*
> *But a white, Celestiall thought,*
> *When yet I had not walkt above*
> *A mile, or two, from my first love,*
> *And looking back (at that short space,)*
> *Could see a glimpse of his bright-face;*
> *When on some gilded Cloud, or flowre*
> *My gazing soul would dwell an houre,*
> *And in those weaker glories spy*
> *Some shadows of eternity;*

> *Before I taught my tongue to wound*
> *My Conscience with a sinfull sound,*
> *Or had the black art to dispence*
> *A sev'rall sinne to ev'ry sence,*
> *But felt through all this fleshly dresse*
> *Bright shootes of everlastingness.*[1]

The state described is clearly similar to that of many ecstasies; in these, as in Angell-infancy, understanding of the world does not exist, the mind is pure, the soul is in contact with God, sees eternity in a flower or a cloud, is assured of eternal life.

But this heaven that lay about us in our infancy may, it is believed by many, be regained in a moment of ecstasy, and an example may again be found in the work of Frances Cornford. Forty years after the poem quoted on p. 107, she wrote another called 'Summer Beach':

> *For how long known this boundless wash of light,*
> *This smell of purity, this gleaming waste,*
> *This wind? This brown, strewn wrack how old a sight,*
> *These pebbles round to touch and salt to taste.*

But this time the answer is not found in pre-Pelasgian terms. 'For how long known...?' she asks again in the last verse, and answers:

> *Since first I laboured with a wooden spade*
> *Against this background of Eternity.*[2]

These two poems, taken together, provide a good example of the fact that very similar experiences may be given different interpretations, even, as appears here, on different occasions by the same person.

There is yet another form of ecstasy in which a unitive symbol triggers an experience of which it is believed that the ecstatic has been translated into time past.[3] In these it is a moment in historical time that the ecstatic believes he has encountered, and in so far as it can be

---

[1] Henry Vaughan, 'The Retreate'.

[2] *Collected Poems*, p. 83.

[3] There is a type of legend in which the ecstatic obliteration of time results in literal translation into the future. In one version, a monk goes out into the fields in spring, hears a lark sing and is transported. When he returns to the monastery no one knows him, and at last his name is found in the records of a hundred years past. 'Time had been blotted out while he listened to the lark.' This legend, which I first met as a child in Arthur Mee's *One Thousand Beautiful Things*, was the direct inspiration of my novel, *The Victorian Chaise-Longue* which, in its turn, gave rise to this book.

accepted that the ecstatic himself creates what he believes he sees, these are knowledge rather than adamic ecstasies, inspirations rather than regenerations; but their obvious similarities to the types discussed above makes it convenient to indicate them here.

Often, in these ecstasies, the trigger is the ruin of something built by men. Jefferies tells of a visit to the ruins of a Roman wall at Pevensey.

> 'and immediately the ancient wall swept my mind back seventeen hundred years to the eagle, the pilum, and the short sword. The grey stones, the thin red bricks laid by those whose eyes had seen Caesar's Rome, lifted me out of the grasp of house-life, of modern civilisation, of those minutiae which occupy the moment. The grey stone made me feel as if I had existed from then till now, so strongly did I enter into and see my own life as if reflected. My own existence was focussed back on me; I saw its joy, its unhappiness, its birth, its death, its possibilities among the infinite, above all its yearning Question. Why? Seeing it thus clearly, and lifted out of the moment by the force of seventeen centuries, I recognised the full mystery and the depths of things in the roots of the grey grass on the wall, in the green sea flowing near.' [1]

A more simply expressed but, I believe, very similar feeling is that of Q 44 in an ecstasy in what was (though he does not say so) the *ruins*[2] of an Augustinian abbey, seen in brilliant moonlight with a long spire of mountains behind it,

> 'and I had this feeling, there's been no plainchant here for four hundred years, and I sang it'.

Dr. Arnold Toynbee accepts such experiences as these as preliminaries to greater experiences. He believes that 'the historian's inspiration is preparing him for an experience that has been described as "the Beatific Vision" by souls to whom it has been vouchsafed', and that an initiatory stage on this pilgrimage is

> 'the experience of a communion on the mundane plane with persons and events from which, in his usual state of consciousness, he is sundered by a great gulf of Time and Space'.

---

[1] *The Story of My Heart*, ch. ii, p. 34-5.
[2] There exist so many apparently ecstatic experiences triggered by ruins that this trigger may be retrieved from the *miscellaneous* heading of my analyses, and accepted among the more common triggers.

He speaks of

'moments in his [*sc.* an historian's] mental life—moments as memorable as they are rare—in which temporal and spatial barriers fall and psychic distance is annihilated'.

He gives several examples. Some such experiences came to him when reading; others, in places with historical associations. On one of the twin summits of the citadel of Pharsâlus he saw Philip of Macedon's phalanx; in Crete, on the coast of Laconia, at Port Arthur, Gettysburg, Ephesus, he 'had been rapt into a momentary communion with the actors in a particular historic event'.[1]

A feeling that the past is or can be accurately re-created is often described without any feelings of ecstasy at all, though taking place in undoubted trigger-surroundings. A classic example is

'It was at Rome, on the 15th of October, 1764, as I sat musing amidst the ruins of the Capitol, while the barefooted friars were singing vespers in the Temple of Jupiter, that the idea of writing the decline and fall of the city first started to my mind.' [2]

Toynbee is however in no doubt that this was an experience similar to his own.[3]

Two oddly similar experiences of what seem to have been time-ecstasies may be mentioned here, one an experience of Toynbee's, the other of Wordsworth's. Both show the situation I postulated earlier,

---

[1] *A Study of History* (Oxford, 1954), Vol. X, pp. 128–39. An admirable comment on this particular variety of ecstatic experience is Lewis Carroll's:

> *Where life becomes a Spasm,*
> *And History a Whiz:*
> *If that is not Sensation,*
> *I don't know what it is.*
>
> from *Phantasmagoria* (1869; Nonesuch edn., 1939), p.793.

[2] Edward Gibbon's *Autobiography* (1796; World's Classics, 1907), p. 160.

[3] Dr. Toynbee's supposition, which derives (as he has told me) from considering the result of the experience, might receive some confirmation from the fact that when in Rome at this time Gibbon does seem to have been enjoying what I call a unitive state: 'My temper is not very susceptible of enthusiasm, and the enthusiasm which I do not feel I have ever scorned to affect. But, at the distance of twenty-five years, I can neither forget nor express the strong emotions which agitated my mind as I first approached and entered the *eternal city*. After a sleepless night, I trod, with a lofty step, the ruins of the Forum; each memorable spot where Romulus *stood*, or Tully spoke, or Caesar fell, was at once present to my eye; and several days of intoxication were lost or enjoyed before I could descend to a cool and minute investigation' (Ibid., pp. 156–9).

where an experience takes place in non-trigger conditions but is identified as similar to others that have taken place under trigger conditions (see p.40); in both these cases surprise is expressed that such experiences should be known under such apparently unpropitious conditions.

Toynbee recounts this experience immediately after those referred to above, saying that this was 'a larger and a stranger experience' and expressing surprise that 'this incongruously prosaic scene should have been the physical setting of a mental illumination'. The scene was the Buckingham Palace Road, and there he

> 'found himself in communion, not just with this or that episode in History, but with all that had been, and was, and was to come. In that instant he was directly aware of the passage of History gently flowing through him in a mighty current, and of his own life welling like a wave in the flow of this vast tide... An instant later, the communion had ceased'. [1]

Wordsworth was coming into London on the top of the Cambridge coach:

> *Never shall I forget the hour*
> *The moment rather say——*

Like Toynbee, he expresses his surprise at having such an experience in such apparently unpropitious surroundings:

> *With vulgar Men about me, vulgar forms*
> *Of houses, pavement, streets, of men and things,*
> *Mean shapes on every side: but, at the time...*
>
> *A weight of Ages did at once descend*
> *Upon my heart; no thought embodied, no*
> *Distinct remembrances; but weight and power,*
> *Power growing with the weight...*
>
> *All that took place within me, came and went*
> *As in a moment, and I only now*
> *Remember that it was a thing divine.* [2]

As Mrs. Moorman comments, what Wordsworth believed he had felt in that moment was 'the accumulated weight of human history'. [3]

[1] *A Study of History*, Vol. X, p. 139.

[2] Prel., viii, ll. 688–709. Unless otherwise stated, references are to the earlier version.

[3] *William Wordsworth, the Early Years*, by Mary Moorman (Oxford, 1957), p. 126. Wordsworth, like Toynbee, also knew more specific historical experience:

Toynbee's insistence that this was a larger and stronger experience than his more specific historical visions provides useful confirmation of a point I made earlier, that knowledge of all, of everything—in this case, all time, all history—is derived from experiences felt to be greater than those in which knowledge of something only is gained (see pp. 91-2).

These later examples have, however, taken us a long way from the simple models by means of which the man who has enjoyed adamic ecstasy expresses his feeling that the experience recovered for him such an idyllic past as that of Adam, the child, the savage, etc. In these later examples the feeling of having encountered past time is strongly laden with feelings of knowledge gained and sometimes of contacts made, and it is to the ecstasies characterized by such feelings that I now turn.

in a momentary revelation at Stonehenge he 'had a reverie and saw the past' which included ancient Britons in wolfskin vests and Druids performing their rites; see *Prel.*, xii, 312 et seq.

CHAPTER X

Knowledge

People's beliefs that they can identify their experiences or what they believe they have encountered in their experiences I have called knowledge by identification, and do not count as constituting a knowledge ecstasy. For knowledge ecstasies I require that people make claims that can be entered—in terms of my headings, under *mystical knowledge* or *new knowledge*.

The identifications made are, however, interesting. The experiences described by the people in the questionnaire group were all ones they identified with the name *transcendent ecstasy*. This name does not imply anything much about the experience which was, as I explained earlier, one of my reasons for choosing it.

Many people in the questionnaire group made it plain that they accepted ecstasy as an experience in which one encountered—or felt one had encountered—say, reality or God. No one compared ecstasy with other experiences in which they felt they had encountered, say, reality or God. It would seem that they accepted ecstasies as reality-encountering or God-encountering experiences and that in ecstasy they could know by experience what hitherto they had known only by description.

In the literary group some people felt able to name the experience they described—Lawrence identifies his as ecstasy, Koestler as Freud's 'oceanic feeling'—and most accepted the experience described as one in which it was proper to feel that one had experienced or come to have knowledge about, say, reality or God or something else that could not be experienced otherwise.

In the religious group everyone apparently knew of the experience described whether they themselves had previously encountered it or not and, by whatever name they called it, knew this to be a type of experience in which a man could encounter God.

A very few people, mostly in the questionnaire group, compared some of the feelings of ecstasy with feelings known in other experiences—for instance, 'associated with sensations of physical flying, like going to sleep or in dreams' (Q 29), 'a mixture of physical attack and cerebral confusion' (Q 52). Only one person identified ecstasy as something at least potentially expressible, analysable, and explicable. This was Q 4, whose answers to the first part of the questionnaire were not analysed because, having answered in this way, what he said was unrelated to my categorization.[1] This apart, no one identified his experience of ecstasy with anything capable of verification; nor, apart from a few physical happenings—for instance, tears—did they so identify any of its feelings.

In this category of knowledge by identification, then, I entered those statements which imply that in an experience of ecstasy something is encountered which is not to be encountered in any other kind of experience, something whose existence cannot be experimentally verified unless the feeling of its being encountered in this experience is itself a verification.[2]

But for an experience to be a knowledge ecstasy in my sense, more is required than the ecstatic's ability to identify (or believe he can identify) the experience or what is encountered in the experience. What is required is that he shall believe that in the experience or as a result of the experience he gained new knowledge, whether of a communicable kind or not.[3]

Sometimes the knowledge seems to dawn spontaneously. Sometimes it seems to be communicated by someone or something else, in which case we have what I call a knowledge-contact ecstasy.[4] For my present purpose, which is to examine the kinds of knowledge claimed, there is nothing to be gained by separating simple knowledge ecstasies from knowledge-contact ecstasies.

[1] Q 4 described ecstasy as an 'euphoric state with slight pathologic undertones, contemplative in origin, transient and forgotten, not sustained'.

[2] For my justification for including here analogical statements such as 'like being in touch with the Creator', see pp. 244-5.

[3] It will be remembered that James regarded 'noetic quality' as an essential character of his mystical states: 'mystical states seem...to be also states of knowledge'. See p. 44.

[4] There are in the groups 34 knowledge-contact ecstasies—that is, texts providing entries under both *feelings of contact* and feelings of *new and/or mystical knowledge*. The results of analysing these as a group can be seen in Appendix D, Table 5; these results seem to be very similar to those of the mean of the three groups.

Broadly it can be said that two kinds of knowledge may be claimed: occasionally, knowledge of something; frequently, knowledge of everything.

The former claim, to have gained knowledge of something, may be expressed in any of three ways. First, the ecstatic may claim indefinite and unspecific knowledge. Thus Q 6 speaks of 'perception of a pattern', C. E. Montague of

> 'keener perceptions...new doors of understanding—wonderful enlightenments, still unreceived, are on their way to you' (L 20).

Hugh of St. Victor writes,

> 'my intellect is illuminated—I seem to have become possessed of something, and I know not what it is' (R 12).

Then the ecstatic may claim to have received limited and specific knowledge but does not say what it is, whether because it is of its nature incommunicable or for any other reason. St. Ignatius Loyola claims that

> 'in one moment, and without any sensible image or appearance, certain things pertaining to the mysteries of the Faith, together with other truths of natural science, were revealed to him' (R 15).[1]

Finally, the ecstatic may claim to know something limited, specific, and communicable. Nichols 'was being told' a poem, wrote it down and published it (see L 5). Berenson discovered a test he could apply to the artifacts he believed he admired, and was able to communicate its nature (see L 10). Similar claims are made by those creative people in the questionnaire group who assimilate ecstasy and inspiration, or who say (as Q 26 does) 'with inspiration one can have ecstasy'. In these cases the inspired piece of work was, presumably, communicated or capable of being communicated to the public.

I think we may include here claims of having acquired limited and putatively communicable knowledge, even where we are not told what this knowledge is. Such is Q 57's 'I feel immensely creative, full of ideas', and Nietzsche's

> 'unexpectedly answers drop into my lap, a small hailstorm of ice and wisdom, of problems solved' (L 6).

[1] St. Teresa often made similar claims: while reciting the Athanasian Creed, 'Our Lord made me comprehend in what way it is that God can be in three persons', and on another occasion 'it was given to St. Teresa to see and understand in what wise the Mother of God had been assumed into her place in Heaven'; see James: V.R.E., p. 403.

Reconstructions of specific moments in history, as discussed in the last chapter, obviously belong here.

Claims to knowledge of everything are far more common. To try to categorize these claims must be arbitrary but may be useful. Variants often found include:

—the simple claim that the ecstatic has seen everything, 'everything' often being implied by the device of a selective list (see pp. 242–3). Thus Tennyson (in text L 2) claims to see everything, naming objects on a list which includes grains of earth, atoms in the air, the moon, the galaxy, people in other worlds.

—the claim that the ecstatic has seen everything and knows how it works. Q 61 says

'you suddenly discover a faculty working with effortless efficiency which enables you to hold in the forefront of conscious feeling both knowledge of the smallest bacteria in the field, how the blade of grass works, and the universe, in the same detail.'

This is similar to the claim made by Boehme in text R 16:

'I saw and knew the being of all things...I saw and knew the whole working essence...and likewise how the fruitful bearing womb of eternity brought forth.'

It may be such experiences as these that St. Thomas Aquinas had in mind when he said that some philosophers, from whom he did not dissent,

'thinking of the natural perfection of man, have said that his final happiness is found when the whole order of the universe is displayed to him in his soul.'[1]

Sometimes the ecstatic limits the field in which he knows everything and also how everything works. Thus Fox, in the passage quoted on pp. 90–1, seems to limit the field of his knowledge to such understanding of creatures as would enable him to practise physic. Boehme, on another occasion than that cited above, makes a very similar claim: at the age of twenty-five he was

'surrounded by the divine light, and replenished with the heavenly knowledge; insomuch as going abroad into the fields...he there sat

[1] Quoted by Kirk: V.G., p. 389.

down, and viewing the herbs and grass of the field, in his inward light he saw into their essences, use, and properties'.[1]

—the claim that the ecstatic perceives that all things are one. Q 20 speaks of 'a sense of the oneness of things', Richard Church writes,

'All was one, with the word as the verbal reality brought to material life by Mind, by man' (L 23b).

—the claim that the ecstatic knows all things because he himself is a part of them and of their unity. Margiad Evans writes,

'that joy of being oneself contained in all one sees! Feeling with the leaves, travelling with the clouds... It is the strangest sensation for the mind to fix itself in the contemplation of one single natural thing; and one of its most singular phenomena is the amazing quality of universal perception which takes place in the thinker at the same time' (L 4).

And Jacquetta Hawkes,

'it grants man a state of mind in which I believe he must come more and more to live: a mood of intensely conscious individuality which serves only to strengthen an intense consciousness of unity with all being. His mind is one infinitesimal node in the mind present throughout all being, just as his body shares in the unity of matter... I found myself comprehending every physical fact of [the camels'] passage as though it were a part of my own existence... I knew the blood flowing through the bodies of men and beasts and thought of it as echoing the life of the anemones which now showed black among the rocks' (L 19).

—the claim that the ecstatic sees all things and in them the presence of something else. Wordsworth speaks of his awareness of a presence, a motion, a spirit

> *that impels*
> *All thinking things, all objects of all thought,*
> *And rolls through all things* (L 1a).

Angela of Foligno says

'I did comprehend the whole world...and the abyss and ocean and all things. In all these things I beheld naught save the divine power' (R 5a).

[1] Quoted by James: V.R.E., p. 401n.

C. P. Snow makes his hero say

> 'It was as though I had looked for a truth outside myself, and finding it had become for a moment part of the truth I sought; as though the world, the atoms and the stars, were wonderfully clear and close to me and I to them, so that we were part of a lucidity more tremendous than any mystery' (L 25).

—the claim that the ecstatic perceives final knowledge, outside or beyond or transcending created things. Sometimes he claims both to perceive and to become part of this knowledge, as Snow's hero does in the example given above. Sometimes he claims only to perceive, not to become part of the knowledge. Thus Q 22 speaks of 'hovering on the edge of seeing right beyond'. Emily Brontë writes 'Then dawns the Invisible, the Unseen its truth reveals' (L 21), and St. Augustine, 'the perspicuous truth is perceived' (R 19).

Claims to knowledge often, of course, spill over the headings under which I have tried to confine them. Thus St. Alphonsus Rodrigues claims both knowledge of God—i.e. final knowledge—and that God gave him 'great light concerning the knowledge of God and self', which seems to be a more limited claim (see R 14). Bucke had 'an intellectual illumination impossible to describe' about the cosmic order, which may certainly be called knowledge of everything; but also

> 'I did not merely come to believe but I saw that the universe is not composed of dead matter, but is, on the contrary, a living Presence' (R 17),

and this seems to be a limited and specific piece of knowledge about the composition of the universe. To say that Bucke's statement is inaccurate or meaningless is to value it, not to say what kind of a statement it is supposed to be.

As I have already pointed out, in many cases knowledge is believed to have been gained through a contact believed to have been made, and the next chapter examines the kinds of contacts claimed in my texts.

CHAPTER XI

Contact

In considering claims of contact, two main points are worth considera-tion: firstly, the closeness of any contact said to have been made; and secondly, the nature of the contact.

The former point is of interest for two reasons. In the first place the closeness of the contact claimed provides a means of estimating the nature and *greatness* of the ecstasy, in terms of the scale I set up in Chapter VII. Sometimes the contact is felt to pass information to the ecstatic and we have what I have called a knowledge-contact ecstasy. Sometimes the contact is felt to be closer than this and no information is passed; sometimes this contact is one of union in which the ecstatic and what is believed to have been encountered become more or less one. These I have called union ecstasies, and all ecstatics who have known these and other varieties of ecstasy regard these as the *greatest*. In these, no information is passed, though the contact made may be named 'the Truth'.

Different degrees of closeness are claimed by the various ecstatics of my texts, and before examining these it will be useful to have some orthodox views on the kinds of contact that may properly be claimed by Christians.

Butler writes,

'the Catholic mystics are insistent in asserting that the soul retains its own individuality and full personality in the unions either of this life or of eternity',

and explains that 'any seeming pantheistic tendency' is due to the 'obscurity and apparent extravagance of their [*sc.* the mystics'] lan-guage' which, in its turn,

'is due to their courage in struggling with the barriers and limitations of human thought and language in order to describe in some fashion what they experienced in the height of the mystic state.'[1]

In the article on 'Mysticism' in the *Oxford Dictionary of the Christian Church*, we find,

'And in place of all notions of absorption of the soul into the divine ("Thou art in me and I am in Thee: and Thy attributes are my attributes' in the Egyptian *Book of the Dead*; much Oriental and Neo-Platonic religion), it [*sc.* Christian mysticism] posits that the union is one of love and will in which the distinction between Creator and creature is permanently retained.'

From this it might appear that something less than orthodoxy was implied by such statements as Ruysbroeck's 'We behold that which we are and we are that which we behold' (R 7) and St. Teresa's 'God visits the soul in a way that prevents it doubting that it has been in God and God in it' (R 10b). But this is not necessarily so, since Catholic theologians may explain any seemingly pantheistic statement by an accepted Catholic mystic as not really meaning what it seems to mean. Thus Poulain explains that though mystics 'sometimes go as far as to say that they not only feel *union* with God in this state, but that there is *oneness with Him*. This is only a manner of speaking.' They thus describe, he says, 'what *we believe* ourselves to feel'; but this is only 'the language of appearances'.[2]

Christian mystics know the orthodox and permissible language, and to the outsider it must seem significant that sometimes the orthodox and permissible language is not felt to be appropriate, even by those people most desirous of accepting as orthodox only those experiences certifiable as orthodox. There is plenty of evidence that even the most respectable Christian mystics do describe experiences that are not doctrinally acceptable. The excuse 'They thus describe what *we believe* ourselves to feel... This is only a manner of speaking' has to be proffered in those cases where the uninitiated might believe the mystic to be saying that he had completely lost his senses or had become completely one with God or the All. Sometimes, indeed, the utmost extension of charity cannot certify the mystic as meaning other than what he says, and then an Eckhart must recant, a Molinos be condemned.

But bearing in mind that, at least in the case of the orthodox Catholic mystics, the right vocabulary is known and the desire for orthodoxy

[1] W.M., p. 5.   [2] G.I.P., ch. xix, 14.

great,[1] I may accept, for my purposes, what people believed themselves to have felt as evidence of their feelings; it is not possible to get behind sincere reports of feelings to 'true feelings'. And taking people's statements of what they believed themselves to have felt supplies ample evidence that orthodox Christian mystics do sometimes have experiences that are not doctrinally acceptable. The frequent warnings against claiming complete loss of sense or complete oneness with God are sufficient proof that such statements are liable to occur, and they are easy enough to find.

A fair example of the kind of experience impermissible to Christians is shown by my text R 4, an experience of Plotinus who was not, of course, a Christian, though his influence on Christian mysticism is generally agreed to have been great. Underhill, for instance, writes that 'Countless mystics, from St. Augustine to St. John of the Cross, echo again and again the language of Plotinus.' [2]

Christian mystics may not, as we have seen, say that they feel oneness with God (e.g. 'Thou art in me and I am in Thee: Thy attributes are my attributes') but the soul must retain its own individuality and full personality' (see p.122). These conditions would not seem to be fulfilled by Plotinus's

'Then the soul neither sees, nor distinguishes by seeing, nor imagines that there are two things... It belongs to God and is one with Him...in this conjunction with Deity there were not two things, but the perceiver was one with the thing perceived'.

Again, Christians may not say 'The person thinks of nothing' or 'he loves God and possesses Him without knowing anything about it' (see p. 59). Plotinus seems, then, to be using a form of expression impermissible to Christians when he writes,

'then nothing stirred within him, neither anger, nor desire, nor even reason, nor a certain intellectual perception'.

But Inge, while necessarily decrying Plotinus's 'strange aspiration to rise above Reason and Intelligence' states that he describes the conditions under which the vision is granted in exactly the same manner as

---

[1] 'The soul always tries to act in conformity with the Church's teaching...and acting as one already so deeply grounded in those truths that no imaginable revelation, even if it saw the heavens open, would cause it to swerve an inch from the doctrine of the Church' (Teresa : Life, ch. xxv, p. 178).

[2] E.U: M., p. 106.

do some of the Christian mystics, and instances St. John of the Cross.[1] Kirk points out that experiences such as these, involving complete loss of sense, were advised by Dionysius the Areopagite, and had 'a profound influence upon the language and practice of private devotion'.[2]

Underhill goes so far as to say that the Christian insistence that the mystic must never feel wholly one with God is inconsistent with the mystic's experience. She quotes such phrases as 'For to me to live is Christ' (*Phil.* i. 21), 'Thou art in me, and I in Thee, glued together as one and the selfsame thing' from Gerlac Petersen, and 'My *me* is God, nor do I know my selfhood save in Him' from St. Catherine of Genoa,[3] saying that 'All mystics in the unitive state make equivalent declarations' and that 'These are plainly reports of that...condition of consciousness, often called by the dangerous name of "deification".'[4] It seems that for Underhill the danger lies in the name; she does not doubt that the condition is known to Christian mystics.[5]

There can, I think, be little doubt that in the *greatest* ecstasies both loss of sense and loss of self are total and any contact felt to have been made is believed to be complete to the point of unification. And to forbid, as the Church does, such ecstasies, is not to conceal the fact that they do occur, both for Christians and for non-Christians.

In my texts there are instances in all three groups of claims in which the mystic becomes one with someone or something else. What the someone or something else is, varies, and it is this variation that is said by Professor Zaehner to constitute the prime difference between Christian and what he calls 'pan-en-henic' experiences. This point I will come to later in the chapter, but for the moment I am concerned only to establish that unifying contact is claimed, no matter whom or what with. Here is an example from each group:

'I am part of the thing that has set it off, and I enclose the universe or it encloses me...both inextricably mingled' (Q 24); 'being oneself

[1] C.M., p. 97.   [2] V.G., p. 303.

[3] Certainly this latter does seem very similar to the phrase 'Thou art in me and I am in Thee: and Thy attributes are my attributes' quoted by the O.D.C.C. (see p. 123); and also to Ruysbroeck's 'We behold that which we are and we are that which we behold...made one with the Truth which is God' (R 7).

[4] M.W., p. 187.

[5] St. Catherine of Genoa claimed not only this forbidden state but also that of complete loss of sense; 'it would be impossible', says Von Hügel, 'to press those of her sayings in which her true self appears as literally God, or her state of quiet as a complete motionlessness or even immovability' (M.E.R., Vol. I, p. 229).

contained in all one sees—lost in the one' (Margiad Evans, L 4); 'united to the well-Beloved—entirely mingled with and steeped in Him' (St. Francis of Sales, R 21).[1]

Of these three people, Q 24 says that she has no religion, St. Francis of Sales is, of course, Catholic, and Margiad Evans's religion I do not know.

Other people from all groups speak of contact less than the one illustrated above, of feelings of being in touch with, in communion with, approaching, in the presence of; for example,

'communion with something else before reason enters' (Q 27); 'being in the presence of extraordinary possibilities' (C. E. Montague, L 20); 'she is already near her God…if she draws a little nearer, she will become by union one with Him' (St. Teresa, C 10a).

Both union and contact less than union are, then, claimed by people in all three groups, by Christians and by non-Christians, by people of religious faith and by people of none. The next consideration must be of that with which contact or union is said to have been made.

Broadly speaking these contacts may be divided into three kinds: contact with a transcendental 'someone' or 'something'; contact with an object or objects; and contact with an immaterial 'all'.

For certain purposes it would, of course, be proper to assume that all the people in the religious group, no matter what forms of expression they use, intend to imply 'God'. But for my purposes this is insufficient, and I shall divide my material on the basis of the claims people actually make, not on what they may be presumed to have intended.[2]

In the questionnaire group, contact with God ('the Creator') is claimed by Q 15, a Christian; in the literary group by Wordsworth (in L 1b) who was, at the time of writing, a pantheist, by H. Warner Allen (L 11) and by Richard Church (L 23b). In the religious group contact with God, named as such, is claimed by many people.

Contact with transcendental beings or things who are not called God and who do not seem to be intended as God is claimed in the questionnaire group by Q 3 (who believes that good is stronger than evil) and by Q 27 who has no faith; and in the literary group by Tennyson, Nichols, Meredith, and Emily Brontë. Wordsworth, in

[1] For other examples, see Appendix E, pp. 497–500; also for the different ways in which this union or meeting is said to take place.
[2] See Appendix E, p. 499, for details of the claims made.

text L 1a, perceives 'a motion and a spirit, that impels All thinking things, all objects of all thought, And rolls through all things'.

Contact with material objects is claimed in the questionnaire group by Q 24, who has no faith; she speaks of 'the thing that has set it off', which recalls Underhill's and St. Teresa's recipes for inducing ecstasy by gazing at trigger-objects (see p. 50). Q 36, also of no faith, speaks of 'living in the object', presumably the trigger-object, and George Eliot's Daniel Deronda of an 'identification of himself with the objects he was looking at' (L 15). In the religious group Plotinus speaks of the perceiver being one with the thing perceived, though he makes it plain that 'the thing perceived' is a synonym for 'Deity' (R 4).

Where identification with a material object is concerned, I believe we have an ecstasy of the type discussed in Chapter IV, initially achieved by withdrawal (whether voluntary or involuntary), the withdrawal being achieved, as Underhill puts it, by looking 'in a special and undivided manner, at some simple, concrete, and external thing' (see p. 49). There is no need to suppose that an initial withdrawal must always be as apparent as in the ecstasies discussed in that chapter.

It is characteristic of ecstasy that nearly all its feelings are nearly always total, infinite, and measureless—due, I believe, to a loss of the sense of difference or distinction, of the faculty of making distinctions.[1]

These feelings of totality, so frequently expressed in ecstasy, are, I believe, important and deserve some comment. What is believed to have been felt or perceived in ecstasy tends to be expressed as feelings of 'that than which nothing greater can be conceived' in the class concerned. Such expressions I shall call *totality expressions* or phrases, and of these the obvious example is *God*

'since by the very notion of God we mean "that than which nothing greater can be conceived" (*id quo nihil majus cogitari possit*)'.[2]

God or synonyms for God are named in many texts, but other unlimited totalities may be indicated. Thus, the author of text L 27 says

---

[1] What Wordsworth, with the ecstatic's typical distaste for the characteristics of non-ecstatic conditions, called,

> *that false secondary power, by which,*
> *In weakness, we create distinctions*
> *Prel.*, ii, ll. 212-2.

[2] O.D.C.C., quoting St. Anselm under 'Ontological Argument'.

that his hero saw 'nothing and everything', Boehme that he 'knew the being of all things' (R 16), Q 17 that he had a sense of union with 'external reality'. Or the class may be a comparatively limited one: Berenson, for instance, says that he 'beheld a world where every outline, every edge, and every surface' was in a living relation to him (L 10). Or it may be the emotions felt that are expressed in totality phrases: happiness is supreme, union sublime, bliss touched at its highest point.[1] In the questionnaire group totality phrases are used in 58 per cent. of the texts; in the literary group in 90 per cent. and in the religious group in 98 per cent. of the texts. It was, of course, to a large extent because totality was felt that the texts in the literary and still more in the religious group were written down for publication.

In the last chapter I have shown how much more common it is to claim that knowledge gained in ecstasy is knowledge of 'everything' than merely knowledge of 'something'. It is similarly much more common to find claims of totality contact than merely of contact with 'something'. And what may begin by feeling like identity with a single object or group of objects is likely to end by feeling like identity with the total cosmos. Thus Q 24's initial feeling of identity with 'the thing that has set it off' becomes a feeling of identity with the universe. Margiad Evans's initial fixing of the mind 'in the contemplation of one single natural thing' also becomes a feeling of identity with the universe (L 4). Jacquetta Hawkes's immediate feeling of identity with specific camels and anemones is simultaneously a feeling of unity with all matter (L 19).

Many people, apparently without passing through a stage of feeling unity with an object or objects, immediately believe their contact to be with a totality of objects. Q 37 (an agnostic) speaks of the universe, and so does Bucke from the religious group (R 17); Angela of Foligno speaks of 'the All' (R 5b), Q 42, an agnostic, of 'the totality of nature' and Joël (L 9) of 'the world'.

In all three groups there are people who identify what they believe they have encountered not with a material but with an abstract totality, and one other than God. Thus Q 1 (who believes in God) and Q 33 (a Christian) both speak of 'reality', and Q 17 (no faith) of 'exter-

---

[1] In Appendix E, pp. 500–2, I give examples of at least one totality phrase from each text in which these occur. In Ch. XXII, which is concerned with the language of ecstasy, I consider some of the ways in which feelings of totality may be expressed.

nal reality'. C. P. Snow's hero (L 25) and Ruysbroeck (R 7) both encounter 'the truth'. Q 44 (a Christian) encounters 'the fringe of eternity'
and a clergyman (R 3) 'the Infinite'.

All these very varied claims are of particular interest in view of
Zaehner's theory that a study of such claims enables one to distinguish
Christian mystical experience from other kinds. He states that 'the
nature of the particular experience is at least *indicated* by the words
used'[1] and that the three types of experience he distinguishes 'can be
pin-pointed, by studying the terminology used'.[2] I also believe that study
of the terminology used enables one to distinguish between varieties
of experience, but I do not find that studying the terminology used
necessarily enables one to distinguish between Christian and non-
Christian experience.

Zaehner writes that the common factor in all mystical experiences
is 'a unitive experience with someone or something other than oneself'.[3]
It is the nature of this 'someone or something other than oneself' that
apparently enables him to distinguish Christian from non-Christian
mystical experiences.

He postulates 'at least three distinct mystical states which cannot be
identical'. First, there is the 'natural mystical' experience or, as he
usually prefers to call it,

> 'the pan-en-henic where all creaturely existence is experienced as one
> and one as all; [secondly] the state of pure isolation of what we may
> now call the uncreated soul or spirit from all that is other than
> itself; and thirdly the simultaneous loss of the purely human per-
> sonality, the "ego", and the absorption of the uncreate spirit, the
> "self", into the essence of God, in Whom both the individual person-
> ality and the whole objective world are or seem to be entirely
> obliterated'[4]

The first would seem to have many correspondences with the type
of experience I call adamic; indeed Zaehner says of it that

> 'In Christian terms the first might be regarded as the reversion of
> the individual soul to a state of original innocence, the oneness that
> the human race enjoyed in Adam who is the whole Man and there-
> fore undifferentiated psychologically'.[4]

[1] M.S.P., p. 7.   [2] Ibid., p. 30.
[3] Ibid., p. 32. But as an example of non-Christian mystical experience he cites
the passage from Proust that is my text L 26, and in which there is no feeling of
contact; nor is there in what I call adamic ecstasies, nor in several of the experiences
in my religious group; see also pp. 45–6.   [4] Ibid., p. 168.

Certain of these states, he says are 'also characteristic of lunacy, whether criminal or otherwise'[1], and almost identical with the manic phase of manic depressions[2]. They may be nothing more than an up-rush from what Jung calls the collective unconscious.[3] Most nature mystics do not connect their experiences with God.[4]

Zaehner's second type of experience, which he associates with certain forms of eastern mysticism, seems to me to bear many resemblances to the desired ends of withdrawal ecstasies. His third type substantially corresponds with what I have called union ecstasies. Of the third type he says that 'communion with God is impossible until sin is eradicated', whereas, of the first type, 'communion with Nature is attainable without any effort and without any moral perfection'[5].

The last condition would seem to be a modification of the method earlier avowed, that of 'studying the terminology used'. The method is still further modified by such statements as the one that 'the only method we have of judging between divine and "natural" mysticism' is that the former can effect 'a total transformation and sanctification of character which no merely praeternatural agency could bring about'[6] and later,

> 'it would seem that the mystic who is genuinely inspired by the divine love, will show this to the world by the holiness of his life and by an abiding humility in face of the immense favours bestowed which always he will see to be God's doing, not his own. Only such criteria can enable us to distinguish between the genuine state of union with God and the "natural" or rather "praeternatural" phenomena we have been discussing'[7].

In these statements Zaehner seems to have moved from judgement by studying the terminology used to judgement by results, and any attempt to pinpoint types of experience by studying the words used seems to have become hopeless. John Custance, extensively quoted by Zaehner as showing the diseased state allied to pan-en-henic experiences, frequently claims contact with God. But Zaehner puts him out of court as having theistic experience because he is (or was) a certified manic-depressive. 'We do not know what exactly he means when he uses the term "God"', Zaehner says[8]; but do we know exactly what anyone means by that term? Wordsworth uses the term

[1] M.S.P., p.101.   [2] Ibid., p. 44.   [3] Ibid., p. 106.   [4] Ibid., p. 90.
[5] Ibid., p. 104.   [6] Ibid., p. 105.   [7] Ibid., p. 193   [8] Ibid., p. 90.

God in the passage that is my text L 1a; but Zaehner refuses to accept Wordsworth as any kind of a mystic, since

> 'to judge from his writings, he does not seem to have had a "unitive" experience of any of the types we have discussed'.[1]

Jefferies, on the other hand, appears as 'an unwilling witness on Christianity's behalf' because he draws a clear distinction between 'the animating power in Nature' and 'the "higher than deity" to which his soul constantly aspires'.[2] He did not attain communion, but he perceived the existence of that with which communion could be attained.

But in addition to the unlikelihood of people who do not believe in God naming God as their contact, no matter what kind of experience they have enjoyed, it is also a fact, as we have seen, that Christian mystics do not always use such terms as must lead us necessarily to assume that their contact was with God or a transcendental spirit. C. P. Snow's hero claimed he had become part of the truth he sought; this is not claimed as Christian experience, and Snow is, I understand, an unbeliever. St. Augustine frequently gives to his contact such names as 'the unchangeable Truth itself', 'Eternal Wisdom', 'That Which Is';[3] in my text R 19 it is 'the perspicuous truth' that he perceives. So persistently does he use such phrases, says Butler, that

> 'we may well wonder whether, under such cold intellectual and philosophical terms, he really describes the same religious experiences as do the mediaeval and later mystics...Are they not, rather, the language of an exalted Platonism describing only the higher operations of the intellect?'[4]

But it is unthinkable that St. Augustine should be rejected as not having known Christian theistic experience; and Butler resolves the doubt, with particular reference to the passage which is my text, commenting that

> 'commencing in what seems to be mere Platonism, it develops quite naturally into a mysticism of the highest type'.[5]

The term 'reality' is, in my texts, used only by the questionnaire

[1] M.S.P., p. 35. This criticism of Wordsworth is discussed on pp. 360-2.
[2] Ibid., pp. 48-9.   [3] All cited by Butler: W.M.
[4] Ibid., pp. 41-2.   [5] Ibid., p. 42.

group, but there by both Christian and atheist. The term is, however often used by orthodox Christian mystics, and Butler states that

'for the Christian and the Theist, "The Absolute", "Absolute Being", "Absolute Reality", "Transcendental Reality", are God'.[1]

We must assume that when Q 33, a Christian, speaks of encountering reality, he is having Zaehner's theistic experience, but that when Q 17, an atheist, does the same, he is having one of Zaehner's other kinds of experience: that when St. Augustine speaks of encountering truth, he is doing so in theistic experience, but Snow's hero in some other kind of experience.

I have already shown earlier in this chapter that experiences, which seem extraordinarily similar to Zaehner's non-Christian types of experience, are often claimed by orthodox Christian mystics.

Zaehner seems further to assume that a person will, on all occasions, enjoy the same type of experience, but this is very far from being the case (see p. 93 and n.). Jefferies, in my text L 3, makes no claim of contact and describes what is, in my terms, an adamic ecstasy; in Zaehner's terms I suspect this would be his first type of experience. But on the basis of other experiences Zaehner accepts him as an unwilling witness for Christianity, and Butler describes him as

'feeling after, if haply he might find, the transcendental God of the mystics and of the theologians'.[2]

St. Catherine of Genoa often claimed experiences more orthodox than those referred to earlier, and both Wordsworth and St. Teresa enjoyed many different types of experience. It was by generalizing from people's comparisons of their varied experiences that I was able to produce the differentiations I made in Chapter VII.

I would, then, agree with Zaehner that study of the terminology used enables us usefully to differentiate between types of mystical experiences. I would further accept his third kind of experience, his Christian experience, as being the type that should—at least eventually —be enjoyed by Christians, and very often is; and his first type, the pan-en-henic experience, as he calls it, as being the type most usually available to 'ordinary' people. (His second type, which I associate with withdrawal experience and, as Zaehner does, with forms of eastern mysticism, I do not feel competent to discuss. The type that

[1] W.M., p. 5.   [2] Ibid., p. 232.

I call knowledge ecstasy—for instance, the experience of St. Ignatius Loyola (R 15)—finds no place in Zaehner's classification.) What, from study of the terminology used, I reject is Zaehner's contention that we are hereby enabled to distinguish Christian experiences from others. Rather I find that study of the terminology used imposes on us the belief that experiences of different kinds are available both to Christian and to non-Christian. I also reject the suggestion, which Zaehner also rejects, that 'sectarian dogma necessarily modifies the actual nature of the mystic's experience',[1] since people's persistent claims to experiences inconsonant with their accepted dogma shows this not to be the case. Indeed, I should think it more likely that dogma often derives from the nature of a mystic's experience.

A more extensive inquiry than I have been able to make might, however, show that individuals tend to have one kind of experience more than another kind, and possibly even that certain culture-patterns tend to produce—or in some measure to be produced by—mystics who show a persistent tendency to describe one or other type of experience.

[1] M.S.P., p. 205.

CHAPTER XII

Ecstasy in Children

There are many beliefs, ranging from accepted myth to apparent statements of fact, about the ecstatic experiences of children. By a fortunate chance I was able to examine some seventy experiences of children in this field, and these have some suggestive implications for the subject of children and ecstasy.

The passage from Richard Church's *Over the Bridge* that is my text L 23a was quoted in an examination-paper set to two parallel forms of high-school girls of average age fifteen years; they had not had, in class, any earlier contact with a similar subject. After answering some short comprehension questions (e.g. 'Explain the reference to Savonarola') they were told to 'Write an account of any event which may have had the same kind of significance in your own life. (It may have been going into the country, reading a book, seeing a picture, hearing a poem, etc.)' [1]

Forty-six girls answered this question; and by kind permission of the headmistress and of the mistress setting the paper, I was allowed (after names had been removed) to see their essays. Later, due to the extremely kind co-operation of the mistress concerned, the same question was given to two other forms, of average ages 14 years and 12 years. In these cases the text was briefly discussed in class before the homework essays were written. Of the younger group I saw only one essay, but was assured that the rest were merely descriptive accounts of, say, pleasant holidays. I saw all essays from the older group. The essays from all groups that seem of interest in the context of ecstasy I have summarized in Appendix F, calling this group of texts Group C (for children).

Not all those I have summarized can I call ecstasies. Many, particularly among those from the 14-year-olds, are accounts of the opposite experiences, those that I call desolations and discuss in Chapter XVI. It

---

[1] I should explain that I saw the examination-paper by chance, after it had been answered. The illustrative triggers were given spontaneously by the mistress setting the paper.

is of interest that some children proffered such experiences when given an exemplar of ecstasy.

Of some others that tell of happy occasions one cannot know whether or not ecstasy in my sense was felt. Did C 4 feel ecstasy the first time she went sailing? She may well have done so, but there is nothing in her account of her experience that could justify my calling it an ecstasy. Nor can we say of these children, as we can of the questionnaire group, that since they were being asked about ecstasy, what they gave must be what they thought was ecstasy. It all depended what kind of experience they identified in Richard Church's account, and many obviously took it (as those I have not summarized obviously did) that all they were being asked for was an account of any pleasant experience.

But it can be said with some assurance that many of these children were telling of ecstatic experiences in my sense. The range of triggers they give, though great, is similar to the range given by the adults in the questionnaire group, and seems to have been little influenced by the trigger shown in the text or by the four illustrative triggers provided. One is often reminded of other experiences in the questionnaire and literary groups. C 15, in the dark cottage like a cavern, seems to have felt very much as Carlo Levi did (L 12), though without the final intensity that completed his experience. C 33, recalling childhood pleasures through taste, reminds one of Q 50 and of Proust (L 26). C 9 gave an historical vision of the fighting in the Pass of Glencoe (I have not summarized this) which recalls those ecstasies with specific historical overbeliefs discussed earlier (see pp. 111–14).

It is commonly believed that adolescence is a time of frequent ecstatic experiences, but none of the children gave any indication that they knew frequent ecstasies at the time of writing or earlier. Nor did the three children in the questionnaire group.[1] Of the adults in the questionnaire group, two people said they had known ecstasy more frequently in adolescence. Q 55, in her early twenties when questioned, spoke of an earlier period when ecstasies were more frequent; in early youth, she said, 'anything' could induce ecstasies and in those days she had known it in 'tens', now in very rare units. Q 4 said that in adolescence he had known ecstasy 'fairly frequently—now in units'. J 2 (see Appendix J, p. 528) claimed frequent ecstasies in adolescence

---

[1] The 10-year-old said he had known ecstasy about 10 times, the 14-year-old girl said she had known ecstasy in 'units', and the 15-year-old girl said 'up to about 15 times very intensely'.

No one suggested that an earlier period than adolescence was one of frequent ecstasies, and the evidence for adolescence usually being a time of frequent ecstasies is slight.[1]

Not only did these children provide no evidence that ecstasy was frequent with them now or earlier. Not one of them identified the experience she was asked to parallel (and often did parallel) as one that recalled an earlier period of childhood when life was like this all the time. Several of them did write of their experiences as being those of a new and paradisical world—in my terms, adamic experiences. It was 'another world, a world of paradise' (C 37); 'I felt that I was in a dream-like world' (C 11); 'everything was fresh and new' (C 14); 'the beginning of everything; the beginning of a new and happy world' (C 52). But these are common feelings of ecstasy (see p. 92), and neither these children nor those of the questionnaire group related the experience they described to a state they had once known. Nor did Church himself do so; his reference was to the legendary state of Adam, an image of such an adult as he was when he wrote.

These children, then, give no indication of remembering a state such as Vaughan described (in the poem quoted on pp. 110–11). Yet adult writers do very often tell us that their own childhoods felt like almost continuous states of ecstasy. Wordsworth's *Intimations of Immortality* ode provides an obvious example, as does Traherne's meditation on his childhood:

'All appeared new, and strange at first, inexpressibly rare and delightful and beautiful... My knowledge was Divine. I knew by intuition those things which since my Apostacy, I collected again by the highest reason... All things were spotless and pure and glorious... Heaven and Earth did sing my Creator's praises, and could not make more melody to Adam, than to me. All Time was Eternity... The corn was orient and immortal wheat, which never should be reaped, nor was ever sown... The green trees when I saw them first through one of the gates transported and ravished me, their sweetness and unusual beauty made my heart to leap, and almost mad with ecstasy.' [2]

The reference to seeing through one of the gates is helpful as showing

---

[1] This need not, of course, affect the possibility that of adolescents who do have ecstasies, a high proportion give religious interpretations to them. Conversions usually take place during the teens (see Michael Argyle, *Religious Behaviour* (London, 1958), p. 59 et seq.), though as these typically occur at revival meetings, they are probably not the results of ecstasies in my sense; see pp. 194–5 and pp. 205–6.

[2] *Centuries of Meditation*, The Third Century, Nos. 2 and 3.

that Traherne was referring to a genuine childhood memory and not making a supposition that the period between baptism and self-consciousness *must* have felt like this.

There can be little doubt that adults have sometimes felt, looking back, that their childhoods were periods of almost continuous ecstasy. But even these people do sometimes reveal that in fact their childhoods were not so untainted as passages like the above might lead one to suppose. Traherne at the age of four was wondering why, if God was so good, he himself was 'so poor? Of so scanty and narrow a fortune, enjoying few and obscure comforts?' [1] He seems to have been about the same age when

'in a lowering and sad evening, being alone in the field, when all things were dead and quiet, a certain want and horror fell upon me, beyond imagination. The unprofitableness and silence of the place dissatisfied me; its wideness terrified me; from the utmost ends of the earth fears surrounded me.' [2]

Wordsworth was, as we know, unhappy for a considerable part of his childhood, and in *The Prelude* recalls

The terrors, all the early miseries
Regrets, vexations, lassitudes, [3]

The general impression is rather of some early ecstasies in some children than a period of almost continuous ecstasy as a common childhood occurrence.

This impression is strengthened by the fact that many of the children write about the moment when they first gained awareness of those aspects of the world that ecstasy momentarily expunges. In accounts of experiences that often closely recall Traherne's account of childhood terror, they tell of their first realizations of sickness and death, isolation, loneliness and fear, madness, number, difference. But they do not say that before they became aware of these things they were living in almost continuous states of ecstasy.

Of course many a fortunate childhood may contain long periods of ecstatic happiness, such unitive states as those discussed earlier (see Chapter V). Many a childhood may be remembered as a period of happiness something less than this, but still almost continuous. But the belief that childhood is normally a Golden Age of ecstasy is, I think, a myth, one of the many myths to which ecstatic experiences give rise.

[1] *Centuries of Meditation*, The Third Century, No. 16.
[2] Ibid., The Third Century, No. 23. [3] Vol. I, ll. 356-7.

CHAPTER XIII

Ecstasy and Childbirth

As between the content of the ecstatic experiences of men and of women there seem to be no appreciable differences. It is not possible to say that one or other type of experience is more common in men than in women, or that certain varieties of experience are available to men or to women only.[1]

Comparison of the triggers that induce ecstasy in men and in women in the groups show a few differences that could, perhaps, have been guessed. Thus, while similar numbers of men and of women are moved to ecstasy by nature, sexual love, religion, art, appreciably more men than women are moved to ecstasy by scientific knowledge and slightly more men than women by exercise; slightly more women than men are moved to ecstasy by recollection and introspection.[2]

But there is one trigger effective for women and not, apparently, for men and this is childbirth. No man in the groups or, so far as I know, elsewhere describes ecstasy induced by the first sight of his child or by the thought of fatherhood. It may be significant that, as Walter de la Mare points out, we have no word *father-love* to match our *mother-love*.[3]

Evidence for ecstasy at childbirth in women is, however, astonishingly scanty. There may well be serious novels and poems in which such ecstasies are described by women writers, but I do not know of any. In the questionnaire group five women gave childbirth as a

---

[1] See Appendix D, Table 6, where analyses of the experiences of men and of women in the groups are compared.

[2] See Appendix D, Table 7.

[3] *Love* (London, 1943), p. xxxvii. In the questionnaire group, Q 12 said that news of the recovery of his child from illness had induced ecstasy in him. He was unable to describe 'ecstasy', but that this was what he meant is indicated by his also giving sex as a trigger and then saying that he had known this experience only twice in his life. This is my only example of an ecstasy whose trigger derived from fatherhood, and the occasion was not the birth of the child.

trigger to ecstasy, and in another very small group questioned later, one woman did so.[1]

Some extremely helpful evidence was however provided by the response to a programme broadcast in the B.B.C.'s Woman's Hour (October 8, 1957). In this programme there was broadcast a recording of the birth of a child assisted by the methods of Dr. Grantly Dick-Read who, together with the husband of the woman, was present at the birth. On subsequent days there were broadcast several letters from listeners to this programme. These were clearly of considerable evidential interest to me, and I am much obliged to the B.B.C. for making available to me the information I asked for on the correspondence as a whole.

Some five hundred letters had been received, one of the largest post-bags for any Woman's Hour programme. The writers were apparently from all classes and varied in age from young to elderly women. About 10 per cent. of these letters protested against the programme, some because they found it disgusting, others because they felt, as one woman put it, that 'childbirth is sacred and should not be commercialized like this'. This reason for protest is interesting, since protests against the commercialization of objects, events, and ideas is often a useful guide to what people feel to be triggers (see p. 179).

About a third of the remaining letters were from women who had not had children and whose response was, therefore, directly to the programme. Many of these letters were, in my sense of the word, ecstatic, indicating that the idea of childbirth can act as a trigger to ecstasy, at least for women.[2]

But in the present context the most interesting letters were those from women whose own experiences of childbirth were recalled by the programme and who often described in some detail these experiences and their reactions to them. Many of these letters recalled extreme joy, using such phrases as 'glorious exultation', 'overwhelming feeling of elation', and—interesting in view of the feelings of loss of worldliness so often expressed in ecstasy—'At the moment of my daughter's birth I would have given all I had away.' 'Never before or since have I experienced the wonderful feeling of spiritual freedom which followed the birth of my first child', wrote one woman. Only a few,

[1] For the composition of this group, see Appendix J.
[2] Among the group of children discussed in the last chapter, one—C 39—chose to describe, in ecstatic terms, seeing the birth of a chicken for the first time.

perhaps twenty, of these letters fulfil all the criteria I have demanded for labelling an experience an ecstasy, but the cumulative impression of many joyful letters of this kind is that ecstatic experiences in my sense are being, however haltingly, expressed, an impression heightened by contrast with other letters which, while accepting childbirth as a happy experience, give no hint of ecstatic feelings.

From all these letters and from the women in the questionnaire group it is possible to reach some tentative conclusions about childbirth in relation to ecstasy.

Not all women experience ecstasy with childbirth. Some negative evidence of this is provided by the women with children in the questionnaire group—there were several of these—who did *not* mention childbirth as a trigger. The B.B.C. group (as I shall call them) were often more positive.

A small number wrote that their own experiences of childbirth were positively distressing: 'conscious only of fear, loneliness and pain', 'the hours I spent in the labour ward are among the most distressing I remember'. A few indicated that their responses to their babies were inhibited by these distressing experiences. One wrote:

> 'The only feeling I had on sight of my baby was revulsion for the object which had caused such distress and misery...the joys of motherhood are over-rated.'

and another,

> 'She was born without joy but lots of pain...and only recently has she felt really mine, she is now six.' [1]

Others described childbirth as a natural function not worth making a fuss about, or even as a jolly occasion without any hint of ecstatic feelings: for instance, 'Childbirth should be an occasion for plenty of smiles and normality.'

A woman may receive ecstasy from the birth of only one child, often but not necessarily the first, out of two or more births. In the questionnaire group, Q 18 and Q 28 say they experienced ecstasy at the births of their first babies, Q 3 at the birth of her fourth baby. In the B.B.C. group,

---

[1] I wonder whether those occasional cases in which a mother rejects one of her children might sometimes prove to be where the conditions of birth were particularly distressing (not necessarily painful), or where the conditions in which the mother first saw her child were particularly inhibiting of response?

ecstatic feelings were described at the birth of first, second, third, and fourth babies—that is to say, women wrote that these particular births had qualities of feeling over and above another or others; for instance, the woman quoted above who said that the feelings that accompanied the birth of her first child were known only that once, another who wrote 'my first childbirth was truly the work of God', and another 'the birth of my second baby was indeed the greatest joy I ever had'.[1]

Ecstasy is as readily felt after comparatively painful as after comparatively painless births. There have been suggestions that there is a relation between painless or comparatively painless birth and the mother's ability to feel ecstasy. Professor Alexander Kennedy was quoted as saying of hypnosis that 'it leaves the mother free to enjoy an ecstatic experience of labour well done and the arrival of a new child'.[2] The whole tendency of the B.B.C. recording was to assume that this form of 'natural' child-bearing, being comparatively painless, enabled the mother to have a joyful experience that other more painful forms either could not or were less likely to give.

Some of the women in the B.B.C. group accepted this implicit supposition and assumed that the reason they had not enjoyed ecstatic experience at the birth of their children was because the births had been painful or, sometimes, because the mother had been anaesthetized.[3]

---

[1] The following was said to me in conversation by Q 5, some years after she had answered the questionnaire, and afterwards written down by her at my request:

'I can still remember the moment when my son was born—when all the stress was over, and they put him in my arms. It was a moment of incomparable elation, and has lost none of its quality over the years, so that when I pass the nursing-home now, my heart fills with the same emotion. It wasn't anything like the same quality when the second child was born.'

Four points here are worth notice: (a) that ecstasy was felt with only one of two children, which Q 5 did not make clear when she answered the questionnaire; (b) that ecstasy took place when the baby was put into the mother's arms; (c) that it was momentary; (d) that a similar emotion is recaptured every time she passes a place that symbolizes the event for her—in my terms, a response experience. This last point was also made by one of the B.B.C. group who wrote that whenever she passes the hospital where her child was born, her eyes fill with tears at the memory.

[2] *The Times*, June 14, 1957.

[3] For instance, three women gave descriptions of ecstatic reactions to the broadcast, commenting that as their own had been painful forceps births, they had had no such feelings as those of the woman in the recording or those they now experienced while listening. Another wrote that she had two children and 'my only

But I do not think that the relations between comparatively painless birth and ecstasy, comparatively painful birth and no ecstasy, can be sustained.

In the first place, ecstasy is most often said to have been felt at the birth of the first child. All other things being equal, a first birth is likely to be more painful than subsequent ones.

In the questionnaire group, so far as I know (and in some cases I do know) none of the births referred to was undertaken with hypnosis or by Dr. Grantly Dick-Read's methods, and so far as I know (and in some cases I do know) all were normally painful.

Then, in the B.B.C. group some of the women who claimed quick and comparatively painless childbirth positively denied having ecstatic feelings or described feelings in no way ecstatic. For instance, one woman wrote, 'the experience wasn't painless but it was so quick it meant nothing at all', and another simply wrote that she 'felt very happy and comfortable all the way through'.

Most significantly, some women in this group did describe ecstatic feelings after painful childbirths and even after caesarean births. For instance,

> 'I know what I missed [she had a forceps delivery and is referring to the pleasure of co-operating in the actual birth] but I don't fret about it now because I *know* what the end of all the labours must mean. When I first held [my baby], the joy, the wonder was indescribable.'

One woman described two births in detail, the first a very painful one followed by ecstasy, the second apparently a cheerful social occasion with the District Nurse. She concludes, 'Do we not lose a lot, in losing the pain?'

Ecstasy is usually felt when the child is first placed in the mother's arms; this may not be until the day after the birth. Less often the ecstasy is induced when the baby's first cry is heard.

In the questionnaire group, Q 28 speaks of 'the first sight of my first baby', Q 18 of holding her baby the day after she was born; Q 3 says that the ecstasy took place two days after the birth. In the B.B.C. group by far the largest number speak of having their babies in their arms for the first time; a few speak of the moment of hearing the baby's

regret is that I didn't have the advantage of Natural Birth tuition. I feel that I missed something wonderful', and another, 'Unfortunately an experience I shall never have as my two Babies were both caesarean births.'

first cry; there is no evidence here that the actual moment of birth is the moment of ecstasy.

One woman describes an ecstasy at the moment of feeling the first birth-pang. The trigger is a compound one; she looked out of a window overlooking fields and trees and 'It was then that I *knew*.' [1]

Certain conditions may inhibit childbirth ecstasy, and others be propitious to it. Some—perhaps half a dozen of the women—wrote of having experienced fear and loneliness because of neglect and lack of kindness in the labour-wards of hospitals, and associated this with their inability to feel the joy expressed by the mother in the recording. In contrast, one or two wrote to say that having a baby at home was an integral part of the joyful emotions they experienced: 'it was a wonderful experience having a child at home' said one, comparing it with a less satisfactory first occasion when she had had her baby in a hospital, and another said that to bear a child at home 'makes the baby part of the family immediately'.

One or two women said that the presence of their husbands at the births had enhanced the occasions:

'My husband was with me... We would not have missed that tremendous event for the whole world.'

Others said they wished the broadcast could be repeated on a Sunday so that husbands could hear it: '—this recording will enable them [*sc.* husbands] to recapture some of the thrill and wonder of the moment of birth'.

After childbirth unitive periods, lasting from hours to days, are not uncommon. One woman from the B.B.C. group wrote that

'the miracle of seeing my two babies born and the satisfaction of the days after were on a plane far above the level of normal life'.

Two women told how they stayed awake all night after their babies were born, the one 'wonderfully happy, spiritually elated and free of my body', the other 'marvelling at the wonderful feeling of being a mother'.

Relevant to this is an article that appeared in the *Manchester*

[1] In one of Rebecca West's novels she describes an ecstasy at the moment of feeling the child quicken for the first time; *The Thinking Reed* (London, 1936), ch. v.

Guardian.[1] The writer is describing her state of mind in the maternity hospital where she then was:

> 'It is not the rest: it is the retreat from life, or, to put it properly... the embracing of life that a retreat from one's normal world makes possible... No martyr's death has moved me so deeply as St. Bernard's distress that his many duties as abbot kept him from a life of meditation.'

Why in ordinary social life, she asks, does one never decide, instead of going out and seeing people, to stay at home 'listening to music, or taking down one of the art books one has saved so long to buy, or just communing critically with oneself—all spiritual refuelling?'—or, in my terms, trigger activities. She goes on,

> 'What is wrong with me or my organisation that I have to have a baby in hospital to hear birds for the first time in years, to watch a crocus come into being, grow and die, to watch an evening sky race past the window, to taste food—not particularly good food— with separate sensations of texture, wetness, solidity...'

This state, she feels, is not merely release—it is 'more positive'. She feels it releases her from the 'isolation', the 'terrible transiency' of being human, and desires to share her feelings with others. She is insistent that her present feelings (which have many similarities with Gissing's on going into the country—see p. 64) have nothing to do with just having had a baby, but we may reasonably suppose that this, as well as the enforced 'retreat from life', played its part in inducing this frame of mind.

[1] 25 February, 1955.

CHAPTER XIV

Ecstasy and Sexual Love

Among contemporary secular people of the kind that composed my questionnaire group sexual love appears to be a common trigger. In this group sexual love was named as a trigger by 43 per cent. of people (18 women and 8 men).[1] Eleven of these people (6 men and 5 women) made unmistakable references to sexual intercourse, and of other references to 'love', 'being in love', etc., sexual intercourse was probably implied in several cases.[2]

It is certain that the people who claimed ecstasy from sexual intercourse did not confuse ecstasy with the pleasures of sexual orgasm. Many of those questioned were married people, yet they did not claim to have known ecstasy more often than people who named only other triggers. In the questionnaire group, of those who said that ecstasy had been induced in them by intercourse and named no other trigger, none claimed ecstasy more often than in tens, while two people claimed it once only and one person twice. Of the people who gave sexual intercourse together with other triggers, none claimed ecstasy more often than in tens, and most people in units.

If then my respondents are not all abnormally low in their sexual responses, the feelings that they identify as *ecstasy* cannot be equated with the feelings they normally derive from sexual intercourse, and this is true both for men and for women.

The evidence that ecstasy is a rare phenomenon is not, then, modified

[1] Of 5 very similar people (see Appendix J), 3 people, one man and two women, named sexual love, the man specifying 'sexual intercourse'. Lawrence's experiences (L 17a and 17b) seem to me to be so peculiar in so many ways that I omit them in trying to establish what is common and generic; I will consider them later in this chapter.

[2] One mention that certainly did not imply sexual intercourse was that of the girl of 14 who said 'Love—for people I've been cracked on and boys I've liked' (Q 49); but it does imply that homosexual attraction can as well act as a trigger as heterosexual attraction—if, indeed, the point needed any more support than it has received from several writers, ancient and modern.

by consideration of ecstasies induced by sexual intercourse. Ecstasies with this trigger, at least among the kind of contemporary secular people of the kind I questioned, are no more or less rare than ecstasies induced by nature or by art.[1]

Nor do they appear to differ appreciably in content. Analyses of the texts according to whether ecstasies were triggered by nature, religion, art, or sexual love, show that ecstasies triggered by religion and by nature are most similar to each other and to the mean of the three groups. Ecstasies triggered by art show comparatively low loss of feelings of difference and of self, comparatively high gain of feelings of release, renewal, etc. Ecstasies triggered by sexual love show a comparatively high loss of feelings of difference and of self, a comparatively high gain of feelings of renewal, etc., and a comparatively low gain of feelings of knowledge. This picture must, however, be to some extent distorted by the fact that several of the people who gave sexual love gave other triggers as well (this accounts for a single entry for feelings of withdrawal for ecstasies triggered by sexual love) and should be accepted with reserve.[2]

I think it is now possible to dispose of the theory that ecstasy is largely if not wholly a phenomenon of sexual repression, a theory often put forward by people sceptical of religious explanations.[3]

Of the people in the questionnaire group who gave sexual love as a trigger, most were married and apparently happily married. Several of the people who gave this trigger gave other triggers as well; a useful example is Q 19 who included among her triggers both 'love, physical passion' and 'real religious experience'. It seems clear that for these people ecstasy is not a result of sexual deprivation. It is my belief that it is the language in which some experiences are described that is the phenomenon of sexual repression, the overbelief and not the experience itself.

Since however it is the experiences of celibate religious people and

---

[1] See Appendix D, Table 3.   [2] See Appendix D, Table 8.

[3] Leuba, for instance, comments that 'Not one of the prominent representatives of mysticism lived a normal married life' and that 'many of the curious phenomena to which most great mystics owe in part their fame or notoriety are due to perturbations of the sex function consequent upon its repression', P.R.M., pp. 119–20. See also pp. 137–53, where, *inter alia*, he writes that 'the virgins and the unsatisfied wives who undergo the repeated "love-assaults of God"...suffer from nothing else than intense attacks of erotomania' and 'the delights said by our great mystics to transcend everything which the world and the senses can procure, involve some activity of the sexual organs'.

not those of happily married secular people that form the material for most studies of mysticism, it is not surprising that a supposition should have arisen that ecstasy is, in some if not all cases, a phenomenon of sexual repression. Often the ecstatic experiences of the religious are described in terms of a love-relationship between the mystic—or, more properly, his or her soul—and God. An example in the texts is the experience of St. Francis of Sales (R 21) and others, often less restrained in their transports, are easily found.[1]

Such expressions of a love-relationship between **the** mystic, or his soul, and God are accepted as proper by the Church. As is well known, until comparatively recent times supererogatory pleasure in even married sexual intercourse was forbidden by the Church.[2] But lately sexual intercourse in Christian marriage has come to be accepted as a type of the love of God, and such statements as that of Zaehner, quoted below, should serve the purpose of explaining why ecstasies derived from sexual love and ecstasies derived from the love of God may 'feel' the same and be described in similar terms:

> 'There is no point at all in blinking the fact that the raptures of the theistic mystic are closely akin to the transports of sexual union, the soul playing the part of the female and God appearing as the male...the human relationship is the symbol of the divine, not, as the psychologists hold, the divine of the human.' [3]

But the explanation will not hold, and for two reasons. In the first place, as Zaehner points out, the religious mystics describe their love-relationship with God as one in which God plays the part of the male and the soul of the mystic that of the female. In sexual intercourse, whether ecstatic or not, no male, so far as I know, feels himself to be playing the part of the female and his female that of the male. The religious language colours a feeling that the ecstatic is merged in something greater than himself, and to express this the feelings of the male, dominant in sexual intercourse, would not be appropriate, whereas

---

[1] Leuba quotes a speech of God to St. Mary Margaret Alacoque, reported by herself when she was protesting at the pains of the bridegroom's love: 'Let me do my pleasure,' he said, 'There is a time for everything. Now I want you to be the plaything of my love, and you must live thus without resistance, surrendered to my desires, allowing me to gratify myself at your expense.' P.R.M., pp. 113-14.

[2] See, for instance, Peter Lombard's 'omnis ardentior amator propriae uxoris adulter est'—passionate love of a man's own wife is adultery; quoted by C. S. Lewis, *The Allegory of Love* (Oxford, 1936), p. 15.

[3] M.S.P., p. 151.

E.—F   147

the feelings of the submissive female provide a suitable image. Thus where Q I speaks of flowing over the lines of her personality and merging into the experience, St. Francis of Sales speaks of the soul letting herself flow into what she loves, of being mingled with and absorbed in her God.

The second reason why this explanation will not hold is that descriptions of ecstasy in terms of a love-relationship are found only in celibate ecstatics and those who, like Madame Guyon, were deprived of normal sex-life. Apart from Lawrence (to whom I will soon return), no one in the questionnaire or literary groups used the imagery of sex to describe ecstasy, not even those people in the questionnaire group who gave sex as a trigger, whether alone or with others. In the latter cases people apparently assumed that a single description of ecstasy, and that one without sexual imagery, would serve, no matter how the experience was triggered. I have already referred to Q 19 who gave as triggers both physical passion and religious experience; she also gave other triggers, but a single description of ecstasy, and one wholly without sexual connotations, apparently seemed to her sufficient, no matter which of these triggers induced the ecstasy.[1]

Since it appears that for people of normal sex-life, as for many, both secular and religious, who are deprived of normal sex-life, it is both possible and usual to describe ecstatic experience without using sexual imagery, it would seem probable that the use of sexual imagery in descriptions of ecstasy is a matter of overbelief. The nature of ecstatic experiences is such that the image of a love-relationship between the ecstatic as the female and that which is believed to have been encountered as the male may sometimes seem appropriate. But, so far as I know, such images are not in fact used by people of normal sex-life.

We may now turn to D. H. Lawrence whose two experiences

---

[1] Another useful example comes from a novel, *The Devil Rides Outside*, by John Howard Griffin (London, 1953). The hero, a musicologist staying at a Benedictine Abbey, has an enormous sexual appetite which he half-longs, half-dreads to exchange for the consolations of religion. After a period of continence he sleeps with a woman and his second coupling with her, said to be unique in his vast experience, is lushly and lengthily described as a typical ecstasy, in no way specifically sexual in imagery; some 200 pages later the whole passage is repeated, this time to serve as a description of the hero's first ecstasy from religion. The author draws no attention to the fact that he uses the same passage twice. For him, it seems, having described an ecstasy as best he could, he saw no reason to vary the description (except in minute and unimportant particulars, such as feeling the wood of the pews and not the flesh of the body), whether the trigger was sex or religion.

(L 17a and 17b) differ from what appears to be the norm in several particulars. I have already pointed out that Lawrence is the only secular mystic I know of who associates *up* and *darkness* (see pp. 73 and 75). His references to sex are equally unusual.

In the first place, sexual imagery is not, as I have just shown, used by secular mystics of normal sex-life. But in Lawrence's description of an ecstasy in Lincoln cathedral (L 17a), the image is a sexual one throughout.[1]

Then, where the image in ecstatic descriptions is a sexual one, the ecstatic or his soul, as already shown, plays the part of the female. But Lawrence, uniquely, sets his hero's soul in the part of the male, 'every jet of him' straining and leaping to the 'fecundity' in the close embrace.

Lawrence's apparent frequency of ecstasy is also peculiar. In text L 17a, the ecstasy in Lincoln cathedral, he describes two immediately successive ecstasies or—in the imagery he uses—two immediately successive sexual orgasms. Two immediately successive sexual orgasms are not impossible; two immediately successive ecstasies are, so far as I know, unique.

Then in the second text (L 17b), where the ecstasy—a word Lawrence himself uses of both experiences—was in fact triggered by sexual intercourse, Lawrence tells us that this experience takes place 'as a rule' when his hero starts love-making. But ecstasy triggered by love-making, as by other triggers, is, as we have seen, not the rule but a very rare exception.

The peculiarities in the first text seem to me to be such as to make one doubt whether Lawrence had, at the time of writing, ever known any of the intense experiences I have called ecstasy. A deep interest in such experiences need be no assurance that such experiences are personally known. It may even be that, as with sex, the contrary is often the case, but, confining ourselves to ecstasy, we may recall the instance of Aldous Huxley who was very much interested in ecstasy for many years before he came to believe he had known, through mescalin, such an experience, and who used a contrived description of an ecstasy as the climax of one of his novels (see p.73n). That Lawrence, like Huxley, had known many lesser experiences on the same scale we need not doubt; but had he ever known ecstasy?

The statement in the second text, that the experience described was

[1] 'leapt up in a manifold, clustered desire...to the ecstasy, the touch, to the meeting and the consummation, the meeting, the clasp, the close embrace', etc.

known 'as a rule' when engaged in love-making, gives rise to another possibility, which is that the language commonly used to describe sexual orgasm may be indistinguishable from the language used to describe ecstasy, and that all that Lawrence intended, in this passage, was to describe satisfactory sexual orgasm.

As we have seen, the people in the questionnaire group do not confuse the *feelings* of sexual orgasm and of ecstasy. Men and women who must often have known the former maintain that they have derived ecstasy from sexual intercourse only a very limited number of times. But if they were asked to describe the satisfactions of sexual orgasm, would their descriptions be distinguishable from descriptions of ecstasy?

To discover whether this is so is peculiarly difficult. Not only is there paucity of evidence, honestly written descriptions of sexual orgasms being scarce; there is also great confusion of evidence owing to the conventions prevailing at various times as to the relationship of love and ecstasy. However, at any given time 'true love' may be defined, this is accepted as a source of ecstasy. True homosexual love is accepted as capable of giving ecstasy to the platonic lover, while the modern Christian accepts both the love of God and love in Christian marriage as being capable of inducing ecstasy. To the medieval churchman ecstasy could be derived only from the love of God, while to those who accepted the medieval secular love-ethic, ecstasy could be derived from love undertaken inside that ethic. But whichever convention prevails, it is conventional to describe the relationship with the chosen trigger in ecstatic terms.

This may be shown by a brief consideration of the medieval love-ethic and its development today. Where Chaucer describes the coupling of Troilus and Cressida, prototypical hero and heroine of the medieval love-ethic, the description is couched in the language of ecstasy:

> *O blisful nyght, of hem so longe isought,*
> *How blithe unto hem bothe two thow weere!*
> *Why nad I swich oon with my soule ybought,*
> *Ye, or the leeste joie that was theere?*
> *Awey, thow foule daunger and thow feere,*
> *And lat hem in this hevene blisse dwelle,*
> *That is so heigh that al ne kan I telle...*
> *That where his spirit was, for joie he nyste.*[1]

[1] *Troilus and Criseyde*, Bk. III, ll. 1317 et seq.

We should notice that Chaucer feels bound to say that such delights are more than he has known himself. And when he comes to describe the couplings of 'common people' who could not, by the convention, experience true love, there is no hint of ecstasy in his language; he is unmistakably describing the coupling of a man with a woman and no other experience:

> Withinne a while this John the clerk up leep,
> And on this goode wyf he leith on soore.
> So myrie a fit ne hadde she nat ful yoore;
> He pricketh harde and depe as he were mad.
> This joly lyf han thise two clerkes lad[1]

This was, we read, the best time the goodwife ever had; but it was not an ecstatic time. Even the Wife of Bath who certainly felt, in modern terms, 'true love' for Jankyn, her fifth husband, never describes love-making in ecstatic terms, though no one would deny her full enjoyment of it. And many people would surely agree that, as those and other Chaucerian passages suggest, love-making can be on occasion an extremely enjoyable experience which still has no significant similarities to ecstatic or response experiences; the same, as we have seen, can be true of childbirth.

A far wider range of people is now allowed to feel 'true love', and in modern popular literature what such people feel when they couple is always ecstasy—a convention demonstrably distressing to many who discover that, as it seems to them, they alone fail to find the ecstatic pleasures of love an inevitable sequel to the assurance of being in love. I may sum up the contemporary popular convention by quoting a collection of novelists' clichés gathered together in a publisher's house-magazine:

> 'Love-making is accompanied (figuratively) by rising to the crests of tremendous waves or soaring towards blinding light, followed by slow descents to ineffable peace or a gradual floating down from mountain-tops to plains of golden bliss.' [2]

But in more serious writing, efforts are occasionally made to tell what sexual intercourse feels like and it is possible, though extremely difficult,

---

[1] *The Reeve's Tale*, ll. 4228–31.
[2] *Now and Then* (Cape, Spring, 1958). Even this short passage of humorous intent demonstrates how difficult it is to 'fake' an ecstasy. Ecstatics may 'come back to earth', even 'come back to earth with a bump'; I do not know of any who float down to plains of golden bliss.

to find examples that suggest, as Chaucer suggested, that great sexual pleasure is obtainable without ecstasy and can be described in terms distinguishable from those of ecstasy. From the very few examples I have been able to find, I have the impression that sexual pleasure without ecstasy tends to be described in terms of sexually local physical sensation, male or female as the case may be, while in descriptions of ecstasy derived from love-making, as from other triggers, sexually local physical sensation is never described and descriptions of men's and women's experiences are indistinguishable from each other.[1]

The contemporary American writer, Edmund Wilson, confirms this with descriptions of love-making undertaken both from lust and from 'true love'. In his story *The Princess with the Golden Hair*,[2] the narrator-hero is romantically obsessed with a married woman called Imogen who reminds him of Mélisande, Isolde, and Arthurian romances generally. Until she is ready to go to bed with him he makes do with Anna, a girl from the slums, several couplings with her being described in detail; 'Anna's visit relieved my tension' is their keynote, and so far Mr. Wilson seems to be following the same convention as Chaucer. But eventually Imogen 'like some creature of enchantment in a fairy-tale' goes to bed with him, and this coupling is described with at least as much physical detail as Lawrence provided in *Lady Chatterley's Lover*. Despite the extreme suitability of the lady, this description could not possibly be taken for one of ecstasy, nor could this possibly be taken as an account as well of a woman's as of a man's feelings; it is a specific account of male sexual pleasure.

The point is again made in a seriously intentioned how-to-do-it book.[3] The author provides, from evidence he says he has collected

---

[1] This impression seems also to be that of Mr. E. C. Pettet, who argues that Keats's descriptions of love-making in *Endymion* are unmistakably descriptions of physical love-making and not descriptions of 'neo-platonic ecstasy' or 'the mystical communion with ideal or essential Beauty. *On the Poetry of Keats* (Cambridge, 1957), p. 154 et seq.

[2] In *Memoirs of Hecate County* (London, 1951).

[3] Not so seriously intentioned how-to-do-it books tend to follow the accepted convention: 'This is it. This is the moment of ecstasy when a woman soars along a Milky Way among stars all her own. This is the high mountain-top of love of which the poets sing. Her whole being is a full orchestra playing the fortissimo of a glorious symphony.' Though the young bride is warned that this does not happen every time, it seems clear that no more than the normal pleasures of orgasm are intended since on a later page this experience is equated with the relief afforded by masturbation. *The Sexual Responsibility of Woman*, by Maxine Davis (London, 1957).

from women, a description of what intercourse with orgasm should feel like for a woman. Though the epithets are enthusiastic to an embarrassing degree, the description is very different from a description of an ecstasy. It is essentially a description of local physical sensations in a woman.[1]

Thus what scanty evidence there is tends to show that it is possible to describe the feelings of sexual orgasm without using the language of ecstasy; and this supposition is reinforced by the ability of the people in the questionnaire group to distinguish between orgasm and ecstasy. We must assume that Lawrence's intention was to write truthfully about love-making and not to follow popular convention, and it is therefore surprising that he apparently takes ecstasy in love-making to be the rule and not a rare exception. It is possible that he thought that ecstasy in love-making *should* be the rule for his hero; but the singularities of his writing, about love-making as about ecstasy, must lead one to wonder whether, at least by the time he came to write *Sons and Lovers*, he had ever known satisfactory love-making.

There is one other point about love-making and ecstasy on which Lawrence provides singular evidence. After the climactic ecstasy in *Lady Chatterley's Lover*, Mellors is made to say that this happened because 'We came off together that time'[2]. I know of no other evidence suggesting that this is necessary for ecstasy from love-making, nor is there any evidence to suggest that when one partner to intercourse experiences ecstasy, the other must too. Such few inquiries as I have been able to make suggests that this is not necessarily the case.

Apart from sexual intercourse or physical contact, ecstasies may be induced by other aspects of love—by thinking of the loved one, by seeing the loved one, or just by being in love.

[1] Theodore Van de Velde, *Ideal Marriage* (London, 1928; 1934 edn.), p. 184. It is interesting in this context to note that when Lawrence describes Connie's climactic experience, said to be uniquely pleasurable and certainly intended to be an ecstasy, what he provides is a description of local female sensations; see *Lady Chatterley's Lover* (1928; Penguin edn., 1960), ch. x, pp. 138-9.

[2] *Lady Chatterley's Lover*, ch. x, p. 139.

CHAPTER XV

Revelation Ecstasies

Some ecstasies have as their result the ecstatic's discovery for the first time of such value in the trigger that a new and continuing focus of value is created for him. Such ecstasies I shall call *revelation ecstasies*.

The phrase *for the first time* is important. Revelation ecstasies must be distinguished from conversion ecstasies (discussed in Chapter XXVII) which represent the culmination of accrued interest in a focus of value. A revelation ecstasy may often be the first step in the process of mutation that can end in an experience, often an ecstatic experience, properly called conversion. Speaking of the relation of such experiences to conversion, de Sanctis writes that the *coup de foudre*—i.e. such an experience —is 'either the point of departure or the point of arrival'.[1] Revelation ecstasies are points of departure; a point of arrival may never be reached.

Revelation ecstasies are often the experiences of children or young people. Richard Church, reading the Bible in school at the age of eight, suddenly experienced ecstasy in which he 'saw a new skyline defined... Everything was now contained, for me, in the power of the Word.' (L 23b). Richard Church became a writer. Einstein's biographer tells of Einstein's point of departure:

'He was impressed most, however, when at about the age of twelve he obtained for the first time a systematic text-book on geometry... Having begun to read the book, he became absorbed in it. The clarity of the exposition and the proof given for every statement...impressed him with an orderliness and straightforwardness that he had not encountered before. The world with its disorder and uncleanliness suddenly appeared to him to contain an element of intellectual and psychological order and beauty.' [2]

The points of arrival of the children discussed in Chapter XII will

[1] R.C., p. 65.
[2] Philipp Frank, *Einstein, His Life and Times*, (London 1948), p. 24.

usually be less spectacular and indeed may never come. But many of them describe experiences, often ecstatic ones, whose result was the discovery of new value in the trigger. 'It was this walk that made me realise that...I could never really enjoy myself unless I was surrounded by hills, moors and crags,' wrote C 36, and C 6, 'That moment made me appreciate the beauty of the mountains.' C 20 had always disliked the idea of listening to music before she went to the concert described; now, 'it is an episode in my life which I shall never forget'. C 41, 'enthralled' by her first visit to the opera, 'began to be an ardent opera fan'. C 34 says that at the age of three, from looking at the stones in the pavement, she suddenly realized the multitudes of people in the world, the endlessness of the human race; 'So on I walked, puzzling over numbers, as I have still been doing to the present day.'

A form of experience often described in ecstatic terms is that of falling in love.[1] When the moment of falling in love, on the first occasion of seeing or being aware of the loved one, is described in ecstatic terms, then such an experience is what I should call a revelation ecstasy.

Ecstasy very quickly imposes conventions of behaviour and language, and seldom more forcefully than in the field of love. For a long time now it has been accepted as proper that 'falling in love' shall be accompanied by some such *coup de foudre* as Dante's on first seeing Beatrice, and we find it natural to ask, as Marlowe and Shakespeare did, 'Who ever loved that loved not at first sight?' and to denigrate love less dramatic than this. But behind convention lies experience, and the experience of falling in love has been, for some people, a moment of ecstasy at the first sight or awareness of what was to be the loved one.

Another group of ecstasies I regard as essentially of the revelation kind are those triggered by childbirth. As Chapter XIII has shown, women do not confuse ecstasy at childbirth with the normal pleasures of the birth of a child, and sometimes regard the child at whose birth they had ecstasy as being of especial value.[2]

This result of an ecstasy, that value should thereafter be felt to inhere

[1] 'The nearest parallel in normal human life [to mystical ecstasy] is that other spiritual sensation which we call "falling in love", in that early beatific stage of the process when all beauty and all wonder seem to be concentrated in some one other person. In those moments of pure adoration the lover enjoys for the time being an essentially mystical rapture'. Gerald Bullett, *The English Mystics*, p. 39.

[2] Revelation ecstasies after childbirth, like those triggered by a person of the opposite sex, might seem to have biological value, and the triggers, in these cases, to be what Tinbergen calls 'sign stimuli' releasing biologically desirable responses. (N. Tinbergen, *The Study of Instinct* (Oxford, 1951).) But the response seems

in its trigger, seems so obvious and probable that it is worth pointing out that it is far from usual. In many of the ecstasies in the texts, the nature of the trigger is irrelevant to the overbelief. The result of St. Ignatius's ecstasy was not that he thereafter found value in rivers (R 15) or of M.E.'s that he found new value in mountains (R 11); the result of Koestler's ecstasy was not the inception of a new devotion to public parks or to the theory of relativity (L 7), or of Richard Feverel's a new and continuing appreciation of shrines (L 16).

It is of course likely that what has proved to be an effective trigger will be regarded as valuable, and a usually unexplained recognition of value is in fact a characteristic of attitudes to triggers. But in other than revelation ecstasies it is not the first discovery of value in the trigger that constitutes the major result of the ecstasy. Both Warner Allen (L 11) and Forster's Helen Schlegel (L 18) obviously set high value on Beethoven's music; but discovery of that value was not the major result of their experiences.

Nor, because result and trigger are closely related, should such experiences as Nichols's and Berenson's (L 5 and L 10) be taken as revelation ecstasies. In both cases we see not the point of departure but the point of arrival. Both men had long since established their foci of value and accrued the material that culminated, with these ecstasies, in the one case in a poem and in the other in a theory of aesthetics. 'For years I had been inquiring, excavating, dredging my inner self, and searching in my conscious experience for a satisfying test,' wrote Berenson, and for years Robert Nichols had been a poet, collecting, consciously and unconsciously, the material for his poetry—for instance, 'there was presented to my consciousness a favourite picture postcard I had twice or thrice bought at the British Museum'. But in revelation ecstasies, as I have defined them, there is no previous awareness of value in the triggers, no previous questions consciously asked. Although we might guess that the revelation comes when the ecstatic is in some way ready for it[1] and to that extent represents a point of

excessive to the need. With responses less intense than ecstatic ones, men and women will wish to mate, and mothers to protect and tend their children. Yet without some such response, would they inhibit their natural repugnances (see p. 257) and obtain the unselfish love without which these relationships cannot prosper?

[1] 'no seemingly instinctive joy or revelation can be purely casual... Each of us perhaps has an innate inclination to, and therefore a delight in a certain type of face, of temperament, and nature... These trends and partialities and prepossessions must travel back pretty far into our past lives.' Walter de la Mare, *Love*, p. lxxvii.

arrival, so far as the ecstatic is consciously aware, an entirely new focus of value has been brought into his life by contact with the trigger to his ecstasy.

It is worth noting the existence of experiences similar to revelation ecstasies in triggers and results but lacking the descriptions of feeling that entitle us to call an experience an ecstasy. Whether in such cases ecstatic feelings were known but not described, or whether the experience itself, though fulminant in its results, was something less than an ecstasy, one cannot know. Again, these experiences seem to be particularly common among children and young people. Two examples will suffice:

St. Augustine was nineteen when at Carthage, in the ordinary course of study,

> 'I fell upon a certain book of Cicero... This book of his contains an exhortation to philosophy, and is called "*Hortensius*". But this book altered my affections, and turned my prayers to Thyself, O Lord; and made me have other purposes and desires. Every vain hope at once became worthless to me; and I longed with an incredibly burning desire for an immortality of wisdom.' [1]

This experience, which it is not justifiable to call an ecstasy, was still the 'point of departure' for the process that led to St. Augustine's conversion ten years later.

Richard Hakluyt was a schoolboy at Westminster when, calling on his cousin in the Middle Temple, he 'found lying open upon his boord certeine bookes of Cosmographie, with an universall Mappe'. The cousin, seeing the boy's interest, began to instruct him in the geography and commerce of the world, and then read him the 23rd and 24th verses of the 107th Psalm:

> 'Which words of the Prophet together with my cousins discourse (things of high and rare delight to my yong nature) tooke in me so deepe an impression, that I constantly resolved...I would by Gods assistance prosecute that knowledge and kinde of literature, the doores whereof (after a sort) were so happily opened before me.' [2]

Here is no description of ecstasy; but the event set the course of Hakluyt's life.

[1] *Confessions*, iii. 7.
[2] *The Principal Navigations, Voiages, Traffiques and Discoveries of the English Nation* (1598–1600; World's Classics edn., 1958), pp. 1–2.

It is characteristic of what I have called revelation ecstasies that the ecstatic should encounter or be aware of the trigger for the first time. It is worth noting how often the fact that the trigger is encountered for the first time is said to be prepotent in inducing an ecstasy, whether the result is a revelation ecstasy or not. In the questionnaire group five people specifically mention 'first times' (apart from childbirth triggers)—the first time of reading *The Golden Bough*, of hearing a piece of music, of seeing ballet, of encountering Italian primitive art. The people in this group do not usually describe any results their ecstasies may have had, but it seems probable that in some cases these ecstasies were, in my terms, revelation ones. But with music at least, people do sometimes say that the first encounter was not the most impressive. Thus Q 44 says that whereas with new music there is 'a bit of me being conscious and surprised, the analytical side not completely submerged', with music he knows 'it's deeper'. And Wesley:

'I could never relish a tune at first hearing, not till I have almost learned to sing it; and as I learn it more perfectly, I gradually lose my relish for it. I observe something similar in poetry, yea, in all the objects of imagination. I seldom relish verses at first hearing: till I have heard them over and over, they give me no pleasure; and they give me next to none when I have heard them a few times more, so as to be quite familiar.' [1]

Some people, like Wesley, draw attention to the fact that triggers whether eventually or after the first encounter, lose potency; in each of these cases the trigger is a man-made one. The child C 16 describes an ecstasy at her first sight of the Venus de Milo, then continues,

'the second time something seemed to be missing. I don't know what it was but I doubt if ever again I shall feel the wonderful "lifted" feeling she gave me.'

C 24 says of a book that she will read it again many times, 'but I will not get the same thrill as when reading it for the first time'. C 19 says of *La Bohème* that she has 'never since been moved quite so much' as she was the first time she heard it.

To discover that emotional force diminishes on repeated impact is

[1] *Journal*, July 3, 1764.

not, of course, confined to ecstatics.[1] But the more similarities one can show between ecstatic and non-ecstatic experience, the more probable it seems that the former is an exaggeration of the latter.

[1] Shakespeare provides a pleasant example:

> So am I as the rich whose blessed key,
> Can bring him to his sweet up-locked treasure,
> The which he will not ev'ry hower survay,
> For blunting the fine point of seldome pleasure.
>
> Sonnet 52

CHAPTER XVI

Desolation

'That which this anguished soul feels most deeply is the conviction that God has abandoned it, *of which it has no doubt*; that He has cast it away into darkness as an abominable thing . . . the shadow of death and the pains and torments of hell are most acutely felt, and this comes from the sense of being abandoned by God, being chastised and cast out by His wrath and heavy displeasure. All this and even more the soul feels now, for a terrible apprehension has come upon it that thus it will be with it for ever. It has also the same sense of abandonment with respect to all creatures, and that it is an object of contempt to all, especially to its friends.'

'The soul is conscious of a profound emptiness in itself, a cruel destitution of the three kinds of goods, natural, temporal, and spiritual, which are ordained for its comfort. It sees itself in the midst of the opposite evils, miserable imperfections, dryness and emptiness of the understanding, and abandonment of the spirit in darkness.' [1]

This is an account of the state known to the religious as aridity or 'the dark night of the soul'.

'Instead of the light of ineffable revelation I seem to be in perpetual fog and darkness. I cannot get my mind to work; instead of associations "clicking into place" everything is an inextricable jumble; instead of seeming to grasp a whole, it seems to remain tied to the actual consciousness of the moment. The whole world of my thought is hopelessly divided into incomprehensible water-tight compartments. I could not feel more ignorant, undecided or inefficient. It is appallingly difficult to concentrate, and writing is pain and grief to me.

'As for wickedness, although my mind has not reached the stage of regarding itself as the most wicked person in the world and responsible for all the sin and evil afflicting mankind, I know too well

---

[1] St. John of the Cross, *Noche Escura del Alma*, quoted by E. U: M., pp. 389–90 and 391.

that it can do so. That appalling self-centredness is the reverse of the delusions of grandeur and power. It leads to the uttermost depths.' [1]

This is an account of the depressive stage of manic-depression.

'In its original state the soul, made in the image of God, was beautiful and glorious, filled with burning love and spiritual light. But through the sin of Adam it was disfigured and deformed into a different likeness... For it lost this spiritual light and heavenly support, and fell into grievous darkness and a perverted longing for this wretched life. It was exiled and cast out from the heritage of heaven which it would have enjoyed had it stood firm: it was cast down into the sorrows of this earth, and later into the prison of hell, doomed to remain there for ever.' [2]

This describes the condition of the sinful soul.

The first state described is accepted by the religious as in fact constituting a state of prayer.[3] Its similarity to the state described in the second passage is evident. Zaehner relates the mystical experiences he calls pan-en-henic or nature mysticism to manic-depression, but not those he accepts as theistic.[4] But the acceptance and documentation of these sad states in religious mysticism suggest that if some mystical states do have a relation to manic-depressive psychoses, such a relation is not confined to the experiences of people identified by Zaehner as *not* having had theistic experiences.

[1] John Custance, *Wisdom, Madness and Folly* (London, 1951), p. 62.

[2] Walter Hilton, *The Ladder of Perfection* (Penguin edn., 1957), Bk. I, ch. i, p. 113.

[3] *'First:* the mind is roughly stricken, as it were, with a kind of paralysis; it is powerless to devote itself to things divine, or to have any experience of them... *Secondly:* the same phenomenon appears in the senses; the heart is absolutely dry; far from experiencing sweet delightful emotions which direct it towards God, it more often feels only aversion (from prayer) and disgust. But *thirdly:* the will, on the other hand, is strongly attracted towards God; it feels the need of Him...the heart and mind are by no means powerless with regard to creatures; on the contrary, the imagination often runs at random, and the senses feel attracted to earthly things: the will alone is drawn towards God.

'When these three signs are found together, it is impossible to have any doubt. The Holy Spirit is present, and bestowing the grace of prayer... Remain peacefully in this state. It is a prayer and a most excellent one.' From *The Science of Prayer*, by Fr. de Besse, quoted by Butler, W.M., pp. xii–xiii.

[4] 'The term "expansion" does in fact accurately describe what the nature mystics conceive happens to the soul. Contraction is the opposite condition, the phenomenon of extreme depression and sense of utter abandonment to oneself in oneself... These states are now recognised as being the manic and depressive poles of what we now call a manic-depressive psychosis.' Zaehner: M.S.P., p. 85.

I had hoped that in writing this book it would not be necessary to take these states into account. As discussed by the religious, they are of their nature prolonged, not momentary,[1] and it seemed to me that they should be contrasted rather with unitive states than, as they usually were, with momentary ecstasies. But I gradually became aware of the probable existence of, not only these prolonged and well-documented states, but also of similar yet brief or momentary states, nowhere referred to in the documentation of mystical conditions. It further seemed to me that such brief or momentary states occurred not only as isolated experiences but also, sometimes, as forming part of and contributing to momentary ecstasies. I will call the prolonged states *desolate states*, and the brief or momentary states, whose existence I hope to establish, *desolations*, or *desolation experiences*.

I want first to establish that these states, whether momentary or prolonged, may properly be regarded as the opposite to ecstatic states. It will be noticed that each of the writers quoted on pp. 360–1 assumes that the state he is describing is the opposite to a more desirable one and I want to show, by examination of the words used, that this state is the opposite to ecstasy.

For feelings of unity, we find feelings of uncoordinated diversity: e.g. 'an inextricable jumble'.

For feelings of eternal continuance we find feelings of time and death: e.g. 'the shadow of death', 'the actual consciousness of the moment'.

For feelings of liberation, we find feelings of restriction: e.g. 'seems to remain tied', 'the prison of hell'.[2]

For feelings of joy we find feelings of grief: e.g. 'anguished', 'hopelessly', 'sorrows'.

For feelings of salvation, perfection, we find feelings of sin, imperfection: e.g. 'an abominable thing', 'imperfections', 'all the sin and evil', 'disfigured and deformed', 'perverted'.

---

[1] 'Such an interval of chaos and misery may last for months, or even for years'. E.U: M., p. 387.

[2] Compare 'When the visionary experience is terrible and the world is transfigured for the worse, individualization is intensified and the negative visionary finds himself associated with a body that seems to grow progressively more dense, more tightly packed... It is worth remarking, that many of the punishments described in the various accounts of hell are punishments of pressure and constriction. Dante's sinners are buried in mud, shut up in the trunks of trees, frozen solid in blocks of ice, crushed beneath stones.' Aldous Huxley, *Heaven and Hell* (London, 1956), p. 50.

For feelings of a new world, another life, we find feelings of the horrors of this world and of hell: e.g. 'the pains and torments of hell', 'this wretched life'.

For feelings of contact we find feelings of loneliness and isolation: e.g. 'abandoned', 'cast out', 'an object of contempt to all, especially to its friends', 'appalling self-centredness', 'exiled and cast out'.

For feelings of knowledge we find feelings of ignorance: e.g. 'emptiness of the understanding', 'cannot get my mind to work', 'could not feel more ignorant', 'lost this spirited light'.

For feelings of 'up' we find feelings of 'down': e.g. 'cast away', 'the uttermost depths', 'fell', 'cast down'.

For feelings of light we find feelings of darkness: e.g. 'darkness', 'the shadow of death', 'perpetual fog and darkness', 'grievous darkness'.

For feelings of enlargement, improvement, we find feelings of emptiness and loss: e.g. 'a profound emptiness', 'lost this spiritual light'.

For feelings of liquidity we find feelings of dryness: e.g. 'dryness...of the understanding'. The whole state is often known as aridity.

For feelings of peace we find feelings of turmoil and anguish: e.g. 'a terrible apprehension', 'pain and grief'.

The only characteristic of ecstasy equally found in these desolation states is feelings of totality; what is felt is total and absolute, affects the whole life, is the most of its kind, lasts for ever: e.g.

> 'thus it will be with it *for ever*...abandonment with respect to *all* creatures...an object of contempt to *all*', 'I *could not feel more* ignorant, etc....the *uttermost* depths', 'doomed to remain there *for ever*'.

I was not aware of these states when I began to question my original group. Consequently I asked no questions about them and no evidence for their existence spontaneously appeared. When I first read about these states in relation to religious experience they did not, as I have explained, seem necessarily relevant to a study of ecstasy. I was first forced to consider them after reading the essays of the schoolchildren in Group C who, when asked for examples of ecstasies, in many cases spontaneously gave accounts of feelings that seemed to be the opposite to ecstasies. Once having noticed these states, I found that it was principally in childhood that they seemed to occur. Here are some examples from different sources of the kind that seem to me to establish the existence of brief or momentary as opposed to prolonged experiences of desolation; many others will be found in Group C.

'My first sight of the mountains was right up close, my parents not having woken me before, and immediately I was overpowered by them. They gave me the feeling that I was very small and insignificant, which, having a younger sister to boss around, I had not experienced much. The weather was appalling...and all the mountains looked dark and unfriendly as if I were an enemy and they were hiding all their secrets from me... The rain started to pelt down again and the unwanted feeling I had arrived at by then was magnified by a roll of thunder which sounded as though it would split the tops of the mountains and they would come crashing down to crush me' (C 5).

Notice the attribution of hostile feelings to the mountains, and contrast with this the attribution of 'good' feelings to the French countryside in the experience of C 10 when she wrote: 'Everything was contented, happy, gleaming. The whole world glowed, and the warm round sun smiled over France...' The apparent transference of feelings from the person to what is perceived is common in accounts of both ecstasy and desolation, and noticeably so in accounts written by children; it is further discussed on pp. 243–4. We find it again in the experience of Thomas Traherne at the age of four, already cited on p. 137, but here usefully quoted again:

'in a lowering and sad evening, being alone in the field, when all things were dead and quiet, a certain want and horror fell upon me, beyond imagination. The unprofitableness and silence of the place dissatisfied me; its wideness terrified me; from the utmost ends of the earth fears surrounded me.'

To confirm this as a desolation experience, and also to show the part played by the transference of feeling from person to scene, I shall attempt the exercise—which may be tried with any other ecstasy or desolation—of replacing the words and phrases that imply desolation (or ecstasy) with their opposites, thereby achieving, in this case, a description of an ecstasy:

'in an uplifting and joyful evening, being alone in the field, when all things were alive yet at peace, a certain satisfaction and assurance flowed into me, beyond imagination. The abundance and tranquillity of the place delighted me; its limitless beauty entranced me; from the utmost ends of the earth confidence poured into me.'

The quasi-physical feelings claimed in experiences of desolation seem to bear out the assumption that these experiences are in all or most respects described in terms which are the antonyms to those used of ecstasies; that is to say, in many desolation experiences we find descriptions of feelings of falling, darkness, seeing things as lacking colour; the 'mind' felt to be oppressed, the heart dry, hard, cold,[1] dejected; feelings of contraction, of being shut in; general depression; lack of interest or enthusiasm; feelings of isolation.

Several of the children in Group C explain that as a result of experiences of this kind they came to knowledge—often for the first time—about aspects of human life, knowledge which contrasts with the kinds of knowledge often claimed to be gained through ecstasy. Two children give accounts of adults falling down, apparently dead, and one of them comments,

'It seemed after that, that nothing would be strong as before. I had thought that grown-ups were never ill; always there, like safe walls on which one could lean; but now one of those walls had fallen, and I was cowering back against three walls and where the fourth had been was the entrance to a frightening exciting world' (C 45).

One child told of her sudden bewilderment and grief at her mother's distress when a sick little sister was taken to hospital. Another encountered a slum for what seems to have been the first time; she used 'nasty' adjectives throughout—wrinkled, ugly, cruel, black, decayed, broken, dirty, smeary, rusty, narrow, dark, old, ragged, and comments on a 'clashing' colour—and ends, 'I was shocked at the sight and very much afraid.' One child remembers seeing her brother and sister being sick on a channel crossing, another her distress at being told she was not

---

[1] The image of the fires of hell seems to have derived from the idea of a purifying fire, but the persistent association of light and warmth with ecstasy, cold and darkness with desolation, makes it seem surprising that there should still be flames in hell. It seems that the paradox has long been felt as puzzling. W. P. Ker explainated that the flames of hell traditionally gave no light, and that torment by fire alters nated with torment by cold (*The Dark Ages* (1904; Mentor edn., 1958), ch. iv, pp. 166–7). For 'bad' conditions, *cold* and *darkness* phrases seem to be the ones that come naturally: 'I am lukewarm and in complete darkness', said St. Teresa of a period of desolation (*Life*, ch. xl, p. 312), and Underhill, of the forbidden negative mysticism which may yet yield rewards to such as St. John of the Cross, describes it as feeling for other people like 'the icy darkness of perpetual negations' (E.U : M., p. 73)—a significant association of what would seem to be withdrawal ecstasy with desolation.

really her mother's child. One read a book that appalled her with realization of the cruelty in the world, led her to contrast her own secure life with those affected by the horrors of war, and made 'my own life seem so insignificant, and what happened to me didn't affect the world at all'.

Ecstasies bring belief in knowledge of unity, eternity, perfection, loving contact, etc. By contrast, desolations bring knowledge, usually and inevitably frightening knowledge of just those facts about human life that the knowledge brought by ecstasies seem to expunge again.[1] What the children learned in these experiences of desolation—which, be it remembered, they proffered when given a model of ecstasy—was the discovery of lonely individuality in a world that could be ugly and terrifying, the discovery of their own insignificance, of the insecurity of their props and the eventual certainty of death—'I, a stranger and afraid In a world I never made.'

These sad discoveries arose as a result of desolations that occurred as isolated experiences. But sometimes what begins as desolation seems to culminate in ecstasy, and then the knowledge believed to have been gained as a result of the experience is of an ecstatic, not a desolation kind. Two straightforward examples of this come again from children. The first is that experience of Traherne's quoted earlier where, after the unmistakable account of desolation there given, he soon continues,

'I was a weak and little child, and had forgotten there was a man alive in the earth. Yet something also of hope and expectation comforted me from every border. This taught me that I was concerned in all the world'.

The second is from Group C:

'For what seemed an eternity I pushed my way through the bracken, half blinded by the rain. Suddenly I became aware of the presence of something; at first I could not tell what it was; then lifting my head...I saw that I had come to the end of the bracken and was looking on to the lake. Two enormous menacing peaks towered above me, and as I saw them through the swirling mist, I seemed to hear a mass of orchestras all playing a triumphant sinister minor chord. I was petrified. I wanted to scream but my throat seemed to be choked. Still the mountains glared malevolently at me;

[1] But one child, gaining knowledge of diversity, was not frightened but pleased. This is C 34, who valued her discovery, at the age of three, of difference and separation by means of number.

I felt I was being lifted from my feet, and drawn by some mysterious power towards them... For how long I stood there I don't know, but gradually I calmed myself, and took a few timid steps nearer the edge of the crag that rose from the lake. Here I saw a huge pit of choppy black water, that seemed to dance in horrible glee at the sight of my terrified bedraggled body... It was not until we had returned to our hotel...that I realised how much I had enjoyed the weird sinister walk over the moor, and the horror of the hills that rose from Lake Ullswater. It was this walk that made me realise that I would never be able to bear the classic holiday of a fortnight at some gaudy holiday town swarming with holiday makers... I knew I could never really enjoy myself unless I was surrounded by hills, moors and crags, and the ancient Roman roads that ramble endlessly over them' (C 36).

In both these accounts the feelings of desolation are very marked, and in the first very few, in the second no phrases descriptive of ecstasy are used. But in both cases the result is similar to the results of an ecstasy, in the second case to a revelation ecstasy.

Viginia Woolf, on the other hand, rather emphasizes the ecstasy than the desolation, though the latter is unmistakably there:

'had a religious retreat; of great agony once; and always some terror; so afraid one is of loneliness; of seeing to the bottom of the vessel. That is one of the experiences I have had here in some Augusts; and got then to a consciousness of what I call "reality"... beside which nothing matters; in which I shall rest and continue to exist... I fancy sometimes this is the most necessary thing to me: that which I seek' (L 8).

Again, the result is an ecstatic one, with an impulse towards creativeness.

In accounts of feelings evoked by listening to music, such mixtures of desolation and ecstasy are very common. We find it in Forster's account of feelings evoked by listening to Beethoven's Fifth Symphony (L 18) where the rather unfortunate image of the goblins is introduced to stand for the terror with which the final building of ramparts is contrasted. This mixture is also shown in two critics' accounts of the same concert, a performance of Beethoven's Ninth Symphony conducted by Klemperer:

'the opening allegro can rarely have assumed the epic grandeur it had on Tuesday, or its wild conflicts have sounded more terrible, so that in the development section it sounded as though one were staring into the very bowels of chaos.' [1]

'From its mysterious opening to that culminating moment, as awful as any "Last Judgment", when the undertow of the flowing chromatic bass seems likely to sweep away the foundations of the universe, the *allegro* was given such spaciousness...' etc.[2]

I do not think it is an over-elaborate gloss on these two comments to say that both critics feel that at moments the *allegro* of the Ninth Symphony arouses feelings of what I have called desolation, although the final effect is ecstatic; and further, that the satisfactions are enhanced by the contrast of the desolation.

These mixed experiences, which I shall call *desolation-ecstasies*, are surely the kind of experience we may hope to derive from tragedy. Certainly C. E. Montague seems to be describing something very similar when he writes,

'we know we shall get from the tragedy, while we are there, a certain stir and glow in our minds; we want to induce in ourselves a specific mood of intense, if fugitive, exaltation—a mood sombre, no doubt, and perhaps sharing with actual sorrow such symptoms as tears, but still exultant and bringing with it a sense of heightened powers in heart and mind.' [3]

Zaehner is not alone in relating mystical states to the manic-depressive psychosis, but other people seem equally ready to relate them to schizophrenia.[4] I have wondered whether it is particularly these desolation-ecstasies that the people who refer to schizophrenia have in mind. The following passage, for instance, which is a description of a schizophrenic condition, does seem to me to have many resemblances to desolation-ecstasies:

'There arises a compelling sense of great metaphysical connections, a profound oneness with the universe and with godliness. Everything

---

[1] Peter Heyworth in the *Observer*, November 17, 1957.

[2] Dyneley Hussey in the *Listener*, November 21, 1957.

[3] 'Delights of Tragedy' in *A Writer's Notes on His Trade* (1930; Pelican edn., 1949), p. 167.

[4] For instance, in a B.B.C. television discussion, *Sainthood and Sanity*, broadcast on June 5, 1957, one speaker assumed that the states discussed were caused by God, another by manic-depression, a third by schizophrenia, while the fourth said the power concerned was the collective unconscious which inspires poets and saints but goes sour in mental patients.

is brilliantly lit up, clear as the edge of a precipice, and strangely threatening. Recoiling from a state of horrible fear into one of ecstatic rapture, the patient now believes in his own annihilation, in a twilight of the gods, in weirdly threatening catastrophes and the destruction of all the world, from which he will arise like a phoenix from the ashes, as saviour, as prophet, indeed as God and Christ Himself, to lead forth his fellow-men to renewed life. Like the mystic he perceives a constant interplay of microcosm with macrocosm, sees everywhere unexpected relations, strange, dreadful, enchanting connections.' [1]

Although desolation-ecstasies do not seem to be so common as ecstasies untinged by desolation, they are frequently found and apparently at varying levels of intensity. I would suggest that desolation-ecstasies of a not very intense kind are to be found in such experiences as that of the child, C 21, who was listening to a poem read over the wireless about the dead in Flanders Field; here, although the trigger included thoughts of death, the experience is described in ecstatic terms—she forgot what she was doing, was one with the people she heard of and the words were like music in her ears.

It may be that the usual contrast of momentary ecstasies with desolate states rather than with brief or momentary desolations is due to the observable fact that an ecstasy may often arise gloriously to transform such states, as it did for Suso (R 1) and for Brainerd (R 13). (But an ecstasy may equally arise from happy states or, as it did for M.E. (R 11), from 'a state of equilibrium'.) I. A. Richards seems to recommend attempts artificially to induce feelings of desolation in order to test the effectiveness of poems as triggers to feelings that will expunge awareness of loneliness, temporality, insignificance, and ignorance:

'When our response to a poem after our best efforts remains uncertain...we may perhaps help ourselves by considering it in a frame of feelings whose sincerity is beyond our questioning. Such are the feelings that may be aroused by contemplation of the following:
  i. Man's loneliness (the isolation of the human situation).
  ii. The facts of birth, and of death, in their inexplicable oddity.
  iii. The inconceivable immensity of the Universe.
  iv. Man's place in the perspective of time.
  v. The enormity of his ignorance.

[1] Ernst Kretschmer, *The Psychology of Men of Genius*, trans. R. B. Cattell (London, 1931), p. 167.

Taking these not as targets for doctrine, but as the most incomprehensible and inexhaustible objects for meditation, while their reverberation lasts pass the poem through the mind, silently reciting it as slowly as it allows. Whether what it can stir in us is important or not to us will, perhaps, show itself then.' [1]

Before leaving the subject of desolation in relation to ecstasy, I should like to draw attention to an oddity of apparent pattern which may be significant. We have already seen that Koestler contrasts anger with what I have suggested is withdrawal ecstasy, and that it seems as if these polarities of anger and withdrawal ecstasy may be some people's normal experiences in these fields (see pp. 54-6). In these cases, anger, the 'bad' polarity, is the tumescent experience, and ecstasy, the 'good' polarity, the diminution of normal responses. More commonly we find people contrasting normal intensity ecstasy with desolation. In these cases ecstasy, the 'good' polarity, is the tumescent experience and desolation, the 'bad' polarity, the diminution of normal responses.

Of course intensity ecstasies and anger differ fundamentally in that intensity ecstasies are regarded as pleasant, anger unpleasant; and similarly withdrawal ecstasies and desolation differ fundamentally in that withdrawal ecstasies are regarded as pleasant and desolations unpleasant. But just as there are some similarities between anger and intensity ecstasies, so there are similarities between desolations and withdrawal ecstasies, for instance:

—some triggers, notably those with *down, dark* qualities, may induce either desolation or withdrawal; and both withdrawal and desolation may be described in terms of *down, dark* feelings.

—both desolation and withdrawal are conditions achieved by diminution of normal responses.

—experiences culminating in normal intensity ecstasy may begin by being either the pleasing experience of withdrawal (see Ch. IV.) or the unpleasant experience of desolation.

I do not know what the significance of these similarities may be, but suspect they may imply a closer relationship between withdrawal and desolation than is suggested by the pleasure of the one experience, the unpleasantness of the other.

[1] P.C., pp. 290-1.

CHAPTER XVII

Nomenclature

Epithets are very often applied to mystical experiences including ecstasies without, apparently, any clear idea about the distinctions that are being made. Thus we find experiences given such names as nature, religious, aesthetic, neo-platonic, sexual, etc. experiences, where in some cases the name seems to derive from the trigger, sometimes from the overbelief, sometimes from the known standing and beliefs of the mystic, and sometimes, though rarely, from the nature of the experience.

Ecstasies enjoyed by accepted religious mystics are usually called religious experiences no matter what the nature of the ecstasy or the trigger inducing it. Thus St. Teresa's experiences induced by books and pictures would certainly be called religious experiences, St. Ignatius Loyola's ecstasy (R 15) would certainly be called a religious experience though it seems to have been induced by looking at a river, contains no feelings of contact and is distinguished by feelings that wonderful new knowledge has been attained—in my terms, a knowledge ecstasy with a nature trigger. But no one would think of calling a religious experience that of Nietzsche (L 6) or of Q 54, the one induced by music, the other by nature and poetry, and both distinguished by feelings that wonderful new knowledge had been attained.

Experiences resulting in religious beliefs would generally be called religious experiences, at least by those who did not find the resulting beliefs unacceptable. The experience of H. Warner Allen (L 11) would be called a religious experience by many people and so would that of M.E. (R 11), induced by a walk in the mountains. But the often very similar experiences of Wordsworth which resulted in pantheist beliefs are usually called nature ecstasies.[1]

We have seen that St. Augustine's insistence on naming as 'Truth' the object of his mystical encounters has led to the suspicion that his

[1] For some examples see pp. 360–1.

experiences were neo-platonic rather than religious ones, only 'the higher operations of the intellect' and not such experiences as those of later religious mystics (see p.131). Here it is apparently the nature of the experience that is in question; but no more is needed than the assurance that by 'Truth' St. Augustine meant God for his experiences to be accepted as religious ones.

Madame Guyon and St. Teresa provide examples of judgement by the standing and beliefs of the mystics. When Madame Guyon met Father Lacombe after a long absence, she felt, she said, an inner peace and joy never before known:

> 'It seemed to me that a great wave of grace swept from him to me, passing through our inmost souls, and returning from me to him, so that he experienced the same feeling. But it was a grace so holy, so pure, so clear, that it was as a wave ebbing and flowing and then losing itself in the divine unity.' [1]

Knox, who, like most Catholics, distrusts Madame Guyon's quietism, stresses the peculiarities of her relationship with Father Lacombe.[2] I do not think that he, or most other Catholics, would accept the above as an account of true religious experience or name it such. But they would accept St. Teresa's account of her meeting with Father García de Toledo:

> 'Once when I was with him in the parlour, my soul and spirit became aware of such a mighty love burning in him that I became almost rapt away, as I thought of the greatness of God, who had raised a soul to this state in so short a time... It helped me so much to be with him that there seemed to kindle in my soul a new fire of longing to serve the Lord afresh.' [3]

Since, for Knox, Madame Guyon's standing is already in question, the trigger is considered relevant in judging her experience not to be a true religious one; in the case of St. Teresa, accepted as an orthodox mystic, the trigger is irrelevant. But when we turn to Inge, who, like most Protestants, accepts Madame Guyon as a genuine religious mystic, we find that he says of her that 'Her Mysticism is identical with that of St. Teresa'.[4] He would certainly be prepared to name her experiences religious ones; to him, as to the Catholic judging St. Teresa, the nature of the trigger is irrelevant.

---

[1] Quoted Leuba: P.R.M., p. 81. [2] *Enthusiasm*, p. 319 et seq.
[3] *Life*, ch. xxxiv, p. 255. [4] C.M., p. 234.

Demonstrably there is no necessary connexion between the nature of the trigger and the nature of the overbelief, at least in so far as religious or non-religious overbeliefs are concerned. Religious overbeliefs can arise from ecstasies triggered by religious objects, events, and ideas, from nature (e.g. R 11, R 15), from art (e.g. L 11), from sexual love,[1] and from other triggers. Conversely, religious triggers may induce ecstasies in people whose overbeliefs are in no way religious. In the questionnaire group, several people who are not Christian name triggers with inescapably Christian connotations. Q 18, an atheist, gives among other triggers, Beethoven's *Missa Solemnis*; Q 24, an atheist, gives Newman's defence of faith[2]; Q 48, whose faith is 'a vague belief in something that makes patterns', says that she once had an ecstasy from religion; Q 60 gives among her triggers being in a cathedral and seeing a picture in a Roman church, and told me that it was experiences of this kind that had made her a pantheist. But a religious person, experiencing ecstasy induced by any of these triggers, would almost certainly regard his experience as a religious one and name it so.

I think we must conclude that as these epithets—nature, religious, aesthetic, neo-platonic, etc.—are generally used, what is meant by a religious experience is an experience, no matter how triggered and no matter what its nature, that results in what the giver of the epithet regards as orthodox religious belief; while by nature, aesthetic, neo-platonic, etc. experiences are meant either experiences triggered by nature, art, knowledge, etc. that do not result in accepted religious beliefs, or else experiences, no matter how triggered, that result in beliefs about the value of nature, art, knowledge, etc. I do not think that the use of such epithets provides an illuminating way of distinguishing ecstasies, however helpful they may be when considering mystical experiences that are not ecstasies.

It must then be asked what *is* the most illuminating nomenclature for distinguishing ecstasies, and I believe that they are best named according to the nature of the experience. It is probable that the nature of the experience is strongly influential on the nature of the overbelief, whether this is expressed in religious terms or not; I shall try to establish such connexions later. But before deciding to name experiences according to their natures, we must consider how far that nature is affected by the nature of the trigger.

[1] See p. 147   [2] See p. 383n,

As I explained earlier, I attempted analyses of the texts grouped according to the most frequent triggers—nature, religion, art, and sex. Some differences did appear (see p. 146) but the results should be accepted with reserve, since in the questionnaire group, which is numerically predominant, several people gave several triggers, and in this group and in the other ones, several were compound triggers, cutting across categories.[1] I have pointed out earlier that most people in the questionnaire group assumed that a single description of ecstasy would suffice, no matter what triggers they adduced (see p. 148 and n.); only one person, the child Q 34, said that 'it differs a bit with what induces it.'

I believe and hope it will become increasingly apparent that ecstasies do in fact differ according to what induces them, but that the differences are not such as one could hope to discover by a categorization so coarse as one that separates, say, art, nature, religion, sex as triggers. I think one would have to distinguish between ecstasies induced by such music as, say, Gregorian chant, and ecstasies induced by such music as, say, the *Tuba mirum* from Verdi's *Requiem Mass*;[2] between ecstasies induced by still water and ecstasies induced by fast-flowing water; between ecstasies induced by water in sunlight and ecstasies induced by water in shade. I have not the material to make such distinctions, and without having made them cannot think it useful to name and distinguish ecstasies by their triggers—i.e. to speak of nature ecstasies, art or aesthetic ecstasies, etc.

It has however been possible to show that, irrespective of trigger or overbelief, irrespective of the sex or religion of the ecstatic, ecstasies have certain characteristics and can, on the basis of these characteristics, be divided into kinds. One such division is that between intensity and withdrawal ecstasies, and to name ecstasies as such is helpful. I have shown that some ecstasies begin by being withdrawal ecstasies and then become intensity ones (the reverse process, intensity into withdrawal, does not appear to take place[3]), and these may be called withdrawal-

---

[1] For instance, sexual love and nature provided compound triggers for some people in the questionnaire group, while the people in the religious group, all of whom I assumed had religion as triggers, often had nature as well.

[2] See note[2] on p. 230.

[3] Unless this is the experience of Louis of Blois (R 20—see p. 47), and part of the experience Keats is describing in the 'Ode to a Nightingale'. But I am not alone in finding it abominably difficult to analyse the experience described in that poem; see E. C. Pettet, *On the Poetry of Keats*, pp. 251–81.

intensity ecstasies. Similarly, ecstasies may start by being experiences of desolation (again, the reverse process, ecstasy into desolation, does not appear to take place[1]), and these may be called desolation-ecstasies

By another method of categorization I have divided ecstasies into *lesser* and *greater* ones, ranging from adamic ecstasies through knowledge and knowledge-contact ecstasies to union ones. Thus one might speak of Emily Brontë's ecstasy (L 21) as being a withdrawal-intensity ecstasy of a knowledge-contact kind. But it should always be remembered that distinctions may be less clear-cut than names must suggest.

I have also distinguished experiences which have triggers similar to the more common ecstatic ones, which are described in language similar to but less enthusiastic and intense than that of ecstasy, and are often said to be the experiences normally to be expected on contact with such triggers. These I have called response experiences. I have also named as unitive periods or states prolonged periods of ecstatic feelings, and have categorized these, like ecstasies, as being adamic unitive states, knowledge unitive states, etc.

Then I have distinguished a kind of ecstasy in which the effect on the ecstatic of first contact with or awareness of the trigger is to create a focus of continuing value in the trigger. These I have called revelation ecstasies, and here it might sometimes be useful to include the trigger in naming the ecstasy, to speak, for instance, of a childbirth revelation ecstasy or an art revelation ecstasy. This would however be insufficient to indicate whether the revelation ecstasy was of, say, an adamic kind or a knowledge kind, or whether it was a straightforward intensity ecstasy or a withdrawal-intensity ecstasy or a desolation-ecstasy.

Apart from revelation ecstasies one may sometimes wish to indicate the nature of the trigger when speaking of an ecstasy, and in such cases I would speak of a childbirth-induced ecstasy, a nature- or religion-induced ecstasy.

[1] But Koestler in text L 7 describes anger turning into his 'oceanic feeling.'

CHAPTER XVIII

Anti-Triggers

To some extent what does or does not act as a trigger must be a matter of personal idiosyncrasy, and there may be almost no limits to what can be shown to have acted as a trigger to ecstatic experience in one or another individual case. It still remains true that certain objects, events, and ideas—substantially, those that form the headings to my analysis of triggers—are most commonly effective, and that to objects, events, and ideas of these kinds is given a common high status and prestige of almost a sacred character.[1]

Among the ways in which it is possible to show that the kinds of things that are commonly effective triggers are regarded as a group and as a group of high prestige is to show the outrage expressed when triggers are felt to be profaned. For there are, it appears, certain other objects, events, and ideas in whose presence ecstasy is hardly to be expected and whose effect, in an ecstatic context, is usually to inhibit ecstatic response.

These inhibiting objects, events, and ideas I call *anti-triggers*. Generally speaking they consist in anything that is inalienably associated with ordinary social life, and a useful general impression of them is gained by putting together what people in the groups felt they had escaped during their ecstatic experiences—ordinary everyday things, cares, commerce, conventionalities, ridiculous desires and purposes, worldly enjoyments, crowds. It is important to notice that outside an ecstatic

---

[1] Auden's 'sacred beings and sacred events' which are, he says, the only concern of the Primary Imagination and which rouse 'a passion of awe' that may range from 'joyous wonder to panic dread' come very near to identity with my triggers, though as he describes them, they include the triggers to desolation as well as the triggers to ecstasy. He says of them, as I should say of triggers, that 'Some sacred beings seem to be sacred to all imaginations at all times' and 'Many of us have sacred landscapes which probably all have much in common, but there will almost certainly be details which are peculiar to each.' W. H. Auden, *Making, Knowing, and Judging* (Oxford, 1956), pp. 27–8.

context there is no reason to condemn all these as such, and that many of them can be, in some circumstances, sources of pleasure and satisfaction. From these derive the enjoyments of social life, the comforts of a high standard of material living, many of the advantages we gain by being members of societies, large and small. But what is fitting and even enjoyable in a social context becomes abhorrent in an ecstatic one.

Perhaps the best-documented anti-trigger is that which forms the very basis of societies—the presence of other people. It is clear from the texts that most people were in fact alone when experiencing their ecstasies, and several speak of their need to be. Q 26, gave among other triggers, 'being alone in a very lonely place', Q 47, as part of a compound trigger including scientific work by the sea, added 'complete isolation', and Q 63 said 'I must be by myself.' Q 31, who gave as his single trigger, 'love in its fullest sense, spiritual and physical', gave as part of his description of ecstasy, 'almost, except for one other person, alone in the world'. We may compare with this the clergyman (R 3) who wrote 'I stood alone with Him who made me,' and the abbot Allois who wrote, 'Except a man shall say in his heart, I alone and God are in this world, he shall not find peace.'[1]

But for the most part we best discover the anti-trigger when its presence is felt to profane the trigger. Literature teems with examples of the anti-trigger, the presence of other people, felt to profane the trigger, nature, in various of its aspects, of which I give three examples.

Gerard Manley Hopkins, in the Swiss mountains, wrote in his Journal on July 25, 1868,

'then the cold feet, the spectacles, the talk, and the lunching came in. Even with one companion ecstasy is almost banished; you want to be alone to feel that'.

Wordsworth, visiting the Caves of Staffa in 1833, wrote four sonnets. The first began,

> We saw, but surely, in the motley crowd,
> Not One of us has felt the far-famed sight;
> How could we feel it? each the other's blight,
> Hurried and hurrying, volatile and loud.[2]

Wordsworth added a note to the next sonnet:

'The reader may be tempted to exclaim, How came this and the

---

[1] Quoted by Helen Waddell in *The Desert Fathers* (London 1936), p. 13.
[2] P.W., Vol. IV, Sonnet XXVIII, p. 40.

two following sonnets to be written, after the dissatisfaction expressed in the preceding one? In fact...I returned to the cave, and explored it under circumstances more favourable to those imaginative impressions which it is so wonderfully fitted to make upon the mind.' [1]

Rupert Brooke's poem 'The Voice' describes an ecstatic experience in woods, when,

> *slowly the holy three,*
> *The three that I loved, together grew*
> *One, in the hour of knowing,*
> *Night, and the woods, and you——*
>
> *And suddenly*
> *There was an uproar in my woods...*
> *...a Voice profaning the solitudes...*
> *You came and quacked beside me in the wood...*
> *By God! I wish—I wish that you were dead.* [2]

I find it hard to confirm the anti-trigger, presence of other people, in relation to other triggers than nature, and perhaps not unreasonably. We take it for granted that we must be alone for creative work and for love. We have had, until recently, to take it for granted that without the presence of other people—albeit people suitably hushed and reverent—art was not available for us to enjoy. Nowadays however there are many people who say that they prefer to listen to music alone at home because disturbed by the presence of other people in concert-halls.

Commerce as an anti-trigger can be confirmed in the context of almost all triggers. The prototypical example of outrage at the presence of commerce in a trigger-context is to be found in the Bible:

'and Jesus went up to Jerusalem, And found in the temple those that sold oxen and sheep and doves, and the changers of money sitting: And when he had made a scourge of small cords, he drove them all out of the temple, and the sheep, and the oxen; and poured out the changers' money, and overthrew the tables; And said unto them that sold doves, Take these things hence; make not my Father's house an house of merchandise.' [3]

The spirit of commercialism in religion, Meister Eckhart believed, was a serious impediment to the entry of God to the soul;[4] and the

---

[1] P.W., Vol. IV, p. 407.
[2] *Collected Poems* (London, 1918), pp. 103–4.   [3] *John* ii. 13–16.
[4] James W. Clark, *Meister Eckhart*, p. 70.

spirit of commercialism in any trigger-context is, it seems, felt as a serious impediment to response. But as compared with conditions in the past, the massive intrusion of commerce into trigger-contexts—and, indeed, the intent to apply the lustre of trigger-contexts to commerce— is a phenomenon of recent times, dependent on mass-production and mass-communications. The most obtrusive manifestation of commerce today is advertising, and protests against the presence of advertising in certain contexts serve to confirm both anti-triggers and triggers. Equally enlightening are the fewer occasions when protests do not need to be made because of the advertisers' acceptance, without any felt need for explanation, that there are certain contexts in which the presence of advertising would be damagingly offensive.[1]

In the next example the complaint is not against commerce or people as such, but against the presence of the kind of people who bring to mind the everyday world of fashion and commercial values:

'There are many disfigurements to this Lake—not in the way of land or water. No; the two views we have had of it are of the most noble tenderness—they can never fade away—they make one forget the divisions of life; age, youth, poverty and riches; and refine one's sensual vision into a sort of north star which can never cease to be open lidded and stedfast [sic] over the wonders of the great Power. The disfigurement I mean is the miasma of London. I do suppose it contaminated with bucks and soldiers, and women of fashion—and hatband ignorance.' [2]

That an anti-trigger need be no more than an idea and a mistaken idea at that, the following quotation shows:

'I was sitting with [a] city friend in the middle of splendid desolation. While purring with content at the peace of it all, he grimaced suddenly. Towards the Coniston fells a speck drifting through the

[1] The opening of the commercial television service in Britain provides many examples of both. From the start it was agreed that advertising would not interrupt or immediately precede or follow royalty or religion; after some dispute the same was conceded for educational programmes. Programmes of artistic or intellectual merit have seldom been shown without subsequent protests at the intrusion of advertising. I have examined this situation in some detail in an article 'Sacred and Profane' in *The Twentieth Century*, February 1959.

It seems, incidentally, to have occurred to no one when a commercial television service was mooted, that since such a service must live by advertising revenue, it was unlikely often to give programmes in whose context advertising was felt to be offensive—i.e. programmes of artistic or intellectual merit.

[2] *Selected Letters o John Keats* (World's Classics edn., 1954), p. 124.

sky in the far distance had uttered "pronk, pronk". He never noticed the speck. He said with a sigh, "What a pity you can hear a car hooting even up here." ' [1]

A mistaken idea may, however, work in the opposite direction:

'I am tempted to raise a question...namely, *why* we dislike litter? That our distaste is largely a matter of association was brought home to me by my momentarily mistaking a piece of blue paper on a hillside for a flower. My disillusion was a shock that set me wondering... Ancient Roman or mediaeval "litter" doesn't trouble us... Why should amphorae be so much more respectable than old tin cans?' [2]

I would suppose the answer to be that Roman litter, like ruins, is purged of anti-trigger associations and can itself, like so many objects from the past (see pp. 106–13) act as a trigger; while contemporary litter is too much associated with contemporary life to be other than an anti-trigger; and that the writer's shock was caused by finding that he had responded to anti-trigger litter as if it were trigger flower.

An article in the *Architectural Review* makes it plain that almost any contemporary man-made activity in natural surroundings is to be regarded as anti-trigger. No explanation of this wholesale condemnation is given:

'[In] WILD [country]—nature must win. If a landscape contains *any* man-made activity that isn't cringing in subservience it ceases to be wild.'

'Seats—none: sit on the landscape... If you want to experience raw nature, that means accepting the discomforts—no car parks, no tea bar, no w.c.—along with the air and the views.'

'No shelters in the wild because the point of going there is to submit to nature: physical discomfort is as much a part of that as "mental liberation".'

'In open country and the wild advertising is alien anyway because it is an urban import'. [3]

The middle paragraphs make it plain that comforts are to be regarded as anti-triggers; this stressed importance of asceticism is nowhere explained (but see pp. 313–4).

[1] Dudley Hoys in *Country Life*, July 11, 1957.
[2] Letter in the *New Statesman*, March 31, 1956.
[3] 'Counter-Attack', the *Architectural Review*, December 1956, pp. 363, 365, 373, 391.

Not all anti-triggers are as obvious and as widely accepted as the foregoing. In a few cases, what is a trigger to one or, indeed, to many people may be an anti-trigger to another or others, and of these perhaps the most surprising is 'natural objects' which—at least under the general heading of 'nature'—is in my texts and almost certainly elsewhere the most common trigger of all.

But at least two people whose opinions in these matters must be respected speak of natural objects as if they were anti-triggers. One is Bernard Berenson:

> 'Natural objects, whether animate or inanimate, because they stimulate activities that are greedy, predatory, or coldly analytical, entailing excitement and exhaustion, with the resulting feeling of lowered vitality, cannot be life-enhancing. To be life-enhancing, visible things—with which we are here concerned—must be presented in a way to make us feel that we are perceiving them more quickly, grasping them more deeply than we do ordinarily... It follows that only works of art can be life-enhancing, for merely visible things by themselves are not—except when we have learnt to enjoy them as if they were already works of art, as is the case with landscape for many of us.' [1]

Berenson believed that the experience described in my text L 10 did teach him to enjoy nature as if it were a work of art: 'it emancipated me from the need for art, for I had become my own artist, as it were, and saw in terms of art'.

The other person is William Blake whose annotation to the title of Wordsworth's poem, 'Influence of Natural Objects In calling forth and strengthening the Imagination in Boyhood and Early Youth', is as follows:

> 'Natural Objects always did & now do weaken, deaden & obliterate Imagination in Me. Wordsworth must know that what he Writes Valuable is Not to be found in Nature.'

Blake then refers with approbation to Wordsworth's own translation of Michelangelo's sonnet:

> *Heaven-born, the Soul a heaven-ward course must hold;*
> *Beyond the visible world She soars to seek,*
> *(For what delights the sense is false and weak)*
> *Ideal Form, the universal mould.* [2]

[1] *Aesthetics and History*, London, 1950, p. 59.
[2] *The Writings of William Blake* (Nonesuch edn., 1957), p. 783.

One can only say rather helplessly that despite Blake's condemnation of natural objects as deadening, he did seem himself on occasion to be able to find in them Ideal Form, the universal mould.

Another considerably less common trigger that we often find treated as an anti-trigger is the exercise of reason and with this the reasonable use of language.[1] It was partly because he believed that natural objects led to 'coldly analytical' activities that Berenson objected to them, and it is not possible to read far in mystical and even in poetic literature without finding reason and the reasonable use of language rejected as inhibiting mystical experience:

> 'At its very best, a mind enclosed in language is in prison... The mind which is enclosed within language can possess only opinions. The mind which has learned to grasp thoughts which are inexpressible...has reached the point where it already dwells in truth. It possesses certainty and unclouded faith.'[2]

> 'It is a matter of experience that in our moments of deep emotion, transitory though they be, we plunge deeper into the reality of things than we can hope to do in hours of the most brilliant argument. At the touch of passion doors fly open which logic has battered on in vain... It is the lover, the poet, the mourner, the convert, who shares for a moment the mystic's privilege of lifting that Veil of Isis which science handles so helplessly, leaving only her dirty figermarks behind.'[3]

This aversion from the exercise of reason seems strange in view of the fact that the exercise of reason can act as a trigger. But I will suggest some reasons why reason is often felt inimical in ecstatic contexts.

---

[1] One should, of course, distinguish between reason and *right reason*, as the Church uses the phrase. Right reason, Wordsworth felt, 'lifts The Being into magnanimity' and purges the effects of anti-triggers:

> Holds up before the mind, intoxicate
> With present objects and the busy dance
> Of things that pass away, a temperate shew
> Of objects that endure,

as contrasted with the ordinary exercises of 'self-applauding intellect' which give rise to impatient or fallacious hopes, heat of passion, excessive zeal, and vain conceits (*Prel.*, xii, ll. 26–37).

[2] Simone Weil, 'The Fallacy of Personal Rights', trans. Richard Rees, in *The Twentieth Century*, June 1959, pp. 547–8.

[3] E.U: M., p. 48.

First, the exercise of reason as a trigger is rare,[1] The pleasures of reason—cold reason, as it is often significantly called—are as yet available to only a few people and are irrelevant if not inimical to the enjoyment of many triggers, and in particular of poetic truth. 'Every feeling loses its strength in the measure that it becomes intellectual,' said Ribot.[2] There can hardly be a schoolchild responsive to poetry who has not complained that the apparatus of criticism 'spoilt' the poetry, and even scholars, it seems, may want not to know:

'The truth perhaps is that the imagination would not be what it is if we could say what it was; *si deprehenditur, perit*—its grandeur would be departed in being known.'[3]

'I am thankful to believe that the connexion between artistic creation and the physical and mental state of the artist remains a mystery.'[4]

Then, in the very moment of ecstasy, the faculty of reasoning is suspended. What is lost in ecstasy comes to be judged as bad—and it is not possible to experience ecstasy and retain the power of reasoning, even though it may have been the exercise of reason that induced the ecstasy.

Two other reasons why ecstatics denigrate reason are concerned with overbelief, but it will be convenient to discuss them briefly here, even if this means making some as yet unwarranted assumptions.

Firstly, then, the overbeliefs to which ecstasy gives rise most usually consist of propositions which, if submitted to the test of reason, could not be sustained.[5] If the desire for a given overbelief is prepotent, then among the tests to which it is submitted—and all overbeliefs are submitted to tests (see Ch. XXXVI)—the test of reason will not be one. More, since reason is the obvious test to which to submit a proposition,

[1] In the questionnaire group no religious person gave 'scientific knowledge' of any kind as a trigger; see Appendix D, Table 9.

[2] Quoted by de la Mare, *Love*, p. lxxv.

[3] H. W. Garrod, *Wordsworth* (Oxford, 1923; 2nd edn., 1927), p. 171.

[4] Helen Darbishire, *The Poet Wordsworth* (Oxford, 1950), p. 6.

[5] 'To oppose the torrent of scholastic religion by such feeble maxims as these, that *it is impossible for the same thing, to be and not to be*, that *the whole is greater than a part*, that *two and three make five*; is pretending to stop the ocean with a bull-rush. Will you set up profane reason against sacred mystery? No punishment is great enough for your impiety.' David Hume, *The Natural History of Religion* (1757), Section XI.

reason must needs be strongly denigrated in order to explain why it is not used.[1]

The last reason follows from the above. Almost everybody would prefer to hold a belief that can be sustained by reason and most intelligent persons seek such a belief. Thus St. Augustine wrote,

> 'I wished to be as assured of the things I saw not, as I was that seven and three are ten.'[2]

and Wordsworth:

> *Dragging all passions, notions, shapes of faith,*
> *Like culprits to the bar, suspiciously*
> *Calling the mind to establish in plain day*
> *Her titles and her honours...*
> *   ...demanding proof,*
> *And seeking it in everything,* [3]

But reason proved incapable of justifying such beliefs as were sought by Wordsworth and St. Augustine and, apparently, by most men, and eventually Wordsworth and St. Augustine, like most men, were satisfied to accept beliefs whose only disadvantage for intelligent men was that they could not be justified by reason.

> *To think that two and two are four*
> *And neither five nor three*
> *The heart of man has long been sore*
> *And long 'tis like to be.*[4]

But most men, unwilling to live with sore hearts, need justification for accepting, at will, three or five as their chosen answers, and so must inevitably denounce the faculty of reason which would forbid their acceptance. For such people, reason must be an anti-trigger.[5]

---

[1] 'When, therefore, we find ourselves entertaining an opinion about the basis of which there is a quality of feeling which tells us that to inquire into it would be absurd, obviously unnecessary, unprofitable, undesirable, bad form, or wicked, we may know that that opinion is a non-rational one, and probably, therefore, founded upon inadequate evidence.' W. Trotter: *Instincts of the Herd in Peace and War* (London, 1916), p. 44.

[2] *Confessions*, vi. 6.   [3] *Prel.*, x, ll. 890–8.

[4] A. E. Housman, *Last Poems* (London, 1928), xxxv, p. 52.

[5] See Kathleen Nott's book, *The Emperor's Clothes* (London, 1953) where what she calls the 'two truths' theory is intelligently demonstrated with useful examples of the mystical aversion from reason. Also Rupert Crawshay-Williams's book, *The Comforts of Unreason* (London, 1947), p. 13 et seq.

In instancing as anti-triggers such reminders of everyday life as commerce and the presence of other people and even natural objects and reason, I have deliberately avoided other anti-triggers which would in all circumstances be regarded as distasteful by most people—for instance, ugliness, brutality, war. It is easy enough to give examples that would show these to be especially offensive because of their contrast with other and trigger conditions;[1] but it would be equally easy to show that these are regarded, by many people, as offensive in all contexts. The significant thing about the anti-triggers I have chosen to display is that it is only in trigger-contexts that they are found offensive—though there are, of course, a few people who seek to live their entire lives in trigger-contexts and would always find offensive all reminders of contemporary social life.

It is important that anti-triggers should be distinguished from desolation-triggers which are not found offensive in ecstasy contexts, presumably because from desolation ecstasy may arise. Certainly it is not always possible to draw a clear distinction between the two: a bleak and desolate mountain may be certainly a desolation-trigger, not an anti-trigger, a car-park an anti-trigger and not a desolation-trigger. But much contemporary writing at least leads one to suppose that at least certain anti-triggers accepted as symbolizing the doleful condition of contemporary man may as readily act as desolation-triggers as the Cross has come to do for Christians.[2]

I believe that the value and prestige attached to triggers, as compared with other objects, events, and ideas, could be further substantiated by examining the attitudes of different societies to, say, such frequently effective triggers as nature, art, knowledge, sexual love. I think it could be shown that the more authoritarian the society, the more rigidly it sought either to anathematize private exploration of the pleasures of these triggers, or inalienably to charge them with associations of the society.

I think, too, that if we look around us we can see further substantiation

[1] For instance: 'the blackened brick dwellings, the black slate roofs glistening their sharp edges, the mud black with coal-dust, the pavements wet and black... The utter negation of natural beauty, the utter negation of the gladness of life, the utter absence of the instinct for shapely beauty which every bird and beast has, the utter death of the human intuitive faculty was appalling.' D. H. Lawrence, *Lady Chatterley's Lover* ch. xi, p. 158.

[2] For Suzuki, who is not a Christian, the Cross is merely terrible: 'The crucified Christ is a terrible sight and I cannot help associating it with the sadistic impulse of a physically affected brain.' *Mysticism, Christian and Buddhist*, p. 136.

of triggers as a class in the uses made of them as objects of social prestige—and not only of triggers themselves but of manufactured objects having the superficial appearance of triggers but not necessarily possessing any of the powers of real triggers to induce even response-experiences. Both subjects, the manipulation of triggers by authority and the manufacture of surrogate triggers which are bought for purposes of prestige are, I think, worth considerable study.

CHAPTER XIX

Some Common Triggers

Taken as a whole the people in the groups responded most frequently to *nature*, and next to nature art, though in the questionnaire group there was a slight preference for art over nature.[1]

Several people spoke of being moved by nature generally, or by landscape, scenery, etc., but of specific aspects of nature named, by far the most common were water and heights, sometimes in combination. It had been suggested to me by a Freudian psychologist that I would find that men tended to be moved by mountains, women by water, but this did not prove to be the case.[2]

Contemporary circumstances must make some difference to the availability of triggers, both physically and emotionally. Women, for instance, would have been less likely than men to climb mountains until comparatively recent times, and considerably less likely to record their emotional responses, whether on mountains or elsewhere. Then, as compared with safe if impressive inland waters, the sea receives comparatively few mentions in trigger-contexts before about 1790, possibly because its associations of danger and toil were prepotent over its ecstasy-inducing qualities; something very similar is, I think, true of winter. Mountains, on the other hand, have a substantial tradition as inducing mystical experiences which were often, no doubt, ecstasies in my sense. The greatest religious leaders of the west all had mystical experiences on mountains. Moses spoke with God on Horeb (Sinai), 'the mountain of God'[3] and later received the ten commandments

[1] See Appendix D, Table 3, for frequencies of trigger-mentions in the groups.
[2] In all groups, mountains (or hills) and water together were mentioned by 3 men and 3 women; mountains or hills only by 7 men and 5 women; and water only by 8 men and 4 women. Mountains, water, and sometimes both together were mentioned by several of the girls in Group C.
[3] *Exod.* iii, 1.

there; Elijah, too, spoke with God on Horeb.[1] Mahomet received his revelation in a cavern on Mount Hara.[2] And Jesus was transfigured on 'an high mountain'.[3]

Trees and flowers receive comparatively frequent mention, both in the texts and elsewhere. Both the flight and the song of birds could be copiously illustrated as triggers to ecstasy. Wild animals are mentioned by inference in one text (L 12), and play an important part in the ecstasy of Jung quoted on p. 109.[4]

Scent—the odour of flowers, trees, the earth, etc.—is often mentioned in accounts of trigger circumstances, and notably by Keats. Q 30 unusually gives scent as a trigger on its own. (Can scent to any extent act as an intoxicant in inducing ecstasy?)

The indications given as to weather, season, time of day are of interest. There is little doubt that, at least when out of doors, fine weather is most apt for ecstasy. It is implied in references to stars, blue sky and, I think, to clouds. In the groups three people mentioned fine daytime weather or specifically named sunshine; Q 61 gave three instances of trigger-conditions, and in each case named sunlight.

Dramatically bad weather is however sometimes mentioned as a trigger; three people in the texts spoke of storms at sea. Bad weather precedes the ecstasy of text L 16, and here the intention is to enhance an atmosphere of pre-ecstatic desolation.

Seven people speak of sunrise and three of sunset (Q 61 twice); eight people speak of night-time and six of these indicate, by mention of moon or stars, a fine night; three people speak of dusk. In

---

[1] I *Kings* xix.

[2] Washington Irving, *The Life of Mahomet* (1849–50; New York, n.d.), ch. vi, pp. 53–4.

[3] *Mark* ix. 2. To read the Gospels is to gain the impression that Jesus was very much attracted by mountains when seeking spiritual experience. When in the wilderness he was led by the devil up a high mountain and there, 'in a moment of time', shown all the kingdoms of the world (*Luke* iv. 5). Matthew (xv. 29) tells how, after Jesus had come to the sea of Galilee, he 'went up into a mountain, and sat down there'. Luke (vi.12) tells how 'it came to pass in those days, that he went out into a mountain to pray, and continued all night in prayer to God'; and the next day he chose his disciples. Elsewhere we are told how he went to the wilderness or to solitary places, which may perhaps sometimes indicate mountains, since of the incident quoted from Matthew above, John also speaks of a mountain (vi. 3) but Luke of a desert place (ix. 10).

[4] Domestic animals are seldom mentioned as triggers, the characteristic of the cat being, as Jacquetta Hawkes comments (see p. 108), that although domesticated it still seems wild.

none of the texts is noon on a sunny day given as the time of the ecstasy.[1]

The seemingly greater aptness of early morning or night-time for ecstasy agrees with Harding's impressions of the times most favourable to creative work. 'On the whole', she writes, 'it appears that morning or night hours are the most favourable to the flow of ideas.' [2] This is not to say, of course, that ecstasies may not occur at other times of day, but that the people in my groups did not find other times of day significant in inducing ecstasies.

Ecstasy may, it seems, be felt at any season, but from the evidence of poets we should expect spring to be most apt for it, and in the groups five people mention spring. Summer is mentioned by only two people, autumn by three, and winter is mentioned or implied by three people.

Wind, breeze, or air are mentioned by eight people.

Colour is seldom specifically mentioned as an element in natural triggers. Q 61, who refers to colour in each of the three experiences he describes, is idiosyncratic in this respect; it may be relevant that it was he who in all three experiences mentioned the presence of sunlight.

In view of the preponderant mention of sunlight as the weather most apt for ecstasy and in view, too, of the possibility (to which I shall return) that certain inherent qualities in triggers may correspond with certain feelings of ecstasy, it is worth noting how often effects of light are mentioned when describing triggers. Apart from specific mentions of sunlight, moonlight, or starlight we find the following:

'when the light and the smell and the scene is just right' (Q 1); 'sudden appearance of light' (Q 30); 'Vesuvius had a red light glowing' (Q 61); 'bathe the world in light' (L 1b); 'the newly-risen sun sent flickering...a series of elastic reflections' (L 5); 'the shining waters glittering in my dreamy eyes' (L 9); 'flickering red flames' (L 12); 'the double glow of the sky and the river' (L 15); 'steady white light' (L 19); 'an eerie glow on the snow' (C 8); 'the lights of the sun shining on the metal of the cars was dazzling' (C 11); C 15 gazed into the fire. Lightning may have been involved in Q 16's storm at sea. Though man-made not natural light, I may add here

[1] Perhaps not surprisingly, since the Psalmist sang of 'the destruction that wasteth at noonday' (xci. 6)—our 'noonday devil'—and Cassian of *accidia* 'disturbing the monk especially about midday'. Helen Waddell, *The Desert Fathers*, p. 157.
[2] A.I., p. 40.

Q 56 who mentioned a pinpoint of light in a cathedral as being relevant in inducing his ecstasy.

No doubt there are many other aspects of nature that could be shown to be effective on a few people or on a single person, but in relation to nature ecstasy seems most commonly to be induced by mountains, hills, and water, by starlit nights, fine dawns and sunsets, by spring and autumn days, by trees and flowers, by the flight and song of birds, by light and by wind and by the sweet smells of the countryside.

In the questionnaire group several people named a branch of *art* before or instead of giving specific instances. They named music (15 times), poetry (8 times), drama (twice), literature, ballet, film; and six people spoke generally of 'art' or 'aesthetic things'.[1]

All the art named is art of 'good' quality. The music for instance may range from Tchaikovsky and Rachmaninov on the one hand to Bach and Beethoven on the other and includes spontaneously created jazz. But no one was moved to ecstasy (or admitted being moved to ecstasy) by creations of a kind that most informed people would agree were 'phoney', commercialized, trivial. It seems that it is 'good' art, not surrogate art, which may induce ecstasy.

In both the questionnaire and the literary groups music was the most frequently named art-trigger (there were no art-triggers in the religious group). I believe that of all the more common triggers to ecstasy, music would be the most rewarding to study in any attempt to find a relation between the qualities of triggers and the effects produced.[2]

Of the other forms of art named as triggers by people in the groups, the only one on which I must comment is sculpture which in one respect I find a puzzling trigger. If there is, as seems probable, an empathetic element in the response to some triggers, one could expect that with sculpture the feelings—or imagined feelings—of the hand on the

---

[1] For details of the specific art forms named in the three groups, see Appendix G.

[2] Dr. Ian Oswald, investigating E.E.G. responses of subjects listening to music, found that 'after a period of raucous cacophony...when perhaps the rhythm was a little difficult to follow...a clear and pleasing clarinet solo with a background of regular drum beats...by a world-famous clarinettist...produced the nearest approach to ecstasy' ('Experimental Studies of Rhythm, Anxiety and Cerebral Vigilance', *Journal of Mental Science*, Vol. 105, No. 439, April 1959, pp. 280-1). Unfortunately Dr. Oswald does not explain how he identified ecstasy or what he means by it, beyond saying that 'Ecstasy necessarily must involve withdrawal from prosaic reality' and, by implication, that this involves 'feelings of delight, with inner peace'.

carved surface would be expressed as feelings of the ecstatic experience. But no feelings of touch with the hands play any part in any descriptions of the feelings of ecstasy, whether triggered by putatively tactile objects or otherwise.

With the possible exception of film (named by two people), all the forms of imaginative creation named fall into the general group that we call art—music, literature, painting, sculpture, drama, ballet. It seems to be accepted that any object created within this group belongs to the kinds of things recognized as capable of giving ecstatic or response experiences, whether or not any particular object proves effective for any particular person. Art objects, in fact, are identified as potential triggers, and I think we could equally say that what we call art are those forms of imaginative creation that we identify as potential triggers.

Architecture does not seem to be treated in the same way. No one named 'architecture' as a group inside which ecstasy-inducing objects might be sought, as they named music, poetry, etc. As a matter of fact, only two kinds of architectural objects are commonly named as inducing ecstasy and these are religious edifices and ruins. The edifices or ruins in question are always specifically named; no one in the questionnaire group, for instance, answered 'cathedrals' and then proceeded to give instances. The religious edifices given are always those of acknowledged beauty; no one named the kind of mid-Victorian church now so much admired by Mr. John Betjeman. The ruins named are always those with historical or emotional associations.

In view of the strong anti-trigger effects of the presence of other people and reminders of contemporary social life, this does not seem surprising. Buildings are, after all, essentially for the use of people in a social context. In the case of ruins, the contemporary social context is expunged and links with past time are evoked. With churches it seems reasonable to suppose that religious and even ecstatic associations are predominant over others, though, unless beautiful, even churches are not, it seems, effective; and when effective, they are as readily so on people whose faith is not associated with that of the church as on people whose church this is.[1]

Nor is it surprising that in the few cases when we do find buildings other than churches inducing ecstasy or spoken of as if they were triggers, these are usually buildings in some way associated with other

[1] In the questionnaire group ecstasies in cathedrals were claimed by a nonconformist, a pantheist, and a Jew.

triggers—university buildings, for instance, monasteries, old castles, and palaces—always remembering, however, the apparently necessary desideratum of beauty.[1]

Architecture is however relevant to another trigger occasionally given, and this is a town or city as a whole. Venice was one of several triggers to ecstasy for Q 19,[2] and Q 22 gives walking at dusk in an eastern city. Wordsworth and Jefferies, both finding cities generally hostile to ecstatic feelings, yet had ecstatic experiences in cities. Wordsworth, though with surprise, experienced ecstasy when entering London on top of a coach (see p. 114); and when leaving London on top of a coach wrote the sonnet in which he says that earth has nothing to show more fair than London at dawn. Jefferies, usually frustrated and unhappy in the city, still managed to find some ecstatic moments in London—at sunset in the streets and once, fulminantly, on London Bridge.[3] An account of what was at least response experience at the sight of a city comes from Villehardouin, who wrote that the Crusaders were so much moved by the beauty of Constantinople seen from the sea that 'il n'i ot si hardi cui la chars ne fremist'.[4]

The fact that people do—albeit often with surprise—obtain ecstasy in and from cities would seem to contradict what I said earlier about the presence of people and contemporary social life acting as anti-triggers and about the general inability of buildings to induce ecstasy because of such associations. I believe I can explain this apparent contradiction.

It is not, in most cases, an ordinary everyday city that gives ecstasy. Venice is a city of outstanding beauty and historical associations; so is—and even more so, was—Constantinople (and it is noteworthy that when the Crusaders entered the actual city, no memory of flesh shiver-

---

[1] This is not to say that occasionally and idiosyncratically a building with no trigger associations may not be effective for one or other individual. For instance: 'The most impressive building in New York is Radio City. Is it "beautiful"? Certainly not in a traditional sense, because it does not trouble itself about tradition and "beauty." It has the power and the security of a natural object... The building may create a future concept of beauty. Certainly the architect must be familiar with the pyramids of Egypt and the Gothic cathedrals and the dome of Michaelangelo; but he has forgotten them again, like one who is asleep' (A. Einstein, *Greatness in Music* (Oxford, 1941), pp. 287-8). Notice how Einstein links Radio City with accepted triggers—natural objects, Gothic cathedrals, etc.— and ends by attributing to it the quality of 'beauty'.

[2] And, by recollection, for Proust; see p.203 n.

[3] *The Story of My Heart*, ch. ii, p. 24 and ch. v, pp. 86-7.

[4] Quoted by Toynbee, *A Study of History*, Vol. X, p. 133.

ing at the sight of its beauty seen from the sea inhibited a sack that was 'unparalleled in history '.)[1] Sunsets, and the river seen as 'the narrow valley grooved out in prehistoric times' which moved Jefferies, are not the ordinary everyday characteristics of the city. Q 22 went to her city because she found employment in a firm that exported ivory, frankincense, and myrrh; with such associations an Arab city (even if, as the *Economist* once described this one, 'incomparably the least attractive city in the Arab world')[2] would not be, at dusk, a surprising trigger to ecstasy. And London at dawn, its noticed features ships, towers, domes, theatres, temples glittering in smokeless air, is not that everyday city in which we are pent but an ideal city rich in triggers.[3]

Thus a city may act as a trigger if it has outstanding beauty; or if it has such associations as may, however momentarily, expunge other anti-trigger associations; or if—as I now want to suggest—it can be seen as an ideal city.

Adamic ecstasies, as we have seen, tend to result in beliefs about reversion to a simpler state (see Ch. IX), and this is often figured as a Garden of Eden or a rural arcadia. *Greater* ecstasies may, I believe, result in beliefs that look to the future rather than to the past (see p. 301) and figure it in terms of an improved form of human social organization of which an ideal city is often the model. The Christian City of God is an obvious example, but there are others; the planning of urban utopias is a common fantasy of our own times, whether in the dreams of political theorists or of science-fiction writers. That the Golden Place of the future is almost always seen in terms of a city and the life of a city is sufficient to ensure that the ideal city shall be a concept of trigger quality; and we must remember that the people who will live in the ideal city are not those ordinary people who act as anti-triggers in the everyday world, but people changed in heart in such ways as to expunge their anti-trigger qualities.

The Christian City of God provides a prototype of the ideal trigger-decked city. The richest model I know, based, as many such are, on the twenty-second chapter of *Revelation*, is found in the Elizabethan

---

[1] Stephen Runciman, *A History of the Crusades* (Cambridge, 1954), Vol. III, p. 123.

[2] August 4, 1956.

[3] Of the view of London from Westminster Bridge which was the occasion of Wordsworth's sonnet, Dorothy Wordsworth wrote, 'there was even something like the purity of one of nature's own grand spectacles'. *Journals*, ed. E. de Selincourt (London, 1952), Vol. I, p. 173.

poem 'Jerusalem, my happy home' by F. B. P.[1] In the 'city of the Saints' here described, there is no toil, no sorrow, no sickness, fear of death, or bad weather; the streets and buildings are decked with gold and precious stones and the gardens bloom continually with flowers and perfumed herbs; silver streams flow through the streets and fruiting trees line their banks; and there is music continually.

Before leaving the general subject of art, it is worth noticing that craft-objects—that is, objects directly expressing the creative impulse of the maker but intended for social use—only very rarely appear as triggering ecstasies. In some ways I find this surprising since I have myself been moved to at least near-ecstasy by some fabrics and ceramics and jewels. But I must admit that those which move me are either old and out of use, or seen in relation to utopia, and I suppose that for most people the immediate association of craft-objects with usefulness in daily life ensures that the responses they evoke will be well below ecstatic levels.

The number of people in the groups for whom *religion* acted as a trigger is swollen by the fact that I included under this heading all mention of art with religious significance. That it is thereby somewhat artificially swollen is shown by the fact that triggers of this kind were named by people of no religion or of a religion different from that expressed by the art in question (see p. 173). The religious associations may have played some part in inducing these ecstasies but it seems doubtful whether it was the religious associations that were prepotent.

Ecstasies induced by communal prayer seem to be rare and only doubtfully appear in my texts. There are none such in the religious group. Communal worship may have been relevant in the case of Q 26, a Christian, at a carol service, but probably not in the case of Q 56, a Jew, watching but not participating in a Christian service. A function of communal worship is undoubtedly to make people feel members one of another but not, it would appear, to induce ecstasies.[2]

The feelings that are induced in crowds at religious revival meetings are sometimes spoken of as if similar to the ecstasies I am concerned

---

[1] *Elizabethan Lyrics*, ed. Norman Ault (London, 1928), pp. 317–20.

[2] The O.D.C.C. comments that though Jesus participated in the public worship of the synagogue, 'When He expressly mentions prayer, however, it is always of a private kind'. See under 'Prayer'.

with.[1] What evidence I have suggests that rarely if ever do such experiences conform to my criteria for ecstasy.[2]

Ecstasies clearly and obviously induced by private prayer are not common in my groups. In the questionnaire group there are four people for whom private prayer may have been a trigger: Q 19 gave 'real religious experience', Q 48 'once from religion', Q 53 'religious feeling', and Q 39 had his Zen experience.[3] Though these people may have meant that their ecstasies followed and were induced by private prayer, they may equally well have been referring to the overbeliefs they derived from these particular experiences. As I have shown, such names as 'religious ecstasy', as commonly used, may as well refer to ecstasies with religious overbeliefs, however triggered, as to ecstasies induced by religious triggers (see Ch. XVII).

In the religious group, only Brainerd (R 13) refers specifically to prayer; he says that he had been 'endeavouring to pray' when 'unspeakable glory seemed to open'. There is a way of speaking in which anything that induces mystical experience may be spoken of as a prayer; and, in addition, states of mind like that of Brainerd before his ecstasy, which to the layman would seem the antithesis of prayer, may by theologians be identified as prayer (see p. 161 n.).

Christians accept, of course, that 'ordinary prayer' (i.e. discursive meditation, affective prayer and contemplation) may lead to 'extraordinary prayer' comprising 'mystical and supernatural experiences'.[4] Butler describes the process:

> 'It is a common teaching of mystic writers that introversion is effected by a successive silencing of the faculties of the mind and of the powers of the soul, till the actuations become blind elevations to God; and in the 'Quiet' thus produced, the very being of the soul—the 'Ground of the Spirit', the later mystics call it—comes into immediate relation with the Ultimate Reality which is God.' [5]

Whatever may be the experiences produced by this method it is my

[1] Accounts of some of these movements will be found in Knox's *Enthusiasm* and in William Sargant's *Battle for the Mind*, (London, 1957).

[2] The experiences described by Wesley, whose always commendable curiosity led him to ask people what they had felt at his meetings, can certainly not be called ecstasies. Wesley himself came later to believe that most of them were sent by the Devil to bring discredit on his work. See Wesley's *Journal* for December 30, 1742, May 30, July 29, August 6, 1759, August 27, 1763.

[3] J 3 and J 6 claimed ecstasy from prayer; see pp. 528 and 531.

[4] See O.D.C.C. under 'Prayer'.   [5] W.M., p. 33.

impression that fewer intensity ecstasies are thereby induced than by accidental contact with other triggers. Even among the religious, it is far easier—at least for the layman—to find examples of ecstasies with religious overbeliefs induced by non-religious triggers than by prayer. It might seem that the mystics who describe such methods do so rather as a means of helping other people than as the usual preliminary to their own intensity ecstasies. St. Teresa, who formulates at length the stages of prayer from recollection to union, admits,

'I could make no use at all of my imagination in the way that others do who can induce recollection by calling up mental images' [1]

but instead found it helpful to look at 'fields, water, or flowers' or a book. She often speaks of rapture or 'ecstasy' overtaking her when in orison but not what I call an intensity ecstasy.

There are some other circumstances, religious in character, that some-times induce ecstasies, but often it is hard to be sure how far it is the religious character of the circumstances that is the prepotent factor. Thus St. Teresa couples with the suggestion of a walk in the country, 'a really religious conversation' as helpful in inducing a mystical state [2] and there are other examples of ecstasies following 'really religious' conversations, among them the most beautifully told ecstasy I know, that which came to St. Augustine as he talked with his mother at a window in Ostia shortly before her death; and he implies that ecstasy came to her too. [3]

But ecstasy is as well induced by secular conversation with one or a few friends. [4] Rupert Brooke describes an ecstasy which seems to have been intense and *great* induced by the company over a tea-table ('Dining-Room Tea'). One of the women in the questionnaire group

---

[1] *Life*, ch. ix, p. 68.　　　　　　　　　　　　[2] Ibid., ch. xi, p. 82.

[3] *Confessions*, ix. 23–5. Mystical experiences less surely to be called ecstasies, were enjoyed by Catherine of Genoa and her friends through religious conversa-tions: 'This soul remained henceforth many a time in company with its many spiritual friends, discoursing of the Divine Love, in such wise that they felt as though in Paradise, both collectively, and each one in his particular way... He who spoke and he who listened, each one fed on spiritual food of a delicious kind; and because the time flew so swiftly, they never could attain satiety, but all on fire within them, they would remain there, unable at last to speak, unable to depart, as though in ecstasy.' Quoted from the *Vita* of St. Catherine of Genoa by Hügel: M.E.R., Vol. I, pp. 160–1.

[4] This will not surprise followers of G. E. Moore: 'By far the most valuable things, which we know or can imagine, are certain states of consciousness, which may be roughly described as the pleasures of human intercourse and the enjoy-ment of beautiful objects.' *Principia Ethica* (Cambridge, 1903), ch. vi, cxiii.

told me that she had known ecstasy when working with a small group of people for a common cause, and C. P. Snow's hero said that he had known moments similar to but less than ecstasy perhaps twice in his life when he had lost himself among friends 'in a common purpose' (L 25). And meetings with one or a few friends are sometimes mentioned as preceding if not as immediately triggering ecstasies. Q 56 thinks it relevant to mention that before his ecstasy he had been having lunch with a very good friend, Bucke that he had spent the hours before his ecstasy 'with two friends, reading and discussing poetry and philosophy' (R 17).[1]

It does, then, seem that the connexion between religion and ecstatic experience is not so obvious as might superficially appear; that communal worship is not likely to induce individual ecstasy; that private prayer is no more likely to induce ecstasies with religious overbeliefs than are other triggers with no religious significance; that religious surroundings and religious art are not only able to rouse ecstasies with no religious overbeliefs in religious people, but equally in people of no religion or of a religion other than that with which the art is associated. It also appears that for many religious people, for a St. Teresa as well as for the Christians of the questionnaire group, religious and non-religious triggers are put on a level in relation to their capacity to induce ecstasy, whether ecstasy with religious overbeliefs or without them.

The kinds of *exercise* or *movement* that seem to be relevant to ecstasy are two: regular rhythmical movement such as walking, jogging along on a horse, riding in a carriage, etc.; and swift movement, such as running, flying, galloping, etc.

The former, the regular rhythmical movement, seems distinctly conducive to inspiration; and Harding, after giving several examples, comments,

'It is possible that the rhythmical movement of a carriage or train, of a horse and to a much lesser degree of walking, may produce on sensitive minds a slightly hypnotic effect conducive to that state of mind most favourable to the birth of ideas.' [2]

It is however comparatively seldom that I have found such forms of regular rhythmical movement apparently playing a part in inducing

[1] Compare the woman who experienced ecstasy on a night walk after 'the warmth of friends, of meeting, of doing war work'; see Appendix J, p. 532.
[2] A.I., p. 43.

not only inspiration but also ecstasy. Bucke was driving in a cab when ecstasy overtook him (R 17) and it was on the top of a coach that Wordsworth had the ecstasy cited on p. 114 which surprised him by its occurrence in such apparently unpropitious surroundings.[1] The movement of a steamship seems to have been significant in inducing Nichols's experience (L 5). Earlier his ship had been in harbour, and he had then tried to write a poem and could not. In the night the ship had got under way again and, half-waking in his cabin, 'phrases in faint rhythm began to turn over in my head with the insistence of a litter of mechanical toys in action'.[2] Next morning he had the experience—ecstasy accompanied by inspiration—that is recounted in my text.[3]

Swift movement, however, seems to be a far commoner trigger to ecstasy, and fast riding to be an effective form of such movement. Of his first race at a local point-to-point Siegfried Sassoon wrote, 'life became lyrical, beatified, ecstatic, or anything else you care to call it.'[4] Wilfred Blunt's sonnet 'St. Valentine's Day' describes hunting on the Downs near the sea, the song of the thrush, the feeling that spring has come, a loved, imagined face, and ends 'My horse a thing of wings, myself a god.' It does not seem surprising that a winged horse became symbolic of poetic inspiration.[5]

---

[1] Wordsworth seems to have been particularly susceptible to regular rhythmical movement in inducing both inspiration and ecstasy. The sonnet 'Westminster Bridge' was composed on the top of a coach; four other poems ('Chatsworth, thou stately mansion', 'Elegiac Musings in the Grounds of Coleorton Hall', 'The Warning', and 'Among all lovely things my love has been') were composed on horseback; and of walking F. W. Bateson writes: 'Even falling in love…was conceived by Wordsworth in terms of country walks. It is significant that his poetry too was almost all of it composed on his feet…And the quasi-mystical experiences described in *The Prelude*—the climb to the raven's nest, the crossing of the Alps… the ascent of Snowdon, for example—all occurred to him when walking, running or climbing.' *Wordsworth, A Re-interpretation* (London, 1954; 2nd edn., 1956). pp. 53–4.

[2] Harding: A.I., p. 150.

[3] Jung's Miss Miller, on whose experiences his book *Psychology of the Unconscious* is largely based, enjoyed on a ship a series of what seem to me often to be ecstasies, one of them resulting in a poem about the experience; once, on dry land, she had 'an extraordinarily plastic memory of the sea, evoked by the sight of a steamship' and remarked, 'Je sentais les pulsations des machines, le soulèvement des vagues, le balancement du navire.' *Psychology of the Unconscious*, trans. B. M. Hinkle (London, 1919), chs. iii and iv.

[4] *Memoirs of a Fox-Hunting Man* (London, 1928), p. 189.

[5] Veblen, intent on discovering why horses had a higher honorific value than cows, decided that this was because cows 'are to an appreciable degree industrially

As fast riding to jogging, so running to walking:

'I remember a moment [in childhood] when I stood barefoot on firm dry sand by the sea. The air had a special quality as if it had a life of its own. The sound of breakers on the shore shut out all others. I looked up at the clouds, like great white-sailed galleons, chasing proudly inland. I looked down at the regular ripples on the sand, and could not absorb so much beauty. I was taken aback—each of the myriad particles of sand was perfect in its way...there was nothing to detract from all this beauty.

'In this supreme moment I leapt in sheer joy. I was startled, and frightened, by the tremendous excitement that so few steps could create... A few more steps—self-consciously now and firmly gripping the original excitement. The earth seemed almost to move with me. I was running now, and a fresh rhythm entered my body. No longer conscious of my movement I discovered a new unity with nature. I had found a new source of power and beauty, a source I never dreamt existed.

'From intense moments like this, love of running can grow.' [1]

For Dr. Bannister, as a child, this was a revelation ecstasy; notice, incidentally, his awareness of the noise of the waves and of rhythm. His experience is very similar to that described by C. H. Sorley in his poem 'The Song of the Ungirt Runners', with its similar wealth of triggers—the great wide air, the big bare sky, the stormy sea, the tempest in the trees,

> *And we run because we like it*
> *Through the broad bright land.*

I have not read any accounts of ecstasy while playing in team-games, but the following was said to me in conversation with one of the women in the questionnaire group:

'I had an ecstasy from netball when I was a child; you don't get it from any other game because you're earthbound. You seem to be jumping up out of yourself in a queer way. You felt all uplifted and

---

useful to the community' (*The Theory of the Leisure Class* (New York, 1899 ; Mentor edn., 1953), ch. vi, p. 102). It is true that objects that are useful for any but the single purpose of inducing ecstasy are very seldom triggers (see p. 194), but horses shared the prestige common to triggers when very much more useful than they are today, and I suggest that some part of the honorific superiority of horses over cows may be due to the fact that one cannot ride to ecstasy on a cow.

[1] Roger Bannister, *First Four Minutes* (London, 1955), pp. 11–12.

happy, real ecstasy. [In answer to a question] No, it's nothing at all to do with being in a team.'

Certain forms of swift movement, often with little or no personal effort, give feelings of not being earthbound and sometimes ecstasy. Ecstasy is almost certainly described in the following poem:

> *The air goes by in a wind.*
>
> *Swifter and yet more swift,*
> *Till the heart with a mighty lift*
> *Makes the lungs laugh, the throat cry:—*
> *'O bird, see; see, bird, I fly!*
>
> *'Is this, is this your joy?*
> *O bird, then I, though a boy,*
> *For a golden moment share*
> *Your feathery life in air!'*
>
> *Say, heart, is there aught like this*
> *In a world that is full of bliss?*
> *'Tis more than skating, bound*
> *Steel-shod to the level ground.*[1]

Notice the comparison with skating and the implication that the less earthbound, the greater the bliss. Wordsworth's description of skating at night is well known; 'It was a time of rapture' he says.[2] Other forms of swift movement given in the groups are ski-ing, flying in aeroplanes, and driving in a fast car.[3]

Swimming was mentioned by four people in the questionnaire group. It would be interesting to know whether these ecstasies were induced when people were swimming strongly or when they were floating; the latter is a common image for the feelings of withdrawal ecstasy (see p. 69).[4]

The distinction I intend between *scientific knowledge* and *poetic know-*

---

[1] H. R. Beeching, 'Going Downhill on a Bicycle'.   [2] *Prel.*, i, 457.

[3] That this last trigger may not be uncommon is perhaps suggested by the quasi-mystical devotion often given to some classic models of racing-cars and old motor-cars. An article in the *Manchester Guardian* Motoring Supplement (October 16, 1957) spoke of a 'Golden Age' of motor-cars, and of certain vintage models as being 'each a work of art that inspires those who come into contact with it'.

[4] An article describing the feelings of a group of amateur underwater swimmers suggested that this form of exercise may be an effective trigger; see *The New Yorker*, May 12, 1957.

ledge, is that in scientific knowledge I include not only mathematical truths but also truths potentially verifiable by observation of objective phenomena; by poetic knowledge I mean conviction of the truth of a statement (often metaphysical and often implying a value judgement) in cases where its verification is not possible or even considered relevant.

In the groups seven triggers were entered under *scientific knowledge*, and two kinds of circumstances are involved. In some cases there is the acceptance of what is believed at the time to be objective truth; such is Q 11 reading *The Golden Bough* for the first time. In other cases, what induces ecstasy is the working out or verification of an objective truth; for instance, Q 45's 'solving mathematical problems'. These latter cases have an obvious claim to inclusion under the heading of creative work. But they differ from the kinds of creative work spoken of by non-scientific people in the implication that it is the conclusion of the work, or the assurance that the work could be concluded and found, by objective tests, satisfactory, that induced the ecstasies.

Of the people in the questionnaire group who gave scientific triggers, all but one gave other triggers as well—mountains, poetry, sex, art, creative literary work—and thus treated scientific knowledge as similar to other triggers to ecstasy.

C. P. Snow's belief that the feelings aroused by assurance of scientific knowledge are the same as the feelings known to the religious mystics (see text L 25 and p. 102n.) is also held by Einstein, who is quoted by his biographer as saying,

> 'The most beautiful emotion we can experience is the mystical. It is the sower of all true art and science. He to whom this emotion is a stranger...is as good as dead. To know that what is inpenetrable to us really exists, manifesting itself as the highest wisdom and the most radiant beauty, which our dull faculties can comprehend only in their most primitive forms—this knowledge, this feeling, is at the centre of true religiousness. In this sense, and in this sense only, I belong to the ranks of devoutly religious men.' [1]

Frank continues in his own words,

> 'According to Einstein's conception, it is particularly the scientist in the field of natural science, and especially in the field of mathematical physics, who has this mystical experience.'

[1] Philipp Frank, *Einstein, His Life and Times*, p. 340-1.

None of the people giving this trigger in the questionnaire group is religious; Q 6 and Q 11 are agnostics, the rest have no religion.[1]

There are five entries for *poetic knowledge* in the analyses of the groups. Poetic knowledge, in the sense in which I am using it, must often have been the trigger in the ecstasies of religious people, since religious truth is essentially knowledge of this kind. But in the religious texts we have here, we more often find poetic knowledge as the result of than as the inducement to ecstasy.

Creative work was, in the texts, a trigger for fifteen people, including five of the people who gave scientific knowledge and who, as I suggested on the previous page, in any case have a strong claim to inclusion here. The nine people in the questionnaire group who gave non-scientific creative work all gave other triggers as well.

Of the four people from the questionnaire group who gave scientific knowledge as triggers, two believed that ecstasy had something in common with inspiration and two did not. Of the nine people who gave non-scientific creative work, eight believed that ecstasy had something in common with inspiration, four of them suggesting that the similarity was very close, sometimes to the point of identity:

interchangeable (Q 9); very difficult to distinguish (Q 20); with inspiration one can have ecstasy (Q 26); the same as ecstasy (Q 38).

In this group as a whole, irrespective of the trigger named, 78 per cent. of creative people said they believed there to be something in common between inspiration and ecstasy, as did 57 per cent. of the people I called intellectual, but only 22 per cent. of those who were neither intellectual nor creative.

Recollection must clearly play some part in the impact of most if

[1] Leuba cites a statistical investigation undertaken in the United States in 1921 as to the existence of religious belief among physical scientists, biologists, historians, sociologists, and psychologists. He writes: 'A study of the charts, with regard to the kind of knowledge which favours disbelief, shows that the historians and the physical scientists provide the greater; and the psychologists, the sociologists, and the biologists, the smaller number of believers.' Each group was divided into 'greater men' and 'lesser men' and 'In three of these groups (biologists, historians and psychologists) the number of believers among the men of greater distinction is only half, or less than half, the number of believers among the less distinguished men. I do not see any way to avoid the conclusion that disbelief in a personal God and in personal immortality is directly proportional to abilities making for success in the sciences in question.' P.R.M., pp. 324-5.

not all triggers. But by *recollection* as a trigger, I refer neither to this nor to the special religious sense of the word.[1] I use the word only to refer to those occasions when ecstasy is induced by recollection of a previous ecstasy or of a previously effective trigger. By *introspection* as a trigger, I mean a process of bringing to mind an effective trigger-situation, whether one previously known or not. (*Introspection* in this sense would seem to have much in common with *recollection* as religious writers use it.)

In some cases the previous ecstasy or trigger was involuntarily recalled, as it was for Proust (L 26) when a physical object actually present jogged the memory.[2] Sometimes the previous ecstasy or trigger is deliberately recalled; Q 27 said that she could call up recollections of the picture that gave her ecstasy and regain ecstasy at will; Q 61 said he could recapture feelings of ecstasy when he repeated a poem he had written as a result of the original ecstasy. Sometimes it is not clear whether ecstasy was known on the original occasion though it was enjoyed in the recall; thus of Q 1, who said that ecstasy had been induced when 'sitting outside a château in France, writing to someone I loved very much', it is not known whether a previous encounter with the loved one had induced ecstasy.

I have already noted that (at least) man-made triggers, after a time of maximum effectiveness (often that of the first encounter), seem gradually or suddenly, to lose their potency (see pp. 158-9). This does not seem to apply to recollected triggers.

One entry under this heading is rather different from those discussed above, Q 61's mention of 'introspection' which refers to the situation he describes—being on a troopship in Naples harbour, looking at the red glow of Vesuvius, and knowing that in twelve hours he will be in battle for the first time. This I should call a desolation-ecstasy, induced by the poignancy of the contrast between the actual scene and the immediate battle.[3]

[1] 'RECOLLECTION. A term used by spiritual writers to denote the concentration of the soul on the presence of God.' O.D.C.C.

[2] Another ecstasy of Proust's was similarly induced by recollection. Stumbling one day on an irregularity in some paving-stones in Paris, he suddenly enjoyed an ecstatic experience which he compared with others previously known, including the incident of the madeleine. And just as, on that occasion, he had recalled Combray, so on this he recognized Venice where he had, in the past, stumbled on two such paving-stones. *Time Regained*, trans. Stephen Hudson (London, 1931; 1957 edn.), ch. iii, pp. 210-11.

[3] Siegfried Sassoon describes an experience which closely resembles Q 61's, a

The objects, events and ideas discussed above together with sexual love and childbirth represent the most common triggers in my groups and, so far as my experience goes, outside them. There are some others, less often mentioned, which are of a certain interest and seem as if they may be more than idiosyncratically effective.

Food—generally sweet food—seems as if it may sometimes play a part in inducing ecstasies. Both Proust and Q 50 recalled ecstatic feelings as children by eating the same sweet foods as on the previous occasion.[1]

Sweet is certainly a 'good' or pro-word, and as such is often used in descriptions of the feelings of ecstasy, for instance,

> the sweetness of Eternal Life (Suso—C 1); accompanied by so much sweetness (St. Teresa—C 10a); the sweetness of inward contemplation (St. Gregory).[2]

Sometimes the pleasures of ecstasy are compared with the pleasures of eating, as they are by St. Alphonsus Rodriguez (R 14), and in this fine passage from St. Augustine:

> 'But what do I love, when I love Thee? not beauty of bodies, nor the fair harmony of time, not the brightness of the light, so gladsome to our eyes, nor sweet melodies of varied songs, nor the fragrant smell of flowers, and ointments, and spices, not manna and honey, not limbs acceptable to embracements of flesh. None of these I love, when I love my God; and yet I love a kind of light, and melody, and fragrance, and meat, and embracement, when I love my God, the light, melody, fragrance, meat, embracement of my inner man: where there shineth unto my soul, what space cannot contain, and there soundeth, what time beareth not away, and there smelleth, what breathing disperseth not, and there tasteth, what eating diminisheth not, and there clingeth, what satiety divorceth not.'[3]

'A very good meal with a very good friend' was apparently thought by Q 56 to be relevant to his subsequent ecstasy.

This last incident recalls the conversations between friends already discussed as a trigger (see pp. 196–7). There are other circum-

---

moment of ecstasy one evening on the Western Front in the 1914–18 War; there is even a red glow in the sky. *Memoirs of an Infantry Officer* (London, 1930), p. 45.

[1] For the part played by wine in inducing ecstasy, see pp. 259–60 and nn.

[2] Quoted by Butler: W.M., p. 81.   [3] *Confessions*, x. 8.

stances in which the presence of other people can, it seems, act as triggers.

Q 7, particularizing the kinds of beauty that moved him, gave 'certain beautiful people'. He did not say whether he had in mind only those of the opposite sex, but it is a commonplace that among the qualities of a loved one, beauty is usually found.

But beauty need not be the only personal quality that makes for trigger effectiveness, and not only the impact of a real but also of an imagined personality can act as a trigger. One need hardly stress the fact that what is imagined to be the personality of the Incarnate Christ has often proved an effective trigger.[1]

Running counter to the general principle that crowds are anti-triggers is the fact that a few people seem to be moved to ecstasy by the presence of folk-heroes for whose very existence as such the actual or recalled or implied presence of a crowd is necessary. Q 32 identified as ecstasy the experience she had had on seeing Churchill and Stalin in Moscow. It may or may not have been, but here are two more likely examples:

> 'Qui considérera que le visage du prince fait toute la félicité du courtisan, qu'il s'occupe et se remplit pendant toute sa vie de le voir et d'en être vu, comprendra un peu comment voir Dieu peut faire toute la gloire et tout le bonheur des saints.' [2]

> 'Jayne Mansfield told reporters in New York yesterday how she met the Queen at the Royal Film Show... "The Queen's soul is pure gold. She has an inner radiance. I was shivering and trembling with ecstasy. I looked at her the way some of my friends look at me.' [3]

Whether oneself to form part of a crowd is ever or can often be an ecstasy-inducing experience I do not know. There seem to exist almost no accounts of what it feels like to be a participant in what Le Bon calls a psychological crowd;[4] but the near-impossibility of finding such

---

[1] Similar in kind, I think, are the often intense devotions expressed towards, say, a saint, a writer, or an historical character.

[2] La Bruyère, *Les Caractères*, 'De la Cour', no. 75. Harold Nicolson's translation of this passage contains the phrase 'all his life he devotes his days to the ecstasy of seeing and being seen by His Majesty'. *Good Behaviour* (London, 1955), p. 169.

[3] *News Chronicle*, October 7, 1957.

[4] Le Bon distinguished under this name a group of people in whom 'a collective mind is formed' as against any gathering of people brought together by chance. Gustave Le Bon, *The Crowd* (London, 1896), pp. 25-6.

accounts, the general insistence on isolation as a pre-condition for ecstasy, and the observable fact that those people who voluntarily communicate their ecstasies are not the kind we should expect readily to seek participation in crowds makes me suspect that crowd-induced feelings can seldom if ever be assimilated to ecstatic ones.[1]

I have not been able to find any clear instances of ecstasies triggered by thoughts of the community or nation to which people belong. It is comparatively easy to find, say, England or a symbol of England spoken of *as if it were* a trigger, but less easy to find the ecstasies that could justify this way of speaking. Undoubtedly thoughts of one's nation do, in many people, arouse feelings believed to be highly if not supremely valuable; such feelings may often be ecstatic ones but I have no evidence that they are.

It is of course always possible that ecstasies may arise without any obvious trigger being present, as, for instance, Toynbee's did in the Buckingham Palace Road (see p. 114). Often, too, people whose ecstasies take place in common trigger-conditions do not apparently regard these conditions as having had any necessary relation to their experiences of ecstasy—and sometimes they may be right. But the preponderance of ecstasies taking place under such conditions as those discussed in this chapter and in chapters XIII and XIV, the widespread prestige accorded to these conditions, the relative lack of ecstasies taking place under conditions other than these, suggest that ecstasies are most likely to be triggered by contact with a limited range of objects, events, and ideas, of which the most common are nature, art, religion, sexual love, childbirth, knowledge, creative work, certain forms of exercise, and the recollection of and introspection about such objects, events, and ideas as these.

---

[1] Le Bon says that 'by the mere fact that he forms part of an organised crowd, a man descends several rungs in the ladder of civilisation. Isolated, he may be a cultivated individual; in a crowd he is a barbarian—that is, a creature acting by instinct' (*The Crowd*, p. 36). The condition Le Bon describes is a regressive one; I hope eventually to show that ecstasy results in improvement.

CHAPTER XX
Some Desolation Triggers

As compared with ecstasies I have only a few examples of momentary desolation, and these mostly from the children's essays discussed in Chapter XII (for texts see Appendix F). The circumstances inducing these fall into a few simple groups and are worth some brief consideration. In giving examples, I shall include not only those circumstances which seem actually to trigger desolations but also similar circumstances which appear in desolation-ecstasies or are given apparently to create contrast with a subsequent ecstasy. (It should always be remembered that the children proffered these desolation-experiences when given an exemplar of ecstasy.)

Death, Illness: C 45 and C 46 both described women falling down in the street, apparently dead. C 47 gave an incident when her little sister was ill and her mother crying, and C 35 offered a brother and sister being seasick. C 21 described her reactions to a poem about death, C 22 to a poem about madness.

Carlo Levi expresses surprise at his experience of ecstasy when 'death was in the house' (L 12).

Ugly People: C 36 speaks of her own 'terrified, bedraggled body' as seen by the 'black waters'. C 42 writes about a street-violinist with 'grey, unbrushed and tangled hair', a hare-lip, and a lame dog. Of the two women who fell down in the street, C 45 says that the face of the woman she saw 'was the colour of her dirty white coat, with sunken-in cheeks. I felt repelled, because my mother's cheeks were plump, homely and rosy.' C 46 says of *her* woman that her face was 'strangely like parchment. Her eyes were sunken...they were black and beady. Her thin lips were pale as if lacking in blood... Her body was thick and flabby.' C 47 speaks of her mother's face being sad with tears rolling down it, and the little sister's 'flushed cheeks and glassy eyes' as showing 'she was none too well'. C 48, who describes her first sight of a slum,

207

writes of 'a short, fat woman' who was 'wrinkled, ugly', with a cruel mouth, teeth that were black, decayed and broken, and hard eyes.

Forster uses the traditionally ugly figure of the goblin to stand for bad things (L 18); and Church stresses the ugliness of the man who made the music that moved him (L 23a).

C 45 contrasts the ugly face she describes with her mother's plump and rosy one which she finds pleasing.[1] She says specifically that she was 'repelled' by the woman she saw, and the appearance that she, like C 46, finds repellent, is one of pale face, sunken cheeks and eyes; the other children obviously found repulsive the ugly people they describe. At the time of these incidents C 46 was under eight years old, and some of the others seem equally to be describing events that took place some years earlier. Were these feelings of revulsion from appearance of ill-health and ugliness instinctive in these young children or the result of social conditioning? James speaks of 'The ordinary motives to antipathy, which usually set such close bounds to tenderness among human beings'.[2] Do we see in these children's experiences an exaggerated form of such antipathy motivated by an unconscious recognition of another human being's condition being, in relation to themselves, something less than life-enhancing?

Dirt, squalor: C 42 speaks of 'a cold filthy wall with half-torn and blown away public notices...grey, unbrushed and tangled hair...unshaved face'; C 45's woman is said to be in a dirty white coat, and her face the colour of her coat; C 48 describes a house with 'dirty and smeary windows and rusty locks...a row of washing, old and ragged' and a woman with teeth that were 'black and decayed and broken'.

Bad weather: 'The weather was appalling,' writes C 5. 'The rain started to pelt down again, and the unwanted feeling I had arrived at by then was magnified by a roll of thunder.' C 10 mentions the bad weather in the French village which preceded the sunlight. Rain and swirling mist were the background of C 36's experience, and C 45, when she saw the woman fall down in the street, mentions that it was raining.

Meredith provides the aftermath of a tempest—'a pale grey light...

---

[1] Some people associate ecstasy with rosy faces (see p. 86). Once at a papal audience I saw several women who seemed as if transported by the occasion and unaware of their surroundings; their faces were flushed and plumped up, as if the lines and hollows had been smoothed out from underneath.

[2] V.R.E., p. 269.

green drenched weeds...raindrops pattering'—to match Richard Feverel's pre-ecstatic mood (L 16). Traherne's childhood desolation took place on 'a lowering and sad evening' (see p. 164).

Loneliness: C 5 speaks of 'the feeling that I was very small and insignificant... the unwanted feeling that I had arrived at'. 'I saw that my family were still far behind...I felt utterly helpless,' writes C 36, and C 44, 'I felt as though as I was right in the middle of a tremendous expanse of water...I was alone.' C 45 felt that whereas before her experience grown-ups had always been strong and safe, like surrounding walls, 'now one of those walls had fallen, and I was cowering back against three walls'.

Traherne was unhappily aware of 'being alone in the field... The unprofitableness and silence of the place dissatisfied me; its wideness terrified me'.

'I was conscious only of fear, loneliness and pain,' said one of the women who wrote about their childbirth experiences to the B.B.C. Several others attributed the fact that childbirth was not happy for them to being left alone and feeling lonely and neglected during labour (see p. 143).

Falling, drowning, being crushed: C 5 felt 'overpowered' by the mountains, as if 'they would come crashing down to crush me'; C 36 speaks of 'two enormous menacing peaks' that towered above her and a huge pit of choppy black water. C 44 speaks of 'water pressing down on me from all sides' and C 45 describes her feeling of loss of security in terms of a wall falling down.

To one critic the *allegro* of Beethoven's Ninth Symphony 'sounded as if one were staring into the bowels of chaos', to another, as though 'likely to sweep away the foundations of the universe' (see pp. 167–8). In contrast with these, C 36 describes her terror of the menacing mountains in terms of 'a mass of orchestras all playing a triumphant, sinister minor chord'.

War: War was involved in the experiences of both C 21 and C 29. The prospect of battle contrasts with the actual trigger in the desolation-ecstasies of Q 61 and of Siegfried Sassoon, mentioned on p. 203 and n.

Cold, darkness: In these desolation pictures we never find mention of warmth or light, and often cold and darkness are specified. C 5 says the mountains looked dark and unfriendly, and C 36 speaks of blinding rain, swirling mist and a huge pit of choppy black water. C 42 mentions a 'cold, filthy wall' and C 48 a narrow dark passage.

Meredith describes the chapel as standing cold and still in the twilight (L 16), and to describe her pre-ecstatic state of despair Emily Brontë uses the word *gloom*, which has connotations of both darkness and *down*.[1]

After ecstasy people often feel as if they can see colour and light with newly clear eyes (see p. 86) ; the feeling that colour and light are not there to be seen is apparently apt for inducing desolation.

This very short list of examples, taken only from texts already cited in this book, suggests that some things which are often triggers to ecstasy may, in different circumstances, be triggers to desolation. Mountains and lakes in bad weather may trigger desolation, in good weather ecstasy. Darkness shot with light may induce ecstasy, unmitigated darkness desolation—and perhaps withdrawal ecstasy. Thoughts of death bring desolation to C 45 and C 46; for C 19 it is accompanied by music and brings ecstasy. To be alone is almost necessary for ecstasy, but to feel loneliness is intolerable.

I think however we may say that unmitigated by other and ecstatic triggers, the following may be triggers to desolation: death, loneliness, dirt, darkness, illness, cold, the apparent possibilities of falling, being crushed, being drowned; and bad weather and other natural phenomena that can be taken as models for any of the preceding.[2]

It may appear that all I am trying to show is that sad and frightening things arouse sad and frightened feelings. I think it is a little more than this. Let us grant a range of ideas that must inevitably be frightening and awful to thinking men—say, I. A. Richards's list comprising man's loneliness, birth and death, the inconceivable immensity of the universe, man's place in the perspective of time, his enormous ignorance (see p. 169). Ideas of this kind, we may agree, almost certainly must be frightening and awful. There is still no necessary awe and fear in some of the triggers to desolation. Though our linguistic practices show that

---

[1] *Gloom*: M.E. *gloumen*, to lower; cf. provincial Modern English *glum*, overcast. From *Concise Etymological Dictionary of the English Language*, by W. W. Skeat (Oxford, 1882; 1956 imp.).

[2] 'The wilderness in which St. Paul has found release from the world is of a desolation never again attempted in painting, and Grünewald has discovered, in the ragged fingers of moss which drip from every leafless twig, a perfect symbol of decay. Their repeated verticals impose a ghastly stillness broken only by the fall of a rotten branch.' Sir Kenneth Clark, *Landscape into Art* (London, 1949; Pelican edn., 1956), ch. iii, pp. 51–2.

we habitually treat cold as worse than heat, darkness as worse than light, continuous cloud and rain as worse than continuous sunshine and blue sky,[1] it is hard to find substantial reasons why we should do so, since each, in excess, would be as disastrous to us as its opposite. There is no obvious reason for *down* habitually to be worse than *up*.[2] There is no obvious reason for music in a minor key to be sadder than music in a major key.

Clearly, bad weather, cold, darkness, minor music, etc., if of their nature tending to induce desolation, will readily become so much associated with it that it comes to look absurd to inquire why these things are felt to be sad and nasty. My suggestion is that some of these things are thought of as sad and nasty because they have some innate capacity to induce feelings of desolation.

I have earlier quoted Leuba's suggestion that feelings of an ecstatic kind may be induced at a low level by trivial stimuli (see pp. 100-1). A passage from D. H. Lawrence reinforces this suggestion with its implication that to many kinds of thing we respond, at however low a level, with feelings of being quickened and enlivened or deadened and depressed:[3]

> 'We have to choose between the quick and the dead. The quick is God-flame, in everything. And the dead is dead. In this room where I write, there is a little table that is dead: it doesn't even weakly exist. And there is a ridiculous little iron stove, which for some unknown reason is quick. And there is an iron wardrobe trunk, which for some still more mysterious reason is quick. And there are several books, whose mere corpus is dead, utterly dead and non-existent. And there is a sleeping cat, very quick. And a glass lamp that, alas, is dead.

[1] It is difficult to describe weather without using adjectives that imply value: lowering, downcast, miserable, bad; fine, lovely, beautiful, good.

[2] The sun, which is *up*, warms and lights us; also scorches us and our crops and makes labour more arduous. From *up* come rains which can flood as well as succour, hail, snow, lightning. The ground, where crops grow and herds feed, is *down*; our necessary water runs ever downwards. We lie down to die; but also to rest, to bear children, to copulate. We sit down to eat and talk with friends. We may look for safety up on a hill or down in a hollow. The circumstances of our daily lives do not provide obvious reasons for regarding *up* as a pro-word and *down* as a con-word.

[3] I feel a little embarrassed at quoting Lawrence after impugning his ecstatic veracity earlier. But on these lesser responses his feelings are so close to my own that I naturally accept what he says. I judge most encounters, human or otherwise, as being enlivening or deadening.

'What makes the difference? *Quien sabe?* But difference there is. And I *know* it.' [1]

To return to the more intense feelings, I have the impression that in some cases feelings of desolation are themselves taken as indicating the presence of deity.[2] Lucan's description of the sacred grove amounts to a list of desolation symbols, including even dirt.[3] I speak from almost complete ignorance of classical literature, but it seems to me that the surroundings in which Romans felt the presence of later less brutish gods were still of a kind to evoke desolation rather than ecstasy:

'If you're confronted by some dense grove of aged and giant trees shutting out every glimpse of sky with screen upon screen of branches, the towering stems, the solitude, the sense of strangeness in a dusk so deep and unbroken, where no roof is, will make deity real to you. Again, the cavern that holds a hill-side poised on its deep-tunnelled galleries of rock...will strike some hint of sanctity into your soul...there are lakes hallowed by their dark inscrutable waters and unplumbed depth.' [4]

Was the expected feeling desolation only? Or was it, as for David Brainerd (R 13) in a thick grove, desolation overcome by ecstasy. The classic conditions of imprisonment—darkness, dirt, isolation, close confinement—amount to a summation of desolation triggers and an absolute void of ecstatic ones; but so do the classic conditions of the rigorist anchorite where, presumably, states induced by these conditions should ultimately lead to ecstasy. [5]

---

[1] 'The Novel' in *Sex, Literature and Censorship* (London, 1955), pp. 69–70.
[2] It will be remembered that Christians accept desolate states as states of prayer; see p. 161n.
[3] *Bellum Civile (Pharsala)*, V.
[4] Seneca, *Epistulae Morales*, 41 (iv. 2), trans. E. P. Barker.
[5] This would suggest that people of anchorite temperament should be well fitted to resist brain-washing techniques whose preliminaries consist of inducing loss of identity through isolation in unpleasant surroundings. Such a person would, presumably, be seeking rather than disturbed by loss of self-awareness and, if religious, his isolation might be mitigated by feelings of contact with God.

CHAPTER XXI

Some Qualities of Triggers

By definition triggers are circumstances preceding ecstatic experiences and probably standing in a causal relationship to such experiences. Apart from this I believe it would at present be a waste of time to seek for some factor or factors that triggers must have in common. To base a question on an analogy that I think is apt, what is there in common between mushrooms and milk and salt and bread and eggs, apart from the fact that they can all be eaten? It was necessary to discover the effects of the provision and deprivation of foodstuffs before it was possible to discover the factors in different foodstuffs that made them effective for purposes of nourishment. Similarly, I assume it would be necessary to discover and value those effects of triggers which are ecstatic and response experiences, in empirical terms before attempting to find out what qualities in triggers contribute to these effects.

But if we cannot find a single quality in all foodstuffs beyond the defining quality of serving as food, we can still classify foodstuffs in various ways that bring certain common factors to light—although such factors may not be relevant to their values as foods. We can say, for instance, that milk and carrots both contain Vitamin A; that milk and orange-juice are both liquids; that orange-juice and carrots are both a yellowish-red in colour; that milk and beef both come from cattle.

In the same way we can classify certain triggers on the basis of certain common factors. The difficulty is to know what classifications it might be useful to make in relation to ecstasy. I think it might be useful to notice that certain triggers give the appearance of flickering lights. I do not know if it is useful to notice that at least two triggers, sexual love and childbirth, are necessary to the propagation of the race. It certainly is not useful to notice that trees and flowers grow in the ground unless we can find in them other qualities which differentiate them from noxious weeds, never cited as triggers.

I have tried throughout to base my comments on what people say they feel, and I think it may be useful to attempt a few classifications of triggers on the basis of what people say they feel about them. There are ways in which people speak of some triggers and not others, ways in which they never speak of things that are not triggers, and from such statements a few tentative classifications may be made.

Many triggers are felt to have qualities that correspond with quasi-physical feelings often claimed in ecstasy, and I think it may be useful to relate some of the quasi-physical feelings of ecstasy to such triggers.

Feelings of *up* are often described in terms of springs and fountains (see pp. 67–8 and 78–9); such comparisons usually relate to a postulated flow in the heart or breast.

Being on tops of mountains or in aeroplanes or watching the flight of birds have obvious *up* connotations. The woman who said she had known ecstasy from playing netball directly related the trigger to the experience, comparing with netball other games in which 'you're earthbound' (see p. 199). Beeching, in the poem quoted on the page after, compares the feeling of going downhill on a bicycle with a bird's flight, and says that it is more than the feeling to be derived from skating because skating is 'steel-shod to the level ground'. The daffodils' movement in the wind was felt by Wordsworth to correspond with the dancing of his heart.[1]

We commonly speak of music as going up and down, and *up*-feelings are by several people compared with music. Q 44 compares mountain-peaks with a blast of trumpets, C 36, describing a desolation-ecstasy, with a triumphant sinister minor chord. Nietzsche and the jazz-player of text L 27, both with music as their triggers, imagine themselves on peaks in their ecstacies.

Feelings of *sinking down into* are characteristic of withdrawal ecstasies and the most usual image used to describe this feeling is one of still water. I have already noted that withdrawal ecstasies of Wordsworth and of Daniel Deronda were induced while gazing on still water (see p. 79), and to describe the feeling of withdrawal ecstasies images of still water are often introduced, for instance, by Koestler with Freud's 'oceanic feeling' and by Suzuki quoting Lao-Tzu. Other images used by Suzuki for this feeling of sinking into depth are those of a valley and of an abyss (see p. 71).

Jung, contrasting western and eastern mystical experiences, gives

[1] 'I wandered lonely as a cloud', P.W., Vol. II, pp. 216–17.

being lifted above the ground as an image for the former and a womb for the latter:

> 'The West is always seeking uplift, but the East seeks a sinking or deepening...the European seeks to raise himself above the world, while the Indian likes to return into the maternal depths of Nature.' [1]

There is however a significant difference between Suzuki's depths and Jung's. Suzuki's depths are always empty—'the silent valley of Absolute Emptiness', 'the abyss of nameless nothingness'—whereas a womb is necessarily an image of fecundity. Whether or not Jung intended this difference from more usual Eastern images I do not know, but images of fecund depths are often used by Europeans in connexion with inspiration. The best-known example probably is Livingston Lowes's use of Henry James's image of the deep well of unconscious cerebration into which the creative man lowers his material for processing and whence, unified, he eventually draws it up. [2]

The situation figured in such images appears as part of the actual trigger in an experience of Wordsworth's. He is climbing Snowdon on a dark night when suddenly the moon comes out and shines on the ocean beneath:

> *All meek and silent, save that through a rift...*
> *Mounted the roar of waters, torrents, streams*
> *Innumerable, roaring with one voice!*

What he then saw and heard reflected, as it seemed to him,

> *the type*
> *Of a majestic intellect...*
> *There I beheld the emblem of a mind*
> *That feeds upon infinity, that broods*
> *Over the dark abyss, intent to hear*
> *Its voices issuing forth to silent light*
> *In one continuous stream;* [3]

Here the abyss, far from containing 'nameless nothingness', as Suzuki's does, stands for the source of creation; indeed, in the earlier version Wordsworth had written that in

> *That dark deep thoroughfare had Nature lodg'd*
> *The Soul, the Imagination of the whole.* [4]

[1] *Eranos Jahrbuch*, 1940-1.   [2] *The Road to Xanadu* (Boston, 1927).
[3] *Prel.* (1850), xiv, ll. 56-74.   [4] *Prel.*, xiii, ll. 64-5.

It will by now have become apparent that not only may actual triggers have some apparently empathetic relation to the feelings of ecstasies, but that the images of appropriate triggers not actually present may be introduced into descriptions of ecstasies to elucidate by metaphor the feelings described.

Some people claim that in ecstasy they had an impression of seeing sustained light. Others use sustained light as an image for mental illumination, and may describe this in terms of light that has been present in the trigger to their own experience or of light effects often found as triggers to other people's experiences.

Feelings of seeing sustained light are by Jacquetta Hawkes directly related to the trigger—'the moonlight had ceased to be a physical thing and now represented a state of illumination in my own mind' (L 19). Berenson speaks figuratively—he felt he had 'emerged into the light after long groping in the darkness of an initiation' (L 10). The sustained light of sunshine is, as we have seen, more apt for ecstasy than dull weather (see p. 188).

Both Tennyson and Emily Brontë believe they see superhuman figures robed in light or shining with light. It is characteristic of good supernatural figures that they should appear bright, shining, gleaming, and often they come to bring mental illuminations; thus the visitant to St. John the Divine. It may also, it appears, be characteristic of real-life folk-heroes that they seem to shine with light; Jayne Mansfield describes the Queen of England as having 'an inner radiance' (see p. 205).[1]

Flashes of light appear as readily in the triggers themselves as in metaphors used to describe feelings. Nichols describes reflections 'flickering' on the water which seemed to flash through him (L 5); Nietzsche spoke of the grey sky of abstraction as being thrilled by flashes of lightning (L 6). A storm at sea, given as a trigger by Q 16, probably implied the presence of lightning-flashes; Tennyson's seraph flew down in 'a curve of whitening, flashing, ebbing light' (L 2). The effects of sunlight flickering through leaves is mentioned in trigger-contexts by many poets; fires flickering in grates apparently helped to

---

[1] Another example appears in an account by Gustave Thibon of an incident with Simone Weil—not, in this case, a folk-hero but a personality felt to have trigger quality: 'She was commenting on the Gospel. Her words did not so much translate the truth as pour it into me whole and unadulterated. I felt as though transported beyond space and time, so that I virtually fed upon light.' G. Thibon and J. M. Perrin, *Simone Weil as we knew her*, tras. E. Crauford (London, 1953), p. 132.

induce the experiences of Carlo Levi (L 12) and of the child C 15. Starlight flickering is another common trigger.

Darkness lit by light or contrasted with light is a circumstance that often moves Wordsworth, and is also an image often used by him to describe the illuminations of ecstasy. We find in the passage quoted on the previous page both the actual appearance of sudden moonlight shining on the ocean and the voices of the mind emerging to silent light; here, as for Jacquetta Hawkes, actual light in the trigger circumstances is felt to correspond with feelings of mental illumination.

Two light images are used by H. Warner Allen (L 11). He compares the fast movement of Beethoven's Seventh Symphony with stars. Then, describing his feelings of mental illumination in terms of an ever-widening stream, he introduces the image of 'a sunbeam striking with iridescence the spray above a waterfall'.

It would be possible to multiply almost indefinitely examples of sudden or flashing light appearing both in actual triggers to ecstasy and in images used to describe the feelings of ecstasy.

The feelings of thrills, shudders, tingling, sometimes associated with flashes, seem to have less correspondence with qualities of actual triggers. But since they are sometimes described in terms of electric shocks (see p. 81), it may be relevant that stormy weather, which without any necessary feelings of ecstasy, sometimes induces such thrills, is occasionally named as a trigger. These feelings may also be induced by hearing deep notes on organs (see p. 83n.); organ-music is a not infrequent trigger and the organ is the preferred instrument in churches.

Earlier I quoted Harding's suggestion that rhythmical movements might create an hypnotic effect which, she suggested, would be conducive to inspiration (see p. 197). This may well be true, but often, I suggest, rhythmical movements may rather correspond with or be conducive to those feelings of pulsation often characteristic of intensity ecstasies. People are, as we have seen, sometimes moved towards intensity ecstasy by such things as the throb of a ship's engine, by walking, jogging on a horse, or being moved in vehicles.

In descriptions of ecstasies by far the most usual image for feelings of pulsation is that of waves of the sea, which are themselves one of the most common of triggers. Sometimes the pulsation is felt to 'thunder' in the ear—another relationship with stormy weather as a trigger—and then the sea-waves may be felt appropriate to express both the feelings of pulsation and the noise it is felt to make. Tennyson—who was actually overlooking the sea—seems with the words *note* and *beat* to link sea-waves and noises in the ear with music:

> *notes of busy lives in distant worlds*
> *Beat like a far wave on my anxious ear* (L 2).

The jazz-player of text L 27, actually hearing music, figures the noises in his ear as rushing wind, waves on sand, thunder and a waterfall.

In so far as rhythm in the trigger corresponds with rhythm or pulsation felt in ecstasy, one can suppose the rhythm of music and of poetry to show an obvious correspondence of this kind.

The noises heard in the ear or head are compared with water noises, wind noises and thunder. All these and others may figure as communicative voices. Wordsworth, in the passage quoted earlier, speaks of the water as 'roaring with one voice' and later, when the scene has become 'the type of a majestic intellect', is 'intent to hear' voices issuing from the dark abyss of water. Tennyson, who, as shown above, links noises in the ear, sea-waves and music, says that what he was in fact hearing was

> *the hum of men,*
> *Or other things talking in unknown tongues...*

The jazz-musician links *his* noises (wind, waves, waterfall) with 'the voice of the world'. The voice of the visitant to St. John the Divine was 'as the sound of many waters'.[1] Wind and babbling brooks are both common triggers and common types for communicative voices.

Water is one of the most common of triggers and feelings of liquidity are almost always described in concrete water images. Those most often found are: the spring or fountain, felt to correspond with liquid surging in the heart or breast; swift streams or torrents, felt to correspond with (*a*) a swift internal flow suddenly released, and (*b*), less often, a stream of newly flowing thoughts—see the ever-widening stream of H. Warner Allen's text (L 11) and the continuous stream of waters in the Wordsworth passage on p. 215 above; slow and gentle flow, often into a body of still water (or either slow flow or water alone) felt to correspond with feelings of withdrawal ecstasies.

Fire-images are so common in descriptions of ecstatic feelings that I

---

[1] *Rev.* i. 15.

find it strange that I cannot substantiate fire as a trigger. Thoughts may be described, as they are by Tennyson, as 'rapid as fire'. Supernatural visitants may have eyes that burn like fire, as did those of the visitants to Tennyson and to St. John the Divine. Fire is a symbol of vitality and life, of purification;[1] burning ardour is a common image of love and feelings of heat are common in ecstasy. More, fire would seem to have many qualities that could make it an effective trigger: it is bright and shining, it burns upwards, it roars as it burns.[2] But no instance of actual fire serving as a trigger to intensity ecstasy has ever come my way.

Looking into a safe domestic fire may bring about feelings of withdrawal, perhaps through a mild hypnosis occasioned by the flicker, as in the cases of Carlo Levi and C 15, though in the former case the initial withdrawal was succeeded by an intensity ecstasy.

Feelings of enlargement, which may include mental enlargement, are expressed by the image of a tributary-fed stream by H. Warner Allen (L 11) and as 'one swelling harmony' by the clergyman of text R 3. People sometimes feel enlarged as by air inside them (see p. 80) and creative energy may be figured as a wind or breeze, as it often is by Wordsworth. Wind or breeze is mentioned as a trigger by several people in the groups and Wordsworth, we may note, was said by his sister to delight in 'starlight walks and winter winds'.[3]

It is not only with quasi-physical feelings that certain qualities of triggers are felt to correspond. The more purely mental feelings characteristic of ecstasies are also shown to have some relation with qualities sometimes felt to be of the very nature of the trigger, sometimes imaginatively attributed to it.[4]

Time-ecstasies, as I have shown earlier (see p. 106 et seq.), are almost always triggered by what I call unitive symbols—objects, events, and ideas which can be seen as long-enduring, sometimes even ever-enduring, older than the life of man and sometimes of mankind. Such are

[1] See Hügel: M.E.R., Vol. II, pp. 239–40 and 244.
[2] The identification by Freud of fire as a phallos-symbol would, if correct, seem to make it likely that fire would be a trigger, particularly if, as Dr. Robert Plank suggests, ecstasy is 'a triumphant assertion of the phallos'. 'On Seeing the Salamander' in *The Psychoanalytic Study of the Child*, Vol. XII (New York, 1957).
[3] Quoted by Helen Darbishire, *The Poet Wordsworth*, p. 18.
[4] 'if a dead object elucidates animate behaviour, the reason is that the inanimate object is itself viewed anthropomorphically...human behaviour is made clear only through reference to something else which is in turn explained by analogy with human behaviour.' Bruno Snell, *The Discovery of the Mind*, trans. T. G. Rosenmeyer (Oxford, 1953), ch. ix, p. 200.

mountains, stars, sea; primitive and barely changing forms such as fossils, pebbles; ruins; ideas such as Art, Beauty, the Word, Truth, God, which can by a hundred quotations be demonstrated as enduring, eternal, indestructible; and growing things such as flowers, trees, babies, seen as capable of perpetual renewal. And all these are common triggers not only to time-ecstasies but to others as well.

Mathematics and abstract sciences are often seen as having, of their nature, qualities that imply timelessness and perpetuity. Wordsworth writes how, from sloth, he

> turned to abstract science, and there sought
> Work for the reasoning faculty enthroned
> Where the disturbances of space and time...
> ...find no admission.[1]

And Sir Thomas Browne,

> 'All things began in order, so shall they end, and so shall they begin again; according to the ordainer of order and mystical mathematics of the city of heaven.' [2]

And Plato:

> ' "it must, I think, be admitted that the objects of that knowledge are eternal and not liable to change and decay." '
> ' "Yes, there's no question of that: the objects of geometrical knowledge are eternal." ' [3]

The feelings of adamic ecstasies are often expressed in terms of symbolic people or things, felt to correspond with the state of the ecstatic after he has lost his normal worldliness, sinfulness, and intellectual capacity and been renewed in joy; such are children, simple people, some animals, flowers, etc., and all these can, as actualities, act as triggers.

Ecstatic feelings often arise when leaving the town for the country, an act felt to correspond with the feelings of release so characteristic of ecstasy. We find such feelings in the Gissing passage given on p. 64, in Keats's sonnet 'To one who has been long in city pent' and in Wordsworth leaving (probably) Bristol for (probably) Racedown.[4] Both Wordsworth and Keats speak of the city as a prison or pen, and it is worth pointing out that this is far from as inevitable an image as

---

[1] *Prel.* (1850), xi, ll. 328–33.   [2] *The Garden of Cyrus* (1658), ch. v.
[3] *The Republic*, trans. H. D. P. Lee (Penguin edn., 1955), Bk. 7, 527, p. 294.
[4] *Prel.*, i, ll. 6–9.

it may seem in an ecstatic context. For many people the city has always stood for a richer, freer life than the countryside can give.

In this context we must distinguish between feelings of contact in the sense of making contact with, being in touch with (someone or something), and tactile sensations. I have already commented that no feelings of touch with the hands play any part in any descriptions of ecstasy (see pp. 190–1), though one would imagine that tactile sensations were a considerable part of the satisfaction to be gained from many triggers—certainly from caressing the loved one and, whether in fact or imagination, from sculpture, flowers, water—who sits in reach of water and fails to put his hand in it?—and from fleecy clouds.

We do however find ecstasy figured as an embrace of love, and because of this ecstasy is often said to be a type of or a surrogate for sexual intercourse. But those who have known sexual intercourse do not emphasize feelings of contact[1] or use the language of love in describing ecstasies derived from it (see p. 148).

It is characteristic of knowledge believed to have been gained in ecstasy that it should feel as if it had come from elsewhere; when noises in the trigger are figured as communicative voices, a feeling of contact with someone or something may be implied.

That mountain-tops and bright light should often be felt to symbolize feelings of knowledge seems reasonable enough; we do in fact see more from a mountain-top than a valley, more in bright light than in dullness or darkness. To figure knowledge in terms of a flash of light is not perhaps so obvious; flashes of light may be and in ecstasy often are described as blinding. New knowledge may also be figured in terms of wind or ever-widening water, used also to figure feelings of enlargement.

A very common feeling of ecstasy is that a new mental unification has been made. For this, both Wordsworth and Nietzsche use images of something falling from the skies, Nietzsche of answers falling like hail, Wordsworth of words falling like snowflakes to take their proper place in the poem he was making (see p. 85); I do not know an instance of hail triggering an ecstasy though snow is not uncommon. Then Nietzsche gives, as a feeling of his experience, that of 'problems solved'; Q 45 gives as a trigger 'solving mathematical problems'. The verbal correspondence here is close, and it is not, I think, straining the

[1] Feelings of contact are no more common in sex-triggered ecstasies than in ecstasies triggered by other means; see Appendix D, Table 8.

possibility of a relation between qualities of triggers and feelings of ecstasies to notice that the unification of mental material is frequently a trigger and the feeling that mental material *has* been unified a frequent feeling of ecstasy.

For this feeling that a new mental unification or pattern has been achieved the image of harmony is often used. Wordsworth writes:

> The mind of Man is fram'd even like the breath
> And harmony of music. There is a dark
> Invisible workmanship that reconciles
> Discordant elements, and makes them move
> In one society.[1]

In *Tintern Abbey*, on the other hand, it is the power of harmony in the trigger that, says Wordsworth, 'quiets our eye' and enables us to 'see into the heart of things'. A feeling that there is harmony in the trigger may induce ecstasy which, in its turn, enables us to achieve harmony.

Things felt to typify harmonious relations we should, then, expect to find as triggers to ecstasy. The word *harmony* implies, of course, music, one of the most commonly effective of all triggers, but harmonious relations may be felt to be characteristic of other triggers than music. *Harmony*, says the dictionary, is 'Combination or adaptation of parts, elements, or related things, so as to form a consistent and orderly whole'. Harmony in this sense is felt to be characteristic of almost all effective man-made triggers.[2]

The relations felt ideally to prevail among members of a society are another interpretation of harmony; in the quotation given above Wordsworth relates this image both to music and to the workings of the mind. The ideal city, can be as we have seen, an idea of trigger force (see pp. 192–4).

Feelings of renewal, of new life are attached to such triggers as childbirth and spring, with the growth of flowers and trees. Feelings of satisfaction are often expressed in terms of eating satisfying foods and these, in their turn, may help to trigger ecstasies (see p. 204).

---

[1] *Prel.*, i, ll. 351–5.
[2] I have wondered whether this was a consideration that Berenson had in mind when demanding an understanding of art as a pre-requisite to appreciating beauty in nature (see p. 181). If for him the essential quality of a trigger was visually harmonious relations, then it seems reasonable that he should need to be able to translate nature into these terms before he could enjoy it. But visually harmonious relations are not the only ecstasy-inducing qualities that natural objects are felt to provide.

Some triggers, then, have or are felt to have qualities corresponding with feelings of the experiences they may induce. A waterfall may correspond with feelings of a swift flow of liquid, of flickering or flashing light, of enlargement, of communicative noises; a mountain-top may correspond with up-feelings, feelings of enhanced knowledge, and so on. But I do not know whether these correspondences are in fact relevant to the ability of some triggers to induce ecstasy, or, if they are relevant, what the relation is.

Some triggers, notably works of art and natural objects, are described as beautiful, and some people say or imply that being beautiful is what makes a trigger effective for them.

Few people would, I think, refuse the epithet *beautiful* to a work of art that had moved them to ecstasy. Some but not all natural objects are found beautiful by people on whom they are effective, and some people imply that beauty is what they seek in nature. But the word *beautiful* is not normally used to describe some effective natural triggers, such as the wind or the noise of waters. Occasionally it is the quality of *not* having beauty that makes an object an effective trigger; the grain of sand in which Blake saw a world, the meanest flower that moved Wordsworth to thoughts too deep for tears, have of intention no such qualities of beauty as one might find in a diamond or a rose.

Mental constructs need not take the form of works of art to be seen as having beauty. Frank writes,

'For the mathematician, Einstein's new concept of gravitation was characterised by beauty and logical simplicity.' [1]

But this may not be a usual way of speaking, and certainly many other triggers are not seen as beautiful. We should not describe copulation or childbirth or creative work as beautiful, though we might well so characterize the *ideas* of sexual love and childbirth and creative work. We should not normally speak of our own movements in exercise as beautiful or of food as beautiful or of a conversation with friends as beautiful, even on the occasions when these things induced ecstasy.

It seems that the quality of being beautiful or being found beautiful may be necessary to some triggers but certainly is not to all, though it may be that some people are moved to ecstasy only by things they find beautiful.

[1] *Einstein, His Life and Times*, p. 168.

It is possible, then, that in the case of many triggers, some properties which are of that trigger's very nature or some ideas which are almost inalienably attached to it may be significant in inducing an experience characterized by feelings corresponding to properties or ideas felt to be inherent in the trigger. It is however demonstrably true that associations which may accidentally become attached to an object, event, or idea may be equally potent in inducing or inhibiting ecstatic response, irrespective of the actual nature of the trigger. Two obvious examples appeared on p. 179-80, where a bird-cry was assumed to be a motor-horn and responded to as such, and a piece of blue paper was taken to be a flower and momentarily responded to as if it had been a flower.

There can hardly exist for any culturally conditioned human being any object, event, or idea that is not more or less loaded with associations, and where ecstasy and response-experiences are concerned, it is obviously important that potential triggers shall not become loaded with anti-trigger associations. In Chapter XVIII I have shown some of the protests, both individual and social, that are made when this happens or seems likely to happen, and in the next chapter I shall indicate the reverse process, the attempt to give to non-trigger or even anti-trigger things some of the lustre and prestige we normally attach to triggers (see p. 231). The point I want to stress here is the probability that the associations attached, either inalienably or accidentally, to things may be as important in inducing or inhibiting ecstatic response as is the nature of the things themselves.

This chapter has not attempted to do more than indicate a few areas in which there seems to be a relationship, which may be significant, between the properties of some objects, events, and ideas and the nature of experiences with which they are almost certainly causally connected. All I can usefully add are a few questions to which I do not begin to know the answers or where or how the answers should be sought:

Can all triggers induce all varieties of ecstasy for people on whom they are effective? Or do different triggers necessarily induce different varieties of experience?

Could some triggers usefully be categorized as minor or secondary ones in that—for most people, at least—they can induce only response experiences but not ecstasy?

Can what most 'cultured' people would regard as surrogates for nature or art—e.g. Palm Court music, calendar art, municipal gardening—give to some people experiences assimilable to ecstatic or response experiences?

Can the same trigger be equally effective on the same person on more than one occasion?

What constitutes readiness to respond to a trigger?

What is the significance of the fact that many apparent triggers to withdrawal ecstasies may also be triggers to desolation-experiences—for instance, things with *dark* and *down* connotations like valleys, forests, chasms?

The analogy with food is, I believe, a useful one. Until we know the needs of the body we do not know what properties to look for in food-stuffs. Until we understand the nature of the psycho-physical events that accompany ecstatic experiences, we do not know what properties to look for in the triggers that induce them.[1]

---

[1] Investigators may, perhaps, be encouraged by the thought that it is only some two hundred years since Hume wrote: 'nature...has afforded us only the knowledge of a few superficial qualities of objects; while she conceals from us those powers and principles on which the influence of these objects entirely depends. Our senses inform us of the colour, weight, and consistence of bread; but neither sense nor reason can ever inform us of those qualities which fit it for the nourishment and support of a human body.' *Inquiry Concerning Human Understanding* (1748), Section IV, Part II.

CHAPTER XXII

Language and Ecstatic Experience

(i) Rhetorical Devices

A number of rhetorical devices seem to derive from the existence and nature of ecstatic and response experiences. Sometimes these devices are used in descriptions of what an ecstatic (or response) experience feels like. Sometimes they are used as a reference to or an ideograph of such an experience, where the experience itself is not described but the idea of it, with its associated values and implications, is to be conveyed.

In the latter case such uses are mostly to be found in imaginative writing and notably in poetry. The massive subject of poetic imagery is beyond my scope and I shall touch on it only in so far as it is necessary to do so in order to show how some of these devices 'work'. My examples are taken from writings in English; it would be interesting to know how far similar devices exist in other languages of the same culture-group.

I do not say that where these devices are used, specific and concrete references to ecstatic experiences are always intended. Often these devices are weakened to the point of formality and intended only to make vague references to feelings universally recognized as beneficial and valuable. It is, however, my suggestion that it is from ecstatic and response experiences that these devices derive, and that to notice them adds to comprehension of the context in which they are used and, in the many cases when these devices involve the mention of common triggers, helps to establish the fact that there is a widespread recognition of such triggers as forming a limited group whose members can be invoked almost indiscriminately for the purpose of inducing similar emotions or conveying similar impressions.

I have given names to these devices because in special relation to ecstasy (and in most cases outside it) names for them do not exist, and the first, and a very common one, I call *trigger-lists*.

More or less extended lists of objects, events, and ideas are given to indicate a single range of feelings to which they all give rise. Their capacity for inducing such feelings is the only or the most significant characteristic which the objects on the list have in common.

In the questionnaire group trigger-lists were often elicited by the question 'What has induced [ecstasy] in you?' In these cases we know that the things on such lists as 'mathematics, mountains, poetry' (Q 6) or 'natural beauty, writing something new, sex' (Q 9) have in common the quality of being able to induce ecstasy for the people concerned.

But where we encounter such lists in literature or in general usage, the specific quality of ability to induce ecstatic or response experiences is seldom mentioned. I believe this is always implicit but the person proffering the list may suggest only that the things on it are valuable for unnamed reasons or because encounter with them brings beneficial results without reference to the experiences from which such results derive.

Where one encounters a list of objects, events, and ideas containing the kinds of things that are most commonly triggers, one can often confirm the intention of a trigger-list by considering the insertion of other objects, events, and ideas that might seem to fall within the general pattern of the group being presented but whose inclusion would palpably distort the intention.

'For the experiences with which criticism is concerned are exceptionally accessible, we have only to open the book, stand before the picture, have the music played, spread out the rug, pour out the wine, and the material upon which the critic works is presently before us.' [1]

This group is, we are told, one of things which are the material for criticism, and all the objects on it may be found in living-rooms. But if we added to it, say, a telephone or a lamp-shade, both proper material for criticism in terms of industrial design, or perhaps a cup of cocoa, we should distort the intention. The rug, it is made clear, is an *objet d'art*, not a useful object for standing on, such a rug as Zaehner chose, with other art objects, to look at when under the influence of mescalin

---

[1] Richards : *Principles* p. 5.

(see p. 267), and, incidentally, a useful and rare example of a craft-object, albeit, not one in use, being indicated as a trigger.

> *yes, in spite of all,*
> *Some shape of beauty moves away the pall*
> *From our dark spirits. Such the sun, the moon,*
> *Trees old, and young, sprouting a shady boon*
> *For simple sheep; and such are daffodils*
> *With the green world they live in; and clear rills*
> *That for themselves a cooling covert make*
> *'Gainst the hot season; the mid forest brake,*
> *Rich with a sprinkling of fair musk-rose blooms:*
> *And such too is the grandeur of the dooms*
> *We have imagined for the mighty dead;*
> *All lovely tales that we have heard or read:*
> *An endless fountain of immortal drink,*
> *Pouring unto us from the heaven's brink.*[1]

The function of the things named is to move away the pall from dark spirits. This could often be achieved by going to a music-hall or a party. But a music-hall or a party would not be congruous in this list; neither could be spoken of as 'a shape of beauty'; more, the principal function of a music-hall is to provide something funny that will make you laugh, and seldom if ever is something funny that will make you laugh named as a trigger to ecstatic experience. But there is no incongruity in grouping natural objects with memories of tragedies and of lovely tales, for we recognize all these as capable of triggering ecstatic experience.

'the child...was perfectly quiet now, but not asleep—only soothed by sweet porridge and warmth into that wide-gazing calm which makes us older human beings, with our inward turmoil, feel a certain awe in the presence of a little child, such as we feel before some quiet majesty or beauty in the earth or sky—before a steady glowing planet, or a full-flowered eglantine, or the bending trees over a silent pathway.'[2]

The common quality is named—that of arousing awe. It is hard to think of anything else significantly in common between a child, a planet, an eglantine, and some trees.

[1] John Keats, *Endymion*, Bk. I, ll. 11–24.
[2] George Eliot, *Silas Marner* (London, 1861; Everyman edn., 1906), ch. xiii, pp. 160–1.

'[The doctor] thought a little and then said:

'"I have found the Zoological Gardens of service to many of my patients. I should prescribe for Mr. Pontifex a course of the larger mammals... Then...I should send him, say, to morning service at the Abbey before he goes. He need not stay longer than the *Te Deum*. I don't know why, but *Jubilates* are seldom satisfactory. Just let him look in at the Abbey, and sit quietly in Poets' Corner till the main part of the music is over... then next day send him down to Gravesend by boat. By all means let him go to the theatres in the evenings..."

'As soon as we were out of the house we took a cab to Regent's Park, and spent a couple of hours in sauntering round the different houses. Perhaps it was on account of what the doctor had told me, but I certainly became aware of a feeling I had never experienced before. I mean that I was receiving an influx of new life, or deriving new ways of looking at life—which is the same thing'. [1]

The activities listed are all recommended as being life-enhancing. The group into which they fall could be that of recreations available in London, but the inclusion of evening-parties or, again, of music-halls would palpably distort the intention. What are recommended are the trigger activities of looking at wild animals, going on the river, visiting theatres, thinking of poets and listening to religious music—not, be it noted, taking part in a religious service.

'She deliberately summoned up images that she knew would help her; Stalin's face of monumental assurance, Lenin's face of eager, out-thrust force, Turner's *Crossing the Brook*, a line out of Meredith: "The rapture of the forward view." Then without thought she hummed the opening of Beethoven's *Fifth Symphony*.' [2]

This last example is, as trigger-lists go, perhaps rather specialized.

The device I call *trigger comparison* is simply an aspect of the use of metaphor and simile, and one that we usually take for granted, the comparison of two or more things whose only significant common feature is their presumed ability to arouse similar feelings. When Burns writes that his love is like a red, red rose and a melody that's sweetly played in tune, we do not assume that his love is red or sweetly played in tune, nor yet that she is petal-soft or goes up and down a scale. Burns's love

[1] Samuel Butler, *The Way of All Flesh* (London, 1903; Travellers' Library edn., 1926), ch. lxxix, pp. 387–8.
[2] Jack Lindsay, quoted *Times Literary Supplement* leader, April 29, 1955.

and the rose and the melody have in common the quality of rousing similar emotions, and love and flowers and music have in common only the quality of being triggers to ecstatic or response experiences.

In the next example the writer himself makes it clear that the ability to arouse similar emotions is what cricket and poetry (with its subjects) and music have in common, all being properly called beautiful:

'cricket by Woolley which has inexplicably found me murmuring to myself (that I might get the best out of it):
> Lovely are the curves of the white owl sweeping,
> Wary in the dusk lit by one large star.

I admit, O reader, that an innings by Woolley has nothing to do with owls and dusk and starlight. I am trying to describe an experience of the fancy. I am talking of cadences, of dying-falls common to all the beauty of the world.' [1]

Explaining the quality of one potential trigger in terms of the feelings known to be roused by another is a device frequently, indeed almost inevitably, used in criticism:

'Raphael's little group has the flowing rhythm of a formal 15th-century lyric, a *villanella* or *terzetto*, both naïve and elaborate. It is far from the ethereal music of Botticelli.' [2]

Sometimes not a particular range or intensity of ecstatic feelings are compared but rather the feelings of a major ecstatic experience:

'He is Himself the poem, the symphony, which expresses His unique vision of truth.' [3]

Often many devices involving triggers are combined in one passage: the following example shows both trigger-list and trigger comparison, and presents the latter device in various ways:

'I send you some of the most wonderful whiskey that ever drove the skeleton from the feast, or painted landscapes in the brain of man.

[1] Neville Cardus, *Autobiography* (London, 1947), Pt. I, pp. 129–30.
[2] Kenneth Clark, *The Nude* (London, 1956), p. 103. That such comparisons can be made does, I think, support my earlier suggestion that ecstatic and response experiences vary with what induces them, though in ways probably too subtle for analysis (see p. 174). These comparisons would be meaningful only if Clark and many of his readers could identify the feelings evoked by Raphael's group and a formal fifteenth-century lyric as similar to each other and different from feelings evoked by Botticelli.
[3] E.U: M.W., p. 149.

It is the mingled souls of wheat and corn. In it, you will find the sunshine and the shadow that chased each other over the billowy fields, the breath of June, the carol of the lark, the dew of night, the wealth of summer, and autumn's rich content, all golden with imprisoned light. Drink it, and you will hear the voices of men and maidens singing the "Harvest Home," mingled with the laughter of children. Drink it, and you will feel within your blood the star-led dawns, the dreamy, tawny dusks of many perfect days.' [1]

Trigger assimilation is a deceitful device which will, when successful, appear as an example of a trigger-list, a trigger comparison, or some other device involving triggers. The method is to compare a trigger with something not usually accepted as a trigger or to insert such a non-trigger in a list of triggers. The aim is that by association with triggers the non-trigger may pass itself off as a trigger and so gain some of the lustre and prestige we accord to triggers. This device is much used for the purposes of politics and commerce. The trigger-list by Jack Lindsay (quoted on p. 229) which associates Lenin and Stalin with Turner, Meredith, and Beethoven, is, no doubt, perfectly sincere; but in a writer of whose credentials we were less assured, we might suspect that the aim of such a list was to rub off on Stalin and Lenin some of the lustre we accord to the other names.

In political speeches and in commercial advertising the device is ubiquitous. One example must suffice:

'How can a lover describe his beloved? How may a mystic communicate his vision? How does a mother describe her child? We are faced with the same inadequacy of language when we try to tell you of the superlative qualities of the Citroën D.S.19... You'll know no rest, no content, until this proud gleaming heaven-on-earth is your own... It's beyond praise because praise, spoken, sung or exquisitely rhymed, can only present a pale shadow of the magic of a car that takes you, as you slide under the steering-wheel, ten years into the future.' [2]

Notice how, in addition to triggers, feelings of ecstasy are introduced—feelings of ineffability, seeing light, being in heaven, and timelessness practicably translated into 'ten years into the future'.

Trigger assimilation may as well be conveyed visually as in words.

[1] Quoted by William James in *Principles of Psychology* (1890), Vol. II, p. 469.
[2] Advertisement in the *Sunday Times*, April 13, 1958.

The use of children is common in posters and advertisements for political parties and—perhaps rather oddly—for manufacturers of steel and primary chemical products; but as a specific instance, I would adduce a recent advertisement presenting a dew-besprinkled rose beside a roll of lavatory paper. More, I think, that the quality of softness was supposed to be common to both.[1]

The intent to deceive is not, of course, always deliberate. Sometimes what seems like trigger assimilation may stem from an idiosyncratic judgement:

> 'And the message of Mozart in music is strikingly akin to that of Barrie in literature. It is the message of the wind, and the flowers of the field.' [2]

The *inserted trigger* device was to some extent demonstrated in the last chapter where I tried to show that certain triggers have or are felt to have qualities that correspond with certain feelings of ecstasy. In this device, such triggers are used illustratively to 'stand for' such feelings in descriptions of ecstasies.

I shall give three sets of examples, all taken from my texts. In the first, the inserted triggers are all mountains or hills, and in none of these cases was mountains or hills the trigger actually inducing the experience; these inducing triggers included music, nature, poetry, recollection.

> the world is surveyed as if from a mountain-top (L 6); she reaches a station scarcely lower than that whence angels looked down on the dreamer of Bethel, and her eye seeks, and her soul possesses the vision of life as she wishes it (L 14); coming to it round the side of a hill—and he was alone on the hill, blasting and challenging the sky—the force of the hill I was on, where I saw nothing and everything and it was beautiful (L 27).[3]

The feelings of ecstasy for which hills and mountains are here introduced as appropriate images are up-feelings, feelings of knowledge, feelings of intensity followed by release.

In the next set of examples the inserted triggers are all water; the

---

[1] My article 'Sacred and Profane' in the *Twentieth Century*, February, 1959, gives many more examples of the use of this device in advertising.

[2] Thomas Moult, *Barrie* (London, 1928), p. 181.

[3] Other examples are provided by Q 50, L 7, R 18.

inducing triggers include music, a mountain-top, art, 'beauty', and in one case (L 2), water:

> the cup is being filled (Q 35); the hum of men, Or other things talking in unknown tongues... Beat like a far wave on my anxious ear (L 2); a wordless stream of complex feelings in which the experience of Union combined with the rhythmic emotion of the music like a sunbeam striking with iridescence the spray above a waterfall—a stream that was continually swollen by tributaries of associated Experience (L 11); that spring whose bright fresh bubbling in her heart keeps it green (L 14).[1]

The feelings for which water-images are here felt appropriate are, of course, feelings of liquidity, and also feelings of intensity, enlargement, satisfaction, knowledge, pulsation, renewal.

In this last set of examples, music is the inserted trigger; the inducing triggers include mountains, water, religion:

> Nanda Devi like a blast of trumpets (Q 44); Glistening and foaming, flowing and fanning and roaring, the entire symphony...becomes one thought, which becomes one with feeling (L 9); [the experience] was like the effect of some great orchestra when all the separate notes have melted into one swelling harmony (R 3); Two enormous menacing peaks towered above me, and as I saw them through the swirling mist, I seemed to hear a mass of orchestras all playing a triumphant sinister minor chord (C 36).

All these music-images 'stand for' feelings of intensity; all but the last stands for joy; L 9 and R 3 powerfully convey feelings of unity as well as of enlargement.

In some desolation-ecstasies (e.g. that of C 36) only desolation triggers seem to be present but the experience none the less changes from desolation to ecstasy. In others, ecstasy triggers suddenly appear in a formerly desolate scene. An example is Richard Feverel's sudden discovery of the chapel with its statue of the Virgin in a dank, desolate forest. It is this latter form that has, I believe, given rise to the device of *trigger contrast* in which the effect of an ecstasy trigger is enhanced and made more poignant by its relationship to triggers to desolation.

---

[1] Other examples are provided by Q 24, L 23a, L 26, L 27, R 8.

The device is extremely common in poetry. To begin with a simple example:

> *I did not lose my heart in summer's even,*
> *When roses to the moonrise burst apart:*
> *When plumes were under heel and lead was flying,*
> *In blood and smoke and flame I lost my heart.*[1]

The trigger love is here associated not with the triggers of roses and moonlight but with such triggers to desolation as cruelty, death, dirt, darkness.

Another simple example:

> *The nightingales are singing near*
> *The Convent of the Sacred Heart,*
>
> *And sang within the bloody wood*
> *When Agamemnon cried aloud,*
> *And let their liquid siftings fall*
> *To stain the stiff dishonoured shroud.*[2]

The contrasts here are too obvious to need pointing out; the nightingale is in any case one of those triggers which must, of its nature, imply the device of trigger contrast since the nightingale, with traditionally the most beautiful song of all birds, traditionally sings in the dark, her breast against a thorn, lamenting her ancient sorrow.

The intention behind poetry which makes use of this device is often a moral one and particularly so, I believe, when the contrasting desolation trigger is not natural but man-made:

> *A Robin Red breast in a Cage*
> *Puts all Heaven in a Rage.*[3]
>
> *Oh hush thee, my baby,*
> *Thy cradle's in pawn:*
> *No blankets to cover thee*
> *Cold and forlorn.*
> *The stars in the bright sky*
> *Look down and are dumb*
> *At the heir of the ages*
> *Asleep in a slum.*[4]

[1] A. E. Housman, *More Poems* (London, 1936), xxxvii, p. 55.
[2] T. S. Eliot, 'Sweeney Among the Nightingales'.
[3] William Blake, 'Auguries of Innocence'.
[4] Cecil Day Lewis, 'A Carol'.

In such cases as these the contrast is more than between ecstasy and desolation; it is contrast between good and evil, right and wrong.

But by a paradoxical inversion the 'bad' thing may come to be seen as good. Christ was born in a stable, the robin is in a cage, the heir of the ages in a slum. We set up what Wright Mills has called a 'counter-élite' and believe that it is to stables and cages and slums, to places where poverty and misery abound, that we must go to seek what is good.[1]

I said earlier that models for the adamic state must be able to be seen as (a) perfectly happy, (b) as uncorrupted by knowledge, (c) as in a lower state than one believed to be possible when perfect knowledge has been attained (see p. 105). These types are what I am calling *symbols of innocence*.

The obvious symbol is the mythical Adam himself. Three others that readily come to mind and are often written of in very similar ways are children, flowers, wild animals:

> —*A simple Child,*
> *That lightly draws its breath,*
> *And feels its life in every limb,*
> *What should it know of death?*[2]

> *This season's Daffodil,*
> *She never hears*
> *What change, what chance, what chill,*
> *Cut down last year's:*
> *But with bold countenance,*
> *And knowledge small,*
> *Esteems her seven days' continuance*
> *To be perpetual.*[3]

> *Their kind across the desert range*
> *Where tulips spring from stones,*
> *Not knowing they will suffer change*
> *Or vultures pick their bones.*

---

[1] 'In western society...there is a long tradition and varied images of the poor, the exploited, and the oppressed as the truly virtuous, the wise and the blessed. Stemming from Christian tradition, this moral idea of a counter-elite, composed of essentially higher types condemned to a lowly station, may be and has been used by the underlying population to justify harsh criticism of ruling elites and to celebrate utopian images of a new elite to come.' C. Wright Mills: *The Power Elite* (New York, 1956; Galaxy edn., 1959), ch. i., p. 14.

[2] Wordsworth, 'We are Seven', P.W., Vol. I., p. 236.

[3] Rudyard Kipling, 'Cities and Thrones and Powers'.

Their strength's eternal in their sight,
They rule the terror of the night,
They overtake the deer in flight,
And in their arrogance they smite;
But I am sage, if they are strong:
Man's love is transient as his death is long.[1]

Other such symbols are, as indicated in Chapter IX, pre-pelasgian man, pre-cortical man (if one can call him man), the Noble Savage; and simple man in various forms such as the Arcadian shepherd, the craftsman, the Worker of the World.

Each of these symbols has its Golden Time—childhood, antiquity, the middle ages; and each has its Golden Place—a garden, an Arcadia, a tropic isle. Often the writer who makes use of these types is concerned to make of the world a place fit for symbols to live in, a timeless and unchanging society that itself symbolizes a state of ecstasy.

A frequent property of symbols of innocence is their possession of simple wisdom valued more highly than cultivated wisdom. This was, of course, a property of many of the characters in whom Wordsworth found subject-matter.

A symbol of innocence is often used to heighten the effectiveness of a trigger contrast. A simple example is Blake's poem, 'The Little Boy Lost'. A little boy is a symbol of innocence who should be, as the poem suggests, safe with his father; or he might find safety on the Echoing Green, Blake's Golden Place for children. Instead he is lost, alone in the dark night.

In discussing trigger contrast above, I suggested that by a kind of paradoxical inversion the 'bad' thing may come to be seen as good, since it is in contrast with the bad that the good is most apparent. This is often particularly effective when the good thing, the trigger, is a symbol of innocence. When the Holy Child lies in a stable, the heir of the ages in a slum, then we are especially moved to value the slum and the stable as the places where we must go to seek the good and, perhaps, seek to restore it to its proper place:

> *As Tom was a-sleeping, he had such a sight!*
> *That thousands of sweepers, Dick, Joe, Ned, & Jack,*
> *Were all of them lock'd up in coffins of black.*

[1] Victoria Sackville-West, 'The Greater Cats'.

And by came an Angel who had a bright key,
And he open'd the coffins & set them all free;
Then down a green plain leaping, laughing, they run,
And wash in a river, and shine in the Sun.[1]

Trigger mutability is to some extent a variant of trigger contrast, though the beliefs usually related to it are of a rather different kind. It arises from the paradox that many triggers which can induce feelings of immortality or eternity are themselves subject to decay.

Thus the device of trigger contrast is implicit in examples of trigger mutability, since the idea of mutability implies contrast with those feelings of perpetuity so common in experiences of ecstasy which may themselves be introduced by triggers that are mutability-images. Sometimes, as in the example that follows, the trigger contrast is explicit— the beautiful woman contrasted with her necessary decay:

> *No rose but fades: no glory but must pass:*
> *No hue but dims: no precious silk but frets.*
> *Her beauty must go underneath the grass,*
> *Under the long roots of the violets.*[2]

'Beauty vanishes, beauty passes—' Examples crowd to the memory. There are few triggers that cannot be seen as images of mutability.

It is from the fact that they are inevitably images of mutability that ruins, I believe, derive much of their effectiveness as triggers. Shelley includes them in a trigger-list of the mutable:

> *Follow where all is fled!—Rome's azure sky,*
> *Flowers, ruins, statues, music, words, are weak*
> *The glory they transfuse with fitting truth to speak.*[3]

But ruins, like many triggers, relate to several of these devices, and several devices may be combined in a very few lines of poetry:

> *Time and fevers burn away*
> *Individual beauty from*
> *Thoughtful children, and the grave*
> *Proves the child ephemeral:*

---

[1] William Blake, 'The Chimney Sweeper' from *Songs of Innocence*.
[2] John Masefield, 'Waste'.
[3] From *Adonais*, verse lii.

But in my arms till break of day
Let the living creature lie,
Mortal, guilty, but to me
The entirely beautiful.[1]

The first four lines combine three devices: trigger mutability—the child is ephemeral ; trigger contrast—the thoughtful child and the grave ; and the child, the symbol of innocence. The second four lines also use three devices: that of trigger contrast (the living creature, mortal and guilty, contrasted with the entirely beautiful), and two devices I have not yet described—the *totality* device with 'the entirely beautiful' and the *definite article* device, in the same phrase.

This device of trigger mutability may as well be used as shorthand for the belief that there is nothing immortal, nothing lasting in life, as to convey that somewhere, as ecstasy promises, beyond the world of mutable triggers there exists Beauty beyond the appearances of beauty, the Rose that cannot wither, thy God, thy life, thy cure— 'It is the search for Something not subject to change, that leads the soul up to God'.[2]

The *unitive symbol* device is the converse of the last discussed in that it is not the ephemeral but the enduring nature of the trigger that is stressed. In its most typical form the writer takes a symbol of the unchanging and timeless and contrasts it with the transitory that fades and passes while the unitive symbol continues to exist. A simple example is Housman's 'Then 't was the Roman, now 't is I'[3] where I and the Roman and Uricon stand for transitoriness, the wind, that blew, as it blows today, when Uricon stood, for the unitive symbol.

Certain symbols tend to recur: primitive forms unchanged through the life of mankind—jelly-fish, fossils, rocks, stars, the sea, etc. (see p. 106 et seq.); words or the Word, both in its fundamental religious expression (Richard Church, in text B 23b, finds his trigger in *John* i. 1), and as used by the poets—'The word, and nought else, in time endures' (Humbert Wolfe); time itself, in personified or idealized form (e.g. 'Time, you old gipsy man, Will you not stay...?' (Ralph Hodgson)); art and the artist ('Art is the currency of the infinite... Nothing lasts, but there will always be Louvres in the world, so long as people are

---

[1] W. H. Auden, 'Lullaby'.
[2] Butler: W.M., p. 34.
[3] *A Shropshire Lad*, (London, 1896), no. xxxi.

human beings and so long as there are people like Picasso to fill them' [1]); and the symbols of religion have an obvious and compelling part here.

Many triggers may stand, as ruins do, at one time as unitive symbols, at another as symbols of trigger mutability. One poet may write 'No rose but fades', another,

> *Oh, no man knows*
> *Through what wild centuries*
> *Roves back the rose.* [2]

Or in a single poem a trigger may be seen at one and the same time as a symbol of mutability because it must decay and as a unitive symbol because it has the power of self-renewal:

> *Cities and Thrones and Powers*
> *Stand in Time's eye,*
> *Almost as long as flowers,*
> *Which daily die:*
> *But, as new buds put forth*
> *To glad new men,*
> *Out of the spent and unconsidered Earth*
> *The Cities rise again.* [3]

Here, Time's eye is a unitive symbol only; but cities, thrones, powers, flowers, and men serve both as examples of trigger mutability and as unitive symbols.

Although occasionally used outside descriptions of and comments on ecstasy, the *capital letter* device has, in these, a particular significance. It is habitually used by those who have derived from ecstasy metaphysical beliefs of an ontological kind, necessarily, that is to say, extrarational in their implications. The capital letters are used for the initials of hypostasized nouns, for their related adjectives, and for adjectives used as nouns in order to indicate the Real Existence of the ideas for which the words are symbols. This device is hardly ever used with verbs, and with prepositions and adjectives only when these are used as nouns.

[1] Picasso in 'Art Means Business', written for *Modern Telephones*, 1957.
[2] Walter De La Mare, 'All That's Past'.
[3] Rudyard Kipling, 'Cities and Thrones and Powers'.

In the texts L 11 provides some nice examples of this device. Here are some others:

From *Mysticism* by Evelyn Underhill: Absolute Reality—the Transcendental World—Unitive State—Undifferentiated Light—Mystic Way—this supernal Thing—the atmosphere of Eternity—the state of Sweetness and Song—the absolute World of Pure Being and the unresting World of Becoming—the Sempiternal Rose—Eternal Life—the Absolute Itself.

From *The Mystical Element in Religion* by Friedrich von Hügel: a completely unchanging Here and Now—in the Moral and Spiritual consciousness of the Perfect and Eternal—Ethics are englobed by Religion, Having by Doing and Doing by Being—Divine Lodger and Sustainer—that Infinite Country, that great Over-Againstness—the soul's life Here and Now...to the soul's life Then and There—the Natural Conformity between God and Rational Creatures.

From *The Doors of Perception* by Aldous Huxley: the Absolute—Suchness—the divine Order of Things—the Clear Light of the Void—the mystic Rose—the Other World—Enlightenment, the Beatific Vision—this Door in the Wall—Infused Contemplation—pure Being—the Inner Light—the Idea—my Not-Self—unmitigated Reality—that Archetypal World—Mind at Large.

From *The Outsider* by Colin Wilson: a great Abstract Universal System—the Universal Scheme—Heidegger's hair-splitting about Existence and Time—the unconditioned Will—the question, Ultimate Yes or Ultimate No—the Man Outside—instinctive, absolute Yea-saying—life is an eternal Pro and Contra—The Outsider has his proper place in the Order of Society—to Will on [notice this rare verbal use of the device].

In English writing today among literate people this practice seems to be almost confined to those who are writing to prove that ecstatic experiences prove the existence of a Supernatural Reality, and to meet with this device is to know with reasonable assurance what kind of book it is one has encountered.

A variant of the capital letter device is the *definite article* device, which consists of preceding unsupported adjectives with the definite article; an example comes from Auden's poem quoted on pp. 237-8. 'The entirely beautiful'. Often the capital letter device and the definite article device are combined for greater impressiveness. For instance, in text L 27 occurs the phrase 'I saw nothing and everything'. In text R 5b comes the more impressive 'she sees nothing and she sees All'. But more impressive still is yet another phrase from text R 5b in which the claim is to see 'the All'.

Propositions in which phrases so expressed occur are supposed to stand outside and above normal processes of verification.

I have already referred briefly to the *totality* device (see p. 127). I must now try to demonstrate its use more fully since it is, I believe, of prime importance and so very characteristic of descriptions of ecstasy and desolation as to constitute an aid to recognition of these experiences.

What I have called totality words and phrases are those whose function is to convey 'than this nothing more' in the class to which they refer. The obvious example of a totality word is God. But, as I have already explained, I do not mean by totality words and phrases only those which, like God, imply the top closure of all classes, but equally those which may imply the top closure of more limited classes such as 'happiness' or 'knowledge' or even 'what one can see' or 'edges and surfaces'.

Here are five examples from each group, in which I have italicized the word or words that identify the totality device:[1]

complete peace—*completeness, wholeness—reality* (Q 1); *timeless* bliss—*complete* separation from trouble—should be like this *for ever* (Q 18); *everything* fits in—*all* creation comes into harmony (Q 23); happiness that takes you *right out of* the world, so *supreme* that you forget *everything* (Q 28); *all* you know about nature, *the whole thing* (Q 61).

a spirit, that impels *All* thinking things, *all* objects of *all* thought, And rolls through *all* things (L 1a); to know *each separate thing* while lost in *the one* (L 4); *all* the details of things—*the world* is surveyed (L 6); *every* outline, *every* edge, and *every* surface—*everywhere* I feel the ideated pulsation...as if *all* served, etc. (L 10); *all* that had happened or could happen—could *never* be superseded (L 18).

the seeing of...*all* joyful things—*all* fulfilled—*Eternal* Life (R 1);

[1] I give in Appendix E, p. 500-2, at least one phrase from each text in which this device appears.

perfect unison—*all* the separate notes have melted into *one*—*highest* faith—*truest* idea (R 3); I knew *all* I longed to know, possessed *all* I longed to possess, I saw *all Good*—sees nothing and sees *All*—surpasses all good—this *Good*...is *the All* (R 5b); knew the being of *all* things— *the whole* working *essence*—had a *thorough* view of the *universe* (R 16); *the perspicuous truth*—the *sole and all-embracing* virtue—*supreme* happiness (R 19).

This device can often be identified by such epithets as *all, wholly, complete,* etc. On other occasions words like *universe, eternity, reality,* etc. sufficiently imply 'than which nothing more' in the class referred to. Totality is also implied by at least three rhetorical devices: the capital letter device and its variant, the definite article device; and *unitive enumeration* and *the ineffability* device, which are discussed below.

The device of *unitive enumeration* is not confined to descriptions of ecstasy. It consists in making lists of objects felt fittingly to symbolize the whole group to which the objects belong. Any selective catalogue is an example of unitive enumeration, from Autolycus's enumeration of his wares to the latest catalogue from Harrods.

But whereas the totalities implied by the above examples are concrete—*all* the contents of a pedlar's pack or of a department store—those implied by unitive enumeration in descriptions of ecstasy are usually abstractions, however concrete the samples named. This is best shown by example:

'both knowledge of the smallest bacteria in the field, how the blade of grass works, and the universe, in the same detail' (Q 61).

Here the unitive enumeration stands for all knowledge.

> the light of setting suns,
> And the round ocean and the living air,
> And the blue sky, and in the mind of man (L 1a).

Here we have good and beautiful things everywhere (or all good and beautiful things). This example shows how unitive enumeration may be and often is a trigger-list.

(i) 'the martyred infants and castrated pioneers', (ii) 'of stars bursting into novae, of sunspots erupting, of rocks decaying into swamps, and primeval forests being transformed into coal' (L 7).

The first phrase stands for all cruelty, sorrow, the second for all time.

'I knew the blood flowing through the bodies of men and beasts and thought of it as echoing the life of the anemones' (L 19).

I.e. contact with and knowledge of all.

'I saw and knew the being of all things, the Byss and the Abyss, and the eternal generation of the Holy Trinity, the descent and original of the world and of all creatures... I knew and saw in myself all the three worlds...and I saw and knew the whole working essence, in the evil and in the good, and the mutual origin and existence; and likewise how the fruitful bearing womb of eternity brought forth' (R 16).

I.e. all knowledge.

Outside these texts examples abound. A well-known if simple one is C. F. Alexander's hymn 'All things bright and beautiful' which is, in the five verses after the first, nothing but unitive enumeration of all things bright and beautiful, all things wise and wonderful, and all creatures great and small. (The limitation of God's creative powers to things bright and beautiful, wise and wonderful, rather smacks, however, of dualism.)

In descriptions of ecstatic experience, *ineffable* (and similar words like *unutterable, unspeakable, indescribable*) come to be little more than identifying adjectives (see p. 31). Their use implies (*a*) that the experience in question is indeed a mystical one, and (*b*) the existence of a totality, since when *ineffable*, etc. is attached to a noun, 'supreme of its kind' or 'than which nothing greater' seems always to be implied. The *ineffability* device is particularly common among religious writers. Some examples in the texts include:

unutterable love (L 1b); unutterable, shining orbs—ineffable smile (L 2); ineffable peace—exults in a sovereign and ineffable manner (R 12); joy unspeakable, peace inconceivable (R 18).

The device of *floating attributions* is very common, as much in common speech as in ecstasy. In it, feelings properly inhering in the experiencing person are attributed to what induced the experience or, very frequently in ecstatic descriptions, hypostasized as what was perceived in the experience. To notice the device is of some importance in identifying ecstatic experiences since one may have to amass the feelings of

the experience from adjectives applied to objects or from hypo-
stasizations.

I will take as examples feelings of knowledge and feelings of joy.
First, the expression of feelings of knowledge and of joy in the
ecstatic:

'the sensation you understand everything to which you turn your
mind' (Q 54). 'you feel...very happy' (Q 21).

Next, attached to the trigger:

> One impulse from a vernal wood
> May teach you more of man,
> Of moral evil and of good,
> Than all the sages can.[1]

'Everything was contented, happy, gleaming. The whole world
glowed, and the warm round sun smiled over France' (C 10).

Finally, as, or in what is perceived:

'we...in swift thought touched on that Eternal Wisdom, which
abideth over all.' [2]

'Enter thou into the joy of thy lord.' [3]

Most if not all the feelings of ecstasy can be attributed in totality form
to God. He is perfection's self, the Inexpressible Light, the Prince of
Peace. He is the One and the All, omnipresent, omnipotent, eternal.
He is the Resurrection and the Life, the Truth and the Word.

The *quia impossible* device consists of a positive statement set in appo-
sition to a negative one, the positive statement claiming that knowledge
has been gained, the negative claiming that normal ways of knowing
have been lost, and the two together implying the gain of a new way
of knowing, i.e. mystical knowledge. This device is fully illustrated
in the content analyses (Appendix B) and an example from each text
will be found on p. 28.

In the *impossible simile* device, something unknown is described in
terms of something that could not possibly be known, unless it were
itself the something for which a simile is being sought. Thus when

---

[1] Wordsworth, 'The Tables Turned', P.W., Vol. IV, p. 57.
[2] St. Augustine, *Confessions*, ix. 25.   [3] *Matt.* xxv. 21.

Q 15 says that ecstasy feels 'as if being borne into heaven itself', he is comparing his feeling with something he has no means of knowing unless the feeling he is trying to describe *is* that of being borne into heaven itself. Some other examples—there are very many—are,

> 'It was as though I had looked for a truth outside myself, and finding it had become for a moment part of the truth I sought' (L 25).
>
> 'It was, as it were, a manifestation of the sweetness of Eternal Life' (R 1).
>
> 'He found himself as it were in another region, alone with God' (R 14).

The phrase *as it were* (which implies, I cannot help feeling, a certain dubiety) is a likely pointer to the use of this device.

Louis of Blois uses this device with his phrase 'like a living fountain, flowing with streams of eternal sweetness' (R 20). The fact that the image is more or less concrete should not lead us to confuse this usage with that of such similes as 'My heart is like a singing-bird'. We may have encountered singing-birds; we have never encountered living fountains flowing with streams of eternal sweetness, unless we have done so in ecstatic experience.

The last literary use of ecstasy to which I want to refer here is hardly a rhetorical device but often a major part of a novelist's plot-making. By giving a character an ecstasy—and by almost no other means—it is possible credibly to change his entire disposition and aims, and a study of the use of ecstatic experiences by novelists would be worth making.[1]

(ii) SOME COMMON VERBAL USAGES

I suggest that in many words and phrases in common use the original metaphor may refer back to ecstatic experiences or to similar experiences of lesser intensity such as were discussed in Chapter VIII (p. 97 et seq.), and that our use of such words and phrases is determined, at least in part, by such references. Certainly these usages suggest that at least the less intense experiences are widely known, since if the metaphors were not felt congruent with common experience they would

---

[1] I have in Appendix H attempted an analysis of a poem in terms of some of the devices described in this chapter.

not have gained acceptance while still perceived as metaphors; now, of course, perception of the metaphor implied by use of the word or phrase may well be dead to all but etymologists.

I shall give examples of common words and phrases used to describe 'good' feelings of a kind it is not unreasonable to link with ecstatic ones, and group them according to the ecstatic feelings apparently expressed by them.

Up-feelings: up in the air—walking on air—up in the clouds—up-lifted—carried away—sublime[1]—supreme—exalted—exultant[2]—peak of perfection—head in the air—head in the clouds—high-flown—high-minded—elevated—wings to thought—unearthly—supernal

Contrast: feet on the ground—bring back to earth—come down to earth—depths of despair—weighed down—depressed—dejected—downcast

Light feelings: the flash of an idea—flashed across my mind—came to me in a flash—blinding revelation—a lucid moment—bright ideas—by the light of nature—see things in a rosy light—a brilliant person—splendour[3]

The word *glory* often used in descriptions of ecstatic feelings is today, I think, for most people an abstract noun, meaning (in the words of the *Concise Oxford Dictionary*) exalted renown or resplendent majesty. But it had until recently a more concrete meaning in English and this, and its general history is of interest in the context of ecstasy.

The Greek word from which our *glory* derives carried the original meaning of worldly fame; but even in Greek times this worldly fame had taken on a transcendent tinge (which might have some relation to the fact that people of high worldly fame can act as triggers). By the sixteenth century in England *glory* had become associated with 'An effulgence of light such as is associated with our conceptions of heaven' (O.E.D.). When, in the seventeenth century, *glory* began to stand for a halo or the nimbus of light round a holy figure, it had done so, says Sir Thomas Browne, after the French model—'Radiant Halo's... which after the French expression are usually tearmed [*sic*], the Glory'.[4]

---

[1] Though *sublime* looks like a down-word, it is not; the O.E.D. gives the derivation thus: ad. L. *sublīmis*, prob. f. *sub* up to + *līmen* lintel.

[2] *Exult* from L. *ex(s)ultā-re*, freq. of *exsilīre* to leap up.

[3] From L. *splēndere*, to be bright.   [4] *Pseudodoxia Epidemica*, V. ix. 247.

By the end of the seventeenth century *glory* was sufficiently associated with radiance for it to mean any circle or ring of light and to be used as such in nineteenth-century scientific works.

In common language *glory* meant halo or nimbus at least up to about 1860. Today, except in a few specialist fields, this meaning seems to be forgotten, and few contemporary people, encountering the word *glory*, would think of a halo.[1]

So when we find *glory* in texts written before about 1860, there is almost certainly an association with light, if not specifically with haloes, in the mind of the writer. This is explicit in text R 13 where Brainerd writes (referring to an occasion in 1739), 'unspeakable glory seemed to open…I do not mean any external brightness'.

There was no evidence that *glory* was associated with light by people in the questionnaire group, and since it was on this group that the analyses were based, I have not entered *glory* references under the heading of light. But in accepting *glory* as an expression of value, it should be remembered that an association with light was once explicit and may sometimes be intended.

Heat feelings: to burn or be on fire with enthusiasm—to be ardent—to glow with happiness—to speak warmly—to have a warm manner

Contrast: to speak coldly—to have a cold manner—to be tepid or lukewarm—to blow hot and cold—cold reason, cold facts

Breathing: to draw one's breath in wonder—to catch one's breath, to sigh with emotion—to hold one's breath in awe—to take one's breath away—to take a deep breath (in order to believe something; see the quotation from Lewis Carroll on p. 81)[2]

Tears: so beautiful it brings tears to one's eyes

[1] For instance, Keats's line 'And on her hair a glory, like a saint' (*The Eve of St. Agnes*, xxv) obviously refers to the appearance of a halo cast by the light through the stained glass windows. But Mr. Robert Gittings says of this line only that St. Paul's description of his conversion in *Acts* xxii may well have something to do with it (*John Keats, The Living Year* (London, 1954), p. 207). St. Paul speaks of being blinded by 'the glory of that light' so it is not possible to know whether Mr. Gittings independently associated *glory* with light; he certainly does not seem to have associated it with a halo.

[2] In a recent stores catalogue the colour of a blouse was named 'Breathless pink'; I take it that this name was unconsciously recognized by the inventor as 'all right', and I identify in it a remote reference to ecstasy. Those who doubt this may ask themselves why, say, 'Breathing mauve' would obviously be unacceptable.

Liquidity: heart is full, overflowing with emotion—emotion wells up—
well-spring of feeling—ideas flow

Contrast: a dry subject, a dry manner—an arid personality

Enlargement: largeness of feeling—magnanimity—heart swells with
emotion—swelling harmonies—big-hearted

The Heart: light-hearted—high-hearted—pluck up heart—heart leaps
with joy—lift of the heart—heart too full for words—a soft place
in the heart—soft-hearted—a melting heart—heart stands still—
heart swelling with emotion—heart on fire—ease the heart—heart
is moved, stirred

Contrast: down-hearted—heavy-hearted—heart sinks—one's heart in
one's boots—hard-hearted—cold-hearted—to have little heart for

Appearance: to be radiant—starry-eyed—glowing with happiness—
bright face—flashing eyes—parted lips—open-mouthed

Loss of place: out of this world—to be miles away—lost in a dream—
unearthly—ecstasy[1]—unworldly

Contrast: commonplace, mundane

Loss of time: people identified as unworldly are often also said to have
no idea of time—people are also often said to forget about time when
outstandingly happy or absorbed

Contrast: everyday—temporal—secular[2]

Loss of self: to be taken out of oneself—to be lost in something pleasant
—selfless

Contrast: to come to oneself again—selfish

Depth: to feel something important deep inside—profound or intense
emotion—depths of erudition or knowledge—a deep saying or
matter

Contrast: shallow—superficial

Pattern-making: something clicks, falls into place.

[1] From Gk. εχστασις, a displacement.
[2] From L. *sēculum*, a generation, an age, the world.

CHAPTER XXIII

Inducing Ecstatic Experiences

There is general agreement that mystical states of the kind to which intensity ecstasies belong cannot be induced. Indeed, many Christians deny the name *mystical* to any state that *can* be induced:

'We apply the word mystic to those supernatural acts or states which our own industry is powerless to produce, *even in a low degree, even momentarily*.' [1]

All that can, in religious terms, be achieved by oneself, are those initial acts of preparation described in Chapter IV, which *may*, if divine grace intervenes, lead to the desired experience. In my terms, withdrawal can be voluntarily achieved which may sometimes—and I do not know why—lead to an intensity ecstasy.

But though a normal intensity ecstasy cannot deliberately be induced it can sometimes, when a positive need for it is felt, be, so to speak, released. I can best illustrate this by reference to Richard Jefferies who is usefully verbal both about the existence of a felt need and the means found effective in relieving it. First, to describe the feeling of need:

'For I thirst with all the thirst of the salt sea, and the sun-heated sands dry for the tide, with all the sea I thirst for beauty... My throat and tongue and whole body have often been parched and feverish dry with this measureless thirst'. [2]

With Jefferies the need seems to have been so great that, sometimes, almost despite himself, he must take steps to relieve it. In his earlier

[1] Poulain: G.I.P., ch. i, 1.
[2] *The Story of My Heart*, ch.v, pp. 88–9. Similar expressions of need are a commonplace of poetry, and often in terms that suggest a need to relieve dryness. For instance, 'As the hart panteth after the water brooks, so panteth my soul after thee, O God. My soul thirsteth for God, for the living God' (*Psalms* xlii. 1–2).

years, in the country, this was easy. After telling of the experience given here as text L 3 he continues,

> 'I went there every morning, I could not exactly define why...
> There was a feeling that I must go somewhere, and be alone. It was a
> necessity to have a few minutes of this separate life every day'. [1]

He does not claim that every day he had an experience as intense as that of text L 3; presumably the response-experiences, which we may assume he had, gave him that measure of refreshment and renewal that were 'a necessity' to him.

When Jefferies came to London trigger conditions were less easily found, though he sought for such as were available—an aspen by a brook, the National Gallery, the Greek sculpture galleries in the British Museum. But these were not enough:

> 'There was a time when a weary restlessness came upon me, per-
> haps from too-long-continued labour. It was like a drought—a moral
> drought—as if I had been absent for many years from the sources of
> life and hope. The inner nature was faint, all was dry and tasteless;
> I was weary for the pure, fresh springs of thought. Some instinctive
> feeling uncontrollable drove me to the sea; I was so under its
> influence that I could not arrange the journey so as to get the longest
> day. I merely started, and of course had to wait and endure some
> inconvenience. To get to the sea at some quiet spot was my one
> thought; to do so I had to travel farther, and from want of pre-
> arrangement it was between two and three in the afternoon before
> I reached the end of my journey. Even then, being too much pre-
> occupied to inquire the way, I missed the road and had to walk a long
> distance before coming to the shore. But I found the sea at last; I
> walked beside it in a trance away from the houses out into the
> wheat... There, alone, I went down to the sea—' [2]

Aud there, at the sea, Jefferies had his ecstasy.

The movement to the sea seems unreasoned, almost animal—'Some instinctive feeling uncontrollable drove me to the sea—to get to the sea at some quiet spot was my one thought—too much preoccupied to inquire the way'. One may compare Gissing's 'maddening desire for country-side and sea-beach' and the 'irresistible impulse' on which he suddenly decided to go (see p. 64); in his case not momentary ecstasy but a unitive period ensued. I suggested earlier that the simple

---

[1] *The Story of My Heart*, ch. v, p. 78.　　　[2] Ibid., ch. vi, p. 111 et seq.

feeling that we need a change may, if we act on it, bring us to a condition that seems like a less intense unitive state (see p. 101); the state of tension described by Jefferies is surely often known to many of us at a less intense level and often relieved by such simple means as we have found effective—listening to music, going for a walk alone, or even, as Leuba suggests, by a hot bath or a cup of tea.

I do not say that an ecstasy must always be preceded by consciously recognized feelings of tension or need or, indeed, that preliminary tension or need must always exist, only that, when such tension or need *is* recognized and steps are taken to encounter appropriate trigger-conditions, an intensity ecstasy may ensue.[1]

But although need and tension may be felt and trigger-conditions encountered, not even response experiences may ensue, as the quotation from Byron on p. 98 makes clear. What inhibits release in such cases I do not know; I have tried to show that normally to confront appropriate trigger-conditions is for some people to obtain a measure of refreshment and release, if at a very much lower than ecstatic level.

I have come across only one account of an attempt to induce from scratch, as it were, an experience which seems as if normal intensity ecstasy is intended. It is described by Wordsworth. Walking one day with De Quincey he bent down and laid his ear to the road to hear whether a cart was coming; then, straightening up, he spoke as follows:

'I have remarked, from my earliest days, that, if under any circumstances the attention is energetically braced up to an act of steady observation, or of steady expectation, then, if this intense condition of vigilance should suddenly relax, at that moment any beautiful, any impressive visual object, or collection of objects, falling upon the eye,

[1] Since I am anxious to stress similarities between ecstasy and inspiration, I may point out that inspiration is often felt to be the release of accumulated tension. Q 54's description of inspiration 'similar to an urgent need to get something off your chest, similar to the urgent need of women to give birth', is typical of many statements by writers, even to the analogy with childbirth. And some writers try deliberately to build up the tension before starting; thus Virginia Woolf writes: 'As for my next book, I am going to hold myself from writing till I have it impending in me: grown heavy in my mind like a ripe pear' (*A Writer's Diary* (London, 1953), p. 138). Indeed, Southey's apparent inability to feel such a burden was thought by Coleridge and Wordsworth to be part of the explanation for the lacks in his poetry. Coleridge wrote, 'Wordsworth complains, with justice, that Southey writes *too much at his ease*—that he seldom "feels his burthened breast Heaving beneath th' incumbent Deity" ' (Quoted by Moorman in *William Wordsworth, the Early Years* p. 310).

is carried to the heart with a power not known under other circumstances. Just now, my ear was placed upon the stretch, in order to catch any sound of wheels...at the very instant when I raised my head from the ground...at the very instant when the organs of attention were all at once relaxing from their tension, the bright star hanging in the air above those outlines of massy blackness fell suddenly upon my eye, and penetrated my capacity of apprehension with a pathos and a sense of the infinite, that would not have arrested me under other circumstances.' [1]

We are not told what, if anything, happens if, after the steady observation is relaxed, the eye falls on an object that is not beautiful and impressive.

Other attempts to induce mystical experiences seem mostly to tend towards withdrawal ecstasies, an impression heightened by warnings attendant on their use or suspicions of mystics who use them. Thus Underhill warns that 'the more controllable ingoing experience' which can be approached by contemplating trigger objects is not an opportunity of pretty and pantheistic mediation' and Butler assures us that St. Gregory's and Jefferies's methods lead to 'no Asiatic or neo-Platonic infusion' (see p. 51). Christians insist that contemplation of Christ shall not become contemplation of God which is liable to lead to such statements as Ruysbroeck's 'so far as distinction of person goes, there is no more God nor creature' and 'we have lost ourselves and been melted away into the unknown darkness'. Such, says Inge, are 'the disastrous consequences which follow from the method of negation and self-deification'.[2]

Quietism, another method of approach which has been condemned, is, says the *Oxford Dictionary of the Christian Church*,

'a certain form of mental prayer in which the soul consciously refuses not only all discursive meditation but any distinct act such as desire for virtue, love of Christ, or adoration of the Divine Persons, but simply rests in the presence of God in pure faith...The moral consequences of such teaching are almost indistinguishable from those of pantheism.' [3]

Other methods sometimes adduced are gazing at a bright object,

---

[1] Quoted by Bateson, *Wordsworth, A Re-Interpretation*, p. 25.
[2] C.M., pp. 170–1.
[3] Von Hügel points out that in the *Guida* of the Quietist Molinos who was forced to recant and was imprisoned for life, there were 'literal reproductions of the teachings of such solemnly approved authorities as Saints Teresa, Peter of Alcantara, John of the Cross, Francis de Sales and Jane Frances de Chantal,—

repeating one's own name over and over again, control of breathing, relaxation. None of these seems to produce intensity experiences.[1]

Some morbid conditions of health undoubtedly facilitate experiences that have been accepted as genuinely mystical, and sometimes such experiences—apart from the lack of a conventional trigger—fulfil my criteria for ecstasies. Obvious ill-health is, of course, no bar to acceptance of experiences as genuine religious ones. 'It is certain that the abnormal and highly sensitized type of mind which we call mystical does frequently, but not always, produce or accompany strange and inexplicable modifications of the physical organism with which it is linked,' writes Underhill,[2] and certainly some of the ecstatics from my religious group were often in states far removed from good health. Such are Angela of Foligno (see p. 76 n) and Catherine of Siena.[3]

Today a probable casual link between ill-health and at least some of these experiences can hardly be denied, and even religious commentators often accept ill-health as a sufficient explanation at least for experiences they cannot certify as genuinely religious. Thus Thurston accepts hysteria as the explanation of the claims and behaviour of many putative mystics whose experiences he rejects as truly religious ones. He comments that when hysteria develops consistently and uniformly along religious lines, then

'it is extremely difficult to decide how much of that which purports

passages which, of course, remained uncondemned even in Molinos's pages, but which it would often be difficult to distinguish from the parts of his book that were censured' (M.E.R., Vol. II, p. 143).

[1] Boehme's first mystical experience came to him after gazing into sunlight, reflected on a pewter vessel; his writings are often called 'pantheistic or dualist' (O.D.C.C.). Tennyson, as a youth, used to be able to induce 'a kind of waking trance' in which 'individuality itself seemed to dissolve and fade away into boundless being' by repeating his own name to himself silently (James: V.R.E., p. 374n.); and Kipling makes Kim achieve a similar experience which is, he says, available to 'a very few white people, but many Asiatics' by repeating his own name silently to himself (Kim, ch. xi). Jefferies believed, according to his biographer, that he could achieve his desired experiences by breath-control (see p. 80 n.); but breath-control is usually associated with eastern mysticism.

[2] E.U : M., p. 59.

[3] Poulain says that Catherine of Siena had 'thousands' of 'ecstasies', sometimes lasting three days (G.I.P., ch. xviii, 7 and 10); that she was unmercifully beaten or bitten by demons and on several occasions thrown into the fire by the demon, though without being hurt (ibid., ch. xxiv, 81 and 82); and Inge says that she was betrothed to Christ with a ring which always remained on her finger, though visible to herself alone (C.M., p. 371).

to be of divine origin may be due to mental disorder and how much is really prompted and suggested by the Holy Spirit.'[1]

Inevitably some people among those who do not accept supernatural explanations for mystical experiences have concluded that all such experiences are causally linked with morbid states of health, and often the discovery that any one pathological condition may induce some of the symptoms of ecstasy tends to make the discoverer believe that all ecstatic states are linked with that single condition. I cited earlier the television discussion in which one speaker assumed that the states in question were caused by God, another by manic-depression, the third by schizophrenia, while the fourth said that the power concerned was that of the collective unconscious (see p. 168 n).

An alternative approach is to assume that while no one pathological condition is responsible for all ecstasies, all ecstasies are caused by one or other pathological condition:

'Medical materialism finishes up St. Paul by calling his vision on the road to Damascus a discharging lesion of the occipital cortex, he being an epileptic. It snuffs out St. Teresa as an hysteric, St. Francis of Assisi as an heriditary degenerate. George Fox's discontent with the shams of his age, and his pining for spiritual veracity, it treats as a symptom of a disordered colon, Carlyle's organ-tones of misery it accounts for by a gastro-duodenal catarrh.'[2]

While some pathological states can undoubtedly produce experiences in some or many ways similar to what I have called intensity ecstasies, it seems to me certain that these ecstasies are typically produced in people of good mental and physical health.

Among the pathological states in which such experiences sometimes arise, epilepsy is undoubtedly one. Dostoievsky, for instances, gives two accounts of experiences which he recognizes as linked with the epileptic seizures that follow them, both of which can—apart from the absence of conventional triggers—be accepted as typical ecstasies.[3] But such experiences do not precede all or even most epileptic fits. Some time after the publication of her ecstatic book *Autobiography* (from

---

[1] S.M. passim, and esp. p. 217. Leuba concludes that 'St. Catherine of Genoa, Santa Theresa, Mme. Guyon and St. Marguerite Marie suffered from hysterical attacks'. P.R.M., p. 191.

[2] James: V.R.E., p. 14.

[3] In *The Possessed*, trans. C. Garnett, ch. v, p. 537; and in *The Idiot*, trans. C. Garnett, Vol. II, ch. v, p. 224.

which text L 4 is taken), Margiad Evans became an epileptic and describes her life as such in a book called *A Ray of Darkness*[1]. She never suggests that her appalling disability was mitigated by any such experiences.

Sir James Crichton-Browne points out such an experience—a 'dreamy mental state', as he calls it—is not caused by the epileptic seizure that follows it, but that

> 'it depends on the heightened activity and increased energising of nervous arrangements intimately linked with those in which the true epileptic discharge begins.'[2]

Such experiences, he says, are 'precursors and not integral parts of epileptic fits'.

The experience of the Boston woman who was converted to 'mind-cure' (R 8), although self-induced, seems possibly to have been facilitated by the fact that she had influenza at the time. I have not seen it stated elsewhere that simple fevers of this kind may facilitate ecstasies and perhaps the feverish state was not, after all relevant. But that it may have been is suggested by a very similar experience of John Wesley's when he took to his bed with a fever:

> 'The fever came rushing upon me as a lion, ready to break all my bones in pieces; my body grew weaker every moment, but I did not feel my soul put on strength. Then it came into my mind, "Be still, and see the salvation of the Lord; I will not stir hand or foot; but let Him do with me what is good in his own eyes." At once my heart was at ease; my mouth was filled with laughter, and my tongue with joy: my eyes overflowed with tears, and I began to sing aloud.'[3]

Dying may, I suppose, be considered a morbid state; the approach of death seems sometimes to be apt for ecstatic experiences:

> 'Pat had a second stroke a year later... It seemed that, according to the doctors, he had actually died during this attack for a time, but had managed to pull himself back into life because he felt he had one more message to deliver. Death, he told us, was nothing to fear. It was a natural culmination to life as we know it and was an experience of indescribable happiness. The release from the bondage

---

[1] Pub. London, 1952.
[2] 'Dreamy Mental States', *The Lancet*, 1895, 2, pp. 1–5 and 73–5.
[3] *Journal*, November 6, 1741.

of life—even from the bondage of love—brought with it an ecstasy and an understanding beyond anything known to living man.' [1]

'Once when I was seriously ill and not expected to recover, I experienced that spiritual elation and awareness of the presence of God described in your broadcast... It seemed to me afterwards, when I could reason coldly and clearly, that as the body sank into nothingness, the spirit strengthened and would survive.' [2]

Leuba comments that illusions of levitation may take place just before death and often in elaborate form, some people believing that they are carried to heaven by angels, others, 'presumably burdened with an evil conscience', that they are being dragged away by demons.[3]

Sometimes ecstatic experiences take place in conditions related to sleeping: on falling asleep, in dreams, or at the moment of waking. The only example I have of the first is the one I put in my novel, and this I found to my surprise, when I looked at it later in the light of this book, was a withdrawal ecstasy; I was not at the time of writing consciously aware of a distinction, but certainly a withdrawal ecstasy seems a more probable experience than an intensity ecstasy when on the point of falling asleep.[4]

Ecstasies in dreams are not infrequent. Q 25 is one of three or four people who have told me of this experience, and I have referred earlier to the dream ecstasy—a desolation-ecstasy—of J. B. Priestley (see p. 72n.). The dream-ecstasy quoted in Appendix J (pp. 532–3) I regard as a most useful and archetypal account of an ecstasy in that it is set down almost raw and without subsequent rearrangement or overbelief.

I have also come across a few instances of ecstasy at the moment of waking before full consciousness is re-established; these are often recollected experiences of childhood.[5]

---

[1] Patricia Hastings, *Life of Sir Patrick Hastings* (London, 1959), pp. 229–30.
[2] Letter received by Christopher Mayhew after the B.B.C. television programme *Sainthood and Sanity*, June 1957.
[3] P.R.M., p. 259.
[4] *The Victorian Chaise-longue* (London, 1953), pp. 40–1.
[5] For an account of such an ecstatic experience, said to have been known several times, see the article 'On Seeing the Salamander' by Robert Plank, where he quotes O. Spitteler (*The Psychoanalytic Study of the Child*, Vol. XIII, 1957). For a child's desolation-ecstasy at the moment of waking, see *So Much Love So Little Money* by Lyn Irvine (London, 1957), pp. 91–2.

Poulain tells of several saints in whom the transforming union (i.e. unitive states) was not interrupted even in sleep.[1] The same seems to have been true for Margiad Evans:

'Even in sleep it does not leave me—the least thrill in the chord recalls me, and in the morning it is there directly the day is felt on my eyelids. Yes, even before I wake, I come to it' (L 4).

Mentally disturbed states like schizophrenia and manic-depression are often held to account for some if not all mystical experiences. Zaehner, for instance, relates manic-depression very closely to experiences he is not prepared to accept as genuinely religious ones (see p. 161). But it does seem to me important to notice some major differences between ecstatic experiences and schizophrenic or manic-depressive states. Ecstasy is momentary while these other states are more or less prolonged; the connexions should surely be sought rather with unitive (or desolate) states than with momentary ecstasy (or desolation). And ecstatics usually are and remain convinced of the value of any beliefs they may derive from their experiences; beliefs derived when in states accepted as those of mental disease are not usually regarded as valuable once the patient is cured.

If however John Custance is a typical manic-depressive, his account of that condition in his book *Wisdom, Madness and Folly* provides some suggestive similarities between manic-depression and ecstasy. In his manic-state, says Custance, his usual feelings of repulsion to things normally regarded as disgusting or distasteful are inhibited; he relates this to the inhibition of a sense of repulsion discussed by William James in connexion with saintliness[2] and draws attention to such actions as St. Francis of Assisi kissing the lepers' sores, writing, 'In the manic phase...it would give me the greatest pleasure to do the same.' He connects our normal feelings of aversion from dirt with the association of dirt and sin; in the manic state he loses all sense of sin.[3]

It is common for ecstatics to feel that through their experiences they have been purified and lost all sense of sin. Sometimes ecstasies, notably adamic ones, and response-experiences result in a generalized love for

---

[1] G.I.P., ch. xix, 8 *bis*.
[2] V.R.E., p. 269; see also my p. 208.
[3] *Wisdom, Madness and Folly*, pp. 42–4. Dirt is a common trigger to desolation; see p. 208.

all creatures, those found normally repulsive being specifically included.[1]

General feelings of love and absence of distaste towards all are necessary features of those altruistic utopias whose formulation seems to result from the nature of some adamic ecstasies (see Chapter XXVIII), and for these utopias a 'change of heart' is usually stipulated as a necessary prerequisite. And of the inhibition of instinctive repugnance, which James finds characteristic of saints, he says that if it became widespread in humanity, it could alter the whole basis of human relations; 'we should be born into another kingdom of being'.[2]

Some physical symptoms described by Custance also bear a close resemblance to those given in many accounts of ecstasies:

'As I sit here in the ward writing, I know that if I get a shiver in my back after puzzling about something for a minute or two, it means that the connection has been established. And if the shiver is really intense, it indicates that the line of thought leads to a large tract of related associations, as though the link or contact involved the passing of an electric current proportionate to the extent of the associations... Now and then, when it really appears as though some vital missing link had been revealed to me, I get an additional feeling as though something had clicked or fallen into place in my head'.[3]

Here, linked in the context of mental improvement, are the shivers, the electric shocks, the feelings of something falling into place so often characteristic of ecstatic experiences. Similarities between Custance's depressive state and states of desolation will be apparent in the passage quoted on pp. 160-1.

Mystical experiences of one kind or another are often sought through drugs, and a radio talk by Morris Carstairs suggested that it is basically two different kinds of experience that drugs can provide; these two kinds of experience, I suggest, correspond closely to the distinction I

[1] For instance, after the dream-ecstasy given in Appendix J, the ecstatic says that everything in daily life seems temporarily enhanced and 'I welcome the wasps into the kitchen even! All defects, neglects still there, but something over the whole lifts it up.'

[2] V.R.E., pp. 278-9.

[3] *Wisdom, Madness and Folly*, p. 54.

have made between intensity and withdrawal experiences. I shall summarize briefly the relevant passages of this talk:[1]

Every known human society has discovered or borrowed from its neighbours substances which are eaten or drunk or inhaled, not to allay hunger but to recreate a mental state which has been found agreeable. Communities choose certain drugs to the exclusion of others, praise these, often invent legends of their supernatural origins; and denounce alien drugs 'with a ferocity which betrays a fear of their powers'.

Carstairs instanced a village he had known in Northern India, where the warrior Rajputs drank wine and despised the local *bhang* or hashish, and the Brahmins took *bhang* and proscribed wine.

He then discussed the French *Club des Haschishins* (of which Baudelaire, Gautier, Daumier, Delacroix were members) who found that after varying initial responses, the one central experience of taking hashish was 'the sense of detachment from oneself, of loss of all impulse towards action, and of widespread indifference to other persons as to all worldly ties'. This is closely akin to 'the climax of a devout Hindu's religious life, the attaining of *samadhi* and direct intuition of the Divine Brahmin'.

But hashish was finally rejected by Baudelaire and Gautier as by most Westerners. 'Western man, like the Rajput, is committed to a life of action and self-assertion; for us, alcohol, which facilitates these tendencies, is inevitably the stimulant of choice.'

Carstairs's description of the final state of the hashish-trance is similar to descriptions of the final state of withdrawal ecstasy, consistently condemned by Christians as nihilistic, negative, and eastern in type. Both the chosen drug and the chosen religious experience of the west are of kinds that lead to increased activity with condemnation for both drugs and religious experiences that tend to diminish it.

Alcohol, the chosen drug of the west, has been thoroughly institutionalized; its supernatural origins are recounted in myths and it plays and has played a substantial part in the religious ceremonies of Greek, Jew, and Christian.[2]

---

[1] It was called *Drugs of Election* and was given in the B.B.C.'s Third Programme, January 31, 1955. It was not reprinted in the *Listener*, but the producer very kindly lent me the script.

[2] An interesting book in this context is *Wine in the Ancient World* by Charles Seltman (London, 1957). A recent example of a quasi-mystical approach to wine in English literature is to be found in the works of a group of Catholic writers of some fifty years ago—Belloc, Chesterton, Machen. Of particular interest is

Wine is occasionally instanced as a trigger[1] and is generally treated as one; wine—and in Scottish and Irish contexts, whisky—finds a place in trigger-lists, trigger comparisons, etc. where other drugs would seem blasphemously out of place. Ecstatics often describe their feelings in terms of being drunk. Q 16 spoke of 'intoxication, if you can think of it as extremely clarity' and Suso, in text R 22, spoke of feeling, 'in an eneffable degree, that which is felt by an inebriated man'. Religious mystics often use the word 'inebriated' of their condition; compare Novalis's description of Spinoza as 'a God-intoxicated man' ('ein Gott-betrunkener Mensch').

Whether wine does very often or to any very great extent induce feelings similar to intensity ecstasy I do not know, but it is in ecstatic terms that James describes its effects:

'The sway of alcohol over mankind is unquestionably due to its power to stimulate the mystical faculties of human nature, usually crushed to earth by the cold facts and dry criticisms of the sober hour. Sobriety diminishes, discriminates, and says no; drunkenness expands, unites, and says yes. It is in fact the great exciter of the *Yes* function in man. It brings its votary from the chill periphery of things to the radiant core. It makes him for the moment one with truth. Not through mere perversity do men run after it. To the poor and the unlettered it stands in the place of symphony concerts and of literature.' [2]

It is again needful to point out a significant difference between the experiences induced by alcohol and those induced by conventional triggers, that the revelations of alcohol-experiences are seldom held for gospel in subsequent sobriety while those of conventionally induced ecstasy tend to hold their value afterwards.

Of all the drugs I have read about, those that seem most often capable of inducing states with most resemblances to intensity ecstasy are some anaesthetics and particularly nitrous oxide. Many instances of

Machen's discussion of the novel in *Hieroglyphics* (London, 1902) where he maintains that novels should be divided into those that give entertainment and those that give ecstasy, that the latter must necessarily be Catholic in feeling, and that *Pickwick Papers* is an example of the ecstatic novel, Mr. Pickwick's milk-punch being derived by direct descent—if weakened in the process—from the wine of Dionysian orgies.

[1] For instance, by Q 48; and we may assume that wine played a part in the 'very good lunch' that Q 56 believed relevant to his subsequent ecstasy.

[2] V.R.E., pp. 377–8.

such experiences are available to the layman,[1] but the example I give is one that has not been published before:

> 'Whilst under the anaesthetic for a short operation, I had a complete revelation about the ultimate truth of everything. I understood the "entire works". It was a tremendous illumination. I was filled with unspeakable joy... When I came round I told the Doctor I understood the meaning of everything. He...said "Well, what is it?" and I faltered out, "Well, it's a sort of green light."' [2]

This experience fulfils many of my criteria for ecstasy: feelings of joy, of new knowledge, of light and, by implication, a rare if not unique experience. But the *green* light is untypical: lights seen in ecstasy seem always to be white (see p. 72).

This experience also shows clearly another distinction I have already pointed out in connexion with the revelations of mentally disturbed states and of wine, that in contradistinction to beliefs arising from ecstasy proper, this kind of 'revelation' is usually regarded as nonsense when looked at in the light of day, even though its subject-matter—knowledge of 'everything'—is the same as that of many ecstatic revelations. The lady's 'sort of green light' recalls the professor who was determined to read the riddle of the world, took chloroform, and with tremendous mental effort just before unconsciousness overtook him, managed to write 'A strong smell of turpentine pervades the whole'.[3]

But William James, though he admitted that any words in which the revealed truth seemed to clothe itself appeared 'the veriest nonsense' when the experience was over, did believe there was a genuine metaphysical significance in these experiences:

> 'the sense of a profound meaning having been there persists... Looking back on my own experiences, they all converge towards a kind of insight to which I cannot help attributing some metaphysical significance.' [4]

---

[1] See, for instance, *A Drug-Taker's Notes* by R. H. Ward, pp. 26–32; *Wisdom, Madness and Folly* by John Custance, p. 14; Leuba: P.R.M., pp. 253–4; James: V.R.E., pp. 378–84.

[2] Letter received by Christopher Mayhew after an article describing mescalin experience, *Observer*, October 28, 1956.

[3] Related by Crichton-Browne, 'Dreamy Mental States', *The Lancet*, 1895.

[4] V.R.E., pp. 378–9.

To receive ecstatic or even pleasant experiences from anaesthetics is, of course, by no means the rule. Some people have experiences of horror;[1] others may have no remembrance of any feelings while under anaesthetics.

The drug which has, in relation to mystical experiences, received most publicity of late is mescalin, and this I shall discuss in the next chapter.

[1] 'My experience was of everlasting hell... I lost all consciousness of my surroundings till suddenly consciousness registered pain...which was interpreted by my consciousness as *everlasting*. There was no consciousness of myself as the subject of suffering, but only an experience of suffering itself, outside of time. It was this experience of being "caught in eternity" which...I shall never forget so long as I live.' An experience of having teeth out under nitrous oxide, described in a letter to Christopher Mayhew.

CHAPTER XXIV

Mescalin and Ecstasy

There have lately become available to the layman several descriptions of mescalin-induced experiences, and on the evidence of seven of these I shall try to establish what appear to be fairly constant differences between mescalin experiences and ecstatic ones. The experiences in question are:

Aldous Huxley's book, *The Doors of Perception* (London, 1954)
Rosalind Heywood's article in the *Manchester Guardian* (May 29, 1954)
Alice Marriot's article in the *New Yorker* (September 25, 1954)
Raymond Mortimer's article in the *Sunday Times* (August 14, 1955)
Christopher Mayhew's article in the *Observer* (October 28, 1956)[1]
Professor R. C. Zaehner's Appendix B to his book *Mysticism, Sacred and Profane* (Oxford, 1957)
R. H. Ward's book *A Drug-Taker's Notes* (London, 1957)[2]

The first difference I shall try to establish is one to which I have already drawn attention in connexion with other drugs. Ecstatics are almost unanimous about the high value of their experiences. Mescalin-takers are not.

The seven people listed above differed in their motives for taking mescalin and differed in their judgements of results. Aldous Huxley sought to find out what mystical experience felt like and came to believe he had attained the Beatific Vision. Rosalind Heywood acted

[1] Mr. Mayhew has very kindly enabled me to see the transcript of the television film made of his experience and shown on December 12, 1955; I shall refer to this also.

[2] The drug taken by Mr. Ward was not mescalin but lysergic acid—d-lysergic acid diethylamide tartrate or LSD 25. I have included his experiences because they have many similarities to those induced by mescalin, and he, like the mescalin-takers, was seeking ecstasy. But where I refer generally to 'mescalin' in this chapter, it should be remembered that in Mr. Ward's case, this other drug was involved.

as guinea-pig for a group of scientists, but does not report her motives for doing so; she ended by doubting whether everybody was ready for a dose of 'Mind at Large'. Alice Marriot, a graduate student of ethnology, was working among an Indian tribe in South Dakota, and took mescalin in a tribal ceremony specially prepared for her when she became ill from the heat; she was cured of her feeling of illness. Raymond Mortimer took mescalin because he had been deeply impressed by Mr. Huxley's book; he found his own 'the most horrifying experience I have ever known' and his 'personal opinions and beliefs remained unchanged'. Christopher Mayhew's motives were similar to Mr. Mortimer's, though he also hoped the experience would make an interesting television film; he came to believe that religious experience could be produced by this means, and wrote 'the mystery of what was revealed fills me with great wonder'. Professor Zaehner hoped to find fundamental differences between religious experience and mescalin experience, and was afterwards satisfied that the mescalin experience was 'not conformable with religious experience or in the same category'. Mr. Ward hoped to find some kind of religious experience through the different state of consciousness induced by the drug, but decided that true religious experience was not to be come by this way, and that use of the drug was 'inappropriate...to the end which the writer of the following [that is, my text L 24] had achieved'.

Compared with ecstatics' virtual unanimity about the high value of their experiences, the divergency of these views is striking, and would seem generally to have some relation to previous expectations.

So far as duration and feelings of duration are concerned, ecstasies and mescalin experiences have almost nothing in common.

Ecstatic experiences are typically momentary and ecstasies often stress the extreme brevity of these experiences. Very occasionally an ecstasy is said to last longer—up to, say, half an hour or so.[1] But however long an ecstasy may be said to last, we never find that a succession of often widely different events and moods is felt to take place. Ecstasies may involve a single change of feeling from dread to delight (see p. 174), never the reverse; they may begin with feelings of withdrawal which change to feelings of intensity (see Chapter IV); most

[1] I have suggested in Chapter V that such apparently longer ecstasies may often consist of an ecstatic moment and a more or less prolonged preliminary withdrawal and/or afterglow.

often only a single if progressively deepening tone of feeling is involved. For the duration of the ecstasy the ecstatic is out of touch with normal life and is capable neither of communication with other people nor of undertaking normal actions.

The taking of mescalin induces a condition that usually lasts for several hours. During this time the subject is capable, despite his altered consciousness, of more or less normal behaviour. He can eat and drink, walk about, communicate with other people. And, in all my examples, he is shown to have successive states of feeling varying very considerably in mood and content. To take only two of the shortest and simplest accounts: Rosalind Heywood (i) saw patterns and had blissful experiences, (ii) saw people cast down and had 'terrible experiences', (iii) encountered a celestial female figure. Raymond Mortimer (i) had a great increase in visual perceptiveness, (ii) lost all capacity for emotion while retaining thought and memory, (iii) felt 'a generalized apprehension amounting to panic'.

The mescalin-takers' feelings about time differ considerably from the feelings of ecstatics. Mr. Huxley remarks of time at one point, 'There seemed to be plenty of it', and speaks of his 'indifference to time'. This casual attitude seems far removed from the ecstatics' 'loss of a sense of time' or gain of a feeling of timelessness or eternity. Elsewhere Mr. Huxley does speak of 'timeless bliss', a common phrase in ecstatic accounts; but it must always be remembered that Mr. Huxley is unusually well versed in the language of mysticism and that 'what the mystics were talking about' was what he consciously sought.

Mr. Mayhew was very much interested in his feelings about time which was, he says at one point, 'behaving strangely. I was not experiencing events in the normal sequence of time . . . but in an apparently capricious sequence which was outside my own control'. He often had the feeling that he was leaving and then returning to ordinary time. These are not the kinds of thing that ecstatics say about time.

But during some of the intervals in which he felt he had left ordinary time, Mr. Mayhew does describe his feelings in terms not dissimilar to those of ecstasy:

'I would become unaware of my surroundings and enjoy an existence conscious of myself, in a state of breathless wonderment and complete bliss, for a period of time which—for me—simply did not end at all. It did not last for minutes or hours, but apparently for years.' [1]

Though the mention of specific periods of time is untypical, this might pass for a description of ecstasy.

Mr. Ward speaks of 'changes in the time-sense' under the influence of lysergic acid. To the other mescalin-takers, changes in time-perception do not seem to have been significant.

Differences in response to triggers are, I think, among the most interesting and probably most significant differences between ecstatics and mescalin-takers.

Ecstasy almost always takes place after contact with something regarded as beautiful or valuable or both. It seems to be characteristic of mescalin that the kind of things that can act as triggers to ecstasy lose their normal power to be found moving in any degree, while objects not of this kind take on the significance and evoke the appreciation normally accorded to triggers.

I find it significant that so many of the mescalin-takers arranged beforehand that they would be confronted while under the drug with objects they normally found beautiful and valuable without in any case giving their reasons for doing so.

Mr. Huxley found that music gave him pleasure, but 'nothing comparable to my seen apocalypses of flowers or flannel'. Instrumental music left him 'rather cold'. Alban Berg's *Lyric Suite* sounded 'rather funny'. Cézanne's self-portrait made him laugh.

Mr. Mortimer writes:

'I was shown photographs of Italian architecture; I listened to Chopin on a gramophone; I repeated lines from a favourite poem: though I recognised the excellences of these works, I was entirely unmoved by any of them.'

Mr. Mayhew was shown a picture of the Madonna and Child from Leningrad and told to comment on it; he said, 'no, the painting has no significance for me' (from the transcript).

Professor Zaehner was shown *The Adoration of the Magi* by Gentile da Fabriano and broke into uncontrollable laughter. He began to read

---

[1] The word 'conscious' is surprising here. I have asked Mr. Mayhew whether it might be a misprint for 'unconscious', but after a lapse of years he does not remember.

Du Côté de chez Swann and broke off in laughter. Michelangelo's *Holy Family* left him unmoved, but Raphael's *Deposition* and a Piero della Francesca were, he felt, holy things and 'not to be looked at when you're drugged'. A Picasso 'doesn't seem to fit together much', a Persian carpet ('the best of my Persian rugs—a Feraghan of extraordinarily rich design with a basic colouring of deep, glowing russets') produced no reaction. Berlioz's *Te Deum* ('Almost my favourite work in all music') would not, he felt, be improper to hear as the drug was wearing off and this, he said, brought him back to the real world without violent transition, although 'the full strength and beauty... was lacking'.

Mr. Ward listened to music in his fifth experiment but says little about it and seems to have been unmoved by it, and confused music by Beethoven and by Mozart which, he assures us, he would not normally have done. Alice Marriot left the tepee briefly to look at the stars and found them glowing with colour as she had found the fire inside. Rosalind Heywood does not seem to have confronted anything she normally found beautiful.

It appears, then, that for people under mescalin the kinds of things that would normally act as triggers for that person, whether to ecstasy or to response-experiences, lose their usual power to move. (Could this be because the person is already in something of the physiological condition to which such triggers usually move him?)

On the other hand things not usually of a trigger kind, whether to this person or to anyone else, often affect the mescalin-taker as if they were triggers. Mr. Huxley's vision of his trouser-legs has become famous. Equally transfigured for him were some flowers in a vase, the books on the wall, chair-legs, drapery in a Botticelli picture and a stucco wall—'blank but unforgettably beautiful, empty but charged with all the meaning and the mystery of existence'. Mr. Mortimer saw 'with unprecedented acuteness' the room he was in, the leaves in a vase, the hair on people's heads and the folds of their clothes—'I felt that I had been lent the eyes of a great painter'. Mr. Ward saw astonishing beauty in a plain distempered wall,[1] and found 'a beautiful note' in a

---

[1] One feels there may be something in these people's beliefs that they were seeing things as great painters saw them; da Vinci advised artists to look at damp walls in order to see the likeness of divine landscapes in the blots and stains (see *Selections from the Notebooks of Leonardo da Vinci*, ed. Irma A. Richter (World's Classics edn., 1952), pp. 181–2.

bell ringing in a hospital corridor. In addition, nearly all these people found beauty in their colour and movement hallucinations.

Apparently for mescalin-takers their normal responses to triggers are, so to speak, reversed: during the experience what usually seems beautiful to them does not move them but they are moved by what does not usually seem to them beautiful. For ecstatics, however, it is after the event that the range of their responses to beauty is sometimes enlarged to include not only what they usually find beautiful but what they usually do not.

In addition to these aesthetic responses there are some notable differences between what ecstatics and mescalin-takers claim to see during or after their experiences.

A close similarity between the visual impressions of mystics and of mescalin-takers is often claimed (for instance, by James).[1] I do not believe that in relation to ecstasies at least there is any significant similarity.

Ecstatics often claim to see bright light, whether as a flash or as sustained brightness, during their experience; and they often claim that afterwards everything seems brighter, as if they were looking at the world with a newly cleansed vision (see p. 86).

Three of the mescalin-takers spoke of seeing light during their experiences. Rosalind Heywood saw a clear white light on top of a mountain that was also somehow within herself. Mr. Mayhew, of one of the periods he describes in terms similar to those of ecstasy, writes,

'During this period I would be aware of a pervasive bright light, like a kind of invisible sunlit snow.'

Though flashes are more common than sustained light, neither of these, in a description of ecstasy, would be out of place. The lights seen by Mr. Huxley at an early stage of his experience are very different:

'I became aware of a slow dance of golden lights. A little later there were sumptuous red surfaces swelling and expanding from bright nodes of energy that vibrated with a continuously changing, patterned life. At another time the closing of my eyes revealed a complex of grey structures, within which pale bluish spheres kept emerging into intense solidity.'

No such patterns of light, let alone of coloured light, ever appear in descriptions of experiences that are in all other respects ecstasies.

[1] V.R.E., p. 248.

Still more typical of mescalin are its famous colour and shape hallucinations where actual colours are seen as glowing with intense or
prismatic effects and actual objects may seem to move in patterns. For
Mr. Huxley, things 'glowed, when I looked at them, with brighter
colours, a profounder significance'. He speaks, for instance, of a deck-
chair with 'stripes of a deep but glowing indigo alternated with stripes
of iridescence so intensely bright that it was hard to believe that they
could be made of anything but blue fire'. Alice Marriot saw colours in
the fire, 'colours my eyes had never till then beheld. They whirled and
turned and blended...revolving before me in a wheel of richness and
brilliance.' Mr. Mayhew found that his curtains took on 'a dozen
ethereal shades of mauve and purple'. Mr. Ward saw many glowing
colours. For Mr. Mortimer 'colour took on a prodigious intensity'.
Professor Zaehner, instead of the intense colour-hallucinations he had
expected, found a rhythmic movement of objects, 'forming and re-
forming of patterns'.

In the transformed world that ecstatics sometimes believe they see
after their experiences, they may speak of colours being brighter, though
not to the degree of intensity claimed by mescalin-takers; more, they
see all, not specific things as brighter in colour. Ecstatics do not claim
this changed vision *during* their experiences; they cannot, because one
of their claims is that perception of the outside world is momentarily
suspended. Ecstatics do not speak of the prismatic effects described by
mescalin-takers or of movement-hallucinations. They never, so far as
I know, claim to see coloured lights.

Mr. Mortimer added that 'form appeared more three-dimensional';
I do not know of an ecstatic who says this. Mr. Huxley at one point
closed his eyes and saw what he describes as a curiously unrewarding
inscape on which he commented, 'Cheap. Trivial. Like things in a Five
and Ten.' If inscapes appear to ecstatics they are never regarded as
unrewarding ones.

Another profound difference between ecstatics and mescalin-takers
is in their attitudes to pleasure. Ecstatics rejoice and feel delight at perfection. Mescalin-takers enjoy and often burst out laughing at what is
awry.[1]

---

[1] Sir Philip Sidney makes the distinction clear: 'For delight wee scarcely doo,
but in things that have a conveniencie to our selves, or to the generall nature:
Laughter almost ever commeth of things moste disproportioned to our selves, and
nature.' *The Defence of Poesie* (1595).

Among the mescalin-takers we find Mr. Huxley often expressing a sense of merriment at what is awry. He started to laugh at Cézanne's head when it 'came to life as a small goblin-like man'; 'What pretensions!' he said, and 'Who on earth does he think he is?' remarking that the question was addressed to the human species at large. Alban Berg's music he found 'rather funny' and commented 'with a derisive lack of sympathy' on its 'essential incongruity'. He was overcome by 'enormous merriment' at the sight of a large blue car; 'Man had created the thing in his own image... I laughed till the tears ran down my cheeks.' Professor Zaehner describes himself as frequently succumbing to uncontrollable or manic or hysterical laughter. He did so when looking at Gentile da Fabriano's *Adoration of the Magi*—'the poor Magus's predicament seemed to me wildly amusing'. Reading Proust he commented, laughing, 'It's the sort of thing I *read* in my dreams. I wish Proust was half as funny as that', and spoke of *The Golden Bough* as 'One of the great comic classics'; 'The idea that there were actually people who believed in causes and effects' seemed to him grotesque and exceptionally funny. So did a book of Picasso drawings.

Ecstatic experiences bring perception of perfection, not of hitherto unnoticed incongruity. Ecstatics find delight in proportion and harmony, not humour in what is awry. Nothing humorous is ever a trigger to ecstasy. In ecstasy there is no fun whatsoever.

One of the most characteristic ecstatic claims is of a feeling of upness. In all seven mescalin examples the only up-expression is Rosalind Heywood's belief that she saw clear light on top of a mountain. In no consecutive seven of the 114 ecstasy texts is there only one up-expression; up-expressions appear in 50 per cent. of the texts.

Some of the mescalin-takers speak of physical symptoms unknown in accounts of ecstasies. Both Mr. Mortimer and Mr. Mayhew suffered from recurrent attacks of nausea. Professor Zaehner felt very thirsty and at one point had a pronounced sensation of cold in his extremities and genitals. Mr. Mayhew does however speak of a curious feeling in the top of his spine, and ecstatics sometimes do so too (see pp. 81 and 88).

Some mescalin-takers speak of feelings of fears of a kind that are not paralleled in descriptions of ecstasies. There are some varieties of ecstatic experience in which ecstasy follows and seems to be enhanced by earlier feelings of fear or awe (see pp. 166–9). The fears expressed by mescalin-takers seem very different.

Mr. Huxley at one point in the middle of his experience found himself 'all at once on the brink of panic'; he interprets this fear 'in theological language' as 'due to the incompatibility between man's egotism and the divine purity'. I do not know of an ecstasy where panic is felt between two periods of bliss. Mr. Mortimer found that taking mescalin 'eventually proved the most horrifying experience I had known... I now began to suffer a generalised apprehension amounting to panic... I was suffering the tortures caused by some forms of madness.' Rosalind Heywood passed through a period of terror and found the whole experience had become unendurable when she was rescued by a celestial figure. These panics may be characteristic of some kinds of religious experiences; they certainly do not occur in ecstatic ones.

It is fairly common in ecstatics after their experiences to feel a generalized love towards everything and everybody, and notably to what is normally repulsive to them (see p. 258). To Mr. Huxley during his experience fellow-creatures had become 'enormously irrelevant' and, as his comment on Cézanne in the same sequence shows, pretentious and ridiculous. Ecstatics do feel momentarily, as Mr. Huxley for longer, that they are removed from human concerns; but at no stage do they find humans contemptible or ridiculous.

Mr. Mortimer writes that 'thought and memory remained' while 'emotion entirely vanished', which certainly cannot be assimilated to the ecstatics' descriptions of their feelings of loss of sense. He continues, 'My mind had become neither less individual nor weaker, but emotionally I had ceased to be a person...the inability to feel suddenly became alarming in the extreme.' This is not the ecstatics' feelings of loss of self—indeed, he specifically says 'I remained highly conscious of self'—but it does seem as if it might be similar to those described by Mr. Huxley when he writes that his ability to 'think straight' remained but that he had no room for 'the ordinary, the necessary concerns of human existence, above all for concerns involving persons'. Then Mr. Mortimer says that he knew but did not feel the difference between right and wrong, love and hate; this is neither the ecstatics' loss of feelings of sin nor their gain of feelings of salvation.

I conclude, then, that though mescalin may occasionally give momentary ecstatic feelings, as it may have done to Mr. Mayhew, it does not typically do so and that mescalin experiences do not feel like ecstatic experiences. This is not affected by the fact that some people may believe that what they have experienced under mescalin *is* religious experience; but I should have thought that for anyone seeking the Beatific Vision (which was, before Mr. Huxley, granted only to Moses and St. Paul)[1] there were surer and pleasanter ways of attaining it than by taking mescalin.

With these conclusions in mind I want to consider my text L 24. This experience is quoted in Mr. Ward's book. It is said to be an account written by someone referred to as A which came into Mr. Ward's hands at the time he was experimenting with lysergic acid. It was, Mr. Ward says, largely this experience which made him discontinue his experiments, since he himself was seeking just such religious experience as A found, and he became convinced that this could not be attained by use of a drug which, as he puts it, rather disintegrates than integrates.

Mr. Ward explains that we have, by permission of A, 'an edited version...relating its terminology to my own'. This must explain why A's style is so very similar to Mr. Ward's, even to the idiosyncratic use of italics and inverted commas and occasional turns of expression. A is as much interested in the mechanism of this kind of experience as Mr. Ward is, and like Mr. Ward he believes that mystical experience is connected with an excess of adrenalin in the blood-stream. Like Mr. Ward, A strives throughout his experience to retain an observer's detachment; we cannot know how far any such experience is affected by determined self-observation. As Mr. Ward experimented with lysergic acid, so A experiments with psycho-physical control; he has been practising that not uncommon trick of 'shutting off pain' and it seems to be this which triggers off his experience. Mr. Ward assures the reader that A's experience is 'unconnected with narcotics or any other artificial stimulus',[2] but in several respects it seems to me rather to resemble the drug-experiences just examined than ecstasy.

Similar to many ecstatic experiences are his feelings of up-ness, of enlargement, that thought and feeling became one, that he had received an important communication about 'everything' which was incapable of adequate translation in words. Dissimiliar are:

—the duration and continuity of his experience. For the half-hour

[1] See Butler: W.M., p. liv.   [2] *A Drug-Taker's Notes*, p. 194.

that it lasted, he was walking to the station and 'the intensity of this new state fluctuated'. Sometimes he felt it was dying down, then 'some other thought or feeling, a fresh access of awe and wonder at the marvels I perceived in the outside world or understood in the world within' would renew it. And, as my very much abridged text shows, the feelings experienced during this half-hour were, like those of mescalin or lysergic acid, various and successive, not, as with ecstasies, a single if progressively deepening feeling.

—his feeling that 'time had very little significance' which, as shown above, is more similar to the mescalin-taker's than to the ecstatic's attitude.

—his reaction to what was 'according to one's ordinary perceptions' 'rather an ugly little suburban villa'. This ability suddenly to perceive beauty in what would not usually be regarded as beautiful is more typical of mescalin-takers than of ecstatics.

Mr. Ward seems himself to accept the experience of A as genuine religious experience because its overbelief was religious. But from mescalin people may derive genuine religious overbeliefs yet not have had the kind of experiences generally regarded as religious ones. Mr. Huxley believed he had attained the Beatific Vision. The female figure seen by Rosalind Heywood is described by her as 'celestial' and as a messenger of 'the High Gods'. Alice Marriot describes her vision as 'Paradise' and Mr. Mayhew accepts the possibility of deriving religious experience from mescalin. Only Mr. Mortimer and Professor Zaehner altogether deny that mescalin experiences are related to or can be assimilated to religious ones.

The experience of A is puzzling. The obvious guess would be that while experiencing what in someone else might have been ecstasy he was still affected by some such drug as mescalin taken earlier, but since Mr. Ward tells us that A's experience was unaffected by drugs, this cannot be the right explanation. But I do not think it would be proper unreservedly to accept A's experience as an ecstatic one or to draw on it, save very tentatively, for evidence about ecstasies.

CHAPTER XXV

The Distribution of Ecstatic Experience

After describing one of her ecstatic experiences—the one that is my text L 8—Virgina Woolf continued, characteristically,

> 'Now perhaps this is my gift; this perhaps is what distinguishes me from other people: I think it may be rare to have so acute a sense of something like that'. [1]

Writers on religious mystical experiences are not agreed as to whether such experiences are rare or common. Kirk assumes they are known to all:

> 'we all experience from time to time—though perhaps rarely—moments which can fairly be called ecstatic.' [2]

Butler, quoting Bishop Hedley of Newport, rather suggests that the ability to enjoy such experiences can be acquired;[3] and Underhill in *Mysticism* adopts what is perhaps the most usual point of view in assuming that ordinary people may know something similar to but less than the experiences of the classic religious mystics.[4] In her later book, *The Mystic Way*, however, she takes the interesting position of suggesting that the ability to enjoy these experiences is the privilege of people more developed than others in an evolutionary sense; she says that in the mystic we see

> 'creative evolution at work; engaged in the production of species as sharply marked off from normal humanity as "normal" humanity supposes itself to be marked off from the higher apes... In the mystics we seem to have a fortunate variation of the race'. [5]

---

[1] *A Writer's Diary*, p. 132. Charlotte Brontë, too, assumed that few people know the experience she described: '[Shirley] does not know her dreams are rare—her feelings peculiar' (L 14).

[2] V.G., p. 206.
[3] W.M., p. xxiii.
[4] E.U: M., p. 73.
[5] M.W., pp. 11-12.

Inge would seem to agree; he writes:

'If some have objected that they themselves have had no such experiences...they are answered by the reply that a genius for religious experience is like other exceptional endowments...and that in all other branches of human effort the average man is content to sit at the feet of the masters of an art or science.' [1]

Many of the religious experiences discussed by these writers are in my sense ecstasies. The evidence provided by my questionnaire group does suggest that the ability to enjoy ecstatic experiences is widespread among intelligent, well-educated, and creative people. It gives no indication as to how far this ability is usual among other kinds of people, though the information would not be difficult to acquire. A more professional approach, probably with modified techniques and special consideration of possible semantic difficulties, could easily discover whether ecstatic experiences are widespread among all kinds of people or, if not, among what kinds of people, and I believe that this information could be extremely useful in many fields. [2]

But without this information there are still certain indications, too slight to be called evidence, about the probable distribution of this ability in the population at large.

In the first place it seems to me likely that only certain kinds of people enjoy ecstasies *greater* than adamic ones. I base this on the following facts: that, in the questionnaire group, only those people who were intellectual or creative enjoyed *greater* than adamic ecstasies; that the ecstasies of children tend to be adamic; and that the ecstatic experiences of women who wrote to the B.B.C. (see Chapter XIII) were almost entirely of an adamic kind, and I do not think it probable that many creative or intellectual women would have been among them. So my guess is that knowledge and contact ecstasies tend to be confined to or to be more common among people of developed intellect or creative capacities.

This guess is, I think, to some extent supported by findings of Crichton-Browne and of Sir Humphry Davy when investigating

---

[1] C.M., p. vii.

[2] Clearly, the sooner such inquiries are undertaken the better. Although no model descriptions of ecstasy existed to guide my questionnaire group (see p. 11), such descriptions could all too easily become accepted and widely known. I did myself make some sporadic forays of inquiry into other groups but none of them was successful. Those that seem to have some interest are described in Appendix J.

nitrous oxide experiences which, as I have explained, seem to me of all drug-induced experiences to be the nearest to ecstatic ones (see pp. 260-2). The feelings induced by inhaling nitrous oxide gas, says Crichton-Browne, may vary

> 'from a simple sense of well-being and enjoyment up to the most magnificent conceptions, their complexion and amplitude being apparently a good deal determined by the personal equation. In persons of average mental calibre, they are pleasant and stimulating but in no way remarkable; but in persons of superior mental power, they become thrilling and apocalyptic. A working man who inhales the gas intimates on his recovery that he felt very happy, just as if he had had a little too much beer, and a philosopher announces that the secret of the universe had been, for one rapt moment, made plain to him.' [1]

Of dreamy mental states—those 'I have been here before' or *déjà vu* feelings which, as he describes them, seem similar to such experiences as Proust's (L 26)—Crichton-Browne says that these will be found to abound 'amongst the educated, the refined and the neurotic classes' but to be 'comparatively rare amongst the unlettered, the prosaic, and the solid masses of our people'. Crichton-Browne's conclusions confirm those of Sir Humphry Davy, who earlier made observations on the effects of inhaling nitrous oxide gas, and commented that in persons of intellectual training and distinction,

> the thoughts are in nine cases out of ten connected with some great discovery, some supposed solution of a cosmic secret',

while in 'humdrum' people the feelings, though pleasant, are 'in no way remarkable'.[2]

The conclusions of these men do indeed suggest the possibility that ecstatic experiences of all kinds may tend to be restricted to only certain kinds of people—the intellectual and the creative, the 'refined and the neurotic'. It seems to me that with extreme caution one might adduce in favour of this possibility the visible preferences of a minority of the population, and that palpably composed of people of these sorts, for trigger conditions where a choice of leisure avocations is

---

[1] 'Dreamy Mental States', *The Lancet*, 1895.
[2] Quoted by Leuba: P.R.M., pp. 272-3. Among the persons of 'intellectual training and distinction' upon whom Davy experimented were Coleridge and Southey.

available; and the preference of a larger section of the population—'the unlettered, the prosaic, and the solid masses'—for leisure conditions of a kind that do not generally trigger ecstasy and would, by ecstatics, often be regarded as anti-trigger conditions. At the very least this does suggest that some people feel they derive benefits from trigger conditions while others do not; and if this is so, it would be interesting to know whether the ability to derive such benefits is innate or acquired.[1]

[1] Supposition might go so far as to wonder whether not only ecstatic but also response experiences are enjoyed by all or only, to any considerable extent, by some; and a limited study, that might be helpful in this context, could be made of a broadcasting episode in 1952 when George VI died. As I remember it, the B.B.C. immediately cancelled all its lighter programmes and broadcast only matter of high artistic value—e.g. 'good' poems and music—such as would normally be heard often on the Third Programme, rarely on the Home, and almost never on the Light. A popular protest arose almost immediately, and long before they had intended to do so, the B.B.C. felt compelled to restore the usual light entertainment.

Not the least interesting part of this episode was the B.B.C.'s feeling, which was never verbalized, that only 'good' art was appropriate at a time when the nation was supposed to feel desolated. It will be remembered that to contemplate the fact of death while silently reciting a good poem is an exercise recommended by I. A. Richards, see pp. 169-70.

PART THREE

CHAPTER XXVI

Inspiration

The following chapters are frankly speculative. In them I try to examine the probable processes of overbelief-formation; to assimilate the process of inspiration to the process of forming overbeliefs; and to sustain the hypothesis that overbelief generally represents the most desired answer to an urgently asked question.

Leaving aside, now, the quasi-physical feelings of ecstasy, what ecstatics said they felt was that they had lost certain feelings and gained certain feelings. The headings under which these feelings of loss and gain were classified were evolved by me solely on a basis of convenience, but there did seem to emerge some pattern of relationship between what was felt to be lost—difference, time, place, limitation, worldliness, desire, sorrow, sin, self, words and images, sense—and what was felt to be gained—unity, eternity, an ideal place, release, a new life or another world, satisfaction, joy, salvation or perfection, glory, contact, knowledge.

The feelings of loss did not however necessarily entail the feelings of gain. To lose a feeling of difference is not necessarily to gain a feeling of all being one, to lose feelings of desire is not necessarily to gain feelings of satisfaction and to lose one's senses is not necessarily to gain knowledge.

But most of the statements of gain do entail, without being synonyms for, the statements of loss. To gain feelings of all being one is necessarily to lose feelings of difference, to gain feelings of satisfaction is necessarily to lose feelings of desire. One cannot feel oneself in a transformed world and, at the same time, in the everyday one; one cannot gain feelings of timelessness and eternity and retain one's sense of time. And though one can gain a feeling of knowledge without necessarily losing the means of expressing it, one cannot gain feelings of knowing everything without in fact, if not in logic, losing some of one's senses.

We may then infer that expressions of loss and gain are not alternatives, the one or the other being arbitrarily or aesthetically chosen. I think we may further infer that feelings of gain are, in these experiences, chronologically sequent to feelings of loss. This second inference is supported by the fact that the common procedure of trying to bring about intensity ecstasy is to induce loss in the hope that gain may follow;[1] and by the fact that after an ecstasy the ecstatic feels himself to be in a state of gain not loss, gain statements typically outnumbering loss statements by two to one.

This related pattern of loss and gain and the nature of the gains felt to have been made as a result of ecstatic experiences leads me to suppose that in these experiences we have a loss of the normal sense of relationships by which we assess our perceptions and a regaining of that sense of relationships in improved form; and that ecstatic experiences are manifestations (probably exaggerated manifestations) of processes facilitating improved mental organization.

The gains of ecstatic experiences are various but all, I believe, are compatible with this hypothesis. At its simplest the ecstatic may feel that he has gained generalized mental or emotional benefits.[2] Or he may feel he has gained a new focus of value, as in revelation ecstasies. Or he may believe that knowledge, whether religious or otherwise, has been gained or confirmed, and the expression of that knowledge may take the form of artistic or scientific creation. Or ecstatic experience may, to borrow an admirable phrase used by Kirk of the power of contemplation, 'inspire to action and...renew ideals'.[3]

I shall try to show that these results of ecstatic experiences do indeed represent improved mental organization and are such as could reasonably be expected from experiences of the kind we are concerned with. I shall begin by trying to establish a relationship between ecstasy and inspiration. That some relationship exists is often taken for granted, but attempts to find out precisely what it is are far less common.

The word *inspiration* is used very variously and it is desirable, at least to start with, to confine its meaning. The first figurative definition given by the dictionary is

A special immediate action or influence of the Spirit of God (or of

---

[1] I am strongly inclined to believe that all intensity ecstasies probably involve an initial withdrawal of no matter how brief a duration.

[2] For instance, 'strengthened in my appreciation of life' (J 1); 'several such experiences may make a person more mature, less insecure, and more at ease with himself' (J 2—see Appendix J).

[3] V.G., p. 353.

some divinity or supernatural being) upon the human mind or soul; said *esp.* of that divine influence under which the books of Scripture are held to have been written.

This definition, though it has an obvious bearing on some of the communications believed to have been received by some religious ecstatics, is too limited for my present purposes. The next definition given by the dictionary, which can include the first, is more useful:

A breathing in or infusion of some idea, purpose, etc. into the mind; the suggestion, awakening, or creation of some feeling or impulse, *esp.* of an exalted kind.

The first part of this definition refers to a supposed process by which ideas or purposes may be formed. I shall use the phrase *processes of inspiration* to refer both to such a supposed process and also to the processes by which new ideas and purposes are translated into communicable form. But it is rather the moment at which the new idea or purpose is first perceived in potentially communicable form that I wish to define as the moment of inspiration, and I shall use the word *inspiration* to denote the new idea or purpose at the moment when it is first perceived.

It is next needful to restrict the use of *inspiration*, as these dictionary definitions do and as common usage tends to restrict it, only to certain ideas and purposes and those 'of an exalted kind'. It would not be thought proper to call an inspiration any sentence spoken in conversation, any intention expressed in everyday life, although in so far as every situation is a new situation, every such sentence and intention must represent a new idea or purpose at some moment perceived for the first time. It is only by courtesy which I am not at present prepared to extend that a new political or advertising slogan may be spoken of as an inspiration; the common usage I seek is not so common as that. I think it would generally be agreed that *inspiration* is properly confined to new ideas and purposes accepted as having value, such new ideas as result in works of art or scientific theories, and some might go further and insist that the work of art or theory must be effective and good. Thus it might well be considered improper to apply *inspiration* to a scientific theory that on testing proved invalid, while of literature Bowra has written,

'Most of us, sooner or later, discriminate between authentic poetry and mere verse, between the real thing and the manufactured article, between *le vers donné* and *le vers calculé*, between what has a strangely unreckonable power and what is merely apt and adequate. In all such distinctions the notion of inspiration lurks somewhere in the background.' [1]

Whether we should properly distinguish between a process that results in good work and one that results in bad we cannot yet say. Common usage does however so distinguish and generally reserves *inspiration* for ideas accepted as valuable—or, to use my own terminology, for ideas which, when communicated, are potentially capable of acting as triggers. We have ample evidence that new ideas of this kind are often the result of ecstatic experience, and in such cases it seems reasonable to assume that the experience of ecstasy in some way facilitates the process of inspiration, the process, that is, of fusing the accumulated material that constitutes the valuable new idea into potentially communicable form.

So far I have illustrated *inspiration* only with reference to art and science. It may equally be referred to expressions of religious belief.

Most writers on religious mysticism allow there to be some relationship between artistic (or scientific) creation and mystical revelation, although artistic creation is naturally regarded as inferior to the processes leading to religious constructs. Thus in Underhill's systematization of the mystic way under five stages, she writes of the third, which she calls Illumination, that

'Many mystics never go beyond it; and, on the other hand, many seers and artists not usually classed amongst them, have shared, to some extent, the experiences of the illuminated state.' [2]

and later,

'So far as the machinery employed in it is concerned, there is little real difference except in degree between Wordsworth's imaginary vision of the "dancing daffodils" and Suso's of the dancing angels...though in the first the visionary is aware that the picture seen is supplied by memory, whilst in the second it arises spontaneously like a dream from the subliminal region, and contains elements which may be attributed to love, belief, and direct intuition of truth.' [3]

[1] *Inspiration and Poetry*, p. 2.   [2] E.U: M., p. 169.
[3] Ibid., p. 285.

Leuba, as an unbeliever, would not admit even this difference, and is positive in relating inspiration and mystical revelation. He maintains that the process that produces 'great thoughts' (he is quoting Goethe) is the same as that which produces mystical inspirations, and he comments,

'*All* kinds of ideas, and ideas of all degrees of puerility and importance, appear in our minds under the conditions which we have found to be those of revelation.' [1]

Now whether or not we accept God as the ultimate source of communications made by religious mystics as a result of ecstatic experiences, I cannot see any grounds for arguing that such communications must or need be produced by processes different from those which result in artistic or scientific communications. If we accept God as the ultimate source of these religious communications, we may still accept, as theologians do, that the form in which they are communicated to the world is largely the product not of God's voice, but of the personality, capacity, limitations, environment of the person to whom God communicated them:

'The most refined mysticism, the most exalted spiritual experience is *partly* a product of the social and intellectual environment in which the personal life of the mystic has formed and matured. There are no experiences of any sort which are independent of preformed expectations or unaffected by the prevailing beliefs of the time... Mystical experiences will be, perforce, saturated with the dominant ideas of the group to which the mystic belongs, and they will reflect the expectations of that group and that period.' [2]

To achieve the form in which they are communicated to the world, inspiration, as I have defined it, is essential.

If however we do deny that God is the ultimate source of Suso's vision, its communication is a creative event of a similar kind to Wordsworth's. If we deny God as the ultimate source of all the religious overbeliefs of ecstasy, then these overbeliefs appear as creative communications differing from other creative communications only in subject-matter. In other words, we can say that the religious communications resulting from ecstatic experience are, just like artistic and

[1] P.R.M., p. 240 et seq. Disappointingly, Leuba does not mean by 'all kinds of ideas' all kinds of ideas but only bad art as well as good, taking *The Ballad of the Schooner Hesperus* as an example of what apparent inspiration can produce.

[2] Jones: S.M.R., p. xxxiv.

scientific communications resulting from ecstatic experience, inspirations whose formulation is apparently facilitated by ecstasy. And by accepting religious communications as such, we have greatly enlarged the range of instances where the result of ecstasy is inspiration, the perception of a new idea or purpose in potentially communicable form.

We may enlarge it still further, for more often in the texts than appears at first sight the result of ecstasy was inspiration. Clearly this was so in Robert Nichol's case (L 5), and we may notice that both Virginia Woolf and Charlotte Brontë (L 8 and L 14) assumed that the result of ecstasy should be to take a pen and write. But surely Berenson's new understanding of art (L 10) is properly called an inspiration? Inspiration is surely the proper name for the beliefs that came to H. Warner Allen and Jacquetta Hawkes and Richard Church as results of ecstasy (L 11, L 19, and L 23b)? In each of these cases what ecstatic experience brought was a moment of perception of a new idea, belief, or purpose, subsequently translated into the form in which we read it.

But if inspiration is frequently the result of an ecstatic experience, an ecstatic experience is not a necessary or even a usual precursor of a creative communication. Ecstasies are typically rare; creative communications, even of an exalted kind, are comparatively frequent. What of the cases when inspirations come unheralded by ecstasy?

It is of course possible that though inspiration is sometimes a result of ecstasy and apparently facilitated by it, in other cases inspiration results from processes that cannot reasonably be shown to have any kind of relationship with ecstasy. I think this is doubtful, and suggest that consideration of the response-experiences which I postulated earlier (see p. 97 et seq.) may help to explain why inspiration sometimes results from ecstatic experiences and sometimes not.

Two examples of response-experiences, similar to ecstasies in taking place in trigger-conditions and to knowledge ecstasies in resulting in inspirations, are as follows:

'Having drunk a pint of beer at luncheon...I would go out for a walk of two or three hours. As I went along, thinking of nothing in particular, only looking at things around me and following the progress of the seasons, there would flow into my mind, with sudden and unaccountable emotion, sometimes a line or two of verse, sometimes a whole stanza at once.' [1]

[1] A. E. Housman, *The Name and Nature of Poetry*, p. 49.

284

'I loved to take my violin with me on my summer rambles, so that whenever I felt inspired, I could express it in music. During the summers in Sääksmäki I selected a platform, for preference, consisting of a stone in Kalalahti with an enchanting view... There I gave the birds endless concerts. The neighbourhood of Lovisa inspired me quite as much. When sailing I often stood in the bows with my violin and improvised to the sea.'[1]

Both these fulfil my criteria for response-experiences in that the feelings of new knowledge gained were apparently the expected response to the chosen trigger-surroundings. And if I am correct in assuming that response-experiences are less intense forms of ecstatic ones, then it may be supposed that what we have in these and innumerable similar cases are response-experiences that are a less intense form of knowledge ecstasies or knowledge-contact ecstasies; that these are the expected responses supports my earlier suggestion that ecstasy is rather an exaggeration than a manifestation of the normal processes facilitating mental reorganization.

It may then be that such rarer experiences as those of Gibbon in the ruins of the Capitol (see p. 113), St. Augustine reading Cicero, and Hakluyt's first encounter with geography (see p. 157), each a moment of perception of a new idea, belief or purpose, each taking place in trigger-conditions but lacking the descriptions of feeling that would justify counting it as an ecstasy, represent experiences similar to both ecstasies and response-experiences but less intense than the former and more so than the latter.[2]

There are however other occasions when inspiration arises in situations unlike any of the common trigger-conditions and without any descriptions of ecstatic feelings; for instance,

'Mark Twain describes his working in Twichell's house with the noise of children and carpenters all around him. "It's like a boiler factory for racket," he declares, "and in nailing a wooden ceiling on the room under me the hammering tickles my feet amazingly...but I am never conscious of the racket at all" '.[3]

'Schubert wrote his song *Ständchen*, sitting at a table in the gardens

---

[1] Sibelius, quoted Harding: A.I., p. 85.
[2] One may, of course, suppose that on occasions such as these ecstasy was felt but, for various reasons, not described; but this is a dangerous supposition.
[3] Harding: A.I., pp. 38–9.

of "Zum Biersack", Währing, surrounded by "a regular Sunday hubbub", waiters running about, fiddlers and chatter.'[1]

It is of course possible that such noises may have been triggers, at least to response-experiences, for both men, though most people would surely regard such conditions as anti-trigger ones. But there is a sense in which trigger-conditions may always be present for the experienced creator, for he has it within himself to create the trigger of creative work. The questionnaire group shows that creative work may properly be included among the more common triggers to ecstasy, and every creative worker knows that creative work can be a trigger to response-experiences as well, that to begin to work, no matter how unwillingly or laboriously, will almost always act as a trigger to set inspiration going. For creative work, once started, acts as a recurrent trigger, each new pattern formed with each stroke of the pen (or brush, etc.) acting as a new trigger to ever-renewed inspiration. And here I am using *inspiration* to denote not a major and exalted idea at its first moment of perception but rather a series of evolving flashes on a tiny scale, constantly guiding and shaping the communicated form.

That this process may be accompanied by feelings of continuous ecstasy, of a unitive state, is shown by the quotation from Bowra given earlier (p. 95). But if creative work, like other common triggers, may sometimes induce ecstasy or ecstatic states, we need not assume that creative work, any more than any other trigger, must always do so. We need only assume that creative work, like other triggers, usually induces experiences or states similar to ecstasy but less intense, and that such experiences or states are associated with processes facilitating improved mental organization.

Up to this point I have used *inspiration* to refer only to 'exalted' ideas and purposes, those generally judged to be of high value. But this is not a position that can be sustained, for it could lead us to suppose that quite different processes account for inspirations judged as of high value and those judged as low. Yet if we do not accept that some inspirations but not others have an ultimately supernatural source, we surely must suppose that similar processes account for the inspirations of Joseph Salmon the Ranter (see R 18) and those of St. Augustine, for Wordsworth's vision of the dancing daffodils and Suso's of the dancing angels, for *The Ballad of the Schooner Hesperus* and for Goethe's

---

[1] Harding: A.I., p. 39.

greatest works. And though the scientific inspiration that proved invalid can never have had value for anyone who knew its falsity, it would be absurd to suppose that the process by which it was made was essentially different from one resulting in a theory that could stand up to test.

Then we have to consider not only good work and bad but also major work and minor. I earlier rejected the possibility of regarding a new political or advertising slogan as a product of inspiration. But here, as in all trivial creative products, we still have examples of new ideas that were, at some moment, first produced in communicable form. Either we must say that exalted ideas and purposes probably spring from one kind of process and trivial ideas and purposes from another, or we must accept the probability that similar processes lie behind all inspirations, no matter what their scale or value.

I think however it would be fair to say that the inspirations which result from ecstatic experience are seldom if ever those that would be judged trivial in scale even though they may prove to lack value—that is, to prove ineffective as triggers. It might then be reasonable to suppose that the more exalted inspirations are likely to result from more intense experiences, which such trivial inspirations as political and advertising slogans are not likely to spring from even those less intense forms I have called response-experiences.[1]

It is however only those inspirations which result from ecstatic or response experiences with which I am concerned. I have suggested that in ecstatic experiences we have a loss of the normal sense of relations by which we assess our perceptions and a regaining of that sense of relations in improved form, and that inspiration, the newly perceived idea or purpose, represents the communicable form of that mental improvement. But not all such gains need be even potentially communicable. The new and improved mental organization may take place at a level below the conscious and be expressed, if at all, only in feelings that the experience has had value, that harmony and satisfaction have replaced stress and dis-ease.[2] But when the results of ecstatic

[1] In my own experience, trigger-conditions are neither sought nor found suitable for writing journalism; but are noticeably useful if not necessary when seeking a new idea for a serious book and in the early stages of thinking it out.

[2] 'We should not forget that finer organisation is the most successful way of relieving strain, a fact of relevance in the theory of evolution. The new response will be more advantageous than the old, more successful in satisfying varied appetencies.' Richards: *Principles*, pp. 196–7.

experiences are what we can properly call inspirations, then it is the conscious perception of the new mental organization or unification that *is* the moment of inspiration. How the material which composes the new unification is collected, how the inspiration is translated into communicable form will be considered later. On the nature of the physical processes that must accompany the mental processes of inspiration I cannot even speculate.

CHAPTER XXVII

Conversion

The word *conversion* is, it appears, properly used to refer only to substantial and lasting improvements in outlook and personality. De Sanctis is emphatic that conversion must not be confused with invention or faith or inspiration. As an example of the first he cites Henri Poincaré discovering the solution to a mathematical problem and comments 'his personality did not undergo, on this account, the least mutation.' Inspiration, he says, 'is an illumination which clarifies a truth already perceived, or reveals a new truth'; work done under its impact is done without effort, and this is not true of conversion. Lastly, 'Conversion, most emphatically, must not be identified with belief' which is 'only a moment of the conversion'.[1]

Underhill seems to restrict the word to conversion to a specific variety of the mystical life,[2] but her general account of the process is capable of wider application:

'All conversion entails the abrupt or gradual emergence of intuitions from below the threshold, the consequent remaking of the field of consciousness, an alteration in the self's attitude to the world.'[3]

Lastly, William James says that *conversion* denotes

'the process, gradual or sudden, by which a self hitherto divided, and consciously wrong, inferior and unhappy, becomes unified and consciously right, superior and happy, in consequence of its firmer hold upon religious realities.'[4]

[1] *Religious Conversion*, p. 66 et seq.
[2] She gives Richard Jefferies as an example of a man who failed to achieve conversion, writing of 'the Life known to the great mystics, which Richard Jefferies apprehended in these moments of insight, yet somehow contrived to miss'. E.U: M., p. 192.
[3] E.U: M., p. 177.
[4] V.R.E., p. 186.

I shall then take *conversion* to refer to a lasting and substantial mental reorganization, spontaneously achieved and accepted as beneficial. By *lasting* I mean usually of permanent, always of considerable duration. By *substantial* I mean relating to those beliefs that the person concerned holds to be the most important part of his mental life, which entails, in effect, that most though not necessarily all conversions will be concerned with religious belief. And by *spontaneously achieved* I mean to exclude such 'conversions' as those examined by Sargant in his book *Battle for the Mind* which are changes in belief deliberately and enforcedly brought about or imposed by the will of some person or persons other than the one whose belief is to be changed; all mass-conversions are therefore excluded.

I want first to establish the fact that the 'moment of conversion', referred to by de Sanctis, may also be the moment of an ecstatic experience.

Some of the texts in the religious group are presented as conversions by the writers from whom I took them. Suso's experience (R 1) is given by Underhill as an example of conversion, and James presents as examples of conversion the experiences of David Brainerd and of the woman who adopted the religion of healthy-mindedness (R 13 and R 8). Outside this group it is easy to find examples when a moment of religious conversion was also a moment of ecstatic experience.

If however we accept conversion as entailing a lasting and substantial alteration in the self's attitude to the world, there are other examples in the groups that must be accepted as such. The clergyman of text R 3 comments on his experience,

> 'My highest faith in God and truest idea of him were then born in me.'

and Bucke, of his experience,

> 'the memory of it and the sense of the reality of what it taught has remained during the quarter of a century which has since elapsed... That view, that conviction, I may say that consciousness, has never, even during periods of the deepest depression, been lost' (R 17).

Confining myself, for the moment, to religious beliefs if not necessarily to orthodox ones, we may fairly add to these H. Warner Allen who clearly intended his experience to be accepted as a conversion (L 11), and Q 56 and Q 60 both of whom told me that their respective and lasting religious beliefs had resulted from the experiences described.

But though the most important part of a person's mental life is likely to be his religious beliefs—or rather his attitude to the questions with which religion concerns itself—this is not necessarily so, and I think it proper to accept as a conversion the experience of Berenson which completely changed his outlook on what was, to him, the most important part of his mental life. He says, 'I acquired faith in my vision... This faith has never abandoned me' (L 10)—words similar to those used by Bucke, and certainly indicative of a lasting and substantial change in mental organization.

I do not of course claim that all conversions are accompanied by ecstasies. Sometimes, as with inspiration, we find a moment of conversion in trigger-conditions but lacking all description of ecstatic feelings; sometimes there are no trigger-conditions and no ecstatic descriptions. Sometimes, de Sanctis suggests, the process of conversion may be so gradual that the exact moment when the new belief is established may not be perceptible. My claim is only that sometimes ecstasy accompanies and appears to facilitate the realization of conversion.

It is clear that the wholly new life adopted by such a religious convert as Suso and representing, after the moment of conversion, years of unremitting effort, must eventually represent a much more complete reorganization of the personality than that effected in a person who, as a result of ecstatic experience, henceforth believes in God or in an aesthetic vision but does not therefore deliberately seek to change his personality or way of life. We are forced to consider how much change in 'the self's attitude to the world' can be considered a sufficiently substantial one to justify the name *conversion*. What is the minimum of change in personality and outlook that can warrant this name, and when should we use some other name or say that some other process has taken place?

Walter de la Mare speaks of falling in love as a conversion:

> 'There is a conversion, a sudden and complete reorientation as it were, of the self. There may also be a similar conversion of the mind, when some new and reviving idea, ideal or cause seizes upon it and deflects its future course into a new channel. This "falling" in love may be called a conversion of the heart, equally unforeseen and complete.' [1]

[1] *Love*, p. lxxiii.

I earlier mentioned falling in love in connexion with revelation ecstasies, those ecstasies whose result is the discovery of a new focus of value in the trigger, and said then that revelation should not be confused with conversion which is the end, not the beginning of the process and represents the culmination of accrued interest in a focus of value (see p. 156). No conversions, says de Sanctis, are in fact fulminant and unprepared, even though they may seem so, and nothing could seem more fulminant and unprepared than the apparently totally unexpected discovery of value in a hitherto unencountered trigger. But, as I have already suggested, such revelations may well be less unprepared than they look (see p. 156 n), and in so far as revelation experiences bring about a lasting change, felt as valuable, in the self's attitude to the world, they have much in common with conversions.

It would probably be convenient to accept the word *conversion*, as I defined it earlier, for experiences that represent mental reorganization on a substantial scale affecting the whole personality. *Revelation*—the discovery of a new focus of value in a trigger—names experiences which result in a reorientation of outlook believed to be valuable, but not necessarily affecting the whole or even a substantial part of the personality; the new purposes derived from revelation may, however, come so to dominate the personality that eventually, whether with or without accompanying ecstasy, conversion will be achieved. *Inspiration*, as de Sanctis says, need effect no personality mutation; but it will still, no matter how transiently and on how small a scale, effect a change from a self 'hitherto divided' to a self unified.

Thus these three names, *conversion*, *revelation*, and *inspiration*, represent differences in degree rather than in kind. To some degree any mental reorganization must change the personality and outlook of the person experiencing it, and conversion, revelation, and inspiration all represent some degree of mental reorganization. Indeed *some* mental reorganization takes place, I have suggested, in all ecstatic experiences and probably in many other experiences far below the level of intensity I have accepted as ecstatic. Change from 'a self hitherto divided, and consciously wrong, inferior and unhappy' to a self 'unified and consciously right, superior and happy', though of a kind neither lasting nor substantial, may be seen in the fleeting changes from despondency to happiness effected in Carlo Levi and in Meredith's and Gissing's heroes, in the finer organization that Richards claims as the benefit to be derived from art (see p. 287 n), in the enhanced well-being and

292

appreciation of life claimed by the people in Group J, even, as Leuba suggests, in the relief to be obtained from a hot bath or a nice cup of tea (see pp. 100–1). Conversion, in short, need not be viewed as other than the most dramatic and substantial of the forms of mental reorganization effected through ecstatic experience.

CHAPTER XXVIII

Primary Overbelief (i)

THE SEEDS OF UTOPIA

Ecstatic experience will be described in some or most of the following terms:

feelings of a new life, another world, satisfaction, joy, salvation, glory; of new and/or mystical knowledge; of loss of words, images, sense; of unity, eternity, heaven; of up-feelings; of contact; of loss of worldliness, desire, sorrow, sin; of enlargement and improvement; of loss of self; of inside-feelings; of loss of feelings of difference, time, place, of light and/or fire feelings; of peace and calm; of liquidity; of ineffability; of release; of pain.[1]

To believe one has had some or most of these feelings is belief warranted by ecstatic experience. If we were to postulate the most probable unwarranted beliefs that would be held as a result of ecstatic experience, we could reasonably surmise that they would include belief in the existence of a joyful and satisfactory condition in which, purified, one could enter a glorious new world or life; in which one gained ineffable knowledge aided by losing the impediment of normal perceptions; in which all was timelessly one; in which worldliness, desire, sorrow, sin were unknown; to which one was raised or elevated; in which one made contact with Someone or Something or everyone or everything; by which one was enlarged or improved; to which all differences, all divisions or time, all localized places were irrelevant; by which one was illumined and warmed; was at peace; felt a beneficial flow; endured delicious pain.

A great many people do indeed believe this or some part of this, and such beliefs, if not formed by experience of ecstasy, are often believed to be confirmed by it. Those who through the ages have

---

[1] See Appendix D, Table 4*b*; the order is that of the percentages of people in the groups reporting these feelings. *Intensity* and *withdrawal* are omitted.

hammered out the vocabulary in which such beliefs could be expressed have believed they were making a fully justified *emprise sur le réel*. An alternative possibility is that an adequate explanation of such beliefs is to be found in the nature of ecstatic experiences.[1]

But whatever may be the ultimate source of these beliefs, which I shall call primary overbeliefs, it is generally accepted that their expression must at least partially be a temporal, local and natural matter, 'saturated', as Rufus Jones put it, 'with the dominant ideas of the group to which the mystic belongs'.[2]

'When men search into the unknowable, they naturally arrive at very different results,' said Leslie Stephen,[3] and some such differences may arise from the total nature of the different mystical systems which impose different expectations upon their followers. But the expressions that will be chosen by any given mystic to express his primary overbelief will depend both on what is culturally available to him and on the particular nature of his experiences which, as we have seen, may vary from one occasion to another. In this chapter I want to consider some of the beliefs which seem as if they may arise from the nature of adamic ecstasies and knowledge (but not knowledge-contact) ecstasies.

Adamic ecstasies are, in my terminology, those characterized by feelings of new life, etc. and loss of feelings of worldliness, etc.; feelings of sense are often lost but, by definition, neither feelings of knowledge nor of contact are gained; feelings of loss of self are typically not mentioned; feelings of difference, time, place are often lost, feelings of unity, eternity, heaven often gained. Feelings of kindness and love

---

[1] Bertrand Russell describes the beliefs which, he says, characterize mystical philosophy 'in all ages and in all parts of the world' as belief in knowledge by intuition or insight as contrasted with sense, reason, analysis; in a Reality behind the world of appearances; in unity and the absence of division; a denial of the reality of Time; that evil is an illusion produced by the divisions and oppositions of the analytic intellect; in joy and a feeling of infinite peace. 'This attitude', he says, 'is the direct outcome of the nature of the mystical experience'. *Mysticism and Logic* (London, 1918; Pelican edn., 1953), pp. 15–17.

[2] See p. 283; compare also 'Catholics, but not Protestants, may have visions in which the Virgin appears; Christians and Mohammedans, but not Buddhists, may have great truths revealed to them by the Archangel Gabriel; the Chinese mystics of the Tao tell us, as a direct result of their central doctrine, that all government is bad, whereas most European and Mohammedan mystics, with equal confidence, urge submission to constituted authority.' Bertrand Russell, *Religion and Science* (London, 1935), p. 180.

[3] *An Agnostic's Apology* (London, 1893), p. 94.

to others seem to belong to this stage, and this I tentatively linked with Inge's statement that it is to this stage that the social and civic virtues belong (see p. 93). In these ecstasies the sense of self and of environment are not so much lost as transformed. The ecstatic's self, freed from all taint of worldliness, desire, sorrow, sin, is made joyful and purified and renewed. He tends to feel that this translation is back to an earlier state, once known, now lost, and recurrent images of this state—which I have called symbols of innocence—are the state of Adam before the Fall, of childhood, of pre-cortical man, of the Noble Savage; or of simpler forms of life which, although they die, need not bear the intolerable burden of knowing it—animals and flowers. Similarly suitable images arise for the transformed environment—the Garden of Eden, the Echoing Grove, the glades of Arcadia.

'Life should be like this for ever,' said Q 18, and it is often the wish of the ecstatic to attain the unitive state in which the feelings of ecstasy may be continuously enjoyed. It is, I suggest, the postulation of a continuous state of adamic ecstasy that has led to so many constructs of communities where the lives, values, and surroundings of the inhabitants symbolize the feelings of adamic unitive states.[1] I will instance a few such models and then show how aptly they represent the feelings of a postulated condition in which life should be, for ever, like the feelings of adamic ecstasy.

The basic Christian model is, of course, the Garden of Eden where Adam and Eve were innocent and unashamed and untainted by knowledge, could gather their food without painful labour, loved one another and lived in perfect amity with all created things. Secular models are numerous.[2] The simplest form, which corresponds with the Christian Garden of Eden, postulates a secluded place—typically an island—untainted by civilization where simple people live without law, property, labour, commerce, holding all things in common in perfect innocence and love. A succint description of such a society is Gonzalo's in *The Tempest*:

> *Had I plantation of this Isle my lord,*
> *I'th' Commonwealth I would (by contraries)*

[1] The ostensible authority for an adamic society will, of course, vary according to the thought of a period. At one time it may be God, at another, the General Will or the Logic of History.

[2] For several such models in early Greek thought, see W. K. C. Guthrie's *In the Beginning* (London, 1957), pp. 69–78.

Execute all things: For no kinde of Trafficke
Would I admit: No name of Magistrate:
Letters should not be knowne: Riches, poverty,
And use of service, none: Contract, Succession,
Borne, bound of Land, Tilth, Vineyard none:
No use of Mettall, Corne, or Wine, or Oyle:
No occupation, all men idle, all:
And Women too, but innocent and pure:
No Soveraignty.
All things in common Nature should produce
Without sweat or endevour: Treason, fellony,
Sword, Pike, Knife, Gun, or neede of any Engine
Would I not have: but Nature should bring forth
Of its owne kinde, all foyzon, all abundance
To feed my innocent people.
I would with such perfection governe Sir:
T'Excell the Golden Age.[1]

For the past two hundred years the adamic society has been a political concept of considerable importance and recent models have been more apparently practical, more nearly related to the supposed possibility of transforming the actual society into the model. One of the most influential of these models, at least in British Socialist thought, has been that depicted in William Morris's *News from Nowhere*, published in 1891; and it so well incorporates all the typical features of the secular adamic society that it will be useful to draw attention to some of its salient points:

It is winter when the narrator goes to bed in contemporary London; when he wakes up it is 'a beautiful bright morning, seemingly in early June'. The Thames water is no longer muddy but crystal-clear; the manufacturies along its banks have gone and now gardens stretch down to the river. The straggling city has gone; what was once London is now small villages with wooded well-watered country between them. All the big manufacturing towns have gone too with the factories that sustained them; craft goods are made at home or in small workshops. There is no more money, no trade of any kind, not even barter; goods are given for love. And all the goods, everything that is made, is beautiful; 'none of that sickening vulgarity' of the narrator's own time.

The people are beautiful too and very long-lived. A woman of

[1] II. i. 150-75; I have omitted the interjections of other characters.

forty looks like a contemporary girl of twenty and a man is lively and active at well over a hundred. No one looks sad or ill or dirty. Everyone is beautifully dressed. No one despises or envies another.

There are no laws, no punishments, no crime. True, a man may occasionally murder for passion but 'remorse will certainly follow transgression'. The former Houses of Parliament are used to store manure; 'the whole people is our parliament'.

There are no schools and the children play in the woods. By watching the happy work of their elders they naturally come to want to perform the simple crafts needed by the community; 'I don't think we need fear having too many book-learned men.'

Oxford and Cambridge still exist but now they cultivate the Art of Knowledge (it is not made clear what this is), not the 'commercial learning of the past'. They are no longer 'the breeding-places of a peculiar class of parasites, who called themselves cultivated people'. A few people do have more or less intellectual hobbies but these are gently laughed at; 'mathematics and antiquarian novels stand on much the same footing'.

There is no mention of major art. What art or craft there is has direct communal use. Neighbours—for so the inhabitants address each other—are called to meals by 'silvery chimes playing a clear sweet tune...like the song of the first blackbird in spring'. People sing together, carve lintels and weave tapestries for communal halls. Hospitality is immediate and unstinted, and a delicious wine is constantly drunk. A mill is said to be 'as beautiful in its way as a Gothic cathedral'.

All neighbours are equal. Once, we are told, it used to be believed that the use of machinery could free the energies of the more intelligent part of mankind to follow the higher arts and science and history. 'It was strange, was it not, that they should thus ignore that aspiration after complete equality which we now recognise as the bond of all happy human society?'

The neighbours look much to the past and particularly to periods that can be seen as similar to their own such as—in Morris's view—the Middle Ages. They never look to the future. 'This is not an age of inventions,' says one of them, and they express lack of interest in what is to come. 'We have got back our childhood again,' says Hammond, the wise old man.

The relation of such models to the feelings of adamic ecstasies is clear. That this is a social model derives from the retention of feelings of self, but of a self no longer lonely, sorrowful, guilty, but filled, instead, with loving-kindness towards others in an environment gloriously transformed. Inhibition of normal feelings of repulsion and their replacement by feelings of *agape* ensure a model of complete equality as 'the bond of all happy human societies', with especial warmth for the counter-elite, the normally repulsive, 'the poor, the maimed, the lame, the blind' [1] who, transformed, inhabit the new environment.[2] Loss of feelings of worldliness ensures a world from which attitudes typical of that condition are absent—feelings of competitive social status based on worldly standards. It also ensures that the anti-triggers typical of the world-as-it-is are absent—commerce, money, dark satanic mills, etc. Instead we find superabundance of triggers—unspoiled nature, beautiful people and things—in whose constant presence ecstatic feelings cannot but be enjoyed.

One of the most interesting aspects of adamic societies is the low and even contemptuous value set on education, intelligence, creativeness, invention. It will be remembered that the adamic is the least valued stage of ecstasy to those who have known others and that there is some probability that no *greater* stage than the adamic is available to those who are neither creative nor intellectual (see p. 275). I have by definition excluded feelings of knowledge from the ecstasies I call adamic, and in adamic societies knowledge is neither valued nor sought.

The pursuit of knowledge could not, in such models, be consonant with the dream. The inhibition of repulsion, the extension of brotherly love to all, ensures that the most cherished inhabitants are those formerly despised;[3] for some people to pursue knowledge would be to set these people above others, endow them with mysteries and powers that others could not share. 'La république n'a pas besoin de savants,'

---

[1] *Luke* xiv. 13.

[2] Sometimes *agape* is extended to the animal world, even to the normally repulsive animal world, like Sister Wasp and Brother Fly:

> Am not I
> A fly like thee?
> Or art not thou
> A man like me?
> (William Blake, *The Fly*)

Compare J 9's 'I welcome the wasps into the kitchen even!' and the Biblical version of the ideal place, where 'The wolf also shall dwell with the lamb, and the leopard shall lie down with the kid; and the calf and the young lion and the fatling together; and a little child shall lead them.' *Isaiah* xi 6.

[3] He hath put down the mighty from their seats, and exalted them of low degree.' *Luke* i. 52.

said Coffinhal in 1794, justifying the death sentence on Lavoisier at one of those moments when it seemed as if a society based on adamic ideals could be established on earth.[1]

The concept of the adamic society would be worth some study in the context of past and current political thought. The doctrine of the change of heart is also of interest. It is generally accepted that people as they are cannot be expected to respond to adamic ideals and that a change of heart (or, as some Marxists put it, of human nature) will be needed. But there is a puzzling paradox. If the adamic society were established, then people's hearts could not help but be changed as a result of living in trigger-conditions which would bring about the experiences that give the change of heart. But only people who have known ecstasy and have had their hearts changed will dream of the adamic society and seek to bring it about.

Periodically, however, enough people have envisaged and pursued the model to make sporadic attempts to create the adamic society here and now. That of the Christians immediately after the death of Jesus was such an attempt:

'And all that believed were together, and had all things common;
'And sold their possessions and goods, and parted them to all men, as every man had need.
'And they, continuing daily with one accord in the temple, and breaking bread from house to house, did eat their meat with gladness and singleness of heart.'[2]

Throughout Christian history there have been periodic attempts to set up communities on this model; the Hutterites in the United States can still provide an example.

In secular societies recent revolutionary movements have shown the influence of the model. 'All men are created equal' is an adamic statement, 'Liberté! Egalité! Fraternité' an adamic slogan. Citizen and comrade, like brother and friend and neighbour, are adamic forms of address. And not only in revolutionary times, when the hearts of all but the incorrigible (and therefore justly punishable) are changed,

[1] An article on Karl Barth in *The Times Literary Supplement* (May 23, 1958) explained that in *Genesis* iii. 22, 'And the Lord God said, Behold, the man is become as one of us, to know good and evil', the Hebrew words for *good* and *evil* 'simply mean things useful and harmful, what we regard as scientific knowledge, which Adam was forbidden to acquire'. Most adamic models show a distrust of science.
[2] *Acts* ii. 44–6.

but, as a protest against the perennial failure to establish the ideal, small adamic societies periodically emerge, on paper or in fact— Fourier's phalansteries, Robert Owen's projected Villages of Co-operation, Southey's Pantisocrasy on the Susquehanna, the Brook Farm Institute of Agriculture and Education, the early kibbutzim in Palestine.

I am not, of course, suggesting that any adamic ecstasy will result in belief in the value of some or other form of adamic community, only that such belief is likely to be acceptable to those who have known adamic ecstasies. But since adamic ecstasies do not themselves result in feelings that knowledge has been gained or in creative expression, it is not from adamic ecstasies that the creation and planning of these models can ensue. They must arise from experiences that bring feelings of creative expression, whether ecstatic or less intense.

There is however another form of ideal place in many ways similar to the adamic model but in significant ways different from it, and this form seems like an expression of knowledge ecstasies when both these and adamic ones have been known.

Where adamic ecstasies usually feel like reversion to simpler states, knowledge ecstasies feel like advance to more developed, more complicated ones. The ideal place of the knowledge ecstasy is more often set in the future than in the past. Where adamic ecstasy feels like a gain of simplicity at the expense of complication and organization, the knowledge ecstasy feels like the organization of increased complexity, and the ideal place of the knowledge ecstasy is figured rather as a city than as a village or small group. And, where both adamic and knowledge ecstasies have been known, comparative values come into play. The knowledge ecstasy is regarded as more valuable than the adamic ecstasy, and in the ideal place of the knowledge ecstasy, those who pursue knowledge must not only be given conditions sympathetic to the pursuit but are set apart from and regarded as superior to simpler people who have not these capacities and needs. The postulated society is now a developing not a static one, and its development is led by the seekers after knowledge. Examples of such models are rarer than those of adamic societies; the *greater* ecstasies are agreed to be rarer than the *lesser* ones.

Moses Maimonides provides an example of the ideal future ensuring ideal conditions for the scholar:

'It is not because they desired to have dominion over all lands and nations, and be honoured by all people, or because they desired to have plenty to eat and drink, and other pleasures, that the wise men and the prophets longed for the Messianic days, but because they would then be at leisure to study the Law and its teaching without being interrupted by any oppressor'. [1]

In More's *Utopia* wise men are given 'a perpetual licence from laboure to learninge', and clever children, who are few, are early set apart:

'there be not many in every citie, which be exempte and discharged of all other laboures, and appointed only to learning, that is to saye: suche in whome even from theire very childhode they have perceaved a singular towardnes, a fyne witte, and a mind apte to good learning.' [2]

Those people who were the sole inhabitants of the adamic utopia are now set, kindly, but firmly, in their lesser places:

'The wisdom of the scribe cometh by opportunity of leisure; and he that hath little business shall become wise. How shall he become wise that holdeth the plough...and whose discourse is of the stock of bulls?... So is every artificer and workmaster...

'All these put their trust in their hands; and each becometh wise in his own work. Without these shall not a city be inhabited... They shall not be sought in the council of the people, and in the assembly they shall not mount on high; they shall not sit on the seat of the judge, and they shall not understand the covenant of judgment: neither shall they declare instruction and judgment... But they will maintain the fabric of the world; and in the handywork of their craft is their prayer.' [3]

Both the last two writers speak of cities and cities imply laws, organization, hierarchy. Plato and St. Augustine both saw the ideal place in terms of civic organization, and to Sir Thomas Browne mathematics significantly pertained to the *City* of Heaven (see p. 220) and was not, as for Morris, a derided pursuit classed with antiquarian novels. In that scientists' paradise, Francis Bacon's city of New Atlantis, mathematicians have their honoured place with other inventors in Salomon's House where the aims are

'the knowledge of causes, and secret motions of things; and the

---

[1] Quoted by M. Friedländer, *The Jewish Religion* (London, 1891; 2nd edn., 1900), pp. 229–30.
[2] *Utopia*, trans. Ralph Robinson (1556; English Reprints edn., 1899), Bk. II, pp. 86 and 104.
[3] *Ecclesiasticus* xxxviii.

enlarging of the bounds of human empire, to the effecting of all things possible'.

There is no question of equality here; we are told of 'a great number of servants and attendants, both men and women'. More, the use of the knowledge gained is determined exclusively by the wise—'some [secrets]...we do reveal sometimes to the State, and some not'.[1]

A transition from the adamic model to this one is interestingly shown by the early Christians. I have cited a passage showing how that society created itself on an adamic model (see p. 300) but a little later disputes arose, the Greeks saying that Greek widows were neglected in favour of Hebrews in the daily ministrations:

'Then the twelve called the multitude of the disciples unto them, and said, It is not reason that we should leave the word of God, and serve tables.

'Wherefore, brethren, look ye out among you seven men of honest report, full of the Holy Ghost and wisdom, whom we may appoint over this business.

'But we will give ourselves continually to prayer, and to the ministry of the word.'[2]

Though this model is an unpopular one in current political thinking it would, I believe, be wrong to assume that the knowledge society, because hierarchical, can be assimilated to models for the form of society we nowadays call fascist. In the knowledge society many features of the adamic society are retained. The simple are respected and well treated; aesthetic values are cherished and commercial values despised;[3] the societies are altruistic and peaceable, and no individuals seek secular glory. If one is looking for a form of ecstatic experience that could provide the source of the fascist ideal, it might perhaps be sought in such experiences as those I have discussed on pp. 101-2, whose

---

[1] *The New Atlantis* (1627; World's Classics edn., 1906), pp. 265 and 274.

[2] *Acts* vi. 2-4.

[3] I have never come across an ideal society in which men of commerce had high prestige. 'Tradesmen and merchants shall not enter the places of my Father,' said Jesus (*The Gospel According to Thomas* (London, 1959), p. 37) and of royal levées we are told that 'were a person actually engaged in trade to obtain a presentation, his presentation would be cancelled as soon as the Lord Chamberlain was made aware of the nature of his occupation' (*Manners and Rules of Good Society*, by A Member of the Aristocracy (24th edn., London, 1900), p. 79). Men of commerce are however often the rulers of cacotopias postulated by contemporary science-fiction writers.

characteristics are feelings of power and glory derived from success in the eyes of the world.

Models of ideal communities are not of course the only possible results of ecstasies, nor is it necessary that knowledge felt to be gained through an ecstatic experience should be an interpretation of the feelings of the ecstasy. Where the knowledge sought and gained is knowledge of neutral truth the nature of the ecstatic experience will usually be irrelevant. Nor is imaginative creation necessarily based on the nature of ecstatic experience, though it does seem that, directly or indirectly, ecstatic experience is the subject most often treated in imaginative creation.

CHAPTER XXIX

Primary Overbelief (ii)

COMMUNICATION AND CONTACT

Knowledge-contact ecstasies are characterized by feelings that knowledge has been gained through a contact believed to have been made. It is characteristic of inspirations, whether preceded by ecstasy or not, that the new idea or purpose feels as if it had arrived independantly of the creator's volition and often as if it were communicated by someone or something else. I want now to consider some of the ways in which inspiration is felt to 'arrive'.

The new knowledge is formed by the creator: This is the least usual way of expressing feelings that new knowledge has been gained. In the questionnaire group there are only three examples of this kind of expression and all relating to *doing* rather than *knowing*—'wanting to do something and feeling you can do it' (Q 9); 'succeeding in doing something you've never been able to do till now' (Q 11); 'done something you haven't done before' (Q 21). These were all answers to questions about inspiration not ecstasy.

The new knowledge is spontaneously created by itself: 'it suddenly comes' (Q 14). Two examples from outside the groups are:

'I don't know what put the Leonides family into my head—they just came. Then, like Topsy, "they growed".' [1]

'They [*sc.* musical ideas] are simply there, flashlike, unprepared and absolutely distinct. I have nothing to do but write them down.' [2]

The notion of two parts to the creative act, the self-creating knowledge and the person who receives and communicates it is by far the most usual expression of inspiration in the questionnaire group. Three people here use the image of childbirth; the 'I' must deliver the spontaneously created idea.

[1] Agatha Christie in the Foreword to *Crooked House* (London, 1949).
[2] Ernest Toch, quoted in *On Inspiration*, by Frank Howe (undatad).

The new knowledge derives from an unnamed and unpersonified source: The questionnaire group provides some examples: 'something urgent that has got to be communicated…not from myself, me only the channel' (Q 18); 'something which appears to be *given* to you' (Q 35).

The new knowledge is communicated by a faculty whose function this is: From the questionnaire group: 'the creative faculty descends' (Q 19); 'an inward power that surges to the surface' (Q 46). From outside the groups, two examples are:

> 'the writer who possesses the creative gift owns something of which he is not always master—something that, at times, strangely wills and works for itself'.[1]
>
> 'The themes have been dictated to him, intuitively and unconsciously, by his inner being, his native genius, his inspired soul.' [2]

The new knowledge is created by a special faculty, as above, but this faculty is personified: 'I couldn't have done what I had done if I hadn't been inhabited by someone other than myself,' said Q 2; 'given to me by a being who was a poet' said Nichols (L 5), and outside the groups this form is extremely common. George Eliot told J. W. Cross

> 'that, in all that she considered her best writing, there was a "not herself" which took possession of her, and that she felt her own personality to be merely the instrument through which this spirit, as it were, was acting'.[3]

Dickens spoke of 'some beneficient power' that, when he sat down to his book, showed it all to him,[4] Stevenson of his 'Brownies' that did all his work for him while he slept.[5] Kipling named as his Daemon the creative voice that spoke to him, and commented, 'When your Daemon is in charge, do not try to think consciously. Drift, wait, and obey.'[6] Goethe is said to have put his own experience into the mouth of Wilhelm in *Die Wanderjahre* when he wrote,

> 'It often seems to me as though an invisible genius were whispering something rhythmical to me'. [7]

'It often seems to me as though——' None of these people believed more than that when they were inspired *it seemed to them as though*

---

[1] Charlotte Brontë in the Preface to *Wuthering Heights* (1849).
[2] Charles Koechlin, quoted in *On Inspiration* by Frank Howe.
[3] Harding: A.I., p. 16.   [4] Ibid., p. 17.
[5] Ibid., p. 113.   [6] *Something of Myself* (London, 1937), pp. 208–10.
[7] Quoted Harding: A.I., p. 65.

someone other than themselves was 'giving' the material, and this impression was so strong that it seemed natural to give this 'someone' a personality and a name.

The new knowledge is believed to be communicated by someone else: It is believed that the communication does in fact come from someone other than the inspired person, which is to say that it comes from a supernatural being. Sometimes the belief may be no more than a matter of poetic imagery, as with the seraph who spoke to Tennyson (L 2), the Spirit of Life that illumined Richard Feverel (L 16) and the messenger of Hope who came to Emily Brontë (L 21).

But these are literary texts, and in the religious texts such claims are more than a matter of poetic imagery. Of text R 2, Underhill explains that St. Catherine of Siena attributed 'the intuitive perception of the deeper self' to 'the Divine Voice speaking in her soul'. We cannot doubt that Angela of Foligno believed it was indeed God who conversed with her (R 5a) or that Joseph Salmon believed he heard a voice 'that came from the throne of the heavenly Almightiness' (R 18).

Not only pregnant sentences but entire books may be believed to be communicated by divine voices and written at their behest.

> 'When our Divine Lord revealed to the saint [*sc.* St. Gertrude] it was His will she should commit her revelations to writing, her humility was exceedingly amazed.' [1]

Boehme professed to write only what he had 'seen' by divine illumination[2] and comments to God,

> 'Thou didst make me write with so great a detachment that I was obliged to leave off and begin again as Thou didst choose...suddenly Thou wouldst cause me to write, then at once to cease, and then to begin again.' [3]

---

[1] Quoted by Poulain: G.I.P., ch. xxv, 27.   [2] Inge: C.M., p. 277.

[3] E.U: M., p. 295. Like many who obey a less exalted source Boehme had difficulty in keeping up with his inspiration: 'Art has not wrote here, neither was there any time to consider how to set it punctually down, according to the Understanding of the Letters, but all was ordered according to the Direction of the Spirit, which often went in haste, so that in many words Letters may be wanting, and in some places a Capital Letter for a Word... And though I could have wrote in a more accurate, fair and plain Manner, yet the Reason was this, that the burning Fire often forced forward with Speed, and the Hand and Pen must hasten directly after it' (Ibid., pp. 296–7). It is difficult to see why a supernatural spirit who has chosen to make a communication should do so at too fast a dictation speed.

Jones describes how Rulman Merswin, the fourteenth-century mystic and author of the *Book of the Nine Rocks*, was commanded to write by 'a Divine Voice', and how he resisted at first and then gave in. Jones comments,

> 'This resistance against the command to put revelations into writing is almost universal with mystics. It appears in quite similar form in the writings of Hildegarde, Elizabeth of Schoenau, and Matilda of Magdeburg.' [1]

Sometimes the divine spirit is believed to appear in person to lay his commands on the inspired. One of the best-known examples is the revelation of God that came to St. John the Divine when he was 'in the Spirit on the Lord's day', appearing as 'one like unto the Son of man' and saying,

> 'What thou seest, write it in a book, and send it unto the seven churches which are in Asia... Write the things which thou hast seen, and the things which are, and the things which shall be hereafter'. [2]

And through the twenty-two chapters of the book rings periodically the admonitory voice crying, 'Write!' 'Write!'

It does appear that inspiration, whether it comes with ecstasy or without it, tends to feel as if presented to the understanding rather than consciously created by it. When it comes thus with ecstasy, we have the form of ecstatic experience I have called knowledge-contact ecstasy. I have already surmised that it is from the more intense experiences that the more exalted inspirations spring (see p. 287), and possibly the more intense the experience the more the feeling of contact with another personality impresses itself as real and not a mere as-though. But to some extent people's readiness to personify this feeling of creative power, as also the names they give it, must be governed by their needs, their environment, the nature of the revealed message and their sense of decorum. We would not expect Agatha Christie to claim that her detective-story was revealed to her by a messenger of God any more than we should expect Angela of Foligno to talk to Brownies. But since the same person may, on different occasions, use different forms of expression, we may suspect that the different forms of expres-

---

[1] Jones: S.M.R., p. 267 and p. 268n. Unwillingness to begin a book is not confined to those who have received a divine command to write it.
[2] *Rev.* i. 11 and 19.

sions listed above refer to fundamentally similar feelings if of varying intensity.[1]

From knowledge-contact ecstasies we should, then, expect the following primary overbeliefs:

Belief that contact has been made with a personality capable of communicating valuable knowledge; and, when the knowledge gained is mystical—i.e. largely incommunicable—which arises at a *greater* stage of ecstasy than that in which communicable knowledge is believed to be gained, the belief that this knowledge is comprehended by other faculties than those of the normal understanding and is either incomprehensible to the normal understanding or capable of being apprehended by it only imperfectly and with loss of meaning. Such an overbelief is well exemplified by St. Augustine in text R 19.[2]

Where the knowledge gained is of a limited or comparatively trivial kind, or where the gainer of knowledge is a sceptic, the belief in contact with another personality will be hardly more than playful, and accepted as deliberate personification of a faculty whose workings make it feel as if it were something other than oneself. But where the knowledge gained is exalted and the gainer a believer, we may reasonably guess what the nature of the supposed communicator will be, and that to it will be attributed, in totality form, all the felt gains of ecstasy—unity, eternity, omnipresence, omniscience, perfection, loving-kindness, joy. And those who had known adamic ecstasies as well might be expected to set this personification in an ideal place of light and beauty 'with all the company of heaven'.

Greater than those ecstasies in which knowledge is felt to have been communicated by someone or something else are those in which union with the someone or something else is believed to be achieved. It will be remembered that Christians are forbidden those experiences in which complete union with God are claimed and also those in which all sense is lost. The Christian must retain sufficient sense to receive

[1] For instance, Dickens on one occasion spoke of 'some beneficient power' that showed his book to him; on another he simply declared that 'he *saw* his stories and wrote them down'. Harding: A.I., p. 30.

[2] The belief that 'intelligence' in the religious sense, as opposed to the less perceptive reason, can grasp spiritual truths immediately and in their essence was well expressed by Richard of St. Victor: 'As we are wont to see corporeal things by corporeal senses, as visible, present, and corporeal, so also can this intellectual sense grasp the invisible, indeed as invisible, but immediately and essentially.' Quoted by Gordon Leff, *Mediaeval Thought* (Penguin, 1958), p. 139.

knowledge and must seek contact not with the ineffable God but with Christ, significantly called the *Logos*.

But, as we have seen, some Christians do claim the forbidden experiences and Underhill states that the two methods of approach to mystical experiences (in my terms, intensity and withdrawal) meet in

> 'that consummation of love..[when] distinctions between inward and outward, near and far, cease to have any meaning'.[1]

But by whichever method it is achieved, writers who disapprove of this variety of experience (as Underhill, apparently, does not) stigmatize it as oriental, buddhistic, pantheistic, negative, etc. It would seem that at this stage withdrawal and intensity ecstasies feel the same and are likely to be described by ecstatics in the anathematized phrases about total oneness without distinction, total loss of feeling and sense, etc. But I think we may expect a difference in primary overbelief according to whether the ecstatic habitually approaches this stage by way of intensity or withdrawal.

I must be tentative about withdrawal ecstasies since I have barely examined them, but they do not seem to induce feelings of knowledge gained or of contact with a communicative personality suitable for personification. In withdrawal ecstasy one seeks to or may involuntarily 'Fade far away, dissolve, and quite forget' and, in doing so, have that feeling of oneness with the trigger which almost always becomes a feeling of oneness with all or perhaps, if the ecstasy is deep enough, of nothingness with nothing. The feelings of contact that arise in intensity ecstasies are different.

But since it is only withdrawal ecstasies that can be deliberately induced, it must follow that the possibility of the forbidden beliefs will arise in any religion where means of attaining ecstatic experience are practised. And if it is true that the *greatest* stages of both withdrawal and intensity ecstasy feel the same, then from people who habitually enjoy only the *greatest* stage of intensity ecstasy we should expect the forbidden beliefs characteristic of those who practise withdrawal ecstasy. But I think it improbable that there would be many people who *habitually* attained this stage of intensity ecstasy without on other and probably more frequent occasions knowing those *lesser* stages I have called adamic and knowledge-contact ecstasies. And if ecstasies of all stages are known, then the resulting overbeliefs are likely to

[1] E.U: M., p. 304.

synthesize in a single system the beliefs appropriate to each stage. How far this is true of Christianity, the system in which we are likely to find such a synthesis most fully worked out, I cannot judge.[1]

I have toyed with the idea—though I will not proffer it as more than a toy—that the first seeds of the Renaissance might be sought at the end of the eleventh century with the invention of courtly love when ecstasies induced by sexual love became, for the first time in the Christian era, ecstatic experiences that could be interpreted without reference to God. Before art or knowledge could take forms unconnected with religion, sexual love became almost a counter-religion.[2]

[1] Some confirmation of the above may be found in the fact that Von Hügel finds it necessary to criticize St. Catherine of Genoa for holding eschatological beliefs which, he admits, derive from the nature of her mystical experiences and which involve, in my terms, extrapolation from only the *greater* stages of ecstatic experience. Thus her concept of the after-life presents 'a markedly unsocial, a *sola cum solo* picture' corresponding with 'her strongly ecstatic, body-ignoring, body-escaping type of religion [which] tended to starve the corporate, institutional conceptions and affections'—that is, in my terms, she ignored adamic models. This, says Von Hügel, is a defect of most mystical outlooks; but to believe that the soul attains its full personality 'in and by direct intercourse with God alone' must not lead to neglect of 'the social constituent of the soul's life both here and hereafter'. M.E.R., Vol. II, pp. 201–2.

[2] I refer only tentatively to Table 8, Appendix D, which shows the shape of ecstasies induced by sexual love, because the mention of other triggers by some people may have blurred the pattern. But the shape they seem to assume, with comparatively high mention of feelings of unity, etc., comparatively high feelings of loss of self, and comparatively low gain of feelings of knowledge, seems similar to that which we might expect from union ecstasies.

CHAPTER XXX

Primary Overbelief (iii)

Ecstasy and Conduct

People who accept ecstatic experiences or the results of ecstatic experiences as of high if not supreme value may well find that this evaluation tends to modify their views of right conduct. For they may come to seek, more or less single-mindedly, a way of living that reproduces as far as possible the feelings of ecstatic experiences and to avoid the conditions likely to inhibit such experiences.

Among feelings frequently lost in ecstasy are those of what I have generically called worldliness, worldliness itself being a condition felt to inhibit ecstasy. The ecstatic will, then, seek to keep himself 'unspotted from the world',[1] to 'Free fro the prees, and dwelle with sothfastnesse'.[2] For 'whoever is resolved to live an inward and spiritual life must, with Jesus, withdraw from the crowd. No man can live in the public eye without risk to his soul'.[3] He will reject the competitive standards of worldly approbation, taking no thought for raiment or possessions, for 'How hardly shall they that have riches enter into the kingdom of God' and 'where your treasure is, there will your heart be also'.[4] He will seek to be rid of the self and the gratification of the self, turning aside from 'the devices and desires of our own hearts', giving alms in ways unattended by worldly approbation,[5] and ready even to sever bonds of worldly affection:

'If any man come to me, and hate not his father, and mother, and wife, and children, and brethren, and sisters, yea, and his own life also, he cannot be my disciple.'[6]

[1] *James* i. 27.　　　　　　　　　　　[2] Chaucer, 'Balade de Bon Conseyl'.
[3] Thomas à Kempis, *The Imitation of Christ*, trans. Leo Sherley-Price (Penguin, 1952), Bk. I, ch. xx, p. 50.
[4] *Luke* xviii. 24 and xii. 34.　　　　　　　　[5] See *Matt.* vi. 1.
[6] *Luke* xiv. 26. Schweitzer concludes that 'The teaching of the historical Jesus was purely and exclusively world-renouncing,' Quoted by Kirk: V.G., p. 57.

There is authority for seeking to lose sense, for 'which of you with taking thought [*cogitando*] can add to his stature one cubit?' [1] St. John of the Cross may sum up:

'That thou mayst have pleasure in everything, seek pleasure in nothing. That thou mayst know everything, seek to know nothing. That thou mayst possess all things, seek to possess nothing.' [2]

To some extent, of course, the standards of conduct derived from ecstatic experience must depend on the types of experience known, the intensity with which they are enjoyed, and the conclusions that are drawn from them.

'If we know how [a man] conceives of God we shall have a clue to his probable conduct; his conduct illumines—to some extent at least—not merely the genuineness but even the type of his creed. Nor can conduct or creed be separated from experience. If there is such a thing as experience of God...then it is bound to have reactions both with creed and conduct. Thought about God must in the end correspond with experience of God'. [3]

Not all ecstatic experiences, as we have seen, bring thoughts about God, and not all people who have known ecstatic experiences will seek to adopt such rigorous rules of conduct as those above. Many will be content with setting high value on triggers and condemning excessive devotion to 'getting and spending'. But even this to some extent, as the religious values to a greater extent, is to reject the common worldly standards based on social and pecuniary values, and to be some way towards being an ascetic which the dictionary defines as 'One who is extremely rigorous in the practice of self-denial, whether by seclusion or by abstinence from creature comforts.' James distinguishes six possible motives for asceticism:

(i) expression of organic hardihood (ii) love of purity, shocked by the sensual (iii) sacrifices made to the Deity (iv) penances arising from pessimistic feelings about the self, coupled with theological beliefs concerning expiation (v) psychopathic obsessions (vi) perversion of bodily sensibilities whereby normally pain-giving stimuli are felt as pleasures.[4]

[1] *Luke* xii. 25.　　　　　　　　　[2] Quoted by E.U: M., p. 206.
[3] Kirk: V.G., pp. 9–10.
[4] V.R.E., pp. 291–2. Kirk suggests that the competitive spirit should be added to these; V.G., p. 194n.

Perhaps there should be added the suggestion that the conditions in which ecstatic experiences are enjoyed and the feelings they give are such that asceticism may seem the way of life most consonant with them.

But to whatever extent conduct is based on ecstatic experience, it will in the first instance tend to run counter to conduct socially based. 'Morality is the herd-instinct in the individual,' said Nietzsche[1] and the suggestion has often been repeated.[2] To lose all thought of self and of the worldly standing of self is to live outside the pecking-order context in which human societies seem to be founded. To regard love of spouse or children as a clog is to disavow the duty of continuing the race. To refuse to seek wealth or the possessions and comforts that money can buy is to undermine the economic framework by which society is sustained.[3] To refrain from taking part in public affairs or ordinary social life suggests that group instincts have been, to whatever extent, inhibited or atrophied. Exclusively to follow such compulsions is to reach a point where, as Kirk put it,

'The normal is the evil: only the supremely abnormal is divine. Religion is the reverse of all that is natural.' [4]

And if to these compulsions is added deliberate cultivation of those forms of ecstatic experience which lead to negative overbeliefs, the situation is reached in which (as Kirk said would have been that of the Church had it endorsed the teachings of Dionysius the Areopagite) the group

'would have dwindled to a tiny sect of anti-social hermits, devoid of all interest in life, art, morality—indeed in everything except what has been called "a static absorption in an unconditioned Reality."' [5]

But, continues Kirk, 'the Church knew a better way' as indeed the Church must if it was to survive. What the Church did was not only

[1] *The Joyful Wisdom*, trans. by T. Common (London, 1910), p. 161.

[2] For instance, by Veblen, who spoke of 'that instinct of race solidarity which we call conscience' (*The Theory of the Leisure Class*, ch. ix, p. 150) and by Trotter, Conscience, then, and the feelings of guilt and of duty are the peculiar possessions of the gregarious animal' (*Instincts of the Herd in Peace and War*, p. 40).

[3] The owner of a clothing store in South Dakota, asked his opinion of the local Hutterite community, said, 'You've seen the way they dress, those old rags they wear... Maybe if they'd fix themselves up and support the retail business and do something for the community, they'd be all right.' *Harper's Magazine*, December 1958, p. 73.

[4] V.G., p. 214.

[5] Ibid., p. 303.

to endorse but to insist upon those forms of ecstatic experience that I have called intensity ecstasy and more, to insist, that these must not be cultivated to the point where 'spiritual vacancy and spiritual fulness are almost indistinguishable'.[1] By insistence that ecstasy must be positive, not negative, it is possible to reconcile the mystic with the world. What may be considered the proper fruits of ecstasy may differ; but it is consistently characteristic of Western thought and not only inside the Church that it gives moral approbation to positive ecstasies with visible fruits, moral condemnation to negative and barren experiences:

> 'unless an alleged experience of God brings with it a call to disinterested action of some kind or another—unless there is reaction, response, reciprocity—we shall scarcely be able to avoid the conclusion that something is amiss.' [2]

> 'the emphasis and decision have to lie with, and to depend upon, the mental and volitional work and the spiritual truth and reality achieved in and for the recipient, and, through him, in and for others.' [3]

> 'An improvement of response is the only benefit which anyone can receive, and the degradation, the lowering of a response, is the only calamity.' [4]

> 'Everything that is good makes me productive. I have gratitude for nothing else, nor have I any other touchstone for testing what is good.' [5]

To seek the experience for its own sake and not for its fruits is consistently decried:

> 'We have seen already how in much pagan thought such a subjective experience—as, for example, ecstasy—was taken as constituting the *whole* end of human endeavour; we shall see the same idea obtruding itself from time to time with disastrous results in the history of the Church...the emotional experience here and now is secondary, and is never to be made the final test of genuine Christianity. What *matters* is that a man should have the right attitude—should love God and his neighbour.' [6]

> 'It is not the intensity of the conscious experience, its thrill, its pleasure, or its poignancy which gives it value, but the organisation of its impulses for freedom and fullness of life.' [7]

[1] Kirk: V.G., p. 199.   [2] Ibid.
[3] Hügel: M.E.R., Vol. II, p. 46.   [4] Richards: *Principles*, p. 237.
[5] Nietzsche, text L 6.   [6] Kirk: V.G., pp. 104-5.
[7] Richards: *Principles*, p. 132.

In the west, then, it is generally accepted that the right and proper function of ecstatic experiences is to lead to improvement—improvement for the individual as he achieves finer organization, sees more truth, develops his intellect and his creative capacity; and improvement for the group as a result of the contribution the improved individual is able to make,[1] whether in the form of service or in the form of communicating new ideas that may lead to more successful mastery of the environment or which may act as triggers to lead to improvement in others. In this light ecstatic experience can be seen as a self-perpetuating process leading to more and more improvement, and as such it has been seen in several quasi-poetical interpretations of the experience or of what is believed to have been encountered in the experience:

> 'Men have given different names to these "obstinate questionings of sense and outward things." We may call them, if we will, a sort of higher instinct, perhaps an anticipation of the evolutionary process; or an extension of the frontier of consciousness; or, in religious language, the voice of God speaking to us.'[2]

> 'the movement which He [Jesus] initiated, the rare human type which He created, is in essence a genuinely biological rather than a merely credal or intellectual development of the race. In it, we see life exercising her sovereign power of spontaneous creation'.[3]

The improvement that the ecstatic has to offer will however often be rejected by the group, at least at first, for change is antithetical to stability, and to seek to change the group is to seek to destroy what at any given moment seems a stable form. But, as Shaw remarked,

> 'in the sphere of thought, Anarchism is an inevitable condition of progressive evolution. A nation without Freethinkers—that is, without intellectual Anarchists—will share the fate of China.'[4]

and (at least until recently) we have all taken it for granted that fifty years of Europe is better than a cycle of Cathay.

[1] Plato was insistent on the duty of improved individuals to contribute to the group: ' we shan't be unfair to our philosophers, but shall be quite justified in compelling them to have some care and responsibility for others.' *The Republic*, Bk. 7, 520: see also Bk. 8, 540: 'they will spend most of their time in philosophy, but when their turn comes they will turn to the weary business of politics and do their duty as Rulers'.

[2] Inge: C.M., p. 5.

[3] E.U: M.W., p. 35.

[4] G. B. Shaw, *The Perfect Wagnerite* (1898), reprinted in *Major Critical Essays* (London, 1932), p. 223.

But to whatever extent the group accepts or rejects the offerings and ideals of the ecstatics, it still is true that ecstatic experiences are likely to give rise to ideals and conduct substantially in conflict with the standards of society as a whole. The standards of the group are denied by the nature and needs of ecstatic experience. More, many of the activities of ordinary social life act spontaneously as inhibiting anti-triggers and also divert time and energy from more creative activities.

Yet ideals drawn from ecstatic experience do undoubtedly influence contemporary social life, though to differing extents in different periods. Indeed I would say that many people judge contemporary social issues by the standards of their chosen ecstatic models, and today we can often see the influence of such a model—usually an adamic one—in judgements made on issues as various as foreign policy, education, town-planning, and the proper functions of mass media. But, to take a more limited and concrete example, I suggest we can see the influence of ecstatic models in the stereotypes we make for certain groups in our society.

Thus we have a stereotype for a group of people who, although in a position to profit from worldly standards, choose to devote their lives to 'the poor, the maimed, the lame, the blind'—nurses, social workers, missionaries, foster-parents, elementary school-teachers. Such people are said to have had a call or vocation to do jobs for which love must have replaced instinctive repulsion. We are shocked when they ask for limited hours of work or sufficient financial reward for them to be able to enjoy worldly pleasures; they should, it is felt, be above such mundane considerations as time and money. We feel that to reward the work in financial terms would be to corrupt the vocation—the wrong people, it is often said, would then go into it.[1]

Then we have stereotypes for creative artists, living in poverty in garrets, carelessly dressed, inconsiderate of time and of conventional social standards, whom we readily think of as corrupt when successful and conforming to conventional display of success.[2] And we have stereotypes for those whose duty to the community is to provide

[1] Socialist reformers often express the hope that in a socialist community all citizens would have such attitudes to their work and to their fellow-citizens.
[2] It has for a long time been accepted that rich men of commerce acquire merit by giving money to such trigger activities as religion, art, scholarship; no one expects successful artists or scholars to make donations to commerce.

spiritual guidance or knowledge—the poor parson, the unworldly absent-minded professor.[1]

Interest and value would, I believe, derive from extended study of the influence of ecstatic models on social life.

[1] 'One feature common to the classical philosophers and their disciples—a feature linking them closely to the ascetic element in Christianity—was their sense of detachment from the phenomenal world of change around them. The characteristic was heightened by popular fancy which, while it often gave the philosopher the "nimbus of a demi-god" and expected miracles of him, could also insist upon the nebulous character of his speculations and the unpractical dreaminess of his life.' Kirk: V.G., pp. 477–8.

CHAPTER XXXI

The Formation of Overbelief (i)

THE GENERAL PROCESS

I must now try to sustain my hypothesis that overbelief represents the most desired answer to an urgently asked question. These two parts, the asking of a question and the desire for a certain kind of answer are, I suggest, the most important factors in the formation of overbelief. There are, of course, others, and for convenience in discussion we may represent the chronological order of overbelief formation as follows:

(i) the asking of the question
(ii) the collection of material
(iii) the fusing of the collected material
(iv) the translation of the fused material into communicable form
(v) the testing of the answer

Before going on to consider these stages separately I will adduce some necessarily lengthy examples in which all or most of them can be seen. In my first examples both the question and answer are known and what is sought is the experience which, it is believed, will validate the answer.

First I have extracted from St. Augustine's account of his progress to his conversion those passages that seem especially relevant in this context:

'To Carthage I came, where there sang all around me in my ears a cauldron of unholy loves. I loved not yet, yet I loved to love, and out of a deep-seated want, I hated myself for wanting not...

'...in that unsettled age of mine, learned I books of eloquence, wherein I desired to be eminent... In the ordinary course of study, I fell upon a certain book of Cicero... This book of his contains an exhortation to philosophy, and is called "*Hortensius*." But this book altered my affections, and turned my prayers to Thyself, O Lord; and made me have other desires and purposes. Every vain hope at once became worthless to me; and I longed with an incredibly burning desire for an immortality of wisdom, and began now to arise, that I might return to Thee... For with Thee is wisdom. But the love of wisdom is in Greek called "philosophy," with which that book inflamed me...

'For this space of nine years then (from my nineteenth year, to my eight and twentieth) we lived seduced and seducing, deceived and deceiving, in divers lusts; openly, by sciences which they call liberal; secretly, with a false named religion... In those years I had one,—not in that which is called lawful marriage, but whom I had found out in a wayward passion...

'In those years when I first began to teach rhetoric in my native town, I had made one my friend, but too dear to me, from a community of pursuits, of mine own age, and, as myself, in the first opening flower of youth... Thou tookest that man out of this life, when he had scarce filled up one whole year of my friendship, sweet to me above all sweetness of that my life... At this grief my heart was utterly darkened; and whatever I beheld was death... I became a great riddle to myself, and I asked my soul, *why she was so sad, and why she disquieted me sorely*: but she knew not what to answer me. And if I said, *Trust in God*, she very rightly obeyed me not; because that most dear friend, whom she had lost, was, being man, both truer and better, than that phantasm she was bid to trust in...

'I loathed exceedingly to live, and feared to die... For I bore about a shattered and bleeding soul, impatient of being borne by me, yet where to repose it, I found not. Not in calm groves, not in games and music, nor in fragrant spots, nor in curious banquettings, nor in the pleasures of the bed and the couch; nor (finally) in books or poesy, found it repose...when I thought of Thee, Thou wert not to me any solid or substantial thing. For Thou wert not Thyself, but a mere phantom, and my error was my God...

'I wrote "on the fair and fit," I think, two or three books... and "fair," I defined and distinguished what is so in itself, and "fit," whose beauty is in correspondence to some other thing: and this I supported by corporeal examples. And I turned to the nature of the mind, but the false notion which I had of spiritual things, let me not see the truth...

'And for almost all those nine years, wherein with unsettled mind I had been their [*s.c.* the Manicheans'] disciple, I had longed but too intensely for the coming of this Faustus. For the rest of the sect... when unable to solve my objections about these things, still held out to me the coming of this Faustus, by conference with whom, these and greater difficulties, if I had them, were to be most readily and abundantly cleared. When then he came, I found him a man of pleasing discourse, and who could speak fluently and in better terms, yet still but the self-same things which they were wont to say. But what availed the utmost neatness of the cup-bearer to my thirst for a more precious draught?...

'To Milan I came, to Ambrose the Bishop... To him was I unknowingly led by Thee, that by him I might knowingly be led to Thee... I began to love him, at first indeed not as a teacher of the truth, (which I utterly despaired of in Thy Church,) but as a person kind towards myself... I hung on his words attentively; but of the matter I was as a careless and scornful looker-on...and yet was I drawing nearer by little and little, and unconsciously...

'My mother had now come to me...when I had discovered to her, that I was now no longer a Manichee, though not yet a Catholic Christian, she was not overjoyed, as at something unexpected...but, as being assured, that Thou, who hadst promised the whole, wouldest one day give the rest...she replied to me, "She believed in Christ, that before she departed this life, she should see me a Catholic believer." '...

'I kept my heart from assenting to anything, fearing to fall headlong... For I wished to be as assured of the things I saw not, as I was that seven and three are ten...

'And I, viewing and reviewing things, most wondered at the length of time from that my nineteenth year, wherein I had begun to kindle with the desire of wisdom, settling when I had found her, to abandon all the empty hopes and lying phrenzies of vain desires. And lo, I was now in my thirtieth year, sticking in the same mire, greedy of enjoying things present, which passed away and wasted my soul; while I said to myself, "To-morrow I shall find it; it will appear manifestly, and I shall grasp it..."

'Meanwhile my sins were being multiplied, and my concubine being torn from my side as a hindrance to my marriage, my heart which clave unto her was torn and wounded and bleeding.'...

'I was constrained against my will to conform myself to a married life, to which I was given up and inthralled.'

'Upon a day...there came to see me and Alypius [his friend], one Pontitianus...we sat down to converse, and it happened that upon a table for some game, before us, he observed a book, took, opened it, and contrary to his expectation, found it the Apostle Paul... Whereat smiling, and looking at me, he expressed his joy and wonder, that he had on a sudden found this book, and this only before my eyes. For he was a Christian, and baptized... He told us then how one afternoon at Triers, when the Emperor was taken up with the Circensian games, he and three others, his companions, went out to walk in gardens near the city walls, and there as they happened to walk in pairs, one went apart with him, and the other two wandered by themselves; and these, in their wanderings, lighted upon a certain cottage, inhabited by certain of thy servants...and there they found a little book, containing the life of Antony. This one of them began to read, admire, and kindle at it...and read on, and was changed inwardly, where Thou sawest, and his mind was stripped of the world...

'Such was the story of Pontitianus; but Thou, O Lord, while he was speaking, didst turn me round towards myself...that I might see how foul I was, how crooked and defiled, bespotted and ulcerous... For many of my years (some twelve) had now run out with me since my nineteenth, when, upon the reading of Cicero's Hortensius, I was stirred to an earnest love of wisdom; and still I was deferring to reject mere earthly felicity... Thus was I gnawed within, and exceedingly confounded with an horrible shame, while Pontitianus was so speaking. And he...went his way...

'Then in this great contention of my inward dwelling, which I had strongly raised against my soul, in *the chamber* of my heart, troubled in mind and countenance, I turned upon Alypius. "What ails us?" I exclaim: "what is it? what heardest thou? The unlearned start up and *take heaven by force*, and we with our learning, and without heart, lo, where we wallow in flesh and blood! Are we ashamed to follow, because others are gone before, and not ashamed not even to follow?" Some such words I uttered, and my fever of mind tore me away from him, while he, gazing on me in astonishment, kept silence. For it was not my wonted tone; and my forehead, cheeks, eyes, colour, tone of voice, spake my mind more than the words I uttered. A little garden there was to our lodging... Thither had the tumult of my breast hurried me, where no man might hinder the hot contention wherein I had engaged with myself, until it should end as Thou knewest, I knew not. Only I was healthfully distracted and dying, to live; knowing what evil thing I was, and not knowing what good thing I was shortly to become. I retired then into the garden, and Alypius, on my steps. For his presence did not lessen my privacy; or how could he forsake me so disturbed? We sate down as far removed as might be from the house. I was troubled in spirit, most vehemently indignant that I entered not into Thy will and covenant, O my God, which *all my bones cried out* unto me to enter...

'Thus soul-sick was I, and tormented, accusing myself much more severely than my wont, rolling and turning me in my chain... For I said within myself, "Be it done now, be it done now." And as I spake, I all but enacted it. I all but did it, and did it not: yet sunk not back to my former state, but kept my stand hard by, and took breath. And I essayed again, and wanted somewhat less of it, and somewhat less, and all but touched and laid hold of it; and yet came not at it, nor touched, nor laid hold of it: hesitating to die to death and to live to life... The very toys of toys, and vanities of vanities, my ancient mistresses, still held me; they plucked my fleshly garment ...a violent habit saying to me, "Thinkest thou, thou canst live without them?" But now it spake very faintly. For on that side whither I had set my face, and whither I trembled to go, there appeared unto me the chaste dignity of Continence... This controversy in my heart was self against self only. But Alypius sitting close by my side, in silence awaited the issue of my unwonted emotion.

'But when a deep consideration had from the secret bottom of my soul drawn together and heaped up all my misery in the sight of my heart; there arose a mighty storm, bringing a mighty shower of tears. Which that I might pour forth wholly, in its natural expressions, I rose from Alypius: solitude was suggested to me as fitter for the business of weeping; so I retired so far that even his presence could not be a burthen to me... I cast myself down I know not how, under a certain fig-tree, giving full vent to my tears; and the floods of mine eyes gushed out, an *acceptable sacrifice to Thee.* And, not indeed in these words, yet to this purpose, spake I much unto Thee: *And Thou, O Lord, how long? how long, Lord, wilt Thou be angry, for ever? Remember not our former iniquities,* for I felt that I was held by them. I sent up these sorrowful words; How long how long? "to-morrow, and to-morrow?" Why not now? why not is there this hour an end to my uncleanness?

'So was I speaking, and weeping in the most bitter contrition of my heart, when lo! I heard from a neighbouring house a voice, as of boy or girl, I know not, chanting, and oft repeating, "Take up and read; Take up and read." Instantly, my countenance altered, I began to think most intently, whether children were wont in any kind of play to sing such words: nor could I remember ever to have heard the like. So checking the torrent of my tears, I arose; interpreting it to be no other than a command from God, to open the book, and read the first chapter I should find. For I had heard of Antony, that coming in during the reading of the Gospel, he received the admonition, as if what was being read, was spoken to him... And by such oracle he was forthwith converted unto Thee. Eagerly then I returned to the place where Alypius was sitting; for there had I laid the volume of the Apostle, when I arose thence. I seized, opened, and in silence read that section, on which my eyes first fell: *Not in rioting and drunkeness, not in chambering and wantonness, not in strife and envying: but put ye on the Lord Jesus Christ, and make not provision for the flesh*, in concupiscence. No further would I read; nor needed I: for instantly at the end of this sentence, by a light as it were of serenity infused into my heart, all the darkness of doubt vanished away.' [1]

It is comparatively rare to find all the stages I have set out so well displayed as here. Thus we have, unusually, the moment at which the question was consciously asked, the need formulated—the 'incredibly burning desire for an immortality of wisdom'. We see twelve years spent in collecting material for the answer with premature and unsatisfactory attempts at syntheses—the mistaken acceptance of Manichaeism which proved unable to answer all the questions asked, the attempts at limited pattern-making on 'the fair and the fit'. We see common triggers at first giving and then failing to give satisfaction, for these could not, as the required answer must, conquer the fear of death and expunge the sense of sin which concupiscence brought. The Christian answer, which can satisfy these needs, comes increasingly before Augustine's mind, with the constant pressure of his mother and the impact of St. Ambrose. The mistress is lost, all other consolations are gone, the story of just such a conversion as he seeks presents itself. The accumulated material fuses in a belief which was indeed the most desired answer, tested not by such proof as is required to show that seven and three are ten (see p. 184), but only by the improbability of a real child saying the words he believed he had heard. And that St. Augustine did indeed find his most desired answer is shown by the names he tended to give to that which he found—Eternal Wisdom, the eternal light of Wisdom, the light of the Wisdom of God, the unchangeable Truth itself, That Which Is, etc. (all cited by Butler). Indeed so persistently does he use such names that it has been wondered whether his experiences were not perhaps Platonic rather than Christian (see p. 131).

St. Augustine himself was in no doubt that the answer he had found

---

[1] *Confessions*, iii 1—viii 29.

was the Christian answer; and I hope I have managed to show that this was the most desired answer to an urgently asked question, achieved by the process I have outlined.

My second example is of an experience in many ways similar to St. Augustine's. It concerns the conversion of John Wesley; and consists of passages from his *Journal*:

'Sat. Feb. 7 [1736, in Georgia] Mr. Oglethorpe returned from Savannah, with Mr. Spangenberg, one of the Pastors of the Germans. I soon found what spirit he was of; and asked his advice with regard to my own conduct. He said, "My brother, I must first ask you one or two questions. Have you the witness within yourself? Does the spirit of God bear witness with your spirit, that you are a child of God?" I was surprised, and knew not what to answer. He observed it, and asked, "Do you know Jesus Christ?" I paused and said, "I know he is the Saviour of the world." "True; replied he; but do you know he has saved you?" I answered, "I hope he has died to save me." He only added, "Do you know yourself?" I said, "I do." But I fear they were vain words...
'Sat. 4. [March 1738] I found my brother at Oxford...and with him Peter Böhler: by whom (in the hand of the great God) I was, on Sunday the 5th, clearly convinced of unbelief; of the want of that faith whereby alone we are saved.

'Immediately it struck into my mind, "Leave off preaching. How can you preach to others who have not faith yourself?" I asked Böhler, whether he thought I should leave it off, or not? He answered "By no means." I asked, "But what can I preach?" He said, "Preach faith till you have it; and then, because you have it, you will preach faith."...
'Thur. 23. [March 1738] I met Peter Böhler again, who now amazed me more and more by the account he gave of the fruits of living faith, the holiness and happiness which he affirmed to attend it...
'Sun. 2. [April 1738]... I see the promise; but it is afar off...
'Sat. 21 [May 1738] I met Peter Böhler once more. I had now no objection to what he said of the nature of faith, viz. that it is (to use the words of our Church) "A sure trust and confidence which a man hath in God, that, through the merits of Christ, his sins are forgiven, and he reconciled to the favour of God."... But I could not comprehend what he spoke of an instantaneous work. I could not understand how this faith should be given in a moment... I searched the Scriptures again... But, to my utter astonishment, found scarce

any instances there of other than instantaneous conversions; scarce any so slow as that of St. Paul, who was three days in the pangs of the new birth. I had but one retreat left, viz. "Thus: I grant, God wrought in the first ages of Christianity; but the times are changed. What reason have I to believe, he works in the same manner now?"

'But on Sunday 22, I was beat out of this retreat too, by the concurring evidence of several living witnesses, who testified, God had thus wrought in themselves; giving them, in a moment, such a faith in the blood of his Son, as translated them out of darkness into light, out of sin and fear into holiness and happiness... In the day or two following, I was much confirmed in the "truth that is after godliness," by hearing the experiences of...two living witnesses, that God can (at least, if he does not always) give that faith whereof cometh salvation in a moment, as lightning falling from heaven...

'What happened on Wednesday the 24th, I think best to relate at large, after premising what may make it the better understood. [Wesley then recounts how in childhood and up till this time he had obediently kept the outward forms of religion, by which he hoped to be saved, but had no notion of inner holiness. He read William Law, lived purely, yet had no assurance of acceptance by God. 'Soon after a contemplative man convinced me...that outward works are nothing, being alone; and in several conversations instructed me how to pursue inward holiness, or a union of the soul with God.' But still he found no comfort, was fearful of death, convinced of his sinfulness, yet sought after the Grace of God.]

'I continued thus to seek it, (though with strange indifference, dullness, and coldness, and usually frequent relapses into sin,) till Wednesday, May 24. I think it was about five this morning that I opened my Testament on those words..."There are given unto us exceeding great and precious promises, even that ye should be partakers of the divine nature." (2 Pet. i. 4.) Just as I went out, I opened it again on those words: "Thou art not far from the kingdom of God." In the afternoon I was asked to go to St. Paul's. The anthem was, "Out of the deep have I called unto thee..."[etc.]

'In the evening I went very unwillingly to a society in Aldersgate-street, where one was reading Luther's preface to the Epistle to the Romans. About a quarter before nine, while he was describing the change which God works in the heart through faith in Christ, I felt my heart strangely warmed.[1] I felt I did trust in Christ, Christ

---

[1] The peculiar effect which Luther had on Wesley seems to have been potent only at this psychological moment, for on June 15, 1741, he wrote in his *Journal*, 'I set out for London; and read over, in the way, Martin Luther's Comment on

alone, for salvation; and an assurance was given me, that he had taken away *my* sins, even *mine*, and saved *me* from the law of sin and death... But it was not long before the enemy suggested, "This cannot be faith; for where is thy joy?" Then was I taught, that peace and victory over sin are essential to faith in the Captain of our salvation; but, that as to the transports of joy that usually attend the beginning of it, especially in those who have mourned deeply, God sometimes giveth, sometimes withholdeth them, according to the counsels of his own will.

'After my return home, I was much buffeted with temptations; but cried out, and they fled away... And herein I found the difference between this and my former state chiefly consisted...then I was sometimes, if not often, conquered: now I was always conqueror.

'Thur. May 25. The moment I awaked, "Jesus, Master," was in my heart and in my mouth... Being again at St. Paul's in the afternoon, I could taste the good word of God in the anthem... Yet the enemy injected a fear, "If thou dost believe, why is there not a more sensible change?" I answered (yet not I,) "That I know not. But this I know, I have 'now peace with God'..."

'Sat. 27. Believing one reason for my want of joy was, want of time for prayer, I resolved to do no business till I went to church in the morning, but to continue pouring out my heart before Him. And this day my spirit was enlarged; so that though I was now assaulted my many temptations, I was more than conqueror...

'Sun. 28. I waked in peace, but not in joy...

'Sun. 4. [June 1738] Was indeed a feast-day. For, from the time of my rising till past one in the afternoon, I was praying, reading the Scriptures, singing praise, or calling sinners to repentance. All these days I scarce remember to have opened the Testament, but upon some great and precious promise. And I saw more than ever, that the Gospel is, in truth, but one great promise, from the beginning of it to the end.' [1]

The similarities with St. Augustine are obvious though, as befits a simpler man, the whole thing is on a simpler scale. Wesley knows what question he is asking, what answer he desires. He is moved by appropriate influences at significant moments, had in detail investigated the moment he sought and knew what it must feel like. As Augustine

the Epistle to the Galatians. I was utterly ashamed. How I have esteemed this book, only because I heard it so commended by others!...he is deeply tinctured with mysticism throughout, and hence often dangerously wrong.'

[1] From the Everyman edition, Vol. I, pp. 21-104.

took the step of becoming a catechumen before his conversion, so Wesley continued preaching before his, following the advice given by Böhler, and almost always found to be effective.[1] Wesley's tests differed slightly from Augustine's; characteristically, he refused to be assured that this experience was indeed the one he sought until he felt he had received sufficient of the joy which, he had learnt, must accompany it.

My third example of this process where both the question and its most desired answer are known is equally a matter of conversion, but this time of a potential, not an actual one, and where the answer sought is something other than religious belief. The major purpose of Mr. P. W. Martin's book *Experiment in Depth* is to bring to 'men and women [who] are dealing with life in a spirit of responsibility and devotion' experience of 'the deep centre' that in the past has been available 'only to the highly percipient man or woman, the mystic, the saint, the seer'.[2] To Mr. Martin the experience is entirely explicable in Jungian terms, and it is in Jungian terms that the required overbelief will finally be expressed. This is what the process entails:

'To those who decide to undertake the experiment in depth, dangerous and uncharted as it is, can any specific advice be given? ... Alone, without a working group, no one can go far. To seek to do so is to court disaster... It is highly desirable, though not essential, that one or two of the working group should already have gone some way in the experiment...

'Such a group can usefully begin by taking some book bearing upon the experiment and discussing it thoroughly among themselves: James' [*sic*] *The Varieties of Religious Experience*, Jung's *Two Essays on Analytical Philosophy*, Toynbee's *A Study of History*, Eliot's *Four Quartets*, the *Journal of George Fox*, or whatever else may seem to them appropriate. The point of the discussion...is what light this book throws on the experiment as a practical human undertaking.

---

[1] Compare Pascal: 'Vous voulez aller à la foi, et vous n'en savez pas le chemin... apprenez de ceux qui ont été liés comme vous, et qui parient maintenant tout leur bien... Suivez la manière par où ils ont commencé: c'est en faisant tout comme s'ils croyaient, en prenant de l'eau bénite, en faisant dire des messes, etc. Naturellement même cela vous fera croire et vous abêtira.' *Pensées*, Section III, No. 233; and Nietzsche: 'First and foremost let us have the works, that is practice, practice, practice! The requisite faith will come in due time—be sure of that!' *The Dawn of Day*, trans. by J. Volz (London, 1903), p. 20.

[2] *Experiment in Depth* (London, 1955), p. 134.

Throughout recorded time there has been the recurring evidence that it is possible to break through to a deeper realm of being...the direct discovery of the "different spiritual dimension". What is to be our considered judgment on this? Is it no more than wishful thinking? Or is it, perhaps, the meaning of life?

'For most people, some such initial discussion is a necessary first stage... Each individual is given the opportunity, moreover, to find out whether this is something he himself really wants to do... As part of such preliminary training the members of the group will probably find it useful to work out their psychological compass-bearings as they go along—extraversion, introversion, and the four functions...

'Those who, as an outcome, feel they are ready to go further, would do well to start recording their dreams... The value of recording at this stage is twofold. First, as a consequence of the serious attention thus shown to the working of the unconscious, there will normally be an increase (qualitative as well as quantitative) in the flow of material. Second, when a sequence of some dozen, score, or fifty dreams has been built up, a quiet weekend spent in going over them carefully may reveal much of interest not previously apparent. In considering such a dream sequence, concentrate especially upon the positive elements, the helpful figures, the transforming symbols, however insignificant they may appear. By their means, the first constructive contact between consciousness and the unconscious may be made.

'Around this stage, a decision has... to be reached... If the decision is for commitment, then these three things may be worth trying.

'First, get what hints you can from someone who has already gone some distance...

'Second, as and when you are ready for it, try some variety of the Mt. Marcy technique:[1] a night vigil in some place sufficiently remote—hill, mountain, moor, forest, headland, beach; a pilgrimage through the night, over un-peopled country, to some place that has

---

[1] The reference is to a letter from William James to his wife, quoted earlier in Martin's book (p. 234) about a night passed on Mt. Marcy. It is as follows: 'I spent a good deal of it in the woods, where the streaming moonlight lit up things in a magical checkered play, and it seemed as if the Gods of all the nature-mythologies were holding an indescribable meeting in my breast with the moral Gods of the inner life . . . The intense significance of some sort, of the whole scene, if one could only *tell* the significance; the intense inhuman remoteness of its inner life, and yet the intense *appeal* of it; its everlasting freshness and its immemorial antiquity and decay; . . . In point of fact, I can't find a single word for all that significance...'

meaning for you. Or a night watch, spent in your own room, carefully prepared so that you know what you are doing, perhaps with some few objects set out before you symbolizing crucial moments or representative periods of your life, can tell you much between dark and dawn...

'Third, as and when you detect suitable figures and/or material in your dreams, it would be well to try acquiring the other psycho-perceptive methods: active imagination; painting and drawing from the unconscious; the inward conversation. Above all, use these methods whenever, in dream or active imagination, either of the two great integrative factors appears: the Friend and the deep centre. If the Friend is constellated, get in touch with him or her by whatever means you can. If the deep centre, in any of its many forms, makes its appearance, hold on to it and do not let it go. Along with the working group, the Friend and the deep centre are the great safeguards.

'A man or woman who adventures thus far will almost certainly have come upon the shadow, the anima-animus and the archetypal world generally. Sooner or later these figures are likely to become constellated, i.e. appear in a state where they can be directly reached. This is the perilous encounter... It is also the great possibility... The man who is centred in depth, can hold...

'Experience of the phenomena coming from the other side of consciousness goes by us like the wind. We feel it at the time, but afterwards it is as if it has never been. This experience can be held, and seen for what it is, only if record is made of it. One method... is to keep a journal consistently day by day. Another...is to get on to paper what might, perhaps, be called the "life pattern".' [1]

Who can doubt but that 'the Mt. Marcy technique' will work, that something recognizable as the desired experience will be achieved during the vigil, and that its overbelief will be established in Jungian terms? Preliminary training has ensured that those who persist with the experiment know explicitly both the question and the answer; and the steps taken to ensure that the answer will be lasting and felt progressively to deepen in significance are of the same kind as those long since found effective by older disciplines. Future catechumens, one feels, will have their own sectarian 'Confessions' and 'Journals' to get the initial group discussions going along the right lines.

I shall now give a case where it is believed, by the person concerned,

---

[1] *Experiment in Depth*, p. 259 et seq.

that the accepted overbelief arose spontaneously with the ecstatic experience, that no question or answer had been considered, no material collected; and where it is, none the less, possible to show that the material had in fact been collected, and that both question and desired answer were known.

The case is that of Alphonse Ratisbonne, discussed by both James[1] and by de Sanctis.[2] James uses this case to show that conversion may be fulminant and unprepared, de Sanctis to show that though this may superficially appear to be so, it is never in fact the case. My account is condensed from both sources:

Ratisbonne was a free-thinking French Jew whose brother had been converted and was a Catholic priest. At Rome in 1842, M. Ratisbonne 'fell in with a French gentleman who tried to make a proselyte of him, but who succeeded no further after two or three conversations than to get him to hang (half jocosely) a religious medal round his neck, and to accept and read a copy of a short prayer to the Virgin' (James). Wearing his medal, which was one of the Virgin, Ratisbonne entered the church of Sant' Andrea delle Fratte where he experienced, before the statue of the Virgin, a typical ecstasy, saw 'the unspeakable truth', and was converted to Catholicism. James comments, 'The predisposing conditions appear to have been slight', and calls this 'The most curious record of sudden conversion with which I am acquainted'.

In fact, the predisposing circumstances seem to have been uniquely favourable to such a conclusion. One would imagine that Jews with Catholic priests for brothers, diligently proselytizing friends, medallions of the Virgin round their necks and prayers to the Virgin on their lips, must be comparatively rare. De Sanctis adds to these circumstances that Ratisbonne had had a long intimacy with a devoutly Catholic friend with whom he had often visited churches, that 'Christianity, Catholicism, conversions, and even books of devotion were known to his consciousness', and that 'in these days he was continually putting the question of conversion to himself'; that he had hitherto decided in the negative is, says de Sanctis, proof of a very usual 'dissimulation of the conflict'. De Sanctis describes the predisposing circumstances in this case as 'typical' and expressed surprise that the case of Ratisbonne ever came to be considered as exceptional. 'It is certainly strange', he says, 'how almost all converts like to believe

---

[1] V.R.E., p. 219 et seq. and p. 252.
[2] R.C., pp. 76–9 and p. 224.

in the suddenness of their mutation,'[1] but states that 'It is hardly permissible to hold that in the case of "lightning" conversion the consciousness of the subject has never experienced, prior to the crisis, the beginnings of mutation'.[2] In this case there can be no doubt that Ratisbonne knew both his question and his most desired answer, even though, as de Sanctis suggests, he may have 'forgotten', both as a result of a desire 'to enhance the workings of grace' and of a blurring and falsification of the memory due to intense emotion.

As compared with the establishment of religious or quasi-religious belief, accounts of the moments of scientific discovery are rare, and I have not come across a suitable non-fictional example where that moment is accompanied by an experience that can properly be counted as an ecstasy. This is not, for my present purposes, essential, though it would have been preferable; but my example does clearly show a case where the question but not the answer was known before the experience that brought it to light:

'To-morrow will be the fifteenth birthday of the Quaternions. They started into life, or light, full grown, on the 16th of October, 1843, as I was walking with Lady Hamilton to Dublin, and came up to Brougham Bridge, which my boys have since called the Quaternion Bridge, that is to say, I then and there felt the galvanic circuit of thought close; and the sparks which fell from it were the fundamental equations between i, j, k; exactly such as I have used them ever since. I pulled out on the spot a pocket-book, which still exists, and made an entry, on which *at the very moment* I felt that it might be worth my while to expend the labour of at least ten (or perhaps fifteen) years to come. But then it is fair to say that this was because I felt a *problem* to have been at that moment solved—an intellectual want relieved—which had haunted me for at least fifteen years before.'[3]

Leuba adds to this account from a later letter of Sir William Rowan Hamilton's which tells how, shortly before the discovery,

'the desire to discover the laws of the multiplication referred to

---

[1] R.C., p. 72.

[2] R.C., p. 67. Jung seems to agree: 'Although the actual moment of a conversion often seems quite sudden and unexpected, yet we know from experience that such a fundamental occurrence always has a long period of incubation. It is only when the preparation is complete, that is to say, when the individual is ready to be converted, that the new view breaks forth with great emotion.' From *Contributions to Analytical Psychology* (London, 1928), p. 257.

[3] Quoted by Leuba: P.R.M., p. 243.

regained with me a certain strength and earnestness, which had for years been dormant'.

Here we see that an exact and specific question has been asked and that lack of its answer has been for fifteen years 'an intellectual want'. Material had been collected and examined, apparently with increased diligence just before the discovery. The material fused, and the immediate answer proved to be the most desired one—that is, the correct one—though we must suppose it was submitted to appropriate tests before final acceptance.

My last example must be one of artistic creation where, although a general question is asked and a general answer to it believed to be capable of existing, yet the question is not precisely phrased and the specific form of the answer cannot be known until it is, so to speak, revealed. We must assume that a question about the form of future literary (or artistic or musical work) must usually be in the writer's (or artist's or musician's) mind and that he knows that the answer to his question must be some form of literary (or artistic or musical) work, but the specific form that it will take he cannot know. Nichols, in text L 5, provides an example where the specific answer came with ecstatic experience.

The answer in such cases need not take even the general form consciously envisaged by the creator when seeking it. Much of the material in *The Ancient Mariner* was collected by Coleridge with the intention of writing a quite different poem, as Livingston Lowes points out when tracing its sources. He uses Henry James's image of the deep well of unconscious cerebration to illustrate the manner in which the material collected coalesced to emerge as 'Form':

> 'For there enter into imaginative creation three factors which reciprocally interplay: the Well, and the Vision, and the Will. Without the Vision, the chaos of elements remains a chaos, and the Form sleeps for ever in the vast chambers of unborn designs. Yet in *that* chaos only could creative Vision ever see *this* Form. Nor without the co-operant Will, obedient to the Vision, may the pattern perceived in the huddle attain objective reality.' [1]

In this passage Livingston Lowes gives prominence to a factor that has not been demonstrated in these examples, the working of 'the

---

[1] *The Road to Xanadu*, p. 432.

co-operant Will obedient to the Vision' by which the fused material is translated into communicable form. In the following chapter I hope to demonstrate this as well as the other parts of the process which, I have suggested, contribute to the formation of overbelief.

CHAPTER XXXII

The Formation of Overbelief (ii)

THE ASKING OF THE QUESTION

On January 28, 1948, the B.B.C.'s Third Programme broadcast a discussion which became famous, that between Bertrand Russell and F. C. Copleston, S.J., on *The Existence of God*. In the course of the discussion Father Copleston spoke of

'the question of the existence of the whole of this sorry scheme of things, of the whole universe',

and said that

'An adequate explanation must ultimately be a total explanation, to which nothing further can be added.'

Russell commented,

'Then I can only say that you are looking for something which can't be got, and which one ought not to expect to get.' [1]

But for Russell and many other contemporary philosophers to regard such questions as meaningless does not inhibit a widespread desire to ask them. Indeed ecstatic experiences might seem uniquely capable of providing satisfactory answers to such questions and perhaps, even, of ensuring that they are asked. We have already seen how often the ecstatic feels that the knowledge he has gained through ecstasy is totality knowledge, knowledge about everything (see Ch. X). The asking of totality questions is equally common.

The framing of the question may take different forms. Copleston wants an answer to 'the question of the existence...of the whole universe'. Amiel wanted to know all there was to be known:

'what I seek to know is the sum of all different kinds of knowledge'.[2]

[1] *From the Third Programme*, ed. by John Morris (London, 1956) p. 120.
[2] *Amiel's Journal*, trans. Mrs. Humphry Ward (London, 1885; 2nd edn., 1889), p. xviii.

For Nietzsche the most urgent question was about the reason for man's existence:

> 'Man has gradually become a visionary animal, who has to fulfil one more condition of existence than the other animals: man *must* from time to time believe that he knows *why* he exists'. [1]

And it seems reasonable to suppose that desolation experiences, like those of the children who learned that to be human is to be lonely, ignorant, guilty and mortal, must lead to questions demanding answers that could give assurance of comfort, knowledge, forgiveness and immortality. Often the answers to such questions are believed to be known, as St. Augustine and Wesley believed the answer to be different forms of the Christian answer and the woman of text R 8 believed it to be the mind-cure answer, and then what is sought is the experience which, it is believed, can validate the chosen answer.

Where a totality answer has been accepted—whether with or without the warrant of ecstatic experience—what is sought may be the means of expressing that answer in a chosen medium:

> 'No man was ever yet a great poet, without being at the same time a profound philosopher. For poetry is the blossom and the fragrancy of all human knowledge, human thoughts, human passions, emotions, language.' [2]

Nor need the totality answer be an orthodox or systematic one. What is sought may be the means of expressing all that *I* know, all that *I* feel:

> 'My symphonies exhaust the content of my entire existence. Whoever listens to my music intelligently will see my life transparently revealed.' [3]

In such cases the answer sought need not ostensibly be about 'everything'. The creative work, the poem, novel, picture, piece of music may ostensibly seek to convey only a limited part of what is known or what there is to be known; but for a creative artist to interpret the particular is usually to attempt to mirror the general.

> 'The Imagination modifies images, and gives unity to variety; it sees all things in one, *il più nell'uno*.' [4]

---

[1] *The Joyful Wisdom*, p. 35.
[2] S. T. Coleridge, *Biographia Literaria*, ch. xv, p. 179.
[3] Gustave Mahler, quoted in the *Manchester Guardian*, February 2, 1957.
[4] S. T. Coleridge, *Table Talk*, June 23, 1834, in *Table Talk* ed. James Thornton (Everyman, 1934), p. 253.

Then what is sought to be known may be limited to only one aspect of a subject, whether the answer required is one that can be empirically tested or not. Berenson was seeking, for example, a satisfactory test for his aesthetic responses to artifacts (see p. 156), Toynbee was seeking communion with certain historical events (see p. 113). Hamilton felt 'an intellectual want' for his Quaternions (see p. 332), Q 6 and Q 45 sought the answers to mathematical problems.[1]

These seem to be the principal sorts of questions whose answers may come with ecstatic experiences. Ecstasies do not seem to answer specific moral dilemmas—what ought I to do in this particular situation?—or minor practical problems. They need not, of course, bring a coherent answer to anything, but if they do, there seems to be a certain scale and grandeur about the answers they bring; they are the kind of answers that can potentially act as triggers.

As I have shown in the last chapter the person need not be consciously aware that a question has been asked, nor are the questions asked necessarily as clear-cut as those of, say, St. Augustine or Hamilton. Often the question would seem to be so incoherent as better to be called a need than a question, a need—in James's phrase—somehow to transform 'a self consciously divided and consciously wrong' into a more satifactory self.[2]

Even if a question is coherently asked we cannot say that the conscious asking of the question is necessarily the starting-point of the process that leads to its answer. St. Augustine was divided, consciously wrong, inferior, and unhappy when he learned that his need was to find 'an immortality of wisdom', and the discovery posed the new question of how this was to be found. The answer that came in the garden was, then, an answer not only to this question about wisdom—which had, in any case, developed and altered since first being asked—but was also an answer to an earlier question and probably to earlier questions still.

[1] Since most urgently asked questions of these kinds usually find answers ('Ask, and it shall be given you; seek, and ye shall find; knock, and it shall be opened unto you' *Matt*. vii. 7)—though not always answers that will stand up to test—it is worth recording that for two and a half years St. Teresa 'greatly longed to see the colour of His eyes' but always failed to do so, and sometimes found that her efforts lost her the vision altogether (*Life*, ch. xxix, p. 205). There are, it seems, some things which is is not lawful to utter.

[2] 'there is a certain uniform deliverance in which religions all appear to meet. It consists of two parts:—1. An uneasiness; and 2. Its solution.' James: V.R.E., p. 498.

Then to discover the answer to a question may imply not only regressive but also progressive questions. Hamilton was delighted to find that 'it might be worth my while to expend the labour of at least ten (or perhaps fifteen) years to come' on problems to which the discovery of the Quaternions gave rise, while for the creative most successful assaults on the ineffable, whether in art or religion, incite to ever renewed efforts—'to make an end is to make a beginning. The end is where we start from... Every phrase and every sentence is an end and a beginning' wrote T. S. Eliot.[1]

I do not want to suggest that every satisfactorily answered question must give rise to other questions that directly derive from its answer. A satisfactory answer may well complete the pattern of that particular focus of interest and allow new and different questions to come to the fore. What I do suggest is that every overbelief implies a previous question or need, whether consciously formulated or not.

[1] 'Little Gidding', V from *Four Quartets* (London, 1944), pp. 42-3.

CHAPTER XXXIII

The Formation of Overbelief (iii)

THE COLLECTION OF MATERIAL

'We hear only the questions to which we are capable of finding an answer,' wrote Nietzsche.[1] We may, like Russell, choose to reject certain questions; but once we have accepted a question as meaningful to ourselves, then we set about collecting material for the kind of answer we need.

I cannot argue with those who believe that any part of the content of overbelief derives from any other source than that of the experience of the individual creating it, who believe that the individual's experiences provides no more than a cloak for the naked truth that comes from Elsewhere. Usually we find that the less exalted the overbelief, the greater the readiness to admit that it may have been formed without supernatural intervention. Thus Underhill believes that while the mechanism of production was the same, Wordsworth's poem about the daffodils was entirely self-created while Suso's vision of the angels came from another and more exalted source (see p.282). Coleridge accepted that what a man said in a state of excitement 'must have pre-existed in his former conversations' (see below) but of more exalted communications wrote,

> 'It is the glory of the Gospel Charter and the Christian Constitution, that its Author and Head is the Spirit of Truth'.[2]

I myself believe it most probable that pre-formed expectations, prevailing beliefs, and the nature of the fusing experience (including, sometimes, the nature of the trigger) are sufficient to account for all the content of all overbeliefs.

According to the answer he desires the individual will seek for the

---

[1] *The Joyful Wisdom*, p. 195.

[2] 'Aphorisms on Spirtual Religion' No. III, from *Aids to Reflections* (1825; 1884 edn.), p. 97.

material to compose it. The creative artist may look anywhere and compose his answer of anything:

'Every great imaginative creation is a vortex into which everything under the sun may be swept.' [1]

Coleridge's explanation of what is said in a state of excitement must apply to all forms of composition:

'For the nature of a man's words, when he is strongly affected by joy, grief or anger, must necessarily depend on the number and quality of the general truths, conceptions and images, and of the words expressing them, with which his mind had been previously stored. For the property of passion is not to *create*, but to set in increased activity. At least, whatever new connections of thoughts or images, or (which is equally, if not more than equally, the appropriate effect of strong excitement) whatever generalizations of truth or experience the heat of passion may produce, yet the terms of their conveyance must have pre-existed in his former conversations, and are only collected and crowded together by the unusual stimulation.' [2]

We may assume a predeliction for material especially suitable to the creator's purpose. There will be a tendency to notice this potential piece of material as against that, a gradual building up of the mass of potentially related but still discrete material which will eventually fuse in the most desired answer. [3]

Those seeking answers to totality questions cannot fail to know or quickly to discover what fields of search are likely to be most profitable to them. To provide such answers is a function of religion, and one may suppose that at any given time the most successful religion will be the one that most satisfactorily succeeds in providing what seems, to use Copleston's phrase, 'a total explanation, to which nothing further can be added'.

Within the chosen field the area of search may be wide or narrow. We have seen something of the breadth of St. Augustine's range of search, and of the carefully circumscribed reading and experience for

---

[1] Livingston Lowes, *The Road to Xanadu*, p. 426.

[2] *Biographia Literaria*, ch. xvii, p. 199.

[3] '[A] significant fact about Keats's relation to his poetic models is that generally speaking the influences to which he submitted himself were chosen with an instinctive rightness. It is as though some force were at work in him directing him towards the kind of inspiration that would be most beneficial to his own development.' E. C. Pettet, *On the Poetry of Keats*, p. 13.

those who are to find the Jungian answer. Those who seek answers to scientific questions must have, as compared with the artistically creative, a very narrow area of search indeed.

Often, it appears, the trigger is itself the last piece of material needed to complete the jigsaw. Nichols was a poet before he went on his sea voyage. The postcard from the British Museum had entered his consciousness long before. The evening before the experience related in text L 5 he had tried to write a poem and could not, though many uncompleted poems were, he felt, churning through his brain. But to his previous collecting there must be added, it seemed, the dawn and the sun on the sea before all this could fuse into the poem about the sun on the sea that he was then able to write.

Sometimes the trigger is such that it seems positively to communicate a message. Church was reading the Bible when he found suddenly 'a landscape in which objects and words were fused. All was one...' (L 23b). St. Augustine was reading 'Not in rioting and drunkenness...' etc., and 'instantly at the end of this sentence, by a light as it were of serenity infused into my heart, all the darkness of doubt vanished away' (see p.324). Wesley found his heart strangely warmed by Luther's words, and later, after his conversion, that 'All these days I scarce remember to have opened the Testament, but upon some great and precious promise' (see p.327).[1] In such cases the sudden discovery of significance in a few words, often in words previously known, must seem to depend on the fact that these words chime and fuse with material already collected, could themselves be taken as representing a no matter how cryptic statement of the most desired answer and so could appear at that moment to have—in L 24's words —'unbelievable depths of significance'.

Other triggers than verbal ones sometimes seem to communicate a message. Forster explains Beethoven as saying something about goblins and splendour and makes Helen 'read' the music as a 'statement' (L 18). H. Warner Allen, drawing upon the Book of Job (*Job* xxxviii. 7), describes a passage from Beethoven in terms of voices—the morning stars singing together and the sons of God shouting for joy. Where triggers are interpreted in such terms as these, it is likely that the

[1] This ability suddenly to find extraordinary significance in a phrase accidentally encountered would seem to have an obvious connexion with such practices of divination as the *Sortes Virgilianae* and, indeed, the *Sortes Biblicae* to which Wesley occasionally resorted; see Knox, *Enthusiasm*, p. 452.

'message' of the trigger will contribute to the subsequent overbelief; and sometimes it seems likely that the 'message' is ascribed to the trigger after the overbelief is formed, as, for instance, in

> 'I believe in Michaelangelo, Velasquez, and Rembrandt; in the might of design, the mystery of colour, the redemption of all things by Beauty everlasting, and the message of Art that has made these hands blessed.' [1]

In such a case it is presumably the known effects of the triggers that make it possible to see them afterwards as having given messages.

I cannot know what constitutes readiness for fusing. Does fusion take place when the material is ready to make a satisfactory pattern—a pattern, that is, which will be satisfactory to the creator? But sometimes satisfaction is very short-lived, and it may be that the processes of fusion take place independently of the readiness of the material to achieve a lastingly satisfactory synthesis.

[1] G. B. Shaw, *The Doctor's Dilemma* (1906), Act IV.

CHAPTER XXXIV

The Formation of Overbelief (iv)

THE FUSING OF THE MATERIAL

I have shown that the fusing of mental material often accompanies and seems to be facilitated by ecstatic experience. I have not suggested that ecstatic or response-experiences necessarily accompany the fusion of even elevated mental material, for demonstrably they do not. Conversion, for instance, may be sudden and may be accompanied by an ecstasy, or may take place so gradually that the convert cannot say at what moment the new belief was established (see p.291). But however conversion or inspiration of imaginative creation or discovery takes place, these all involve the fusion of mental material and all can be and sometimes are accompanied by or result from ecstatic experience.

Many ecstatic experiences are characterized by or result in the kind of knowledge called mystical—'Spiritual apprehension of truths beyond the understanding' (see p. 31)—which can only imperfectly be translated into words. It is tempting to seek an explanation of this common claim.

If I am right in assuming that the processes which give rise to the feelings described as ecstatic experience may facilitate the fusion of mental material into a satisfactory pattern, then it would seem to follow that at the moment of fusion such material forms the most satisfactory pattern it is capable of assuming. The most satisfactory pattern is, I suppose, the pattern most likely to facilitate the development of the creator in the context of such mental events as the formation of belief.[1] In speaking of *pattern*, here, I am referring to physical

[1] 'Some system of impulses not ordinarily in adjustment within itself or adjusted to the world finds something which orders it or gives it fit exercise. Then follows the peculiar sense of ease, of restfulness, of free, unimpeded activity, and the feeling of acceptance, of something more positive than acquiescence. This feeling is the reason why such states may be called beliefs. They share this feeling with, for example, the state which follows the conclusive answering of a

events which must correspond with the mental event which is the conviction that a question has been satisfactorily answered or a need resolved or a satisfactory belief found.

Such physical events, corresponding with the arrangement of mental material in a satisfactory pattern, might well involve a momentary suspension of the mental functions concerned with differentiating and classifying, the relevant physical functions 'not working' because the mental material was, for the moment, satisfactorily harmonized. Such suspension might be expected to result in feelings of timelessness, placelessness, loss of differences, etc. and also, because the pattern *was* satisfactory, a feeling that knowledge had been gained before any attempt was made to translate it into communicable form.

This suggestion could, I believe, help to explain those feelings of totality so commonly claimed of knowledge believed to have been gained through ecstatic experience. At the moment of fusing, *all* the relevant material falls into place in the satisfactory pattern. At that moment the feeling of knowledge, as of other gains, is a feeling of *all*. But the moment is no sooner there than past. If the question asked was as limited and well-defined as, say, Hamilton's was, then all the answer may be recalled. If it was as total as Copleston's, then it never can be, for though all the material collected may have been fused and that fusion may feel, momentarily, like the answer to everything, in fact all the material necessary to answer the question could never have been collected.

We do in fact have instances of people believing that the very simple statements, which are the 'messages' they received in mystical experiences, are the answer to everything. L 24 believed he had received a message which ran 'There is something perfect'; this, he said, seemed 'to be telling me in those four words everything that it is important and necessary to know', though he realized that to communicate the message to other people 'conveys nothing of the meaning it bore at that moment, for it had unbelievable depths of significance'. Similarly, under anaesthetics the 'meaning of everything' and the 'riddle of the

question... when the required attitude has been long needed, where its coming is unforeseen and the manner in which it is brought about complicated and inexplicable, where we know...that formerly we were unready and that now we are ready for life in some particular phase, the feeling which results may be intense. Such are the occasions upon which the arts seem to lift away the burden of existence, and we seem ourselves to be looking into the heart of things...to be recipients of a revelation.' Richards: *Principles*, p. 283.

universe' were momentarily revealed to a lady and to a professor, in one case as 'a sort of green light', in the other in the phrase 'A strong smell of turpentine pervades the whole' (see p. 261). That both these revelations were quickly rejected as meaningless does not alter the fact that momentarily they seemed like totality answers.

CHAPTER XXXV

The Formation of Overbelief (v)

THE TRANSLATION

What the new pattern represents cannot be known until it is translated into communicable terms, if only to himself, by the creator. These terms may of course be those of words, paint, music, numbers, etc. I shall principally concern myself with translation into words.

Sometimes, though rarely where ecstatic experience is involved, the fusing experience and the translation into communicable terms seem to arrive almost simultaneously:

'there would flow into my mind, with sudden and unaccountable emotion, sometimes a line or two of verse, sometimes a whole stanza at once'. [1]

'I then and there felt the galvanic circuit of thought close; and the sparks which fell from it were the fundamental equations between i, j, k; exactly such as I have used them ever since.' [2]

'I was walking on a hill-side, alone, one bright summer day, when suddenly there came into my head one line of verse—one solitary line—"For the Snark *was* a Boojum, you see." ' [3]

But where ecstatic experience is involved, the most usual post-ecstatic feeling is that something new is known but it is not known what.

I have suggested that ecstatic experiences are often followed by a period of time during which normal feelings are re-established, the period I have called 'ecstatic afterglow', and it appears that often it is in this period that the content of the ecstatic experience is (to quote H. Warner Allen) 'embalmed in thought-forms and words' (see pp. 58–63). We have seen that often it is during this period that the ecstatic

---

[1] A. E. Housman; see p. 284. [2] Hamilton; see p. 332
[3] Lewis Carroll, quoted by Harding: A.I., p. 63.

discovers to himself the content of his feeling that valuable new knowledge has been gained.

But the new knowledge, the new mental unification, does not stay still to be examined and then translated into the ecstatic's chosen medium. The very instant of its possibility of conscious perception is the instant when it must begin to be modified by the balance of other perceptions, now, after the ecstatic moment, re-established. The ecstatic is indeed urgently pressed to communicate if he is to communicate truly. More, his very act of communication must modify the original perception, perhaps—if his first attempt at translation has seemed true —to deepen and enhance it, or—if his first translation has seemed faulty —to mar and distort it. It is, I believe, this part of the process that the people in the questionnaire group are referring to when they speak of the brain working faster than the pen, the urgent need to get something off your chest:

'tremendous excitement, can't get things on paper quick enough' (Q 7); 'your brain works faster than your pen' (Q 30); 'the idea comes when you're not looking for it, it grows very rapidly, you know you must go and write it down or you will lose it' (Q 57).

Compare Boehme:

'And though I could have wrote in a more accurate, fair and plain Manner, yet the reason was this, that the burning Fire often forced forward with Speed, and the Hand and the Pen must hasten directly after it' (see p. 307 n),

and, in another medium, Berlioz:

'My head seemed ready to burst with the pressure of my seething thoughts. No sooner was one piece sketched than another presented itself. Finding it impossible to write fast enough, I adopted a sort of shorthand... Every composer knows the anguish and despair occasioned by forgetting ideas which one has not time to write down and which thus escape for ever.' [1]

What has been perceived in the moment of inspiration had been felt as 'true'—as the most satisfactory unification or generalization that could at that moment be made from the discrete parts composing it. And 'true' is the word that creative people usually use when measuring their success in translation against their original perception:

'One set of words was the truthful mirror of her thoughts; no

[1] Berlioz in his *Memoirs*, quoted in *The Times*, September 15, 1956.

others, however apparently identical in meaning, would do. She had [a] strong practical regard for the simple holy truth of expression... She would wait patiently searching for the right term, until it presented itself to her.' [1]

'I don't see it like that,' people will often say when someone suggests this or that modification of the scheme, but if the translation is felt to be correctly made, to be 'true' to the original perception, then, it seems, each act of correct translation may trigger off ever renewed inspirations (see p. 286).

'when the Lord gives inspiration things go easily and better. Then it is like doing a piece of embroidery with the pattern before one. But if the spirit is lacking, there is no more agreement between the words than in so much gibberish... Therefore it seems to me to be a very great advantage to be in the state of prayer when I am writing. Then I realise that it is not I that speak, nor is it I that am putting the words together with my own understanding.' [2]

'that pleasurable emotion, that peculiar state and degree of excitement which arises in the poet himself in the act of composition... Hence is produced a more vivid reflection of the truths of nature and of the human heart, united with a constant activity modifying and correcting these truths by that sort of pleasurable emotion, which the exertion of all our faculties gives in a certain degree; but which can only be felt in perfection under the full play of those powers of mind, which are spontaneous rather than voluntary, and in which the effort required bears no proportion to the activity enjoyed.' [3]

Both writers convey the impression of working to a pattern that has been presented independently of the writer's volition and which must, for satisfaction, be correctly interpreted. The interpretation need not however always be of the kind we should normally call creative work. Where totality is felt to have been encountered, the ecstatic's task may be less a matter of creation than of choosing from a stock vocabulary those words and phrases that seem best to fit his own experience.

Many of the texts in the religious group demonstrate how readily this stock vocabulary may be drawn from, and, as the questionnaire group shows, it is barely possible to describe an ecstatic experience

---

[1] Mrs. Gaskell, *The Life of Charlotte Brontë* (1857; Everyman edn., 1908), ch. xv, p. 214.
[2] Teresa: *Life*, ch. xiv, p.101.
[3] S. T. Coleridge, *Lectures and Notes of 1818*, Section I.

without using it. Mystical religions and philosophies, together with poetry, have so comprehensively provided the vocabulary in which ecstatic experience is felt to be fittingly described that their words and phrases will perforce be used even by people who do not share the beliefs these words and phrases imply.[1] So many inroads have been made on the ineffable that even an atheist may find *heaven* the appropriate word to describe a feeling of 'not mundane here but happy unified everywhere' and *communion with God* or *union with ultimate reality* the appropriate phrase for a feeling of 'not isolated lonely self but together with something or someone else'. Thus Q 17, an atheist, described ecstasy as a feeling of union with external reality, but told me afterwards that he had no belief in an external reality and thought his phrase meaningless but still the only one available to express the feeling he was trying to describe.

The moment when the translation is felt finally to be completed is of course infinitely variable, ranging from a matter of seconds to a lifetime. But at some point the answer must be tested. What has been received through ecstatic experience is overbelief, belief which has not been warranted. For overbelief to be accepted as belief, it must receive the warrant of having passed appropriate tests.

[1] Thus L 27, describing ecstasy induced by jazz and not, apparently, seeking to convey religious overbelief, still uses many phrases traditionally associated with religion—for instance, 'praise, ecstatic, believing, strong', 'something that was either profanity or a prayer', 'the world's passion', 'the sky opened' (cp. *Mark* i. 10), 'rushing wind' (cp. *Acts* ii. 2).

CHAPTER XXXVI

The Formation of Overbelief (vi)

TESTING THE ANSWER

Before discussing some of the ways in which answers are tested, we may ask why they need to be tested. Why, since so many of the answers provided by ecstatic experiences are meaningless, nonsensical or unverifiable, are they not instantly discarded?

Some part of the answer, I believe, lies in the fact that the answers provided through ecstatic experiences arrive accompanied by a strong sense of certitude, authority, and significance.

But the messages of ecstasy are not the only ones that come so accompanied. This is often true of dreams—which has made dream-interpretation a profitable avocation from earliest recorded times to the present day.[1] It is also often true of what is called the voice of conscience, of premonitions, and, however briefly, of those voices we seem to hear in drowsy states just before going to sleep, sometimes taking the form of a 'heard' voice, more often of sentences or phrases discovered in the mind and seeming, at the instant of their discovery, immensely significant. Why these kinds of messages carry such felt significance I do not know, but why the messages of ecstasy so come it is possible to make guesses.

In the first place, if such answers represent, as I have suggested, the most satisfactory synthesis of all the relevant material, it follows that such answers will seem, at the moment of receipt, satisfactory, which must, at least for that moment, mean true and if true significant.

Secondly the pleasing and satisfying nature of ecstatic experience makes it seem probable that what results from it will be good and valuable. And thirdly, if my previous arguments have been accepted,

[1] One may wonder how much of the success of various theories of dream-interpretation is due to the fact that they enable people to accept their dreams as being as significant as they feel.

the answer received represents, however momentarily, the most desired answer.

There may well be, then, good reason for at least some answers to appear to bring their own verification in the sense of certitude that accompanies them, and instead of asking why such answers are not instantly rejected, we might well ask why, since they come with such certitude, they are submitted to test at all.

The reason, I suggest, is that no matter how much certitude accompanies their coming, the answers given by ecstatic experiences cannot continue to exist *in vacuo*. The rapturous moment of their reception over, they have to take their place inside the whole framework of desires, beliefs, knowledge of the ecstatic, and the tests they must undergo are tests to discover whether, in relation to the whole environment of the ecstatic, they may be accepted as belief or rejected as unwarranted.

The tests to which the overbeliefs are submitted are, of course, the tests to which the ecstatic desires or thinks it appropriate to submit them.[1] Both Wordsworth and St. Augustine looked first for beliefs which could pass the test of reason (see p.184). But needing beliefs that could not pass this test more than they needed belief in the validity of the test, both men discarded reason for other tests which gave results more satisfactory to themselves.

I discuss below some of the tests which may be applied—usually by the people concerned—to overbeliefs received through mystical experiences including ecstasies, in order to decide whether such overbeliefs can be warranted and accepted as beliefs. Sometimes several tests are applied, and there are, undoubtedly, many more than these.

The test of right experience: Certain kinds of beliefs, notably religious ones, are believed to be warranted by experience of ecstasy (and some other mystical experiences), already known to be a kind of experience providing answers which may be accepted. This is a test adopted by both St. Augustine and Wesley: could they be satisfied that the experiences they enjoyed were similar to those of other people which were known to be sufficient to ratify the beliefs in question? The clergyman of text R 3 equally bases his assurance of God's existence, not only on the evidence of his own experience, but also

[1] 'there must be some cases in which we use a set of criteria because, as an empirical fact, they give higher ratings to those objects which we prefer.' P. Nowell-Smith, *Ethics* (Penguin, 1954), p. 174.

'in the conviction, gained from reading and reflection, that something the same has come to all who have found God'.

But only certain kinds of beliefs can be validated by the test of right experience. That it came with ecstasy is nowadays no test of the value of a prophecy or a poem and even less of a scientific theory. Though it is, as I have said, dangerous to assume that people may have had ecstatic experiences even though they do not describe them, this may help to explain why sudden inspirations in aesthetic or scientific fields are often presented without evidence of ecstasy although the conditions in which the inspirations took place make it seem not improbable that ecstasy may have accompanied them. To have described ecstasy in the context of the discovery of the Quaternions would have been supererogatory and even embarrassing. Again, for Gibbon to have described ecstasy in the ruins of the Capitol would for him have added no valid authority to his decision to write about the fall of the Roman Empire; but for Toynbee an accompanying ecstasy *would* have added authority to such a decision, and he assumes that it was with ecstasy that this decision came to Gibbon (see p. 113 and n).

The test of nonsense: When the overbelief received seems to bear no relation at all to the general framework of the ecstatic's previous beliefs, the test of nonsense may lead to the overbelief being instantly discarded, as the 'messages' of drowsy states are usually instantly discarded when looked at in daylight. The best examples I have of messages rejected under such tests are from anaesthetic experience, the answers received by the lady and the professor who momentarily believed that they knew about 'everything' (see p. 261) ; exposure to daylight led, in each case, to realization that the answer was nonsense in relation to everything else they believed they knew and so to immediate rejection.

These instances come from anaesthetic experience because people do not usually communicate the fact that they have received, through an ecstatic experience, an overbelief that they almost instantly rejected as nonsense. Lewis Carroll is unusual in accepting as valuable what he knew to be nonsense: 'I knew not what it meant, then,' he said of his line 'For the Snark *was* a Boojum, you see', 'I know not what it means now.' But he wrote it down and in the next year or so a poem 'pieced itself together' of which this could be the last line.[1] In my groups Q 17

---

[1] Harding: A.I., p. 63.

is the only person who described his overbelief and then rejected it as meaningless (see p.349); but many people would have accepted a belief about a sense of union with external reality as potentially meaningful and important.

We do occasionally hear of overbeliefs that wavered between rejection and acceptance and were then accepted. Of the mystical experience which she eventually accepted as her 'Second Shewing' Juliana of Norwich writes,

> 'mine understanding was led down into the sea-ground, and there I saw hills and dales green, seeming as it were moss-be-grown, with wrack and gravel... This Second Shewing was so low and so little and so simple, that my spirits were in great travail at the beholding,— mourning, full of dread, and longing: for I was some time in doubt whether it was a Shewing.' [1]

But eventually she 'understood truly that it was a Shewing', having been able to interpret it in such a way that it fitted into the framework of her beliefs.

The hedgehog test: This test, which was applied by Juliana of Norwich, almost always gives affirmative results. 'The hedgehog knows one big thing', said Archilochus, and in order that he may be sure of knowing his one big thing, all the little things he knows must be fitted into it. The synthesizing capacity of ecstatic experience, the tendency for expression in totality terms of what is believed to be known, entail the likelihood that ecstatic overbelief will postulate one big pattern into which everything must be fitted in. For Juliana it would have been unaesthetic and unsatisfactory to have known fifteen revelations from God and with them another experience, in many ways similar, that must be accepted as something other than a revelation from God; and which, if accepted as something other than a revelation from God, might have involved re-assessing the overall pattern of revelations from God believed to apply to all the other experiences. The test, then, was 'Can this be fitted in?' and since the overwhelming desire was for an affirmative answer, a way was found of so interpreting the recalcitrant experience that an affirmative answer could be justified.

The hedgehog test of 'Can this be fitted in?' is often applied in order to justify the creation of totality structures on the basis of evidence

---

[1] *Revelations of Divine Love*, ed. Grace Warrack (London, 1901; 13th edn., 1950), pp. 22–3.

that could justify only more cautious and limited statements. 'A sort of green light' is seen; it follows that everything is a sort of green light, that is, if we look at everything in such a way that it can be seen in a sort of green light. Berenson suddenly felt that a stone carving had become alive: 'Since that morning, nothing visible has been indifferent or even dull. Everywhere I feel the ideated pulsation of vitality' (L 10). And everywhere, I must admit, I tend to see evidence of the influence of ecstatic experiences, just as everywhere others—to take instances of theories put forward by self-avowed ecstatics—see evidence of the need for healthy sexuality or of a collective unconscious or of the existence of standard patterns of development in history. There is no evidence so recalcitrant that it cannot, if one really tries, be shown to display a sort of green light:

> 'he selects the instances which will support his theses, or he presents them in the way that suits him, and he does so with an assurance which hardly leaves room for the suspicion, not only that one might quote innumerable others with which his theses would not bear company, but especially that those cases he does mention can be explained or described in a different way so as to disagree no less completely with his theses'.[1]

Ecstatic experiences seem to encourage men to be pattern-making animals, and a negative result to the test of 'Can this be fitted in?' is, as many ecstatics have sadly discovered, more often imposed from outside than spontaneously accepted by the ecstatic himself.

The test of reason: Matters of neutral truth have their appropriate tests which cannot be evaded.

> 'Let us learn to dream, gentlemen. Then, perhaps, we shall find the truth . . . but let us beware of publishing our dreams before they have been put to the proof by the waking understanding.'[2]

No doubt the scientific discovery that fails its appropriate tests may come with the same initial certitude and authority as the one that passes them; but as with most overbeliefs, we seldom hear of the ones that failed.

It may be, as Wordsworth and St. Augustine found, that the test of reason would necessarily lead to rejection of an overbelief that could

[1] Peter Geyl, 'Toynbee's System of Civilisations' in *Debates with Historians* (London, 1955), pp. 97–8.
[2] A. Kekulé quoted by Leuba: P.R.M., p. 242n.

be fitted in to a desired totality system. Or it may be that the test of reason would necessarily lead to acceptance of a result that could *not* be fitted into a prevailing totality system. The last six or seven hundred years have seen the constant modification of totality systems in order to bring them into accordance with beliefs imposed by acceptance of the test of reason.

The test of orthodoxy: Where the ecstatic subscribes to an accepted body of doctrine, religious or otherwise, overbeliefs must be tested by their conformity with it; and how to apply and accept the results of such tests is well explained by St. Teresa:

> 'The soul always tries to act in conformity with the Church's teaching, asking advice from this person and that, and acting as one already so deeply grounded in these truths that no imaginable revelation, even if it saw the heavens open, would cause it to swerve an inch from the doctrine of the Church. If it should ever feel its thoughts wavering on this point, or stopping to say, "If God says this to me, it may well be true, just as what He said to the saints was true", I do not say that it will believe what it is saying, but that the devil will be beginning to tempt it'. [1]

But it may happen that revelations *not* in accordance with received teaching are still so desirable to the ecstatic that their failure to pass the test of orthodoxy is not sufficient for them to be given up. In such cases a test likely to be applied is

The test of feeling it to be true: This test also is well explained by St. Teresa:

> 'Anyone who has had a true vision from God will detect a false one almost immediately... It is the most impossible of all impossibilities that this can be the work of the imagination...I once said to some of these people whom I used to consult: "If you were to tell me that someone I knew well...is not really himself, and that I was imagining things and you knew what the truth really was, I would believe your statement rather than my own eyes. But if this person had left me some jewels as a pledge of his great love, and if I...now found myself rich where I had been poor, I could not possibly believe that this was a delusion, even if I wanted to.' [2]

The test of chosen authorities: Again St. Teresa provides an example. As the passage quoted above shows, the people whose advice she once

[1] *Life*, ch. xxv., p. 178.   [2] Ibid., ch. xxviii, pp. 201-2.

sought became the people she used to consult when she found that they would not ratify her revelations. To those few people who do not find this saint a wholly admirable character, her *Life* seems to display a determined search for authorities who will ratify her revelations, a determined discard of those who will not. There are so many different accepted answers to the unknowable that it is seldom difficult to find an authority who will ratify one's own.

The test of benefit: This test is, in various forms, widely accepted as valid. It is adduced by St. Teresa in the same chapter as the last passage quoted, in support of her contention that she could distinguish true from false visions; if these latter came only from our own minds, she says,

> 'instead of being restored and fortified, the soul will become wearier; it will become exhausted and nauseated. But it is impossible to exaggerate the riches that accompany a true vision; it brings health and comfort even to the body.'

In a secular application of this test, which he uses throughout his book, Richards judges the value that may properly be set on the trigger by the benefits derived from the experience it induces:

> 'Everybody knows the feeling of freedom, of relief, of increased competence and sanity, that follows any reading in which more than usual order and coherence has been given to our responses.' [1]

This test of improved response is widely used by the religious when assessing the experiences of others:

> 'all the great mystics, and this in precise proportion to their greatness, have ever taught that...only such ecstasies are valuable as leave the soul, and the very body as its instrument, strengthened and improved'. [2]

For Kirk the test is for moral benefit:

> 'unless an alleged experience of God brings with it a call to disinterested action of some kind or another...we shall scarcely be able to avoid the conclusion that something is amiss'. [3]

---

[1] *Principles*, p. 235.
[2] Hügel: M.E.R., Vol. II, pp. 46–7. I have already shown Von Hügel's attempts to explain the recalcitrant fact that many accepted mystics seem, as a result of their experiences, to have suffered considerable deterioration in health; see pp. 86–7n.
[3] V.G., p. 199.

He explains, with approval, that for St. Bernard the test of a vision's validity is always a moral one. On the one hand, 'The vision does not terrify but soothe': on the other, is 'the power of contemplation to inspire to action and to renew ideals'.[1]

The possibility of benefiting others is a test by which mystical revelations may be accepted although failing other and, one might suppose, more important tests. Of a group of female ecstatics, each of whose revealed account of events in Jesus's life differed from the others, Thurston comments,

> 'Of course, it would be possible to take the line that one parti-cular mystic, say Anne Catherine, was really a channel of true inspiration, while all the others were deluded, but there seems little reason for giving the preference in this matter to one visionary rather than another. The contemplations of all may be highly profitable to their own souls, and a source of edification for those who in faith and simplicity accept their guidance, but they do not, on the other hand, lead us to any clearer knowledge of the actions of our Saviour or His Blessed Mother, and consequently their historical value is absolutely nil.'[2]

Aesthetic tests: Thurston's comment may usefully serve as the basis for a test of certain works of art, the contemplation of which may be highly profitable to the souls of their creators and even to those who in faith and simplicity seek their guidance. But it must always be the sincere wish of the artist that the tests he is capable of applying to his own work are sufficiently rigorous to enable him to strangle at birth all inspira-tions which would pass only Thurston's test. Every artist knows the inspiration that had had its moment or hour or even years of glory but which must finally be discarded under the test of critical considera-tions in a wider context than the immediate satisfaction inspiration must of its nature give.[3]

I consider that the test most properly applied to aesthetic inspirations is test of their ability to act as triggers. For the creator they must be capable of acting as triggers to ever-renewed inspirations until the desired structure is completed. For those who encounter the completed structure this must act (as suggested by Montague in text L 20 and in the quotation from Richards on the last page) as a trigger to ecstatic

[1] V.G., pp. 352–3. [2] S.M., pp. 79–80.
[3] Q 19 comments that the 'feeling of infinite facility' when 'the creative faculty descends' is 'not necessarily accompanied by one's best work'.

or response experiences, whether for the creator or for others, which will result in improved organization.

An inspiration may of course remain satisfactory to its creator even though it may fail to be effective on those who later encounter it. But it may also happen that the critical opinion of others is one of the tests to which the creator desires to submit his work and in the light of which he may modify it, as Coleridge modified *The Ancient Mariner* in response to the criticisms of reviewers.

I suggest that the aesthetic tests are those most often applied by other people to the revelations of religious mystics. Indeed it is hard to know what other tests *can* be applied by laymen, since they are specifically told that the test of believing the revelations to be true is not required of them:

> 'With regard to the special revelations that have been made to the saints, **belief** in them is **not required** by the Church even when she approves them. By this approbation she only intends to declare that nothing is to be found in them contrary to faith or morals, and that they can be accepted without danger and even with advantage.' [1]

Theologians scan such visions to see whether they pass the test of orthodoxy, but without an ability to act as triggers, that 'strangely unreckonable power' by which Bowra distinguishes inspired from uninspired writing (see pp.281-2) the tests of the theologians would hardly be necessary.

The power so to act seems sometimes to supersede even tests of orthodoxy. Von Hügel can speak of St. Catherine of Genoa's 'delicately psychological, soaring, yet sober-minded Eschatology' [2] even though he has to show that parts of her eschatology were not consonant with orthodoxy (see p. 311 n). Juliana of Norwich is regarded with devotion by many Anglicans, largely, it would seem, because of the impact made on them by a single phrase frequently quoted: 'Sin is behoveable, but all shall be well, and all shall be well, and all manner of thing shall be well'; Inge, who surprisingly finds 'sunny hopefulness and happiness' shining from every page of her book, seems unworried by the fact that her view of human personality 'reminds us of the Neoplatonic doctrine that there is a higher and a lower self, of which the former is untainted by the sins of the latter'.[3] And St. Teresa of Avila and St. John of the Cross are only two among many saints whose writings

[1] Poulain: G.I.P., ch. xxi, 2. [2] M.E.R., Vol. I, p. vi.
[3] C.M., pp. 202-9.

remain uncondemned even though containing passages almost indistinguishable from the writings of Molinos who *was* condemned (see pp. 252–3n.).

The test of deeper meaning:

'How can an artist expect that what he has felt intuitively should be perfectly realised by others, seeing that he himself feels in the presence of his work, if it is true Art, that he is confronted by a riddle, about which he, too, might have illusions, just as another might?'[1]

Leuba cites St. Teresa as saying (in *The Interior Castle*) that divine words possess, in a way she finds impossible to describe, several meanings outside the one they express by their sounds, and that

'A single one of these divine utterances expresses in a few words that which our minds could express only in many.' [2]

This may be compared with L 24's comment on the sentence he believed he had heard, that 'the phrase conveyed nothing of the meaning it bore at that moment, for it had unbelievable depths of significance', and in the sudden discovery of significance in certain phrases (see p. 341).

This readiness to accept a content of incomprehensibility as warrant for beliefs is probably related to the widespread desire that some things should remain unexplained and inexplicable and the belief that rational explanation destroys the numinous (see p. 183).

1 Wagner to Roeckel, quoted by G. B. Shaw in *The Perfect Wagnerite*, reprinted in *Major Critical Essays*, p. 246.
2 P.R.M., pp. 180–1nn.

CHAPTER XXXVII

Some Critical Judgements

Earlier I outlined some of the criteria for mystical experiences accepted by some other writers on these subjects and showed how these differed from my own criteria for ecstatic experiences. It will by now be clear that in many cases where experiences are accepted as mystical ones by these and other writers and as ecstatic experiences by me, my judgement of the way such experiences should be assessed and of the conclusions that can usefully be drawn from them differs in many respects from theirs. To some extent such differences arise from divergencies in basic premises and beliefs; to some extent they are founded on empirical study of the subject-matter. In this chapter I shall examine a few judgements made by other people of texts I have used.

The passage from Wordsworth's *Tintern Abbey* that is my text L 1a is quoted by Zaehner in support of his contention that Wordsworth had not known mystical experience. He writes:

'In these lines there is an intimation, if you like, of something which transcends and informs transient Nature, but it is no more than an intimation. It amounts to little more than that there is a Spirit somewhere which pervades all Nature. There is no trace of an actual experience at all, either of union with Nature or communion with God. There is a dim perception only that there is a unifying principle in the universe. On these grounds Wordsworth can scarcely be classed as a mystic since, to judge from his writings, he does not seem to have had a "unitive" experience of any of the types we have discussed.' [1]

Other Christian writers find no difficulty in accepting Wordsworth as a mystic, albeit of that inferior kind they usually call a nature mystic. Butler regards Wordsworth's lines in *Tintern Abbey* as an example of 'the higher grade of nature ecstasies not produced by artificial means'.[2]

[1] M.S.P., p. 35.   [2] W.M., p. 228.

Inge gives twelve pages to Wordsworth's mystical beliefs and concludes that this 'eminently sane and manly spirit' is 'the best representative' of 'Nature Mysticism'.[1] Underhill says that although Wordsworth cannot be called a pure mystic, he was one of those (with Plato, Heracleitus, Tennyson and Whitman) in whose works we can detect 'indications that they too were acquainted, beyond most poets and seers, with the phenomena of the illuminated life', and later compares Wordsworth's 'certain degree' of 'Cosmic Consciousness' with its full development in the mystical experiences of Boehme, Fox, and Blake.[2]

Among Wordsworth's literary critics both Helen Darbishire and H. W. Garrod are agreed that Wordsworth had mystical experiences and that these were of great value to him.[3] I myself regard Wordsworth as probably the most rewarding study of all secular mystics and contend that many of his mystical experiences, including that of the text under discussion, are in my sense ecstatic ones.[4]

It is of interest that Zaehner alone denies the title of mystic to Wordsworth. To grant it would, however, be destructive of much of the argument of Zaehner's book, which involves there being a fundamental difference between natural and theistic mystical experiences; and one of the ways, he claims, in which this difference can be seen is that nature mystics claim 'an experience of Nature in all things or of all things as being one' but that in such experiences 'there is no mention of God'.[5]

But Wordsworth, long before he had come to Christian belief, was giving the name God to what he believed he had encountered in his mystical experiences. For instance, in a notebook written before 1800 he speaks of

> one interior life
> In which all beings live with God, themselves
> Are God, existing in the mighty whole,

[1] C.M., pp. 305–16.

[2] E.U: M., p. 238 and p. 255. Zaehner also denies Blake the quality of mystic. 'Though superb both as a poet and as a painter, he cannot be strictly classed as a mystic.' M.S.P., p. 35.

[3] See Garrod, *Wordsworth*, p. 105, and Darbishire, *The Poet Wordsworth*, pp. 95–120. F. W. Bateson however sets much less value both on the experiences and on their importance in the creative process. 'An abnormal psychological condition sometimes came to seem important to him simply because he had experienced it and because it was out of "the common track of life"... Wordsworth took these things a good deal too seriously'. *Wordsworth, A Re-Interpretation*, p. 168.

[4] Wordsworth's own name for the wanderer's experience of my text L 1b is ecstasy; see *The Excursion* (P.W., Vol. V), Bk. I, l, 237.   [5] M.S.P., p. 50.

'How far this intense mystical experience is compatible with Christianity let theologians determine' writes de Selincourt,[1] and 'Certainly at this time Wordsworth's faith was in no way tinged with dogmatic Christianity.' Thus long before he had turned to Christianity, at a period when Butler, Inge, and Underhill agree in regarding him as a nature mystic, Wordsworth found that at least some of his experiences must be expressed in terms that would, according to Zaehner's distinction, show him to be speaking of theistic mystical experience, albeit of a possibly impermissible identification with Deity (see p. 123).

But Wordsworth himself does not appear to have believed that there was a fundamental difference between the experiences he enjoyed as a pantheist and Christian mystical experiences, but rather that the same experiences could bear at will either a pantheist or a theist gloss. De Selincourt has shown, with several examples, how in the later text of *The Prelude* the addition or alteration of a few words allowed Wordsworth to use passages previously pantheist in tone to reflect his later theism:

> 'The highest achievement of that Power which he has learnt to reverence in Nature was, in the A text, that it "lifts the being into magnanimity", i.e. to that greatness of soul which raises us above our petty selves to realise the "Godhead that is ours, as natural beings in the strength of nature". In the later version *this same power* [my italics]
> "Trains to meekness and exalts by humble faith." ' [2]

It could be argued that by the time Wordsworth had become an orthodox Christian, his capacity for mystical experience had so much diminished that he never knew what true theistic experience felt like. It must still be accepted that while a pantheist he felt he had encountered in some of his experiences what it seemed to him proper to call God. To me Wordsworth provides one of many demonstrations that a wide range of mystical experiences may be known by a single individual, and that the evidence does not allow the assumption that the experiences of Christians necessarily differ from those of non-Christians.

Zaehner also discusses several experiences of Proust's, and among them the passage from *Swann's Way* that is my text L 26. This experience is not, according to Zaehner, a 'nature' or, as he prefers to call it,

[1] *Prel.*, p. lvii.   [2] Ibid., p. lx.

a pan-en-henic experience; Proust differs from nature mystics in that 'he experiences no enlargement of the personality beyond its natural bounds'. But Proust does not speak of 'an indwelling God', so he is not having, in Zaehner's terms, theistic experience. What he is having, according to Zaehner, is experience of the kind typically enjoyed by eastern mystics, and experience 'in accordance with the Sāṁkhya-Yoga "philosophy"'; 'to use the Jungian jargon, he achieved the integration of his personality or "individuation"'. Zaehner regards the theme of *La Recherche du Temps Perdu* as 'thoroughly oriental, more specifically Buddhistic', and the whole novel as 'one vast illustration of the Buddhist thesis', that is, of 'disillusion and disgust with the world' whose 'transience and instability... can be overcome by the attainment of the state of *nirvāṇa*'.[1]

In my terms Proust's were certainly not withdrawal experiences of the kind for which both Koestler and Gissing found the word *nirvana* appropriate (see p. 55). This particular text describes, in my terms, adamic ecstasy; other experiences of Proust's cited by Zaehner, all, by my criteria, momentary intensity ecstasies, show feelings of knowledge ('the permanent essence of things, which is usually hidden, is set free'; 'I had a thought which, a moment ago had not existed for me and which took on verbal form in my head') and feelings of contact expressed as 'a blinding yet indistinct vision' which seemed to speak to him. For me, Proust, like Wordsworth, enjoys different varieties of ecstatic experience, which cannot, from his descriptions of them, be differentiated from some Christian experiences.

The passage from Joël's *Seele und Welt* which is my text L 9 I took from Jung's *Psychology of the Unconscious*, and this is Jung's comment on it:

> 'Joël paints here, in unmistakable symbolism, the confluence of subject and object as the re-union of mother and child... The sea, devouring the sun and giving birth to it anew, is already an old acquaintance. The moment of the rise of consciousness, the separation of subject and object is a birth...The idea of the jelly-fish is not "accidental." Once when I was explaining to a patient the maternal significance of water...she experienced a very unpleasant feeling. "It makes me squirm," she said, "as if I touched a jelly-fish." Here, too, the same idea!'[2]

[1] M.S.P., p. 52.   [2] *Psychology of the Unconscious*, p. 199.

In my terms this is a withdrawal-intensity ecstasy triggered by the sea, with the idea of the jelly-fish acting as a unitive symbol (see p. 108). I am uncertain whether Jung would relate to a reblending with the mother and subsequent birth all the experiences I call ecstasies or only those which are, in my terms, withdrawal-intensity ecstasies triggered by the sea and/or described in terms of oceanic symbols.[1]

Underhill says of St. Catherine of Siena's experience (my text R 2):

'A healthy ecstasy so deep as this seems to be the exclusive prerogative of the mystics: perhaps because so great a passion, so profound a concentration, can be produced by nothing smaller than their flaming love of God.' [2]

Her assumption, which I do not challenge, is that this is religious 'ecstasy', though the reference to involuntary speech is more typical of intensity ecstasy.[3] My interest here is in Underhill's judgement of this experience as a healthy one, and her apparent use of 'deep' as implying value. St. Catherine would not be regarded by most people as a healthy woman (see p. 253n); and to consider that depth of trance is an indication of value is surely to fall into what Leuba describes as 'the surprisingly coarse error of confusing degrees of ecstatic trance with degrees of moral perfection'. [4]

My text R 8, an experience recounted by a convert to the religion of healthy-mindedness, is included by James in his chapter on that 'religion' where he instances it as an example of conversion to 'Mind-cure' and comments that it is 'exceedingly trivial'.[5]

This judgement is, I suggest, based on the negligible prestige of the woman concerned, the nature of the overbelief (James had small liking for 'Mind-cure'), and the poor prose in which the experience is recounted. But the content of the experience is no more or less trivial

---

[1] Zaehner, who quotes this same text as an example of nature ecstasy, says that Jung has 'given up much of the cruder sexual symbolism of Freud'; we should now take this passage as being about 'the more fruitful ideas of the collective unconscious and the integration of the personality'. M.S.P., p. 40.

[2] E.U: M., p. 366.

[3] As I have indicated earlier (p. 57n), many religious 'ecstasies' are described in terms that could not allow one to distinguish them from momentary ecstasies without a specific statement about prolonged duration and trance.

[4] P.R.M., p. 186.

[5] V.R.E., p. 119.

than that of many better-told conversions of better-known people to more admirable faiths.

Judgements based on criteria similar to James's will enable readers to assess the experiences of the questionnaire group as trivial when compared with those of the religious groups. But these are the very criteria I have tried throughout to eschew in favour of attempting to show that if prestige, style and overbelief are disregarded, the experiences of the questionnaire group must be judged as essentially similar to those of the religious.

For Rufus Jones the experience of Joseph Salmon the Ranter (my text R 18), is part of his evidence for concluding that:

> 'It is at any rate perfectly clear, even when full allowance is made for sectarian misunderstanding and exaggeration, that the Ranter movement was a serious outbreak of mental and moral disorder. The movement...brings forcibly to light the dangers involved in *extreme* mystical doctrines, that is, doctrines by which the individual is assumed to be an infallible embodiment of God, to be superior to all previous revelation, and to be able to arrive at final truth without the help of the Church or the social environment.' [1]

As a judgement of the Ranter movement, which was, says the *Oxford Dictionary of the Christian Church*, 'A fanatical antinomian and pantheistic sect', I cannot comment on this. As a judgement of tendencies displayed in Salmon's description of his experience I find it hard to understand. There is hardly a phrase in this account that is not closely similar to phrases used by mystics who would be accepted by Jones as orthodox, and I shall demonstrate this by trying to match the phrases used by Salmon with phrases used by other people in the religious group:

'as one inspired with a supernatural life': cp. 'I became conscious in myself of eternal life' (Bucke, R 17).

'sprang up far above my earthly centre': cp. 'he was lifted up above all created things' (St. Alphonsus Rodriguez, R 14).

'into a most divine and heavenly enjoyment': cp. 'he had of it a joy such as he might have known in the seeing of the shapes and substances of all joyful things' (Suso, R 1).

'wrapt up in the embraces of such pure love and peace': cp. 'I am

[1] S.M.R., pp. 479-80.

plunged into an ineffable peace...my Love has embraced me' (Hugh of St. Victor, R 12).

'I knew not oft-times whether I were in or out of this fading form': cp. 'whether his soul were in the body or out of the body he could not tell' (Suso, R 1).

'Here I saw heaven opened upon me, and the new Jerusalem': cp. 'If that which I see and feel be not the Kingdom of Heaven, I know not what it can be' (Suso, R 1).

'all my former enjoyments being nothing in appearance to that glory which now rested upon my spirit': cp. 'obliteration of the conventionalities which usually surround and cover my life' (a man cited by James, R 6) and 'changed into...another glory' (Suso, R 22).

'joy unspeakable, peace inconceivable': cp. 'joy unspeakable' (David Brainerd, R 13) and references to 'peace' almost passim.[1]

'what soul-ravishing delights and most divinely infatuating pleasures my soul was here possest with': cp. 'his soul was full of contentment and joy' (Suso, R 1) and 'inebriated' (Suso, R 22).

'I can give you no perfect account of that glory which then covered me': cp. 'the more I seek words...the more I feel the impossibility of describing the thing by any of our usual images' (M.E., R 11).

'whose pure perfection surmounts the reach of the most strenuous and highflown expression': 'I beheld naught save the divine power, in a manner assuredly indescribable' (Angela of Foligno, R 5a).

'I appeared to myself as one confounded into the abyss of eternity': cp. 'my soul opened out...into the Infinite' (a clergyman, R 3).

'nonentisized into the being of beings': cp. 'she is, as it were, entirely dead to the world, the better to live in God' (St. Teresa, R 10b).

'my soul spilt and emptied into the fountain and ocean of divine fullness': cp. 'The outflowing of a soul into her God is a true ecstasy... wholly mingled with, absorbed and engulfed in, her God' (St. Francis of Sales, R 21).

'expired into the aspires of pure life': cp. '[the soul] melts away into God' (Louis of Blois, R 20).

'the Lord so much appeared': cp. 'I felt the presence of God' (M.E., R 11).

'that I was little or nothing seen, but walked at an orderly distance from myself': cp. 'scarce reflected that there was such a creature as myself' (David Brainerd, R 13).

[1] Many such phrases probably echo the 'joy unspeakable' of 1 *Peter* i. 8.

'treading and tripping over the mountains of the heavenly land, where I walked with the Lord' : cp. 'He found himself as it were, in another region, alone with God' (St. Alphonsus Rodriguez, R 14).

'and was not': cp. 'temporary loss of my own identity' (a man cited by James, R 6).

'I have been exalted into the bosom of the eternal Almightiness': cp. 'through the perfect union which the soul has made with Me, she is raised from the earth' (St. Catherine of Siena, R 2).

'where I have seen and heard things unlawful...to be uttered amongst men': cp. 'then did he see and hear that which no tongue can express' (Suso, R 1).

Apart from the last phrase, where the religious group provides no parallel for 'unlawful',[1] the similarities are close enough to make it clear that there was nothing unusual or outlandish in Salmon's experience; and had I sought parallels beyond the compass of this group, I could have found still closer ones among orthodox religious mystics. We must, on authority, accept Salmon as a Ranter and therefore an antinomian and a pantheist. We must accept that his claims to have been 'nonentisized' in God as beyond Christian bounds; but such claims are made by other and orthodox Christians in this group and elsewhere (see p. 94n. and pp. 122-5).

Does Jones's objection to this text spring from an assessment of the way Salmon puts his phrases together, each by itself being a mystical commonplace but amounting, in the order here, to evidence of 'mental and moral disorder'? But I do not think it has ever been suggested that the order in which phrases are arranged in descriptions of mystical experiences is relevant to their orthodoxy.

Two other explanations of Jones's judgement seem more plausible. First, knowing Salmon to be a Ranter and disapproving of the movement, he judged the experience by Salmon's known beliefs and status without reference to the content of the experience; and secondly that he disliked Salmon's style.

The method of comparison used above can be applied to any ecstatic experience. Certainly almost every phrase in every text in all three groups can be paralleled by a phrase in another text and often by a phrase in each of the other two groups.

For some purposes it is obviously proper to value ecstasies according

[1] But this is obviously adapted from 2 *Cor.* xii. 4.

to their orthodoxy, their provenance or their beauty; or, as many religious ecstatics do, according to whether they reveal a simpler, purer life, wonderful knowledge, or the possibility of communion or union with a desired totality. For many people such judgements may be genuinely life-enhancing and creative. But for my purposes value-judgements of all these kinds are irrelevant; and in considering whether it may justly be said that the experiences of people in all my three groups are similar, all such value-judgements must be laid aside.

PART FOUR
CHAPTER XXXVIII
Conclusions

On the basis of the material presented I offer the following conclusions, some firm, some tentative:

Among the experiences generally known as mystical it is possible to isolate a group which I have generically called ecstatic experiences and which can be circumscribed by the language used to describe them. In describing ecstatic experiences people will usually say that they have lost some of a limited range of feelings and that they have felt certain physical or quasi-physical feelings; and will always say that they have gained some of a limited range of feelings.

Ecstatic experiences may be divided into two kinds according to the manner in which they are approached. One manner, which I have called withdrawal and which involves a more or less gradual loss of normal perceptions, I have noted only in passing. Withdrawal experiences, which can be deliberately induced or involuntarily achieved, may sometimes turn into the other kind of experience which I have called intensity experience; indeed I think it probable that all intensity experiences begin by being, to no matter how slight a degree, withdrawal ones.

Intensity experiences, which have been my main subject, cannot be voluntarily induced and are typically rare. They are tumescent experiences, usually, and probably always, of momentary duration; they are sometimes followed by a more or less extended period—up to an hour or so—which I have called ecstatic afterglow, during which the experience is appreciated and interpreted, and normal faculties and perceptions gradually restored.

Intensity experiences may be divided into three kinds, though with infinite possibilities of gradation. Some, which I have called adamic ecstasies, are characterized by feelings of purification and renewal, of life and the world transformed and of loving-kindness to all. Some are characterized by feelings of knowledge gained, often believed to have been communicated from someone or somewhere else; these I have called knowledge or knowledge-contact ecstasies. And some are characterized by feelings of union with someone or something else and these I have called union ecstasies. This scale, which emerged as a tentative postulation from my own material, corresponds with scales set up by religious writers, by whom it is regarded as a scale of ascending value.

Intensity experiences are almost always preceded by contact with one or some of a limited range of objects, events, and ideas which I have called triggers. Contact with a trigger appears usually to be a necessary though not a sufficient cause of ecstatic experience. I have not been able to discover what constitute sufficient pre-conditions for ecstatic experience, or what qualities in triggers are efficacious in inducing these experiences, though it is noticeable that what are felt to be the qualities of many triggers correspond with some of the feelings of these experiences. Triggers form a group to which high prestige is widely accorded, and which are widely accepted as entitled to reverence and freedom from contamination; I have suggested that it would be useful and interesting to examine the importance accorded by societies to triggers, whether this is shown by anathematizing them, by institutionalizing them, or by using them as models for objects of honorific display.

Not all triggers are effective on all people who enjoy ecstatic experiences, but many people usually expect, from certain triggers at least, beneficial experiences which are similar in kind to ecstatic ones, though often felt with a much lesser degree of intensity. I have called these response experiences.

Some ecstasies have as their result the discovery of a continuing and often expanding focus of value in the trigger to the experience. These, which seem most likely to occur in children and young people, I have called revelation ecstasies. They, and almost certainly similar but less intense experiences, may have considerable influence on an individual's tastes, interests, beliefs, and aims. Many of the feelings of momentary ecstatic experiences may be known for more or less prolonged periods ranging from, say, an hour, a day, a week to (ideally) a lifetime. Such states may come unsought after, for instance, childbirth or going away on holiday; they are usually postulated as necessary states for inhabitants of utopias; and they may and even should be sought by the religious as almost continuous conditions. In the last case they are known as unitive states or periods, and I have used this name for all more or less long-continuing feelings of ecstasy.

It is generally agreed that ecstatic experiences are to be valued not for the delight they give—which is great—but for their beneficial results. These results may be generally expressed as improved mental organization, whether this takes the form of replacing uneasiness and dissatisfaction with ease and satisfaction, or of appearing to confirm a sought belief, or of inspiring to moral action or of enabling the expression of a new mental creation.

Many of the beliefs to which ecstatic experiences give rise or which they seem to substantiate appear to be the direct outcome of the nature of the experiences enjoyed. Ecstasies and the pursuit of ecstasies often give rise to ideals and values opposed to those usual in and even necessary for the social life of the community; these ideals and values are none the less influential in contemporary social life.

Some people have experiences which seem to be the obverse of ecstatic ones, and these I have called desolations. It is widely recognized that more or less prolonged states of desolation are not unusual in people liable to ecstatic experiences. These, I have suggested, should rather be regarded as the obverse of the more or less prolonged ecstatic states which I have called unitive states, and I have shown that people may also have brief or momentary desolation experiences; and that some experiences, which I have called desolation-ecstasies, may begin as desolation and end as intensity ecstasy. There are many and possibly significant similarities between desolation experiences and withdrawal experiences.

I do not know whether identifiable physical events accompany ecstatic and desolation experiences, but in descriptions of such experiences the occurrence of physical events is frequently and consistently claimed, sometimes by use of figurative language, sometimes in the form of literal claims.

Both withdrawal and intensity ecstasies may be enjoyed by the same person, though in the western culture-pattern the tendency is to approve intensity ecstasies and not withdrawal ones. The same person may enjoy intensity experiences of different kinds. I have not been able to discover whether ecstatic experiences may be enjoyed by all or by only some people. Some slight evidence suggests that the latter is more probably the case, and also that knowledge-contact ecstasies and union ecstasies may be known only to people who are intellectual or creative.

No variety of ecstatic experience that appears in my texts is available exclusively to Christians; to name an ecstatic experience a Christian one is to name it according to its overbelief and not according to its kind.

I have made a number of other suggestions about the nature and effects of ecstatic experiences, some more or less well founded, others more or less guesswork. Much of what I have said could be confirmed or refuted by further evidence beyond my capacity to collect. Further inquiries that could be made and would, I believe, be fruitful, include the following:

May ecstatic experiences be universally enjoyed or are they available to only some people and, if so, to what kinds of people? To people who can have ecstatic experiences, are all kinds available or only some kinds, and if the latter, what qualities in the people can be distinguished as relevant to the kinds of experiences they can have?

What are sufficient pre-conditions for ecstatic experience, and what qualities in triggers determine their effectiveness as such?

What physical events accompany ecstatic experiences? Do these have any kind of reference to the physical events that ecstatics describe?

Would the conclusions I have drawn from experiences recounted in, or translated into, English hold good for experiences told in other languages, whether of the Indo-European group or outside it?

Do certain varieties of ecstatic experience tend to predominate in certain culture-groups?

Are ecstatic experiences known or usual in simpler, less civilized culture-groups?

Are the feelings of people in 'psychological crowds' (see p. 205 and n.) often or ever assimilable to ecstatic experiences? And does the idea of the actual society—state, city, congregation, school, family—often or ever act as a trigger to ecstatic experience?

Ecstatic experiences are in themselves delightful and have beneficial results. It is not surprising that most ecstatics have regarded their experiences as highly if not supremely valuable. But in so far as ecstasies are, as I have suggested, experiences which accompany and are linked with processes facilitating the synthesis of mental material, then experiences as intense as ecstatic ones seem exaggerated in relation to the need, since the synthesis of mental material may and usually does take place without being accompanied by ecstatic experiences. It is true that the more intense experiences are usually regarded as more pleasurable, and some part of our estimation of the value of ecstasies must depend on our estimation of these forms of pleasure. It may well be that without experiences as intense as these, totality answers would not be sought or found or accepted; and if so, then some part of our estimation of the value of ecstasies must depend on our estimation of the value of totality beliefs. But it is certain that both a high degree of pleasure and satisfaction and the answers to limited questions may be derived from experiences which, if often in many ways similar to ecstatic ones, can be very much less intense.

But I do not believe that any explanations of these experiences can be satisfactory if they suggest that ecstasies are *only* this or *only* that— only a phenomenon of repressed sexuality or only a concommitant of some or other morbid condition. Certainly convictions are an insufficient substitute for evidence, but both people's convictions of the value of these experiences and their substantial influence on outlook and language persuade me that these are of some evidential value in justifying the conclusion that ecstatic experiences must be treated as important outside religious contexts, as having important effects on people's mental and physical well-being, on their aesthetic preferences, their creativity, their beliefs and philosophies, and on their conduct.

I do not think it sensible to ignore, as most rationalists have done, ecstatic experiences and the emotions and ideas to which they give rise. To ignore or to deny the importance of ecstatic experiences is to leave to the irrational the interpretation of what many people believe to be of supreme value. It is, I think, significant that we have no neutral adjective to distinguish the range of emotions, values, moral compulsions, felt truths that arise from ecstatic experience. *Spiritual* implies acceptance of pre-suppositions rejected by rationalists, and those who reject such pre-suppositions have sought rather to deny importance to ecstatic experiences than to examine them on the basis of their own pre-suppositions and to supply a vocabulary in which such examinations could be made.

I myself believe that an adequate explanation of ecstatic experiences would show that Nietzsche made a valid interpretation and prediction when he wrote,

'Perhaps the whole of *religion*...may appear to some distant age as an exercise and a prelude, in like manner as the prelude and preparation of science here exhibit themselves... Perhaps religion may have been the peculiar means for enabling individual men to enjoy but once the entire self-satisfaction of a God and all his self-redeeming power. Indeed!—one may ask—would man have learned at all to get on the tracks of hunger and thirst for *himself*, and to extract satiety and fullness out of *himself*, without that religious schooling and preliminary history?' [1]

I do not believe that to seek a rational explanation of these experiences is in any way to denigrate them, but rather that a rational explanation may prove at least as awe-inspiring as earlier interpretations. Wordsworth was once content to believe that the source of this range of feelings was the human mind, and wrote,

> *For I must tread on shadowy ground, must sink*
> *Deep—and, aloft ascending, breathe in worlds*
> *To which the heaven of heavens is but a veil.*
> *All strength—all terror, single or in bands,*
> *That ever was put forth in personal form—*
> *Jehovah—with his thunder, and the choir*
> *Of shouting Angels, and the empyreal thrones—*
> *I pass them unalarmed. Not Chaos, not*
> *The darkest pit of lowest Erebus,*
> *Nor aught of blinder vacancy, scooped out*
> *By help of dreams—can breed such fear and awe*
> *As fall upon us often when we look*
> *Into our Minds, into the Mind of Man——* [2]

This passage so much upset Blake that it gave him a bowel complaint from which he nearly died ('Does Mr. Wordsworth think his mind can surpass Jehovah?' he asked)[3], and Wordsworth later modified his views. But I should be content and happy to believe that ecstatic experiences are wholly human experiences; that what men have worshipped since ecstatic experiences were known to them was their own creative and generalizing capacity, and that the god they sometimes believed they had perceived in these experiences was indeed the *logos*.

---

[1] *The Joyful Wisdom*, p. 234.
[2] *The Excursion*, 'Preface to the Edition of 1814', P.W., Vol., V, pp. 3-4, ll. 28-40.
[3] Quoted by H. Darbishire, *The Poet Wordsworth*, p. 139.

APPENDICES

INDEX TO AUTHORS OF TEXTS

	text no.	page no.
Allen, H. W.	L 11	409
Alphonsus Rodriguez, St.	R 14	433
Angela of Foligno	R 5a, R 5b	426, 427
Anon	L 24, R 3, R 6, R 8, R 11	418, 425, 428, 428, 431
Augustine of Hippo, St.	R 19	436
Berenson, B.	L 10	408
Boehme, J.	R 16	434
Brainerd, D.	R 13	432
Brontë, C.	L 14	410
Brontë, E.	L 21	416
Bucke, R. M.	R 17	434
Catherine of Siena, St.	R 2	424
Church, R.	L 23a, L 23b	417, 418
Eliot, G.	L 15	411
Evans, M.	L 4	402
Forster, E. M.	L 18	413
Fox, G.	R 9	429
Francis of Sales, St.	R 21	437
Gissing, G.	L 13	410
Hawkes, J.	L 19	414
Hugh of St. Victor,	R 12	432
Ignatius Loyola, St.	R 15	434
Jefferies, R.	L 3	402
Joël, K.	L 9	407
Koestler, A.	L 7	405
Lawrence, D. H.	L 17a, L 17b	412, 413
Levi, C.	L 12	409
Louis of Blois	R 20	436
Meredith, G.	L 16	412
Montague, C. E.	L 20	415
Nichols, R.	L 5	403
Nietzsche, F.	L 6	405
Ovid	L 22	417
Plotinus	R 4	426
Proust, M.	L 26	422
Ruysbroeck, J van	R 7	428
Salmon, J.	R 18	435
Snow, C. P.	L 25	421
Suso, H.	R 1, R 22	423, 437
Tennyson, A.	L 2	400
Teresa of Avila, St.	R 10a, R 10b	429, 430
Woods, F.	L 27	422
Woolf, V.	L 8	406
Wordsworth, W.	L 1a, L 1b	399

APPENDIX A

I. The Questionnaire Texts

To prevent identifications I have omitted the answers to Question 9 ('What is your profession?'), and have also omitted place-names where these might provide clues to people's identities. Some indication of types of people can be gathered from the C, I, O classifications (see p. 24).

The questionnaires are given and numbered in the order in which they were collected. M after the number stands for *male*, F for *female*. Where the respondent is under eighteen, the age is given. References to duration are italicized throughout. The questionnaires collected by E. C. are so marked.

The questions asked were:

1. Do you know a sensation of transcendent ecstasy?
2. How would you describe it?
3. What has induced it in you?
4. How many times have you felt it—in units, in tens, in hundreds?
5. What is your religion or faith?
6. Do you know a feeling of creative inspiration?
7. How would you describe it?
8. Does it seem to you to have anything in common with the ecstasy described above?
9. What is your profession?

The Texts

Q 1 F: 'I'

1. Yes.
2. In a curious way, a sort of merging into the experience—the hard lines round one's individuality are gone, one flows over them—essentially a *moment* of complete peace—the ultimate trademark is a feeling that this does touch reality—allied to this thing of

375

completeness, wholeness, other forms of so-called reality are not wholly real, only particles of reality.

3. Say, at dusk, when the light and the smell and the scene is just right. Sex. *Moments* I can't define, like sitting outside a château in France, writing to someone I loved very much—a completeness.

4. Units.

5. Believe in God in the broadest sense.

6. Doubtful—I think yes.

7. Not in essentials different from ecstasy—some slight approach to making a thing whole, a temporary *moment* of completeness.

8. Yes, certainly.

Q 2 F: 'I'

1. Yes.

2. (Gave no answer.)

3. Love.

4. Under ten times.

5. I believe in good.

6. Yes.

7. I couldn't have done what I had done if I hadn't been inhabited by someone other than myself.

8. Yes.

Q 3 F: 'I'

1. Yes.

2. Release—soaring up to something you've always wanted, always known was there—liberation, release.

3. Being in love on a perfect day, in the sea—visually perfect, everything physical—after my fourth baby was born, the right baby, it was two days after.

4. Twice.

5. Good is stronger than evil.

6. I think so.

7. Something coming out of one's fingers—drive.

8. No.

Q 4 M: 'I'

1. Yes.

2. Euphoric state with slight pathologic overtones—contemplative in origin—transient and forgotten, not sustained.

3. No obvious cause.

4. In adolescence fairly frequently—now in units.

5. Nothing specific—Christian without revelation.

6. Incessantly.

7. Of sustained elation.

8. Very much so, unquestionably.

Q 5 F: 'C'

1. Yes.

2. Transcend your normal limitations, capacity for experience, burst into a wider one.

3. After my son was born, achievement, it was *ten minutes to half an hour*. Once I had been ill, gone away, I walked alone on the Downs absolute ecstasy, particularly a sense of peace and communion—no release of tension but no tension came into it. Always connected with nature—in ecstasy you get direct communication, in art one is put in touch, not oneself in touch—in art, intense pleasure, illumination, tranquillity, but only exalted when something seems to fall into pattern.

4. Before marriage, for two or three years, almost constantly, always in relation to nature, including in town.

5. No faith.

6. Yes.

7. This resemblance to the other, you become airborne suddenly,—the power has taken hold—being written *through*.

8. Yes.

Q 6 M: 'I'

1. Yes.

2. Feeling that the mind has an accurate understanding that it can't conceptualize—suddenly clicked—perception of a pattern—mostly happiness at harmoniousness—if there's a struggle to find the harmony, then something more than harmony's achieved, it affects everything.

3. Mathematics, mountains, poetry—Eliot's 'Prufrock', Tennyson's 'Ulysses'.

4. In waves—dozens of times a year.

5. Agnostic—strongly mystical.
6. Yes.
7. Can conceptualize a pattern that is illuminating.
8. No.

Q 7 M: 'C'

1. Yes.
2. Tremendous sense of life worth living.
3. Second movement of Rachmaninov concerto—the Renoir Exhibition in 1950—certain beautiful people—in a word, beauty.
4. In tens.
5. I believe in re-incarnation—continuity.
6. Yes.
7. Tremendous excitement—can't get things on paper quick enough.
8. Creativeness is a reduction of the other.

Q 8 M: 'C'

1. Yes.
2. The soul leaving the body.
3. Women.
4. A dozen times.
5. Pantheism, Wordsworth's pantheism.
6. Yes.
7. Sudden correlation of one's raison d'être.
8. Quite different.

Q 9 F: 'C'

1. Yes.
2. Outside and above yourself.
3. Nothing—natural beauty—writing something new—sex.
4. In tens.
5. None.
6. Yes.
7. Wanting to do something and feeling you can do it.
8. Yes—interchangeable.

Q 10 M: 'I'

1. No.

5. None.

6. Yes.

7. Most of the feelings of creative inspiration I get are the pattern-making type in the arrangements of certain sets of material—that's the working level, the making of satisfactory patterns, mostly on a low level of material arrangements.

Q 11 F: 'I'

1. Yes.

2. A state of not being oneself.

3. Love—finding ten chromosomes when I knew they ought to be there—reading 'The Golden Bough' for the first time.

4. In tens.

5. Agnostic.

6. Yes.

7. Succeeding in doing something you've never been able to do till now.

8. Yes.

Q 12 M: 'O'

1. Yes.

2. (Gave no answer.)

3. When my child was ill, a phone message that he was all right—sex.

4. Twice.

5. Anything—I'm a mason.

6. Yes.

7. Saw a film newsreel of a floral fete, and I suddenly wanted to know its history.

8. (Gave no answer.)

Q 13 M: 'O'

1. No.

5. Not anything.

6. Yes, creativeness.

7. Do better than other people.

Q 14 M: 'O'

1. No—yes.

2. Removed from consideration of earthly things.

3. Music—Tchaikovsky's Fourth, the pizzicato.

4. (Gave no answer.)

5. Based on progressive re-incarnation—we are here to learn, if we learn sufficient, we go to another sphere.

6. Yes.

7. After thinking how to do a job, it suddenly comes.

8. (Gave no answer.)

Q 15 M: 'C'

1. Yes.

2. As if being borne into heaven itself—it gives complete satisfaction but sometimes it's disturbing—a sense of being in touch with the Creator.

3. Music, Bach's organ music—love.

4. Hundreds.

5. Believe in God, Christian.

6. Yes.

7. Feeling of almost intolerable urge and necessity to put down sounds on paper.

8. Yes.

Q 16 F: 'C'

1. Yes.

2. No words—intoxication if you can think of it as extreme clarity, no muddle.

3. Love—Music (Mozart, Verdi, Beethoven's Ninth once but not now, Vaughan Williams's penultimate)—'King Lear'—landscape—swimming in the sun more than anything—flying—being in a storm at sea —occasionally writing—singing, especially German lieder, Irish folk songs, Italian opera.

4. Under twenty times.

5. Agnostic.

6. Yes.

7. Very physical—not in my head, in my middle—intense excitement, not the same as ecstasy—like wishing to be delivered and labour has begun—totally concentrated, concentrated physical effort.

8. Yes, starting-point the same, both start inside—ecstasy is an enlarging, a self-losing, inspiration the opposite.

Q 17 M: 'I'

1. Yes.
2. Feeling of liberation from ordinary sense-impressions, but heightened awareness and sense of union with external reality—intense feeling of physical well-being.
3. Nature—mountains—music, Beethoven's Fifth—sex.
4. About ten.
5. None.
6. Yes.
7. Sudden excited stream of understanding.
8. Yes, but quite different and I don't know what the connexion is.

Q 18 F: 'C'

1. Yes.
2. Sensation of timeless bliss—complete separation from trouble—life should be like this for ever.
3. Nature—sex—holding my first baby, the day after she was born—music (the Archduke, the Missa Solemnis), listening to Toscanini doing Beethoven and looking at the river—water often, crossing the Thames once—Provence.
4. Ten to twenty times.
5. None—anti supernatural explanations.
6. Yes.
7. Something urgent that has got to be communicated, got down—not from myself, me only the channel—not pleasant but overwhelming and inescapable, more important than real life.
8. Yes.

Q 19 F: 'C'

1. Yes.
2. Sensation of absolute oneness, rightness, the same thing—the whole world falls into place, matches, fits.
3. Love, physical passion—real religious experience—the Flemish primitive paintings in the National Gallery—any Brandenburg, especially the Sixth—Venice.
4. In tens.
5. Protestant.
6. If it means the moment when the creative faculty descends, yes—not necessarily accompanied by one's best work.

7. A feeling of infinite facility.

8. No.

Q 20 M: 'C'

1. Yes.

2. A sense of the oneness of things.

3. (*a*) Minor scientific discovery; (*b*) own literary work coming out (*c*) Sexual love.

4. Four or five times.

5. None.

6. Yes.

7. Differences suddenly becoming one.

8. Yes, very difficult to distinguish.

Q 21 M: (10 years old)

1. Yes.

2. You feel you haven't any cares in the world—very happy—you don't feel anything but ecstasy—floating.

3. Swimming—orchestral music—driving in the sunshine.

4. In tens—about ten times.

5. Atheist.

6. Yes, I think so.

7. Done something you haven't done before—conquered—happiness.

8. Very slightly.

Q 22 F: 'C'

1. Nearly.

2. Mystic sensation—hovering on the edge of seeing right beyond.

3. Evening in the streets of [a Middle Eastern city]—the end of 'Othello' and 'Antony and Cleopatra'.

4. Once.

5. None.

6. Yes.

7. I imagine it's something like having a child, straining at something, bubbling through.

8. No, one is giving out, the other being given.

NOTE: This woman wrote to me from Israel four years later: 'From the first *moment* I sat in the sunshine by the lake at Zurich to the *moment* of near-ecstasy when I walked above the Danube opposite Belgrade on a heat shimmering afternoon, and sitting in the morning sunshine on the Acropolis and by the sea in Marathon Bay, and now, nearly every day in Jerusalem, I feel flooded with deep physical content. That day above Belgrade I thought of your theories of "ecstasy". I do not think it is ecstasy unless you are literally lifted out of yourself, unless you have left yourself behind, so it was not ecstasy in that sense; I was always myself and in myself. It was more the sensation of a poet in the act of creation.'

Q 23 F: 'C'

1. Yes.
2. This is it and everything fits in—all creation comes into harmony.
3. (No answer given.)
4. Ten times.
5. C of E.
6. Yes.
7. Seeing the book.
8. Ecstasy more satisfying.

Q 24 F: 'C'

1. Yes.
2. Absolute physical sensations, terrific constriction in throat and stomach, but it's a mental sensation—it is to me perfectly described in Cassian, when the heart without words leaps like a fountain—a wordless feeling of sudden tremendous expansion, sudden glory, which is the key, so that I am part of the thing that has set it off, and I enclose the universe or it encloses me—it is an end of individuality *for a moment*, because there's sudden glory in both me and the universe, both inextricably mingled.
3. Beauty—scenery—poetry or a passage with a high poetic content— Newman's 'defence of faith',[1] 'The glories of our blood and state'.
4. In tens—about twenty-five times.
5. None.
6. Yes.
7. Being given it, always your best work.
8. No, one is taking, one is given.

Q 25 F: 'C'

1. Yes.

[1] This I eventually discovered to be the passage beginning 'The Church regards the world... as dust and ashes compared with the value of one single soul' from Lecture VIII of *Lectures on Anglican Difficulties* (1850).

2. Indescribable—I know but I can't describe it—a shock of joy—
something perfectly apprehended, not formulated, a recognition.

3. Realization of profound truth or intense beauty, like in Greek
tragedy—'jewels five words long'.

4. Very rarely—once in a transcendental degree, perhaps two or three
times in all—but have approached more frequently without achieving—once I had it in a dream.

5. Christian.

6. Yes.

7. A roll of drums, beginning far off, rising to a crescendo.

8. Yes.

Q 26 F: 'C'

1. Yes.

2. Double realization of perfection with life, but life isn't perfect, so
it's a contradiction.

3. Contemplation of art—Chartres cathedral—the Bodhisatta in the
British Museum—being alone in a very lonely place—the beginning
of King's College Chapel carols with 'Once in royal David's city'.

4. Something under a hundred times, say between fifty and a hundred,
but really intensely, real spiritual ecstasy, say twenty to thirty
times.

5. Christian.

6. Yes.

7. Something wells up in one, prompted apparently by nothing, grows
like a spring.

8. Yes, with inspiration one can have ecstasy.

NOTE: I see this friend seldom owing to distance. The first time I met
her after she gave me these answers, some three years later, she said
spontaneously that she had often been thinking about ecstasy since
then and made the following remarks which, with her permission,
I took down:

'Does it seem to you possible that it could be the same feeling,
whether it's being in love or going downhill on skis or creating a
piece of sculpture? I think it is. Or swimming. You feel you're
literally in another world, outside everything. When it's greatest,
you're entirely unaware, you realize it only when you come back;
if you're conscious of the state when you're in it, it's not so terrific.
But with the great ones, you don't realize till you come back that
you were in heaven.'

Q 27 F: 'C'

1. Yes.
2. Difficult—communion with something else before reason enters.
3. Painting—Giorgione's 'Tempest' in the Accademia in Venice and recollections of that picture—I can call it up.
4. I'm often in a mystical state.
5. None.
6. Yes.
7. Sensation of a critical faculty about oneself.
8. Very much inferior.

Q 28 F: 'O'

1. Yes.
2. A feeling of happiness that takes you right out of the world, so supreme that you forget everything.
3. The first sight of my first baby.
4. A few times.
5. Jewish—love thy neighbour as thyself—I believe in God.
6. I think so.
7. When something I've planned comes off right.
8. No, just satisfaction.

Q 29 F: 'C'

1. I suppose I have.
2. Getting out of myself, associated with sensations of physical flying, like going to sleep or in dreams.
3. The air—walking in wind—a rough day by the sea—some height— water, sea, rivers—in March, black trees before the leaves come out in sunshine.
4. Dozens.
5. Agnostic.
6. Yes.
7. Very exhausted—the book is running away with you—associated with physical exhaustion.
8. Yes, same kind of thing.

Q 30 F: 'C'

1. Yes.

2. Halfway between pleasure and pain—suddenly overwhelms without expectation—standstill feeling.

3. (a) sudden appearance of light—coming into [an Eastern port] in the early morning—clouds—flowers.
   (b) Scent—flowers—the road to [abroad] with mimosa on both sides.
   (c) Sex.

4. (a) Perfectly only about twelve times.
   (b) About five times.
   (c) Rarely.

5. Born C of E.—Very little now.

6. Yes.

7. Sudden glorious moment when your talent is used to the full—your brain works faster than your pen—very pure.

8. Everything—but the brain is working too hard for that standstill feeling.

Q 31 M: 'I' (compiled by E. C.)

1. Yes.

2. Almost, except for one other person, alone in the world—this is the whole world—sensation of timelessness—full of force, wonderful force—completely uplifted.

3. Love in its fullest sense, spiritual and physical.

4. Twice.

5. Belief in the idea of God because it is necessary—not formalized in any sect or church.

6. Yes.

7. Two sorts:—(a) the carefully thought-out and tested evolvement of an idea; (b) sudden flash of an idea, later to be worked out as in (a).

8. Yes, in common with and stemming from it.

Q 32 F: 'O' (compiled by E. C.)

1. Yes.

2. So happy that you don't know what you're doing.

3. Seeing Stalin and Churchill shaking hands in the Bolshoi Theatre, Moscow.

4. Very rarely.

5. C of E.

6. No.

Q 33 F. 'I' (compiled by E. C.)

1. Yes.
2. Complete satisfaction—sense of touching reality.
3. Unexpectedly hearing Mozart's 'Hallelujah' sung for the first time, for instance.
4. In units.
5. Christian.
6. Yes.
7. Similar to ecstasy, but not quite so ecstatic.
8. Yes.

Q 34 F: (16 years old)

1. Yes.
2. I don't know how to put it into words—forgetting oneself, no, oneself ceasing to matter and no longer being connected with everyday things, with the commercial sort of life one lives—a feeling that for the first time you're seeing things in proper proportion—you know that the things in the women's magazines aren't worth anything compared with the leaves on the trees, say,—and time seems to stop, no, not matter—and even if it's because you've seen a particular thing or place, it doesn't matter, you're not anywhere, and despite not feeling anywhere in particular, feeling in unity with everything—no, not with everything, with nature, but not specifically trees, flowers, plants, everything that comes out of nature, like you might say a book was written by a man, but it's still nature,—it feels to a certain extent like a great climax which has built up—this thing has been seething inside you and suddenly it comes out.
3. Poetry and music—a Beethoven symphony, I'm not sure if it's the Fifth or the Seventh—nature—it differs a bit with what induces it.
4. It varies in intensity—one can induce it in oneself, not very intensely, if one's in a suitable mood, place, etc.—up to about fifteen times very intensely.
5. I have a sort of faith in man, I mean in nature, like I said before—I don't believe in God or in anything supreme.
6. Yes.
7. A minor form of ecstasy only slightly different,—generally along a line you may have been thinking of a long time ago, and the right shape, pattern, you suddenly know it, it goes on and on, you may

not get the right thing at first, but you go on, maybe writing it down.

8. Yes.

Q 35 M: 'I'

1. Yes.

2. Sense of complete satisfaction—the cup is being filled—you feel that it is all right—sense of something being perfected, couldn't be better done, the experience couldn't be more perfect.

3. Mantegna's 'Agony in the Garden'—any aesthetic experience is liable to.

4. Constantly.

5. Christian.

6. Yes.

7. Feeling of complete pre-occupation with something which appears to be *given* to you.

8. (Gave no answer.)

Q 36 F: 'C'

1. Yes.

2. A feeling of satisfaction with the actuality of existence—extreme unanalysable excitement—a sensation of pure existence—living in the object—most intense.

3. Poetry—Donne, Shakespeare's Sonnets, the work of the Spanish-American poets, Salinas—rather metaphysical types—I suspect it's erotic in origin.

4. Thousands of times.

5. None.

6, 7, 8. I know a state of mind of intense mental activity, rather what I get from reading good poetry, parallel to the ecstatic one.

Q 37 M: 'I'

1. Yes.

2. I'll have a bit of bother with that one—a feeling of identification with the whole sensible universe.

3. Merely a casual thing, like watching a gardener mowing a lawn.

4. In units.

5. Agnostic.

6. Yes.

7. An idea unconsciously formulated which is coming into conscious formulation—mental gripes.

8. Very little.

Q 38 F: 'C' (compiled by E. C.)

1. Yes.

2. An emotion so intense in its joy as to be almost painful—overwhelming all other senses and superseding thought during its existence.

3. Becoming a mother, after the labour-pains had passed—sexual relations—music—natural beauty, also the memory of certain scenes—writing about beautiful scenes—drawing—certain poetry.

4. In tens.

5. None.

6. Yes.

7, 8. The same as ecstasy.

Q 39 M: 'O'

1. Yes.

2. You can't describe it, because the more you describe, the further you get from it.

3. (Gave no answer).

4. Once.

5. Zen.

6. Yes.

7. A different state of consciousness.

8. No.

Q 40 F: 'I'

1. Yes.

2. What makes sense to me about it is, I think, a complete absence of a sense of specific time and place, complete involvement of one's whole being, at the same time a loss of the sense of being yourself.

3. Love.

4. In units.

5. I can't say that I have none.

6. I think not.

Q 41 M: 'I'

1. Yes.

2. You lose all sense of being yourself, being just nowhere—didn't remember myself, this person, *for a very short time.*

3. Love.

4. Once.

5. None.

6. Yes.

7. Of its nature impossible to describe—satisfaction at having conquered some kind of—at having put things into place.

8. No.

Q 42 M: 'C'

1. Yes.

2. A feeling of oneness with the totality of nature.

3. Being brought face to face with the vast greatness of the universe.

4. Twice.

5. Agnostic.

6. Yes, rarely.

7. The need to establish a nexus between oneself and the oneness.

8. Undoubtedly.

Q 43 F: 'O' (compiled by E. C.)

1. Yes.

2. Great emotion.

3. Love of a particular person—music—drama.

4. In tens.

5. C of E.

6. Yes, in ceramics.

7. Tense, but satisfaction in the completion of the design.

8. Not so great.

Q 44 M: 'C'

1. Yes.

2. Very different in kind from mere pleasure—I know when it's coming—it involves human sensation and body—curious—it's practically impossible to describe—a tingling that goes on—weightlessness—it's coming—complete sense of liberation, a blankness too —tremendous expansion, a different dimension altogether—it's different when it's music I do know or don't know—can't go on, a

bit of me being conscious and surprised, the analytical side not completely submerged—with music I know it's deeper.

3. Music, Mahler's Tenth Symphony—I induced it in myself once, in [abroad], a long spire of mountains, an Augustinian fourteenth-century abbey, brilliant moonlight, a Gothic refectory, and I had this feeling, there's been no plainchant here for four hundred years, and I sung it—in the Himalayas once, seeing Nanda Devi like a blast of trumpets—one passage, written specifically for the purpose, in 'The Dream of Gerontius'.

4. Frequently—in a good year about three times.

5. Catholic.

6. Yes.

7. Induced by all sorts of natural things, wind in the trees—I feel I'm going to write a tremendous play—it's never related to my own writing.

8. Difficult—there's a sort of common factor in both, a sensation of meaningfulness—the opposite of ennui.

Q 45 M: 'I'

1. Yes.

2. Words like 'liberation'—multiplication of possibilities—intense perception would go with it, hardly a part of it—confidence—a feeling of nearness to splendour.

3. Sex—occasionally *lesser* works of art—the first time I saw 'The School for Scandal' with the Oliviers in Australia—solving mathematical problems.

4. In tens.

5. None.

6. Yes.

7. I won't attempt to.

8. Ecstasy has often felt as if it could be described as creative inspiration that didn't result, and, conversely, I've had feelings of creation that didn't turn to ecstasy.

Q 46 M: 'C'

1. Not like the religious ecstatics, but if you don't mean that, yes.

2. Awareness of being so alive you feel in any given *moment* you've almost touched the fringe of eternity which seems to come into life at that *moment*—when living horizontally, you come into

connexion with a kind of vertical eternity, something that can't alter —we are mostly kept from transcendent living by sin.

3. By a river in summer—suddenly able to express something in permanent form—Gloucester Cathedral—in Italy coming into contact for the first time with Italian primitive art—music, Bach and Mozart—'War and Peace', the 'Brothers Karamazov', Shakespeare.

4. Endlessly, in a sense.

5. Protestant—Non-Conformist Christian.

6. Yes.

7. An inward power that surges to the surface at odd times.

8. Yes.

Q 47 M: 'I'

1. Yes.

2. Lord, awfully embarrassed—not sexual—sort of great joyful gusts and a burst, a sudden feeling of complete calm.

3. Not one single thing, a complex of circumstances—a series of experiments at a marine biological station, the lab overlooking the sea, complete isolation.

4. About three or four times.

5. None.

6. Yes, once or twice.

7. A sense of suddenly—of first being aware—one's usually trapped and stopped by environment, being involved in ordinary things, hard to extricate.

8. No.

Q 48 F: 'C'

1. Yes.

2. I think like the transfiguration, only happening within.

3. Fine weather—seeing someone I love—writing—wine at exactly the right *moment*—being in hills near the sea—once from religion.

4. Under twenty times.

5. A vague belief in something that makes patterns.

6. Yes.

7. At the beginning like an electric shock—then something opening, the growth of an idea—like being pushed, partly, but not altogether.

8. Yes.

Q 49 F: (14 years old)

1. Yes.
2. Great joy bubbling up inside—you don't think about the future, the future doesn't matter.
3. Love—for people I've been cracked on and boys I've liked.
4. Units.
5. None.
6. Yes.
7. When you're trying to think of a way to do something, suddenly it comes to you.
8. No.

Q 50 F: 'I'

1. I know a sensation of ecstasy.
2. I always think of it as a peak—as much a memory as an actuality—ecstasy is an extreme—one felt it more in youth, and it was always followed by the longest falls I've ever known in emotion—but I think it's genuine, not self-induced—I've often had it nearly, but not the real fire.
3. A line of poetry, often 'Loveliest of trees—' and 'Look thy last on all things lovely—' and, I know it sounds corny, but 'Magic casements—' —suddenly coming across an unexpected view that stretches for miles with the consciousness that you'll never recapture it, except in the mind.—Once eating thin bread with butter *and* jam as a child: I can recapture it in memory even now.
4. Units.
5. I'm a pantheist, if anything.
6. Yes.
7. The phrase I think of is competent automation—you know very well that what you're doing isn't really you.
8. No.

Q 51 F: 'O'

1. Yes.
2. Butterflies in the tummy and a floating sensation—it can make me feel sick—a wonderful feeling of peace.
3. A really beautiful piece of music, most Beethoven, some Mozart, the night I heard Kathleen Ferrier singing 'Chanson de Mer' [?]— a really beautiful spring or autumn day, mostly autumn—a play

beautifully acted and produced, Shakespeare, Olivier's 'Richard III' and 'Titus' at Stratford—and ballet, the first I ever saw.

4. In tens.

5. C of E.

6. Yes.

7. I get it mostly, because this is my job, when I've done a face, a really sad face, say, with a scar or with acne, and the client has sometimes cried with delight at the result.

8. Yes, it can have—it has had in one case, a child of sixteen with a scar, and when I'd finished she didn't recognize herself in the mirror, she thought it was someone looking over her shoulder.

Q 52 F: 'C'

1. Rarely.

2. I think of it as a mixture of physical attack and cerebral confusion—sadness mixed with joy.

3. Music, more singing than orchestral—poetry, 'Paradise Lost', some of Shakespeare and the Bible, some Auden.

4. In hundreds—five, six, seven times a year since I was eight.

5. None.

6. No.

ADDED LATER: I think of 'inspiration' as meaning something much greater than could ever have anything to do with *my* work.

Q 53 F: 'O'

1. I think so.

2. I couldn't begin to describe it.

3. Religious feeling.

4. Once.

5. C of E.

6. No.

Q 54 M: 'I'

1. Yes.

2. An electric sensation in the chest, spreading over your whole body—the centre of your being is there—always accompanied by intense physical well-being—immediately after one has the sensation of understanding almost everything one puts one's mind to—I frequently don't sleep afterwards and have a feeling it doesn't matter.

3. Going for a walk on a November afternoon, then taking down John Davidson's poems and reading 'St. Valentine's Eve'—it's not a very good poem, but it produced this and it went on *for a day or two*—whenever I'm deeply affected by something beautiful, it produces this state in which you have the sensation you understand everything to which you turn your mind, but any good poem would have done.

4. Units.

5. C of E, but I've not always been.

6. I think I do.

7. Similar to an urgent need to get something off your chest, similar to the urgent need of women to give birth.

8. One flows from the other.

Q 55 F: 'I'

1. I want it analysed first—I don't know—possibly yes.

2. This thing I'm thinking of, it's like an enormous bubble swelling inside the chest, bursting into a soundless shout.

3. In early youth, probably anything—not very high mountains in Switzerland,—love—occasional *moments* in works of art—a perfect *moment* in a film—some music, Mozart—rarely with literature, just occasionally.

4. Once in tens, now in very rare units.

5. An extremely complicated personal one—I'm atheist.

6. Yes.

7. I don't think I can—something coming out right from the mind, which one recognizes to be the thing it ought to be.

8. Not certain—I think it might.

Q 56 M: 'C'

1. Yes.

2. Complete suspension of time, sudden sense of certitude about nothing I can define, exaltation—tears streaming down my face at the force of beauty.

3. Watching vespers in [a foreign] cathedral, after a very good lunch with a very good friend—a pinpoint of light in the middle of the dark, green vestments and chanting.

4. Once.

5. Jewish.

6. Yes.

7. Always a suspension of time and enormous elation, then utter exhaustion at the end—a sense of having got through the sound barrier into a strange kind of calm where all the proportions are different.

8. No. But it has this in common with ecstasy, the sense of certitude and suspension of time, but there's a difference between exultation and elation—and ecstasy isn't exhausting.

Q 57 F: 'C'

1. Yes.

2. I suppose feelings of relief, gratified vanity, a wonderful surprise—you feel immensely light, you feel as if you're not walking on the ground, capable of anything and immensely fortunate—I think this is more delightful to me than a physical thing—I could sit here for ever, listening—when I hear music, etc. I feel immensely creative, full of ideas—there are two feelings, one is the liberation of relief, like work finished, the other you experience while it's happening, and it's rare to enjoy things in the present.

3. Aesthetic things suddenly—a Scotch folk-song—sudden *moments* like seeing a very well-turned sentence, or looking at the film, 'The Member of the Wedding'—a curious sensation, a feeling of ecstasy induced by something that isn't physical, something creeping up your spine.

4. Not units, not hundreds, so I suppose tens—it's very specific when felt—I'm astonished to find it can be induced by aesthetic things.

5. No religion—faith in myself.

6. I suppose yes.

7. The idea comes when you're not looking for it, it grows very rapidly, you know you must go and write it down or you will lose it.

8. Yes.

Q 58 M: 'I'

1. Yes.

2. A sense that, a feeling that everything is right and the world makes sense.

3. One time I particularly remember, ski-ing on top of a hill and it began to snow—definitely connected with outdoors, with nature.

4. A dozen times.

5. No dogmatic faith—what is the faith of Thoreau?

6. This is definitely tied up with occasional writing and drawing.

7. In a minor way, those moments when something goes right, but not so mysterious and exciting as the other—a feeling that the day has been lived, not just passed through.

8. Yes, only less intense, more easily explainable, less mystical.

Q 59 F: 'O'

1. Yes.

2. Extreme happiness—everything I ever wanted falling into place—as if nothing could ever go wrong again.

3. It wasn't just sex, it was everything right at that *moment*—I was going to marry the person I wanted to.

4. Once.

5. I haven't any now, but I have a feeling I will one day.

6. No.

Q 60 F: 'I'

1. Yes.

2. Away from yourself, you feel nothing—you don't feel yourself, away from yourself—it sort of overwhelms you, it hits you, and it's all-powerful.

3. Being in love, out-of-doors—then in [a foreign] cathedral, not really ecstasy, and once, there was a lovely picture in [a Roman] church.

4. Twice.

5. Sort of pantheistic.

6. No.

Q 61 M: 'I'

1. Yes.

2. When you suddenly discover a faculty working with effortless efficiency which enables you to hold in the forefront of conscious feeling both knowledge of the smallest bacteria in the field, how the blade of grass works, and the universe, in the same detail—all you know about nature, the whole thing, you can think about them all simultaneously and not in parts, that knowledge is almost limitless —one's aware objectively of what one's doing but not aware of anything else, not aware of yesterday or tomorrow, just of *the moment*, doing this now.

3. Introspection—on a troopship in the harbour at Naples, and Vesuvius had a red light glowing and in only twelve hours one would be in battle for the first time—in [a foreign country] in the evening in autumn, the fields were flooded, the sun low, sloshing through the fields, and the grass and water had a peculiar colour—sometimes here [in a London office] because the sky is blue and the building is white, you look at it and feel that life is worthwhile, the same kind of feeling, but much less—when I was about eighteen or nineteen [we] drove to a fantastic temple outside High Wycombe, I used to write poetry, I wrote 'Evening sunlight on a blade of grass', if I say that to myself, I can recapture it.

4. Units.

5. I can't put it in a word—I believe in God.

6. Yes.

7. Sense of certainty—things couldn't be otherwise than as they present themselves to you in that *instant* [my italics].

8. Yes.

Q 62 F: 'I'

1. Yes.

2. I can't—it's a most marvellous feeling—whatever words I used would be inadequate.

3. Music, when I play it myself.

4. Units.

5. Protestant.

6. No.

Q 63 F: 'C'

1. Yes.

2. An unbearable knowledge of the reality of things.

3. It happens on mountains—I must be by myself.

4. Tens.

5. Catholic.

6. No.

II. THE LITERARY TEXTS

L 1a. WILLIAM WORDSWORTH. From *Lines written a few miles above Tintern Abbey*. P.W., Vol. II, ll. 93–102.

> 'And I have felt
> A presence that disturbs me with the joy
> Of elevated thoughts; a sense sublime
> Of something far more deeply interfused,
> Whose dwelling is the light of setting suns,
> And the round ocean and the living air,
> And the blue sky, and in the mind of man:
> A motion and a spirit, that impels
> All thinking things, all objects of all thought,
> And rolls through all things.'

L 1b. WILLIAM WORDSWORTH. From *The Excursion*. P.W., Vol. V, Bk. I, ll. 197–218.

> 'Such was the Boy—but for the growing Youth
> What soul was his, when, from the naked top
> Of some bold headland, he beheld the sun
> Rise up, and bathe the world in light! He looked—
> Ocean and earth, the solid frame of earth
> And ocean's liquid mass, in gladness lay
> Beneath him:—Far and wide the clouds were touched,
> And in their silent faces could he read
> Unutterable love. Sound needed none,
> Nor any voice of joy; his spirit drank
> The spectacle: sensation, soul, and form,
> All melted into him; they swallowed up
> His animal being; in them did he live,
> And by them did he live; they were his life.
> In such access of mind, in such high *hour* [my italics]
> Of visitation from the living God,
> Thought was not; in enjoyment it expired.
> No thanks he breathed, he proffered no request;
> Rapt into still communion that transcends
> The imperfect offices of prayer and praise,
> His mind was a thanksgiving to the power
> That made him; it was blessedness and love!'

L 2. ALFRED LORD TENNYSON. From *Timbuctoo. Poems of Tennyson* (Oxford edn., 1923), p. 699 et seq.

'I stood upon the Mountain which o'erlooks
The narrow seas...
                    ...Then I raised
My voice and cried, "Wide Afric, doth thy Sun
Lighten, thy hills enfold a City as fair
As those which starr'd the night o' the elder World?
Or is the rumour of thy Timbuctoo
A dream as frail as those of ancient Time?"

A curve of whitening, flashing, ebbing light!
A rustling of white wings! the bright descent
Of a young Seraph! and he stood beside me
There on the ridge, and look'd into my face
With his unutterable, shining orbs.
So that with hasty motion I did veil
My vision with both hands, and saw before me
Such colour'd spots as dance athwart the eyes
Of those, that gaze upon the noonday Sun...'

[The Seraph says 'Open thine eyes and see']

                'I look'd, but not
Upon his face, for it was wonderful
With its exceeding brightness, and the light
Of the great Angel Mind which look'd from out
The starry glowing of his restless eyes.
I felt my soul grow mighty, and my spirit
With supernatural excitation bound
Within me, and my mental eye grew large
With such a vast circumference of thought,
That in my vanity I seem'd to stand
Upon the outward verge and bound alone
Of full beatitude. Each failing sense,
As with a *momentary* [my italics] flash of light
Grew thrillingly distinct and keen. I saw
The smallest grain that dappled the dark Earth,
The indistinctest atom in deep air,
The Moon's white cities, and the opal width
Of her small glowing lakes, her silver heights
Unvisited with dew of vagrant cloud,
And the unsounded, undescended depth
Of her black hollows. The clear Galaxy

Shorn of its hoary lustre, wonderful,
Distinct and vivid with sharp points of light,
Blaze within blaze, an unimagin'd depth
And harmony of planet-girded suns
And moon-encircled planets, wheel in wheel,
Arch'd the wan sapphire. Nay—the hum of men.
Or other things talking in unknown tongues,
And notes of busy life in distant worlds
Beat like a far wave on my anxious ear.

A maze of piercing, trackless, thrilling thoughts.
Involving and embracing each with each,
Rapid as fire, inextricably link'd,
Expanding momently with every sight
And sound which struck the palpitating sense,
The issue of strong impulse, hurried through
The riv'n rapt brain...
                              ...I know not if I shape
These things with accurate similitude
From visible objects, for but dimly now,
Less vivid than a half-forgotten dream,
The memory of that mental excellence
Comes o'er me, and it may be I entwine
The indecision of my present mind
With its past clearness, yet it seems to me
As even then the torrent of quick thought
Absorbed me from the nature of itself
With its own fleetness...

My thoughts which long had grovell'd in the slime
Of this dull world, like dusky worms which house
Beneath unshaken waters, but at once
Upon some Earth-awakening day of Spring
Do pass from gloom to glory...
Ev'n so my thoughts, erewhile so low, now felt
Unutterable buoyancy and strength
To bear them upward through the trackless fields
Of undefin'd existence far and free...
                                        ...my human brain
Stagger'd beneath the vision, and thick night
Came down upon my eyelids, and I fell.

With ministering hand he rais'd me up:
Then with a mournful and ineffable smile,

Which but to look on for *a moment* [my italics] fill'd
My eyes with irresistible sweet tears...
                                                    ...thus he spake:
"There is no mightier Spirit than I to sway
The heart of man: and teach him to attain
By shadowing forth the Unattainable..." '

L 3. RICHARD JEFFERIES. From *The Story of My Heart* (1883; Swan
Library edn., 1936), ch. v, pp. 76–7.

'I looked at the hills, at the dewy grass, and then up through the elm
branches to the sky. In *a moment* [my italics] all that was behind me, the
house, the people, the sounds, seemed to disappear, and to leave me
alone. Involuntarily I drew a long breath, then I breathed slowly. My
thought, or inner consciousness, went up through the illumined sky,
and I was lost in *a moment* [my italics] of exaltation. This only lasted *a
very short time* [my italics], perhaps *only part of a second* [my italics],
and while it lasted there was no formulated wish. I was absorbed; I
drank the beauty of the morning; I was exalted. When it ceased I did
wish for some increase or enlargement of my existence to correspond
with the largeness of feeling I had *momentarily* [my italics] enjoyed.'

L 4. MARGIAD EVANS. From *Autobiography* (London, 1943; 2nd edn.,
1952), pp. 116–17.

'But the clear *moment* [my italics] which was the prelude, oh, rarely,
rarely have I had that again. Those are the eras, the visions, when the
inner and outer meaning of the earth and sky and all that is in them, fit
exactly the one over the other, when there is no slipping, no edge of
obscurity, no groping. Ah, how impossible it is to keep those *moments*
[my italics], to hold down for more than a *single instant* [my italics] that
joy of being oneself contained in all one sees! Feeling with the leaves,
travelling with the clouds, seeing back from the star, into one's own
breast that is the very essence of perception. It is then that one can live
for *an instant* [my italics] in the million kinds of life which fumble for
the sun, or in the stars which search through space for the earth to
shine on, and on the earth, a spirit to enter.

It is the strangest sensation for the mind to fix itself in the contemplation of one single natural thing; and one of its most singular phenomena
is the amazing quality of universal perception which takes place in the
thinker at the same time. Fixed on one, all things become supernaturally
distinct and detailed. With the mind utterly rapt the eye becomes
abnormally sensitive, but unconsciously, so that in recollection memory
brings back a landscape where one seemed to see only a cloud's broken
suns. Yet not always. Sometimes I seem to know each separate thing

while lost in the one, and it is then that I feel profoundly the almost palpable linking up of the universe. From life to life, from kind to kind, through the mind to the sky and out to each planet, the chain reaches. Ah, who can doubt it? Who that really feels what he sees can fail to be sure, if he thinks at all of what his senses tell him? The air itself is felt to be woven of threads of life. Even in the darkness they are there. Looking up to the moon as it seems to rush backwards across its own white hollow of light, looking at the sun's direct rays on the earth, looking at the stars whose presence reaches us through enormous darkness, who can deny the thought? Even in sleep it does not leave me—the least thrill in the chord recalls me, and in the morning it is there directly the day is felt on my eyelids. Yes, even before I wake, I come to it. And there are millions of spirits like mine. To them I unite because we are still more closely connected. I believe in it. But I have failed to describe it, because language cannot form the thought, because it is wordless and unimaginable and pictureless, an inhabitant unseen.'

FREQUENCY: Earlier of similar experience, Margiad Evans writes: 'More than twenty years with only as many separate unlightened moments' (ibid., p. 77).

L 5. ROBERT NICHOLS. *Birth of a Poem.* Quoted from the Appendix to Harding: A.I., pp. 151–3.

'At that *moment* [my italics] the newly-risen sun sent flickering over the long, low, smooth, glassy mounds of the rolling swells a series of elastic reflections which expanded and contracted and zigzagged and appeared and disappeared and reformed as they travelled in stately and regular motion toward me . . . I became aware of an extraordinary physical exhilaration. "Of course!" I said to myself—"Arabic."

It was at that *moment* [my italics], as I now discern, that I understood I had only to yield to the emotion evoked by what I beheld to discover a poem, the potentiality of which existed not only in the characters propelled toward me but all around me, in the entire sea and sky and, more remotely, in my own solitude which, however, wasn't my unique loneliness as it had existed up to that *moment* [my italics]—the loneliness of Robert Nichols standing on an iron fo'c'sle— but the solitude of any figure beholding the miracle (and in a state to receive it as such) at any period in history. As I realised this, the hieroglyphics upon the waters seemed to flash through me, that is to say, to pass through my body without occasioning any pain. They continued to do this. My eye dwelled upon the scene and the longer it dwelled— though *but a moment passed* [my italics]—the more I was filled with an immense and pure emotion *which was the reflection of what I saw*, that is to say I was conscious of a regular and growing central excitement surrounded by an area of deep, tranquil and joyful satisfaction. This was, I felt, as it should be—I was being told something. Now the existence of this satisfaction, being simply due to the glory of the morning, might have merely remained a state of being for the expression of which words were neither sought nor found, because not felt to be needed, had not the character of the hieroglyphics given a special quality to the emotion possessing me. That change may roughly be defined as a change from the animal to the spiritual. And when I ask myself why that change was effected, I can only reply that the answer lies in the fact that the reflections travelling toward me had the changing shapes that were theirs. Had the reflections been merely blobs of light, had they been written in a script with which I was acquainted, had they for instance formed a succession of capital letters—such as RKP followed by LZO followed by NQT—they would, I fancy, have added little, if indeed anything, to my animal pleasure. But they were recognisable, though not decipherable, as units having the peculiarities of a cursive script, rightly or wrongly taken by me to be Arabic and Arabic, I instantly grasped, of a peculiar kind—golden letters in a holy book... I at the same or nearly the same *instant* [my italics] apprehended that these figures *weren't* in a book but were, at that very *moment* [my italics]...*being written on the sea by the sun*, a being who was a poet. *I did not say to myself "the sun is a poet" but I felt the emotion such a person as myself might be expected to feel were he to find himself in the presence of a being both capable of doing what I now beheld being done and accustomed to doing it.* There was then *a fractional pause* [my italics], a halt in my attention as if that attention didn't wholly apprehend what was presented to it, the halt in fact that precedes recognition. And just as the memory of a name...brings with it the memory of the circumstances in which this person was earlier met...what I may call the *myth* of this person—so *on an instant* [my italics] there was presented to my consciousness a favourite picture-postcard I had twice or thrice bought at the British Museum. Almost simultaneously there formed in my mouth the line

"The sun an ancient, serene poet."

The picture on the postcard—that of a poet, possibly Persian... and the line were indissoluble. They remain indissoluble to this day—in the sense that I cannot repeat the first line of the poem without seeing the picture on the postcard.'

L 6. FRIEDRICH NIETZSCHE. From *The Case of Wagner* (trans. A. M. Ludovici, London, 1911; 3rd edn.), pp. 2–3.

'Has anyone ever observed that music *emancipates* the spirit? gives wings to thought? and that the more one becomes a musician the more one is also a philosopher? The grey sky of abstraction seems thrilled by flashes of lightning; the light is strong enough to reveal all the details of things; to enable one to grapple with problems; and the world is surveyed as if from a mountain top.—With this I have defined philo-sophical pathos.—And unexpectedly *answers* drop into my lap, a small hailstorm of ice and wisdom, of problems *solved*. Where am I? Bizet makes me productive. Everything that is good makes me productive. I have gratitude for nothing else, nor have I any other touchstone for testing what is good.'

L 7. ARTHUR KOESTLER. From *Arrow in the Blue* (London, 1952), ch. xii, pp. 97–9.

'The juvenile quest for the secret of infinity, split into two simul-taneous and in all respects contradictory pursuits.

I can remember fairly clearly *the moment* [my italics] when the arrow split and the two halves began to lead their independent existence. It was on a spring morning in 1924. I was sitting on a bench in the *Volksgarten*, one of Vienna's enchanted parks, with a pile of books beside me. On top lay a pamphlet about the latest Arab riots in Palestine, with appalling details of children put to the sword as in the days of Herod, of Jewish pioneers being killed after having been blinded and castrated, of the passivity of the Mandatory Administration and their refusal to allow the Jews to arm in self-defence.

While I was reading the pamphlet, I felt myself choke and seethe with impotent anger. Moral indignation did and still does affect me in a direct physical manner. Like most people who suffer from Chronic Indignation—as others do from chronic indigestion—I can feel, during an attack, the infusion of adrenalin into the bloodstream, the craving of the muscles, flooded with blood-sugar, for violent action. As the case may be, you begin to tremble, or throw a choleric fit, or write a revolu-tionary tract, or start growing an ulcer. When I had finished reading the pamphlet and had calmed down a little, I fell into one of my habitual reveries about devoting my life to the cause of the persecuted as a fighter and writer of books which would shake the conscience of the world. I must have used up since then tons of adrenalin on that job.

While still in the grip of that dream, and all geared for action, I opened the next book in the pile at its marked page. It was Weyl's introduction to Einstein's theory of Relativity. A phrase suddenly struck me and has remained in my memory ever since. It said that the theory of General Relativity led the human imagination "across the peaks of glaciers never before explored by any human being." This cliché had an unexpectedly strong effect. I saw Einstein's world-shaking formula—Energy equals Mass multiplied by the square of the velocity of light—hovering in a kind of rarified haze over the glaciers, and this image carried a sensation of infinite tranquillity and peace. The martyred infants and castrated pioneers of the Holy Land shrank to microscopic insignificance. Beast had fed on beast in sea and jungle since the beginnings of organic life; it was a law of Nature and of history; there was nothing to get excited about. The fate of these un-fortunates had to be viewed with the same serene, detached, meditative eye as that of stars bursting into novae, of sunspots erupting, of rocks decaying into swamps, and primeval forests being transformed into coal. This change in perspective was accompanied by an equally pro-nounced physiological change. The sensation of choking with indigna-tion was succeeded by the relaxed quietude and self-dissolving stillness of the "oceanic feeling."[1]

I have often since experienced both of these opposite states of mind, but never in such close proximity as on that occasion. They are opposites in every respect—in their physiological mechanism, emotional tone, intellectual outlook, and in the social attitudes which they produce. Moral indignation may be compared to a sudden, or continuous im-plosion which provides the heat and pressure required for action. The effect of the "oceanic feeling," on the other hand, is an expansion of consciousness, its liberation from any pressure and itch, its temporary dissolution in Nirvana.

Though the two states are mutually exclusive at any given moment, they may alternate in time. They may succeed each other in quick oscillation of mood and outlook within a single day, or there may be periods of several years in an individual's life when one or the other is dominant. The institution of the "retreat" known in various forms to all civilisations, was obviously developed under the influence of this duality...the "oceanic experience" to a large extent eludes verbal communication...'

FREQUENCY: From internal evidence, the first experience of its kind.

L 8. VIRGINIA WOOLF. From *A Writer's Diary* (London, 1953), p. 132.

'Often down here I have entered into a sanctuary; a nunnery; had a religious retreat; of great agony once; and always some terror; so

[1] Koestler gives a footnote on 'oceanic feeling': 'The term used by Freud to denote mystic or religious experience.'

afraid one is of loneliness; of seeing to the bottom of the vessel. That is one of the experiences I have had here in some Augusts; and got then to a consciousness of what I call "reality": a thing I see before me: something abstract; but residing in the downs or sky; beside which nothing matters; in which I shall rest and continue to exist. Reality I call it. And I fancy sometimes this is the most necessary thing to me: that which I seek. But who knows—once one takes a pen and writes? How difficult not to go making "reality" this and that, whereas it is one thing.'

FREQUENCY: 'Often'.

L 9. KARL JOËL. From *Seele und Welt* (1912). Quoted from C. G. Jung. *Psychology of the Unconscious* (London, 1919; 6th imp., 1951), ch. vii, pp. 198-9.

'I lay on the seashore, the shining waters glittering in my dreamy eyes; at a great distance fluttered the soft breeze; throbbing, shimmering, stirring, lulling to sleep comes the wave beat to the shore—or to the ear? I know not. Distance and nearness become blurred into one; without and within glide into each other. Nearer and nearer, *dearer and more homelike sounds the beating of the waves*; now, like a thundering pulse in my head it strikes, and now it beats over my soul, devours it, embraces it, while it itself at the same time floats out like the blue waste of waters. Yes, without and within are one. Glistening and foaming, flowing and fanning and roaring, the entire symphony of the stimuli experienced sounds in one tone, all thought becomes one thought, which becomes one with feeling; the world exales in the soul and the soul dissolves in the world. Our small life is encircled by a great sleep—*the sleep of our cradle, the sleep of our grave, the sleep of our home, from which we go forth in the morning, to which we again return in the evening*; our life but the short journey, the interval between the emergence from the original oneness and the sinking back into it! Blue shimmers the infinite sea, wherein dreams the jelly fish of the primitive life, toward which without ceasing our thoughts hark back dimly through eons of existence. For every happening entails a change and a guarantee of the unity of life. At that *moment* [my italics] when they are no longer blended together, in that *instant* [my italics] man lifts his *head, blind and dripping, from the depths* of the stream of experience, from the oneness with the experience; at that *moment* [my italics] of parting when the unity of life in startled surprise detaches the Change and holds it away from itself as something alien, at this *moment* [my italics] of alienation the aspects of the experience have been substantialized into subject and object, and in that *moment* [my italics] consciousness is born.'

L 10. BERNARD BERENSON. From *Aesthetics and History* (London, 1950), pp. 68–70.

'in my own case it is accompanied by an ideated tingling on and in my own skin corresponding to eye movement, both retinal and muscular, but...the feeling as a whole is one of aesthetic identification, as if there were nothing in me that was not living the life of the contour...

This direct contact with an otherness, but for the circumstance that it need have no touch of "uplift", is in essence a mystical experience, no more common perhaps than other mystical experience. I recall when it first came to me. I had already published two books. For years I had been inquiring, excavating, dredging my inner self, and searching in my conscious experience for a satisfying test. I needed a test to apply to the artifacts that I thought I admired but could not hypnotize or habituate myself to enjoy with complete abandon, while the worm of doubt kept gnawing at the felicity of the ideal paradise. Then one morning as I was gazing at the leafy scrolls carved on the door jambs of S. Pietro outside Spoleto, suddenly stem, tendril and foliage became alive and, in becoming alive, made me feel as if I had emerged into the light after long groping in the darkness of an initiation. I felt as one illumined, and beheld a world where every outline, every edge, and every surface was in a living relation to me and not, as hitherto, in a merely cognitive one. Since that morning, nothing visible has been indifferent or even dull. Everywhere I feel the ideated pulsation of vitality, I mean energy and radiance, as if it all served to enhance my own functioning ... The machine alone can turn out artifacts guaranteed to be non-conductors of a vitalizing spark.

The revelation that came to me while looking at the façade of a church at Spoleto fifty years ago did various things for me.

In the first place, it emancipated me from the need for art, for I had become my own artist, as it were, and saw in terms of art...

...this revelation increased my enjoyment of the work of art, and the greater the confidence I felt in my own sensations and perceptions, or, to speak more accurately, in the genuineness of the successive ecstasies I was experiencing, the more I was relieved of uncertainty about their subjective reality and reliability. In other words, as is the case in all mystical experience, I acquired faith in my vision and its revelation of values. This faith has never abandoned me, although often enough one has moments of dryness when, as to the religious mystic, God is out of reach.

Finally this same revelation led me to perceive that while the feeling for movement is perhaps not quite the same as the feeling for quality, the two are nearly the same, in fact quite identical when on the same path, the path, namely, of lines and curves and linear figures...

If the feeling for movement or the feeling for "functional line"...is almost identical with the feeling for quality, and if it is psychologically a condition of ecstasy, it may be as rare as the mystically religious experience and as unintelligible to those who have not had it.'

FREQUENCY: From internal evidence, this is the first experience of its kind.

L II. H. WARNER ALLEN. From *The Timeless Moment* (London. 1946), pp. 30–1.

'an answer came.

It flashed up lightning-wise during a performance of Beethoven's Seventh Symphony at the Queen's Hall, in that triumphant fast movement when "the morning stars sang together and all the sons of God shouted for joy". The swiftly flowing continuity of the music was not interrupted, so that what Mr. T. S. Eliot calls "the intersection of the timeless moment" must have slipped into the interval between two demi-semi-quavers. When, long after, I analysed the happening in the cold light of retrospect, it seemed to fall into three parts: first the mysterious event itself which occurred in *an infinitesimal fraction of a split second* [my italics]; this I learned afterwards from Santa Teresa to call the Union with God; then Illumination, a *wordless* stream of complex feelings in which the experience of Union combined with the rhythmic emotion of the music like a sunbeam striking with iridescence the spray above a waterfall—a stream that was continually swollen by tributaries of associated Experience; lastly Enlightenment, the recollection in tranquillity of the whole complex of Experience as it were embalmed in thought-forms and words.'

L 12. CARLO LEVI. From *Christ Stopped at Eboli* (trans. F. Frenaye; London, 1948), ch. xxii, pp. 222–3.

'I lay in the high bed, which was like a theatre-box suspended in mid-air. Hung on the walls all around me were the bodies of newly killed foxes; I could smell their gamey odour and see their sharp muzzles outlined against the flickering red flames. I had only to stretch out my hands to touch the skin, which had something of woods and caves about them. Through the door I could hear the dying man's continuous wailing, like an endless litany of pain: "Jesus, help me; Doctor, help me; Jesus, help me; Doctor, help me," and the whispered prayers of the women. I looked at the dancing flames, the long, wavering shadows and the dark figures of the three hunters with their hats on their heads, motionless in front of the fire.

Death was in the house: I loved these peasants and I was sad and humiliated by my powerlessness against it. Why, then, at the same time, did a great feeling of peace pervade me? I felt detached from every earthly thing and place, lost in a no-man's land far from time and reality. I was hidden, like a shoot under the bark of a tree, beyond the reach of man. I listened to the silence of the night and I felt as if I had all of a sudden penetrated the very heart of the universe. An immense happiness, such as I had never known, swept over me with a flow of fulfilment.'

FREQUENCY: Apparently the first experience of its kind.

L 13. GEORGE GISSING. From *Born in Exile* (London, 1892), Vol. III, PART VI, ch. iii, p. 180.

'a curious experience befell me,—one I had, long, long ago, in the Whitelaw days. Sitting down before some interesting strata, I lost myself in something like nirvana, grew so subject to the idea of vastness in geological time that all human desires and purposes shrivelled to ridiculous unimportance. Awaking for a minute, I tried to realise the passion which not long ago rent and racked me, but I was flatly incapable of understanding it.'

L 14. CHARLOTTE BRONTË. From *Shirley* (1847; Everyman edn., 1950), ch. xxii, pp. 306–7.

'At last, however, a pale light falls on the page from the window: she looks, the moon is up; she closes the volume, rises, and walks through the room. Her book has perhaps been a good one; it has re-freshed, refilled, rewarmed her heart; it has set her brain astir, furnished her mind with pictures. The still parlour, the clean hearth, the window opening on the twilight sky, and showing its "sweet regent," new throned and glorious, suffice to make earth an Eden, life a poem, for Shirley. A still, deep, inborn delight glows in her young veins; un-mingled—untroubled, not to be reached or ravished by human agency, because by no human agency bestowed: the pure gift of God to His creature, the free dower of Nature to her child. This joy gives her experience of a genii-life. Buoyant, by green steps, by glad hills, all verdure and light, she reaches a station scarcely lower than that whence angels looked down on the dreamer of Bethel, and her eye seeks, and her soul possesses, the vision of life as she wishes it. No—not as she wishes it; she has not time to wish: the swift glory spreads out, sweep-ing and kindling, and multiplies its splendour faster than Thought can effect his combinations, faster than Aspiration can utter her longings. Shirley says nothing while the trance is upon her—she is quite mute...

If Shirley were not an indolent, a reckless, an ignorant being, she would take a pen at such *moments* [my italics]; or at least while the recollection of such *moments* [my italics] was yet fresh on her spirit: she would seize, she would fix the apparition, tell the vision revealed. Had she a little more of the organ of acquisitiveness in her head—a little more of the love of property in her nature, she would take a good-sized sheet of paper and write plainly out, in her own queer but clear and legible hand, the story that has been narrated, the song that has been sung to her, and thus possess what she was enabled to create. But indolent she is, reckless she is, and most ignorant, for she does not know her dreams are rare—her feelings peculiar: she does not know, has never known, and will die without knowing, the full value of that spring whose bright fresh bubbling in her heart keeps it green.'

L 15. GEORGE ELIOT. From *Daniel Deronda* (1876; London, 1877), ch. xvii, p. 140.

'He used his oars little, satisfied to go with the tide and be taken back by it. It was his habit to indulge himself in that solemn passivity which easily comes with the lengthening shadows and mellowing light, when thinking and desiring melt together imperceptibly, and what in other hours may have seemed argument takes the quality of passionate vision. By the time he had come back again with the tide past Richmond Bridge the sun was near setting; and the approach of his favourite hour—with its deepening stillness, and darkening masses of tree and building between the double glow of the sky and the river—disposed him to linger as if they had been an unfinished strain of music. He looked out for a perfectly solitary spot where he could lodge his boat against the bank, and, throwing himself on his back with his head propped on the cushions, could watch out the light of sunset and the opening of that bead-roll which some oriental poet describes as God's call to the little stars, who each answer, "Here am I." He chose a spot in the bend of the river just opposite Kew Gardens, where he had a great breadth of water before him reflecting the glory of the sky, while he himself was in shadow. He lay with his hands behind his head propped on a level with the boat's edge, so that he could see all around him, but could not be seen by anyone at a few yards' distance; and for a long while he never turned his eyes from the view right in front of him. He was forgetting everything else in a half-speculative, half-involuntary identification of himself with the objects he was looking at, thinking how far it might be possible habitually to shift his centre till his own personality would be no less outside him than the landscape,—when the sense of something moving on the bank opposite him where it was bordered by a line of willow-bushes, made him turn his glance thitherward.'

L 16. GEORGE MEREDITH. From *The Ordeal of Richard Feverel* (1859; Everyman edn., 1954), ch. xlii, pp. 461-2.

'A pale grey light on the skirts of the flying tempest displayed the dawn. Richard was walking hurriedly. The green drenched weeds lay all about in his path, bent thick, and the forest drooped glimmeringly. Impelled as a man who feels a revelation mounting obscurely to his brain, Richard was passing one of those little forest-chapels, hung with votive wreaths, where the peasant halts to kneel and pray. Cold, still, in the twilight it stood, raindrops pattering round it. He looked within, and saw the Virgin holding her Child. He moved by. But not many steps had he gone ere his strength went out of him and he shuddered. What was it? He asked not. He was in other hands. Vivid as lightning the Spirit of Life illumined him. He felt in his heart the cry of his child, his darling's touch. With shut eyes he saw them both. They drew him from the depths; they led him a blind and tottering man. And as they led him he had a sense of purification so sweet he shuddered again and again.

When he looked out from his trance on the breathing world, the small birds hopped and chirped'.

L 17a. D. H. LAWRENCE. From *The Rainbow* (1915; Penguin edn., 1949), ch. vii, pp. 204-5.

'Then he pushed open the door, and the great, pillared gloom was before him, in which his soul shuddered and rose from her nest. His soul leapt, soared up into the great church. His body stood still, absorbed by the height. His soul leapt up into the gloom, into possession, it reeled, it swooned with a great escape, it quivered in the womb, in the hush and the gloom of fecundity, like seed of procreation in ecstasy...

Here, the twilight was the very essence of life, the coloured darkness was the embryo of all light, and the day. Here, the very first dawn was breaking, the very last sunset sinking, and the immemorial darkness, whereof life's day would blossom and fall away again, re-echoed peace and profound immemorial silence.

Away from time, always outside of time!... Here in the church, "before" and "after" were folded together, all was contained in oneness...he had pushed open the doors of the cathedral, and entered the twilight of both darknesses, the hush of the two-fold silence, where dawn was sunset, and the beginning and the end were one.

Here the stone leapt up from the plain of earth, leapt up in a manifold, clustered desire each time, up, away from the horizontal earth, through twilight and dusk and the whole range of desire, through the swerving, the declination, ah, to the ecstasy, the touch, to the meeting

412

and the consummation, the meeting, the clasp, the close embrace, the neutrality, the perfect, swooning consummation, the timeless ecstasy. There his soul remained, at the apex of the arch, clinched in the timeless ecstasy, consummated.

And there was no time nor life nor death, but only this, this timeless consummation, where the thrust from earth met the thrust from earth and the arch was locked on the keystone of ecstasy. This was all, this was everything. Till he came to himself in the world below. Then again he gathered himself together, in transit, every jet of him strained and leaped, leaped clear into the darkness above, to the fecundity and the unique mystery, to the touch, the clasp, the consummation, the climax of eternity, the apex of the arch.'

L 17b. D. H. LAWRENCE. From *Sons and Lovers* (1913; Penguin edn., 1954), ch. xiii, pp. 442-3.

'As a rule, when he started love-making, the emotion was strong enough to carry with it everything—reason, soul, blood—in a great sweep, like the Trent carries bodily its back-swirls and intertwinings, noiselessly. Gradually the little criticisms, the little sensations, were lost, thought also went, everything borne along in one flood. He became, not a man with a mind, but a great instinct. His hands were like creatures, living; his limbs, his body, were all life and consciousness, subject to no will of his, but living in themselves. Just as he was, so it seemed the vigorous, wintry stars were strong also with life. He and they struck with the same pulse of fire, and the same joy of strength which held the bracken-frond stiff near his eyes held his own body firm. It was as if he, and the stars, and the dark herbage, and Clara were licked up in an immense tongue of flame, which tore onwards and upwards. Everything rushed along in living beside him; everything was still, perfect in itself, along with him. This wonderful stillness in each thing in itself, while it was being borne along in a very ecstasy of living, seemed the highest point of bliss.'

FREQUENCY: 'As a rule' in love-making.

L 18. E. M. FORSTER. From *Howard's End* (1910; Penguin edn., 1946), ch. v, p. 26.

'Beethoven chose to make all right in the end. He built the ramparts up. He blew with his mouth for the second time, and again the goblins were scattered. He brought back the gusts of splendour, the heroism, the youth, the magnificence of life and of death, and amid vast roarings of a superhuman joy, he led his Fifth Symphony to its conclusion. But the goblins were there. They could return. He had said so bravely, and that is why one can trust Beethoven when he says other things.

Helen pushed her way out during the applause. She desired to be alone. The music had summed up to her all that had happened or could happen in her career. She read it as a tangible statement, which could never be superseded. The notes meant this and that to her, and they could have no other meaning, and life could have no other meaning. She pushed right out of the building, and walked slowly down the outside staircase, breathing the autumnal air, and then she strolled home.'

L 19. JACQUETTA HAWKES. From *Man on Earth* (London, 1954), ch. i, pp. 15–17.

'One night when the land was still fresh from the rain, I was wandering near our camp enjoying the moonlight when an immense exaltation took possession of me. It was as though the White Goddess of the moon had thrown some bewitching power into her rays. It seemed to me that our arid satellite was itself a living presence bounding in the sky—I do not myself understand this use of the word "bounding", but it comes insistently, and I cannot but use it to express some deeply felt vitality. Indeed, the whole night was dancing about me.

It appeared that the moonlight had ceased to be a physical thing and now represented a state of illumination in my own mind. As here in the night landscape the steady white light threw every olive leaf and pebble into sharp relief, so it seemed that my thoughts and feelings had been given an extraordinary clarity and truth.

So powerfully was I moved by this sense of possession that I climbed up on to a high outcrop of rock against the mouth of the wadi and knelt down there. The moonlight swam round, and in, my head as I knelt looking across the plain to the shining silver bar of the Mediterranean.

From far behind me, still muffled in the folds of the mountain, I heard the bronze sound of camel-bells. To my sharpened but converging senses they seemed like a row of brown flowers blooming in the moonlight. In truth the sound of bells came from nothing more remarkable than a caravan, perhaps twenty camels with packs and riders, coming down the wadi on its way northward to Haifa. But even now I cannot recognise that caravan in such everyday terms; my memory of it is dreamlike, yet embodies one of the most intense sensuous and emotional experiences of my life. For *those minutes, and I have no notion how many they were* [my italics], I had the heightened sensibility of one passionately in love and with it the power to transmute all that the senses perceived into symbols of burning significance. This surely is one of the best rewards of humanity. To be filled with comprehension of the beauty and marvellous complexity of the physical world, and for this happy excitement of the senses to lead directly into an awareness of spiritual significance. The fact that such experience comes most surely with love, with possession by the creative eros, suggests that it belongs near the root of our mystery. Certainly it grants man a state of mind in which I believe he must come more and more to live: a mood of intensely conscious individuality which serves only to strengthen an intense consciousness of unity with all being. His mind is one infinitesimal node in the mind present throughout all being, just as his body shares in the unity of matter.

The bells came nearer and another sound mingled with theirs; a low, monotonous chanting. I looked behind me for a moment and saw the dark procession swaying out from behind the last bend in the wadi, then I turned back so that the column should pass me and enter my world of vision from behind. I found myself comprehending every physical fact of their passage as though it were a part of my own exist-ence. I knew how the big soft feet of the camels pressed down upon and embraced the rough stones of the path; I knew the warm depth of their fur and the friction upon it of leather harness and the legs of the riders; I knew the blood flowing through the bodies of men and beasts and thought of it as echoing the life of the anemones which now showed black among the rocks around me. The sound of bells and the chanting seemed rich and glowing as the stuff of the caravan itself.

So the swaying line came from behind, went past, and moved away across the plain. It was a procession of life moving through the icy moonlight. It was coming from the mountain and going towards the sea. That was all I knew, but as the moon leapt and bounded in the sky I took full possession of a love and confidence that have not yet forsaken me.'

L 20. C. E. MONTAGUE. From the essay 'The Last Question of All' in *A Writer's Notes on His Trade* (1930; Pelican edn., 1949), pp. 184-5.

'If we cannot say why we capitulate thus [i.e. to "certain simple groupings of a few ordinary words" in poetry], we may at least try to fix and describe the sensations that visit us while the charm is at work.

For one thing, we are deeply excited. We are shaken or lifted out of our ordinary state of consciousness. Many of our faculties are, *for the moment* [my italics], enhanced. We feel keener perceptions coming into action within us. We are given the use of more than our normal stock of penetrative sympathy: we feel that we can enter into people's feelings and understand the quality of their lives better than ever before.

Another effect of the drug is that, while it is acting strongly, the whole adventure of mankind upon the earth gains, in our sight, a new momentousness, precariousness and beauty. The new and higher scale of power in ourselves seems to be challenged by an equal increase in the size of the objects on which it is exercised. Living becomes a grander affair than we had ever thought.

A third effect on the mind is a powerful sense—authentic or illusory —of being in the presence of extraordinary possibilities. You feel as if new doors of understanding and delight were beginning to open around you. Some sort of mysterious liberation or empowerment seems to be approaching. You are assured, in an unaccountable way, that wonderful enlightenments, still unreceived, are on their way to you, like new stars that are nearing the point in space at which they will come within range of our sight.'

L 21. EMILY BRONTË. From *Julian M. and A. G. Rochelle. The Complete Poems of Emily Jane Brontë*, ed. C. W. Hatfield (New York, 1941), pp. 238-9, ll. 65-99.

'Yet, tell them, Julian, all, I am not doomed to wear
Year after year in gloom and desolate despair;
A messenger of Hope comes every night to me,
And offers, for short life, eternal liberty.

He comes with western winds, with evening's wandering airs,
With that clear dusk of heaven that brings the thickest stars;
Winds take a pensive tone, and stars a tender fire,
And visions rise and change which kill me with desire—

Desire for nothing known in my maturer years
When joy grew mad with awe at counting future tears;
When, if my spirit's sky was full of flashes warm,
I knew not whence they came, from sun or thunderstorm;

But first a hush of peace, a soundless calm descends;
The struggle of distress and fierce impatience ends;
Mute music soothes my breast—unuttered harmony
That I could never dream till earth was lost to me.

Then dawns the Invisible, the Unseen its truth reveals;
My outward sense is gone, my inward essence feels—
Its wings are almost free, its home, its harbour found;
Measuring the gulf it stoops and dares the final bound!

Oh, dreadful is the check—intense the agony
When the ear begins to hear and the eye begins to see;
When the pulse begins to throb, the brain to think again,
The soul to feel the flesh and the flesh to feel the chain!

Yet I would lose no sting, would wish no torture less;
The more that anguish racks the earlier it will bless;
And robed in fires of Hell, or bright with heavenly shine,
If it but herald Death, the vision is divine.'

FREQUENCY: 'every night'.

L 22. OVID. From *Vesta's Day: Account of her Temple and Ceremonial* from *Fasti*, Book VI. ll. 51–6. (translated by J. C. H.)

'I was totally absorbed in prayer. I perceived the heavenly godhead, and the joyful ground shone with purple light. I did not see you myself, O Goddess (farewell to the lies of the poets!) nor were you to be seen by man, but the things that I did not know and of which I was held in error were made known to me without anyone teaching.'

L 23a. RICHARD CHURCH. From *Over the Bridge* (London, 1955), pp. 88–90.

'Then one day a gaunt young man with long hair and a nervous cough came to tune the piano. I noticed his thin, dirty hands, with finger-nails like claws, that rattled on the keys and scratched the face-board behind them. He smoked cigarettes the whole time he was at work: and that was an unusual habit in 1900...

During a pause, after the tuning was done, he [*s.c.* my brother] produced the Beethoven sonata, and asked the tuner to give him an inkling how it should be attacked.

The result was like that of opening a weir. The thin, bow-backed figure of the piano-tuner shook with latent energy. He tossed his hair back, cracked his bony knuckles, and began to play the sonata in G major, Opus 32 No. 1 [*sic*], (published in 1803), which, as music-lovers will recollect, opens with a startling statement, a running gesture, and then the assertion of a theme whose dogma is beyond all doubt.

The tuner emphasized that dogma with the vehemence of a Savonarola castigating the pleasure-loving Florentines. Jack and I swayed like water-weeds in the flood, making the same mesmeric movements under the invisible punches of the music. Then, after the violent assertion and running to and fro, the second part of the sonata, heard by us both for the first time in our lives, came out with a long, rapid melody that tore us up by the roots and flung us downstream; the main stream of the art of music.

The musician was equally touched by his own magic, for as he played this melody, he leaned over it, watering it with his flowing hair, which almost touched the ivories. I was deeply impressed, as much by the spectacle as by the music. All was new to me: the performer, his odd manners and appearance, the nature of the music and

417

the fluidity of the performance. That is why I have never forgotten that *half-hour* [my italics], as long as one of the half-hours spent by Adam and Eve in the Garden, before their Disobedience set the clocks ticking.'

L 23b. RICHARD CHURCH. From *Over the Bridge*, pp. 167–8.

'We had been set to learn a passage from one of Paul's Epistles by heart. I had already got this, and I sat turning the dreary-looking pages of the school edition of the Bible, covered in shiny black. One hand was thrust into my inside pocket, clasping the tiny silver watch as a talisman. The other stopped at the page opening on the Fourth Gospel. I saw the phrase, "In the beginning was the Word, and the Word was with God, and the Word was God."

I felt the hair on my head tingling, and a curtain of red blood appeared to fall before my eyes. I leaned forward, clasping myself close, while the world rocked around me. And as this earthquake subsided, I saw a new skyline defined. It was a landscape in which objects and words were fused. All was one, with the word as the verbal reality brought to material life by Mind, by man. It was therefore the very obvious, tangible presence of the Creator.

Sitting in Surrey Lane School…I received a philosophy which I have never lost, a working faith in the oneness of all life. My fears of evil, the old Satanic dreads due to the division between the flesh and the spirit, vanished in that *moment* [my italics] of revelation. Everything was now contained, for me, in the power of the Word.

…on this sharp and concise symbolism I was to build a concept of universal singleness that gave me authority over the horrors, the divisions, the guilt complexes, that beset us all as we go through life, in a world supposedly split into two, the flesh and the spirit, where civil war rages eternally, in sombre Miltonic gloom and hopelessness.'

L 24. THE EXPERIENCE OF 'A'. From *A Drug-Taker's Notes* by R. H. Ward. (London, 1957), pp.195–201.

'Last night as I was walking home from the station I had one of those strange experiences of "rising up within oneself", of "coming inwardly alive". As it happens, I can remember the comparatively trivial beginnings of it. A minute or so after I had left the station, I was attacked, though not severely, by the indigestion which is always liable to recur when I have been working particularly hard. I thought to myself, though I suppose not in so many words, "I could separate myself from this pain; it belongs only to my body and is real only to the physical not-self. There is no need for the self to feel it." Even as I thought this the pain disappeared; that is, it was in some way left behind because I, or the self, had gone somewhere where it was not; and the sensation of "rising up within" began. (Although I had not yet walked more than a couple of hundred yards, I have the impression that movement encouraged this sensation. It is as if movement has some kind of integrative effect...)

First there is the indescribable sensation in the spine, as of *something mounting up*, a sensation which is partly pleasure and partly awe, a physical sensation and yet one which, if it makes sense to say so, is beginning to be not physical. This was accompanied by an extraordinary feeling of *bodily lightness*, of well-being and effortlessness, as if one's limbs had no weight and one's flesh had been suddenly transmuted into some rarer substance. But it was also, somehow, a feeling of living more in the upper part of one's body than in the lower, a certain rather peculiar awareness of one's head as, appropriately no doubt, the most important and intelligent of one's members. There was also a realization that one's facial expression was changing; the eyes were wider open than usual; the lips were involuntarily smiling. Everything was becoming "more", everything was *going up on to another level*. (What exactly is happening at such a time to one's nervous system, one's endocrine glands, the cells of one's brain; how much a sudden access of adrenalin to the blood stream is involved; whether areas of one's brain which are normally "dark" are being "lighted", neurologists and others might or might not be able to say.)...

I found that I could think in a new way. Or rather, it would be more accurate to say that I could think-and-feel in a new way, for it was hard to distinguish between thought and feeling, since both happened at once and in association. This was like becoming possessed of a new faculty...it was not exactly that [things] were trivial; they had simply got into their proper proportions... This, I realized, was the real meaning of "being at peace with the world"...

I noticed in regard to this thinking-and-feeling in a new way that certain thoughts-and-feelings were dangerous. If I allowed any suggestion of dislike, distrust, fear or contempt to approach, it had to be deliberately put away, or the "rising up" began to be a "falling down"; but once these kinds of thoughts-and-feelings had been put away, then the "rising up" was continued...

It was now (I had gone perhaps a quarter of a mile) that I found myself looking at a certain house, one with which I am very familiar, as if I had never seen it before. There was a cloudy moon, and the house, some of its windows lighted, was outlined against the night sky. According to one's ordinary perceptions, it is rather an ugly little suburban villa; but now it appeared to be quite otherwise. In fact the proper way of putting it is to say that it did not merely appear to be anything: it simply *was*. And the "is-ness" of it was all I knew and all I needed to know. I stood and stared at it, and the mere sight of it filled me with an indescribable joy... It was *another house*, and yet I knew that it was the ugly little villa I pass nearly every day. I realized that, could one always live on the different psychological level on which I was living at this *moment* [my italics], then the whole world would be changed; it would be *another world* in which there could be nothing which we habitually call ugly or evil, and nothing which we habitually call beautiful or good either, since *the truth of things* is beyond these contradictions, and somehow takes them up into itself.

...Time had very little significance, but I must have been in this different state, sometimes more, sometimes less, for *rather over half an hour* [my italics]. Not only did the realization of the truth, the astonishing *new reality*, of everything that I saw persist; everything I saw was mysterious and wonderful... My ability to see, my actual and physical eyesight, was greatly sharpened. Even distant things, the cloud-formations, the moon, were miraculously clear.

The sheer joy I experienced in all this is beyond expression. I felt that the world of nature was *utterly right* and literally *an act* of God's, and that to know this, and to be permitted to appreciate so much of the wonderful and the adorable, was nothing less than bliss. *And this was reality*. That is the whole point. The feelings and the thoughts we usually have are not real by comparison with this new condition of being into which I had moved. My knowledge of this reality *which lies beyond where we normally are* was undeniable and irrefutable...

At one point in this walk, it flashed upon me with the same effect of irrefutable conviction, *Of course there is God...God was here*; he was in everything that I looked at and in me who looked...I was in God's presence...

...the idea of death came to me more than once during *this half hour* [my italics], but it had then quite a different meaning from the one we usually give it. It was not merely that it was not in itself evil and to be feared; more positively, death was "Dear, beauteous death! the jewel of the just"...

As I have indicated, the intensity of this new state fluctuated during the *half hour or so* [my italics] that it took me to go from the station to my house. At times I felt that it was "dying down"; but then some other thought or feeling, a fresh access of awe and wonder at the marvels I perceived in the outward world or understood in the world within, would again renew the peculiar sense of "rising within myself", the sensation of bodily insubstantiality, the extraordinary speed and exactitude of perception. On one of the crests of these waves of renewed intensity, when the aperture of consciousness was at its widest, I heard, vividly, shockingly, and *as instantaneously as one might see a flash of lightning* [my italics], what I can only call an inward voice which said, *"There is something perfect"*. The phrase conveys nothing of the meaning it bore at that *moment* [my italics], for it had unbelievable depths of significance. The voice seemed to be telling me in those four words everything that it is important and necessary to know. "There is something perfect" was a summary of what it is to be in the presence of God who is perfection's self...

I stood still in the road, filled to the brim with this wonderful and joyous realization, that whatever we may have to endure of pain, sickness, grief and man's inhumanity to man, *there is still something perfect within all created things, that ultimately they live by it, and that nothing else matters.* Tears fell from my eyes. I had an impulse to go on my knees, there in the road beneath the stars...'

L 25. C. P. SNOW. From *The Search* (London, 1934; 1958 edn.), pp. 103–4.

(A scientific prediction has been verified after a series of failures)

'Then I was carried beyond pleasure. I have tried to show something of the high moments that science gave to me; the night my father talked about the stars, Luard's lesson, Austin's opening lecture, the end of my first research. But this was different from any of them, different altogether, different in kind. It was further from myself. My own triumph and delight and success were there, but they seemed insignificant beside this tranquil ecstasy. It was as though I had looked for a truth outside myself, and finding it had become for *a moment* [my italics] part of the truth I sought; as though the world, the atoms and the stars, were wonderfully clear and close to me, and I to them, so that we were part of a lucidity more tremendous than any mystery.

I had never known that such a *moment* [my italics] could exist. Some of its quality, perhaps, I had captured in the delight which came when I brought joy to Audrey, being myself content; or in the times among friends, when for some rare *moment* [my italics], maybe twice in my life, I had lost myself in a common purpose; but these *moments* [my italics] had, as it were, the tone of the experience without the experience itself.

Since then I have never quite regained it. But one effect will stay with me as long as I live; once, when I was young, I used to sneer at the mystics who have described the experience of being at one with God and part of the unity of things. After that afternoon, I did not want to laugh again; for though I should have interpreted the experience differently, I thought I knew what they meant.'

FREQUENCY: From internal evidence, an unique experience, although others, similar but lesser, have been rarely known.

L 26. MARCEL PROUST. From *Swann's Way* (trans. C. K. Scott Moncrieff, London, 1922; Phoenix edn., 1929), Vol. I, p. 58.

'Many years had elapsed during which nothing of Combray, save what was comprised in the theatre and the drama of my going to bed there, had any existence for me, when one day in winter, as I came home, my mother, seeing that I was cold, offered me some tea, a thing I did not ordinarily take. I declined at first, and then, for no particular reason, changed my mind. She sent out for one of those short, plump little cakes called "petites madeleines," which look as though they had been moulded in the fluted scallop of a pilgrim's shell. And soon, mechanically, weary after a dull day with the prospect of a depressing morrow, I raised to my lips a spoonful of the tea in which I had soaked a morsel of the cake. No sooner had the warm liquid, and the crumbs with it, touched my palate than a shudder ran through my whole body, and I stopped, intent upon the extraordinary changes that were taking place. An exquisite pleasure had invaded my senses, but individual, detached, with no suggestion of its origin. And at once the vicissitudes of life had become indifferent to me, its disasters innocuous, its brevity illusory—this new sensation having had on me the effect which love has of filling me with a precious essence; or rather this essence was not in me, it was myself. I had ceased now to feel mediocre, accidental, mortal. Whence could it have come to me, this all-powerful joy? I was conscious that it was connected with the taste of tea and cake, but that it infinitely transcended those savours, could not, indeed, be of the same nature as theirs.'

L 27. FREDERICK WOODS. *Session* from *Departure*. Vol. 3, No. 8 (undated).

(The scene is a jazz-club)

'We're there, thought Ray, we've done it. They're roaring, shouting, threshing, but they can't beat us. They can't drown us. He leant the mike into the guts of the open upright, and let Louie come in with the heavy, sharp chords off-rhythm, till they didn't know, any of them, who was playing, who was listening, but they were all playing and all listening, and Larry came in high up in triplets, catching them by the throat and holding them with sweet bitterness, his notes silver and hard, cleanly coming and high again, Ray taking his note and

Larry cutting out, so that the change-over was impeccable. The crowd was gone, its noise the sea's noise or a waterfall, coming to it round the side of a hill, rising and retreating, and he was alone on the hill, blasting and challenging the sky with his lasciviously-toned sax till the sky opened and there was nothing beyond, and the challenge turned to praise, ecstatic, believing, strong. The notes kept coming and the inspiration flowed in Ray like blood, essential. The passion rushed out of him, and then Larry and Louie and Hank were up there with him, all on the hilltop, all praising, and there was nothing beyond nothing, and again nothing. There was rushing wind in his ears, waves on sand, thunder, and the voice of the world in peace. The hillside darkened and split, a negro stumbled up the slope, tears on his face. His pink palms rattled on tight drum skins, giving an edge to the deeper tenor. He swayed like a snake. The bass crashed to the ground and Dix's voice called to the soul wildly, extemporising mad parabolas of sound. Larry hit G in altissimo and held it, a screaming fury, and then shaking on it till the hillside crumbled and the sky came together and they were back in the room with the lights and the crowd and the heat.

There was stillness in the small room... There was no cheering, no applause, just a gentle murmur as [the crowd's] breath escaped. They stared at Ray as though hypnotised, and a little afraid of what they had seen and heard. They had seen Ray crouched over his alto, blind to everything but the music, blowing something that was either profanity or a prayer...

[Ray] lurched to the centre of the dais, still dazed and still on the hill alone, only now instead of nothing, there was poison, evil, staring hatred. He stared back at the evil and the hatred with equal hatred.

"Is that what you wanted? Is that what you were yelling for? Well, you got it. You got what you wanted. Do you know what you got? You got everything, heart, soul, guts and bones. There's nothing else left. Do you understand? You bled me, sucked me dry. You asked for everything and you got it. Do you know what you got? You got the world's passion, the force of the hill I was on, where I saw nothing and everything and it was beautiful..." '

III. THE RELIGIOUS TEXTS

R 1. HEINRICH SUSO. Quoted E.U.: M., pp. 187–8.

'In the first days of his conversion it happened upon the Feast of St. Agnes, when the Convent had breakfasted at midday, that the Servitor[1] went into the choir. He was alone, and he placed himself in

---

[1] Suso refers to himself as the Servitor.

the last stall on the prior's side. And he was in much suffering, for a heavy trouble weighed upon his heart. And being there alone, and devoid of all consolations—no one by his side, no one near him—of a sudden his soul was rapt in his body, or out of his body. Then did he see and hear that which no tongue can express.

That which the Servitor saw had no form neither any manner of being; yet he had of it a joy such as he might have known in the seeing of the shapes and substances of all joyful things. His heart was hungry, yet satisfied, his soul was full of contentment and joy: his prayers and hopes were all fulfilled. And the Friar could do nought but contemplate this Shining Brightness; and he altogether forgot himself and all other things. Was it day or night? He knew not. It was, as it were, a manifest-ation of the sweetness of Eternal Life in the sensations of silence and of rest. Then he said, "If that which I see and feel be not the Kingdom of Heaven, I know not what it can be: for it is very sure that the endur-ance of all possible pains were but a small price to pay for the eternal possession of so great a joy.

This ecstasy lasted from *half an hour to an hour* [my italics], and whether his soul were in the body or out of the body he could not tell. But when he came to his senses it seemed to him that he returned from another world. And so greatly did his body suffer in this short rapture that it seemed to him that none, even in dying, could suffer so greatly in so short a time. The Servitor came to himself moaning, and he fell down upon the ground like a man who swoons. And he cried inwardly, heaving great sighs from the depth of his soul and saying, "Oh, my God, where was I and where am I?" And again, "Oh, my heart's joy, never shall my soul forget this hour!" He walked, but it was but his body that walked, as a machine might do. None knew from his de-meanour that which was taking place within. But his soul and his spirit were full of marvels; heavenly lightnings passed and repassed in the deeps of his being, and it seemed to him that he walked on air. And all the powers of his soul were full of these heavenly delights. He was like a vase from which one has taken a precious ointment, but in which the perfume long remains.'

R 2. ST. CATHERINE OF SIENA. Quoted E.U: M., pp. 365–6.

(Underhill explains that 'the intuitive perceptions of the deeper self are attributed by St. Catherine to the Divine Voice speaking in her soul'.)

'Oftentimes, through the perfect union which the soul has made with Me, she is raised from the earth almost as if the heavy body became light. But this does not mean that the heaviness of the body is taken away, but that the union of the soul with Me is more perfect than the union of the body with the soul; wherefore the strength of the spirit, united with Me, raises the weight of the body from the earth, leaving it as if immoveable and all pulled to pieces in the affection of the soul. Thou rememberest to have heard it said of some creatures, that were it not for My Goodness, in seeking strength for them, they would not be able to live; and I would tell thee that, in the fact that the souls of some do not leave their bodies, is to be seen a greater miracle than in the fact that some have arisen from the dead, so great is the union which they have with Me. I, therefore, sometimes for a space withdraw from the union, making the soul return to the vessel of her body . . . from which she was separated by the affection of love. From the body she did not depart, because that cannot be except in death; the bodily powers alone departed, becoming united to Me through affection of love. The memory is full of nothing but Me, the intellect, elevated, gazes upon the object of My Truth; the affection, which follows the intellect, loves and becomes united with that which the intellect sees. These powers being united and gathered together and immersed and in-flamed in Me, the body loses its feeling, so that the seeing eye sees not, and the hearing ear hears not, and the tongue does not speak; except as the abundance of the heart will sometimes permit it, for the alleviation of the heart and the praise and glory of My Name. The hand does not touch and the feet walk not, because the members are bound with the sentiment of Love.'

R 3. A CLERGYMAN. Quoted James: V.R.E., pp. 66-7.

'I remember the night, and almost the very spot on the hill-top, where my soul opened out, as it were, into the Infinite, and there was a rushing together of the two worlds, the inner and the outer. It was deep calling unto deep—the deep that my own struggle had opened up within being answered by the unfathomable deep without, reaching beyond the stars. I stood alone with Him who had made me, and all the beauty of the world, and love, and sorrow, and even temptation. I did not seek Him, but felt the perfect unison of my spirit with His. The ordinary sense of things around me faded. For the *moment* [my italics] nothing but an ineffable joy and exultation remained. It is impossible fully to describe the experience. It was like the effect of some great orchestra when all the separate notes have melted into one swelling harmony that leaves the listener conscious of nothing save that his soul is being wafted upwards, and almost bursting with its own emotion. The perfect stillness of the night was thrilled by a more solemn silence. The darkness held a presence that was all the more felt because it was not seen. I could not any more have doubted that *He* was there than that I was. Indeed, I felt myself to be, if possible, the less real of the two.

My highest faith in God and truest idea of him were then born in me. I have stood upon the Mount of Vision since, and felt the Eternal round about me. But never since has there come quite the same stirring of the heart. Then, if ever, I believe, I stood face to face with God, and was born anew of his spirit... My most assuring evidence of his existence is deeply rooted in that *hour* [my italics] of vision, in the memory of that supreme experience, and in the conviction, gained from reading and reflection, that something the same has come to all who have found God; I am aware that it may justly be called mystical...'

FREQUENCY: From internal evidence this was an unique experience at the time.

R 4. PLOTINUS. Quoted E.U: M., p. 372.

'Then the soul neither sees, nor distinguishes by seeing, nor imagines that there are two things; but becomes as it were another thing, ceases to be itself and belong to itself. It belongs to God and is one with Him, like two concentric circles: concurring they are One; but when they separate they are two . . . Since in this conjunction with Deity there were not two things, but the perceiver was one with the thing perceived, if a man could preserve the memory of what he was when he mingled with the Divine, he would have within himself an image of God . . . For then nothing stirred within him, neither anger, nor desire, nor even reason, nor a certain intellectual perception, nor, in short, was he himself moved, if we may assert this; but, being in an ecstasy, tranquil and alone with God, he enjoyed an unbreakable calm.'

FREQUENCY: Plotinus is said by his disciple Porphery to have received the vision four times during six years.

R 5a. ANGELA OF FOLIGNO. Quoted E.U: M., p. 252.

'The eyes of my soul were opened, and I beheld the plenitude of God, wherein I did comprehend the whole world, both here and beyond the sea, and the abyss and ocean and all things. In all these things I beheld naught save the divine power, in a manner assuredly undescribable; so that through excess of marvelling the soul cried with a loud voice, saying "This whole world is full of God!" Wherefore I now comprehended how small a thing is the whole world, that is to say both here and beyond the seas, the abyss, the ocean, and all things; and that the Power of God exceeds and fills all. Then He said unto me: "I have shown thee something of My Power," and I understood, that after this I should better understand the rest. He then said "Behold now My humility." Then was I given an insight into the deep humility of God towards man. And comprehending that unspeakable power and beholding that deep humility, my soul marvelled greatly, and did esteem itself to be nothing at all.'

R 5b. ANGELA OF FOLIGNO. Quoted E.U: M., pp. 350–1.

' "Whilst I was questioning her," says her secretary, "Christ's faithful one was suddenly rapt in spirit and seemed not to understand my words. And then was given her a wondrous grace. After a short time . . . she began to tell me what follows. 'My soul has just been rapt to a state in which I tasted unspeakable joy. I knew all I longed to know, possessed all I longed to possess. I saw all Good.' She said further: 'In this state the soul cannot believe that this Good will ever depart from her, or that she will depart from it, or that she will again be separated from it. But she delights herself in that Sovereign Good. My soul sees nothing whatever that can be told of the lips or the heart, she sees nothing and she sees All . . . No good that can be described or conceived is now the object of my hope; for I have put all my hope in a secret Good, most hid and secret, which I apprehend in great darkness.' And as I, the brother, could not receive or understand this dark, Christ's faithful one wishing to explain said: 'If I see it in the dark, it is because it surpasses all good. All, all the rest is but darkness. All which the soul or heart can reach is inferior to this Good. That which I have told hitherto, namely, all the soul grasps when she sees all creatures filled with God, when she sees the divine power, and when she sees the divine will, is inferior to this most secret Good; because this Good which I see in the darkness is the All, and all other things are but parts.' And she added, 'Though inexpressible, these other things bring delight; but this vision of God in darkness brings no smile to the lips, no devotion or fervour of love to the soul . . . All the countless and unspeakable favours God has done to me, all the words He has said to me, all you have written are, I know, so far below the Good I see in that great darkness that I do not put in them my hope' . . . Christ's faithful one told me that her mind has been uplifted but three times to this most high and ineffable mode of beholding God in great darkness, and in a vision so marvellous and complete. Certainly she had seen the Sovereign Good countless times and always darkly; yet never in such a high manner and through such great dark.' "

FREQUENCY: Three times.

427

R 6. A MAN OF 27. Quoted James: V.R.E., p. 69.

'I have on a number of occasions felt that I had enjoyed a period of intimate communion with the divine. These meetings came unasked and unexpected, and seemed to consist merely in the temporary obliteration of the conventionalities which usually surround and cover my life . . . Once it was when from the summit of a high mountain I looked over a gashed and corrugated landscape extending to a long convex of ocean that ascended to the horizon, and again from the same point when I could see nothing beneath me but a boundless expanse of white cloud, on the blown surface of which a few high peaks, including the one I was on, seemed plunging about as if they were dragging their anchors. What I felt on these occasions was a temporary loss of my own identity, accompanied by an illumination which revealed to me a deeper significance than I had been wont to attach to life. It is in this that I find my justification for saying that I have enjoyed communication with God. Of course the absence of such a being as this would be chaos. I cannot conceive of life without its presence.'

FREQUENCY: A number of occasions.

R 7. JAN VAN RUYSBROECK. Quoted E.U: M., p. 423.

'When love has carried us above and beyond all things, above the light, into the Divine Dark, there we are wrought and transformed by the Eternal Word Who is the image of the Father; and as the air is penetrated by the sun, thus we receive in idleness of spirit the Incomprehensible Light, enfolding us and penetrating us. And this Light is nothing else but an infinite gazing and seeing. We behold that which we are, and we are that which we behold; because our thought, life and being are uplifted in simplicity and made one with the Truth which is God.'

R 8. A CONVERT TO THE RELIGION OF HEALTHY-MINDEDNESS. Quoted James: V.R.E., pp. 118–19.

'I went into town to do some shopping one morning, and I had not been gone long before I began to feel ill. The ill feeling increased rapidly, until I had pains in all my bones, nausea and faintness, headache, all the symptoms in short that precede an attack of influenza. I thought that I was going to have the grippe, epidemic then in Boston, or something worse. The mind-cure teachings that I had been listening to all the winter thereupon came into my mind, and I thought that here was an opportunity to test myself. On my way home I met a friend, and I refrained with some effort from telling her how I felt. That was the first step gained. I went to bed immediately, and my husband wished to send for the doctor. But I told him that I would rather wait until morning and see how I felt. Then followed one of the most beautiful experiences of my life.

I cannot express it in any other way than to say that I did "lie down in the stream of life and let it flow over me." I gave up all fear of any impending disease; I was perfectly willing and obedient. There was no intellectual effort, or train of thought. My dominant idea was: "Behold the handmaid of the Lord: be it unto me even as thou wilt," and a perfect confidence that all would be well, that all *was* well. The creative life was flowing into me every instant, and I felt myself allied with the Infinite, in harmony, and full of the peace that passeth understanding. There was no place in my mind for a jarring body. I had no consciousness of time or space or persons; but only of love and happiness and faith.

I do not know how long this state lasted, nor when I fell asleep; but when I woke up in the morning, *I was well*.'

R 9. GEORGE FOX. Quoted by Ronald Knox in *Enthusiasm* (Oxford, 1950), p. 153.

'Now was I come up in spirit, through the flaming sword, into the paradise of God. All things were new, and all the creation gave another smell unto me than before, beyond what words can utter. I knew nothing but pureness, innocency, and righteousness, being renewed up into the image of God by Christ Jesus, so that I was come up into the state of Adam, which he was in before he fell.'

R 10a. ST. TERESA OF AVILA. Quoted E.U: M., p. 321.

'This true orison of quiet has in it an element of the supernatural. We cannot, in spite of all our efforts, procure it for ourselves. It is a sort of peace in which the soul establishes herself, or rather in which God establishes the soul, as He did the righteous Simeon. All her powers are at rest. She understands, but otherwise than by the senses, that she is already near her God, and that if she draws a little nearer, she will become by union one with Him. She does not see this with the eyes of the body, nor with the eyes of the soul . . . It is like the repose of a traveller who, within sight of the goal, stops to take breath, and then continues with new strength upon his way. One feels a great bodily comfort, a great satisfaction of soul: such is the happiness of the soul in seeing herself close to the spring, that even without drinking of the waters she finds herself refreshed. It seems to her that she wants nothing more: the faculties which are at rest would like always to remain still, for the least of their movements is able to trouble or prevent her love. Those who are in this orison wish their bodies to remain motionless, for it seems

to them that at the least movement they will lose this sweet peace . . .
they are in the palace close to their King, and they see that He begins to
give them His kingdom. It seems to them that they are no longer in the
world, and they wish neither to hear nor to see it, but only God . . .
There is this difference between the orison of quiet and that in which
the whole soul is united to God; that in this last the soul has not to
absorb the Divine Food. God deposits it with her, she knows not how.
The orison of quiet, on the other hand, demands, it seems to me, a
slight effort; but it is accompanied by so much sweetness that one hardly
feels it.'

R 10b. ST. TERESA OF AVILA. Quoted E.U: M., pp. 356-7.

' In this state, says St. Teresa, "There is no sense of anything: only
fruition, without understanding what that may be the fruition of which
is granted. It is understood that the fruition is of a certain good, containing in itself all good together at once; but this good is not comprehended. The senses are all occupied in this fruition in such a way, that
not one of them is at liberty so as to be able to attend to anything else,
whether outward or inward . . . But this state of complete absorption,
together with the utter rest of the imagination—for I believe that the
imagination is then wholly at rest—*lasts only for a short time* [my italics];
though the faculties do not so completely recover themselves as not to
be for some hours afterwards as if in disorder . . . He who has had
experience of this will understand it in some measure, for it cannot be
more clearly described, because what then takes place is so obscure. All
I am able to say is, that the soul is represented as being close to God; and
that there abides a conviction thereof so certain and strong that it cannot
possibly help believing so. All the faculties fail now, and are suspended
in such a way that, as I said before, their operations cannot be traced . . .
The will must be fully occupied in loving, but it understands not how it
loves; the understanding, if it understands, does not understand how it
understands. It does not understand, as it seems to me, because, as I said
just now, this is a matter which cannot be understood."...

"Do not imagine," says St. Teresa in another place, "that this orison,
like that which went before [i.e. the quiet] is a sort of drowsiness: (I
call it drowsiness, because the soul seems to slumber, being neither
thoroughly asleep, nor thoroughly awake). In the prayer of union the
soul is asleep; fast asleep as regards herself and earthly things. In fact,
during the *short time* [my italics] that this state lasts she is deprived of
all feeling, and though she wishes it, she can think of nothing. Thus she
needs no effort in order to suspend her thoughts; if the soul can love—
she knows not how or when she loves, nor what she desires . . . she is,
as it were, entirely dead to the world, the better to live in God...".

"The soul," she says, "neither sees, hears, nor understands anything while this state lasts; but this is usually *a very short time* [my italics], and seems to the soul even shorter than it really is. God visits the soul in a way that prevents it doubting when it comes to itself *that it has been in God and God in it*; and so firmly is it convinced of this truth that, though years may pass before this state recurs, the soul can never forget it nor doubt its reality. . . But you will say, how can the soul see and comprehend that she is in God and God in her, if during this union she is not able either to see or understand? I reply, that she does not see it at the time, but that afterwards she perceives it clearly: not by a vision, but by a certitude which remains in the heart which God alone can give." [1]

R 11. M.E. Quoted Leuba: P.R.M., pp. 209–10.

'As to ecstasies, I have experienced one, among others, which I remember perfectly. I will try to tell you when and how it happened and what it was like. I was thirty-six years old. I was climbing with some young fellows from Forclaz to the Croix de Bovine in order to reach Champex. We were following a road bordered by blooming oleanders and looking down over a stretch of country dotted here and there with clumps of firs. The wind scattered the clouds above and below us, sending them down or driving them up in whirling eddies. Now and then, one escaped and floated over the valley of the Rhone. I was in perfect health; we were on our sixth day of tramping, and in good training. We had come the day before from Sixt to Trent by Buet. I felt neither fatigue, hunger, nor thirst, and my state of mind was equally healthy. I had had at Forclaz good news from home; I was subject to no anxiety, either near or remote, for we had a good guide, and there was not a shadow of uncertainty about the road we should follow. I can best describe the condition in which I was by calling it a state of equilibrium. When, all at once, I experienced a feeling of being raised above myself, I felt the presence of God—I tell of the thing just as I was conscious of it—as if His goodness and power were penetrating me altogether. The throb of emotion was so violent that I could barely tell the boys to pass on and not wait for me. I then sat down on a stone, unable to stand any longer, and my eyes overflowed with tears. I thanked God that in the course of my life He had taught me to know Him... Then, slowly, the ecstasy left my heart; that is, I felt that God had withdrawn the communion which he had granted, and I was able to walk on, but very slowly, so strongly was I still possessed by the emotion. Besides, I had

---

[1] The first paragraph of this text comes from the *Life*, the next two from *The Interior Castle*; but Underhill links them, as descriptions of a single kind of experience.

wept uninterruptedly for several minutes, my eyes were swollen, and I did not wish my companions to see me. The state of ecstasy may have lasted *four or five minutes* [my italics], although it seemed at the time to last much longer. My comrades waited for me ten minutes at the cross of Bovine, but I took about twenty-five or thirty minutes to join them; for, as well as I can remember, they said that I had kept them back for about half an hour. The impression had been so profound that in climbing slowly the slope, I asked myself if it were possible that Moses on Sinai could have had a more intimate communication with God. But the more I seek words to express this intimate intercourse, the more I feel the impossibility of describing the thing by any of our usual images.'

R 12. HUGH OF ST. VICTOR. Quoted E.U: M., p. 245.

'*The Soul Says*, "Tell me, what can be this thing of delight that merely by its memory touches and moves me with such sweetness and violence that I am drawn out of myself and carried away, I know not how? I am suddenly renewed: I am changed: I am plunged into an ineffable peace. My mind is full of gladness, all my past wretchedness and pain is forgot. My soul exults: my intellect is illuminated: my heart is afire: my desires have become kindly and gentle: I know not where I am, because my Love has embraced me. Also, because my Love has embraced me I seem to have become possessed of something, and I know not what it is; but I try to keep it, that I may never lose it. My soul strives in gladness that she may not be separated from That which she desires to hold fast for ever: as if she had found in it the goal of all her desires. She exults in a sovereign and ineffable manner, seeking nought, desiring nought, but to rest in this. Is *this*, then, my Beloved? Tell me that I may know Him, and that if He come again I may entreat Him to leave me not, but to stay with me for ever."'

R 13. DAVID BRAINERD. Quoted James: V.R.E., pp. 209–10.

'One morning, while I was walking in a solitary place as usual, I at once saw that all my contrivances and projects to effect or procure deliverance and salvation for myself were utterly in vain; I was brought quite to a stand, as finding myself totally lost...

I continued, as I remember, in this state of mind, from Friday morning till the Sabbath evening following (July 12, 1739), when I was walking again in the same solitary place. Here, in a mournful melancholy state *I was attempting to pray; but found no heart to engage in that or any other duty; my former concern, exercise, and religious affections were now gone. I thought that the Spirit of God had quite left me; but still was not distressed; yet disconsolate, as if there was nothing in heaven or earth could make me happy. Having been thus endeavouring to pray—though, as I thought, very stupid and senseless*—for near half an hour; then, as I was walking in a thick grove, unspeakable glory seemed to open to the apprehension of my soul. I do not mean any external brightness, nor any imagination of a body of light, but it was a new inward apprehension or view that I had of God, such as I never had before, nor anything which had the least resemblance to it. I had no particular apprehension of any one person in the Trinity, either the Father, the Son, or the Holy Ghost; but it appeared to be Divine glory. My soul rejoiced with joy unspeakable, to see such a God, such a glorious Divine Being; and I was inwardly pleased and satisfied that he should be God over all for ever and ever. My soul was so captivated and delighted with the excellency of God that I was even swallowed up in Him; at least to that degree that I had no thought about my own salvation, and scarce reflected that there was such a creature as myself. I *continued in this state* [my italics] of inward joy, peace, and astonishing, *till near dark* [my italics] without any sensible abatement; and then began to think and examine what I had seen; and felt sweetly composed in my mind all the evening following. I felt myself in a new world, and everything about me appeared with a different aspect from what it was wont to do...'

R 14. ST. ALPHONSUS RODRIGUEZ. Quoted Poulain: G.I.P., pp. 268–9.

'Speaking of himself: "This person placed himself in the presence of God, saying to Him lovingly with heart and mouth: 'Lord, let me know Thee, and let me know myself.' And, at once, he was lifted up above all created things. He found himself as it were in another region, alone with God, who gave him great light concerning the knowledge of God and of self . . . His knowledge of God which was without intermediary and reasoning and, consequently, his love for God and his intimate familiarity with Him, rose to such a pitch that it seemed as if the Almighty *desired to make Himself known to him as He does to the Blessed in Heaven* . . . The soul now has but to feed on what she most desires amongst the many divine viands that are served up on the table of the divine perfections, viands that are of an excellent savour, because their *savour is the savour of God Himself.* O heavenly banquet! God invites the soul, and in this banquet of love He giveth Himself! O supreme love! O heavenly love! O precious love! O deep and divine love in which the Master of the feast *gives Himself* as nourishment to the soul . . . The soul forgets all earthly things and forgets her own self also, because she is solely occupied in loving God who *is* so intimately *present* to her and *as though face to face.*" '

R 15. ST. IGNATIUS LOYOLA. Quoted Poulain: G.I.P., pp. 278–9.

(St. Ignatius is speaking of himself in the third person).

'As he was going to pay his devotions at the Church of St. Paul, about a mile out of the town of Manresa, and was sitting on the banks of the Cardenero, or as some say of the Rubricato, his mind was suddenly filled with a new and strange illumination, so that in *one moment* [my italics], and without any sensible image or appearance, certain things pertaining to the mysteries of the Faith, together with other truths of natural science, were revealed to him, and this so abundantly and so clearly, that he himself said, that if all the spiritual light which his spirit had received from God up to the time when he was more than sixty-two years old, could be collected into one, it seemed to him that all this knowledge would not equal what was at that *moment* [my italics] conveyed to his soul.'

R 16. JACOB BOEHME. Quoted James: V.R.E., p. 402n.

'In *one quarter of an hour* [my italics] I saw and knew more than if I had been many years together at an university. For I saw and knew the being of all things, the Byss and the Abyss, and the eternal generation of the holy Trinity, the descent and original of the world and of all creatures through the divine wisdom. I knew and saw in myself all the three worlds, the external and visible world being of a procreation or extern birth from both the internal and spiritual worlds; and I saw and knew the whole working essence, in the evil and in the good, and the mutual original and existence; and likewise how the fruitful bearing womb of eternity brought forth. So that I did not only greatly wonder at it, but did also exceedingly rejoice, albeit I could very hardly apprehend the same in my external man and set it down with the pen. For I had a thorough view of the universe as in a chaos, wherein all things are couched and wrapt up, but it was impossible for me to explicate the same.'

R 17. R. M. BUCKE. Quoted James: V.R.E., pp. 390–1.

'I had spent the evening in a great city, with two friends, reading and discussing poetry and philosophy. We parted at midnight. I had a long drive in a hansom to my lodging. My mind, deeply under the influence of the ideas, images, and emotions called up by the reading and talk, was calm and peaceful. I was in a state of quiet, almost passive enjoyment, not actually thinking, but letting ideas, images, and emotions flow of themselves, as it were, through my mind. All at once, without warning of any kind, I found myself wrapped in a flame-coloured cloud. For an instant I thought of fire, an immense conflagration somewhere close by in that great city; the next, I knew that the fire was within myself. Directly afterward there came upon me a sense of exultation, of immense joyousness accompanied or immediately followed by an intellectual illumination impossible to describe. Among other things, I did not merely come to believe, but I saw that the universe is not composed of dead matter, but is, on the contrary, a living Presence; I became conscious in myself of eternal life. It was not a conviction that I would have eternal life, but a consciousness that I possessed eternal life then; I saw that all men are immortal; that the cosmic order is such that without any peradventure all things work together for the good of each and all; that the foundation principle of the world, of all the worlds, is what we call love, and that the happiness of each and all is in the long run absolutely certain. The vision lasted *a few seconds* [my italics] and was gone, but the memory of it and the sense of the reality of what it taught has remained during the quarter of a century which has since elapsed. I knew that what the vision showed was true. I had attained to a point of view from which I saw that it must be true. That view, that conviction, I may say that consciousness, has never, even during periods of the deepest depression, been lost.'

FREQUENCY: From internal evidence, once in twenty-five years.

R 18. JOSEPH SALMON, a Ranter. Quoted Jones: S.M.R., pp. 475-7.

In this, says Rufus Jones, Salmon relates 'how, as he was coming to maturity, he "...received some quickenings of a Divine principle in him". After going through many stages of religious experience, he heard "a voice that came from the throne of the heavenly Almightinesse (which said), 'Arise and depart, for this is not your rest.'"' Jones then prints Salmon's account of his 'great experience':

'I was made as truly sensible of this inwardly, as the eye is sensible of the light, or the ear of the outward sound. I was suddenly struck dead to all my wonted enjoyment... I then had a clear discovery in my spirit, how far all my former enjoyments came short of that true rest which my soul had all along aimed at. Here I stood for a season weeping with Mary at the sepulchre... When my three dayes (or set time) was expired, I begann to feele some quickening comfort within me...out I came with a most serene and cheerfull countenance, and (as one inspired with a supernaturall life) sprang up farr above my earthly center, into a most heavenly and divine enjoyment. Wrapt up in the embraces of such pure love and peace, as that I knew not oft-times whether I were in or out of this fading forme. Here I saw heaven opened upon me, and the new Jerusalem...all my former enjoyments being nothing in appearance to that glory which now rested on my spirit. Time would faile to tell what joy unspeakable, peace inconceivable, what soul-ravishing delights, and most divinely infatuating pleasures my soul was here possest with... In a word, I can give you no perfect account of that glory which then covered me; the lisps and slipps of my tongue will but render that imperfect, whose pure perfection surmounts the reach of the most strenuous and high-flown expression. I appeared to myselfe as one confounded into the abyss of eternitie, nonentitized into the being of beings, my soul spilt and emptied into the fountaine and ocean of divine fulness, expired into the aspires of pure life. In briefe, the Lord so much appeared, that I was little or nothing seen, but walked at an orderly distance from myself, treading and tripping over the pleasant mountains of the heavenly land, where I walked with the Lord and was not...I have been exalted into the bosome of the eternall Almightiness, where I have seene and heard things unlawful (I say unlawful) to be uttered amongst men'.

R 19. ST. AUGUSTINE. Quoted Butler: W.M., p. 53.

'If, as one is rapt from the senses of the body, so as to be among those images of bodies which are seen by the spirit (imagination); in the same way may one be rapt from them also, so as to be lifted up into that region of intellectual or intelligible things, where without any image of body the perspicuous truth is perceived and is obscured by no mists of false opinions; there the virtues of the soul have no scope for their operations or labours: for neither is there lust to be restrained by temperance, nor adversities to be borne by fortitude, nor iniquity to be punished by justice, nor evils to be avoided by prudence. There the sole and all-embracing virtue is to love what you see, and the supreme happiness to possess what you love... There is seen the brightness of the Lord, not by any symbolic vision, whether corporal or spiritual (imaginary); but by "species", not by enigmas (aenigmata), in so far as the human mind can grasp it, according to the grace of God who takes hold of it, that God may speak mouth to mouth to him whom He hath made worthy of such colloquy: not the mouth of the body, but of the mind.'

R 20. LOUIS OF BLOIS. Quoted Butler: W.M., pp. 9–10.

'It is a great thing, an exceeding great thing, in the time of this exile to be joined to God in the divine light by a mystical and denuded union. This takes place where a pure, humble, and resigned soul, burning with ardent love, is carried above itself by the grace of God, and through the brilliancy of the divine light shining on the mind, it loses all consideration and distinction of things, and lays aside all, even the most excellent images, and all liquified by love, and, as it were, reduced to nothing, it melts away into God. It is then united to God without any medium, and becomes one spirit with Him, and is transformed and changed into Him, as iron placed in the fire is changed into fire, without ceasing to be iron. It becomes one with God, yet not so as to be of the same substance and nature as God ... In the faculty of intellect it perceives the surpassing illumination of the Sun of Justice, and learns divine truth; and in the faculty of love it feels a certain glow of quiet love, or contact of the Holy Spirit, like a living fountain, flowing with streams of eternal sweetness; and thus it is introduced into sublime union with God. The soul, having entered the vast solitude of the Godhead, happily loses itself; and enlightened by the brightness of most lucid darkness, becomes through knowledge as if without knowledge, and dwells in a sort of wise ignorance...'

R 21. ST. FRANCIS OF SALES. Quoted Butler: W.M., p. 11.

'As melted balm that no longer has firmness or solidity, the soul lets herself pass or flow into What she loves: she does not spring out of herself as by a sudden leap, nor does she cling as by a joining or union, but gently glides, as a fluid and liquid thing, into the Divinity Whom she loves. She goes out by that sacred outflowing and holy liquefaction, and quits herself, not only to be united to the well-Beloved, but to be entirely mingled with and steeped in Him. The outflowing of a soul into her God is a true ecstasy, by which the soul quite transcends the limits of her natural way of existence, being wholly mingled with, absorbed and engulfed in, her God.'

R 22. SUSO. Quoted E.U: M., pp. 424–5.

' "Lord, tell me," says the Servitor, "what remains to a blessed soul which has wholly renounced itself?" Truth says, "When the good and faithful servant enters into the joy of his Lord, he is inebriated by the riches of the house of God; for he feels, in an ineffable degree, that which is felt by an inebriated man. He forgets himself, he is no longer conscious of his selfhood; he disappears and loses himself in God, and becomes one spirit with Him... All human desires are taken from them [sc. such people] in an indescribable manner, they are rapt from themselves, and are immersed in the Divine Will...for the true renunciation and veritable abandonment of a man to the Divine Will in the temporal world is an imitation and reduction of that self-abandonment of the blessed, of which Scripture speaks: and this imitation approaches its model more or less, according as men are more or less united with God and become more or less one with God. Remark well that which is said of the blessed: they are stripped of their personal initiative, and changed into another form, another glory, another power. What then is this other form, if it be not the Divine Nature and the Divine Being whereinto they pour themselves, and which pours Itself into them, and becomes one thing with them? And what is that other glory, if it be not to be illuminated and made shining in the Inaccessible Light? What is that other power, if it be not that by means of his union with the Divine Personality, there is given to man a divine strength and a divine power, that he may accomplish all which pertains to his blessedness and omit all which is contrary thereto? And thus it is that, as has been said, a man comes forth from his selfhood." '

APPENDIX B

CONTENT ANALYSIS

As described in Chapter II, the texts were analysed in such a way that what people said they felt could be entered under the heading or headings in which their various statements seemed appropriately to fall. In Group Q, the intention was to be able to enter virtually everything that was said, with almost nothing left over. In Groups L and R, however, people were considerably more wordy. Not only did they provide an average of 12.6 (Group L) and 13.0 (Group R) entries per person as compared with an average of 4.8 entries per person in Group Q; they also often said the same thing several times in different ways.

From the texts in Groups L and R I have extracted at least one statement to justify every entry made; but I have not necessarily put in all statements that would justify only one entry. I have, as with Group Q, ignored overbelief and confined myself 'to what is common and generic (see p. 20). No significant phrase should have been omitted in any group.

The verbal analyses of the texts form the basis of the charts in Appendix C.

I. TRIGGERS

1. Natural scenery, objects, etc.:

Group Q: at dusk, when the light and the smell and the scene is just right—sitting outside (Q 1); on a perfect day, in the sea—visually perfect (Q 3); I walked alone on the Downs—always connected with nature—always in relation to nature, including in town (Q 5); mountains (Q 6); natural beauty (Q 9); landscape—swimming in the sun—being in a storm at sea (Q 16); nature—mountains (Q 17); nature—(listening to music and) looking at the river—water often, crossing the Thames once—Provence (Q 18); swimming—driving in the sunshine (Q 21); scenery (Q 24); being alone in a very lonely place (Q 26); the air—walking in wind—a rough day by the sea—some height—water, sea, rivers—in March, black trees before the leaves come out, in sunshine

439

(Q 29); sudden appearance of light—coming into [an Eastern port] in the early morning—clouds—flowers (Q 30); nature (Q 34); natural beauty (Q 38); a long spire of mountains…brilliant moonlight—in the Himalayas once, seeing Nanda Devi like a blast of trumpets (Q 44); by a river in summer (Q 46); overlooking the sea, complete isolation (Q 47); fine weather—being in hills near the sea (Q 48); suddenly coming across an unexpected view that stretches for miles (Q 50); a really beautiful spring or autumn day, mostly autumn (Q 51); going for a walk on a November afternoon (Q 54); not very high mountains in Switzerland (Q 55); (ski-ing) on top of a hill and it began to snow—definitely connected with outdoors, with nature (Q 58); (being in love) out-of-doors (Q 60); (on a troopship in the harbour at Naples) and Vesuvius had a red light glowing—in [a foreign country] in the evening in autumn, the fields were flooded, the sun low…and the grass and water had a peculiar colour—sometimes here [in London] because the sky is blue (and the building is white) (Q 61); it happens on mountains, I must be by myself (Q 63).

Group L: sunset, ocean, air, blue sky (L 1a); view from high mountains over the sea (L 1b); mountain-top overlooking the sea (L 2); hills, dewy grass, sky through elm branches (L 3); clouds, leaves, stars, moon (L 4); the sun on the sea (L 5); in a park on a spring morning (L 7); downs and sky (L 8); the sea (L 9); the bodies of newly killed foxes (L 12); moonlight (L 14); sunset on a river (L 15); forest, storm, dawn (L 16); moonlight in the desert, mountains, sea (L 19); western wind, evening, stars (L 21); a cloudy moon (L 24).

Group R: on a hilltop at night (R 3); on a mountain-top with ocean and clouds beneath (R 6); a mountain-road on a fine day (R 11); walking in a thick grove in a solitary place (R 13); on the banks of a river (R 15).

2. Sexual love:

Group Q: sex—writing to someone I loved very much (Q 1); love (Q 2); being in love (Q 3); women (Q 8); sex (Q 9); love (Q 11); sex (Q 12); love (Q 15); love (Q 16); sex (Q 17); sex (Q 18); love, physical passion (Q 19); sexual love (Q 20); sex (Q 30); love in its fullest sense, spiritual and physical (Q 31); sexual relations (Q 38); love (Q 40); love (Q 41); love of a particular person (Q 43); sex (Q 45); seeing someone I love (Q 48); love, for people I've been cracked on and boys I've liked (Q 49); love (Q 55); it wasn't just sex, it was everything right at that moment (Q 59); being in love (Q 60).

Group L: love-making (L 17b).

Group R: None.

3. Childbirth:

Group Q: after my fourth baby was born, the right baby, it was two days after (Q 3); after my son was born (Q 5); holding my first baby, the day after she was born (Q 18); the first sight of my first baby (Q 28); becoming a mother, after the labour-pains had passed (Q 38).

Groups L and R: None.

4. Exercise, Movement:

Group Q: in the sea...everything physical (Q 3); I walked alone on the Downs (Q 5); swimming in the sun—flying (Q 16); swimming—driving in the sunshine (Q 21); walking in wind (Q 29); going for a walk on a November afternoon (Q 54); ski-ing on top of a hill (Q 58); sloshing through the fields (Q 61).

Group L: on a moving ship (L 5); walking hurriedly (L 16); walking home from the station (L 24).

Group R: walking in mountains (R 11); walking in a solitary place (R 13); driving in a hansom-cab (R 17).

5. Religion:

Group Q: the Missa Solemnis (Q 18); real religious experience (Q 19); Newman's 'Defence of Faith' (Q 24); Chartres Cathedral—the Bodhisatta in the British Museum—the beginning of King's College Chapel carols with 'Once in royal David's city' (Q 26); Mozart's 'Hallelujah' (Q 33); Mantegna's 'Agony in the Garden' (Q 35); Zen (Q 39); (a long spire of mountains), an Augustinian fourteenth-century abbey, (brilliant moonlight), a Gothic refectory, and I had this feeling, there's been no plainchant here for four hundred years, and I sang it—one passage, written specifically for the purpose, in 'The Dream of Gerontius' (Q 44); Gloucester Cathedral (Q 46); once from religion (Q 48); some of...the Bible (Q 52); religious feeling (Q 53); watching vespers in [a foreign] cathedral (Q 56); in [a foreign] cathedral, not really ecstasy, and once, there was a lovely picture in [a Roman] church (Q 60).

Group L: a little forest chapel (L 16); Lincoln Cathedral (L 17a); in prayer at a religious ceremony (L 22); reading the Bible (L 23b).

Group R: alone in church (R 1); endeavouring to pray (in the country) (R 13); speaking to God (R 14).

6. Art:

Group Q: poetry, Eliot's 'Prufrock', Tennyson's 'Ulysses' (Q 6); second movement of Rachmaninov concerto—the Renoir Exhibition in 1950

(Q 7); music, Tchaikovsky's Fourth, the pizzicato (Q 14); music, Bach's organ music (Q 15); music, Mozart, Verdi, Beethoven's Ninth once but not now, Vaughan Williams's penultimate—'King Lear'—singing, especially German lieder, Irish folk-songs, Italian opera (Q 16); music, Beethoven's Fifth (Q 17); music, the Archduke, the Missa Solemnis—listening to Toscanini doing Beethoven (and looking at the river) (Q 18); the Flemish primitive paintings in the National Gallery—any Brandenburg, especially the Sixth (Q 19); orchestral music (Q 21); the end of 'Othello' and 'Antony and Cleopatra' (Q 22); poetry or a passage with a high poetic content, Newman's 'Defence of Faith', 'The glories of our blood and state' (Q 24); intense beauty, like in Greek tragedy (Q 25); contemplation of art (Q 26); painting—Giorgione's 'Tempest' in the Accademia in Venice (Q 27); Mozart's 'Hallelujah' for the first time (Q 33); poetry and music—a Beethoven symphony, I'm not sure if it's the Fifth or the Seventh (Q 34); Mantegna's 'Agony in the Garden'—any aesthetic experience is liable to [induce it] (Q 35); poetry—Donne, Shakespeare's Sonnets, the work of the Spanish-American poets, Salinas, rather metaphysical types (Q 36); music—certain poetry (Q 38); music—drama (Q 43); music—Mahler's Tenth Symphony—(singing plainsong himself)—one passage, written specifically for the purpose, in 'The Dream of Gerontius' (Q 44); occasionally *lesser* works of art—the first time I saw 'The School for Scandal' with the Oliviers in Australia (Q 45); coming into contact for the first time with Italian primitive art—music, Bach and Mozart—'War and Peace', 'The Brothers Karamazov', Shakespeare (Q 46); a line of poetry, often 'Loveliest of trees'—and 'Look thy last'—'Magic casements—' (Q 50); a really beautiful piece of music, most Beethoven, some Mozart, the night I heard Kathleen Ferrier singing 'Chanson de Mer'—a play beautifully acted and produced, Shakespeare, Olivier's 'Richard III' and 'Titus' at Stratford—and ballet, the first I ever saw (Q 51); music, more singing than orchestral—poetry, 'Paradise Lost', some of Shakespeare and the Bible, some Auden (Q 52); taking down John Davidson's poems and reading 'St. Valentine's Eve'...any good poem would have done (Q 54); occasional moments in works of art—a perfect moment in a film—some music, Mozart—rarely with literature, just occasionally (Q 55); aesthetic things suddenly—a Scotch folk-song —sudden moments like seeing a very well-turned sentence, or looking at the film 'The Member of the Wedding' (Q 57); a lovely picture (Q 60); music when I play it myself (Q 62).

Group L: music, the music of Bizet (L 6); carved scrolls on the door-jambs of a church (L 10); fast movement of Beethoven's Seventh Symphony (L 11); a good book (L 14); Beethoven's Fifth Symphony

(L 18); bells and chanting (L 19); poetry (L 20); Beethoven sonata in G major, Op. 32, No. 1 [*sic*] (L 23a); jazz (L 27).

Group R: None.

7. Knowledge:

a. scientific knowledge:

Group Q: mathematics (Q 6); finding ten chromosomes when I knew they ought to be there—reading 'The Golden Bough' for the first time (Q 11); minor scientific discovery (Q 20); solving mathematical problems (Q 45); a series of experiments at a marine biological station (Q 47).

Group L: Einstein's formula (L 7); a scientific prediction verified (L 25).

Group R: None.

b. poetic knowledge:

Group Q: realization of profound truth...like in Greek tragedy (Q 25); being brought face to face with the vast greatness of the universe (Q 42).

Group L: 'a phrase suddenly struck me' about the theory of general relativity leading the human imagination 'across the peaks of glaciers never before explored by any human being' (L 7); 'the idea of vastness in geological time' (L 13); the phrase 'In the beginning was the word' etc. (L 23b).

Group R: None.

8. Creative work:

Group Q: writing something new (Q 9); occasionally writing (Q 16); own literary work coming out (Q 20); with inspiration one can have ecstasy (Q 26); writing about beautiful scenes—drawing (Q 38); suddenly able to express something in permanent form (Q 46); music, when I play it myself (Q 62).

Group L: playing jazz (L 27).

Group R: None.

9. Recollection, Introspection:

Group Q: writing to someone I loved very much (Q 1); Giorgione's 'Tempest' in the Accademia in Venice, and recollections of that picture—I can call it up (Q 27); the memory of certain scenes (Q 38); once eating thin bread and butter *and* jam as a child, I can recapture it in memory even now (Q 50); introspection—I can recapture it (Q 61).

Group L: recall of a postcard from the British Museum (L 5); fox-skins which 'had something of woods and caves about them' (L 12); recall after tea and cake (L 26).

Group R: memory of a previous ecstatic experience (R 12).

10. 'Beauty':

Group Q: in a word, beauty (Q 7); natural beauty (Q 9); beauty (Q 24); intense beauty (Q 25); a really beautiful (piece of music)—a really beautiful (spring or autumn day) (Q 51); something beautiful (Q 54).

Group L: the beauty of the morning (L 3); the glory of the morning (L 5).

Group R: None.

11. Miscellaneous:

Group Q: a château in France (Q 1); certain beautiful people (Q 7); when my child was ill, a phone message that he was all right (Q 12); Venice (Q 19); evening in the streets of [a Middle Eastern city] (Q 22); once in a dream (Q 25); seeing Stalin and Churchill shaking hands in the Bolshoi Theatre, Moscow (Q 32); merely a casual thing, like watching a gardener mowing a lawn (Q 37); ruins (Q 44); wine at exactly the right moment (Q 48); eating thin bread and butter *and* jam as a child (Q 50); (watching vespers) after a very good lunch with a very good friend (Q 56); on a troopship in Naples...and in only twelve hours one would be in battle for the first time (Q 61).

Group L: death in a peasant's cottage (L 12); a camel caravan (L 19); 'an ugly little suburban villa' (L 24).

Group R: in conversation (R 5b); in bed with 'flu (R 8); in a hansom-cab 'in a great city' (R 17).

II–IV: *What they said they felt*

II: Feelings of Loss

1. Loss of feelings of difference:

Group Q: the hard lines round one's individuality are gone (Q 1).

Group L: undefin'd existence (L 2) ; gave me authority over...the divisions (L 23b) ; beyond these contradictions (L 24).

Group R: the soul neither...distinguishes by seeing, nor imagines that there are two things (R 4) ; [the soul] loses...all distinction of things (R 20).

2. Loss of feelings of time:

Group Q: standstill feeling (Q 30); time seems to stop, no, not matter (Q 34); complete absence of a sense of specific time (Q 40); you don't think about the future, the future doesn't matter (Q 49); complete suspension of time (Q 56); not aware of yesterday or tomorrow, just of the moment (Q 61).

Group L: far from time (L 12); she has not time to wish (L 14); away from time, always outside of time (L 17a); those moments, and I have no notion how many they were (L 19); time had very little significance (L 24); [life's] brevity illusory—I had ceased now to feel...mortal (L 26).

Group R: Was it day or night? He knew not (R 1); I had no consciousness of time—I do not know how long this state lasted (R 8).

3. Loss of feelings of place:

Group Q: outside and above yourself (Q 9); takes you right out of the world (Q 28); you're not anywhere (Q 34); a complete absence of a sense of specific...place (Q 40); being just nowhere (Q 41).

Group L: all that was behind me, the house, the people...seemed to disappear (L 3); distance and nearness become blurred into one; within and without glide into each other (L 9); detached from every earthly thing and place, lost in a no-man's land (L 12); the crowd was gone (L 27).

Group R: the ordinary sense of things around me faded (R 3); above and beyond all things (R 7); I had no consciousness of...space (R 8); it seems to [those in this state] that they are no longer in the world (R 10a); I know not where I am (R 12).

4. Loss of feelings of limitation:

Group Q: transcend your normal limitations, capacity for experience (Q 5).

Group L: when...the flesh [begins] to feel the chain [i.e. afterwards] (L 21).

Group R: the soul quite transcends the limits of her natural way of existence (R 21).

5. Loss of feelings of worldliness:

Group Q: removed from consideration of earthly things (Q 14); you feel you haven't any cares in the world (Q 21); takes you right out of the world (Q 28); almost, except for one other person, alone in the world (Q 31); no longer being connected with everyday things, with the sort of commercial life one lives (Q 34).

Group L: swallowed up his animal being (L 1b); the house, the people, the sounds, seemed to disappear (L 3); a change from the animal to the spiritual (L 5); the martyred infants and castrated pioneers of the Holy Land shrank to microscopic insignificance (L 7); beside which nothing matters (L 8); detached from every earthly thing and place—far from …reality—beyond the reach of man (L 12); all human desires and purposes shrivelled to ridiculous unimportance (L 13); up from the plain of earth—away from the horizontal earth through…the whole range of desire (L 17a); gradually the little criticisms…were lost (L 17b); earth was lost to me (L 21); the vicissitudes of life had become indifferent to me, its disasters innocuous—I had ceased now to feel mediocre (L 26); the crowd was gone (L 27).

Group R: he altogether forgot…all other things (R 1); the ordinary sense of things around me faded (R 3); temporary obliteration of the conventionalities which usually surround and cover my life (R 6); above and beyond all things (R 7); no consciousness of…persons (R 8); no longer in the world (R 10a); fast asleep as regards…earthly things (R 10b); lifted up above all created things—the soul forgets all earthly things (R 14); far above my earthly centre—all my former enjoyments being nothing (R 18); transcends the limits of [the soul's] natural way of existence (R 21).

6. Loss of feelings of desire:

Group Q: None.

Group L: no thanks he breathed, he proffered no request (L 1b); there was no formulated wish (L 3); liberation from any pressure and itch (L 7); all human desires and purposes shrivelled to…unimportance (L 13); she has not time to wish (L 14); thinking and desiring melt together (L 15) ; my own triumph and delight and success…seemed insignificant (L 25).

Group R: nothing stirred within him…[not] desire (R 4); no good that can be described or conceived is now the object of my hope (R 5b); she knows not…what she desires (R 10b); my desires have become kindly and gentle—seeking naught, desiring naught (R 12); neither is there lust…(R 19); all human desires are taken from them (R 22).

7. Loss of feelings of sorrow:

Group Q: complete separation from trouble (Q 18); you feel you haven't any cares in the world (Q 21).

Group L: the martured infants and castrated pioneers...shrank to microscopic insignificance (L 7); the vicissitudes of life had become indifferent to me, its disasters innocuous (L 26).

Group R: I gave up all fear (R 8); all my past wretchedness and pain is forgot (R 12); neither is there...adversities (R 19).

8. Loss of feelings of sin:

Group Q: we are mostly kept from transcendent living by sin (Q 46).

Group L: the goblins were scattered (L 18); as long as one of those half-hours spent by Adam and Eve...before their Disobedience set the clocks ticking (L 23a); my fears of evil, the old Satanic dreads...vanished—gave me authority over the horrors...the guilt complexes (L 23b); nothing which we habitually call ugly or evil (L 24); [afterwards] instead of nothing, there was poison, evil, staring hatred (L 27).

Group R: nothing stirred within him, neither anger... (R 4); I had no thought about my own salvation (R 13); neither is there...iniquity...nor evils (R 19).

9. Loss of feelings of self:

Group Q: the hard lines round one's individuality are gone (Q 1); the soul leaving the body (Q 8); outside and above yourself (Q 9); a state of not being oneself (Q 11); ecstasy is...a self-losing (Q 16); it is an end of individuality for a moment (Q 24); getting out of myself (Q 29); forgetting oneself, no, oneself ceasing to matter (Q 34); a loss of the sense of being yourself (Q 40); you lose all sense of being yourself—didn't remember myself, this person, for a very short time (Q41); away from yourself—you don't feel yourself (Q 60).

Group L: soul...melted—swallowed up his animal being (L 1b); I was lost—I was absorbed (L 3); lost in the one (L 4); wasn't my unique loneliness as it had existed up to that moment (L 5); emancipates the spirit (L 6); self-dissolving (L 7); the soul dissolves (L 9); I felt...lost (L 12); I lost myself (L 13); thinking how far it might be possible habitually to shift his centre till his own personality would be no less outside him than the landscape (L 15); there his soul remained...till he came to himself (L 17a); when...the soul [begins] to feel the flesh [afterwards] (L 21); I was totally absorbed (L 22); I or the self had gone somewhere where [the pain] was not (L 24); further from myself (L 25); they didn't know, any of them, who was playing, who was listening (L 27).

Group R: he altogether forgot himself (R 1); the soul...ceases to be itself (R 4); my soul has just been rapt (R 5b); temporary loss of my own identity (R 6); complete absorption (R 10b); raised above myself (R 11); drawn out of myself (R 12); scarce reflected there was such a creature as myself (R 13); the soul...forgets her own self (R 14); non-entitized—I was little or nothing seen, but walked at an orderly distance from myself—I...was not (R 18); soul...carried above itself...reduced to nothing (R 20); quits herself (R 21); he forgets himself, he is no longer conscious of his selfhood (R 22).

10. Loss of words and/or images:

Group Q: (feeling that the mind has an accurate understanding) that it can't conceptualize (Q 6); no words—intoxication (if you can think of it as extreme clarity) (Q 16); liberation from ordinary sense-impressions (but heightened awareness) (Q 17); the heart without words—a wordless feeling (Q 24); (I know) but I can't describe it—(something perfectly apprehended) not formulated (Q 25); (communion with something else) before reason enters (Q 27); I don't know how to put it into words (Q 34); I couldn't begin to describe it (Q 53); (sense of certitude about) nothing I can define (Q 56); whatever words I used would be inadequate (Q 62).

Group L: form...melted—no thanks he breathed, he proffered no request (L 1b); each failing sense...(grew thrillingly distinct and keen)—a maze of...trackless...thoughts...through the riv'n rapt brain—(the torrent of quick thought) absorbed me from the nature of itself (L 2); no formulated wish (L 3); (the amazing quality of universal perception)...with the mind utterly rapt—(seem to know each separate thing) while lost in the one (L 4); a state of being for the expression of which words were neither sought nor found (L 5); (an expansion of consciousness)...its temporary dissolution (L 7); who knows—once one takes a pen and writes? (L 8); (one thought) which became one with feeling (L 9); (a living relation to me) and not, as hitherto, a merely cognitive one (L 10); a wordless stream (of complex feelings) (L 11); (multiplies its splendour) faster than Thought can effect his combinations, faster than Aspiration can utter her longings. Shirley says nothing while the trance is upon her—she is quite mute (L 14); when thinking and desiring melt together imperceptibly and...argument takes the quality of passionate vision (L 15); (a revelation mounting) obscurely to his brain—What was it? He asked not. He was in other hands (L 16); I cannot recognise that caravan in such everyday terms; my memory of it is dreamlike (yet embodies one of the most intense sensuous and emotional experiences of my life) (L 19); unuttered harmony (that I could never dream till earth was lost to me)—the Unseen (its truth reveals)—my outward sense is gone (my inward essence feels) (L 21);

(made known to me) without anyone teaching (L 22); objects and words were fused (L 23b); hard to distinguish between thought and feeling—the phrase conveys nothing of the meaning it bore (L 24).

Group R: (that which the Servitor saw) had no form neither any manner of being (R 1); the memory is full of nothing but Me—the tongue does not speak; except as the abundance of the heart will sometimes permit it (R 2); the soul neither sees, nor distinguishes by seeing, nor imagines there are two things (R 4); thought, life and being...made one with the Truth (R 7); (she understands) but otherwise than by the senses—(God deposits it with her) she knows not how (R 10a); (fruition) without understanding—(this good) is not comprehended (R 10b); the more I seek words...the more I feel the impossibility of describing the thing by any of our usual images (R 11); carried away, I know not how—(possessed of something) and I know not what it is (R 12); (knowledge)... without intermediary or reasoning (R 14); (illumination)...without any sensible image or appearance (R 15); could very hardly apprehend ...in my external man and set it down with the pen—(had a thorough view of the universe)...but it was impossible for me to explicate the same (R 16); without any image of body (the perspicuous truth is perceived)—obscured by no mists of false opinions—seen...not by any symbolic vision—(God may speak)...not [with] the mouth of the body, but of the mind (R 19); the soul...lays aside all, even the most excellent images—(becomes through knowledge) as if without knowledge and dwells in a sort of wise ignorance (R 20).

11. Loss of feelings of sense:

Group Q: removed from consideration of earthly things (Q 14); you don't feel anything but ecstasy (Q 21); you forget everything (Q 28); so happy that you don't know what you're doing (Q 32); overwhelming all other senses and superseding thought (Q 38); a blankness [with music heard before] the analytical side not completely submerged [with newly heard music] (Q 44); cerebral confusion (Q 52); you feel nothing (Q 60).

Group L: sensation...melted—thought was not...it expired (L 1b); each failing sense—my human brain stagger'd (L 2) ; my thought, or inner consciousness, went up (L 3); the mind utterly rapt (L 4); temporary dissolution [of consciousness] (L 7); to the shore—or to the ear? I know not (L 9); the trance is upon her (L 14); he was forgetting everything (L 15); when he looked out from his trance [afterwards] (L 16); the emotion was strong enough to carry with it everything—reason, soul, blood—in a great sweep (L 17b); we are shaken or lifted out of our ordinary state of consciousness (L 20); when the ear begins to hear and the eye begins to see; when the pulse begins to throb, the brain to think again [afterwards] (L 21); they didn't know...who was playing, who was listening (L 27).

Group R: his soul was rapt—he altogether forgot himself and all other things—whether his soul were in the body or out of the body he could not tell—when he came to his senses [afterwards] (R 1); the bodily powers...departed—the body loses its feeling, so that the seeing eye sees not, and the hearing ear hears not (R 2); the ordinary sense of things around me faded (R 3); neither sees, nor distinguishes by seeing—nothing stirred within him...[not] even reason, nor a certain intellectual perception (R 4); my soul has just been rapt (R 5b); idleness of spirit—uplifted in simplicity (R 7); no intellectual effort, or train of thought (R 8); all her powers are at rest—the faculties which are at rest...wish neither to hear nor to see [the world] (R 10a); the senses [are none of them] at liberty so as to be able to attend to anything else—all the faculties fail now and are suspended in such a way that...their operations cannot be traced—the understanding, if it understands, does not understand how it understands—deprived of all feeling—can think of nothing —the soul neither sees, hears, nor understands anything (R 10b); I knew not oft-times whether I were in or out of this fading form—my soul split and emptied...expired—soul-ravishing (R 18); rapt from the senses of the body—the virtues of the soul have no scope for their operations or labours (R 19); [the soul] loses all consideration (R 20); inebriated (R 21).

III. Feelings of Gain

1. Feelings of unity, of 'everything':

Group Q: allied to this thing of completeness, wholeness, other forms of so-called reality are not wholly real, only particles of reality—a completeness (Q 1); harmoniousness—affects everything (Q 6); sense of union with external reality (Q 17); sensation of absolute oneness, rightness, the same thing—the whole world falls into place, matches, fits (Q 19); sense of the oneness of things—differences suddenly becoming one (Q 20); everything fits in—all creation comes into harmony (Q 23); I enclose the universe or it encloses me (Q 24); this is the whole world (Q 31); feeling in unity with everything, no, not with everything, with nature...everything that comes out of nature, (Q 34); feeling of identification with the whole sensible universe (Q 37); feeling of oneness with the totality of nature—face to face with the vast greatness of the universe (Q 42); a sense that, a feeling that everything is right and the world makes sense (Q 58); everything...falling into place

(Q 59); all you know about nature, the whole thing, you can think about them all simultaneously and not in parts (Q 61).

Group L: through all things (L 1a); I saw [everything] (L 2); lost in the one—the almost palpable linking up of the universe (L 4); reveal all the details of things (L 6); reality…is one thing (L 8); distance and nearness become blurred into one—without and within are one—the entire symphony…becomes one thought, which becomes one with feeling—the unity of life (L 9); beheld a world—everywhere I feel…etc. (L 10); all was contained in oneness—this was all, this was everything (L 17a); everything rushed along in living beside him (L 17b); unity with all being—his mind is one infinitesimal node in the mind present throughout all being, just as his body shares in the unity of all matter (L 19); the whole adventure of mankind upon the earth gains…etc. (L 20); harmony (L 21); all was one—the oneness of all life (L 23b); had become…part of the truth I sought; as though the world, the atoms and the stars…were part of a lucidity—the unity of things (L 25); saw nothing and everything (L 27).

Group R: seeing of the shapes and substances of all joyful things (R 1); a rushing together of the two worlds, the inner and the outer—alone with Him…and all the beauty of the world, and love, and sorrow, and even temptation—all the separate notes have melted into one swelling harmony (R 3); I did comprehend the whole world…and all things—this whole world is full of God (R 5a); I saw all Good—[the soul] sees All—sees all creatures filled with God—this Good…is the All (R 5b); all things were new—all the creation gave another smell (R 9); a certain good, containing within itself all good together at once (R 10b); I saw and knew the being of all things…all the three worlds…the whole working essence—I had a thorough view of the universe…wherein all things are couched and wrapped up (R 16); I saw that the universe is… a living Presence—the cosmic order is such that…all things work together for the good of each and all (R 17).

2. Feelings of eternity:

Group Q: sensation of timeless bliss—life should be like this for ever (Q 18); sensation of timelessness (Q 31); you feel in any given moment you've almost touched the fringe of eternity which seems to come into life at that moment—when living horizontally, you come into connexion with a kind of vertical eternity, something that can't alter (Q 46); I could sit here for ever, listening (Q 57); as if nothing could ever go wrong again (Q 59).

Group L: any figure…at any period in history (L 5); infinite—since the beginnings of organic life (L 7); in which I shall…continue to exist

(L 8); the infinite sea—eons of existence (L 9); 'the timeless moment'—(L 11); lost myself in...the idea of vastness in geological time (L 13); timeless ecstasy—timeless consummation—the climax of eternity (L 17a); eternal liberty (L 21).

Group R: a manifestation of the sweetness of Eternal Life—eternal possession of so great a joy (R 1); my soul opened out...into the Infinite—felt the Eternal (R 3); cannot believe that this Good will ever depart from her...or that she will again be separated from it (R 5b); an infinite gazing and seeing (R 7); allied with the Infinite (R 8); I try to keep it that I may never lose it—stay with me for ever (R 12); inwardly pleased and satisfied that he should be God over all for ever and ever (R 13); became conscious in myself of eternal life—I possessed eternal life then—saw that all men are immortal (R 17); into the abyss of eternity (R 18); flowing with streams of eternal sweetness (R 20).

3. Feelings of an ideal place, heaven:

Group Q: as if being borne into heaven itself (Q 15).

Group L: its home, its harbour found (L 21); [comparison with] Adam and Eve in the Garden (L 23a); reality which lies beyond where we normally are (L 24); the sky opened and there was nothing—I saw nothing and everything and it was beautiful (L 27).

Group R: if that which I see and feel be not the Kingdom of Heaven, I know not what it can be (R 1); I was come up in spirit...into the paradise of God (R 9); in the palace close to their King (R 10a); in another region, alone with God...as...to the Blessed in Heaven (R 14); saw heaven opened upon me, and the new Jerusalem (R 18); lifted up into that region of intellectual or intelligible things (R 19).

4. Feelings of release:

Group Q: release—liberation (Q 3); transcend your normal limitations, capacity for experience, burst into a wider one (Q 5); liberation (Q 17); complete sense of liberation (Q 44); words like 'liberation' (Q 45); the liberation of relief (Q 57).

Group L: free (L 2); emancipates the spirit (L 6); liberation (L 7); as if I had emerged into the light—emancipated me (L 10); new doors... beginning to open—liberation (L 20); eternal liberty—its wings are almost free (L 21); the sky opened (L 27).

Group R: my soul opened out (R 3); the eyes of my soul were opened (R 5a); glory seemed to open (R 13); heaven opened (R 18); transcends the limits of her natural way of existence (R 21).

5. Feelings of a new life, another world:

Group Q: soaring up to something you've always wanted, always known was there (Q 3); burst into a wider [capacity for experience] (Q 5); as if being borne into heaven itself (Q 15); life should be like this for ever (Q 18); whole world falls into place, matches, fits (Q 19); on the edge of seeing right beyond (Q 22); this is it and everything fits in—all creation comes into harmony (Q 23); double realization of perfection with life (Q 26); this is the whole world (Q 31); for the first time you're seeing things in proper proportion (Q 34); you feel that it is all right—something being perfected (Q 35); satisfaction with the actuality of existence—sensation of pure existence (Q 36); a different dimension altogether (Q 44); nearness to splendour (Q 45); almost touched the fringe of eternity (Q 46); like the transfiguration (Q 48); everything is right and the world makes sense (Q 58); everything I ever wanted falling into place (Q 59).

Group L: the trackless fields of undefined existence, far and free (L 2); when it ceased, I did wish for some increase or enlargement of my existence to correspond with the largeness of feeling I had momentarily enjoyed (L 3); change in perspective—nirvana—retreat (L 7); entered into a sanctuary—retreat (L 8); our small life is encircled by a great sleep—our life but...the emergence from the original oneness and the sinking back into it (L 9); I...beheld a world where...etc. (L 10); lost in a no-man's land far from time and reality—penetrated the very heart of the universe (L 12); nirvana (L 13); earth an Eden—the experience of a genii-life—the vision of life as she wishes it (L 14); into the darkness...the unique mystery (L 17a); the gusts of splendour, the heroism, the youth, the magnificence of life and of death (L 18); grants man a state of mind in which I believe he must come more and more to live—near the root of our mystery (L 19); the whole adventure of mankind upon the earth gains...a new momentousness, precariousness and beauty—living becomes a grander affair (L 20); its home, its harbour found (L 21); as long as one of those half-hours spent by Adam and Eve in the Garden (L 23a); a new skyline—a landscape in which objects and words were fused (L 23b); [things] had simply got into their proper proportions—could one always live on the different psychological level on which I was living at this moment, then the whole world would be changed; it would be another world—this reality which lies beyond where we normally are (L 24); the sky opened and there was nothing beyond—the voice of the world in peace—I saw nothing and everything and it was beautiful (L 27).

Group R: Eternal Life—the Kingdom of Heaven—it seemed to him that he returned from another world [afterwards] (R 1); my soul opened out...into the Infinite—born anew (R 3); the soul...becomes as it were another thing (R 4); just been rapt to a state in which...etc. (R 5b); love has carried us...into the Divine Dark (R 7); I was come up...into the paradise of God. All things were new and all the creation gave another smell unto me than before—renewed up (R 9); in the palace close to their King...He begins to give them His kingdom (R 10a); I am suddenly renewed: I am changed—found...the goal of all her desires (R 12); felt myself in a new world, and everything about me appeared with a different aspect from what it was wont to do (R 13); found himself...in another region (R 14); saw in myself all the three worlds—had a thorough view of the universe (R 16); consciousness that I possessed eternal life then—saw...that the cosmic order is such...etc. (R 17); heaven opened upon me, and the new Jerusalem—tripping over the pleasant mountains of the heavenly land (R 18); lifted up into that region...etc. (R 19); transformed and changed—entered into the vast solitude of the Godhead (R 20); changed into another form (R 22).

6. Feelings of satisfaction:

Group Q: something you've always wanted (Q 3); complete satisfaction (Q 15); complete satisfaction (Q 33); complete satisfaction (Q 35); satisfaction (Q 36); gratified vanity—immensely fortunate (Q 57); everything I ever wanted (Q 59).

Group L: satisfaction (L 5); a flow of fulfilment (L 12); life as she wishes it (L 14).

Group R: his heart was hungry, yet satisfied...his prayers and hopes were all fulfilled (R 1); possessed all I longed to possess (R 5b); great satisfaction—wants nothing more (R 10a); the goal of all her desires (R 12); satisfied (R 13); what she most desires (R 14); the supreme happiness to possess what you love (R 19).

7. Feelings of joy:

Group Q: absolute ecstasy—exalted (Q 5); happiness (Q 6); life worth living (Q 7); as if being borne into heaven itself (Q 15); timeless bliss (Q 18); very happy (Q 21); a shock of joy (Q 25); happiness...so supreme (Q 28); so happy (Q 32); intense...joy (Q 38); very different in kind from mere pleasure (Q 44); joyful (Q 47); great joy (Q 49); a wonderful feeling (Q 51); sadness mixed with joy (Q 52); exaltation—exultation (Q 56); a wonderful surprise—delightful (Q 57); extreme happiness (Q 59); life is worthwhile (Q 61); a most marvellous feeling (Q 62).

Group L: joy (L 1a); gladness—joy—enjoyment (L 1b); upon the outward verge...of full beatitude (L 2); exaltation—exalted (L 3); joy (L 4); joyful (L 5); joy (L 11); immense happiness (L 12); delight—joy (L 14); so sweet (L 16); ecstasy (L 17a); joy—ecstasy—the highest point of bliss (L 17b); superhuman joy (L 18); happy—love and confidence (L 19); delight (L 20); joyful (L 22); partly pleasure and partly awe—indescribable joy—nothing less than bliss—wonderful and joyous (L 24); carried beyond pleasure—ecstasy (L 25); exquisite pleasure—all-powerful joy (L 26); praise, ecstatic (L 27).

Group R: joy—sweetness (R 1); ineffable joy and exultation (R 3); unspeakable joy (R 5b); love and happiness and faith (R 8); happiness—so much sweetness (R 10a); ecstasy (R 11); delight—sweetness—gladness—my soul...exults in a sovereign and ineffable manner (R 12); joy unspeakable—pleased (R 13); exceedingly rejoice (R 16); exultation—immense joyousness—happiness (R 17); heavenly and divine enjoyment—all my former enjoyments being nothing in appearance to that glory—soul-ravishing delights (R 18); supreme happiness (R 19); happily (R 20); the joy of his Lord (R 22).

8. Feelings of salvation, perfection:

Group Q: absolute...rightness (Q 19); perfection with life (Q 26); you feel that it is all right—something being perfected—the experience couldn't be more perfect (Q 35); everything is right (Q 58); as if nothing could ever go wrong again (Q 59).

Group L: immense and pure emotion (L 5); sense of purification (L 16); perfect, swooning consummation (L 17a); everything...was...perfect in itself (L 17b); [compared with] Adam and Eve in the Garden, before their disobedience (L 23a); gave me authority over the horrors...the guilt complexes (L 23b); world of nature was utterly right—something perfect—in the presence of God who is perfection's self (L 24).

Group R: I saw all Good—cannot believe that this Good will ever depart from her (R 5b); knew nothing but pureness, innocency, and righteousness—renewed up (R 9); fruition...of a certain good, containing in itself all good together at once (R 10b); His goodness...[was] penetrating me (R 11); renewed (R 12); pure love and peace—pure perfection—pure life (R 18).

9. Feelings of glory; beauty:

Group Q: sudden glory (Q 24); splendour (Q 45).

Group L: pass from gloom to glory (L 2); the swift glory—its splendour

(L 14); the gusts of splendour—the magnificence of life and of death (L 18); comprehension of the beauty...of the physical world (L 19); the whole adventure of mankind...gains...a new momentousness, precariousness and beauty (L 20); death was 'Dear beauteous death! the jewel of the just' (L 24); it was beautiful (L 27).

Group R: unspeakable glory—Divine glory (R 13); that glory which now rested on my spirit—that glory which then covered me (R 18); changed into...another glory...and what is that other glory, if it be not to be illuminated and made shining in the Inaccessible Light? (R 22).

10. Feelings of contact:

Group Q: merging into the experience—touch reality (Q 1); soaring up to something (Q 3); communion—direct communication (Q 5); in touch with the Creator (Q 15); union with external reality (Q 17); I am part of the thing that has set it off, and I enclose the universe or it encloses me (Q 24); communion with something else (Q 27); touching reality (Q 33); feeling in unity with everything (Q 34); living in the object (Q 36); identification with the whole sensible universe (Q 37); oneness with the totality of nature (Q 42); almost touched the fringe of eternity—come into connexion with a kind of vertical eternity (Q 46).

Group L: felt a presence—a sense...of something far more deeply interfused...a motion and a spirit (L 1a); visitation from the living God—rapt into still communion (L 1b); [contact with a seraph, a spirit] (L 2); being oneself contained in all one sees—millions of spirits like mine... to them I unite (L 4); in the presence of a being (L 5); it beats over my soul, devours it, embraces it—the world exales in the soul and the soul dissolves in the world (L 9); direct contact with an otherness—every outline, every edge, and every surface was in a living relationship with me (L 10); Union with God (L 11); penetrated the very heart of the universe (L 12); identification of himself with the objects he was looking at (L 15); he was in other hands—the Spirit of Life illumined him—he felt...his darling's touch (L 16); to the...meeting, the clasp, the close embrace...to the touch, the clasp (L 17a); possession by the creative eros—intense consciousness of unity with all being (L 19); more than our normal stock of penetrative sympathy—a powerful sense...of being in the presence of extraordinary possibilities (L 20); a messenger of Hope comes...to me (L 21); the very obvious, tangible presence of the Creator (L 23b); had become...part of the truth I sought (L 25).

Group R: the perfect union which the soul has made with Me (R 2); my soul opened out...into the Infinite—I stood alone with Him—perfect unison of my spirit with His—a presence that was all the more felt because it was not seen—I stood face to face with God (R 3); [the soul] belongs to God and is one with Him—the perceiver was one with the thing perceived—mingled with the Divine—alone with God (R 4); [converse with God] (R 5a); intimate communion with the divine (R 6); we receive...the Incomprehensible Light, enfolding us and penetrating us—made one with the Truth which is God—we behold that which we are, and we are that which we behold (R 7); allied with the Infinite (R 8); she is already near her God and...if she draws a little nearer, she will become by union one with Him—close to their King (R 10a); close to God—God visits the soul in a way that prevents it doubting...that it has been in God and God in it (R 10b); I felt the presence of God...as if His goodness and power were penetrating me altogether—Moses...could [not] have had a more intimate communion with God—intimate intercourse (R 11); my Love has embraced me— my soul strives...that she may not be separated from That...etc. (R 12); I was even swallowed up in [God] (R 13); in the presence of God— alone with God—intimate familiarity with Him—God...so intimately present to her and as though face to face (R 14); the universe is...a living Presence (R 17); wrapt up in the embraces of such pure love and peace—the Lord so much appeared—walked with the Lord—into the bosom of the eternal Almightiness (R 18); joined to God;—melts away into God—becomes one with God, yet not so as to be of the same nature and substance as God—contact of the Holy Spirit—sublime union with God (R 20); the soul lets herself pass or flow into What she loves...into the Divinity—united to the well-Beloved—entirely mingled with and steeped in Him—out-flowing of a soul into her God—wholly mingled with, absorbed and engulfed in her God (R 21); loses himself in God—the Divine Being whereinto they pour themselves, and which pours Itself into them, and becomes one thing with them—union with the Divine Personality (R 22).

11a. Feelings of mystical knowledge:

Group Q: the mind has an accurate understanding (that it can't conceptualize) (Q 6); (intoxication if you can think of it as) extreme clarity (Q 16); (liberation from ordinary sense-impressions but) heightened awareness (Q 17); mystic sensation (Q 22); (a wordless feeling) of sudden tremendous expansion, sudden glory (Q 24); I know (but I can't describe it)—something perfectly apprehended (not formulated) (Q 25); communion with something else (before reason enters)— mystical (Q 27); sudden sense of certitude (about nothing I can define) (Q 56); (unbearable) knowledge (Q 63).

Group L: communion (that transcends the imperfect offices of prayer and praise) (L 1b); (each failing sense)...grew thrillingly distinct and keen—the hum of men or other things (talking in unknown tongues) beat on my anxious ear—I know not if I shape these things with accurate similitude from visible objects (for but dimly now)...the memory of that mental excellence comes o'er me (L 2); (with the mind utterly rapt) the eye becomes abnormally sensitive (but unconsciously) (L 4); an expansion of consciousness...(its temporary dissolution) (L 7); a thing I see before me...(But who knows—once one takes a pen and writes?) How difficult not to go making 'reality' this and that (L 8); all thought becomes one thought (which becomes one with feeling) (L 9); a mystical experience—every outline...was in a living relation to me and not, as hitherto, in a merely cognitive one (L 10); the mysterious event—(a wordless stream) of complex feelings...continually swollen by tributaries of associated Experience (L 11); thinking and desiring melt together imperceptibly, and what in other hours may have seemed argument takes the quality of passionate vision (L 15); a revelation mounting (obscurely) to his brain (L 16); to...the unique mystery (L 17a); even now I cannot recognise that caravan in such everyday terms; for my memory of it is dreamlike, yet embodies one of the most intense sensuous and emotional experiences—belongs near the root of our mystery (L 19); you are assured (in an unaccountable way) that wonderful enlightenments (still unreceived) are on their way to you (L 20); (unuttered) harmony that I could never dream (till earth was lost to me)—dawns (the Invisible), (the Unseen) its truth reveals—(my outward sense is gone), my inward essence feels (L 21); objects and words were fused—that moment of revelation (L 23b); I could think in a new way...it was hard to distinguish between thought and feeling, since both happened at once and in association. This was like becoming possessed of a new faculty—everything...was mysterious and wonderful—I heard an inward voice which said, 'There is something perfect.' (The phrase conveyed nothing of the meaning it bore at that moment) for it had unbelievable depths of significance (L 24).

Group R: that which the Servitor saw (had no form neither any manner of being) (R 1); in all these things I beheld naught save the divine power (in a manner assuredly indescribable) (R 5a); a (secret) Good, (most hid and secret), which I apprehend (in great darkness) (R 5b); (loss of my own identity) accompanied by an illumination which revealed to me...etc. (R 6); Our thought, life and being are uplifted (in simplicity) and made one with the Truth (R 7); understands (but otherwise than by the senses) (R 10a); fruition (without understanding)—it is understood that the fruition is of a certain good...(but this good is not comprehended) (R 10b); the more I seek words...(the more I feel the impossibility of describing the thing by any of our usual images) (R 11); my intellect is illuminated—I seem to have become possessed of something (and I know not what it is) (R 12); a new inward apprehension or view...of God, such as I never had before—(I was even swallowed up in Him—scarce reflected that there was such a creature as myself) (R 13); his knowledge of God (which was without intermediary and reasoning) (R 14); illumination...(without any sensible image or appearance) (R 15); (I could very hardly apprehend the same in my external man and set it down with the pen)—I had a thorough view of the universe...(but it was impossible for me to explicate the same) (R 16); (without any image of body) the perspicuous truth is perceived (R 19); (loses all consideration and distinction of things, and lays aside all, even the most excellent images)—in the faculty of intellect it perceives the surpassing illumination of the Sun of Justice, and learns divine truth—becomes through knowledge (as if without knowledge) and dwells in a sort of wise (ignorance) (R 20).

11b. Feelings of enhanced mental capacity, new knowledge:

Group Q: some slight approach to making a thing whole (Q 1); something seems to fall into pattern (Q 5); perception of a pattern (Q 6); wanting to do something and feeling you can do it (Q 9); something being perfected (Q 35); sensation of meaningfulness (Q 44); multiplication of possibilities—intense perception (Q 45); the sensation you understand everything to which you turn your mind (Q 54); immensely creative, full of ideas (Q 57); the world makes sense (Q 58); a faculty working with effortless efficiency which enables you to hold in the forefront of conscious feeling both knowledge of the smallest bacteria in the field, how the blade of grass works and the universe, in the same detail—all you know about nature, the whole thing, you can think about them all simultaneously and not in parts, that knowledge is almost limitless (Q 61).

Group L: elevated thoughts (L 1a); my mental eye grew large with such a vast circumference of thought—thoughts...expanding momently—mental excellence (L 2); quality of universal perception...in the thinker (L 4); I had only to yield...to discover a poem—I was being told something (L 5); gives wings to thought—enable one to grapple with problems—answers drop into my lap—problems solved—makes me productive (L 6); as one illumined [with details given of what was known] (L 10); Enlightenment (L 11); she would fix the apparition, tell the vision revealed (L 14); the music had summed up to her all that had happened or could happen in her career. She read it as a tangible statement (L 18); a state of illumination in my own mind—my thoughts and feelings had been given an extraordinary clarity and truth—power to transmute all that the senses perceived into symbols of burning significance—awareness of spiritual significance—comprehending every physical fact of...[the camels'] existence—confidence (L 19); our faculties...enhanced—keener perceptions—new doors of understanding (L 20); the things that I did not know and of which I was held in error were made known to me without anyone teaching (L 22); I received a philosophy—everything was now contained, for me, in the power of the Word (L 23b); my knowledge of this reality...was undeniable and irrefutable—when the aperture of consciousness was at its widest I heard...an inward voice (L 24); [had found] a truth outside myself—as though the world...[was] wonderfully clear—lucidity (L 25); I saw nothing and everything and it was beautiful (L 27).

Group R: my highest faith in God and truest idea of Him were then born in me (R 3); I did comprehend the whole world (R 5a); I knew all I longed to know (R 5b); an illumination which revealed to me a deeper significance than I had been wont to attach to life (R 6); a new inward apprehension or view that I had of God, such as I never had before (R 13); gave him great light concerning the knowledge of God and of self (R 14); certain things pertaining to the mysteries of the Faith, together with other truths of natural science were revealed to him (R 15); in one quarter of an hour I saw and knew more than if I had been many years together at an university. For I saw and knew the being of all things (R 16); an intellectual illumination—among other things, I did not merely come to believe, but I saw...etc. (R 17); I have seen and heard things unlawful...to be uttered amongst men (R 18).

11c. Feelings of knowledge by identification:

Group Q: this does touch reality (Q 1); soaring up to something you've always wanted, always known was there (Q 3); in ecstasy you get direct communication (Q 5); borne into heaven itself—in touch with the Creator (Q 15); union with external reality (Q 17); life should be like this for ever (Q 18); absolute oneness, rightness (Q 19); sense of the oneness of things (Q 20); seeing right beyond (Q 22); everything fits in—all creation comes into harmony (Q 23); I enclose the universe or it encloses me (Q 24); realization of perfection with life (Q 26); this is the whole world (Q 31); touching reality (Q 33); for the first time you're seeing things in proper proportion (Q 34); you feel it is all right —the experience couldn't be more perfect (Q 35); pure existence (Q 36); identification with the whole sensible universe (Q 37); complete involvement of one's whole being (Q 40); oneness with the totality of nature (Q 42); a different dimension altogether (Q 44); nearness to splendour (Q 45); almost touched the fringe of eternity (Q 46); like the transfiguration only happening within (Q 48); everything is right and the world makes sense (Q 58); everything I ever wanted falling into place—as if nothing could ever go wrong again (Q 59); knowledge of the reality of things (Q 63).

Group L: a motion and a spirit, that impels all (L 1a); visitation from the living God (L 1b); shadowing forth the Unattainable (L 2); the inner and outer meaning of earth and sky and all that is in them, fit exactly (L 4); a change from the animal to the spiritual (L 5); reveal all the details of things—the world is surveyed (L 6); nirvana (L 7); reality (L 8); without and within are one (L 9); direct contact with an otherness (L 10); Union with God (L 11); penetrated the very heart of the universe (L 12); nirvana (L 13); experience of a genii-life (L 14); the Spirit of Life (L 16); all was contained in oneness—the climax of eternity (L 17a); everything rushed along in living beside him (L 17b); superhuman joy (L 18); the creative eros (L 19); then dawns the Invisible, the Unseen its truth reveals (L 21); the heavenly godhead (L 22); the very obvious, tangible presence of the Creator (L 23b); [things] had simply got into their proper proportions—knowledge of this reality which lies beyond where we normally are (L 24); become... part of the truth I sought (L 25); I saw nothing and everything (L 27).

Group R: the Kingdom of Heaven (R 1); Me [i.e. God, the Divine Voice] (R 2); the Infinite—Him who made me—God (R 3); —God—Deity—the Divine (R 4); the plenitude of God (R 5a); all Good—the All (R 5b); the divine—God (R 6); the Eternal Word—the Incomprehensible Light (R 7); the Infinite (R 8); paradise (R 9); God (R 10a); God (R 10b); God (R 11); my Beloved (R 12); it appeared to be Divine glory—such a God, such a glorious Divine Being (R 13); God (R 14); I knew...all the three worlds—I saw and knew the whole working essence (R 16); I saw that the universe is...a living Presence (R 17); heaven...and the new Jerusalem—the Lord—the eternal Almightiness (R 18); the brightness of the Lord (R 19); God—the Godhead (R 20); Divinity—God (R 21); Divine Will—God—Divine Nature (R 22);

Feelings of ineffability:

Group Q: indescribable (Q 25); unanalysable (Q 36); you can't describe it, because the more you describe, the further you get from it (Q 39); practically impossible to describe (Q 44).

Group L: unutterable (L 1b); unutterable (L 2); I have failed to describe it, because language cannot form the thought, because it is wordless and unimaginable and pictureless (L 4); to a large extent eludes verbal communication (L 7); mysterious—assured, in an unaccountable way (L 20); not easy to describe (L 23b); indescribable—beyond expression (L 24).

Group R: then did he see and hear that which no tongue can express (R 1); ineffable—impossible fully to describe the experience (R 3); indescribable (R 5a); unspeakable (R 5b); that passeth understanding (R 8); beyond what words can utter (R 9); cannot be more clearly described—a matter which cannot be understood (R 10b); ineffable (R 12); unspeakable (R 13); impossible to describe (R 17); unspeakable—inconceivable—surmounts the reach of the most strenuous and highflown expression—unlawful to be uttered amongst men (R 18); seen...not by any symbolic vision...not by enigmas in so far as the human mind can grasp it (R 19); ineffable—indescribable (R 22).

IV: Quasi-Physical Feelings

1. 'Up'-words and phrases:

Group Q: soaring up (Q 3); become airborne—exalted (Q 5); the soul leaving the body (Q 8); above yourself (Q 9); removed from consideration of earthly things (Q 14); being borne into heaven (Q 15); heightened awareness (Q 17); floating (Q 21); hovering (Q 22); the heart...leaps like a fountain (Q 24); something wells up—grows like a spring (Q 26); supreme—right out of the world (Q 28); associated with sensations of physical flying, like going to sleep or in dreams (Q 29); completely uplifted (Q 31); like a great climax which has built up (Q 34); weightlessness (Q 44); when living horizontally, you come into connexion with a kind of vertical eternity (Q 46); bubbling up (Q 49); I always think of it as a peak (Q 50); a floating sensation (Q 51); exaltation—exultation (Q 56); you feel immensely light, you feel as if you're not walking on the ground (Q 57).

Group L: elevated thoughts—a sense sublime (L 1a); in such high hour (L 1b); I felt...my spirit...bound—my thoughts erewhile, so low, now felt unutterable buoyancy...to bear them upward (L 2); my thought... went up—exaltation—exalted (L 3); gives wings to thought (L 6); hovering (L 7); floats out (L 9); flashed up (L 11); buoyant...she reaches a station scarcely lower than that...etc. (L 14); drew him from the depths (L 16); leapt up—leapt clear into the darkness above (L 17a); licked up—tore onwards and upwards—highest point of bliss (L 17b); superhuman joy (L 18); bounding—dancing—heightened sensibility (L 19); shaken or lifted out of—new and higher scale of power (L 20); earth was lost to me—its wings are almost free—dares the final bound (L 21); tore us up (L 23a); a new skyline (L 23b); rising up within—

something mounting up—bodily lightness—as if one's limbs had no weight—everything was going up to another level (L 24); carried beyond (L 25); the sky opened—on the hilltop...till the hillside crumbled (afterwards) (L 27).

Group R: he walked on air (R 1); raised from the earth almost as if the heavy body became light—intellect elevated (R 2); exultation—soul is being wafted upwards—highest faith—supreme experience—(R 3); surpasses all—the good I see—all...so far below—her mind had been uplifted—in such high manner (R 5b); above and beyond all things— above the light—thought, life and being are uplifted (R 7); come up in spirit—the state of Adam, which he was in before he fell (R 9); being raised above myself (R 11); carried away—my soul exults (R 12); lifted up—rose to such a pitch (R 14); wrapped in a flame-coloured cloud—exultation (R 17); sprang up far above my earthly centre—high-flown expression—tripping over the pleasant mountains of the heavenly land—exalted (R 18); lifted up—supreme (R 19); carried above itself—surpassing—sublime (R 20).

2. Inside and depth words and phrases:

Group Q: [ecstasy and inspiration] both start inside (Q 16); something wells up in one...grows like a spring (Q 26); full of force (Q 31); this thing has been seething inside you (Q 34); the cup is being filled (Q 35); happening within (Q 48); bubbling up inside (Q 49); butterflies in the tummy (Q 51); the centre of your being is [in the chest] (Q 54); like an enormous bubble swelling inside the chest (Q 55).

Group L: something far more deeply interfused—rolls through all things (L 1a); all melted into him (L 1b); my spirit...bound within me (L 2); inner consciousness—drank the beauty (L 3); seeing back... into one's own breast—universal perception which takes place in the thinker—I feel profoundly (L 4); the hieroglyphics upon the water seemed to flash through me—filled with an immense and pure emotion—a regular and growing central excitement, surrounded by an area of deep...satisfaction (L 5); a great feeling of peace pervade[d] me— penetrated the very heart of the universe (L 12); a still, deep, inborn delight (L 14); he felt in his heart...etc. (L 16); deeply felt vitality—near the root of our mystery (L 19); deeply excited—keener perceptions coming into action within us (L 20); 'rising up within oneself'— 'coming inwardly alive' (L 24); an exquisite pleasure had invaded my senses...filling me with a precious essence (L 26).

Group R: all fulfilled—in the deeps of his being (R 1); memory is full of nothing but Me—powers...immersed and inflamed in Me (R 2); deeper significance (R 6); as the air is penetrated...thus we receive...

etc. (R 7); I did lie down in the stream of life—flowing into me—full of the peace (R 8); goodness and power were penetrating me altogether (R 11); plunged into an ineffable peace—my mind is full of gladness (R 12); inwardly pleased and satisfied—inward joy, peace, and astonishing (R 13); deep and divine love—God who is so intimately present (R 14); his mind was suddenly filled (R 15); I knew and saw in myself (R 16); the fire was within myself (R 17); inspired with—confounded into the abyss—emptied into (R 18); engulfed in her God (R 21); immersed in the Divine Will—which pours Itself into them (R 22).

3. Light and/or Heat words and phrases:

Group Q: sudden flash of an idea (Q 31); I've often had it nearly, but not the real fire (Q 50).

Group L: whitening, flashing, ebbing light—his face...with its exceeding brightness, and the light of the great Angel Mind which look'd from out the starry glowing of his restless eyes—each failing sense, as with a momentary flash of light, grew...distinct and keen—thoughts... rapid as fire (L 2); seemed to flash through me (L 5); the grey sky of abstraction seems thrilled by flashes of lightning; the light is strong enough to reveal all the details of things (L 6); made me feel as if I had emerged into the light—I felt as one illumined—a vitalizing spark (L 10); flashed up lightning-wise—Illumination...like a sunbeam striking with iridescence—Enlightenment (L 11); delight glows in her young veins—all verdure and light—glory...sweeping and kindling (L 14); vivid as lightning the Spirit of Life illumined him (L 16); he and they struck with the same pulse of fire—in an immense tongue of flame (L 17b); the moonlight had ceased to be a physical thing and now represented a state of illumination in my own mind (L 19); wonderful enlightenments (L 20); my spirit's sky was full of flashes warm—[the vision] robed in fires of Hell, or bright with heavenly shine (L 21); ground shone with purple light (L 22); it flashed upon me—I heard, vividly, shockingly and as instantaneously as one might see a flash of lightning (L 24); a lucidity (L 25).

Group R: Shining Brightness—heavenly lightnings passed and repassed in the deeps of his being (R 1); these powers...inflamed in Me (R 2); an illumination (R 6); the Incomprehensible Light (R 7); my intellect is illuminated: my heart is afire (R 12); unspeakable glory...I do not mean any external brightness (R 13); God, who gave him great light (R 14); a new and strange illumination—spiritual light (R 15); a flame-coloured cloud—for an instant I thought of fire...the next, I knew that the fire was within myself—intellectual illumination (R 17); there is seen the brightness of the Lord (R 19); burning with ardent love—the brilliancy of the divine light shining on the mind—the Sun of Justice—glow of quiet love—the brightness of most lucid darkness (R 20); illumined and made shining in the Inaccessible Light (R 22).

4. Dark-words and phrases:

Group Q: None.

Group L: leapt clear into the darkness above (L 17a).

Group R: a secret Good...which I apprehend in great darkness—I see it in the dark...because it surpasses all good—this vision of God in darkness—beholding God in great darkness (R 5b); above the light, into the Divine Dark (R 7); the brightness of most lucid darkness (R 20).

5. Enlargement, Improvement words and phrases:

Group Q: transcend your normal limitations, capacity for experience, burst into a wider one (Q 5); tremendous sense of life worth living (Q 7); an enlarging (Q 16) intense feeling of physical well-being (Q 17); full of force, wonderful force (Q 31); like a great climax which has built up (Q 34); great emotion (Q 43); tremendous expansion, a different dimension altogether (Q 44); multiplication of possibilities (Q 45); awareness of being so alive (Q 46); great joyful gusts and a burst (Q 47); like the transfiguration (Q 48); great joy bubbling up inside (Q 49); intense physical well-being (Q 54); like an enormous bubble swelling inside the chest (Q 55); capable of anything and immensely fortunate (Q 57).

Group L: I felt my soul grow mighty—my mental eye grew large with such a vast circumference of thought—thoughts...expanding momently (L 2); largeness of feeling (L 3); an extraordinary physical exhilaration —filled with an immense and pure emotion—growing central excitement (L 5); expansion of consciousness (L 7); everywhere I feel the ideated pulsation of vitality, I mean energy and radiance, as if all served to enhance my own functioning (L 10); a stream that was continually swollen by tributaries of associated Experience (L 11); a great feeling of peace pervade[d] me—an immense happiness (L 12); the swift glory spreads out, sweeping and kindling, and multiplies its splendour (L 14); just as he was, so it seemed the vigorous, wintry stars were strong with life (L 17b); vast roarings of a superhuman joy (L 18); an immense exaltation—some deeply felt vitality—heightened sensibility (L 19); our faculties...enhanced—keener perceptions—more than our normal stock of penetrative sympathy—mysterious...empowerment (L 20); 'coming inwardly alive'—well-being—everything was becoming 'more'—my ability to see, my actual and physical eyesight, was greatly sharpened (L 24); filling me with a precious essence (L 26); strong (L 27).

Group R: the intellect, elevated—the bodily powers...inflamed—the abundance of the heart (R 2); one swelling harmony—the soul... almost bursting with its own emotion (R 3); through excess of marvelling the soul cried with a loud voice (R 5a); our thought, life and being are uplifted (R 7); the creative life was flowing into me (R 8); a great bodily comfort (R 10a); as if His goodness and power were penetrating me altogether (R 11); immense joyousness (R 17); as one inspired with a supernatural life (R 18); changed into...another power—there is given to man a divine strength and a divine power (R 22).

6. Pain and fear words and phrases:

Group Q: sometimes it's disturbing (Q 15); terrific constriction in throat and stomach (Q 24); a shock of joy (Q 25); halfway between pleasure and pain (Q 30); so intense in its joy as to be almost painful (Q 38); sadness mixed with joy (Q 52); unbearable knowledge (Q 63).

Group L: a presence that disturbs me (L 1a); great agony once; and always some terror (L 8); like a thundering pulse in my head it strikes, and now it beats over my soul, devours it (L 9); his strength went out of him and he shuddered—a sense of purification so sweet he shuddered again and again (L 16); his soul shuddered (L 17a); partly pleasure and partly awe—vividly, shockingly (L 24); a shudder ran through my whole body (L 26); a screaming fury (L 27).

Group R: so greatly did his body suffer in this short rapture that it seemed to him that none, even in dying, could suffer so greatly in so short a time (R 1); the throb of emotion was so violent (R 11); moves me with such sweetness and violence (R 12).

7. Liquidity words and phrases:

Group Q: the hard lines...are gone...one flows over them (Q 1); the heart...leaps like a fountain (Q 24); something wells up...grows like a spring (Q 26); this thing has been seething inside you (Q 34); the cup is being filled (Q 35); bubbling up inside (Q 49); an enormous bubble (Q 55).

Group L: all melted into him (L 1b); torrent (L 2); self-dissolving— 'oceanic feeling'—dissolution (L 7); the soul dissolves (L 9); stream (L 11); swept over me with a flow (L 12); that spring...bubbling in her heart (L 14); melt together (L 15); borne along in one flood (L 17b); the result was like that of opening a weir—swayed like water-weeds in the flood—flung us downstream (L 23a); a curtain of red blood appeared to fall before my eyes (L 23b); filling me with a precious essence (L 26); the inspiration flowed in Ray like blood (L 27).

Group R: the bodily powers...immersed...in Me (R 2);I did lie down in the stream of life and let it flow over me—the creative life was flowing into me (R 8); emptied into the fountain and the ocean of divine fullness (R 18); like a living fountain, flowing with streams of eternal sweetness (R 20); the soul lets herself pass or flow into What she loves—gently glides, as a fluid and liquid thing—that sacred out-flowing and holy liquefaction—mingled with and steeped in Him—outflowing of a soul into her God (R 21); the Divine Being, whereinto they pour themselves, and which pours Itself into them (R 22).

8. Feelings of peace; calm:

Group Q: essentially a moment of complete peace (Q 1); a sense of peace (Q 5); standstill feeling (Q 30); complete calm (Q 47); wonderful feeling of peace (Q 51).

Group L: still communion (L 1b); deep, tranquil and joyful satisfaction (L 5); infinite tranquillity and peace—serene—relaxed quietude (L 7); a great feeling of peace (L 12); a still, deep, inborn delight (L 14); solemn passivity (L 15); the neutrality, the perfect, swooning con-summation (L 17a); everything was still—this wonderful stillness (L 17b); a hush of peace, a soundless calm (L 21); at peace with the world (L 24); tranquil ecstasy (L 25).

Group R: sensations of silence and of rest (R 1); the perfect stillness of the night was thrilled by a more solemn silence (R 3); tranquil—an unbreakable calm (R 4); idleness of spirit (R 7); peace (R 8); peace—repose—the faculties...at rest would like always to remain still—sweet peace (R 10a); imagination is then wholly at rest (R 10b); peace—desiring nought, but to rest in this (R 12); inward...peace (R 13); pure love and peace—peace inconceivable (R 18); quiet love (R 20).

V: INTENSITY AND WITHDRAWAL

1. Intensity words and phrases:

Group Q: burst into...suddenly (Q 5); suddenly clicked (Q 6); tremendous (Q 7); intense feeling (Q 17); suddenly (Q 20); terrific constriction—sudden tremendous expansion (Q 24); intense beauty —a shock of joy (Q 25); something wells up...grows like a spring (Q 26); suddenly overwhelms without expectation (Q 30); full of force (Q 31); like a great climax which has built up—this thing has been seething inside you and suddenly it comes out (Q 34); extreme unanalysable excitement—most intense (Q 36); an emotion so intense in its joy as to be almost painful (Q 38); it's coming—tremendous expansion, a different dimension altogether (Q 44); intense perception (Q 45); suddenly (Q 46); great joyful gusts and a burst, a sudden feeling of complete calm (Q 47); great joy bubbling up inside (Q 49); I always think of it as a peak...always followed by the longest falls I've ever known in emotion (Q 50); a mixture of physical attack and cerebral confusion (Q 52); an electric sensation in the chest, spreading over your whole body—intense physical well-being (Q 54); like an enormous bubble swelling inside the chest, bursting into a soundless shout (Q 55); sudden—the force of beauty (Q 56); feelings of relief—the liberation of relief—sudden moments (Q 57); [inspiration said to be 'less intense'] (Q 58); it sort of overwhelms you, it hits you and it's all-powerful (Q 60); you suddenly discover...etc. (Q 61).

Group L: I felt my soul grow mighty, and my spirit with supernatural excitation bound—thrilling thoughts...expanding momently—the issue of strong impulse, hurried through the riv'n racked brain (L 2); a regular and growing central excitement (L 5); like a thundering pulse in my head it strikes (L 9); ideated pulsation of vitality (L 10); it flashed up (L 11); all of a sudden—swept over me with a flow (L 12); the swift glory spreads out, sweeping and kindling (L 14); a revelation mounting obscurely to his brain—vivid as lightning (L 16); leapt up in a manifold, clustered desire (L 17a); the emotion was strong enough to carry...everything...in a great sweep—pulse of fire—licked up in an immense tongue of flame, which tore onwards and upwards (L 17b); the gusts of splendour—amid vast roarings of a superhuman joy, he led his Fifth Symphony to its conclusion (L 18); one of the most intense sensuous and emotional experiences of my life—happy excitement of the senses (L 19); deeply excited (L 20); dares the final bound (L 21); tore us up by the roots and flung us down-stream (L 23a); the world rocked around me—this earthquake (L 23b); something mounting up —everything was becoming 'more'—intensity (L 24); the extraordinary changes that were taking place—an exquisite pleasure had invaded my senses...and at once...etc.—this all-powerful joy (L 26); the inspiration flowed in Ray like blood—rushing wind—screaming fury (L 27).

Group R: of a sudden his soul was rapt (R 1); the bodily powers... inflamed (R 2); a rushing together—one swelling harmony—almost bursting (R 3); through excess of marvelling, the soul cried with a loud voice (R 5a); suddenly rapt (R 5b); all at once...the throb of emotion was so violent (R 11); violence—suddenly—my heart is afire—my soul strives (R 12); at once... rose to such a pitch (R 14); suddenly (R 15); all at once (R 17); quickening comfort—sprang up (R 18); rapt (R 19); burning with ardent love (R 20).

2. Withdrawal words and phrases:

Group Q: a sort of merging into the experience—the hard lines...are gone...one flows over them (Q 1); no release of tension but no tension came into it (Q 5).

Group L: all melted into him (L 1b); relaxed quietude and self-dissolving stillness—Nirvana (L 7); lulling to sleep (L 9); lost myself in something like nirvana (L 13); forgetting everything else in a half-speculative, half-involuntary identification of himself with the objects he was looking at (L 15); a hush of peace, a soundless calm descends; the struggle of distress and fierce impatience ends; mute music soothes my breast (L 21).

Group R: melts away into (R 20); she does not spring out of herself by a sudden leap...but gently glides, as a fluid and liquid thing, into the Divinity (R 21).

APPENDIX C

EXAMPLES OF ANALYSES

Here I present and draw attention to points of interest in a sample half-dozen of the questionnaire texts, which I have selected so as to display not similarities—which will soon become apparent—but something of the range and divergencies shown by different people's answers.

I will also show how the material in the six examples was categorized. When dealing with material as inexact as language it is not to be expected that the categorization will seem to everyone to be in all particulars cogent and justified. I can only insist that so long as phrases are consistently entered, the statistical relation between the three groups remains constant.

EXAMPLE I

Q 1 F: 'I'

Question 1: Do you know a sensation of transcendent ecstasy?
Answer: Yes.

Question 2: How would you describe it?
Answer: In a curious way, a sort of merging into the experience—the hard lines round one's individuality are gone, one flows over them—essentially a *moment* of complete peace—the ultimate trademark is a feeling that this does touch reality—allied to this thing of completeness, wholeness, other forms of so-called reality are not wholly real, only particles of reality.

Question 3: What has induced it in you?
Answer: Say, at dusk, when the light and the smell and the scene is just right. Sex. *Moments* I can't define, like sitting outside a château in France, writing to someone I loved very much—a completeness.

Question 4: How many times have you felt it—in units, tens, hundreds?
Answer: Units.

Question 5: What is your religion or faith?
Answer: Believe in God in the broadest sense.

Question 6: Do you know a feeling of creative inspiration?

Answer: Doubtful—I think yes.

Question 7: How would you describe it?

Answer: Not in essentials different from ecstasy—some slight approach to making a thing whole, a temporary *moment* of completeness.

Question 8: Does it seem to you to have anything in common with the ecstasy you described above?

Answer: Yes, certainly.

Points of interest

1. Notice that references to duration have been italicized.

2. This shows that comparatively rare type of experience, the natural withdrawal ecstasy; see p. 47.

3. Three different triggers are instanced, the third, which is compound, being classified under *Nature, Recollection, Introspection, Sexual Love,* and *Miscellaneous.*

4. These answers show an extremely common feature of ecstatic descriptions, the use of *id quo nihil majus cogitari possit*—that than which nothing greater can be conceived—words and phrases; here, the peace is *complete*, the trademark *ultimate*, the thing is of *wholeness, completeness* contrasted with what is not *wholly* real but only particles of reality. I call these totality words and phrases; see pp. 127-8.

5. Inspiration is described as similar to but less than ecstasy.

Analysis

Q 1's answers were categorized as follows:

SECTION I: *Triggers*

1. *Nature:* at dusk, when the light and the smell and the scene is just right; sitting outside (a château).

2. *Sexual love:* sex; writing to someone I loved very much.

9. Recollection, introspection: writing to someone I loved very much.

11. *Miscellaneous:* a château in France.

SECTION II: *Negative:* Feelings of loss of

1. *Difference:* the hard lines round one's individuality are gone.

9. *Self:* the hard lines round one's individuality are gone.

SECTION III: *Positive:* Feelings of gain of

1. *Unity:* allied to this thing of wholeness, completeness, other forms of so-called reality are not wholly real, only particles of reality.

10. *Contact:* merging into the experience—touch reality.

11. *(b) Knowledge by enhanced capacity, new knowledge:* some slight approach to making a thing whole.
    (c) Knowledge by identification: this does touch reality.

SECTION IV: *Quasi-physical feelings*

7. *Liquidity:* the hard lines are gone...one flows over them.

8. *Peace, calm:* essentially *a moment* of complete peace.

SECTION V: *Intensity, withdrawal*

2. *Withdrawal:* a sort of merging into the experience—the hard lines are gone, one flows over them.

EXAMPLE 2

Q 17 M: 'I'

Question 1: Do you know a sensation of transcendent ecstasy?
Answer: Yes.

Question 2: How would you describe it?
Answer: Feeling of liberation from ordinary sense-impressions, but heightened awareness and sense of union with external reality—intense feeling of physical well-being.

Question 3: What has induced it in you?
Answer: Nature—mountains—music, Beethoven's Fifth—sex.

Question 4: How many times have you felt it—in units, tens, hundreds?
Answer: About ten.

Question 5: What is your religion or faith?
Answer: None.

Question 6: Do you know a feeling of creative inspiration?
Answer: Yes.

Question 7: How would you describe it?
Answer: Sudden excited stream of understanding.

Question 8: Does it seem to you to have anything in common with the ecstasy you described above?
Answer: Yes, but quite different and I don't know what the connexion is.

Points of interest

1. The triggers given fall under three headings. *Nature, Sexual Love, and Art.*

2. Though inspiration is believed to be related to ecstasy, no similarities are adduced; therefore in the analysis the description of inspiration is ignored.

3. Like Q 1 and many other people, Q 17 identified as 'reality' what he believed he had encountered in his experience. But in this case he commented afterwards that he thought his phrase 'sense of union with external reality' was meaningless, but still the only adequate expression he could find for what he had felt.

Analysis

Q 17's answers were classified as follows:

SECTION I: *Triggers*

1. *Nature:* nature—mountains.

2. *Sex:* sex.

6. *Art:* music, Beethoven's Fifth.

SECTION II: *Negative:* Feelings of loss of

10. *Words, images:* liberation from ordinary sense-impressions (but heightened awareness)

SECTION III: *Positive:* Feelings of gain of

1. *Unity:* sense of union with external reality.

4. *Release:* liberation.

10. *Contact:* union with external reality.

11. *(b) Mystical knowledge:* (liberation from ordinary sense-impressions) but heightened awareness.
   (c) Knowledge by identification: union with external reality.

SECTION IV: *Quasi-physical feelings*

1. *Up-words and phrases:* heightened awareness.

5. *Enlargement, improvement:* intense feeling of physical well-being.

SECTION V: *Intensity, withdrawal*

1. *Intensity:* intense feeling.

473

Example 3

Q 26 F: 'C'

Question 1: Do you know a sensation of transcendent ecstasy?
Answer: Yes.

Question 2: How would you describe it?
Answer: Double realization of perfection with life, but life isn't perfect, so it's a contradiction.

Question 3: What has induced it in you?
Answer: Contemplation of art—Chartres cathedral—the Bodhisatta in the British Museum—being alone in a very lonely place—the beginning of King's College Chapel carols with 'Once in royal David's city'.

Question 4: How many times have you felt it—in units, tens, hundreds?
Answer: Something under a hundred times, say between fifty and a hundred, but really intensely, real spiritual ecstasy, say twenty to thirty times.

Question 5: What is your religion or faith?
Answer: Christian.

Question 6: Do you know a feeling of creative inspiration?
Answer: Yes.

Question 7: How would you describe it?
Answer: Something wells up in one, prompted apparently by nothing, grows like a spring.

Question 8: Does it seem to you to have anything in common with the ecstasy you described above?
Answer: Yes, with inspiration one can have ecstasy.

Three years later Q 26 said to me: Does it seem to you possible that it could be the same feeling, whether it's being in love or going downhill on skis or creating a piece of sculpture? I think it is. Or swimming. You feel you're literally in another world, outside everything. When it's greatest, you're entirely unaware, you realize it only when you come back; if you're conscious of the state when you're in it, it's not so terrific. But with the great ones, you don't realize till you come back that you were in heaven.

Points of interest

1. Triggers fall into four categories, *Nature*, *Art*, *Religion*, and *Creative Work*. The later comment adds *Exercise* and *Sexual Love*. It also considerably enlarges the original description of ecstasy. I have not,

however, thought it proper to include it in the analysis, though I have drawn on it as a source of information.

2. In the later comment Q 26 usefully compares what she regards as more and less intense experiences; see Ch. VIII.

3. Although she is a Christian, no religious gloss is placed on the experience.

4. This example shows how a very few phrases can fairly be entered under several different headings.

Analysis

Q 26's answers were classified as follows:

SECTION I: *Triggers*

1. *Nature:* being alone in a very lonely place.

5. *Religion:* Chartres cathedral—the Bodhisatta in the British Museum —the beginning of King's College Chapel carols with 'Once in royal David's city'.

6. *Creative work:* with inspiration one can have ecstasy.

SECTION III: *Positive:* Feelings of gain of

5. *A new life, another world:* double realization of perfection with life.

8. *Salvation, perfection:* perfection with life.

11. *(c) Knowledge by identification:* realization of perfection with life.

SECTION IV: *Quasi-physical feelings*

1. *Up-words and phrases:* something wells up—grows like a spring.

2. *Inside-words and phrases:* something wells up in one—grows like a spring.

7. *Liquidity:* something wells up—grows like a spring.

SECTION V: *Intensity, withdrawal*

1. *Intensity:* something wells up—grows like a spring.

EXAMPLE 4

Q 28 F: 'O'

Question 1: Do you know a sensation of transcendent ecstasy?
Answer: Yes.

Question 2: How would you describe it?
Answer: A feeling of happiness that takes you right out of the world, so supreme that you forget everything.

Question 3: What has induced it in you?
Answer: The first sight of my first baby.

Question 4: How many times have you felt it—in units, tens, hundreds?
Answer: A few times.

Question 5: What is your religion or faith?
Answer: Jewish—love thy neighbour as thyself—I believe in God.

Question 6: Do you know a feeling of creative inspiration?
Answer: I think so.

Question 7: How would you describe it?
Answer: When something I've planned comes off right.

Question 8: Does it seem to you to have anything in common with the ecstasy you described above?
Answer: No, just satisfaction.

Points of interest

1. The people who give childbirth as a trigger do not assimilate to ecstasy the normal pleasure at the birth of a baby, any more than the people who give sex assimilate to ecstasy the pleasures of sexual orgasm. Q 28 is typical in specifying that it was at the birth of only one out of two or more children that she enjoyed ecstasy; see p. 140–1.

2. Like Q 28, most of the people I have classified as 'O' do not believe that ecstasy and inspiration have anything to do with each other, whereas about three-quarters of the creative and about half of the intellectuals believe that the two are connected; see p. 202.

3. The phrase 'takes you right out of the world' is a good example of a phrase that may be literally or figuratively intended. 'Out of this world' is a contemporary cliché of praise, but descriptions of ecstasy characteristically include obviously literally intended phrases about being out of this world and in heaven; compare in the last example, 'You feel you're literally in another world—entirely unaware—in heaven' and, for a phrase that superficially seems no more than a meaningless cliché, 'so happy that you don't know what you're doing' (Q 32).

4. Even in this brief description totality words and phrases are used—'supreme—right out of the world'.

Analysis

Q 28's answers were classified as follows:

SECTION I: *Triggers*

3. *Childbirth:* the first sight of my first baby.

SECTION II: *Negative: Feelings of loss of*

3. *Place:* takes you right out of the world.

5. *Worldliness:* takes you right out of the world.

11. *Sense:* you forget everything.

SECTION III: *Positive: Feelings of gain of*

7. *Joy:* happiness...so supreme.

SECTION IV: *Quasi-physical feelings.*

1. *Up-words and phrases:* supreme—right out of the world.

EXAMPLE 5

Q 46 M: 'C'

Question 1: Do you know a sensation of transcendent ecstasy?

Answer: Not like the religious ecstatics, but if you don't mean that, yes.

Question 2: How would you describe it?

Answer: Awareness of being so alive you feel in any given *moment* you've almost touched the fringe of eternity which seems to come into life at that *moment*—when living horizontally, you come into connexion with a kind of vertical eternity, something that can't alter—we are mostly kept from transcendent living by sin.

Question 3: What has induced it in you?

Answer: By a river in summer—suddenly able to express something in permanent form—Gloucester cathedral—in Italy coming into contact for the first time with Italian primitive art—music, Bach and Mozart—'War and Peace', 'The Brothers Karamazov', Shakespeare.

Question 4: How many times have you felt it—in units, tens, hundreds?

Answer: Endlessly, in a sense.

Question 5: What is your religion or faith?

Answer: Protestant—Non-Conformist Christian.

Question 6: Do you know a feeling of creative inspiration?

Answer: Yes.

Question 7: How would you describe it?

Answer: An inward power that surges to the surface at odd times.

Question 8: Does it seem to you to have anything in common with the ecstasy you described above?

Answer: Yes.

Points of interest

1. This man makes the very usual assumption that the ecstasies of religious mystics differ from his own experience, but does not say wherein he believes them to differ.

2. His reference to religious mystics makes it seem possible that he has read of religious experiences; but his answers seem uninfluenced by this, and notably his answers to question 3.

3. He is the only person in Group Q who introduces the concept of sin.

4. His answer to question 4 is unusual; see p. 100 n.

Analysis

SECTION I: *Triggers*

1. *Nature:* by a river in summer.

4. *Religion:* Gloucester cathedral.

6. *Art:* coming into contact for the first time with Italian primitive art —music, Bach and Mozart—'War and Peace', 'The Brothers Kara-mazov', Shakespeare.

8. *Creative work:* suddenly able to express something in permanent form.

SECTION II: *Negative:* Loss of feelings of

8. *Sin:* we are mostly kept from transcendent living by sin.

SECTION III: *Positive:* Gain of feelings of

2. *Eternity:* you feel in any given moment you've almost touched the fringe of eternity which seems to come into life at that moment —when living horizontally, you come into connexion with a kind of vertical eternity, something that can't alter.

5. *A new life, another world:* almost touched the fringe of eternity which seems to come into life at that moment.

10. *Contact:* almost touched the fringe of eternity.

11. *(c) Knowledge by identification:* almost touched the fringe of eternity.

SECTION IV: *Quasi-physical feelings*

1. *Up-words and phrases:* when living horizontally, you come into con-nexion with a kind of vertical eternity.

5. *Enlargement, improvement:* awareness of being so alive.

478

SECTION V: *Intensity, withdrawal*

1. *Intensity:* suddenly.

EXAMPLE 6

Q 61 M: 'I'

Question 1: Do you know a sensation of transcendent ecstasy?
Answer: Yes.

Question 2: How would you describe it?
Answer: When you suddenly discover a faculty working with effortless efficiency which enables you to hold in the forefront of conscious feeling both knowledge of the smallest bacteria in the field, how the blade of grass works, and the universe in the same detail—all you know about nature, the whole thing, you can think about them all simultaneously and not in parts, that knowledge is almost limitless—one's aware objectively of what one's doing but not aware of anything else, not aware of yesterday or tomorrow, just of *the moment*, doing this now.

Question 3: What has induced it in you?
Answer: Introspection—on a troopship in Naples, and Vesuvius had a red light glowing and in only twelve hours one would be in battle for the first time—in [a foreign country] in the evening in autumn, the fields were flooded, the sun low, sloshing through the fields, and the grass and water had a peculiar colour—sometimes here [in a London office] because the sky is blue and the building is white, you look at it and feel that life is worthwhile, the same kind of feeling, but much less—when I was about eighteen or nineteen [we] drove to a fantastic temple outside High Wycombe, I used to write poetry, I wrote 'Evening sunlight on a blade of grass', if I say that to myself, I can recapture it.

Question 4: How many times have you felt it—in units, tens, hundreds?
Answer: Units.

Question 5: What is your religion or faith?
Answer: I can't put it in a word—I believe in God.

Question 6: Do you know a feeling of creative inspiration?
Answer: Yes.

Question 7: How would you describe it?
Answer: Sense of certainty—things couldn't be otherwise than as they present themselves to you in that *instant*.

Question 8: Does it seem to you to have anything in common with the ecstasy you described above?
Answer: Yes.

Points of Interest

1. Though this is one of the longest texts in Group Q it requires comparatively few entries. Long accounts do not necessarily give more information than short ones, a point that will be very noticeable when we come to Groups L and R.
2. 'Introspection' is actually named as a trigger. Q 61 can also induce ecstasy by recollection. The unusual circumstances of the wartime ecstasy are closely matched by an experience of Siegfried Sassoon; see pp. 203–4n.
3. This man is extremely aware of light as a factor in triggers. Light in connexion with triggers is mentioned by other people in Group Q and notably by Q 30 who gives 'sudden appearance of light' as a trigger on its own. As we shall see, some qualities of triggers seem to have extremely close correspondences with some felt features of the experience; see Ch. XXI. And since the principal difference between Group Q and the other two groups is that people in Group Q make fewer references to light as a felt feature of the experience, it is worth noticing that some of them are aware of it as a feature of triggers.
4. He believes he has gained knowledge of a total kind about the physical world. This is fairly common; see p. 119.

Analysis

SECTION I: *Triggers.*

1. *Nature:* Vesuvius had a red light glowing—in the evening in autumn, the fields were flooded, the sun low...and the grass and water had a peculiar colour—because the sky is blue.
4. *Exercise:* sloshing through the fields.
9. *Recollection, introspection:* introspection—I can recapture it.
11. *Miscellaneous:* on a troopship in Naples...and in only twelve hours one would be in battle for the first time.

SECTION II. *Negative:* Feelings of loss of
2. *Time:* not aware of yesterday or tomorrow, just of the moment.

SECTION III: *Positive:* Feelings of gain of
1. *Unity:* all you know about nature, the whole thing, you can think about them all simultaneously and not in parts.

480

7. *Joy:* life is worthwhile.

11. *(b) Knowledge by enhanced mental capacity, new knowledge:* a faculty working with effortless efficiency which enables you to hold in the forefront of conscious feeling both knowledge of the smallest bacteria in the field, how the grass works and the universe in the same detail—all you know about nature, the whole thing, you can think about them all simultaneously and not in parts, that knowledge is almost limitless.

SECTION V: *Intensity, withdrawal*

1. *Intensity:* you suddenly discover.

All texts in the questionnaire group in which an affirmative answer was given to the first question were similarly analysed; there were 60 of these. The number of entries under each heading in Sections II–V were then expressed as a percentage of the total number of entries in Sections II–V. The actual statements by each person under each heading will be found in the content analyses in Appendix B.

The 30 texts in the literary group and the 24 texts in the religious group were analysed in the same way, the entries under each heading in Sections II–V being similarly expressed as a percentage of the total number of entries in Sections II–V. Again, the statements justifying each entry can be found in the content analyses in Appendix B.

APPENDIX D

TABLE 1

For each group the total number of entries in Sections II–V was counted, and then the total number of entries under each heading was expressed as a percentage of this total.

	Group Q No.	Group Q %	Group L No.	Group L %	Group R No.	Group R %	Mean %
SECTION II: Loss of							
1. Difference	1	0·3	3	0·8	2	0·6	0·6
2. Time	6	2·1	6	1·6	2	0·6	1·4
3. Place	5	1·7	4	1·1	5	1·6	1·4
4. Limitation	1	0·3	1	0·3	1	0·3	0·3
5. Worldliness	5	1·7	12	3·2	10	3·2	2·8
6. Desire	—	—	7	1·9	6	1·9	1·3
7. Sorrow	2	0·7	2	0·5	3	1·0	0·7
8. Sin	1	0·3	5	1·3	3	1·0	0·9
9. Self	11	3·8	16	4·2	13	4·2	4·1
10. Words/images	10	3·4	18	4·8	13	4·2	4·2
11. Sense	8	2·8	13	3·4	13	4·2	3·5
TOTALS	50	17·1	87	23·1	71	22·8	21·2
SECTION III: Gain of							
1. Unity	14	4·8	15	4·0	8	2·5	3·8
2. Eternity	5	1·7	8	2·1	10	3·2	2·3
3. Ideal place/heaven	1	0·3	4	1·1	6	1·9	1·1
4. Release	6	2·1	7	1·8	5	1·6	1·8
5. New life/world	18	6·2	18	4·8	16	5·1	5·3
6. Satisfaction	7	2·4	3	0·8	7	2·2	1·7
7. Joy	20	6·9	20	5·3	14	4·5	5·5
8. Salvation/perfection	5	1·7	7	1·8	6	1·9	1·8
9. Glory	2	0·7	7	1·8	3	1·0	1·2
10. Contact	13	4·5	17	4·5	18	5·7	4·9
11. *a.* Mystical knowledge	9	3·1	16	4·2	15	4·8	4·1
b. New knowledge	11	3·8	16	4·2	10	3·2	3·8
c. Identification	28	9·6	25	6·6	23	7·3	7·7
TOTALS	139	47·8	163	43·0	141	44·9	45·0
Ineffability	4	1·4	7	1·8	13	4·2	2·4

TABLE 1—contd.

	Group Q No.	%	Group L No.	%	Group R No.	%	Mean %
SECTION IV: Quasi-physical							
1. Up	22	7·6	21	5·6	13	4·2	5·7
2. Inside	10	3·4	13	3·4	15	4·8	3·9
3. Light/fire	2	0·7	14	3·7	12	3·8	2·9
4. Dark	—	—	1	0·3	3	1·0	0·4
5. Enlargement/improvement	16	5·5	15	4·0	10	3·2	4·2
6. Pain	7	2·4	8	2·1	3	1·0	1·8
7. Liquidity	7	2·4	13	3·4	6	1·9	2·6
8. Peace/calm	5	1·7	11	2·9	11	3·5	2·8
TOTALS	69	23·7	96	25·4	73	23·4	24·3
SECTION V: Intensity and Withdrawal							
1. Intensity	27	9·3	19	5·0	13	4·2	6·0
2. Withdrawal	2	0·7	6	1·6	2	0·6	1·0
TOTALS	29	10·0	25	6·6	15	4·8	7·0
TOTALS							
SECTION II	50	17·1	87	23·1	71	22·8	21·2
SECTION III	139	47·8	163	43·0	141	44·9	45·0
Ineffability	4	1·4	7	1·8	13	4·2	2·4
SECTION IV	69	23·7	96	25·4	73	23·4	24·3
SECTION V	29	10·0	25	6·6	15	4·8	7·0
TOTALS	291	100·0	378	99·9	313	100·1	99·9

Totals do not add to 100 precisely because of rounding.

In Group Q each person averaged 4·8 entries in Sections II–V.
In Group L each person averaged 12·6 entries in Sections II–V.
In Group R each person averaged 13·0 entries in Sections II–V.

THE SIMPLIFIED ANALYSES

The aim was to present the results of the analyses in a simpler form than that of Table 1 so as to enable comparisons more easily to be made.

SECTIONS II & III: Feelings of gain and loss

The headings, loss of feelings of difference, of time, of place; and gain of feelings of unity, eternity, heaven, have each been condensed in a single group (A in Section II, A in Section III).

What these seem to me to have in common is that they are perceived as external to the ecstatic and that what is normally regarded as limited is now, in ecstasy, regarded as limitless, whether in a negative or in a positive sense. The doubtful entry here is *heaven* since mention of heaven seems often to imply a value-judgement rather than a statement about place; but since heaven *is* thought of as a place and this must be implicit even when a value-judgement is intended, the decision can be justified. To say one is in heaven implies happiness because one is in the ideal place for ever.

Loss of feelings of limitation and gain of feelings of release remain as separate headings (II.B and III.B).

Loss of feelings of worldliness, desire, sorrow, sin; gain of feelings of a new life/another world, satisfaction, salvation/perfection, joy, glory, each become single headings (II.C and III.C).

These seem to be linked statements. The ecstatic is joyful because satisfied and saved, the new life or world is satisfactory because perfect and glorious, and in it the ecstatic is freed from sorrow and sin; he has lost the clogs that usually prevent his enjoying this condition. If sin may be defined, as it often is, as that which keeps us from God (cp. Q 46's 'We are mostly kept from transcendent living by sin'), then in this sense, because keeping us from ecstasy, worldliness, desire, and sorrow may all be seen as aspects of sin and so, by ecstatics, they often are. 'It appeared to be Divine glory' said R 13, and this is the impression that these gains, taken together, do convey.

Loss of feelings of self, and gain of feelings of contact are retained as separate headings (II.D and III.D).

Loss of words/images and of sense; gain of mystical knowledge and of new knowledge are each grouped together (II.E and III.E). Gain of knowledge by identification is kept apart (III.F). This is because I believe and hope to show that claims of mystical and of new knowledge are of importance to an assessment of the value of these experiences, while claims to knowledge by identification are of little or no value for this purpose.

Ineffability now stands alone as an unnumbered heading. As explained in the Notes (p. 31), it is demonstrably untrue to say that these experiences are ineffable, no matter how ineffable they may feel. More, *ineffable* seems often to be used, and noticeably by the religious group, as an identifying adjective—e.g. ineffable peace, ineffable glory—in such a way that its meaning appears to be *total* or *ideal* or *ultimate*, and its original meaning of *unable of its nature to be described* to be relevant only because *total* or *ideal* or *ultimate* anything is meaningless. But where the word is used, we can generally assume that the speaker is using it as a signpost to indicate that it is an experience of this kind that he has in mind.

SECTION IV, quasi-physical feelings, and SECTION V, intensity and withdrawal, remain as in Table 1.

TABLE 2

Simplified entries in Sections II–V of the analyses, expressed as percentages of the total number of entries in each group.

	Group Q No.	%	Group L No.	%	Group R No.	%	Mean %
SECTION II: Negative							
Loss of:							
A. Difference, time, place	12	4·1	13	3·5	9	2·8	3·4
B. Limitation	1	0·3	1	0·3	1	0·3	0·3
C. Worldliness, desire, sorrow, sin	8	2·7	26	6·9	22	7·1	5·7
D. Self	11	3·8	16	4·2	13	4·2	4·1
E. Words/images, sense	18	6·2	31	8·2	26	8·4	7·7
TOTALS	50	17·1	87	23·1	71	22·8	21·2
SECTION III: Positive							
Gain of:							
A. Unity, eternity, heaven	20	6·8	27	7·2	24	7·6	7·2
B. Release	6	2·1	7	1·8	5	1·6	1·8
C. New world/life, satisfaction, joy, salvation, glory	52	17·9	55	14·5	46	14·7	15·5
D. Contact	13	4·5	17	4·5	18	5·7	4·9
E. Knowledge, mystical, new	20	6·9	32	8·4	25	8·0	7·9
F. Knowledge, by identification	28	9·6	25	6·6	23	7·3	7·7
TOTALS	139	47·8	163	43·0	141	44·9	45·0
Ineffability	4	1·4	7	1·8	13	4·2	2·4
SECTION IV: Quasi-physical feelings							
1. Up	22	7·6	21	5·6	13	4·2	5·7
2. Inside/depth	10	3·4	13	3·4	15	4·8	3·9
3. Light/fire	2	0·7	14	3·7	12	3·8	2·9
4. Dark	—	—	1	0·3	3	1·0	0·4
5. Enlargement, improvement	16	5·5	15	4·0	10	3·2	4·2
6. Pain	7	2·4	8	2·1	3	1·0	1·8
7. Liquidity	7	2·4	13	3·4	6	1·9	2·6
8. Peace, calm	5	1·7	11	2·9	11	3·5	2·8
TOTALS	69	23·7	96	25·4	73	23·4	24·3
SECTION V:							
1. Intensity	27	9·3	19	5·0	13	4·2	6·0
2. Withdrawal	2	0·7	6	1·6	2	0·6	1·0
TOTALS	29	10·0	25	6·6	15	4·8	7·0

TABLE 2—*contd.*

	Group Q No.	%	Group L No.	%	Group R No.	%	Mean %
TOTALS							
SECTION II	50	17·1	87	23·1	71	22·8	21·2
SECTION III	139	47·8	163	43·0	141	44·9	45·0
Ineffability	4	1·4	7	1·8	13	4·2	2·4
SECTION IV	69	23·7	96	25·4	73	23·4	24·3
SECTION V	29	10·0	25	6·6	15	4·8	7·0
TOTALS	291	100·0	378	99·9	313	100·1	99·9

Items do not add to 100 precisely because of rounding.

TABLE 3

Frequency of trigger mentions

In Group Q several people mentioned several triggers.

In Group L only one set of preceding circumstances was given for each person but several of these were entered as compound triggers.

In Group R only one set of preceding circumstances was given and that in only 11 out of 24 cases, but some of these were compound triggers.

Group J, Nos. 1–5 (see Appendix J) is added, in order to compare with Group Q another group of similar contemporary people, each naming several triggers.

	Group Q No.	%	Group L No.	%	Group R No.	%	Group J No.	%
1. Nature	27	18·2	16	34·0	5	33·3	4	25·0
2. Sexual love	25	16·9	1	2·1	—	—	3	18·8
3. Childbirth	5	3·4	—	—	—	—	1	6·2
4. Exercise, movement	8	5·4	3	6·4	3	20·0	—	—
5. Religion	14	9·5	4	8·5	3	20·0	1	6·2
6. Art	31	20·9	9	19·1	—	—	2	12·5
7. *a.* Scientific knowledge	5	3·4	2	4·3	—	—	—	—
b. Poetic knowledge	2	1·4	3	6·4	—	—	—	—
8. Creative work	7	4·7	1	2·1	—	—	—	—
9. Recollection, introspection	5	3·4	3	6·4	1	6·7	1	6·2
10. 'Beauty'	6	4·0	2	4·3	—	—	3	18·8
11. Miscellaneous	13	8·8	3	6·4	3	20·0	1	6·2
TOTALS	148	100·0	47	100·0	15	100·0	16	99·9

Totals do not add to 100 precisely because of rounding.

TABLE 4a

Percentages of mentions under the different headings in the order of frequency in each group and in the mean.

Group Q		Group L		Group R		Mean	
	%		%		%		%
III C	17·9	III C	14·5	III C	14·7	III C	15·5
III F	9·6	III E	8·4	II E	8·4	III E	7·9
IV 1	7·6	II E	8·2	III E	8·0	II E	7·7
III E	6·9	III A	7·2	III A	7·6	III F	7·7
III A	6·8	II C	6·9	III F	7·3	III A	7·2
II E	6·2	III F	6·6	II C	7·1	II C	5·7
IV 5	5·5	IV 1	5·6	III D	5·7	IV 1	5·7
III D	4·5	III D	4·5	IV 2	4·8	III D	4·9
II A	4·1	II D	4·2	II D	4·2	IV 5	4·2
II D	3·8	IV 5	4·0	IV 1	4·2	II D	4·1
IV 2	3·4	IV 3	3·7	Ineff.	4·2	IV 2	3·9
II C	2·7	II A	3·5	IV 3	3·8	II A	3·4
IV 6	2·4	IV 2	3·4	IV 8	3·5	IV 3	2·9
IV 7	2·4	IV 7	3·4	IV 5	3·2	IV 8	2·8
III B	2·1	IV 8	2·9	II A	2·8	IV 7	2·6
IV 8	1·7	IV 6	2·1	IV 7	1·9	Ineff.	2·5
Ineff.	1·4	III B	1·8	III B	1·6	III B	1·8
IV 3	0·7	Ineff.	1·8	IV 4	1·0	IV 6	1·8
II B	0·3	II B	0·3	IV 6	1·0	IV 4	0·4
IV 4	—	IV 4	0·3	II B	0·3	II B	0·3
	90·0		93·3		95·3		93·0
Sect. V	10·0	Sect. V	6·6	Sect. V	4·8	Sect. V	7·0
	100·0		99·9		100·1		100·0

Totals do not add to 100 precisely because of rounding.

Translated into words, the feelings of ecstasy in each group, in order of statistical probability, would be as follows:

Group Q

new life, satisfaction, joy, salvation, glory; knowledge by identification; up-feelings; unity, eternity, heaven; new and/or mystical knowledge; loss of words, images, sense; enlargement, improvement; contact; loss of difference, time, place; loss of self; inside-feelings; loss of worldliness, desire, sorrow, sin; pain-feelings; liquidity-feelings; release; peace, calm; ineffability, light and/or fire feelings; loss of limitation.

Group L

new life, satisfaction, joy, salvation, glory; new and/or mystical knowledge; loss of words, images, sense; unity, eternity, heaven; loss of worldliness, desire, sorrow, sin; knowledge by identification;

up-feelings; contact; loss of self; enlargement, improvement; light and/
or fire feelings; loss of difference, time, place; inside-feelings; liquidity-
feelings; peace, calm; pain-feelings; release; ineffability; loss of limitation; dark-feelings.

Group R

new life, satisfaction, joy, salvation, glory; loss of words, images,
sense; new and/or mystical knowledge; unity, eternity, heaven; knowledge by identification; loss of worldliness, desire, sorrow, sin; contact; inside-feelings; loss of self; up-feelings; ineffability; light and/or
fire feelings; peace, calm; enlargement, improvement; loss of difference, time, place; liquidity-feelings; release; dark-feelings; pain-
feelings; loss of limitation.

The Mean

new life, satisfaction, joy, salvation, glory; new and/or mystical knowledge; loss of words, images, sense; knowledge by identification;
unity, eternity, heaven; loss of worldliness, desire, sorrow, sin; up-
feelings; contact; enlargement, improvement; loss of self; inside-
feelings; loss of difference, time, place; light and/or fire feelings; peace,
calm, liquidity-feelings; ineffability; release; pain-feelings; dark-
feelings; loss of limitation.

TABLE 4b

Percentages of the total number of people (112) reporting certain feelings.

Feelings	No. of people	%
new world/life, satisfaction, joy, salvation, glory	82	73 [a]
knowledge by identification	76	68
new and/or mystical knowledge	61	54
intensity	59	53
loss of words/images, sense	57	51
unity, eternity, heaven	56	50
up-feelings	56	50
contact	48	43
loss of worldliness, desire, sorrow, sin	42	38
enlargement, improvement	41	37
loss of self	40	36
inside-feelings	38	34
loss of difference, time, place	29	26
light/fire	28	25
peace, calm	27	24
liquidity	26	23
ineffability	24	21

[a] There is a case for excluding references to *joy* by the questionnaire group on the
grounds that this was entailed by use of the word *ecstasy* in the initial question. If mention
of *joy* by this group are subtracted, then the percentage of mentions for all three groups
under the general heading *new life*, etc., is 61.

TABLE 4b—contd.

Feelings	No. of people	%
release	18	16
pain	18	16
withdrawal	10	9
dark-feelings	4	4
loss of limitation	3	3

TABLE 5

Comparison of adamic ecstasies and knowledge-contact ecstasies

There are 22 adamic ecstasies (i.e. those with an entry under III.C and no entry under III.D or III.E). 17 from Group Q, 4 from Group L, 1 from Group R. There are 34 knowledge-contact ecstasies (i.e. those with an entry under both III.D and III.E). 5 from Group Q, 16 from Group L, and 13 from Group R.

	Adamic No.	Adamic %	Knowledge-contact No.	Knowledge-contact %	Mean %
Section II: Negative					
Loss of:					
A. difference, time, place	5	3·8	11	2·4	3·4
B. limitation	—	—	2	0·4	0·3
C. worldliness, desire, sorrow, sin	11	8·4	19	4·2	5·7
D. self	1	0·8	18	4·0	4·1
E. words/images, sense	10	7·6	46	10·2	7·7
TOTALS	27	20·6	96	21·2	21·2
Section III: Positive					
Gain of:					
A. unity, eternity, heaven	11	8·4	34	7·5	7·2
B. release	—	—	10	2·2	1·8
C. new world/life, salvation, joy, satisfaction, glory	34	25·9	57	12·6	15·5
D. contact	—	—	34	7·5	4·9
E. knowledge, mystical/new	—	—	45	9·9	7·9
F. knowledge by identification	9	6·9	31	6·9	7·7
TOTALS	54	41·2	211	46·6	45·0
Ineffability	—	—	11	2·4	2·4
Section IV: Quasi-physical					
1. up	9	6·9	23	5·1	5·7
2. inside	8	6·1	16	3·5	3·9
3. light/fire	2	1·5	16	3·5	2·9
4. dark	—	—	3	0·7	0·4
5. enlargement, improvement	9	6·9	15	3·3	4·2
6. pain	3	2·3	7	1·5	1·8
7. liquidity	5	3·8	10	2·2	2·6
8. peace, calm	3	2·3	16	3·5	2·8
TOTALS	39	29·8	106	23·3	24·3

TABLE 5—contd.

		Adamic		Knowledge-contact		Mean
		No.	%	No.	%	%
SECTION V:						
1. Intensity		11	8·4	22	4·9	6·0
2. Withdrawal		—	—	7	1·5	1·0
	TOTALS	11	8·4	29	6·4	7·0
TOTALS						
SECTION II		27	20·6	96	21·2	21·2
SECTION III		54	41·2	211	46·6	45·0
Ineffability		—	—	11	2·4	2·4
SECTION IV		39	29·8	106	23·3	24·3
SECTION V		11	8·4	29	6·4	7·0
	TOTALS	131	100·0	453	99·9	99·9

Totals do not add to 100 precisely because of rounding.

TABLE 6

Feelings of men and women compared

The sub-groups consist of all men and all women in all three groups, 66 men and 48 women.

	Men		Women	
	No.	%	No.	%
SECTION II: Negative				
Loss of:				
A. difference, time, place	20	3·0	14	4·3
B. limitation	1	0·1	2	0·6
C. worldliness, desire, sorrow, sin	43	6·5	13	4·0
D. self	26	4·0	14	4·3
E. words/images, sense	45	6·9	30	9·2
TOTALS	135	20·5	73	22·4
SECTION III: Positive				
Gain of:				
A. unity, eternity, heaven	49	7·5	22	6·8
B. release	13	2·0	5	1·5
C. new world/life, satisfaction, joy, salvation, glory	101	15·4	52	15·9
D. contact	31	4·7	17	5·2
E. knowledge, mystical and/or new	53	8·1	24	7·4
F. knowledge by identification	49	7·5	27	8·3
TOTALS	296	45·2	147	45·1
Ineffability	18	2·7	6	1·8

TABLE 6—*contd.*

	Men No.	%	Wemen No.	%
SECTION IV: Quasi-physical feelings				
1. up	38	5·8	18	5·6
2. inside	26	4·0	12	3·7
3. light/fire	23	3·5	5	1·5
4. dark	3	0·5	1	0·3
5. enlargement, improvement	27	4·1	14	4·3
6. pain	12	1·8	6	1·8
7. liquidity	16	2·4	10	3·1
8. peace, calm	17	2·6	10	3·1
TOTALS	162	24·7	76	23·4
SECTION V:				
1. Intensity	39	6·0	20	6·2
2. Withdrawal	6	0·9	4	1·2
TOTALS	45	6·9	24	7·4
TOTALS				
SECTION II	135	20·5	73	22·4
SECTION III	296	45·2	147	45·1
Ineffability	18	2·7	6	1·8
SECTION IV	162	24·7	76	23·4
SECTION V	45	6·9	24	7·4
TOTALS	656	100·0	326	100·1

Totals do not add to 100 precisely because of rounding.
Men averaged 9·9 mentions each: women averaged 6·8 mentions each.

TABLE 7

Triggers of men and women compared

This comparison is based on Group Q only since only in this group were several triggers named by most people. The group consists of 60 people, 23 men and 27 women.

Entries under each heading are expressed as percentages of all mentions by each group.

	Men		Women	
	No.	%	No.	%
1. Nature	9	17·1	18	18·9
2. Sexual love	8	15·1	17	17·9
3. Childbirth	—	—	5	5·3
4. Exercise	4	7·5	4	4·2
5. Religion	5	9·4	9	9·5
6. Art	11	20·7	20	21·0
7. *a.* Scientific knowledge	4	7·5	1	1·1
b. Poetic knowledge	1	1·9	1	1·1
8. Creative work	2	3·8	5	5·3
9. Recollection, introspection	1	1·9	4	4·2
10. 'Beauty'	2	3·8	4	4·2
11. Miscellaneous	6	11·3	7	7·4
TOTALS	53	100·0	95	100·1

Totals do not add to 100 precisely because of rounding.

TABLE 8

Patterns of ecstasies induced by religion, nature, art, sexual love

Religion includes all Group R and that only; *nature* includes all ecstasies in all 3 groups where nature appeared as a trigger; *art* includes all ecstasies in Groups Q and L where *art* appeared as a trigger (it did not appear in Group R); *sexual love* is taken only from Group Q. The picture is to some extent distorted because several people in Group Q gave several triggers.

	Religion		Nature		Art		Sexual love		Mean
	No.	%	No.	%	No.	%	No.	%	%
SECTION II: Negative									
Loss of:									
A. difference, etc.	9	2·8	13	3·1	5	1·9	7	6·2	3·4
B. limitation	1	0·3	2	0·5	—	—	—	—	0·3
C. worldliness, etc.	22	7·1	21	4·9	11	4·1	2	1·9	5·7
D. self	13	4·2	18	4·2	6	2·3	8	7·1	4·1
E. words, images, sense	26	8·4	37	8·7	21	7·9	6	5·4	7·7
TOTALS	71	22·8	91	21·4	43	16·2	23	20·6	21·2

TABLE 8—contd.

	Religion		Nature		Art		Sexual love		Mean
	No.	%	No.	%	No.	%	No.	%	%
SECTION III: Positive									
Gain of:									
A. unity, etc.	24	7·6	23	5·4	12	4·5	9	8·0	7·2
B. release	5	1·6	8	1·9	8	3·0	3	2·7	1·8
C. new life, etc.	46	14·7	59	13·8	50	18·8	19	17·0	15·5
D. contact	18	5·7	22	5·2	11	4·1	5	4·5	4·9
E. knowledge, new, mystical	25	8·0	39	9·1	25	9·4	5	4·5	7·9
F. identification	23	7·3	31	7·3	21	7·9	12	10·7	7·7
TOTALS	141	44·9	182	42·7	127	47·7	53	47·4	45·0
Ineffability	13	4·2	9	2·1	4	1·5	—	—	2·4
SECTION IV: Quasi-physical									
1. up	13	4·2	25	5·9	19	7·1	7	6·2	5·7
2. inside	15	4·8	20	4·7	11	4·1	5	4·5	3·9
3. light, fire	12	3·8	9	2·1	5	1·9	1	0·9	2·9
4. dark	3	1·0	1	0·2	—	—	—	—	0·4
5. enlargement, etc.	10	3·2	19	4·5	18	6·8	7	6·2	4·2
6. pain	3	1·0	9	2·1	5	1·9	3	2·7	1·8
7. liquidity	6	1·9	12	2·8	9	3·4	3	2·7	2·6
8. calm, peace	11	3·5	15	3·5	3	1·1	1	0·9	2·8
TOTALS	73	23·4	110	25·8	70	26·3	27	24·1	24·3
SECTION V:									
1. Intensity	13	4·2	27	6·4	22	8·3	8	7·1	6·0
2. Withdrawal	2	0·6	7	1·6	—	—	1	0·9	1·0
TOTALS	15	4·8	34	8·0	22	8·3	9	8·0	7·0
TOTALS									
SECTION II	71	22·8	91	21·4	43	16·2	23	20·6	21·2
SECTION III	141	44·9	182	42·7	127	47·7	53	47·4	45·0
Ineffability	13	4·2	9	2·1	4	1·5	—	—	2·4
SECTION IV	73	23·4	110	25·8	70	26·3	27	24·1	24·3
SECTION V	15	4·8	34	8·0	22	8·3	9	8·0	7·0
TOTALS	313	100·1	426	100·0	266	100·0	112	100·1	99·9

Totals do not add to 100 precisely because of rounding.

TABLE 9

Trigger mentions of Christians and of non-believers

The Christian group consists of all people in the questionnaire group who described themselves as Christian, no matter of what denomination; it does not include people who merely said that they believed in God. The non-believer group consists of all people in the questionnaire group who described themselves as atheists or agnostics or as having no faith or belief.

In the Christian group there are 16 people, 5 men and 11 women. In the non-believer group there are 32 people, 11 men and 21 women.

The entries for each heading are expressed as a percentage of all trigger mentions by that group.

Triggers	Non-believers		Christians		
	No.	%	No.	%	
1. Nature	16	20·2	6	15·0	
2. Sexual love	17	21·5	3	7·5	
3. Childbirth	4	5·1	—	—	(a)
4. Exercise, movement	6	7·6	1	2·5	
5. Religion	4	5·1 (b)	7	17·5	
6. Art	14	17·7	12	30·0	
7. a. Scientific knowledge	5	6·3	—	—	
b. Poetic knowledge	1	1·3	1	2·5	
8. Creative work	4	5·1	3	7·5	
9. Recollection, introspection	2	2·5	—	—	
10. 'Beauty'	2	2·5	3	7·5	
11. Miscellaneous	4	5·1	4	10·0	
TOTALS	79	100·0	40	100·0	

(a) The lack of childbirth triggers among the Christians may be due to there being fewer married woman among them; I do not know whether this was so.

(b) The religious mentions by non-believers are all of art with a religious theme.

TABLE 10

Frequencies of trigger mentions in various groupings

The questionnaire group

Art (20·9%), nature (18·2%), sexual love (16·9%), religion (9·5%), exercise, movement (5·4%), creative work (4·7%), 'beauty' (4·0%), childbirth and scientific knowledge and recollection, introspection (all 3·4%), poetic knowledge (1·4%).

The literary group

Nature (34·0%), art (19·1%), religion (8·5%), exercise, movement and poetic knowledge and recollection, introspection (all 6·4%), scientific knowledge and 'beauty' (both 4·3%), sexual love and creative work (both 2·1%).

The religious group

Nature (33·3%), exercise, movement, and religion (both 20·0%), recollection, introspection (6·7%).

(For the figures on which the above are based, see Table 3.)

From the questionnaire group only

Men

Art (20·7%), nature (17·1%), sexual love (15·1%), religion (9·4%), exercise, movement and scientific knowledge (both 7·5%), creative work and 'beauty' (both 3·8%), poetic knowledge and recollection, introspection (both 1·9%).

Women

Art (21·0%), nature (18·9%), sexual love (17·9%), religion (9·5%), childbirth and creative work (both 5·3%), exercise, movement and recollection, introspection and 'beauty' (all 4·2%), scientific knowledge and poetic knowledge (both 1·1%).

(For the figures on which the above are based, see Table 7.)

Non-believers

Sexual love (21·5%), nature (20·2%), art (17·7%), exercise, movement (7·6%), scientific knowledge (6·3%), childbirth and religion [a] and creative work (all 5·1%), recollection, introspection and 'beauty' (2·5%), poetic knowledge (1·3%).

[a] The religious mentions by non-believers are all of art with a religious theme.

Christians

Art (30·0%), religion (17·5%), nature (15·0%), sexual love and creative work and 'beauty' (7·5%), exercise, movement and poetic knowledge (both 2·5%).

(For the figures on which the above are based, see Table 9.)

APPENDIX E

1. Up-words and phrases

(a) probably literally intended

floating (Q 21); associated with sensations of physical flying (Q 29); weightlessness (Q 44); a floating sensation (Q 51); you feel immensely light, you feel as if you're not walking on the ground (Q 57).

the sensation of 'rising up within'—bodily lightness...as if one's limbs had no weight (L 24).

[afterwards] it seemed to him that he walked on air (R 1); raised from the earth almost as if the heavy body became light (R 2); I experienced a feeling of being raised above myself (R 11).

(b) probably figuratively intended

soaring up, become airborne, the soul leaving the body, above yourself, removed from consideration of earthly things, being borne into heaven, hovering on the edge of—,the heart leaps, right out of the world, climax which has built up, come into contact with a kind of vertical eternity, bubbling up (all from the questionnaire group).

felt...my spirit...bound—my thoughts...now felt unutterable buoyancy (L 2); my thought...went up (L 3); buoyant—reaches a station scarcely lower than that...etc. (L 14); drew him from the depths (L 16); leapt up (L 17a); bounding—dancing (L 19); shaken or lifted out (L 20); earth was lost to me—wings are almost free (L 21); tore us up (L 23a); going up to another level (L 24); carried beyond (L 25); the sky opened—on the hilltop (L 27).

soul is being wafted upwards (R 3); her mind had been uplifted (R 5b); above and beyond all things—thought, life and being are uplifted (R 7); come up in spirit (R 9); carried away (R 12); lifted up (R 14); sprang up far above my earthly centre (R 18); lifted up (R 19); carried above itself (R 20).

(c) obvious metaphors

built up, exalted, exaltation, exultation, heightened, a peak, uplifted (all from the questionnaire group).

elevated, exaltation, flashed up, heightened, high, higher, highest, lifted out, sublime, superhuman, wings to thought (all from the literary group).

came up, elevated, exalted, exaltation, high, highest, high-flown, renewed up, rose to such a pitch, sublime, supreme, uplifted (all from the religious group).

2. Contact words and phrases

(a) *claims of union*

merging into the experience (Q 1—believes in God); union with external reality (Q 17—no faith); I am part of the thing that has set it off, and I enclose the universe or it encloses me...both inextricably mingled (Q 24—no faith); in unity with everything (Q 34—'a sort of faith'); living in the object (Q 36—no faith); identification with the whole sensible universe (Q 37—agnostic); oneness with the totality of nature (Q 42—agnostic).

being oneself contained in all one sees—lost in the one (M. Evans—L 4); within and without are one (Joël—L 9); Union with God (H. W. Allen—L 11); identification...with the objects he was looking at (G. Eliot—L 15); unity with all being (J. Hawkes—L 19); had become ...part of the truth (C. P. Snow—L 25).

the perfect union which the soul has made with [God] (St. Catherine of Siena—R 2); the perfect union of my spirit with His (a clergyman—R 3); the perceiver was one with the thing perceived (Plotinus—R 4); made one with the Truth (Ruysbroeck—R 7); she will become by union one with Him (St. Teresa—R 10a); [the soul] has been in God and God in it (St. Teresa—R 10b); swallowed up in Him (Brainerd—R 13); united to God without any medium...transformed and changed into Him (Louis of Blois—R 20); entirely mingled with and steeped in Him (St. Francis of Sales—R 21); changed into...the Divine Being... which...becomes one thing with them (Suso—R 22).

(b) *claims of contact without union*

touch reality (Q 1—believes in God); soaring up to something... you've always known was there (Q 3—'good is stronger than evil'); communion...in touch (Q 5—no faith); in touch with the Creator (Q 15—Christian); communion with something else (Q 27—no faith); almost touched the fringe of eternity (Q 46—Christian).

felt a presence (Wordsworth—L 1a); visitation from the living God (Wordsworth—L 1b); (contact with a seraph—Tennyson—L 2); being told something...[by] a being who was a poet (Nicols—L 5); direct contact with an otherness (Berenson—L 10); He was in other hands...

the Spirit of Life illumined him (Meredith—L 16); the meeting, the clasp, the close embrace (Lawrence—L 17a); in the presence of extraordinary possibilities (Montague—L 20); (contact with a messenger of Hope—E. Brontë—L 21); the…presence of the Creator (Church—L 23b); in God's presence ('A'—L 24).

I stood alone with Him who had made me (a clergyman—R 3); (conversation with God—Angela of Foligno—R 5a); intimate communion with the divine ('a man of 27'—R 6); allied with the Infinite (a woman —R 8); close to God (St. Teresa—R 10b); communication with God ('M.E.'—R 11); my Love has embraced me (Hugh of St. Victor—R 12); in the presence of God (St. Alphonsus Rodriguez—R 14); a living Presence (R. M. Bucke—R 17); I walked with the Lord (Joseph Salmon—R 18).

(c) claims of contact with communication

I have, with some doubt, taken *communion* as implying *communication* in the dictionary sense of *intercourse*; it will be noticed that Q 5 and R 6 use both *communion* and *communication*, while R 11 uses both these and *intercourse* as well.

communion…direct communication (Q 5—no faith); communion with something else (Q 27—no faith).

still communion (Wordsworth—L 1b); (conversation with a seraph—Tennyson—L 2); being told something…[by] a being who was a poet (Nichols—L 5); contact with an otherness—revelation (Berenson—L 10); an answer came…union with God (H. W. Allen—L 11); the Spirit of Life illumined him (Meredith—L 16); in the presence of extraordinary possibilities—enlightenments (C. E. Montague—L 20); (communion with a messenger of Hope, the truth revealed—Brontë—L 21); in God's presence—a voice which said… ('A'—L 24); part of the truth I sought (C. P. Snow—L 25).

(universal understanding—speech with God—Angela of Foligno—R 5a); communion with the divine—meetings—communication with God (a clergyman—R 6); creative life was flowing into me—allied with the Infinite (a woman—R 8); communion—communication with God —intimate intercourse ('M.E.'—R 11); my intellect is illuminated—my Love has embraced me (Hugh of St. Victor—L 12); alone with God, who gave him great light concerning the knowledge of God and self (St. Alphonsus Rodriguez—R 14); intellectual illumination—a living Presence (R. M. Bucke—R 17); (received knowledge from God —Joseph Salmon—R 18); becomes one with God—learns Divine Truth—contact of the Holy Spirit (Louis of Blois—R 20).

The next two sub-divisions distinguish between those who claimed to feel the presence of God (or used some term obviously standing for God) and those who felt they had made contact with something other than God. I have added the religious position of those in the question- naire group.

(d) contact with God

claimed by Q 15 (a Christian); Wordsworth (L 1b); H. W. Allen (L 11); Church (L 23b); 'A' (L 24).

We may take it that whatever terms were used by people in the religious group, 'God' was their intended meaning. But terms other than God or obvious synonyms are of interest and include:

the Infinite (a clergyman—R 3); the thing perceived (Plotinus—R 4); the All (Angela of Foligno—R 5b); the Truth (Ruysbroek—R 7); my Love (Hugh of St. Victor—R 12); the universe (R. M. Bucke—R 17); pure love and peace (Joseph Salmon—R 18); the Holy Spirit (Louis of Blois—R 20);[1] the well-Beloved (St. Francis of Sales—R 21); Divine Will, Divine Nature, Divine Being, Divine Personality (Suso—R 22).

(e) contact with something other than God

the experience, reality (Q 1—believes in God); something (Q 3— 'good is stronger than evil'); external reality (Q 17—no faith); the thing that has set it off—the universe (Q 24—no faith); something else (Q 27—no faith); reality (Q 33—Christian); everything, nature (Q 34 —'a sort of faith'; does not believe in God); the object (Q 36—no faith); the whole sensible universe (Q 37—agnostic); the totality of nature (Q 42—agnostic); the fringe of eternity (Q 46—Christian).

a motion and a spirit, that impels all thinking things…and rolls through all things (Wordsworth—L 1a); a Seraph—a Spirit (Tennyson—L 2); all one sees—millions of spirits like mine (M. Evans—L 4); a being who was a poet (Nichols—L 5); the world (Joël—L 9); an otherness (L 10); the very heart of the universe (L 12) ; the objects he was looking at (G. Eliot—L 15); other hands—the Spirit of Life (Meredith—L 16); all being—the creative eros (L 19); a messenger of Hope (E. Brontë— L 21); the truth (C. P. Snow—L 25).

There are four ways in which the contact can be said to take place: I shall call the ecstatic or his soul X, and the contact, whatever it may be, Y.

---

[1] This last is an obvious synonym for *God*, but I include it as a parallel to the use of *spirit* by Wordsworth and Tennyson.

(*f*) X may be said to pass into Y as Y into X: for example:

I enclose the universe or it encloses me (Q 24—no faith); without and within glide into each other (Joël—L 9); [the soul] has been in God and God in it (St. Teresa—R 10b).

(*g*) X may move towards and penetrate or be enclosed in Y: for example:

living in the object (Q 36—no faith); had become...part of the truth I sought (C. P. Snow—L 25); I am drawn out of myself...my Love has embraced me (Hugh of St. Victor—R 12).

(*h*) Y may be said to move towards or penetrate X: for example:

His goodness and power were penetrating me altogether ('M.E.'—R 11).

(There are other examples in the religious group, but none in the other two groups).

(*i*) X and Y may be said to have achieved union without any indication as to how this came about: for example:

sense of union with external reality (Q 17—no faith); the mysterious event...the Union with God (H. Warner Allen—L 11); I did not seek Him but felt the perfect unison of my spirit with His (a clergyman—R 3).

In a few cases the variations may indicate differences in variety or intensity of experience. But for the most part I believe that the choice of expression is arbitrary or aesthetic, and this is supported by the fact that some people use two or more modes of expression; for instance, Q 24 says:

I am part of the thing that has set it off—i.e. (*g*); I enclose the universe or it encloses me—i.e. (*f*); me and the universe, both inextricably mingled—probably (*i*).

And Suso, in text R 22:

loses himself in God—i.e. (*g*); whereinto they pour themselves and which pours itself into them—i.e. (*f*); more or less united with God—probably (*i*).

. Totality words and phrases

The relevant words and phrases are italicized.

Group Q: complete peace—*completeness, wholeness*—*reality* (Q 1); something you've *always* wanted, *always* known was there (Q 3); it affects *everything* (Q 6); borne into *heaven*—the *Creator* (Q 15); *extreme* clarity

(Q 16); union with *external reality* (Q 17); *timeless* bliss—*complete* separation from trouble—should be like this *for ever* (Q 18); *absolute oneness—whole world* falls into place (Q 19); the *oneness* of things (Q 20); haven't *any* cares in the *world* (Q 21); seeing *right beyond* (Q 22); *everything* fits—*all creation* comes into harmony (Q 23); I enclose the *universe* (Q 24); *perfection* with life (Q 26); happiness that takes you *right out of the world*, so *supreme* that you forget *everything* (Q 28); *timelessness*—this is *the whole world—completely* uplifted (Q 31); *complete* satisfaction—touching *reality* (Q 33); seeing things in *proper proportion*—unity with *everything* (Q 34); *complete* satisfaction—something being perfected, *couldn't be better done... couldn't be more perfect* (Q 35); satisfaction with *the actuality of existence—pure existence* (Q 36); identification with *the whole sensible universe* (Q 37); *complete* involvement of *one's whole being* (Q 40); *oneness* with *the totality* of nature (Q 42); *complete* sense of liberation (Q 44); the fringe of *eternity* (Q 46); *a peak* (Q 50); sensation you understand *everything* (Q 54); *complete* suspension of time (Q 56); capable of *anything* (Q 57); *everything* is right—*the world* makes sense (Q 58); *extreme* happiness—*everything* I *ever* wanted—*nothing* could *ever* go wrong again (Q 59); *all*-powerful (Q 60); *all* you know about nature, *the whole thing* (Q 61); a *most marvellous* feeling (Q 62); *the reality* of things (Q 63).

Group L: a spirit, that impels *all* thinking things, *all* objects of *all* thought, and rolls through *all* things (L 1a); visitation from the living God (L 1b); *full* beatitude—*no mightier* Spirit than I (L 2); *universal* perception—lost in *the one* (L 4); the solitude of *any* figure...at *any* period in history (L 5); *all* the details of things—*the world* is surveyed (L 6); *infinite* tranquillity and peace—liberation from *any* pressure or itch—*Nirvana* (L 7); *reality*—beside which *nothing* matters (L 8); *the world* exales in the soul (L 9); *every* outline, *every* edge, and *every* surface—*everywhere* I felt the ideated pulsation—it *all* served to enhance, etc. (L 10); Union with *God* (L 11); penetrated *the very heart of the universe*—happiness such as I had *never* known (L 12); *nirvana*—*all* human desires and purposes shrivelled (L 13); *earth* an *Eden*—pure gift of *God* (L 14); *the Spirit of Life* (L 16); the *perfect*, swooning consummation—*unique* mystery—*the climax of eternity* (L 17a); *all* life and consciousness—*everything—the highest point* of bliss (L 17b); *all* that had happened or could happen—could *never* be superseded (L 18); the power to transmute *all*—comprehension of...*the* physical *world*—unity with *all* being (L 19); *eternal* liberty—then dawns *the Invisible, the Unseen* its truth reveals (L 21); *totally* absorbed—*the heavenly godhead* (L 22); *all* was new to me—*Adam and Eve in the Garden* (L 23a); *all was one*—the *Creator—everything* was now contained, for me, in the power of *the*

Word (L 23b); *proper proportions*—new *reality of everything*—*nothing less than* bliss—*God* who is *perfection's self*—*everything* that it is important or necessary to know (L 24); *the unity of things* (L 25); *all*-powerful joy (L 26); I saw *nothing and everything* (L 27).

Group R: a joy such as he might have known in the seeing of...*all* joyful things—*all* fulfilled—*Eternal* Life (R 1); the *perfect* union which the soul has made with *Me* (R 2); *perfect* unison—*all* the separate notes have melted into *one*—*highest* faith—*truest* idea (R 3); belongs to *God* and is *one* with Him (R 4); I did comprehend *the whole world* (R 5a); I knew *all* I longed to know, possessed *all* I longed to possess, I saw *all Good* —sees *nothing* and sees *All*—*surpasses all* good—this *Good*...is *the All*; (R 5b); communication with *God* (R 6); above and beyond *all* things —the *Eternal Word*—made one with *the Truth* which is *God* (R 7); allied with *the Infinite* (R 8); *all things were new—all the creations* gave another smell—knew *nothing but* pureness, innocency, and righteous-ness (R 9); only *God*—the *whole* soul is united to *God* (R 10a); a certain good containing in itself *all good together at once—complete* absorption (R 10b); the presence of *God*—penetrating me *altogether* (R 11); to keep it, that I may *never* lose it—the goal of *all* her desires;—exults in a *sovereign* and *ineffable* manner (R 12); *God* over *all* for *ever and ever* (R 13); above *all* created things—what she *most desires* (R 14); knew the being of *all* things—the *whole* working *essence*—a *thorough* view of the *universe* (R 16); possessed *eternal* life—the *cosmic* order—*all* things work together—*the foundation principle* of *the world*, of *all the worlds* (R 17); heaven—pure *perfection*—*eternity*—*the Lord* (R 18); *the perspicuous truth* —the *sole and all-embracing* virtue—*supreme* happiness (R 19); learns *divine truth*—*eternal* sweetness—*sublime* union with *God* (R 20);[1] *entirely* mingled with and steeped in *Him* (R 21); union with the *Divine Personality* (R 22).

[1] Notice the tautology, typical of many such; union with God must, presum-ably, of its nature be sublime.

APPENDIX F

GROUP C

SECTION I: average age 15 years

C 1

Circumstances: On the sands with her aunt, running ahead to the point, although warned the tide was turning.

Significant phrases: '...the waves, dashing on the rocks further out, seemed to call me on... I was alone... I stood on a rock and the bay stretched round... At the same *moment* [my italics] there was a lull in the waves and there was *a moment* [my italics] of almost silence, broken only by the solitary call of a lonely seagull... I stood for so long just looking, that it was only the water lapping into my left shoe that reminded me of the oncoming tide... I returned to Auntie, still in such a wondering state that I was quite oblivious to her anxious scolding...'

Result: 'I think the meaning of this will last me all my life because of the utter silence of the *moment* [my italics] when there was a lull in the wind and the long, lonely cry of the seagull.'

C 2

Circumstances: Recall to age of 12. Had gone unwillingly to the seaside in bad weather. One fairly fine day, went to look at the sea and at a rock just off-shore. A violent storm developed.

Significant phrases: 'Suddenly I was excited by the storm and the sea, and the great rock, stubborn yet majestic, defying the waves. I began to sing softly, not a song, just a tune, keeping in time with the waves... Then—"Look, a rainbow..." I became very happy. All the sadness went.'

Result: 'Now I had seen the rock, steady while in trouble till it could emerge smiling. I had no trouble, just a little pain, but when I would have it, I would remember to fight like the rock.'

C 3

Circumstances: Recall to age of 12 or 13. On a cliff above the sea, watching the waves crashing below.

Significant phrases: 'As I watched, I felt as though I was a wave coming in towards shore, bobbing up and down and finally hitting the cliff and being thrown back again... It is a wonderful feeling to feel yourself tossing and turning and having seagulls landing on you and then flying off again like an airport.'

Result: None stated.

C 4

Circumstances: The first time she went sailing.

Significant phrases: 'The sensation was one I shall never forget, for the wind took hold of my hair and whipped it across my face like a lash; the spray flew up and covered me with droplets of shining water and the boat sped across the ruffled water.'

Result: None stated.

C 5

Circumstances: Recall to age of 6. Had never seen mountains. Drove with her family to Wales.

Significant phrases: 'My first sight of the mountains was right up close, my parents not having woken me before, and immediately I was overpowered by them. They gave me the feeling that I was very small and insignificant, which, having had a younger sister to boss around, I had not experienced much. The weather was appalling...and all the mountains looked dark and unfriendly as if I were an enemy and they were hiding all their secrets from me... The rain started to pelt down again and the unwanted feeling I had arrived at by then was magnified by a roll of thunder which sounded as though it would split the tops of the mountains and they would come crashing down to crush me.'

Result: None stated.

C 6

Circumstances: Was afraid of heights. Went on holiday to Wales, and was appalled when taken on a climb of Snowdon.

Significant phrases: 'I remember the *moment* [my italics] well; we were three thousand feet up, near the summit, when I stopped to admire the view. The loveliness took my breath away... The view was so lovely that I forgot my fear of heights and it has never returned since.'

Result: 'That *moment* [my italics] made me appreciate the beauty of the mountains and gave me an added zest to do more climbing. From that *moment* [my italics] onwards I appreciated the beautiful scenery... I love a beautiful landscape, but none that I have seen has been as beautiful as the view from the top of Snowdon.'

C 7

Circumstances: Descending Snowdon on a winter evening as night was falling.

Significant phrases: None—a purely factual account.

Result: '…it opened my eyes to the wonder and mystery of a mountain-side in the dark'.

C 8

Circumstances: Sledging in the snow at night.

Significant phrases: None.

Result: 'It was an experience that I shall never forget, the rushing wind and the half-moon casting an eerie glow on the snow.'

C 9

Circumstances: The Pass of Glencoe.

Significant phrases: '…the Pass of Glencoe which had seen so much but which remained solid and silent, pitying the weak commotions of men… That first impression left me with a strange longing to understand that which would be for ever beyond my grasp. Those indomitable hills gripped my very soul…they awed me into a stunned silence of reverence…the passing years were infinitesimal spaces of time in their long history… They had seen the hand of God on the earth…'

Result: 'These great hills in all their majesty threw out a challenge to me; these must I conquer first and in my conquering be taught the humbleness of my position. Then I must go on to climb the greatest hill of all.'

C 10

Circumstances: After bad weather, climbing up to a hill village in France and looking out of the inn window at the sunset.

Significant phrases: 'I was on top of the village. I was high up, higher than anything else except the ancient belfry… Beyond the village were the wide rolling fields of France. The sun shone on the pink and copper roofs of the village and on the golden window-panes. Everything was contented, happy, gleaming. The whole world glowed, and the warm round sun smiled over France, over the fields and over the villages.'

Result: None stated.

C 11

Circumstances: In Paris, on a beautiful day, going up the Eiffel Tower.

Significant phrases: 'We reached the top and I had a surprising sensation. All was misty and mysterious below... The lights of the sun shining on the metal of the cars was dazzling. It was a wonderful experience, here I was, it seemed, miles above the ground, with the whole of Paris, which I had fallen in love with, stretched out before me. I felt exhilarated and filled with happiness... I felt like a conqueror, I felt that I was in a dreamlike world. There was life down below, but I was here, away from it all, from all the troubles and cares of life. I will always remember that wonderful feeling of light and space.'

Result: None stated.

C 12

Circumstances: 'The time when I really saw a sunset. I did not see it from the ground. I was high in the air, higher even than the swallows in their gay flight—I was on a level with the cloud.' (She was, in fact, in an aeroplane.)

Significant phrases: 'I looked out and drew my breath in wonder... I glanced at my companions; on each face was a rapt, thoughtful expression, and they were no longer laughing and chattering. All gazed together peacefully.'

Result: None stated.

C 13

Circumstances: Had always wanted to fly, even when very small, as a fairy. Now, being given first ride in uncle's aeroplane.

Significant phrases: 'We sailed into the air, like a gigantic bird. Then I was filled with a sudden great exhilaration.'

Result: None stated.

C 14

Circumstances: Staying at a cottage in Snowdonia, looking out of the window early on a beautiful day.

Significant phrases: 'Everything was fresh and new. I shall never forget the solitary feeling of that *moment* [my italics], as I watched the spring morning, and the sense of absolute joy and freedom of staying in the country in the spring.' She lists, as elements of the *moment*, 'the sunlight', 'the cloudless blue sky', 'a shepherd calling in Welsh to his dog', 'the young lambs skipping', 'a blackbird singing', 'the breeze shaking the berries off a mountain ash', 'the bushes and firs rustling'.

Results: None stated.

C 15

Circumstances: First visit to the country. Going into a farmhouse, sitting by the fire.

Significant phrases: 'The room was low and dark, and my first impression was that I was in an underground cavern... This was so different from the London flat, so peaceful and still. I gazed shyly into the fire. I sat, building castles in the air, for *what seemed eternity* [my italics], till the distant roar of a tractor brought me back to life.'

Result: None stated.

C 16

Circumstances: Going to the Louvre in Paris for the first time.

Significant phrases: 'Having arrived at the Louvre, I was too excited to do anything but stare. For looking down a brown stone passage, I saw the wish of my heart, the Venus de Milo. Never in my life will I forget the *moment* [my italics] when I actually touched and felt her exquisitely carved feet... A couple of days later I was taken...to see her again, but came home deflated. My first visit was marvellous, but the second time something seemed to be missing. I don't know what it was but I doubt if ever again I shall feel the wonderful "lifted" feeling she gave me.'

Result: 'That experience has made a landmark in my life. I often think of life before that, but it was different; it was before I grew up.'

C 17

Circumstances: Going to the ballet for the first time. Saw 'a lovely ballet, Swan Lake', then the interval. Decided she was enjoying herself and by the time the music began again, 'I was prepared'.

Significant phrases: 'Slowly the music died away and we waited; waited for one solo cello and harp to swell into being. We were now in total darkness and as the music rose gloriously, higher and higher, one white light traced the prima ballerina's steps across the stage. Suddenly I could see it all, and though I only half understood, the tears rose in my throat as the swan floated away on the langour of its beautiful theme. When it had gone, a great void was left, no one clapped and gradually people rose and left the theatre, carrying with them the beauty that was now forever lost to them.'

Result: None stated.

C 18

Circumstances: Recall to age of 9. Going to the ballet unwillingly, preferring the formerly promised circus. 'Quite enjoying' the first act, but still hankering for the circus.

Significant phrases: 'Just then the second act began and the stage was full of mysterious blue moonlight and ebony shadows.' This is contrasted with the swan maidens who 'drifted out' all in white, until 'the stage seemed full of floating white clouds against the night sky'. The Snow Queen is 'a snowflake, a dewdrop on a flower, as brittle and lacy as a piece of Dresden china... Surely she could float away on her own. I felt sure she was not of this world...she swayed across the stage, borne on the tide of the unearthly music, swaying and flowing in her dance like a fragment of apple blossom blown in a gentle wind...my rapture grew. I nearly wept when the Prince was enchanted by Odile... and I was happy when they both died... I left the theatre enraptured.'

Result: None stated.

C 19

Circumstances: 'When I was very small', went to Covent Garden to hear 'La Bohème' in which her father was singing at short notice.

Significant phrases: 'Then when Mimi was dying and Colline went to sell his coat, I think that was the most moving experience of my life... As my father sang the Coat Song, I was conscious not of the fact that it was my father but that it was Colline... Everything stood still as he finished the beautiful song...the whole theatre was feeling the same... before the clapping broke out the audience took a second to come out of their trance... Everyone chatted gaily as we watched Daddy take his make-up off, but I was still in a trance. I continued to be all the way home.'

Result: 'Although I have never since been moved quite so much by Bohème, I loved the theatre and music even more strongly after that day.'

C 20

Circumstances: A Robert Mayer concert for children, her first concert, having always disliked the idea of listening to music.

Significant phrases: 'Then, the most wonderful music I have ever heard filled the hall and resounded in my mind. I cannot remember the composer or the name of the music but to the end of my life I shall never forget it. It starts with the bells of Rome at dawn and one can imagine the soft, still air, penetrated only by those bells. Then...the music becomes louder, telling of the fields to be ploughed... Then one hears the music of all the fountains...the thought of them makes one cool and refreshed.'

Result: 'I have never felt so moved by a piece of music...it is an episode in my life which I shall never forget.'

C 21

Circumstances: Half listening to a radio programme while doing prep, then heard 'the professor' reading 'Rupert Brooke's "In Flanders Field."'

Significant phrases: 'His words were like music to my ears. With maths and history forgotten, I lived every minute with those brave men fighting, dying and living again amongst the poppies... I thought of their parents, their children, and then the poppies... Suddenly there was silence; the professor had finished, but the audience, and I dare say the majority of the listeners, were still with the poppies, in Flanders Field.'

Result: None stated.

C 22

Circumstances: Listening on the wireless to 'a very famous actor' who was appealing for a society that helps mental defectives.

Significant phrases: 'We listened to his voice, stilled and silenced by his wonderful diction... At the end he read, "Mad, who would be mad."'

Result: 'Those few, beautifully uttered words have stayed in my memory ever since that day. At night, as I am dropping off to sleep, I hear them through the darkness, and my mind shies away from the terrors of madness.'

C 23

Circumstances: Reading Emily Brontë's poems.

Significant phrases: 'I read one of her poems for the first time in the school library, a singularly uninspiring place I admit, but I was fascinated and was soon far away... I went to find a biography... I was soon lost to the world outside, was in the dark and narrow rectangle that was Emily's room; was up on the moors and running with her between earth and clouds.'

Result: 'I cannot tell if this event will have any later significance in my life, as it happened too recently for it to be seen in perspective—but I have been captured and held fast by the character and writings of Emily Brontë.'

C 24

Circumstances: Reading Mark Twain's *The Innocents Abroad.*

Significant phrases: 'I shall read this book again many times, but I will not get the same thrill as when reading it for the first time. In this book Mark Twain visits many places all over the land, and his descriptions of the places make you feel you have been there yourself.' She specifies

(1) looking at Naples from a mountain with the sun shining, (2) 'some of his descriptions of early morning leave you spellbound', (3) Milan Cathedral 'just floating high up on the hill where it stands' (but Milan Cathedral does not stand on a hill).

Result: 'You feel that somehow or other in your lifetime you must see these places with your own eyes.'

C 25

Circumstances: 'I had a similar experience.' 'I was only eight at the time', reading a life of Madame Tussaud.

Significant phrases: 'It's very funny that it's always the terrible things that you can remember most clearly... While I was reading that book I felt all the emotions that I could ever have felt... This had the same kind of significance for me that the piano-tuner and Beethoven's sonata had for the little boy and his brother Jack.'

Result: None stated.

C 26

Circumstances: Picked up a book from the classics department of the school library, resolved to read it whatever it was; it was something unnamed by Dickens.

Significant phrases: 'It inspired me considerably.'

Result: 'I began to read other of his works and other classics.'

C 27

Circumstances: Recall to 12 years old, 'the day I put away childish books'. Used to like Enid Blyton and Arthur Ransome, then, reading a new book of this kind in bed, 'was thoroughly sick of it'. Took out *David Copperfield*.

Significant phrases: None.

Result: 'Perhaps I didn't understand it all; but on that night I vowed I would only read books worth reading.'

C 28

Circumstances: Was devoted to the works of an unnamed woman writer. One day read a biography of this woman and discovered 'she had done none of the wonderful things she had written about...she was like a drowning person who longed to save her body from a watery grave, who did so by imagining the wonderful things she would do when she had'.

Significant phrases: 'It was like the raising of a blind.'

Result: 'This was the first time I realized how easy it had been for me to misinterpret her character. From that day I have been determined not to be jealous of others, but to understand myself and others better.'

C 29

Circumstances: Read a book called *The Long Walk*.

Significant phrases: None.

Result: 'The reason why this story made me have a different outlook on life was the way seven men overcame their difficulties and clung on to life. It made me realize, too, the cruelty there is in the world... I was appalled by the effects of war and it made my own life seem so secure and happy and that I really ought to be grateful for the life I lead. It also made my own life seem so insignificant, and what happened to me didn't affect the world at all.'

C 30

Circumstances: A preacher heard each Saturday in a synagogue.

Significant phrases: 'Everybody listens in silence, their minds seeing the pictures he paints before them, and through his words the pictures come alive and each person fits himself into the picture of right and wrong... His words open up a new life in many people, it is the beginning of a series of new thoughts, on how to understand things, on how to bring up their children in the right way, and how to teach them to do these things so that they can be carried on for generations.'

Result: Included in the above.

C 31

Circumstances: Seeing on the television divers 'like birds, twisting and turning gracefully in the air'.

Significant phrases: 'I have never before wanted to be one of them, like a swallow flying through the air.'

Result: 'At that very *moment* [my italics] I decided I would try to be even as they were... Straightway I went to a swimming-bath.'

C 32

Circumstances: Going to a cricket match.

Significant phrases: 'I was sure I would never compare it with anything else, apart from the arts, of course.'

Result: Not stated.

C 33

Circumstances: Recall to the age of 3, visiting the now dead grand-mother, recounting the pretty possessions remembered and the tasting of the home-made cherry wine.

Significant phrases: None.

Result: 'When I think about those Sunday mornings which I used to love so much...I will always remember grandma as I loved her best and remember the lovely things she kept about her. When I think of the lovely wine which she made, I can taste the delicious beauty of the cherries in my mouth and whenever I drink home-made cherry wine, I remember the Sunday mornings I used to spend with my grand-mother.'

C 34

Circumstances: Recall to the age of 3, when the writer first came to live in London.

Significant phrases: 'I was walking along a pavement, built of many small bricks, and, being very short, I felt near to the ground and to those bricks. There were millions and millions, or so it seemed to my young mind, and I wondered if there could possibly be as many people in the world as there were bricks embedded in that pavement. I thought "poor bricks, will you be here for ever and ever?"... I cannot forget how endless the pavement seemed, going on for ever like the human race. It was by no means a smooth pavement, it had its ups and downs. Once I stepped into a puddle of water and had pity for the poor oppressed bricks underneath; now I compare them to the more un-fortunate people in the world. The bumps on the pavement were also rather unpleasant. They were vain and above themselves... I knew they would be trodden down.'

Result: 'So on I walked, puzzling over numbers, as I still have been doing to the present day.'

C 35

Circumstances: Seeing her brother and sister sick on a Channel crossing.

Significant phrases: None.

Result: 'I shall never forget that night... Never have I been so glad as when that sea journey ended.'

The circumstances given in the other eleven essays in this group are: (1) a drive to a small cove in Cornwall, (2) seeing a pretty house among ugly ones from a train, (3) the film *Reach for the Sky*, (4) the film *East of Eden*, (5) first experience of bell-ringing, (6) first visit to a farm, (7) visit to a beautiful country house, (8) train journey to camp, (9) visit to St. Ives ('It was like stepping back into History'), (10) visit to a cottage in the New Forest, (11) reading Pavlova's life ('I realized how wonderful ballet is').

Obviously any of these might be trigger situations, but there was nothing at all in the descriptions of the experiences to justify belief that anything like escstasy was involved—except for their being proffered in answer to the question.

SECTION II: average age 14 years

C 36

Circumstances: Recall to age of 10. Tramping over the hills of the Lake District with her family on a rainy day, and walking on ahead of them.

Significant phrases: 'For what seemed an eternity I pushed my way through the bracken, half blinded by the rain. Suddenly, I became aware of the presence of something; at first I could not tell what it was; then lifting my head…I saw that I had come to the end of the bracken, and was looking on to the lake. Two enormous menacing peaks towered above me, and as I saw them through the swirling mist, I seemed to hear a mass of orchestras all playing a triumphant sinister minor chord. I was petrified. I wanted to scream but my throat seemed to be choked. Still the mountains glared malevolently at me; I felt I was being lifted from my feet, and drawn by some mysterious power towards them. Looking round, I saw my family were still far behind. This made me panic for a moment, and tears began to spring in my eyes. I felt utterly helpless, as if I were trying to catch a bus in a night-mare, and found my legs had suddenly refused to go. For how long I stood there I don't know, but gradually I calmed myself, and took a few timid steps nearer the edge of the crag that rose from the lake. Here I saw a huge pit of choppy black water, that seemed to dance in horrible glee at the sight of my terrified bedraggled body. This was too much for me. I summoned up all my courage and energy, and ran as hard as I could to my family.'

Result: 'It was not until we had returned to our hotel…that I realized how much I had enjoyed the weird sinister walk over the moor, and the horror of the hills that rose from Lake Ullswater. It was this walk that made me realize that I would never be able to bear the classic holiday of a fortnight at some gaudy holiday town swarming with holiday makers… I knew I could never really enjoy myself unless I was surrounded by hills, moors and crags, and the ancient Roman roads that ramble endlessly over them.'

C 37

Circumstances: Recall to age of 10. In a chair-lift on the Swiss mountains.

Significant phrases: 'It was a thrilling experience to be suspended in space with only the ragged rocks far below. I felt I was in another world, a world of paradise unknown to me before this moment. It was difficult to believe that this was actually happening to me... My mind drifted as I sat moving slowly, rhythmically, on. Suddenly, amidst this haven, peace was interrupted, and as I came to my senses I realized that we had stopped moving. What had seemed like heaven was transformed to hell. There we were, hanging motionless. Looking down there were only the glaciers and the hard jagged rocks which glared challengingly at me... After what seemed like a lifetime of pessimistic imagination there was a sudden jerk and we continued our journey.'

Result: 'I can still remember how petrified I was at the prospect of remaining there or falling.'

C 38

Circumstances: Just learning to play the piano. Found a piece of music 'with a row of mountains drawn across the top of the page'.

Significant phrases: 'I have always been fascinated by mountains, though I have never seen any real ones.' Persuaded her aunt to play the piece to her. After the aunt had left the room, 'I gazed open-mouthed at the mountains drawn across the top of the page, forgetting myself in awe.'

Result: None stated.

C 39

Circumstances: Went to Whipsnade Zoo, and in an outhouse watched a chicken being hatched.

Significant phrases: 'People were now beginning to gather round, and were gazing, enthralled, at this wonderful spectacle. Eventually the shell split open, and with this final effort, the new-born chicken flopped down with exhaustion... No one said a word, but just looked on in wonder... A few people moved away, but I still stayed on watching the chicken's feeble attempts to move. So many millions of others, I thought, had been born, just like this, yet each had to fight his own way out of the shell; each had had just such a struggle into the world. And here was another one. Just another insignificant little chicken being born, but oh so wonderful to me, who had never seen anything like it before... I awoke from my reverie and left... Another tiny creature had been born into this wide, wide world.'

Result: None stated.

C 40

Circumstances: A lost dog on a summer holiday. Went to the ballet to take their minds off it.

Significant phrases: Usually enjoys the ballet, but 'today it all seemed pointless. The dancers were like autumn leaves fluttering in the breeze with no special significance, and the music was like a noise in the distance, such as one might hear a little way from a noisy market-place.' When they return home, the dog is back. The writer goes to her bedroom window and looks out. 'The stars were shining brightly and a full moon was throwing its light on to a calm sea. This, together with the return of our dog, made me feel there could be no nicer ending to our adventure.'

Result: None stated.

C 41

Circumstances: First visit to the opera.

Significant phrases: 'I was enthralled.'

Result: 'From that time on, I began to be an ardent opera fan.'

C 42

Circumstances: Going to a concert, through a street dirty with blown dust and scraps of paper.

Significant phrases: In the street, 'A middle-aged man with a cheap-looking violin' playing by 'a cold filthy wall with half-torn and blown away public notices'. The 'cracked tone was distorted by the busy traffic and barking of the crippled dog'. The violinist had 'grey, unbrushed and tangled hair', 'a hare lip', and 'Altogether his unshaved face was a sorrowful one.'

Result: None stated.

C 43

Circumstances: A service at St. Paul's Cathedral.

Significant phrases: Description of the cathedral largely in terms of contrast of light and dark, but no description of her feelings.

Result: None stated.

C 44

Circumstances: Recall to age of 8. First swimming lesson in deep water.

Significant phrases: 'I had a strange, tense, tied-up feeling... I felt as though I was right in the middle of a tremendous expanse of water, water pressing down on me from all sides. I felt strange and lost, I felt the power of the water and I was alone, struggling against a tremendous force. I gave in and immediately I felt panicky.' She is taken out, 'and suddenly I began to cry... I had had to admit defeat.'

Result: 'The thought of my defeat made me determined to do bigger and better things... I am sure I shall never be satisfied till I have done something really great to counteract the humiliation of my defeat.'

C 45

Circumstances: Standing in the doorway of a shop, with other people, sheltering from the rain. Beside her she sees a woman in a dirty white coat, who kept putting her large bony hand to her forehead.

Significant phrases: 'In some curious way I felt afraid of something and I stared at her face; it was the colour of her dirty white coat, with sunken-in cheeks. I felt repelled because my mother's cheeks were plump, homely and rosy. Again I looked at her face, her heavy puffed eyelids dropped sickeningly over her eyeballs and she swayed on her feet; horrified I saw her fall in a motionless heap at my feet. My mother grabbed me away; I was crying with shock and fright.'

Result: 'It seemed after that, that nothing would be strong as before. I had thought that grown-ups were never ill; always there, like safe walls on which one could lean; but now one of those walls had fallen, and I was cowering back against three walls and where the fourth had been was the entrance to a frightening exciting world.'

C 46

Circumstances: Recall to some age less than 8. Coming home from school with eight-year-old brother, sees a gypsy on a neighbour's doorstep with a basket of wax flowers for sale.

Significant phrases: 'Her face was strangely like parchment. Her eyes were sunken, but pierced like pins; they were black and beady. Her thin lips were pale as if lacking in blood... Her body was thick and flabby... her brown arms bare. For a moment as I looked at them I felt cold, but then after feeling the warmth of my clothes, I realized how lucky I was... She came slowly down the stone steps and as she reached the last two, her foot missed one. The tree, as if struck by lightning, fell; she lay quite still. "She is dead," I thought. I looked at my brother, he too had the same fear... "Run and fetch mummy. Tell her the gypsy's dead," he said softly. And I ran. I ran as if in a dream.'

Result: None stated. The gypsy gets up and goes away.

C 47

Circumstances: With her mother and two-year-old sister went to a hospital. The sister had 'a bad infection in her mouth and her flushed cheeks and glassy eyes showed she was none too well'. The doctor said the child must come into hospital, and the mother cried.

Significant phrases: 'How I remember her sad face with the tears rolling down it.' As they went back through the corridors, 'my bewilderment and sorrow for my mother increased until at last I too was crying... This made an impression on me and for many years I could see the faces of my mother and my sister, in particular that of my mother who seemed to be alone and helpless.'

Result: 'I now have resolved to be a nurse to help people such as her.'

C 48

Circumstances: Walking for the first time down a lane behind a garage, guarded by a notice 'Private—Trespassers Will be Prosecuted'. Saw a 'short fat woman', 'wrinkled, ugly', with 'a cruel mouth, teeth that were black and decayed and broken' and 'hard eyes'. Behind her was a house with 'dirty and smeary windows and rusty locks...while the door was painted a contrasting orange which clashed, and a narrow dark passage could be seen behind. In the garden was a long line on which hung a row of washing, old and ragged.'

Significant phrases: 'I was shocked at the sight and very much afraid.'

Result: None given.

C 49

Circumstances: The house on fire, in the night.

Significant phrases: 'I was petrified, glued to my bed by the invisible grip that attacks all humans at one time or another—fear.'

Result: None stated.

C 50

Circumstances: Recall to age of 5. Is told by the child next door that she (the writer) is not really her mother's child, but was found crying 'on a bonfire patch' in a field at the end of the garden. Is relieved next day to discover this is not true.

Significant phrases and results: None.

C 51

Circumstances: In her grandfather's house, full of Victorian trinkets, picks up a china candlestick and drops it; it smashes into tiny pieces.

Significant phrases: 'I never was so startled in all my thirteen years of life; I burst into tears and ran upstairs to my room... I was very shamed and never forgot the terrible incident.'

Result: None stated.

The circumstances given in the other five essays in this class are as follows: (1) a camping holiday, (2) a first visit to a fair, (3) a holiday in Sark, (4) and (5) return home to discover a new baby has been born.

All are purely descriptive of event, and none convey any of the writer's feelings.

SECTION III: age 12 years

C 52

Circumstances: A walk in the park in early spring, on a sunny day.

Significant phrases: 'The sun was warm and there was a fresh wind that swayed the daffodil leaves to and fro. Buds had just burst and showed tiny green curled up leaves... The bright green grass was short, and dew sparkled on it. Among the grass were snowdrops and crocuses... I stood and watched them as if I expected them to jump out of the soil. When the wind blew more strongly, the trees, which made a canopy of grey with speckles of blue, waved their graceful branches, while birds sang merrily in the bushes. It was a beautiful picture and I felt as though it were the beginning of everything; the beginning of a new and happy world.'

In this class, this was the only essay I saw, but I was assured that the others were irrelevant to my interests.

APPENDIX G

Details of Art Triggers named

(a) Music

BACH	organ music (Q 15)
	any Brandenberg especially the Sixth (Q 19)
	(specific music not named) (Q 46)
BEETHOVEN	Fifth Symphony (Q 17, L 18, J 2)
	Seventh Symphony (L 11)
	Fifth or Seventh, not sure which (Q 34)
	Ninth Symphony (Q 16)
	Archduke Trio (Q 18)
	Missa Solemnis (Q 18)
	Sonata Op. 32, No. 1 (L 23a)[1]
	(specific music not named) (Q 51)
BIZET	(specific music not named) (L 6)[2]
DEBUSSY	*Chanson de Mer* sung by Kathleen Ferrier (Q 51)[3]
ELGAR	The Dream of Gerontius (Q 44)
MAHLER	Tenth Symphony (Q 44)
MOZART	'Hallelujah' (Q 33)
	(specific music not named) (Q 16, Q 51, Q 55)
RACHMANINOV	Second movement of concerto (Q 7)
RESPIGHI	The Fountains of Rome (C 20)—not named, but obviously intended.
TCHAIKOVSKY	Pizzicato from Fourth Symphony (Q 14)

[1] Presumably Op. 31, No. 1 is intended.

[2] L 6 is Nietzsche, and Einstein says that 'Nietzsche's paen of praise for Bizet's *Carmen* is admittedly a malicious joke' (*Greatness in Music* (Oxford, 1941), p. 84). I am not sure if *Carmen* is intended here, but I see no reason to suppose that in text L 6 Nietzsche was not sincere. Paul Henry Laìng certainly assumes that Nietzsche was sincere in his praise of Bizet. (*Music in Western Civilisation* (London, 1942), pp. 907–8.)

[3] Debussy did not write a song called *Chanson de Mer* and I do not know what was intended. But that Kathleen Ferrier's singing could produce ecstatic effects Canon Roger Lloyd bears witness: 'In recent years I should say that the person who has done most to convince all kinds of people that the spiritual order is real and close is Kathleen Ferrier.' (*Manchester Guardian*, April 23, 1956.)

VAUGHAN WILLIAMS   Penultimate symphony (Q 16)
VERDI   (specific music not named) (Q 16)
'Orchestral music' (Q 21)
'More singing than orchestral' (Q 52)
Carols (Q 26)
Plainsong (Q 44)
German *lieder* (Q 16)
Irish folk-songs (Q 16)
Scotch folk-songs (Q 57)
Unnamed jazz (L 27)
Music (unspecified) (Q 43)

(b) Literature

Poetry

W. H. AUDEN   (poems not named) (Q 52)
EMILY BRONTË   (poems not named) (C 23)
JOHN DONNE   (poems not named) (Q 36)
W. DE LA MARE   'Look thy last' from 'A Farewell' (Q 50)
JOHN DAVIDSON   'St. Valentine's Eve' (Q 54)
T. S. ELIOT   'The Love Song of J. Alfred Prufrock' (Q 6)
A. E. HOUSMAN   'Loveliest of trees' (Q 50)
JOHN KEATS   'Magic casements' from 'Ode to a Nightingale' (Q 50)
JOHN MILTON   'Paradise Lost' (Q 52)
SALINAS and other South American poets (poems not named) (Q 36)
W. SHAKESPEARE   Sonnets (Q 36)
                 'the end of *Othello* and *Antony and Cleopatra*' (Q 22)[1]
                 'some of Shakespeare' (Q 52)
                 'Mad, who would be mad' (C 22)
A. TENNYSON   'Ulysses' (Q 6)
                 'jewels five words long' from *The Princess* (Q 25— I do not know whether she meant to suggest that this phrase acted as a trigger or well described triggers)

Poetry (unspecified) (Q 34)   Literature (unspecified) (Q 55)
C 21 named 'Rupert Brooke's poem "In Flanders Field" '; I assume she means John McCrae's poem of that name.

Fiction was mentioned by only one person in the questionnaire group, Q 46, who gave Tolstoy's *War and Peace* and Dostoevsky's *The Brothers Karamazov*.

---

[1] I do not know whether Q 22 intended to refer to private reading or public performance.

The Bible was mentioned by Q 52 (an atheist), and provided the phrase that triggered Richard Church's ecstasy of text L 23b.

Several books were named by the children in their essays: *David Copperfield* and another unnamed novel by Dickens, Mark Twain's *The Innocents Abroad*, the biography of an unnamed woman writer. In two cases books seemed to have aroused desolation rather than ecstatic feelings: these were a life of Madame Tussaud and *The Long Walk*.

(c) Drama

W. SHAKESPEARE   'the end of *Othello* and *Antony and Cleopatra*' (Q 22—as already explained, I do not know whether she was speaking of private reading or public performance)

R. B. SHERIDAN   *The School for Scandal* with the Oliviers (Q 45)

Greek tragedy (Q 25)

'drama' (unspecified) (Q 43)

(d) Painting, drawing, etc.

The Renoir Exhibition of 1950 (Q 7)

Flemish primitives in the National Gallery (Q 19)

Giorgione's *Tempest* (Q 27)

Mantegna's *Agony in the Garden* (Q 35)

Italian primitive art (Q 46)

A picture in a Roman church (Q 60)

(e) Sculpture

The Bodhisatta in the British Museum (Q 26)

The foliage carved on the door-jambs of the church of S. Pietro outside Spoleto (L 10)

The Venus de Milo (C 16)

(f) Film

'a perfect moment in a film' (Q 55)

The Member of the Wedding (Q 57)

(g) Architecture

Since the architecture named is all of a kind with religious associations, I give, where known, the religious position of the people concerned.

King's College Chapel and Chartres Cathedral (Q 26—Christian)

A ruined Augustinian abbey (Q 44—Roman Catholic)

Gloucester cathedral (Q 46—non-conformist)

A cathedral (Q 56—Jew)

A cathedral and a church (Q 60—pantheist)

'A fantastic temple' (Q 61—'I believe in God')
A forest chapel (L 16)
A sacred grove (L 22)
A chapel (R 1—Christian)
Milan Cathedral imagined (C 24)

Two children told of experiences, one in a synagogue and one in St. Paul's Cathedral; but these could not fairly be called ecstasies.

Lincoln Cathedral was the scene of the experience of Lawrence's hero (L 17a) which, for reasons given in Ch. XIV, I do not accept as an ecstasy.

I have chosen a poem of less than outstanding quality, so that if my interpretation of it seems maladroit, it will not mar a poem likely to be highly valued by the reader.

The Reverie of Poor Susan

At the corner of Wood Street, when daylight appears,
Hangs a Thrush that sings loud, it has sung for three years:
Poor Susan has passed by the spot, and has heard
In the silence of morning the song of the Bird.

'Tis a note of enchantment; what ails her? She sees
A mountain ascending, a vision of trees;
Bright volumes of vapour through Lothbury glide,
And a river flows on through the vale of Cheapside.

Green pastures she views in the midst of the dale,
Down which she so often has tripped with her pail;
And a single small cottage, a nest like a dove's,
The one only dwelling on earth that she loves.

She looks, and her heart is in heaven: but they fade,
The mist and the river, the hill and the shade:
The stream will not flow, and the hill will not rise,
And the colours have all passed away from her eyes!

Poor Outcast! return—to receive thee once more
The house of thy Father will open its door,
And thou once again, in thy plain russet gown,
May'st hear the thrush sing from a tree of its own.

(William Wordsworth. P.W., Vol. II, p. 217)

The last stanza, which appears only in the 1800 edition, was omitted by Wordsworth after a protest by Lamb; but since it formed part of the poet's original intention, it seems proper to take it into account.

The first stanza opens with the trigger contrast of the singing bird in the cage. The bird's fate is Susan's too, and both the bird and Susan are symbols of innocence, the simple rural bird and the simple rustic girl, the one pent in a cage, the other in the city.

But it is dawn and the city is silent. In the silence the bird's song can act as a trigger on Susan. By 'what ails her?' I understand, why does she suddenly look as if her senses have left her? The onlooker cannot know, but we know that it is because, in the silence, the presence of the anti-trigger city, its commercial aspects emphasized by the choice of the names Lothbury and Cheap, is replaced by the recollected trigger images of mountains and trees, river and mist.

Because Susan is a symbol of innocence, her proper place is not to be solitary on mountains or in woods. For her, these are the background to the simple rural houselife where she belongs, to engage, not in wearisome toil but with light foot, in her arcadian tasks. She belongs in the domestic cottage as the dove in its nest.

As she gazes her heart is uplifted and she feels she is in heaven. Momentarily she enjoys adamic ecstasy, but inevitably the moment passes; the vision fades and with it the ecstatic feelings of uplift and liquidity and brightness. The city at dawn may in fact be as colourful as the misty scene of the vision, but by contrast with the clear perceptions of ecstasy the city must seem dull and colourless. The rejected last stanza introduces the themes of purification and regeneration. As an ecstatic may feel purged of sin and assoiled, so may Susan, a sinning outcast, be purified if she returns to the adamic simplicity from which she came where she will discard her worldly gauds for her unpretentious russet gown; if she repents and returns to the open door of the church, her Father in Heaven will accept her again to his green pastures where the liberated thrush will sing in his own proper place.

The evidence of ecstasy is as follows:

The trigger is the song of the bird at dawn, and the recollected vision that it evokes.

The feelings of ecstasy intimated are:

Loss of sense: Susan is enchanted, i.e. bewitched, under a spell. I think that the mist, too, may express the bemusement of her senses, a happy bemusement because the vapour is bright. But passers-by would wonder what ailed her.

Feelings of joy, of another world: her heart is in heaven; the city has been replaced by the ideal place.

Feelings of liberation: She is released from the city as the thrush from its cage.

Feelings of salvation: The outcast is once more received in her Father's house.

Up-feelings: Expressed by Susan's heart feeling as if it is in heaven, and by the vision of the mountains which will not rise when the moment is over.

Liquidity-feelings: Expressed by the vision of the stream which will not flow when the moment is over.

Light-feelings: As compared with the colours of the vision, the real city is colourless. A light/dark contrast is suggested by the shade provided by the trees and the brightness of the mist.

As I suggested on p. 234, the device of trigger contrast often implies a moral intention, particularly when the contrast with the trigger is man-made. I think it does so here and that we should take it that thrushes should not be put in cages or Susans enticed to cities.

APPENDIX J

Some Further Investigations

1. Some time after the texts in Groups Q, L, and R had been collected and analysed, a further questionnaire was prepared (this time with expert help), based on that used for Group Q but in some ways simpler—owing to doubts whether words like *transcendent* and *ecstasy* were likely to be known to the people I wanted to question—and in some ways more complicated—i.e. questions were added on age, marital status, education, etc. 100 copies of this were distributed through letter-boxes in a working-class district of London, together with stamped addressed envelopes (with an uninformative name and address) for the return of the completed forms. 11 forms were returned. Of these, 10 gave a negative answer to the first question but provided all the factual details asked for, so presumably took the inquiry seriously. One affirmative answer was received. This respondent was a newspaper-packer whose age was over 50 and who had left school by the age of 15. His answers to the questions relating to ecstasy were as follows:[1]

J 1

Question: Have you ever known a feeling of unearthly ecstasy?
Answer: Yes.

Question: Would you say it was the same as feeling very happy indeed, or different from feeling very happy indeed?
Answer.   Different.

Question: What sort of things have brought this feeling on?
Answer: Sunsets. Beautiful music. Scenery from heights, e.g. from Snowdon, Helvellyn, etc. Also masses of flowers.

Question: How many times have you had it?
Answer: Dozens.

Question: Could you describe what it was like on one of the occasions when you have had this feeling?
Answer: Indescribable. Peace, accompanied by a little heavier breathing and sometimes a feeling of wanting to close my eyes and cry.

[1] I shall number texts quoted in this Appendix and refer to them as Group J.

Question: Was your life in any way changed as a result of feeling like this?

Answer: Not exactly changed but certainly strengthened in my appreciation of life.

Question: Do you remember ever reading about ecstasy in a book?
Answer: No.

Question: What is your religion or belief?
Answer: Rationalist.

Obviously the numbers involved are too small for any conclusions. But one affirmative to 10 negative answers in this working-class group shows a very different proportion from the 3 negative answers—2 people classified by me as 'O' and one as 'I'—to 60 affirmative answers in Group Q.

2. A psychologist friend, experienced in questionnaire techniques, challenged the results I had obtained with Group Q on the grounds that the questions I had asked were of a kind impossible to answer, and to be avoided. She accepted the basic postal questionnaire described above after making some small alterations, and distributed 7 copies of this with stamped addressed envelopes. 4 were given to university colleagues and students, inviting their comments on the questionnaire as well as their answers to it, and 3 to non-academic middle-class people.

Three of the academic respondents gave negative replies to the first questions, together with substantial notes on why it was unanswerable ('difficult to decide on an exact definition'—'depends entirely on context'—'confused terms of reference'; all very similar criticisms to those my friend had made of my own questionnaire); one of these three people did add that he would have given an affirmative answer to a differently arranged and phrased questionnaire, but as his note demanded an exact definition of the word *thinking*, it is hard to believe his reply would have been fruitful. The fourth academic respondent, though troubled by similar scruples (his is text J 2 below) managed to answer the questionnaire. The three non-academic respondents apparently found no difficulty.

The questions asked were as follows:

1. Have you ever had a feeling of 'ecstasy' or bliss or outstanding joy? (If your answer to this is 'no' please skip questions 2–7 and just fill in the answers to question 8.)

2. Would you say it was the same as feeling very happy indeed or different from feeling very happy indeed?

3. What sort of things have brought this feeling on?

4. About how many times have you had it?

5. Could you describe what it was like on one of the occasions when you had it?

6. Was your life or way of thinking in any way changed as a result of feeling like this?

7. Do you remember ever reading about ecstasy in a book? If so, could you name the book or books?

8. (Here people were asked their sex, occupation, religion or belief, whether married or single, age-group, the age at which they left school, and whether they went to a college or university.)

J 2

1. Yes.

2. Different from feeling very happy indeed. This is a purely semantic question. To me, happiness is a prolonged unemotional state. Ecstasy is *momentary* [my italics] and highly charged.

3. Sexual intercourse. Beethoven's 5th. As an adolescent, certain emotional passages in a book, which could bring this feeling on again and again.

4. Maybe 8–12 times.

5. Very intense, with all bodily signs of great emotional imbalance, almost painfully pleasurable, sometimes leading to tears, *short duration*. It seemed to involve much more than just the body—all-enveloping, something to be very grateful for afterwards.

6. No—except that perhaps several such experiences may make a person more mature, less insecure, and more at ease with himself.

7. Only vague stories about Red Indians or Yogis fasting, etc. I have had a number of 24-hour complete fasts, but these never led to any extraordinary experiences.

8. (Married man aged between 31 and 40. University lecturer. Left school at 16, went to college or university. No religion or belief.)

J 3

1. Yes.

2. Different from feeling very happy indeed.

3. Visual beauty, i.e. scenery—The state of complete physical relaxation—Prayer.

4. Approximately half a dozen times.

5. Freedom from the body yet a greater awareness of being alive.
6. Not to my knowledge.
7. No.
8. (Married woman aged between 31 and 40. Shop assistant. Left school at 12, did not go to college or university. Agnostic.)

J 4

1. **Yes.**
2. (This respondent ticked both parts of the answer.)
3. Generally a combination of beauty, exhilarating weather, of loving and being loved, tremendous anticipation. Flowers in perfect weather have done this. The birth of my children.
4. Difficult—maybe 20 instances over about 10 years.
5. Sheer exhilaration as I saw again a place of very happy memories. A feeling of tremendous urgency to do something—quite indefinable.
6. Not directly.
7. Must have done, but can think of no particular instance.
8. (Married woman aged between 21 and 30. Housewife. Left school at 16, went to college or university. Religion or belief: 'A little of something.')

J 5

1. Yes.
2. Same as feeling very happy indeed.
3. Simply a sudden extreme mood for no apparent reason. Thinking of someone you are in love with. A wonderful sunrise in romantic surroundings.
4. About a dozen times within the last ten years.
5. Terrific feeling of undefined hope and gladness.
6. Not really.
7. Yes, but could not name the book.
8. (Single woman aged between 21 and 30. Secretary. Left school at 17, went to college or university. No religion or belief.)

Unfortunately these four people are of similar range, socially and educationally, to those in Group Q. The results did confirm that such questions could be answered, even without interview; that the answers in Group Q were not affected by the questioner's desire for or expectation of certain kinds of answer; and that similar kinds of people knew these experiences. But they were useless as an attempt to find out how far ecstatic experiences were known to the population at large.

3. The children of Group C (see Ch. XII and Appendix F) were all at a high-school to which entrance was obtained by competitive examination. There is no reason to assume that the experiences they described either would or would not be known to children from a secondary modern school or from an exclusive public school.

4. In 1957 I was able to get information about some 500 letters received by the B.B.C. after a programme on childbirth (these are discussed in Chapter XIII). Some 400 of these letters seemed to be describing possibly ecstatic feelings. These women apparently ranged from middle-class to barely literate working-class.

The audience for this programme is over three million. There is no means of knowing whether the 400 women who might have had ecstasy were the only ones among the listeners to have had the experiences described, or, if not, what proportion they were of women who had had these experiences. All that can be said of this group in relation to the ability to have an ecstasy is that it showed that some 400 women of all classes had probably experienced ecstasy either through childbirth or through hearing a programme about childbirth. It is almost certainly significant that only three of these women compared the experiences they were writing about with other experiences induced by other triggers.

5. In August 1958, I took part in a B.B.C. television Brains Trust at which a question was asked on mysticism, and I took the opportunity to ask those watching to write and tell me of mystical experiences they had known. I received 42 letters, most of them from women and many of them dotty—anyone who has received letters after appearing on television will know what I mean. Among experiences claimed as mystical were some concerned with 'Cosmic Law', with 'Radiotonics', with astrology, with supernatural entities; others wrote of hallucinations, sense of presence, visions, automatic writing, experiences of divine healing, of the regular receipt of supernatural answers to everything. Several people, including 4 Jungians (3 men and 1 woman), wrote long dissertations on the value of mysticism, and most of these suggested books I should read.

To 4 people, who seemed to be speaking of ecstasy in my sense though they gave no descriptions, I sent questionnaires of the kind used in (2) above. All were returned. One gave an affirmative answer to the first question but no answer to any of the other questions except the factual ones at the end. Two described their ecstasies in ways typical of literature rather than of other respondents and claimed to have read so many books on the subject as to force one to doubt how far their answers were derived from personal experience. Only one, a Roman Catholic woman, gave answers similar to those derived from the other questionnaires. Her experiences were triggered by prayer, by music, by views, by poetry and by watching her children. She said she had known the experience 'too many times to remember' but that sometimes it was less intense 'and might only be great happiness', and when asked to describe it, wrote:

'This is almost impossible to describe. I know enough about mysticism to know that they are not the ecstasies the saints experience. They are definitely religious even when related to poetry, music, etc. One is extremely uplifted and even oblivious to what is going on round one. Praise of God is inextricably mixed up in these feelings and gratitude to God, too, for making and allowing such beauty.' (J 6)

In her original letter she had written:

'Where does mysticism begin and appreciation of life end? I, for instance, get the same feelings from hearing music that I can get from prayer. I have found no other experience to equal them and, because of my training, I instinctively turn to God in music as in prayer. To what or whom do you turn in such *moments* [my italics]?'

Seven people's letters gave descriptions of ecstasies. Triggers included walking, seeing a sparrow, being on a hill in moonlight, beautiful views, and seeing a dead grandfather. One woman said she had known this experience once when much troubled and in the act of walking from one room to another with two small children tugging on her skirts. Another, arising from feelings of boredom but in trigger surroundings, is worth quoting:

'In 1916 I was walking along the shore road westward out of the Royal Borough of Culross wheeling a pram which contained one child recumbent and one doing everything but lie down. There were three other young children running round me, getting under my feet and asking the silliest questions... The sun was not shining. I looked across the waters of the Firth of Forth over to the hills hiding the town of Linlithgow, studying their outline against the watery sky, and out of the utter boredom and empty meaninglessness of that afternoon came a stab of knowledge. I *knew* and have known ever since that there *is* some Reason, some Plan, some Cause, some Soul, call it what you will, which can be relied upon... For *a split second* [my italics], there upon the shores of the Firth, I *understood*. What I understood I don't know now, but I *know* I understood then and I have remained firm and calm and unshaken upon that rock—i.e. that once I understood—ever since. I do not say that my whole life was altered from that *moment* [my italics], only say that fear departed and I was left with something firm and secure... If everything I can think of were taken away this would still remain. Something so infinitely larger, that the rest, though lost, would be of no account. I do not call this a faith. It is not really so active as that, it is *me*.' (J 7)

Two people gave experiences of desolation as children.

Among these letters there was one of great interest from an obviously intelligent and well-balanced woman who described three experiences. One, a typical intensity ecstasy, took place on a night walk after, she specifies, 'the warmth of friends, of meeting, of doing war work'. Another time, when sitting in the sun, very weak after illness, she found herself with tears pouring down her face.

'—just release. Then a poem, almost complete, came. Tears all the time. I altered the poem very little...it truly expresses my life or feeling or thought at that time, also something universal about it. Then I felt better.' (J 8)

Also, most valuably, this woman sent a dream experience. She explained that she had once belonged to a group whose members wrote down dreams and discussed them together, and that this dream was written down immediately on waking and was not altered:

'This is not perhaps exactly a whole dream at all, an experience, a marvellous feeling, a state, I don't know: Woke, time not known, suddenly, easily, without shock. Just awake, feeling extraordinary, marvellous, as if *everything*, whole answer to everything, all problems of life, were just round the corner, so near, so close, could almost touch it, them, the whole whatever may be: The feeling is impossible to describe. The whole *was* there, so near, just out of sight it is true, but that did not matter. It *was* there. As well as the impossible to describe feeling there was more concrete sight or rather sight and feeling perhaps, as if a star was suddenly broken and out poured showers of light. That does not really quite describe it either. Streams, showers of silver white light, brittle; cascading up (I know) and down (I think). As if a rock, crystal, star, some substance broke, shattered, and all these streams, lines, poured up from it (and down, not sure).

532

Fireworks, perhaps, the nearest description, but unlike fireworks this light was white, light or silver, also it was at the *side* of the dream? That sounds silly, I mean, supposing the dream a cinema screen, then the breaking light, showering light was at the left side rather. But spread all round I think. Several times in the night I woke after this, each time I thought and felt and went over the experience, unconsciously, I mean, and now, on waking, write it down.'

She adds, 'This was dreamt the night of the Brains Trust', and continues:

'Result in daily life: Just that everything for a little while seems wonderful, lighter, brighter, sounds daft. But on going downstairs (house rather shabby) even the carpet seems a better blue. The sunshine coming in through drawing-room windows more, can't describe it, but *more* than sunshine. Everything enhanced somehow. I get my Mother's breakfast, do jobs in very short time. Am light, easy, (usually very happy) but now even happier. I welcome the wasps into the kitchen even! All defects, neglects still there, but something over the whole lifts it up.' (J 9)

I regard the above as probably being as near to a pure description of the feelings of an ecstatic experience as one could hope to get, as nearly as possible unadulterated by overbelief or by subsequent interpretation.

Grateful as I am for these letters, and particularly for the last, they can add nothing as evidence about the distribution of the ability to have ecstatic experiences in the population at large.

INDEX

In the longer entries (with the exception of book titles) the more significant page references are printed in italics.

Acts, 247n., 300, 303, 349n.
Adam, the state of, *91, 95, 105–7, 110,* 115, 136, *235, 296*
Adamic ecstasies, *92–5 pass.,* 97n., *103–15 pass.,* 129, 132, *136,* 175, 193, *220, 257–8, 275, 295–303 pass., 309, 311,* 317, *363, 369*
Adolescence and ecstasy, 135–6
Adonais, 237
Advertising, 6–7, 179, 231–2, 281, 287
Aesthetics and History, 181
Agnostic's Apology, An, 295
Aids to Reflection, 339
Alacoque, St. Mary Margaret, 147n.
Alcohol, 259–60
Alexander, C. F., 243
Allegory of Love, The, 147n.
Allen, H. Warner, *60*, 126, 156, 171, 217, 218, 219, 284, 290, 341, 346
Allois, Abbot, 177
Alphonsus Rodrigues, St., 121, 204, 365, 367
Ambrose, St., 324
Amiel's Journal, 335
Anaesthetics, 260–2, 344, 352
Anatomy of Inspiration, An, 22n., 189, 197, 198, 285, 286, 306, 309n., 346n., 352
Ancient Mariner, The, 333, 358
Angela of Foligno, 73, *75–6*, 84, 120, 128, *253*, 307, 308, 366
Anger, 37–8, 54–5, 170, 174n.
Anima Poetae, 8
Animals as triggers, 108–9, 188, 220, 229, 235
Anselm, St., 127n.
Anti-triggers, 176–86, 191–3, 205, 224, 277, 317
Aquinas, St. Thomas, 119

Archilochus, 353
Architectural Review, 180
Architecture as trigger, 191–4
Argyle, M., 136n.
Aridity. *See* Dryness
Aristotelean Society, Proceedings of the, 18
Art as trigger, *26–7*, 138, *146, 173–4, 178,* 185, 187, *190–1,* 194, 201, 206, 220, *223,* 224, 233, 266–8
Asceticism, 180, 313–14
Auden, W. H., 176n., 238, 240
Augustine of Hippo, St., 57, 59, 79, 82, 91, 121, *131–2, 157, 171–2, 184, 196, 204,* 244, 285, 286, 302, *309, 319–25, 327–8,* 336, *337,* 340, 341, 351, 354
Ault, N., 194
Austen, J., 6
Austin, J. L., 18
Autobiography of Neville Cardus, 230
Autobiography of Margiad Evans, 254
Autobiography of Edward Gibbon, 113

Bach, J. S., 190
Bacon, F., 302
Bannister, R., 199
Barrie, 232
Barth, K., 300n.
Bateson, F. W., 198n., 252, 361n.
Battle for the Mind, 195n., 290
B.B.C., 5n., *65, 139–43 pass.,* 168n., *209,* 256n., 259n., 275, *277n.,* 335
Beatific Vision, The, 112, 263, 272, 273
Beauty as trigger, *26–7, 191–2, 205,* 220, *223,* 230, 233
Beeching, H. R., 200, 214
Beethoven, L. van, 156, *167, 173,* 190, *209,* 217, 231, 267, 341
Belloc, H., 259n.

Bellum Civile, 212
Berenson, B., 81, 118, 128, *156*, *181*, *182*, 216, *222*n., *284*, *291*, 337, 354
Berg, A., 266, 270
Berlioz, H., 267, 347
Bernard, St., 57, 78, 357
Besse, Fr. de, 161n.
Betjeman, J., 191
Bible, 72, 154, 341
Biographia Literaria, 24n., 336, 340
Blake, W., *181–2*, 223, 234, 236–7, 299n., 361, 374
Blue and Brown Books, The, 39n.
Blunt, W., 198
Boehme, J., 57, 61, 74, *119*, 128, 253n., *307*, 347, 361
Böhler, P., 328
Book of the Nine Rocks, 308
Born in Exile, 109
Botticelli, A., 230n., 267
Bowra, C. M., 95, 281–2, 286, 358
Brainerd, D., 60, 169, *195*, 212, 247, 290, 366
Brain-washing, 212n.
Breathing, 77, 79–81, 87, 247, 253
Brontë, C., 48, 54, 62, 67, 78, 79n., 83, *103*, 104, *274*n., *284*, *306*
Brontë, Charlotte, The Life of, 348
Brontë, E., *47–54 pass.*, 87, 121, 127, 175, 210, 216, 307
Brook Farm, 301
Brooke, R., 178, 196
Browne, T., 220, 246, 302
Bucke, R. M., *84*, *121*, 128, 197, 198, *290–1*, 291, 365
Bullett, G., 72n., 155n.
Burns, R., 229
Butler, C., 29, 45, *46*, *50–1*, 53n., 57, 78n., *122–3*, *131–2*, 161n., *195*, 204n., *238*, 252, 272, *274*, 324, *360*, 362
Butler, S., 229
Byron, Lord, 98, 251

Caractères, Les, 205
Cardus, N., 230
Carmina, 72
Carroll, L., 81, 113n., 247, 346, 352
Carstairs, M., 258–9
Cassian, J., 67, 189n.
Catherine of Genoa, St., 57, *69*, 70n., *125*, 132, *196*n., *311*n., *358*

Catherine of Siena, St., 64n., 68, 84, *253*, 307, *364*, 367
Centuries of Meditation, 67, 136–7
Cézanne, P., 266, 270, 271
Change of heart, 65, 193, 258, 300
Chapman, Abbot, 105n.
Chaucer, G., 150–2, 312
Chesterton, G. K., 259n.
Childbirth, 11, 26, *65–6*, *138–44*, 151, 155, 204, 206, *209*, *213*, 222, 223, 251n., 305, 370
Childe Harold, 98
Children and desolation, 163–7, 207–210, 336
Children and ecstasy, 104–7 *pass.*, *110–111*, *134–7*, *154–5*, 220, 235, 256, 275, 370
Christian Mysticism, 51, 52, 71n., 74, 78n., 92n., 93, 125, 172, 252, 253n., 275, 307, 316, 358, 361
Christie, A., 305, 308
Church, R., 57, 78, 81, *84*n., *103–5*, 120, 126, *134–6*, 154, 208, 238, 284, 341
Churchill, W. S., 205
Cities, 192–4, 220–1, 222, 301–3
Clark, J. M., 74, 178
Clark, K., 210, 230
Coffinhal, J. B., 300
Coldness, 85, 165, 209–10, 247
Coleridge, S. T., 8, *24*, 251n., *276*n., *333*, 336, *339–40*, *348*, 358
Collective unconscious, 107, 130, 168n., 254, 354
Comforts of Unreason, The, 184n.
Commerce, 9n., 38, 139, 176, *178–9*, 185, *231*, 299, *303*n., *317*n.
Concise Etymological Dictionary of the English Langiage, 210n.
Concise Oxford Dictionary, 29, 31, 246
Confessions of St. Augustine, 79, 82, 157, 184, 196, 204, 244, 319–24
Constantinople, 192
Contact feelings and words, *30–1*, *45–6*, *91–5 pass.*, *122–33*, 163, 221, *308–9*, *310*, 363
Contributions to Analytical Psychology, 332n.
Conversation as trigger, 75n., *196–7*, 205, 223
Conversion, 154, 289–93, 324, 331–2, 343

Copleston, F. C., 335, 340, 344
Corinthians, 14, 367n.
Cornford, F., 107-8, 111
Country Life, 180
Coveney, P., 105n.
Craft-objects, 194, 228
Crawshay-Williams, R., 184n.
Creative work as trigger, 26, 65, 95,
    201-2, 206, 223, 286
Crichton-Browne, J., 255, 261n., 275-6
Crooked House, 305
Cross, J. W., 306
Crowd, The, 205n., 206n.
Crowds, 38, 176-8 pass., 194, 205-6,
    372
Cupid's dart, 82n.
Custance, J., 130, 161, 257-8, 261n.

Daniel Deronda, 52n., 79, 127, 214
Dante Alighieri, 155
Darbishire, H., 183, 219n., 361, 374n.
Dark Ages, The, 165n.
Dark night of the soul, 160
Darkness feelings and words, 18n.,
    32-3, 72-6, 149, 163, 165, 170,
    209-12 pass., 217, 225, 234
Darwin, C., 106
Da Vinci, L., 267n.
Davis, M., 152n.
Davy, H., 275-6
Dawn of Day, The, 328n.
Day-Lewis, C., 234
Death, 137, 169, 207, 210, 234, 255-6,
    277n.
Debates with Historians, 354
Defence of Poesie, The, 269n.
Déjà vu, 276
De La Mare, W., 138, 156n., 183n.,
    239, 291
De Quincey, T., 251
Desert Fathers, The, 177n., 189n.
De Selincourt, E., 81n., 193n., 362
Desolation experiences, 135, 160-70,
    175, 207-12, 225, 257, 258, 336,
    371
Desolation ecstasies, 168-9, 175, 203,
    207, 212, 233, 256, 371
Desolation triggers, 176n., 185, 207-12,
    234
Devil Rides Outside, The, 148n.
Devils of Loudun, The, 70n.
Dick-Read, G., 139-43 pass.

Dickens, C., 306, 309n.
Dionysius the Areopagite, 73-5, 94n.,
    125, 314
Dirt, 208, 212, 234, 257
Discovery of the Mind, The, 219n.
Doctor's Dilemma, The, 342
Donne, J., 6
Doors of Perception, The, 73n., 240, 263
Dostoievsky, F., 254
Down feelings and words, 70-3, 163,
    170, 211, 214-15, 225, 246
Dreams, 72n., 256, 350
Dreamy Mental States, 255, 261n., 276
Drug-Taker's Notes, A, 80, 261n., 263,
    272-3
Drugs, 16, 41, 258-73 pass.
Drugs of Election, 259n.
Dryness, 42, 160, 163, 165, 248, 249n.
Du Côté de Chez Swann, 267
Duration of ecstasies, 6, 24, 43-4, 57-
    66, 257, 264-5, 272-3, 280n.,
    364n., 369

Ecclesiasticus, 302
Eckhart, Meister, 70-1, 73-5, 123, 178
Economist, The, 193
'Ecstasy' in religious usage, 6, 7, 42,
    57n., 75-6, 84n., 196, 253n., 364
Ecstatic afterglow, 58-63 pass., 66,
    264n., 346, 369
Ecstatic, an defined, 18n.
Einstein, A., 154, 192n., 201, 223
Einstein, His Life and Times, 154, 201,
    223
Elijah, 188
Eliot, G., 79, 127, 228, 306
Eliot, T. S., 234, 338
Elizabethan Lyrics, 194
Ellis, H., 19
Emperor's Clothes, The, 184n.
Encephalography, 190n.
Encounter, 54n.
Endymion, 152n., 228
English Mystics, The, 72n., 155n.
Enthusiasm, 172, 195n., 341n.
Epilepsy, 254-5
Epistulae Morales, 212
Eranos Jahrbuch, 109, 215
Ethics, 351n.
Evans, M., 120, 126, 128, 254-5, 257
Eve of St. Agnes, The, 247n.
Excursion, The, 361n., 374

Exercise as trigger, 26–7, 138, 197–200, 206, 223
Existence of God, The, 335
Exodus, 187
Experiment in Depth, 328–30
Eyeless in Gaza, 73n.
Ezekiel, 71n.

Fabriano, G. da, 266, 270
Faked ecstasies, 14–15, 73n., 151n.
Fallacy of Personal Rights, The, 182
Fever, 255
Fire, 31, 79n., 82, *84–5, 165n.,* 216–17, *218–19,* 247
First and Last Love, 81
First Four Minutes, 199
Flashes of light, 72, 77, *81–3,* 87, *216–7,* 221, 223, 268
Flicker, 213, 216–17, 219, 223
Folk-heroes, 205, 216
Food as trigger, 204, 222, 223
Forster, E. M., 58, 79, 156, 167, 208, 341
Fourier, C., 301
Four Quartets, 338
Fox, G., 79–80, *90–1,* 92, 93n., 103, 105, 119, 361
Francesca, P. della, 267
Francis of Assisi, St., 257
Francis of Sales, St., 45, 69, 79, 126, *147,* 148, 366
Frank, P., 154, 201, 223
Frequency of ecstasies, 5, 7, *23–4, 43,* 48, 54, 94, *97,* 106, 135–6, *145,* 149
Freud, S., Freudian, 29, 54, 69, 116, 187, 214, 219n.
Friedländer, M., 302n.
From the Third Programme, 335

García de Toledo, 172
Garden of Cyrus, The, 220
Garrod, H. W., 183, 361
Gaskell, E. C., 348
Genesis, 91n., 300n.
George VI, 277n.
Geyl, P., 354
Gibbon, E., 113, 285, 352
Gissing, G., *55–6, 64–6,* 87, *95,* 96, 109, *144,* 220, *250,* 292, 363
Gittings, R., 247n.
Gladstone, W. E., 29

Glory, 31–2, 79n., 246–7
God, *116, 123–33 pass.,* 147, 168n., 187–8, 220, 238, *241, 244,* 254, *283,* 291, 296n., *307–11 pass., 313, 349,* 353, *361–3,* 367
Goethe, W., 283, 286, 306
Golden Bough, The, 158, 201, 270
Good Behaviour, 205n.
Gospel according to Thomas, The, 303n.
Graces of Interior Prayer, The, 6n., 21, 46, 59, 63, 74, 75, 76, 123, 249, 253n., 257, 307n., 358
Greatness in Music, 192n.
Gregory the Great, St., 50, 51, 57, 204, 252
Griffin, J. H., 148n.
Guida, 252–3n.
Guthrie, W. K. C., 296n.
Guyon, Madame, 148, 172

Hakluyt, R., 157, 285
Hamilton, W. R., 332, 337–8, 344, 346
Hamlet, 6
Harding, R., 22n., *189,* 197, 198, *217,* 285, 286, 306, 309n., 346n., 352
Harper's Magazine, 314n.
Hashish, 259
Hastings, P., 256
Hawkes, J., 61, *108–10,* 120, 128, 188n., 216, 217, 284
Haydon, B., 87–8, 95
Heart, 67, 77–8, 165, 248
Heat, feelings and words, 32–3, 72, 78, 82, 247
Heaven and Hell, 162n.
Hedley, Bishop, 274
Hell, 163, 165n.
Heracleitus, 361
Hewlett, D., 88n.
Heywood, R., 263–73 *pass.*
Heyworth, P., 168
Hieroglyphics, 260n.
Hilton, W., 161
History of the Crusades, A, 193
Hodgson, R., 238
Homosexuality, 145n., 150
Hopkins, G. M., 177
Horace, 72
Housman, A. E., 80, 82, *88,* 184, *234,* 238, *284,* 346
Howe, F., 305n., 306n.
Hoys, D., 180

Hügel, F. von, 57, *69*, *72*, 82n., 83n., *86n.*, 91n., 93n., *125n.*, 196n., 219n., *240*, *252-3n.*, *311n.*, *315*, *356*, *358*
Hugh of St. Victor, 78, 84, 85, 118, 366
Human Nature in Politics, 83-4n.
Hume, D., 183n., 225n.
Hussey, D., 168
Hutterites, 300, 314n.
Huxley, A., 70, *73n.*, 149, *162n.*, 240, *263-73 pass.*
Hypnosis, 141-2, 197, 217, 219
Hysteria, 253-4

Ideal Marriage, 153n.
Idiot, The, 254n.
Ignatius Loyola, St., 46, 118, 133, 156, 171
Imitation of Christ, The, 312
In the Beginning, 296n.
In the Days of the Comet, 65
Incendium amoris, 78n.
Ineffability, 30-1, 44-5, 243, 349
Inge, W. R., 51, 52, 71n., 74, 92n., *93*, *124-5*, *172*, 252, 253n., 275, 296, 307, *316*, *358*, *361*, 362
Inquiry Concerning Human Understanding, 225n.
Inspiration, 8, *81*, 85n., 87-8, *89-90*, 95-6, 100, *118*, 197-8, *202*, 217, 25In., *279 ff. pass.*
Inspiration and Poetry, 95, 282
Instincts of the Herd in Peace and War, 184n., 314n.
Intensity ecstasies, *18-20*, 32, *47-56 pass.*, *57-63 pass.*, *67-76 pass.*, 89, 108, 135, *170*, 174-5, *195-6*, 217, 219, 232-3, *249-61 pass.*, 264, 280, *310*, *315*, *363*, *369-371 pass.*
Interior Castle, The, 359, 431n.
Intimations of Immortality, 99, 136
Introspection as trigger, 26-7, 138, 203, 206
Involuntary speech, 28n., 84
Irvine, L., 256n.
Irving, W., 188
Isaiah, 299n.

Jacopone da Todi, 82n.
James, Epistle of, 312
James, H., 215, 333

James, W., *20-1*, *44-5*, 66, 80, 117n., 118n., 120n., *208*, 231, 253n., *254*, *257-8*, *260*, *261*, 268, *289*, 290, *313*, *329n.*, *331*, *337*, *364-5*, 366, 367
Jazz, 190, 214, 218, 349n.
Jefferies, R., *51*, 80, 87, *99*, 103-4, 112, *131-2*, *192-3*, *249-51*, 252, 253n., 289n.
Jennings, P., 82n.
Jeremiah, 14
Jesus, 64n., 78n., 105n., *188*, *194n.*, 300, *303n.*, 357
Jewish Religion, The, 302n.
Job., 84n., 341
Joël, K., *47-54 pass.*, 84, 87, 108, 109, 128, *363*
John, 178, 188n., 238
John of the Cross, St., *52*, *91*, 93, 125, *160*, 165n., *313*, *358*
John the Divine, St., 84, 216, 218, 219, 308
John Keats, The Living Year, 247n.
Jones, R., 283, 295, 308, 365-7
Journal of George Fox, The, 90-1
Journal of Mental Science, 190n.
Journal of the Rev. John Wesley, The, 96, 158, 195n., 255, 325-7
Journals of Dorothy Wordsworth, 193n.
Joyful Wisdom, The, 314, 336, 339, 374
Juliana of Norwich, 353, 358
Jung, C. G., Jungian, *107-9 pass.*, 130, 188, *198n.*, 214-15, *328-30 pass.*, 332n., 341, *363-4*

Keats, J., 8, *152n.*, *174n.*, 188, 220, *228*, *247n.*
Keats, John, A Life of, 88n.
Keats, John, Selected Letters of, 179
Kekulé, A., 354
Kempis, Thomas à, 312
Kennedy, A., 141
Ker, W. P., 165n.
Kibbutzim, 301
Kim, 253n.
Kings, 188
Kipling, R., 235, 239, 253n., 306
Kirk, K. E., *51-2*, 63n., 94, 119n., 125, *274*, 280, *312-5 pass.*, 318n., *356-7*
Klemperer, O., 167

Knowledge as trigger, 26–7, 185, 200–202, 206

Knowledge, contact ecstasies, *92–5*, 97n., 103n., 106, 117, 122, 175, *285, 305, 308–9, 311, 370, 371*

Knowledge ecstasies, *92–5*, 106, 109, *116–21 pass.*, 133, 171, 175, *221–2, 301–4 pass.*, *370*

Knowledge feelings and words, *30–1, 44–5, 59–62, 91–2*, 96, 163, *165–6, 221–3, 232–3*, 244, *279, 280, 286, 295, 305–10, 335, 343–5, 347*, 363, *369*

Knox, R., 172, 195n., 341n.

Koechlin, C., 306

Koestler, A., *54–6*, 69, 79, 116, 156, *170*, 174n., 214, 363

Kretschmer, E., 169

La Bruyère, J de, 205

Lacombe, F., 172

Ladder of Perfection, The, 161

Lady Chatterley's Lover, 152–3, 185n.

Lancet, The, 255, 261n., 276

Land, A, 108

Landscape into Art, 210

Language and ecstasy, 10–15 *pass.*, 210–11, 226–48, 348–9

Lao Tzu, 71, 214

Last Poems, 184

Lavoisier, A., 300

Lawrence, D. H., *73–6 pass.*, 84n., 116, 145n., *148–53*, 185n., *211–12*

Le Bon, G., 205n., 206n.

Lectures and Notes of 1818, 348

Leff, G., 309n.

Lenin, V. I., 231

Leuba, J. H., *45–6, 82, 91n., 100–1, 146n.*, 147n., 172n., *202n.*, 211, 251, 254n., *256*, 261n., 276, *283*, 293, 332, 354n., 359, *364*

Levi, C., 48, *53–4*, 78, 135, 207, 217, 219, 292

Levitation, 68n., 256

Lewis, C. S., 147n.

Life of Charlotte Brontë, The, 348

Life of Patrick Hastings, The, 256

Life of John Keats, A, 88n.

Life of Mahomet, The, 188

Life of Saint Teresa, The, 29, 50, 53, 60, 68n., 82, 84, 90, 124n., 165n., 172, 196, 337n., 348, 355, 356

Light, 31, *32–3*, 69, *72–6*, 163, *189–90*, 210, *213, 216–17*, 221, 231, *246–7*, 261, 268–9

Lindsay, J., 229, 231

Lines composed a few miles above Tintern Abbey, 90, 222, 360

Liquidity feelings and words, 19, 32, *47*, 55, *67–9, 78–9*, 87, 163, 200, *214*, *218*, 233, 248

Listener, The, 168, 259n.

Little Gidding, 338

Lives, 6

Livingston Lowes, J. *See* Lowes, J. Livingston

Logos, 310, 374

Lombard, P., 147n.

Louis of Blois, 14, *47*, 69, *73, 75*, 78, *174n.*, 245, 366

Love, 138, 156n., 183n., 291

Love and ecstasy, 65, 82n., *90, 92, 93, 145, 150–3, 155*, 230, 234, *257–8, 271, 291, 295–96, 299, 369*

Lowes, J. Livingston, 215, 333, 340

Lucan, 212

Luke, 188n., 299, 312, 313

Luther, M., 326n., 341

Lysergic acid, 263–73, pass.

Macarius of Egypt, St., 94

Machen, A., 259–60n.

Mahler, G., 336

Mahomet, 188

Maimonides, M., 301

Major Trends in Jewish Mysticism, 71n.

Making, Knowing and Judging, 176n.

Man on Earth, 109

Manchester Guardian, 143–4, 200n., 263, 336n.

Manic-depression, 130, 161, 168, 254, 257

Manners and Rules of Good Society, 303n.

Mansfield, J., 205, 216

Mark, 188, 349n.

Marlowe, C., 155

Marriot, A., 263–73 pass.

Martin, P. W., 328–30

Mary Margaret Alacoque, St., 147n.

Masefield, J., 237

Mathematics, 201, 220, 221, 302, 337

Matthew, 105n., 188n., 244, 312, 337n.

Mayhew, C., 256n., 261n., 262n., 263–73 pass.
Mediaeval Thought, 309n.
Mee, A., 111n.
Meister Eckhart, 74–5, 178
Memoirs of a Fox-Hunting Man, 198
Memoirs of Hecate's County, 152
Memoirs of an Infantry Officer, 203–4n.
Meredith, G., 80, 81, 127, 208, 210, 231, 292
Merkabah mystics, 71n.
Merswin, R., 308
Mescalin, 149, 227, 261n., 262, 263–273
Michelangelo, 181, 267
Mill, J. S., 27n.
Mills, C. Wright, 235
Missa Solemnis, 173
Molinos, M. de, 123, 252–3n., 359
Montague, C. E., 118, 126, 168, 357
Moore, G. E., 196n.
Moorman, M., 114, 251n.
Morbidly-induced ecstasies, 16, 41, 76n., 253–6
More, T., 302
More Poems, 234
Morley, T., 22n.
Morris, W., 297, 302
Mortimer, R., 263–73 pass.
Moses, 187, 272
Motor-cars as triggers, 200
Moult, T., 232
Mountains as triggers, 185, 187–8, 201, 210, 221, 220, 223, 232–3
Mozart, W. A., 267
Music as trigger, 211, 171, 174, 190, 210, 214, 217, 222, 224, 230, 232–3, 266–7
Mystic Way, The, 64n., 86n., 94n., 125, 230, 274, 316
Mystical Element in Religion, The, 57, 69, 72, 82n., 86–7n., 91n., 93n., 125n., 196n., 219n., 240, 252–3n., 311n., 315, 356, 358
Mysticism, 48–51, 74, 75, 78n., 86nn., 94n., 96n., 124, 160n., 162n., 165n., 182, 240, 253, 274, 282, 289, 307, 310, 313n., 361, 364
Mysticism and Logic, 295n.
Mysticism, Christian and Buddhist, 71, 100–1n., 185n.
Mysticism, Sacred and Profane, 105n., 129–33 pass., 147, 161n., 263, 360–3 pass., 364n.

Name and Nature of Poetry, The, 80, 88, 284
Natural History of Religion, The, 183n.
Nature as anti-trigger, 181–2
Nature ecstasies, mystics, 171, 174, 360–2, 363
Nature as trigger, 26–7, 138, 146, 171, 173–4, 178, 181, 185, 187–90, 206, 222–4, 232
Neoplatonists, 74, 171–3 pass.
New Atlantis, The, 302–3
New Men, The, 102
New Statesman, 180
New Yorker, 200n., 263
Newman, J. H., 173
News Chronicle, 205
News from Nowhere, 297–8
Nichols, R., 62, 82, 83, 118, 127, 156, 198, 216, 284, 306, 333, 341
Nicolson, H., 205n.
Nietzsche, F., 82, 85, 118, 171, 214, 216, 221, 314, 315, 328n., 336, 339, 373–4
Nirvana, 55–6, 363
Nitrous oxide gas, 260–1, 262n., 276
Noche Escura del Alma, 160
Notebooks of Leonarda da Vinci, Selections from, 267n.
Nott, K., 184n.
Novalis, F., 260
Now and Then, 151
Nowell-Smith, P., 351n.
Nude, The, 230

Observer, 6n., 82n., 168, 261n., 263
Oceanic feeling, 45, 69, 79, 116, 174n., 214
On Inspiration, 305n., 306n.
On the Poetry of Keats, 152n., 174n., 340
One Thousand Beautiful Things, 111n.
Oswald, I., 190n.
Outsider, The, 240
Over the Bridge, 134
Overbelief, 20–1, 62, 146, 148, 171, 173, 183, 195, 197, 279 ff. pass.
Ovid, 72
Owen, R., 301
Oxford Dictionary of the Christian Church, 2, 92–3, 123, 125n., 127,

194n., 195, 203n., 252, 253n., 365

Oxford English Dictionary, 7, 20, 61n., 70, 71, 82, 222, 246, 280-1

Pain, 32, 87, 141-2
Pantheism, pantheist, 51, 69, 123, 126, 171, 173, 191n., 310, 362, 367
Pascal, B., 328n.
Paul, St., 14, 57, 64n., 69n., 247n., 272
Pensées, 328n.
Perfect Wagnerite, The, 316, 359n.
Perrin, J. M., 216n.
Peter, 366n.
Peter Bell, 99
Petersen, G., 125
Pettet, E. C., 152n., 174n., 340
Phantasmagoria, 113n.
Philippians, 125
Physical Phenomena of Mysticism, The, 78n., 86n.
Picasso, P., 239, 267, 270
Pickwick Papers, 260n.
Piero della Francesca, 267
Plaine and Easie Introduction to Practicall Musicke, A, 22n.
Plank, R., 219n., 256n.
Plato, 220, 302, 316, 361
Platonic love, 150
Plea for Excuses, A, 18n.
Plotinus, 24, 124, 127
Poet Wordsworth, The, 183, 219n, 361 374n.
Poetic knowledge as trigger, 26-7, 183, 200-2
Poetical Works of William Wordsworth, The. See Wordsworth's Poetical Works.
Poetry, 169, 171, 190, 201, 230, 232
Poincaré, H., 289
Poor Monkey, 105n.
Possessed, The, 254n.
Poulain, A., 6n., 21, 45-6, 52n., 59, 63, 74-6, 123, 249, 253n., 257, 307n., 358
Power Élite, The, 235n.
Practical Criticism, 170
Prayer, 27, 161, 194-6, 212n.
Prelude, The, 81n., 114, 127n., 137, 182n., 184, 200, 215, 220, 222, 362
Pride and Prejudice, 6
Priestley, J. B., 72n., 256

Princess with the Golden Hair, The, 152
Principal Navigations, Voiages, Traffiques and Discoveries of the English Nation, 157
Principia Ethica, 196n.
Principles of Literary Criticism, 227, 287n., 315, 343-4n., 356
Principles of Psychology, 231
Private Papers of Henry Ryecroft, The, 64
Proceedings of the Aristotelean Society, 18
Proclus, 93n.
Proust, M., 78, 81, 103-4, 129n., 135, 192n., 203, 204, 270, 276, 362-3
Psalms, 189n., 249
Pseudoxia Epidemica, 246.
Psychoanalytic Study of the Child, The, 219n., 256n.
Psychology of Men of Genius, The, 169
Psychology of Religious Mysticism, 45-6, 82, 91n., 100-1, 146n., 147n., 172n., 202n., 254n., 256, 261n., 276n., 283, 332, 354n., 359, 364
Psychology of Sex, 19
Psychology of the Unconscious, 198n., 363
Pulsation, 83-4, 87, 108, 217-8, 233

Quasi-physical feelings and words, 18, 32-3, 41, 67-88 pass., 100, 104, 165, 214-19 pass., 258, 279, 369
Quietism, 172, 252

Rachmaninov, S., 190
Rain Upon Godshill, 72n.
Ranters, 286, 365, 367
Raphael, S., 230n., 267
Ratisbonne, A., 331-2
Ray of Darkness, A, 255
Read, G. D-, 139-43 pass.
Reason as anti-trigger, 182-4
Recherche du Temps Perdu, La, 363
Recollection as trigger, 26-7, 138, 192n., 202-3, 206, 232
Reeve's Tale, The, 151
Religion as trigger, 26-7, 138, 146, 173-4, 194-7, 202, 206, 233
Religion and Science, 295n.
Religion of Nature, The, 27n.
Religious Behaviour, 136n.
Religious Conversion, 154, 289-92 pass., 331-2
Resnaisance, 311

Republic, The, 220, 316
Response experiences, *98–101, 175, 191, 192,* 213, 224, 226, *230,* 250, 251, *257, 277n., 284–5,* 287, 343, 358, *370*
Revelation, 14, 84, 193, 218, 308
Revelation ecstasies, 154–9, 167, 175, 280, 292, 370
Revelations of Divine Love, 353
Revival meetings, 136n., 194–5
Ribot, T., 183
Richard Jefferies, His Life and Work, 80n.
Richard of St. Victor, 309n.
Richards, I. A., *169–70,* 210, 227, *277n., 287n.,* 292, *315, 343–4n., 356,* 357
Richardson, M., 6n.
Road to Xanadu, The, 215, 333, 340
Rolle of Hampole, R., 78n.
Ruins, 40n., *112n.,* 180, *191,* 220, 237, 239
Rumbold, R., 54n.
Runciman, S., 193
Russell, B., 295nn., 335, 339
Ruysbroeck, J. van, 73–4, 123, 125n., 129, 252

Sackville-West, V., 236
Sainthood and Sanity, 168n., 256n.
Salmon, J., 68, 286, 307, 365–7
Sanctis, S. de, 154, 289–93 *pass.,* 331–2
Sargant, W., 195n., 290
Sassoon, S., 198, 203–4n., 209
Schizophrenia, 168, 254, 257
Scholem, G., 71n.
Schweizer, A., 312n.
Science of Prayer, The, 161n.
Scientific knowledge as trigger, 26–7, 138, 183n., 200–2
Sculpture as trigger, 190–1, 221
Seele und Welt, 363
Selected Letters of John Keats, 179
Selections from the Notebooks of Leonardo da Vinci, 267n.
Selincourt, E. de, 81n., 193n., 362
Seltman, C., 259n.
Seneca, 212
Sex, Literature and Censorship, 212
Sex and ecstasy, *11,* 26–7, *37,* 82, 84, 138, *145–53,* 173, 174, 185, 201, 204, 206, *213,* 221, 223, 311

Sexual Responsibility of Woman, The, 152n.
Shakespeare, W., 155, 159n.
Shaw, G. B., 316, 342, 359n.
Sheean, V., 81
Shelley, P. B., 237
Shocks. *See* Shudders.
Shropshire Lad, A, 238
Shudders, shocks, thrills, 77, 81–3, 87–8, 217, 257
Sibelius, J., 285
Sidney, P., 269n.
Silas Marner, 228
Simone Weil as we knew her, 216n.
Sin, 29, *103–6 pass.,* 162, 220, *257,* 271, 296
Skeat, W. W., 210
Snell, B., 219n.
Snow, C. P., 102, 121, 129, 131–2, 197, 201
So Much Love, So Little Money, 256n.
Socialism, socialists, 297, 317n.
Something of Myself, 306
Sons and Lovers, 153
Sorley, C. H., 199
Soul, 29, 147
Southey, R., 251n., 276n., 301
Spinoza, B., 260
Spitteler, C., 256n.
Stalin, J., 205, 231
Stephen, L., 295
Stevenson, R. L., 306
Story of My Heart, The, 80, 87, 99, 104n., 112, 192, 249–50
Studies in Mystical Religion, 283, 308, 365
Study of History, A, 113, 114, 192n.
Study of Instinct, The, 155n.
Sunday Times, 231, 263
Surprising Mystics, 105n., 254, 357
Suso, H., 14, *57, 58, 63,* 64n., *72,* 78n., *79, 85, 87, 91, 96,* 169, 204, 260, 283, 286, 290, 291, 339, 365, 366, 367
Suzuki, D. T., 70–1, 100–1n., 185n., 214–15
Swann's Way, 362

Table Talk, 336
Talks with Mr. Gladstone, 29
Tchaikovsky, I., 190
Tears 86, 87–8, 99, 100n., 117, 247

Television, 168n., 179n., 254, 256n., 263n.

Tempest, The, 296–7

Tennyson, A., *46, 62,* 68, 72, *82–5 pass.,* 102, 119, 127, 216, 218, 219, 253n., 307, 361

Teresa of Avila, St., 29, *50, 52–4, 59–60,* 64n., 68n., *82,* 84, 90, 93, 118n., 123, 124n., 126, 127, 132, 165n., 171, *172, 196,* 197, 204, 337n., *348, 355–6, 358, 359,* 366

Teresa, St., *Life of. See Life of Saint Teresa*

Theory of the Leisure Class, The, 199n. 314n.

Thibon, G., 216n.

Thinking Reed, The, 143n.

Thomas à Kempis, 312

Thomas Aquinas, St., 119

Thomas, E., 80n.

Thomas, The Gospel according to, 303n.

Thomas of Villanova, St., 76n.

Thrills. *See* Shudders.

Through the Looking-Glass, 81

Thurston, H., 78n., 86n., 105n., 253–4, 357

Time ecstasies, 106–15, 219–20

Time Regained, 203n.

Times, The, 141, 347

Times Literary Supplement, 229n., 300n.

Tinbergen, N., 155n.

Tintern Abbey, Lines composed a few miles above, 90, 222, 360

Toch, E., 305

Tollemache, L. A., 29

Totality beliefs and expressions, *127–8, 163, 241–3, 335–6, 344–5, 348, 353–5, 373*

Toynbee, A., 40n., 112–15, 192n., 206, 337, 352

Traherne, T., 67, 136–7, 164, 166, 209

Triggers, *16–17, 26–7, 38, 39–40,* 49n., 50n., 65, 75n., *79, 98–100,* 113–4, 127, 134n., *138,* 144, *145–6, 154–8,* 169, *170, 171–225 pass., 227–44 pass.,* 250–1, *266–8, 276–7,* 282, 284–7 *pass.,* 291–2, *299–300,* 313, *316, 339, 341–2, 357–8, 370,* 372

Troilus and Criseyde, 150

Trotter, W., 184n., 314n.

Turner, J., 231

Twentieth Century, The, 179n., 182, 232n.

Ugliness, 185, 207–8

Underhill, E., *48–51,* 64n., 74–5, 78n., 84n., 86n., *93, 94,* 96n., 124–5, 127, 160n., 162n., 165n., *182, 230, 240, 252, 253, 274, 282, 289,* 290, 307, 310, 313n., *316, 339, 361, 362, 364*

Union ecstasies, *92–6 pass.,* 97n., 122, *130,* 175, *309–11, 370, 371*

Unitive states, *63–6, 95–6, 101,* 137, 143–4, 162, 175, 250–1, 257, 286, *296, 370–1*

Up feelings and words, 32, *67–76 pass.,* 78, 87, 108, 149, 163, 211, *214,* 223, 232, *246, 270*

Utopia, 302

Utopias, 65, 95, 193–4, 258, 294–304 *pass.,* 370

Van de Velde, T., 153n.

Varieties of Religious Experience, 20, 44, 80, 118n., 120n., 208, 253n., 254, 257, 258, 260, 261, 268, 289, 313, 331, 337, 364

Vaughan, H., 72n., 111, 136

Veblen, T., 198–9n., 314n.

Venice, 192, 203n.

Victorian Chaise-Longue, The, 111n., 256

Villehardouin, G. de, 192

Vinci, L. da, 267n.

Vision of God, The, 52., 63n., *94,* 119n., 125, 274, 280, 312–15 *pass.,* 318n., 356–7

Waddell, H., 177n., 189n.

Wagner, R., 359

Wallas, G., 83n.

Walton, I., 6

Wanderjahre, Die, 306

Ward, R. H., 80, 261n., 263–73 *pass.,*

Warner Allen, H. *See* Allen, H. Warner.

Water as trigger, *79,* 174, *187,* 210, 214, 216, *217–18,* 221, 223, 232–3, 364

Way of All Flesh, The, 229

Weather as trigger, 188–9, 208–11 *pass.*

Weil, S., 182, 216n.
Wells, H. G., 65, 95
Wesley, J., 96, 158, *195n.*, 255, *325–8*, 336, 341
Wesley, The Rev. John, The Journal of. See Journal of the Rev. John Wesley.
West, R., 143n.
Western Mysticism, 29, 45, 46, 50, 51, 53n., 57, 78n., 123, 131, 132, 161n., 195, 204n., 238, 272, 274, 360
Whitman, W., 361
Willey, B., 27n.
William Wordsworth, The Early Years, 114, 251n.
Wilson, C., 240
Wilson, E., 152
Wine, 204n., 259–60, 261
Wine in the Ancient World, 259n.
Wisdom, Madness and Folly, 161, 257–8, 261n.
Withdrawal ecstasies, *18–20*, 32, *47–56*, *58*, *68–76 pass.*, *79*, 108, *127*, *130*, 132, 165n., *170*, 174, 200, 210, 218, 219, *225*, 256, *259*, 264, *280n.*, *310*, *363*, *369*, *371*
Withdrawal-intensity ecstasies, 58, 174–75, 219, 364
Wittgenstein, L., 39n.

Wolfe, H., 238
Woman's Hour, 139
Woolf, V., 61, 167, 251n., 274, 284
Wordsworth, 183, 361
Wordsworth, A Re-Interpretation, 198n., 252, 361n.
Wordsworth, D., 85n., 193n.
Wordsworth's Poetical Works, 85, 90, 99, 177–8, 214, 235, 244, 374
Wordsworth, W., 40n., 79, 80, 81n., 85, *90*, 92, 99, *113–14*, 120, 126, 127, *130–1*, 132, *136–7*, 171, *177–8*, *181*, 182n., *184*, 192, 193n., *198*, 200, 214, *215–23 pass.*, 235, 236, 244, *251–2*, 283, 286, 339, 351, 354, *360–2*, *363*, *374*
Worldliness, *28–9*, *37–8*, 139, *176–7*, 220, 295, *299*, *312–14*
Wright Mills, C., 235
Writer's Diary, A, 251n., 274
Writer's Notes on his Trade, A, 168
Writings of William Blake, The, 181
Wuthering Heights, 306

Zaehner, R. C., 105n., 125, *129–33*, 147, *161*, 168, 227, 257, *263–73 pass.*, *360–3*, 364n.
Zen Buddhism, 24n., 54n., 100–1n., 195